Early American Bicycle Works

Early American Bicycle Works

Exploring the Architecture and Innovation of an Industry

Robert L. McCullough

McFarland & Company, Inc., Publishers
Jefferson, North Carolina

Library of Congress Cataloging-in-Publication Data

Names: McCullough, Robert, 1949– author.
Title: Early American bicycle works : exploring the architecture
and innovation of an industry / Robert L. McCullough.
Description: Jefferson, North Carolina : McFarland & Company, Inc., 2025 |
Includes bibliographical references and index.
Identifiers: LCCN 2024044366 | ISBN 9781476696690 (paperback : acid free paper) ♾
ISBN 9781476654621 (ebook)
Subjects: LCSH: Bicycle industry—United States—History. | Bicycles—Design
and construction—United States.
Classification: LCC HD9993.B543 U544 2024 | DDC 338.4/76292272097309034—dc23/eng/20241205
LC record available at https://lccn.loc.gov/2024044366

ISBN (print) 978-1-4766-9669-0
ISBN (ebook) 978-1-4766-5462-1

Front cover images: (*top*) Bicycle assembly room, Weed Sewing Machine Company, Hartford, Connecticut. *Frank Leslie's Popular Monthly* November 1881 (author's collection); (*bottom*) Eclipse Bicycle Works, Elmira, New York, constructed in 1895 and designed by architects Pierce and Bickford (courtesy Chemung County Historical Society).

Printed in the United States of America

McFarland & Company, Inc., Publishers
Box 611, Jefferson, North Carolina 28640
www.mcfarlandpub.com

For Ruth, my steadfast companion

Table of Contents

Introduction: Factory Remnants

Discovery that humans could balance easily on two wheels by sustaining forward motion, coupled with the invention of a self-propelled driving mechanism to maintain momentum, represented advances of seemingly boundless possibility for personal mobility. For roughly two dozen years, from 1878, the year Albert Pope and the Weed Sewing Machine Company began manufacturing Columbia high wheel bicycles in Hartford, Connecticut, to 1902, the year the American Bicycle Company conglomerate failed and entered receivership, bicycles and bicyclists introduced an independent and dependable means of overland transportation free from predetermined routes and schedules; dramatically shaped and reshaped American social, cultural, commercial, and industrial history; propelled a campaign to improve the nation's sorry network of rural roads; mapped and documented

Figure 1. Weed Sewing Machine Company works on Capitol Avenue in Hartford, c. 1888, where the company produced Columbia high-wheel bicycles for the Pope Manufacturing Company in Boston. Among the buildings shown in the photograph, only the two-story center wing with paired cupolas survives, but in three-story height. Courtesy Hartford Preservation Alliance.

those roads, many of them unnamed, with ingeniously formatted road books; developed complex webs of urban, suburban, and rural bicycle paths; shaped urban form; influenced park planning; redefined travel and tourism; nurtured the talents of important American artists who, in early stages of their careers, illustrated cycling's journals with enticing tour itineraries; promoted heritage tourism nearly half a century before Williamsburg, Virginia, revealed the economic value of preserving historic buildings; dominated the machine tool industry; and set into motion the modern machine and engineering technology essential to the development of automobiles and airplanes. Few inventions can match the bicycle's travels into the far reaches of American culture; fewer still have retained their fundamental form for more than 130 years, a feat accomplished by the true safety bicycle after 1890 (two wheels of equal size, diamond frame, rear-wheel chain drive, and pneumatic tires); and few phenomena of cultural significance equal to that of the bicycle are so poorly recalled in our built and cultural environments.

Figure 2. Standard Columbia high-wheel bicycle. *Frank Leslie's Popular Monthly* 12 (November 1881), and Charles E. Pratt, *The American Bicycler: A Manual* (1880). Author's documents.

Many years ago, I began seeking out the scarce, hidden, and forgotten remnants of nineteenth-century bicycle history on the land, confining that search to the country's northeasterly quadrant—roughly as far west as Ohio and a few cities in Indiana, and as far south as Maryland and Washington, D.C. Places where that history becomes visible can take various forms: clubhouses; rural side paths; bicycle paths in urban parks or along parkways; retail and repair shops; overland routes for important races and tours; and industrial sites—the factories where inventors and investors achieved an often-uneasy alliance in the quest to manufacture one of the world's inspiring inventions. The first account of those travels and explorations, *Old Wheelways: Traces of Bicycle History on the Land*, circulated in 2015 and introduced nineteenth-century cyclists as landseërs, keen observers of American landscapes at a crucial moment in American history, just prior to the arrival of automobiles and the great periods of land-shaping that followed. The documentation of industrial sites, related commercial buildings, and planned urban amenities and worker housing offered here is a successor to that earlier work and explores similarly uncharted terrain.

Estimates vary widely about the number of bicycle manufacturers in America at the height of cycling's booming years during the mid-1890s. Due to the extraordinary growth of the industry during that period, the government supplemented its 1900 census with a special report, identifying 312 companies (compared to twenty-seven in 1890) together with another sixteen limited to bicycle assembly. However, numerous small companies already had failed by 1900, succumbing soon after the bicycle bubble began to lose buoyancy during the 1897 and 1898 seasons. The 1896 bicycle exposition in Chicago, where 400 different firms displayed more than 1,000 models of bicycles, may have provided a more accurate measure. Nor did the report identify many of the manufacturers of specialized parts or accessories, including seamless steel tubing, ball bearings, chains, rubber tires, cyclometers, bells, and lamps—among others. The ranks of these parts-makers increased dramatically as industry leaders adjusted production methods to meet swelling demand, steps that led toward consolidation of the industry. Underscoring this difficulty in tabulating accurate counts, cycling historian Carl Burgwardt from Buffalo has identified nearly five hundred bicycle manufacturers, dealers, repair shops, and parts-makers doing business in just western New York during the 1880s, 1890s and early years of the twentieth century.[1]

About two-thirds of American bicycle manufacturers located their plants in the northeasterly quarter of the country—roughly the dozen states explored here. Excluding most of Indiana, Illinois, and the Upper Midwest (Michigan, Wisconsin, and Minnesota), which accounted for a large number of manufacturers if Chicago is included, barely more than a dozen of the nineteenth-century factories adapted to bicycle production survive. Adding marginally to that surviving count, only about six factories constructed specifically for bicycle fabrication remain, including those for the Eagle Bicycle Manufacturing Company in Torrington, Connecticut; the Keating Wheel Company in Middletown, Connecticut; the Trinity Cycle Manufacturing Company in Keene, New Hampshire; the Crawford Manufacturing Company in Hagerstown, Maryland; the Speirs Manufacturing Company in Worcester, Massachusetts; and the Emblem Manufacturing Company in Angola, New York. In addition, scattered traces of the industrial empire amassed by the Pope Manufacturing Company (including planned worker housing) survive in Hartford and Hagerstown, Maryland. Among those factory complexes, the

Figure 3. Former Ames Manufacturing Company mills, Chicopee, Massachusetts, where Albert Overman first began building Victor high-wheel tricycles and bicycles. For short periods, the Ames company also built high wheel and safety bicycles for several other companies including the King Wheel Company (King bicycles); William Read and Son (New Mail bicycles); Eagle Bicycle Manufacturing Company (Eagle bicycles); Rouse, Hazard and Company (Sylph bicycles); and A.G. Spalding and Brothers (Credenda bicycles). The Chicopee company also manufactured bicycles using its own Ames moniker. In 1985, owners of the complex rehabilitated the factory for housing. Photo by the author.

plant built by the Pope Tube Company in Hartford is significant for its innovative design. Remnants also survive of worker housing related to large factories built by Henry Lozier in Toledo, Ohio, and Westfield, Massachusetts.

Among all surviving bicycle factories, possibly only four or five represent cycling's earliest era in this country, where we can say with certainty that the manufacture of high-wheel bicycles took place: the mills built by the Ames Manufacturing Company in Chicopee, Massachusetts, where Albert Overman first produced Victor tricycles and bicycles; the center wing of Albert Pope's factory complex on Capitol Avenue in Hartford; the Gormully and Jeffery factory on North Franklin Street in Chicago; and possibly the factory of the Western Wheel Works on West Schiller Street, also in Chicago. Ruins of the industrial buildings in Smithville, New Jersey, also survive, where the H.B. Smith Machine Company produced the Star high-wheel; the village and its workers housing are today a well-preserved historic site. One of the principal goals of this study is to encourage other cycling historians to explore remaining states and to lengthen that list.[2]

Adding urgency to this project, several important factories have been demolished during the pendency of this exploration. These include the last remaining building contributing to the enormous works of the Lozier Manufacturing Company in Toledo; the entire factory complex built by Henry Lozier in Westfield;

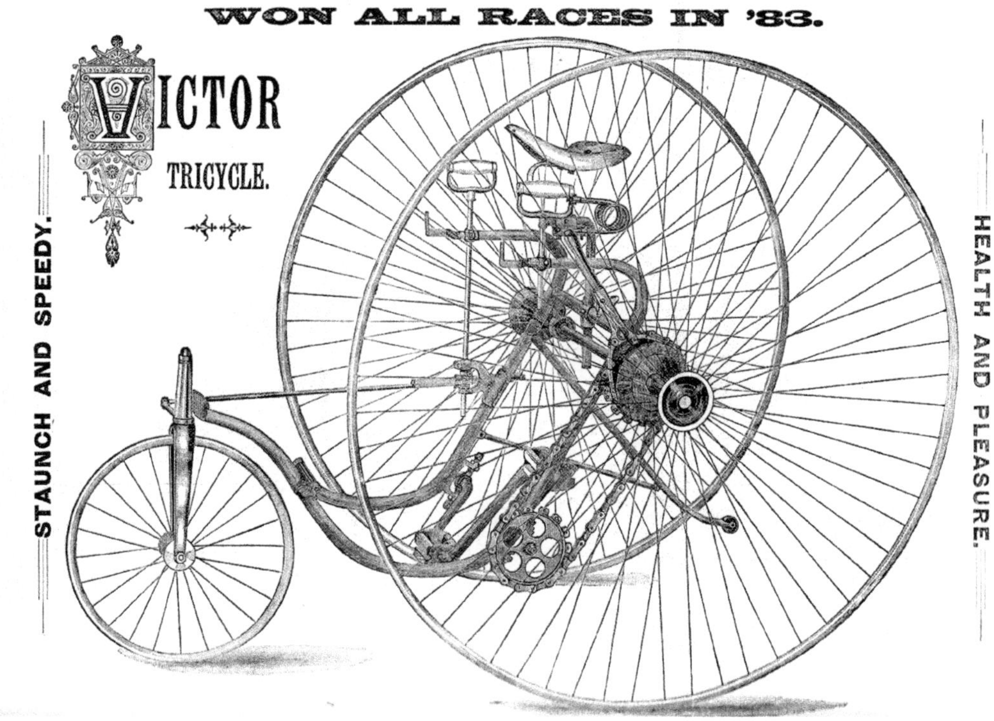

Figure 4. Victor tricycle manufactured by the Overman Wheel Company. From *Harper's Weekly* 28 (May 31, 1884). Courtesy Howe Library, University of Vermont.

the John P. Lovell Arms and Cycle Company factory in South Portland, Maine; the Grand Rapids Cycle Company works in Grand Rapids, Michigan; and the most recent, the well-designed Warwick Cycle Manufacturing Company plant in Springfield, Massachusetts—one of the earliest factories built specifically for the manufacture of bicycles and one of the better examples suitable for historical interpretation; only remnants of its ancillary shops remain.

This compilation is a partial inventory of factories that remain with the hope that greater awareness of the plight faced by these few surviving landmarks, many of them threatened, will encourage more thoughtful planning and forestall further losses. Documentation explains the contributions and historic significance of surviving sites in the context of both nineteenth-century bicycle history and the history of industrial architecture as well as local history. Unavoidably, those historical narratives are concentrated because the period of contribution to cycling history for most of these surviving buildings was short, reflecting the rapid rise and equally swift decline of cycling during that period of inventive development. Although the factories that do survive typically have lengthy histories devoted to other uses, the overriding importance attaching to the bicycle's initial period of invention and popular embrace, coupled with the contributions of those advances to American culture, add import to any assessment about the historic significance of these surviving works.

Although industrial buildings and their structure, architectural form, internal organization, production systems, machine tools, fixtures or trade fixtures, and evolving efficiencies establish the study's fundamental organization, numerous patterns surface, broadening the resulting

Figure 5. In Chicago, the factories of the Gormully and Jeffery Manufacturing Company, facing North Franklin Street and extending along West Institute Place (formerly Pearson Street), have survived. The company erected the oldest of these lofts in 1884, embellishing the cornice with a pedimented parapet, and then enlarged the building in 1885; groundbreaking for the adjoining five-story factory occurred in 1886. G. & J. built high-wheel bicycles in these works, introducing several monikers including Ideal, American Challenge, and American Champion, followed by Rambler safety bicycles. In 1891, the company also acquired a three-story warehouse on the opposite side of Franklin Street and by 1894 had replaced it with an eight-story factory that also survives. Photograph by Tom McGrath.

composition. For example, bicycle factories provide a chance to chronicle many of the subtle improvements to the design of an important nineteenth-century architectural type, *standard mill construction*, as it evolved into concluding stages during the closing decades of that century and early part of the twentieth century. The buildings also provide an occasion to study the important relationships between factory design and production methods specific to a single industry—and the quest by proprietors of that industry to improve efficiency, in turn generating greater profits.

These factories also chronicle the shift from versatile standard mill construction to industrial buildings designed and engineered to achieve maximum production efficiency by integrating building and manufacturing processes into a coherent, unified plan. Although the works of many bicycle companies confirm a continued dependence on standard mill construction at the close of the nineteenth century, and a succession of owners demonstrate the versatility of that building type throughout much of the twentieth century, other factories built to produce bicycles or bicycle parts demonstrate creative departures from that building tradition. Still others illustrate the progression of four evolving structural types utilized by American industry during that same general period: open-floor production sheds framed with iron or steel; urban industrial lofts; load-bearing concrete block;

Figure 6. By 1892, cyclists could order the G & J Rambler with solid, cushion, inflated-cushion, or pneumatic tires (solid tires shown). Advertisement from *The Illustrated American* (1891). Author's document.

Figure 7 (*above*) and Figure 8 (*opposite*). In Keene, New Hampshire, businessman Charles A. Jones constructed an industrial loft for the Trinity Cycle Manufacturing Company, located two blocks from the city's Central Square. Designed by architect Walter Nourse from Worcester, Massachusetts, and completed in 1897, the factory today accommodates a mix of uses. At the start of that 1897 season, the company offered the Trinity Roadster safety bicycle with true diamond frame, rear-wheel chain drive, and pneumatic tires for $100—available in enamel of black, maroon, imperial blue, olive, or canary yellow, with nickel-plated forks. *Above:* photo by the author; *opposite:* courtesy Hagley Museum and Library.

THE TRINITY ROADSTER

and skeletal-frame, reinforced concrete construction.

Although factories provide the framework for each chapter, the overlapping contexts for both the history of industrial architecture and the history of bicycle manufacturing illuminate and inform important aspects of each context, often in unsuspected ways. For instance, cycling's contributions to the industrial built environment extend far beyond the locales of a few, well-known companies linked in one way or another to the high-wheel era, as considered in early chapters, and surface in almost all major cities (and myriad small cities and towns) located in the country's northeasterly sectors. In turn, the industry's broad geographical dispersion—evident in factories both large and small—also mirrors the bicycle's profound cultural influence during that period. Thus, even modest factories erected by short-lived companies help to define the character of those shared regional and local contexts, and our tendency to sequester the exceptional examples of industrial architecture should not relegate lesser buildings to obscurity, at least not for bicycle history.

In similar fashion, the prevalence of standard-mill construction in late nineteenth and early twentieth-century manufacturing, including its ready acceptance by the nascent bicycle industry, reflects the aura of industrialization in America during this period. For a fleeting moment, the bicycle revealed industry's most inventive qualities and illuminated the optimistic temper of management and, in some quarters, labor. Today, when the word "industry" is voiced in conversation, a smudge may linger in mind; however, the word "industrious" is usually expressed in a much more complimentary manner, suggesting diligence, inventiveness, and productivity. Although the bicycle industry was not immune to the country's cultural failings, including harsh racial and economic disparities, a sense of progressivism is nevertheless apparent in historical accounts of work on shop floors as well as in administrative offices, particularly among some of the smaller companies. Such views are important parts of these overlapping historical contexts and should not be overlooked.

These merging contexts also provide unusual opportunities to continue the introduction of talented local architects and builders, whose work thus can be compared or contrasted across an extended region, revealing broad trends but also vernacular traditions. Together, these varied perspectives strengthen the foundation for preserving what precious little remains of cycling's nineteenth-century architectural and industrial heritage.

Numerous other thematic threads also bind these overlapping contexts, adding depth and consistency to the patterns that occur. Especially prominent is the bicycle industry's domination of machine tool production during the decade of the 1890s, creating more innovations in the design and manufacture of specialized, labor-saving machine tools, by far, than in any other sector of small metal manufacturing during that period. The bicycle also drew attention to the central role of patented invention in America's industrial sectors and took center stage in attempts to enforce patents through litigation. All the while, the often-tenuous relationships between inventor and investor in converting creativity into profit moved sharply into focus. Company accounting ledgers also tell us much about management practices during this period of industrious activity: the cautious approach to making corporate ends meet by some company owners; the imaginative and increasingly desperate financial maneuvering by many others; and the frequently insistent demands for largesse from public sources made by numerous bicycle firms—a very practiced strategy that contrasted with proud self-reliance by other builders of bicycles. In Hartford, too, Albert Pope, George Day, and architect George Keller gave industrial works a burnished public façade, extending the influence of the World's Columbian Exposition in 1893 into an overlooked sector of the City Beautiful movement.[3]

The organizational approach to this study, that of isolating a collection of surviving factories employed to manufacture bicycles, offers an unexpected contribution to cycling history by providing opportunities to compare or contrast companies of varying sizes and origins, adding much clarity to our picture of the entire industry during its early period. Previous studies of bicycle manufacturing often have focused on primary firms such as the Pope Manufacturing Company or the American Bicycle Company. In this work, comparisons illuminate the shadowed corners of company offices or shops, and sharpen our focus on factors such as financial capitalization; willingness or circumspection regarding debt; the skills, engineering expertise, and foresight of company officials or floor superintendents; the hard or deceptive practices that occasionally surface; the emerging assembly of automobiles in many of these factories; the clouded circumstances surrounding formation the American Bicycle Company trust, particularly the murky criteria used to select companies to join that conglomerate; and the narrowly confined sectors of bicycle manufacturing that developed following collapse of the bicycle boom.

Several chapters of this work build on the foundations established by earlier studies, including Bruce Epperson's *Peddling Bicycles to America: The Rise of an Industry* (Jefferson, NC: McFarland, 2010). Overlap with some of Epperson's discussion is unavoidable, notably that involving the Pope Manufacturing Company, the Pope Tube Company, the Westfield Manufacturing Company, and the Columbia Manufacturing Company, to provide a supporting context for arguments that the surviving buildings are historically significant or to fill chronological gaps. When that overlap occurs, however, the text is supported by primary sources whenever possible, and the Pope chapters supplement and in some places clarify Epperson's earlier study, particularly regarding the influence of the World's Columbian Exposition in Chicago on the development of Hartford's industrial district.

This study also draws from two other books—Lindy Biggs' *The Rational Factory: Architecture, Technology, and Work in America's Age of Mass Production* (Baltimore: Johns Hopkins University Press, 1996) and Betsy Hunter Bradley's *The Works: The Industrial Architecture of the United States* (New York: Oxford University Press, 1999)—to explain the bicycle industry's contributions to the history of industrial architecture. I am indebted to Betsy Bradley for her review of Chapters 1 and 2.

Similarly, David Hounshell's *From the American System to Mass Production, 1800 to 1932* (Baltimore: Johns Hopkins University Press, 1984) and Glen Norcliffe's "Bridging the American System and Mass Production: Albert Pope's System of Bicycle Manufacture," in *Tools and Technology: Newsletter of the American Precision Museum* (Windsor, Vermont: Summer 1997), together with Epperson's study, provide a foundation for the argument advanced in Chapter 2 that bicycle manufacturing revolutionized American industry in ways supplemental to those discussed in the three studies.

During the long pendency of this project, Robert K. Keating published an excellent biography of Robert M. Keating, *Wheel Man: Robert M. Keating, Pioneer of Bicycles, Motorcycles and Automobiles* (Jefferson, NC: McFarland, 2014), and contextual overlap is again unavoidable. As with the Epperson work, my text is supported by primary sources whenever possible. Ironically, Keating's book cites my earlier work regarding the design of the Middletown factory.

Most of the structure for this study is founded in local history—the records available from city clerks, town libraries, archival organizations, historical societies, registries of deeds, and engineering or public works departments. The availability of digitized newspapers has increased the scope of this type of research dramatically, as has the availability of online trade journals. Nevertheless, the study remains unfinished because the limited geographical scope of this search has resulted in pages that are already too lengthy. My hope is that others will continue to rummage for surviving examples and focus more attention on preserving traces of those factories. Chicago, alone a Mecca of bicycle manufacturing, deserves its own exhaustive study. For now, the task is to use these pages to place readers inside and outside the nineteenth-century factories where workers built bicycles.

1

Versatile Factory

Factories (and bicycles, too) can be described as complex, working assemblages of inter-related parts. For standard mill construction, the manner of structural support, dimension of roof span, spacing for interior columns, availability of natural lighting and ventilation, type of motive power, protections against fire waste, and manufacturing methods (among various other factors), all influence building form. Changes to improve one facet of design often require a corresponding adjustment to other features. Although such factories qualify as ordinary because standard mill construction became a very common building type, the simple austerity of these industrial facades belies the breadth and complexity of the

Figure 9. Adopting a practice common among bicycle manufacturers, that of moving from place to place, the Eclipse Bicycle Works left Indianapolis for Beaver Falls, Pennsylvania, and then relocated to Elmira, New York, where investors offered the company financial incentives. There, the company built this factory in 1895, to the design of architects Pierce and Bickford. Among the last new industries to rely on standard mill construction, bicycle companies tested the limits for the size of window openings in load-bearing brick walls, an effort to maximize the admission of natural light. The company was eventually swallowed by the Bendix Corporation and the building demolished. Courtesy Chemung County Historical Society.

many factors studied by their designers or builders. Understanding these relationships improves our ability to read the history of industrial buildings, evident in their physical form, and we can compare specific buildings by considering the ways in which designs respond to these assorted concerns.

Consider, for example, the relationship between structure, light, and building width. Bearing wall design, which relies on the weight and mass of masonry or brick walls to provide principal structural support, dominated nineteenth-century industrial buildings. Walls needed to be strong enough to support the weight of floors; roofs and the top floors sometimes suspended from roof frames; exterior forces such as wind and snow; the burden of any materials and machinery placed on floors; and heavy mill shafting hung from ceilings where it distributed motive power to machinery. The strength, rigidity, and elasticity required of a factory building fluctuated according to the construction materials used, the span of floor beams, the weight resting upon the floors, the type of machinery used, and the speeds at which machinery operated. Vibrations or juddering emanating from machinery and shafting, as well as the oscillations that sometimes resulted—two very different types of motion—placed severe demands on timber floor beams, walls, joinery, and roof assembly, and these concerns developed into a critical aspect of structural design. Durable stone and brick, typically the latter, addressed these matters for most of the nineteenth century, and added protection against fire in the bargain.[1]

Factory interiors also required as much daylight and ventilation as possible, aspects controlled principally by the size and location of windows. However, the number and dimension of window openings remained limited by the extent of structural mass required for bearing walls. Constraints to building width were a direct consequence, and even bright sunlight faded too quickly to reach the middle of buildings much wider than fifty or sixty feet. Uniform sources of light helped, accomplished with long rows of identical, evenly-spaced windows placed as high above floors as possible. As well, the elongated, orderly facades of brick punctuated by precisely aligned voids of glass became the most visually dominant features of an aesthetic canon sanctified by industry notables and sought by its aspirants.

The quest for larger windows accompanied practically the entire evolution of bearing wall structures for industry and pushed design in several different directions. After mid-nineteenth century, builders began consolidating walls into rows of piers spaced to support floor beams, reducing the load-bearing requirements of spandrel walls principally to that of their own weight. Engineers occasionally modified the design by tapering the depth of piers supporting upper floors, where bearing weight decreased (see Chapter 11).[2]

With spandrel walls relieved of bearing loads, the size of window openings could be enlarged. However, window size also depended on the methods used for structurally supporting the weight of spandrel walls above each window, and on the type of window sash used. That weight increased with building height, even as it decreased as windows became larger. Builders employed a variety of structural devices, but segmental arches of brick offered greater strength than flat arches or lintels and eventually became characteristic features of bearing-wall factories in mature form. Often, the radii of these arches corresponded to the widths of window openings, and arch springing points could be contained by adjoining piers. In addition, these arches could be stiffened by iron tie rods threaded through cast-iron molds called skewbacks, encased in the piers; rods could be concealed by wood panels placed above the sash.[3]

Figure 10. Keating Wheel Company factory, Middletown, Connecticut. As measured from pier-center to pier-center, a ten-foot interval, wall space is about 270 square feet. Window openings comprise about 137 square feet, or roughly half the wall space—but far less than the image appears to show. Sash mullions, muntins, casing, and rails further reduce the amount of light reaching the interior. The round iron plates secure floor-beam anchor bolts. Photo by the author.

Despite these improvements, factory walls with long rows of large window openings can be deceiving about the amount of light reaching building interiors. For example, if piers and floor beams are center-spaced at ten-foot intervals (a common span), window openings typically might occupy only 50 percent of the wall surfaces between pier centers, and substantially less if one measures just the panes of glass. A drawing titled "Modern Mill Building" and included in a report first published in 1902 by the Boston Manufacturers Mutual Insurance Company suggests the maximum window size possible for standard mill construction, as does the two-story Eclipse Bicycle Company factory in Elmira, New York, built in 1895 but no longer standing. By 1902, however, this building type was far from modern.[4]

Roof lighting contributed to these designs, and monitors or lanterns of varying height, width, length, and sash size became the industrial equivalent of basilica clerestories, washing the top floors of gable or hipped-roofed factories with light and venting rising heat. However, the attics and monitors of these roofs created pockets of space vulnerable to fire, and flat or very low-pitched gable and hipped roofs gained dominance for many types of industrial buildings during the post–Civil War years. Engineers and architects also adapted monitors and lanterns to these roofs, but saw-tooth skylights in various forms soon offered greater advantages, leading to expansive, one-story buildings.

The relationship between structure, light, and building width is just one of many ways to ponder the complexities of factory design. Just as the need for natural light limited building width, the difficulty of distributing power over extended distances constrained building length and forced the careful positioning of buildings in relation to power sources, whether water wheels, turbines, steam engines, or combinations of all three. Overhead mill

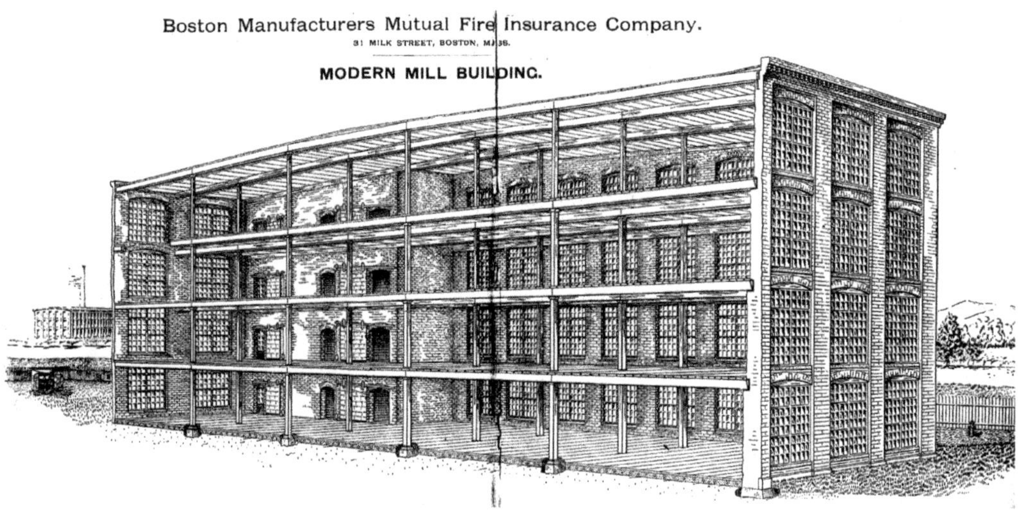

Figure 11. In 1902, the Boston Manufacturers Mutual Insurance Company published this model design for a "Modern Mill Building," suggesting the maximum window size feasible with standard mill construction's load-bearing brick walls. By that time, however, engineers and architects had turned to other more advanced structural designs, including skeletal frames of steel or reinforced concrete. Report No. 5, Slow Burning or Mill Construction, by Boston Manufacturer Mutual Fire Insurance Company, 1908.

Figure 12. General machine room, Liberty Cycle Company, Rockaway, New Jersey, c. 1895. The overhead mill shafting used in nineteenth-century factories, powered initially by water, then by steam engines, followed in turn by electricity, distributed power to machines via wheels, belts, and pulleys. Eventually machines driven by individual electric motors made this system of power distribution redundant. The timber trusses carrying the weight of the roof and mill shafting are strengthened by iron tension rods. *Engineering Magazine* 9 (May 1895).

shafting, a complex system of shafts, gears, rods, pulleys, wheels and belts, delivered power both vertically and horizontally from its source to its destination—the machinery operated by workers. However, the movement of gears required to change the direction of power from vertical to horizontal and again from horizontal to vertical created friction, and the combined weight of equipment caused resistance to motion, as did torsional stresses on long revolving shafts. Ultimately, a substantial amount of power being generated failed to reach the machinery, and that loss of power increased as mill shafting lengthened. Moreover, the main shafting revolved continuously regardless of load, a very inefficient system if workers needed to operate only a few machines. These limitations also had a direct influence on manufacturing processes, dictating the placement of machinery in relation to the alignment of both overhead shafting and windows.

Although steam power alleviated some of the shortcomings of direct-drive water power by generating greater and more consistent power, not until the advent of electric motors, initially driving individual main shafts and ultimately each unit of machinery, were these challenges surmounted. With electric motors attached to main shafts at measured intervals, building length could be increased. In addition, motors could be attached to secondary shafts, allowing machinery operated in unison to be arranged into groups (known as group drive) and reducing power consumption. With more advanced design of machinery powered by individual motors (unit drive), mill shafting became redundant, efficiency improved, and factory design evolved with much greater freedom, pointing again to sprawling, one-story structures with roof lighting.

Standard mill construction also addressed concern for fire, an aspect that became one of the most important and lasting determinants of factory design. The genesis of a science devoted to preventing fire waste in industry traces to 1835 when a small cadre of Yankee textile capitalists embraced communal enterprise and formed factory mutual fire insurance companies. Managers of these factory mutuals pursued two objectives from the outset. One involved offering insurance at actual cost, made possible by sharing all losses and expenses equally among members of a single mutual company. The second concerned recognition that through prevention and control of fires, mill owners could reduce fire waste dramatically. Focus turned to the methods of detecting, containing, and suppressing fire when it occurred, which in turn led to testing the length of time that building materials resisted fire.

The prototypical factory developed by the factory mutual companies became a standard for industrial design in many manufacturing sectors, including bicycles, and the model continued to be built during the early years of the twentieth century until skeletal-frame steel or reinforced-concrete construction superseded it. The terms fire-resistive construction, slow-burning construction, or standard mill construction (especially the latter two) described that prototype, and these phrases settled comfortably into industrial vocabulary during the early 1880s when treatises for architects and builders began to include drawings and excerpts from company reports. Familiarity with both the terminology and building type also extended to lending institutions. With manufacturers, engineers, architects, builders, lenders, and insurers all in accord, the manner of factory design acquired a widely accepted uniformity, as the term standard-mill construction implies.

The factory mutuals sought economy as well as protection against fire waste, and building specifications were thorough. In addition to incombustible brick bearing walls, insurers favored heavy timber for vertical posts and floor beams, with each floor sealed as much as possible from adjoining floors to resist fires long enough, or to keep flames burning slowly enough, to be extinguished before spreading. Traditional floor joists, which created inaccessible pockets of dust and debris, yielded to thick floor planks nailed directly to floor beams and extending across two bays in an alternating, interlocking pattern to create rigidity. Builders then secured a top layer of floorboards, usually hardwood, at right angles to the floor planks. Flat, or slightly pitched roofs of three-inch plank replicated floor construction. Tarred paper and gravel sufficed for an exterior roof surface, and brick parapets limited the risk of fire from nearby buildings. Slate roofs also added protection, but at greater cost and weight.

The principal point is that the more conversant we become with these features, the greater our appreciation for industrial buildings. We can also look past the superficial layers of wear from heavy use or neglect and see these buildings more clearly in terms of their potential; we can also recognize subtle traces of innovation.[5]

Smart Factory Owners

Among several studies that explore the history of industrial architecture in America, two of those books create a useful dialogue for assessing the contributions of bicycle manufacturers and the works they erected. In her 1996 book, *The Rational Factory: Architecture, Technology, and Work in America's Age of Mass Production*, Lindy Biggs argues that the design of industrial buildings as integral parts of production technology—the rational factory—achieved maturity during the first quarter of the twentieth century. She observes accurately that two lines of progress advancing during the late nineteenth century, namely mechanized techniques for processing materials and automation made possible by special purpose machines demonstrated that the speed of production (and corresponding profits), depended heavily on both the handling of materials and the flow of work. Those two aspects of manufacturing became cornerstones for the rational planning of twentieth-century factories by engineers and architects, who fashioned a newly-defined, specialized field of practice. In Biggs' words, factories became "the master machine for organizing and controlling work."[6]

However, in her 1999 book, *The Works: The Industrial Architecture of the United States*, Betsy Bradley disagrees with Biggs' assessment that nineteenth-century factories were passive shells intended principally to shelter an allotted number of machines, tools, and workers. For Bradley, the term "master machine" depends on the "technological integration of machinery and the structure that housed it, not on rationalized planning and management," and she argues forcefully that those who built nineteenth-century industrial works constantly adapted the designs and inter-relationships of those buildings to respond to changing technology, competition, and opportunities for expansion as American industry evolved. Without a doubt, the bicycle industry and its factories filled with machine tools substantiate Bradley's observations.[7]

Both authors develop their arguments in greater depth, but two aspects of these studies warrant further consideration. One is that the dialogue voiced by Biggs and Bradley gives us convenient vantage points for identifying and measuring efficiencies in the design of industrial buildings, the inventive engineering and placement of machine tools, and the organization of manufacturing systems. Stated differently: If factories are complex assemblages of interrelated parts, machines by another name, to what extent does the original or adapted design of any building accommodate a careful integration of the building's structural form and the manufacturing processes occurring inside? Clearly, the ability to answer that question depends heavily upon knowledge of the forces that governed production in the bicycle industry, aspects illuminated by the close study of individual companies, in turn enabled by access to local history.

The second is that the conversation begun by Biggs and Bradley is unfinished because neither author intended to investigate a specific industry in sufficient depth to unearth the sometimes-subtle factors that shaped decisions about factory plans and investment in machine tools. Several of the surviving bicycle works considered here clearly negate Biggs' descriptions of standard mill construction as passive shells, but at the same time reveal conventions that both Biggs and Bradley may have overlooked. In some instances, practices establish clear patterns. For example, neither author considered the frequency with which companies moved from one place to another, bargaining with municipal governments or local investors to obtain financial inducements and then constructing new plants that improved or refined existing operations, or replicated already efficient systems. Some owners repeated the process several times, a strategy that surfaced frequently in the burgeoning bicycle sector—even to the point of dependence on plans that became templates. Contractors erected these buildings with astonishing speed, as well.

Moreover, neither author considers the seasonal nature of many types of manufacturing, bicycles among them, and the need for versatility in building design to accommodate the fabrication of different types of products during different times of the year; passive building shells become rationally designed by default in that context. Nor is the economic specter of industry consolidation or demise, and its influence on factory investment, given full attention. In many instances, the versatility of buildings easily adapted to other uses provided a measure of assurance—a factor well understood by provident owners, chary financiers, or prudent local subscribers alike. The saga of the two tube manufacturing factories erected by Albert Pope in Hartford is a perfect illustration, the first built in 1893 and an example of standard mill construction, and the second erected in 1896, superseding the first and exemplifying a supremely rational design. However, consolidation of the country's tube industry forced closure of the latter building four years after it was built, and it remained unused for more than a decade, before being acquired at a tiny fraction of its construction cost and consigned to the banal storage of paper waste. Meanwhile, the first tube factory continued to serve diverse industrial uses for most of the twentieth century, underscoring the versatility of standard mill construction.

Nor are the complexities inherent in the selection of factory design, choice of machine tools, organization of production systems, and day-to-day management easy to unravel without local records—and can be very difficult even with that advantage. For instance, Biggs by chance uses the Lozier Manufacturing Company works in Toledo, a plant first constructed in 1885 to manufacture sewing machines and one that exploits standard-mill construction, to support her observation that "nineteenth-century industrialists did not so much rethink the factory as expand it to suit growing and varying needs," thus inviting more sophisticated designs by architects and engineers. Many manufacturers certainly did expand in kind, and the Lozier works steadily grew into a large manufacturing complex where fabrication of Cleveland bicycles occurred, seeming to corroborate Biggs' general conclusions.

However, closer study of the Lozier works reveals her selection of that factory to be an awkward one for several reasons. Biggs borrows from a series of six essays by engineer Horace L. Arnold titled "Machine Shop Economics" published in *Engineering Magazine* from April to September 1896. The May article focuses on the requisites of machine shop construction and includes images of both the Lozier factory and a plant erected in 1895 by the Sterling Cycle Works in Kenosha, Wisconsin—juxtaposed on the same page. Arnold marvels at the rise of bicycle manufacturing and its machine shops, and he uses the latter plant to demonstrate the trend of placing large machine works on a single open floor without partitions, similar to what Bradley calls a production shed. The low, one-story building, with brick bearing walls that allow large expanses of glass, is radically different from the standard-mill construction displayed by the Lozier works, although timber posts and trusses support the roof span of the former, rather than iron framing. Thus, Arnold is interested primarily in showing two approaches to the design of machine shops, and his intentional comparison of those very different factories suggests that some bicycle manufacturers did consider alternate types of industrial buildings such as production sheds in the quest for economic advantage.[8]

More importantly, the story of Lozier's swift rise to prominence in the bicycle industry places his company's far-flung plants in a more instructive light, revealing his emphasis on improving the manufacturing process, introducing automated machinery, employing a template for machine shop design (albeit occupying more than one story), and organizing multiple buildings into quadrangular complexes. Even as Arnold's articles were being published, Lozier already had begun

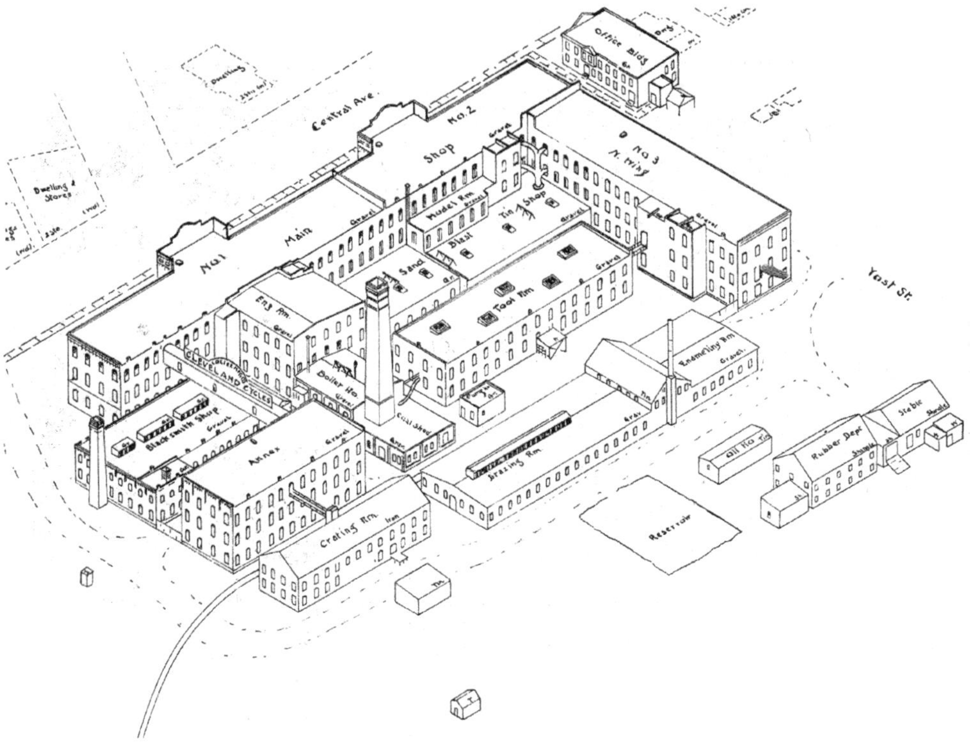

Figure 13 (*top*) and Figure 14 (*bottom*). In 1896, engineer Horace L. Arnold penned a series of essays for *Engineering Magazine* titled "Machine Shop Economics" and compared two different bicycle factories: the multi-story works owned by the Lozier Manufacturing Company in Toledo (top), and a plant erected in 1895 by the Sterling Cycle Works in Kenosha, Wisconsin, the latter displaying what Arnold regarded as a desirable trend toward one-story, open floor plans with monitor or clerestory windows. The radically different designs for each building confirm that bicycle manufacturers explored alternatives for factory design in the quest for economic advantage. None of the buildings depicted survives. *Engineering Magazine* 11 (May 1896).

planning two other factories, one in Thompsonville, Connecticut, and one in Westfield, Massachusetts, relying on comparable designs and similarly advanced manufacturing processes. Despite his preference for one-story plants, Arnold acknowledged Lozier's Toledo factory to be an exceptionally good example of a multi-floored shop—narrow, well-lighted, well heated, and ventilated.[9]

Selection of the Lozier plant is awkward for another reason, but one ascertainable only from reports in local newspapers or cycling's various journals. In November 1894, much of Lozier's plant burned to the ground, and thus the image of the works used by Arnold in his 1896 article for *Engineering Magazine* (and later borrowed by Biggs) shows a factory complex rapidly constructed in two or three months during the winter of 1894 and 1895. Arnold knew of the fire, but only his articles for another journal, *American Machinist*, under the pen-name Hugh Dolnar reveal that awareness.[10]

True, the fire might have provided an opportunity to exploit more advanced theories of factory planning during reconstruction. However, the bicycle industry's crucial production calendar loomed large, and the fire had crippled the business precisely when all bicycle companies were preparing for the coming season by estimating demand, purchasing materials to meet anticipated quotas, tooling patterns for new models, and assembling demonstration prototypes for dealers. Even the slightest delay in those tasks would have been disastrous for Lozier. In 1894 and 1895, demand for bicycles far exceeded supply, and Lozier, who averaged 300 finished bicycles each day in 1894 and who

MACHINE SHOP OF VEEDER MANUFACTURING COMPANY, HARTFORD, CONN.

Figure 15. Manufacturers of bicycles or bicycle parts explored progressive alternatives for factory design. In 1898, the Veeder Manufacturing Company in Hartford, makers of bicycle cyclometers, retained the Berlin Iron Bridge Company to erect a three-story shop of steel, glass, and brick spandrel walls, foretelling trends that would supersede standard mill construction. The shop has not survived. *Engineering Record* 38 (July 10, 1898). Courtesy Howe Library, University of Vermont.

anticipated record numbers for 1895, hoped to sell all the bicycles he could build, at great profit; or, face an equally-great loss of economic opportunity, thus placing his capital investment in peril. The desperate nature of his plight became clear when, two days after the fire, Lozier departed for Boston to negotiate with rival Albert Pope, who generously had offered one of his idle Hartford buildings for temporary use. Under those circumstances, reconfiguring factory design would have been both impractical and unnecessary for Lozier, who had developed a well-integrated production system prior to the fire.[11]

Granted, the circumstances surrounding the Lozier factory and its loss by fire can be regarded as an anomaly, certainly so in the context of Biggs' and Bradley's expansive and very valuable studies. Yet by 1893 the bicycle craze had begun to expand with such astonishing momentum that any manufacturers who erected bicycle factories during this period focused intently on the calendar of production, with speed of construction a critical concern. Thus, Lozier was far from alone in his single-minded approach to hurried factory planning.

Nevertheless, the Lozier example is important primarily to emphasize that circumstances specific to sites or to individual companies frequently yielded outcomes that greatly expanded practices in factory design relating to production systems. Even among the scarce surviving works erected by bicycle companies during the 1890s, several examples confirm that reconsidering factory design is precisely what owners of those enterprises and their builders set out to do—sometimes assisted by architects or engineers, but often not. In Connecticut alone, Pope's second tube factory, the Keating Wheel Company works in Middletown, the Eagle Bicycle Manufacturing Company plant in Torrington, and the machine shop designed by the Berlin Iron Bridge Company for the Veeder Manufacturing Company in Hartford (makers of bicycle cyclometers) are all good cases in point.

The histories of the bicycle companies and their factories contained in the chapters that follow create contexts in which the quests by bicycle-company owners to achieve efficiencies in factory design and production can be measured in the broader context of advancing trends in American architecture, engineering, and invention. In addition, those stories add depth to our understanding of the bicycle industry's boom years, calling attention all the while to the scarce remnants of bicycle history in our built environments.[12]

2

Bicycle Factory

Architectural and engineering historians who observe that the builders of nineteenth-century industrial works consistently adapted the designs and inter-relationships of buildings and their interior arrangements to respond to changing technology, competition, and opportunities for expansion—striving all the while to integrate machinery and building—might easily be describing bicycle manufacturers. The story of the bicycle's contributions to American industry, industrial architecture, machine tool technology, and production systems during the late nineteenth century begins with an original invention, expands at an extraordinary pace, declines abruptly, and is condensed into a brief period lasting little more than two decades. The result is a remarkably complete, compact, and sharply-focused picture of precisely the types of adaptations and integrations that these historians describe—progressing literally from one bicycle season to the next.

To identify the bicycle industry's specific innovations, a concise restatement of America's industrial originations becomes essential. The list is a long one and includes the *American System* of precision machinery capable of producing interchangeable parts, thus encouraging standardization; the stamping and pressing of metal parts with dies—an alternative to the milling machines that removed extraneous metal; escalating mechanization and automation, leading to labor-saving specialized machines capable of completing several tasks at once; the resulting growth of subsidiary parts-industries; the rise of skilled labor followed by division of labor; a sequestering of well-defined departments; emphasis on an efficient, linear flow of materials and production, leading to the development of mechanized assembly; and scientific testing to achieve quality control.

Other advances increased the size of industrial works, including the growth of large factory complexes and the need for efficient generation and distribution of power, achieved initially by improvements in steam technology, succeeded in turn by electricity; and advances in structural engineering coinciding with the growth of steel and glass manufacturing, as well as reliance on reinforced concrete during the early 1900s.

Still other developments extend far beyond factory walls and include vertical integration to achieve economies of scale essential for mass production and mass consumption; control of proprietary technology through litigious enforcement of patents; market segmentation delineated by cost and quality; industry-wide trade exhibitions; corporate branding through advertising; knowledgeable contributions to professional, trade, and popular journals—informative but often promotional as well; anticipation of obsolescence; planned worker housing; and industry consolidation.[1]

Although many of these nineteenth-century advances led to well-defined

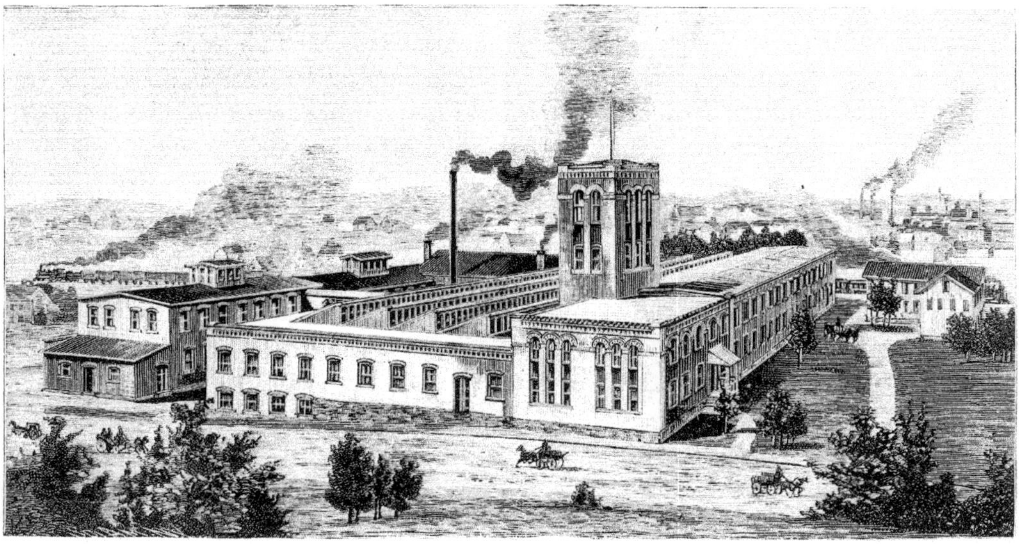

Figure 16. In 1896, editors of *Scientific American* published an illustration of the Eagle Bicycle Manufacturing Company's newly completed factory in Torrington, Connecticut, designed by Waterbury architect Theodore Peck. Peck's design combined traditional standard mill construction with an expansive one-story machine shop capped by northern roof-lights. However, the illustrator reversed the direction of the skylights' glazed facades, probably to explain the purpose of the saw-tooth roof configuration. *Scientific American* 74 (January 1896).

responses in the design of industrial buildings and complexes, and to the integration of machinery and buildings, not all belong exclusively to the second half of that century—some originate before mid-century and others continue to evolve after 1900; not all occur from one industry to the next; not all fall into sequential order within specific industries; and not all advance uniformly.

Nor, with several notable allowances, can the bicycle industry be credited with the origins of any one specific innovation on that long list. Those exceptions, however, deserve mention and include the Pope Manufacturing Company's scientific testing of steel to determine the optimum balance of strength and light weight, resulting in a reliance on fifty-carbon tubular steel (an alloy of steel having one-half of 1 percent carbon); and that company's sophisticated scripting of travel literature to promote the sale of bicycles. In addition, by introducing the commercial production of bicycles in America, Albert Pope and George Fairfield, president of the Weed company, launched America's ball-bearing industry, although credit for inventing the machines that produced those bearings efficiently belongs elsewhere. Yet the bicycle, more than any other machine in use at the time, demonstrated the inherent usefulness of ball bearings. In Chicago, the methods refined by the Western Wheel Works for stamping and pressing metal parts foretold eventual reliance on that practice by the automobile and other industries.[2]

Instead, bicycle manufacturers orchestrated nearly all those innovations into a concerted arrangement that rises to originality in manner and scope, a creative product of the astonishing public demand for bicycles. Equally important, America's industries noticed. The convergence of several key factors set the stage for that imaginative exploitation, beginning with a wheeled machine that, in one capacity, managed to capture public fascination with a promise of self-propulsion constrained by neither route nor schedule nor horsepower; but in another capacity, to spark intense curiosity among those who inclined toward mechanical invention. Rapid rise of the industry followed, encouraging entry into the industry by a host of new companies, in turn creating dogged competition and a frenzied scramble to capture a share of profits.[3]

Forging Arms into Bicycles

When Pope and Fairfield began building bicycles in Hartford, they consciously adopted America's use of precision tooling to fabricate interchangeable parts, advances that machinists in the Springfield Armory in Massachusetts had introduced during the early nineteenth century. However, not until 1851 when owners of the Robbins and Lawrence Company in Windsor, Vermont, exhibited at the Great Exhibition of the Works of Industry of all Nations at the Crystal Palace in London's Hyde Park, did the imperative of true precision tooling become widely apparent. At that exposition, the Windsor company displayed numerous disassembled rifles, with parts mixed, and invited observers to reassemble the weapons in random order. From that success, the company began exporting not only Windsor rifles but also the machine tools designed to produce those armaments.[4]

The line of connectivity from arms and precision machine tools in Windsor to bicycle manufacturing in Hartford has nary a twist nor turn. Mechanical engineer Richard Lawrence and investor Samuel Robbins formed the Robbins and Lawrence Company in 1850, a successor to an earlier partnership between Robbins, Lawrence, and gunsmith Nicanor Kendall. Listed among the company's roll of employees were gunsmith Christian Sharps, machinist and gunsmith George Fairfield, and apprentice die-sinker Charles Billings. In 1851, Lawrence and Sharps formed the Sharps Rifle Manufacturing Company, a subsidiary of the Robbins-Lawrence concern, to produce a rifle patented by Sharps. The partners acquired land in Hartford in 1852, erected a factory on Rifle Avenue (later Capitol Avenue), and established the beginnings of an industrial complex that would form the nucleus of Pope's bicycle empire three decades hence.[5]

By 1857, Fairfield and Billings also had moved to Hartford to work for the Colt Patent Firearms Manufacturing Company, which produced precision machine tools in addition to weaponry. Confronting the declining demand for armaments after the Civil War, Fairfield became founder and president of Weed Sewing Machine Company in 1866, with Billings as superintendent. The company rented the upper floors of a small Pratt and Whitney Company factory across the Park River from the Sharps complex and soon convinced the owners of the Sharps firm to produce sewing machines as well as rifles. Fairfield began acquiring land on Rifle Avenue in 1869, and in 1874 purchased the entire Sharps factory, eventually enlarging the complex. The company also acquired adjoining land in 1881—three years after Pope's bold proposal to build bicycles. Pope's company finally absorbed the Weed firm in 1890, and Ned Lawrence, the son of Richard Lawrence, served as plant superintendent during part of that transitional period.[6]

Hartford's machine tool industry sprouted immediately and quickly flourished as the bicycle's popularity grew, creating a booming industrial district along Capitol Avenue. By 1885, Fairfield had become one of the founders of the Hartford Machine Screw Company, which built its first factory on the westerly side of Pope's Capitol Avenue complex. Francis Pratt and Amos Whitney, who established the Pratt and Whitney Company, drew inspiration from the precision tools developed by both Colt and Sharps, and they expanded their factory on the easterly side of Pope's factories, along both sides of the Park River. Billings, who left the Weed company after the Civil War, collaborated with inventor Christopher Spencer to form a tool-making business, the Billings-Spencer Company, with a factory located at the corner of Russ and Lawrence Streets, two blocks from Pope's factory complex. The Hartford Machine Screw Company, Pratt and Whitney, and the Billings-Spencer Company all played key roles in the evolution of Pope's sprawling factory complexes and bicycle production.[7]

Bicycles Propel Innovation in American Industry

Three studies establish preludes for gauging bicycle manufacturers' creative orchestration of the lengthy tally of innovations owed to American industry. In his incisive 1984 study of this country's manufacturing history, *From the American System to Mass Production, 1800 to 1932*, David Hounshell credits the bicycle with contributing an important transitional chapter to that story, an industry that illuminates—but does not resolve—the complex system for mechanized assembly so essential to mass production. Hounshell's view is framed by the contributions of Pope's company and the Western Wheel Works, the latter founded by Adolph Shoeninger as the Western Toy Company but later headed by R. Lindsay Coleman, and although Hounshell credits the bicycle with several innovations, including improvements to ball bearings and to the use of electric resistance welding to join the ends of wheel rims, he argues that bicycle manufacturers simply refined the armory system, differing in degree rather than practice, and thus stopped short of revolutionizing manufacturing technology and systems of work in America.[8]

However, cycling historian and geographer Glen Norcliffe chooses a broader vantage point, likening the bicycle industry to a carrier wave—meaning an important invention that spawns related innovations, which diffuse into other closely-connected industries, and in turn cause important cultural shifts; by definition, a revolutionary consequence. To support his cogent argument that Hounshell's conclusions are understated, Norcliffe points to numerous innovations, including: selective improvements to the American System of precision-tooled interchangeable parts; advances in specialized machine tools; division of labor; the replacement of labor with automation necessitating capital investment; and the technological advances credited to the bicycle that later proved essential to the development of automobiles, including: lightweight wire wheels with tensioned spokes; tangential rather than radial spokes; pneumatic tires; wheel bearings; gears; spring suspensions; lightweight tubular frames; and various braking devices.[9]

A third, perceptive study authored by economic historian Bruce Epperson, *Peddling Bicycles to America: The Rise of an Industry*, offers additional insight, concluding that bicycle manufacturers did not pursue the goal of mass production and thus should not be judged as falling short of revolutionary advances in that context. Instead, they sought to match supply with rapidly-rising demand by building bicycles in batches, hoping to avoid the accumulation of either unused raw materials or unsold finished products, both of which idled capital. Thus, company owners focused less on economies of scale than accuracy in calculating the number of potential buyers, allowing small firms with carefully identified markets to compete with large companies.[10]

Epperson also observes that the challenges of manufacturing a product with many small parts for various models, and in batches of calculated size, added complexity and negated many of mechanized assembly's advantages. If final assembly lacked mechanization, explanation rested not in a failure to grasp the possible advantages of such a system, but rather recognition that mechanized assembly cost too much or didn't work well for the specialized nature of bicycle production.[11]

Wheel Works Idealized

The manufacture of Columbia bicycles by Pope and the Weed company in 1878 marks a logical starting point for illuminating the complex relationships among bicycle design, machine tool engineering, production systems, and factory architecture or engineering—and the roles of each in the larger orchestration of innovative practices. From that start, no aspect of production—whether bicycle, or bicycle component, or machine tools, or factory design escaped study as the industry expanded, and by July 1893—barely the start of the bicycle boom—inventors had secured roughly 3,600 patents related to bicycles or bicycle parts; one cycling historian has calculated that by 1900 that figure had risen astoundingly to as many as 11,000 patents. The architectural manifestations of those advances became evident in at least three ways: the physical form of buildings; the relationships of multiple buildings to one another; and the internal arrangements of buildings to accommodate machinery and production systems.[12]

Given the light weight and manageable size of parts and finished products, the multiple stories of standard mill construction (if cumbersome at times), posed only minor burdens for the bicycle industry, and most bicycle factories rose two or three stories in height; industrial lofts, with power typically shared by several small manufacturers, might include an additional story or two. Varying dimensions (100, 200, or 300 feet long by 50 or 60 feet wide) were common.[13]

By the spring of 1895, when *Wheel and Cycling Trade Review* published advice about "The Ideal Cycle Factory," editors had begun encouraging industry aspirants to build small factories and to purchase rather than manufacture certain parts to reduce costs, cautioning that factories erected during the industry's early years were unavoidably large to provide space for materials and machinery, thus requiring a long investment of capital. Although recommending that owners invest only an amount needed to start production and generate profits, the journal's editors also noted that new businesses could choose between low costs or high quality to compete, but they recommended the latter.[14]

For calculating the proper amount of capital outlay, editors urged owners to compare the cost of buying or fabricating each part, both finished and rough, then prioritizing that list according to cost savings. Once the cost of operations had been stabilized, the company then could maximize efficiency for the most expensive parts to produce, preferably including at least one proprietary feature to add a marque of quality to the finished bicycle. Cost savings also could be achieved by completing unfinished parts purchased in rough form.[15]

Unavoidably, certain aspects of production necessitated capital investment, for example equipment for nickel and enamel finishing, easily marred in transport; tools for brazing, thus avoiding the cost of freight for transporting unfinished frames; and labor-saving tools or machinery. Editors recommended paying labor by the piece when special skills were essential, yielding a savings to the company and higher wages to skilled workers, and observed that production units should follow one another in distance as well as time.[16]

Whether or not aspirants to the industry heeded that advice, or that offered by editors of *Cycle Age and Trade Review*, who in 1898 published a system for estimating the expense of operating a bicycle factory, numerous small or moderately sized companies began manufacturing bicycles in varying capacities. For those enterprises joining the industry as the safety-bicycle era boomed, expansion into new or larger factories often proved to be irresistible, and numerous companies repeated those steps more than once. Late arrivals sometimes remained cautious, opting to diversify and limiting production to manageable quotas. Still others remained content to produce parts.[17]

Although practices for integrating production systems varied, adequate space, light, and power became principal considerations, with labor-saving circulation managed well enough by careful organization. Factories evolved into industrial complexes as owners sequestered certain aspects of production into separate buildings, for example work requiring heat such as forging, smithing, welding, brazing, or enameling. Other detached units often included fire-proof storehouses for finished bicycles—literally vaults protecting capital needed for the following season; power plants; administrative offices; and gate houses.

Specialized Machine Tools

Invention extended not only to parts, whether to improve quality or to distinguish one company's bicycles from another's (or both), but also to the specialized machines that gave companies economic advantages. Horace Arnold, a journeyman machinist who began his career in engine and railroad shops before becoming a designer for the Pratt and Whitney Company in Hartford, provided an authoritative documentation of the bicycle's contribution to machine tool technology. Arnold turned to journalism and traveled from the Midwest to New England to study seventeen of the country's bicycle factories and, using the pen-name Hugh Dolnar, authored an instructive, thirty-one-part series for *American Machinist*. The numerical articles, which began in October 1895 and concluded in September 1896, are titled simply "Bicycle Tools."[18]

Arnold's series is an exhaustive photographic and written description of those advances, and he stressed that the rise of machinery designed exclusively for bicycle manufacturers had far outstripped that of the bicycle itself. Arnold justified the journal's decision to launch the lengthy series by proclaiming that bicycle factories were better equipped and presented more innovations in small metal manufacturing than any other shops. He also concluded that elaborate and costly special tools would continue to be introduced whenever small savings in labor could be gained. During that same period, many advertisements placed by machine tool companies in trade journals such as *American Machinist* or *Iron Age* touted only special machines being built for bicycle manufacturing, confirming Arnold's observations.[19]

Astonished by the rapid installation of specialized machine tools in bicycle works, he proclaimed that bicycles dominated the machine tool industry, but he also observed that practices and machine tools varied from city to city and from region to region. Those variations became evident in the provenance of technology, the repute of companies designing the machinery, the amount of capital invested, and the examples of comparatively simple machine tools invented by shop mechanics—inexpensive but also serviceable. Arnold highlighted two traditions in particular: the armory system developed in the Northeast; and stamping and pressing techniques developed by the Western Wheel Works. Thus, although certain commonalities existed, that all-important picture of bicycle factory interiors is by no means a uniform one. Arnold's two important points, that the bicycle craze fueled growth of the machine tool industry, and that practices employed to build bicycles varied significantly among manufacturers, are essential to any visualization of factory floors and the machine tools arranged in those spaces—one of the most challenging aspects of reconstructing cycling history in our built environments.[20]

Arnold documented a third manufacturing practice during his factory inspections (supplementing the armory and stamping methods), describing them as "home constructions." These devices represented improvised specialized machinery to meet the challenges of manufacturing an invention much in demand—contrivances sometimes roughhewn but nevertheless inexpensive and supremely functional.[21]

Aided by Arnold's written descriptions and comprehensive photographs, the inner workings of bicycle factories move into sharper focus. A second journalist-engineer, Englishman Robert Perkins, contributed to that picture with an 1895 article for *Engineering Magazine*, "A Marvel of Mechanical Achievement," which traced the technological development of the bicycle but also provided photographs of shop floors at the Liberty Cycle Manufacturing Company in Rockaway, New Jersey, where Perkins served as vice president.[22]

Departmental Factory

The versatility of standard mill construction often aided the process of orchestrating production into departments, whether well-defined by separate building or room, or less formally arranged on open floors. The small size and large number of bicycle components presented challenges, but practical considerations and the quest for cost-efficiency generally governed the allocation of factory spaces. Ultimately, decisions to segregate production departments caused a corresponding division of labor according to skill. Although many divisions created during the high-wheel era survived the transition to safety models, the advantages of automated machinery prompted shop managers to rearrange production systems frequently, exploiting yet another aspect of the versatility inherent in standard mill construction.[23]

By 1881, Pope and Fairfield already had segregated production into more than sixteen discrete departments (see Chapter 5). Pictorial and written records of the manufacturing systems and machine tools employed at the Weed works are documented by several articles, the first published in *Scientific American* in 1880, followed by *Bicycling World* in April 1881, and *Frank Leslie's Popular Monthly* in November 1881. All contain wood-block engravings, possibly crafted from photographs. Although not as pictorial, articles in the *L.A.W. Bulletin*, such as those published in February 1886 and February 1888, and catalogs published by Pope and by the few other companies manufacturing high-wheel bicycles during the 1880s, add fragments of information about bicycle manufacturing systems and machine tools during later stages of that period.[24]

At the Weed factory, workers fabricated the first high-wheel ordinaries using more than 150 different machine tools, many of them general-purpose in type such as drop-forges, grinding machines, lathes, or milling machines, which could be adjusted easily to produce a great variety of parts. The extent to which bicycle manufacturers may have introduced specialized machinery during the high-wheel era remains difficult to assess, but both the 1881 articles in *Bicycling World* and *Frank Leslie's Popular Monthly* mention a corps of machinists who designed special machinery for bicycle parts. That same year, one of Fairfield's toolmakers,

Henry T. Russell, patented several inventive dies to forge key parts of the Columbia ordinary, including wheel fellies joints, rear forks, neck and spindle blanks, and head-set blanks—the last two parts joining front forks, steering spindle, handlebars, and backbone or perch. Moreover, if factory machinists were prone to extemporaneous solutions during the safety-bicycle era, as Arnold confirms, presumably similar problem-solving occurred during the high wheel era. Elsewhere, Iver Johnson's tinkering with machine tools for high wheel bicycles supports that assumption, as does Perkins' respect for American aptness at devising special tools, particularly because he was well-positioned to compare English and American practices.[25]

Although Arnold establishes that only after the safety bicycle captured the public's imagination did the machine tool industry take full notice, some of the credit for those inventive devices also belongs to the bicycle industry's machinists who encouraged improvement. Invention flowed from overwhelming demand for bicycles by the mid–1890s, but also from continuing advances in bicycle technology and the added complexity of safety bicycles. For example, Pope's Standard Columbia contained more than 300 parts (seventy-seven solitary parts); by 1894, the Columbia safety bicycle used more than 800 total parts; the woman's model more than 1,000.[26]

The resulting demand for specialized machines capable of completing several tasks at once focused attention on the design and fabrication of specific parts; the ability to produce those parts cheaply; and the origins of subsidiary manufacturers capable of offering high-quality parts at the lowest-possible cost. However, Arnold noted that while superintendents constantly sought reductions in operating costs by purchasing more sophisticated grinding or milling machines to pare away metal efficiently, the outlays for that equipment often negated cost savings.[27]

Arnold's emphasis on varying practices among bicycle manufacturers is important because despite the thoroughness of his study, he observed only a small fraction of the hundreds of bicycle companies doing business in 1895 and 1896. Thus, only general observations are possible here, supplemented by descriptions of practices by those companies considered in subsequent chapters. For each department, the descriptions of machine tools that follow, whether general or specialized, trace developments from the high-wheel era to the safety-bicycle era during the mid–1890s; most from the latter period are drawn from the articles by Arnold and Perkins. Befuddled by the many different approaches to production that he observed, even Arnold found it difficult to compose a uniform description of exactly how skilled workers transformed raw materials into bicycles. Although descriptions of the machines designed for the fabrication of parts are unavoidably technical and much condensed here, a glimpse of bicycle factories floors becomes possible.[28]

Forge and Blacksmith Shops. During the high-wheel era, following completion of design, pattern, or model work, machinists began production of precision-tooled parts in forge or blacksmith shops. By 1881, the Weed company's forge housed a dozen large drop forges, with smaller pony or power hammers of various sizes placed in available space. An adjoining room contained cabinets for the storage of dies, which workers cut in a separate area. The largest of those dies required two men to lift, and the dies developed by Russell for the head-set blanks took six weeks to cut and finish. Forgings shaped blanks for hubs, cranks, head-sets, and front and rear forks, and the forging process occurred in several stages to minimize the amount of metal to be removed later during machine tooling. Case hardening and tempering also became necessary for some parts such as hubs, yokes (handlebars) and cranks, and by the early 1890s Pope had erected a separate shop for those purposes. By 1895, both Pratt and Whitney and Billings and Spencer advertised the ability to produce

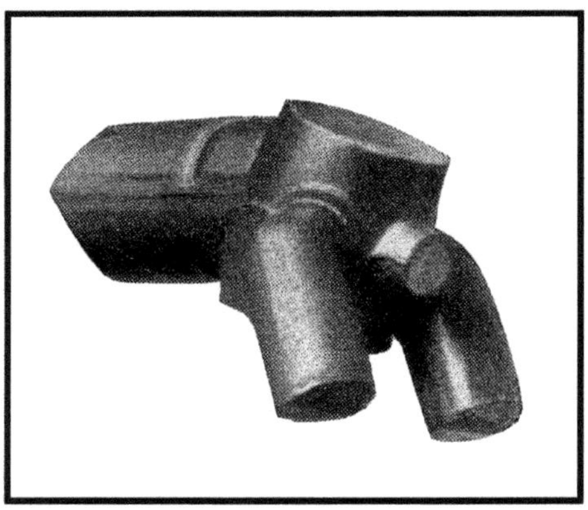

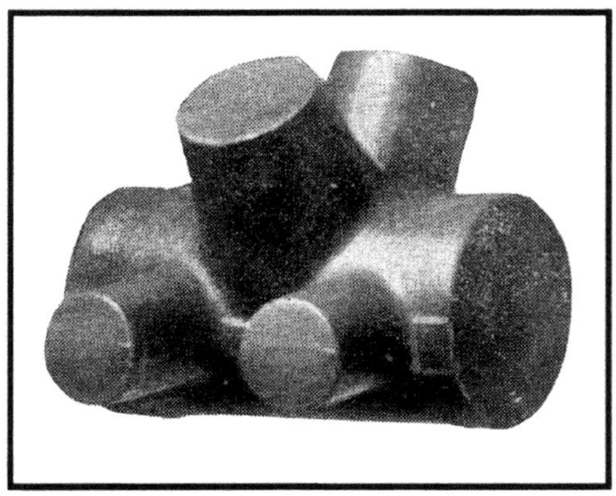

Figure 17 (*top*) and Figure 18 (*bottom*). Forge and blacksmith shop, Weed Sewing Machine Company (top). During the high-wheel era, bicycle manufacturers adopted the American System of armory manufacturing reliant on machine tooling to fabricate interchangeable parts. For bicycles, the parts that joined sections together such as front and rear forks and headsets, or the parts subject to considerable stress such as hubs, axles, and crank arms, required forging—a repetitive and alternating process of heating and pounding using dies and drop hammers. Once the molecular integrity of the metal achieved consistency, increasing its durability, precise machine tools removed extraneous metal and refined the parts. Some bicycle manufacturers, including the Iver Johnson Arms and Cycle Works (*bottom*), continued to use that practice during the safety bicycle boom. From *Scientific American* 42 (March 20, 1880) (top), with thanks to Amanda Ciampolillo, and the Iver Johnson Catalog (1897). Both are author's documents.

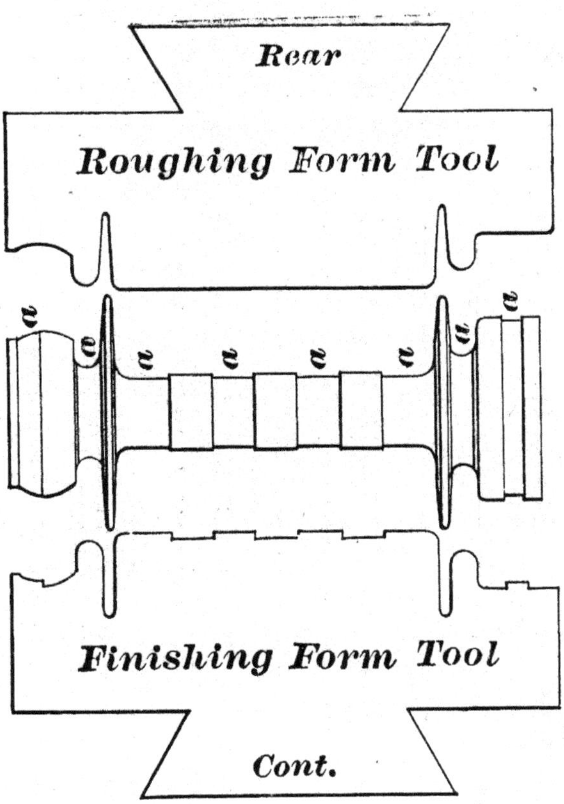

Figure 19 (*above*) and Figure 20 (*left*) Removing extraneous metal to achieve the requisite precision needed for interchangeable parts required numerous steps, leading to machines designed to perform several tasks automatically, either simultaneously or in succession, thereby reducing the cost of producing each part. The milling of hubs presented several challenges, and machine-tool companies devised different approaches. The Garvin Machine Company in New York City designed a hub-forming machine that shaped the exterior dimensions of the hub from a round bar using a spindle lathe with two simultaneous cuts, the first rough and the second finishing to produce a hub blank. *American Machinist* 19 (March 5, 1896).

complete drop-forging plants, including all necessary dies and tools.[29]

General Machine Rooms. From the forging or case-hardening shops, the blanks or castings moved to various departments where workers used various machine tools including lathes and drills as well as screw, milling, and grinding machines to cut or bore away metal to achieve the requisite precision. During the high-wheel era, Pope and the Weed company organized most aspects of production into well-defined units, including departments for hubs, spokes, ball bearings, cones and cups, bolts, nuts and screws. However, some of those departments may have been arranged in close proximity on shop floors, notably those producing parts having cylindrical form. By the mid–1890s, however, smaller companies had consolidated many of those divisions into one or two general machine rooms, such as that of the Liberty Cycle Company (see Chapter 1) devoted to small parts, which by then included sprockets, chains and the all-important crank-hanger bracket (today called a bottom bracket).

Hub Fabrication. Among the bicycle's many small parts, hubs illustrate the shift from general purpose machine tools to more specialized, automated designs. During the early 1880s, workers fabricated hubs for Columbia ordinaries by boring the centers of the forged, case-hardened blanks with drills, turning the blanks on a lathe, and then drilling small holes in the flanges for the spokes. Fifteen years later, Arnold observed four or five standard methods, giving greatest attention to the Garvin Machine Company's hub-forming machine, a powerful hollow-spindle lathe that converted round-bar stock into hub blanks, with roughing and finishing cuts completed simultaneously with two forms, one above the hub blank and one below. The hub then moved to Garvin drilling machines for rough boring, followed by lathe turning for accurate finishing of internal surfaces and threaded parts.

Figure 21 (*opposite*) and Figure 22 (*above*). Machinists then transferred the hub blank to a Garvin four-spindle bank of drilling machines (*opposite*) for rough boring, followed by finish machining on a Garvin double-turret screw machine or lathe for accurate tooling of the internal surface and threaded parts (*above*). Pratt and Whitney developed a single, specialized hub machine that combined the steps required by three Garvin machines into an automated succession of steps to produce a finished hub, other than a counter bore at one end. Amos Whitney prohibited engineer-journalist Horace Arnold from publishing a description of its internal workings. *American Machinist* 19 (March 5, 1896).

Pratt and Whitney also produced specialized hub machines, but Amos Whitney restricted Arnold to a photograph and to explanation that the machine produced a completed hub, other than finishing the counter bore at one end.[30]

The Pratt and Whitney machine was likely an improvement to the company's standard screw machines developed under the guidance of William Wallace Tucker, one of the city's well-known machinists and inventors who had begun working for the company in 1861. Initially foreman of the screw machine department, Tucker expanded that business from small beginnings and patented numerous labor-saving devices that earned him acclaim from bicycle manufacturers.[31]

At the Lozier works in Thompsonville, Connecticut, workers demonstrated a third system, using "Spencer Automatic" screw machines manufactured by Pratt and Whitney under contract with the Hartford Machine Screw Company. The Spencer machines made the full outside cuts to give the hub its shape, bored a hole through the middle, and formed one of the ball-bearing chambers at one end. Machinists then moved the hubs to another Pratt and Whitney screw machine for final tooling, followed by shaving and polishing on lathes.[32]

By contrast, Gormully and Jeffery produced hubs using a fourth method, from a solid bar of steel turned on a lathe in twenty-one separate steps, presumably including drilling, which yielded a uniform concentricity that hubs fabricated from drop-forged blanks on screw machines could not achieve, thus justifying the higher cost of so many steps. Both the Western Wheel Works and the Sterling Cycle Manufacturing Company employed a fifth method reliant on presses, cutting and drawing dies to form tubes from sheet metal strips, followed by brazing, and then built-up with drawn or cup-flanged collars, also brazed.[33]

Shops also used various methods to drill spoke holes in the hubs, ranging from single-spindle drills operated by hand to banks of single-spindle automatic drills, to widely used, multi-spindle automatic drills manufactured by Pratt and Whitney. Some companies such as the St. Nicholas Manufacturing Company in Chicago (St. Nicholas bicycles) improvised by designing their own machines with automatic feeds and automatic indexing, serviceable as well as inexpensive. Similarly, practices varied for fashioning the cups and cones to seal hub ends or secure ball-bearing chambers.[34]

Ball-Bearings. As early as 1869, European inventors had introduced ball bearings to the design of velocipedes, and by 1878 patents protected bearing devices in use on English high-wheel bicycles, most relying on a single row of balls in some type of threaded, coned case. In America, Fairfield and Pope initially copied the English bicycles, likely cutting short lengths of case-hardened iron rod and turning them by hand on lathes. Between 1886 and 1901 George Simonds of Fitchburg, Massachusetts, patented rolling machines with dies that could produce up to 18,000 bearings per day, and by 1895 Arnold had concluded that all bicycle manufacturers were purchasing ball bearings from one of three concerns: Simonds Rolling Machine Company; the Excelsior Machine Company in Buffalo; or the Cleveland Machine Screw Company. Pope eventually lost patent infringement litigation with Simonds, who then licensed his machines to Pope. Arnold also identified laborious methods used by several companies to gauge the accuracy of ball-bearings, including hand-sorting by women at the Lozier works, at a rate of 6,000 ball-bearings per day with payment by the piece.[35]

Pedals. By the early 1880s, ball bearings had improved the efficiency of pedals, as well, and by the end of that decade pedal design had achieved uniformity. By the mid–1890s, automated machinery also had reached that corner of bicycle factories, and the Langelier Manufacturing Company of Providence developed two different machines: one for simultaneously facing and counterboring both ends of the pedal hubs for ball-bearing cases; the second, a drill press to bore and cut to size the four arms of pedal hubs.[36]

Sprockets. Among small parts, Arnold found that sprockets generated the greatest variations in fabrication techniques and machine tools, including casting; drop-forging; milling machines; screw machines; turning on lathes; punching from sheet metal using turret machines; two-stage presses (roughing and shaving) with perfect results but at high initial cost; or cutting on vertical profiling machines; teeth also could be shaped on gear cutters. Emphasis on some specialized machine tools such as milling machines led to a greater number of cutting edges brought into simultaneous action on pieces of limited size, thus reducing production steps. For example, the Warwick Cycle Manufacturing Company turned to F.E. Reed and Company in Worcester to supply a modified Lincoln milling machine, the latter representing an important advance in machine tooling for firearms during the mid–1850s and developed by the Lincoln Foundry and Machine Company in Pittsburgh.[37]

Chains. Although various models of high-wheel bicycles and tricycles used chain drive in one form or another, rather than direct front-wheel drive, safety bicycles added a new and challenging element to the manufacturing process. Those bicycle companies making chains typically produced one or two types, block or roller, both developed by a Swiss engineer, Hans Renold, during the 1880s. Complex in fabrication, demanding in accuracy, and usually requiring considerable hand-labor, chains confirmed the wisdom offered by editors of *Wheel and Cycling Trade Review* who discouraged industry entrants from producing parts that could be purchased less expensively elsewhere. The Indianapolis Chain and Stamping Company became one of the country's largest chain producers and relied on a battery of automatic block drilling, reaming and counterboring machines (a single machine) designed by the Woodruff Manufacturing Company in Hartford in 1894.[38]

Generally, machinists cut chain blocks from steel bars drawn to shape by Lincoln milling machines, or cut side links from sheet-metal strips. By the mid–1890s, inventors had transformed the riveting process by developing machines that spun rather than hammered rivets, and another Hartford business, the L.E. Rhodes Company, had developed a versatile machine that automatically headed the rivets notwithstanding variations in distances between each rivet. The extent of automation varied from company to company, but hand assembly dominated at the Lozier shops at the time of Arnold's inspection, with much of the assembly paid by the piece, under rigorous inspection to acceptable margins of 0.001 inch for chain parts and exacting pitch (the distance between drive links). Following riveting, Lozier's workers straightened the chains with mallets and then loaded them into wooden tumblers for polishing.[39]

Frames. Hand work also governed frame assembly during both the high-wheel and safety bicycle eras. At the Columbia works in Hartford, assembly of high-wheel bicycles required joining the backbone or perch, shaped from cold-drawn seamless steel tubes, to the arm of the forged steering head, followed by brazing of that coupling. Workers welded the front forks to the arms extending downward from that steering head, and also welded rear forks to the base of the backbone. Forged units and drawn tubes were sturdy enough to permit threading, and parts fit together sturdily, if at the expense of weight.[40]

However, the increasingly light gauge

of tubes together with the large number of tube sections, joints with lugs, and brackets required for safety bicycle frames added complexity to the assembly process, which depended entirely upon skilled labor for the exacting tasks of brazing and truing frames. Companies resorted to various types of brazing furnaces and placed those heating units in any of several locations but usually near frame fitting and filing. Excluding frame jigs and various milling machines used to cut and burr tubes to length, specialized machine tools contributed very little to the frame-assembly process.[41]

However, the quest to control the quality of brazing and the resulting uniformity of the brazing process developed by Pope in Hartford yielded what may have been bicycle manufacturers' closest approximation of assembly-line production during this period, albeit non-mechanized. Workers placed the frame's seven tubular units in a jig mounted on a wheeled table and served by a stationary drill spindle. The jig held the frame units in a true horizontal position while workers drilled pin holes through the joints and tubes and then drove temporary wire pins through the holes to secure the frame during brazing. Attendants

then shuttled the frame through a series of twenty brazing stations (one for each frame joint), each station's cast iron top fitted with a V-shaped notch to accept a specific joint. Two braziers usually managed each station, working simultaneously and using the minimum of heat and spelter compound of brass, copper, tin, and zinc required to secure a solid joint. Attendants quickly wiped away the still-hot excess spelter, thus avoiding the added step of cleaning with sandblast and minimizing finish filing.[42]

Pope's process of moving product to worker exemplifies the type of instinctive response to evolving product design and increasing competition that led to the improved integration of factory and manufacturing systems. For his part, Arnold proclaimed the brazing process in Hartford to be superior in cleanliness, uniformity, and efficiency to any he had seen, and he also commended the company's frame-truing fixtures as magnificent examples of the art of improvisational tool making.[43]

The evolving design and complexity of safety-bicycle frames led to another

Figure 23 (*opposite*) and Figure 24 (*above*). Assembling frames in true required skilled hand work and the use of jigs to hold frame parts in place before drilling and pinning to secure the frame prior to brazing. Companies often devised their own methods of frame assembly and jig design, and in Hartford, the Pope Manufacturing Company used wheeled carriages to move the frames pinned in jigs to a succession of brazing stations, each station configured for a specific frame joint. The process in Hartford represented one of the bicycle industry's few instances of moving parts to stationary workers via a mechanical (wheeled) device during this period, a rudimentary precursor to assembly line production. *American Machinist* 19 (August 6, 1896, and November 19, 1896).

adaptation to the manufacturing process, that of fabricating the joints, brackets, lugs or sleeves required to assemble the tube sections into a completed frame. Among those parts, the bottom bracket or crank hanger best demonstrated the inefficiency of the armory forging process because the solid forged unit required excessive drilling, boring, and reaming to create the hollow section for the crank and its bearings, as well as the hollow tubular openings to receive the seat tube, down tube, and chain stays; ultimately, machinists removed about 80 percent of the metal in that part. As emphasis on minimizing bicycle weight grew, forged parts earned another demerit.[44]

In Chicago, however, the Western Wheel Works shifted to a process of punching, cupping, pressing, and stamping of thin sheet steel using a series of steps with die-presses, each pass followed by annealing to restore metallurgical integrity, followed by the cutting of teeth on a milling machine for parts such as sprockets; the process concluding with brazing or electric resistance welding. By the mid–1890s, the company had adopted that process to produce most of the parts for its Crescent bicycles, including bottom brackets, and had pioneered a dramatic shift from the armory tradition. By the close of that decade, even Pope had implemented the practice for some parts, and Arnold acknowledged that the best stamped joints, cheaper than solid joints, could be considered high-quality components.[45]

Fabrication of Wheel Rims and Spokes, and Wheel Assembly. The bicycle's arrival depended greatly on a novel awakening concerning the design of wheels. Paradoxically, wire wheels with thin rims and a sufficient number of delicate spokes secured in tension are structurally more efficient than typical carriage wheels with heavy rims and spokes that function entirely in compression, the former capable of achieving a requisite load capacity with far less material and weight. Thus, the large, tensioned, lightweight spider wheel, patented by French mechanic and racer Eugene Meyer in 1868, assured the full potential of two-wheeled balance during the high-wheel era.[46]

In their meticulous study of the bicycle's technical evolution, *Bicycle Design: An Illustrated History*, cycling historians Tony Hadland and Hans-Erhard Lessing, the latter also a physicist, analyze the structure of Meyer's invention, explaining

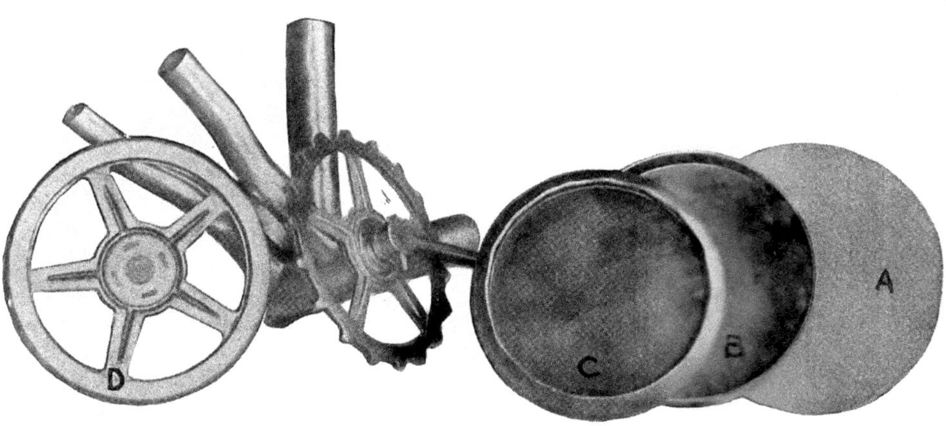

Figure 25. In Chicago, the Western Wheel Works fashioned sprockets with several stages of punching, cupping, pressing, and stamping, followed by the cutting of teeth on a milling machine. *American Machinist* 19 (September 17, 1896).

that tension-spoked wheels function in suspension, with the load-distributing hub hanging from the connection of rim and upward spoke rather than supported in compression from the downward spoke. The tension of additional spokes prevents distortion of the rim as the load absorbed by the wheel hub is transferred to the ground. Despite its advanced design, Meyer's driving wheel often succumbed to broken spokes, which were configured radially and thus vulnerable to flexing stresses caused by force exerted from pedal strokes. In 1870, Englishmen James Starley and William Hillman improved Meyer's design by aligning spokes tangent to, or parallel with, the rider's driving thrust and thus minimized spoke failure. The Ariel bicycle with tangent spokes produced by Starley and Hillman helped to elevate the elegant high-wheel bicycle to its remarkably advanced state of engineering during the 1880s.[47]

Yet even with such fundamental advances, the bicycle wheel continued to evolve, whether from efforts to adapt to the revolutionary introduction of pneumatic tires or, instead, simply to perfect the wheel's many intricate parts—hubs, cones, bearings, spokes, connections, felloes or rims, and tires. Arnold acknowledged the complexity of wheel manufacture, a process exacerbated by the shifting preferences for wood and metal rims during the mid–1890s, by the industry's varying practices, heavy reliance on hand labor, and the demands of experimentation. Consequently, only Arnold's two central themes remain constant: first, the economic law of hand labor dictating that conversion to automated machine work lowered product costs, leading to many types of specialty machines; and second, the ingenuity of American machinists concerning both manufacturing methods and mechanical problems, the former to improve the bicycle and the latter to improve the machines that produced the bicycle's numerous parts.[48]

Many of the specialty machines developed for wheel production modified existing technology to meet the specific demands of the bicycle, for instance the use of rolling mills developed by the iron industry and adapted to shape wheel rims. Cycling's inventors soon modified those mills to fabricate several crescent-shaped rims capable of securing the round, solid rubber tires for high wheels without stretching off the rim, all the while providing space for the spoke connection and its washer beneath the tire. By 1886, Pope had shifted to imported seamless tubes for wheel felloes, rolled into a hollow crescent form. Gormully and Jeffery machinists responded to the development of pneumatic tires for safety bicycles by devising a complex set of five rolling mills, each a separate machine, requiring separate passes to shape thin, narrow flats of steel into trough-shaped rims with intricately curled edges to secure the detachable outer tire firmly, but also to permit its easy removal for repair or replacement of the inner tube. Arnold also marveled that the mills could be adjusted to roll the rim to any desired diameter.[49]

In a few instances, companies turned to advanced technology for certain aspects of wheel production—for example, Pope's use of electric resistance welding to join rim ends. However, Arnold devoted most of his attention to the brazing methods still used for that same purpose by Gormully and Jeffery in 1895, the rim ends overlapping with scarf joints.[50]

Among the many inventive specialty machines that Arnold documented, he seemed especially impressed by automatic rim-drillers, which improved the accuracy and speed of drilling angled spoke holes in both metal and wooden rims. Safety bicycles rims, with as many as thirty-two holes, required accurate spacing of spoke holes; a correct angle of the hole in relation to the corresponding hole on the hub; countersinking for the spoke

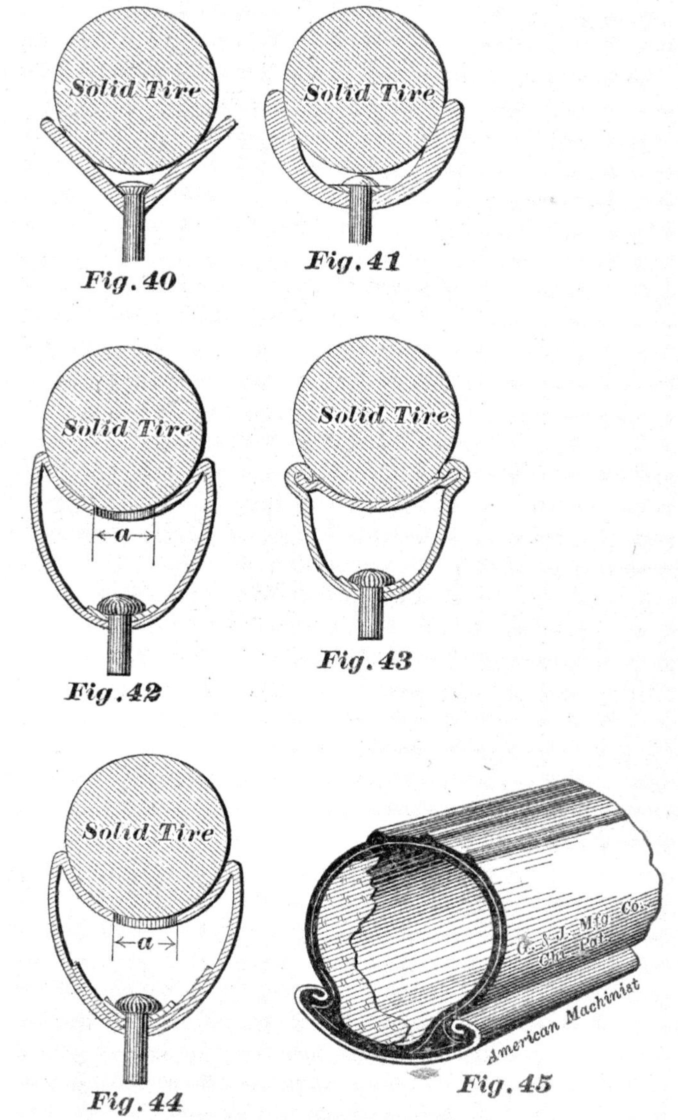

nipple washer; and a separate and larger valve-stem hole. Variations in wheel sizes and the general intricacy of tangent spoking, which demanded a uniformly recurrent sequence of four holes, each at a distinct angle different from the angle of any other hole in that group of four, added complexity.[51]

The Wilmarth and Mormon Company in Grand Rapids, Michigan, designed a machine with four adjustable spindles capable of drilling at the four different angles required for tangent spokes, needing only a single turn of the wheel; the spindles also could be adjusted for radial spokes. In addition, the company added a fifth spindle for the valve-stem, the only machine observed by Arnold to do so, and placed the machine's capacity at 800 to 1,000 rims during a ten-hour period.[52]

Arnold commended two other machines, one manufactured by the Rudolphe and Krummel

Figure 26. To manufacture wheels, bicycle companies turned to technology developed by the iron industry to shape metal, primarily rolling mills requiring multiple passes, often accompanied by heating or annealing, or both. However, the many intricate parts of bicycle wheels added to the complexity of wheel manufacture, and inventors created machines to meet the specific demands of wheel fabrication and assembly. Evolution in the design of rolling mills for the metal rims of high-wheel bicycles began with angles (Fig. 40); followed by crescent rims better to secure solid tires (Fig. 41); followed by seamless tubes rolled into a crescent shape with hole drilled to accommodate the washer for the spoke nipple, thus separating the spoke nipple from the tire but also weakening the rim (Fig. 42); a two-piece crescent rim that eliminated the washer hole (Fig. 43); followed by a seamless tube rolled into crescent shape but reinforced at the spoke nipple with brazed stock, a design patented by Englishman Thomas Warwick (Fig. 44); followed by a wheel rim of sheet steel for detachable pneumatic tires, with hooked edges to secure the outer tire firmly before inflating the inner tube, a design developed by Gormully and Jeffery in Chicago. *American Machinist* 18 (November 14, 1895).

shop in Chicago, and the other designed and built by Willis J. Perkins for his company in Grand Rapids, Michigan. The former, commissioned by the Sterling Cycle Company to speed the process of wheel production at their works, employed two spindles but introduced a device to adjust spindle angles and distance, making it the only two-spindle machine in the industry capable of drilling two adjacent holes and thus complete rim drilling in a single turn of the wheel for radial spokes. Although drilling for tangent spokes required reversing the wheel for a second pass, the machine also became the industry's only machine capable of either single or double-pass drilling. Rudolphe and Krummel continued to improve the design of their rim-driller with a sophisticated indexing mechanism, estimating capacity at 600 rims in ten hours.[53]

Arnold reserved special praise for the Perkins machine, calling it an original conception and a mechanical novelty, the only machine he studied capable of perfectly uniform work. Perkins devised a system that automatically varied the angle of a single drill spindle for every hole drilled, doing so in a regular sequence of changes guided by specially designed cams. The machine also could drill valve-stem holes with a separate spindle. Perkins demonstrated that his machine could drill a thirty-two-hole rim in forty seconds, with

Figure 27. Machinists faced special challenges when drilling spoke and valve holes in rims. Tangent spoking demanded a uniformly recurrent sequence of four holes, each at a distinct angle different from the angle of any other hole in that group of four. Automatic rim-drillers developed by Perkins and Company in Grand Rapids, Michigan, provided the requisite accuracy and speed, as well as reducing the tedium of drilling as many as thirty-two holes in each rim for safety bicycles. *American Machinist* 19 (March 26, 1896).

a daily capacity of 1400 rims with one operator managing two machines simultaneously. An especially skilled operator who could manage six machines concurrently could increase that capacity to 3,600 rims per day.[54]

Transformative Factory

With a better understanding of the machines designed to fabricate bicycle parts, only briefly sampled in this chapter, and a clearer picture of the methods employed to assemble bicycles, we can join the analysis developed by Hounshell, Norcliffe, and Epperson concerning criteria to determine when and how technological inventiveness precipitates revolutionary change, and whether the bicycle satisfied such criteria in the context of American industrial history. From the spark of awareness that mastering two-wheeled balance could transform personal mobility, the bicycle rolled into nearly every sector of American society. Bicycle manufacturers pursued technological inventiveness to the fullest in every aspect of design and production, and one ingenious improvement after another guided the bicycle's evolution, with many of those inventions transforming other sectors of American manufacturing. Ironically, Arnold complained that inventors were designing new bicycle machines so rapidly that the length of time he needed to study bicycle factories made some of the devices he described redundant before publication of the year-long series had ended.[55]

Context is an equally important criterium. Measuring the bicycle industry's contributions by turning to later manufacturers who perfected other industrial systems, for example mechanized assembly-lines to achieve mass production, and who in turn revolutionized American industry, gives too little consideration to the objectives, demands, constraints, and many other factors that influenced development of the bicycle industry decades before. A far better standard would be the extent to which bicycle manufacturers consistently met their objectives through progressive, technological and strategic invention, and the extent to which others who followed borrowed from those advances, whether specifically or as part of collective knowledge. In the chapters that follow, the descriptions of factory interiors and patented improvements to bicycle design enlarge that context.

3

Overman Wheel Company

Chicopee and Chicopee Falls, Massachusetts

Stories about the companies devoted to the manufacture of bicycles, and about the factories where production whirred, can tell us much about that industry's two-decade era of phenomenal growth and precipitous decline: the speed with which companies organized, entered into construction contracts, and erected factories in time to secure a share of seasonal production; the relationships among company owners and local governments—and the optimistic concessions often granted by the latter; the intense competition among company owners—some of them self-serving but others idealistic; the shifts in production methods as the industry matured—and the frequent efforts to refine manufacturing systems by improving industrial space; the challenges faced by many small concerns trying to sustain loyalty among local cyclists; and the ever-present financial manipulations and contrivances that contributed to the industry's rapid downfall.

The saga of the Albert H. Overman and the Overman Wheel Company is apropos, partly because it establishes a chronology of the industry's rise and fall during the late nineteenth and early twentieth centuries; partly because it involves several of the industry's principal protagonists and their conflicts; partly because it illustrates much of the context into which the stories of other companies and their owners can be placed; and partly because one of America's three or four surviving buildings in which the manufacture of high-wheel bicycles took place is linked to Overman's company and to several other bicycle manufacturers.

Ames Manufacturing Company and Victor Bicycles

The interconnected mills of the Ames Manufacturing Company in Chicopee (also called Chicopee Center) offer a perfect starting point for touring the bicycle industry's surviving nineteenth-century manufactories. The rows of narrow buildings—most of which date from 1847 to 1870 and are thus among the oldest surviving works adapted to bicycle production—represent archetypal standard mill construction at mid-century. Many of the buildings are credited to Charles McClallan, who at age seventeen began working as an apprentice bricklayer in nearby Springfield and developed into an accomplished builder-designer of industrial works, one of New England's most important. His large firm, McClallan and Son, erected numerous mills in Chicopee, Chicopee Falls, Holyoke, and South Hadley Falls, but also engaged in the construction of other building types, including commercial blocks; workers' housing; masonry dams; power canals; railroad contracts; and residential commissions.[1]

Figure 28. Former Ames Manufacturing Company mills, Chicopee, Massachusetts, c. 1984, prior to rehabilitation for housing. Traces of the Overman Automobile Company sign painted on the façade are visible. Courtesy Massachusetts Historical Commission, MHC No. CHI.A.

McClallan's mills in Chicopee are characterized by unpretentious brick façades dominated by regiments of moderately-small windows, most with stone windowsills and flat stone lintels. The primary elevation fronts a power canal and is punctuated by a prominent tower and belfry, the latter embellished by arches and elaborate brick corbelling. The tower is functional, providing access to upper stories for workers and materials (and separation from open floors in the event of fire), but its crowning belfry is both practical and symbolic, a very visible counterpoint to the spires of the city's churches and one proclaiming reward to the industrious—its bell tolling a secular, workday pilgrimage by laborers.[2]

Several of the buildings' features also reveal the evolving design of American factories. When built, many of the Ames shops stood three stories tall with steeply-pitched gable roofs. However, fourth stories added later to several of the mills increased floor space but reduced fire hazards by replacing the gable roofs with low-pitched, nearly flat roofs favored by factory mutual insurance companies. Facades of the Ames mills also display floor-beam anchor bolts and plates, designed to secure the beams to brick walls and to prevent the loosening of those joints by the vibrations or oscillations of heavy machinery. The designs of those anchor bolts and floor-beam pockets also evolved to prevent the collapse of walls caused by failure of beams during fire.

The buildings, adapted to apartments in 1985, are well preserved and orderly in appearance, the current owners having vanquished the grit, clutter, pollution, and wear that attended industrialization and its corresponding urban transformation. Nevertheless, that same orderliness offers a valuable glimpse of American industry's water-powered beginnings during the early nineteenth century, a period accompanied by disciplined ingenuity and idealism that today is often forgotten. The surviving buildings in Chicopee also call attention to the sometimes-unavoidable tension between hopeful aspiration and the drudgery of day-to-day labor. Yet the principal value of the Chicopee buildings in the context of cycling history is that one of the country's most important bicycle firms, the Overman Wheel Company, established its manufacturing division at the Ames mill complex in 1882, before relocating to nearby Chicopee Falls and there erecting an impressive factory complex.

Nathan Peabody Ames, patriarch of an edge-tool business founded in Chelmsford, Massachusetts, relocated to Chicopee in 1828 and began manufacturing swords for the United States government. His sons, Nathan Peabody Ames, Jr., and James Tyler Ames, expanded the manufactory to produce an array of implements, including cutlery, lathes, water wheels and turbines, and castings for bronze statuary. Between 1836 and 1860, the company erected many of its principal buildings including several three-story machine shops fronting the Chicopee Power Canal, and foundries for both brass and iron. Production burgeoned during the Civil War, bolstered by government contracts for swords, light artillery, and ordnance, and the company continued to enlarge its works following that conflict, adding fourth stories to the machine shops. However, the firm's economic prospects ebbed, and the advent of bicycles during the early 1880s proved timely.[3]

Albert H. Overman arrived in Chicopee at this precise moment, a very energetic but also idiosyncratic figure, most often recalled as the dogged rival of Albert Pope and as the outmatched adversary of baseball hero Albert G. Spalding. Born in Normal, Illinois, in 1850, Overman worked for a Chicago publishing and stationer house, Janson, McClurg and Company, before succumbing to the roll of the wheel and its manufacture. Seeking skilled machinists, he journeyed to Hartford and with assistance from local investors chartered the Overman Wheel Company in February 1882. In April of that year, armed with patents assigned to him by inventor James McKenzie of Galesburg, Illinois, Overman announced plans to produce a high-quality tricycle (see illustration on page 5), the Victor, to be built by the Ames Company and finished with a superior enameling process licensed by an English firm headed by John Harrington. During the fall of 1883, Overman moved his administrative offices to Chicopee Falls to simplify production, and the following fall announced plans to produce a Victor high-wheel bicycle to be available in the spring of 1885. In February of that same year, he also moved the general office and sales rooms to Tremont Street in Boston, and not quite two years later, January 1887, announced the arrival of the Victor safety bicycle that coming spring, touted for its spring fork to reduce vibrations during the days before pneumatic tires.[4]

By then, Overman had created an amicable business relationship with Edward C. Hodges, a wealthy Bostonian and one of cycling's Old Guard, who had begun publishing *Bicycling World* and who shared Overman's antipathy toward Albert Pope, especially the latter's efforts to enforce royalties from various patents, including those involving ball bearings. Hodges became a shareholder in Overman's company, and his journal, aided by revenue from Overman's advertising, launched salvos in Pope's direction, tilting editorial columns in favor of Overman's

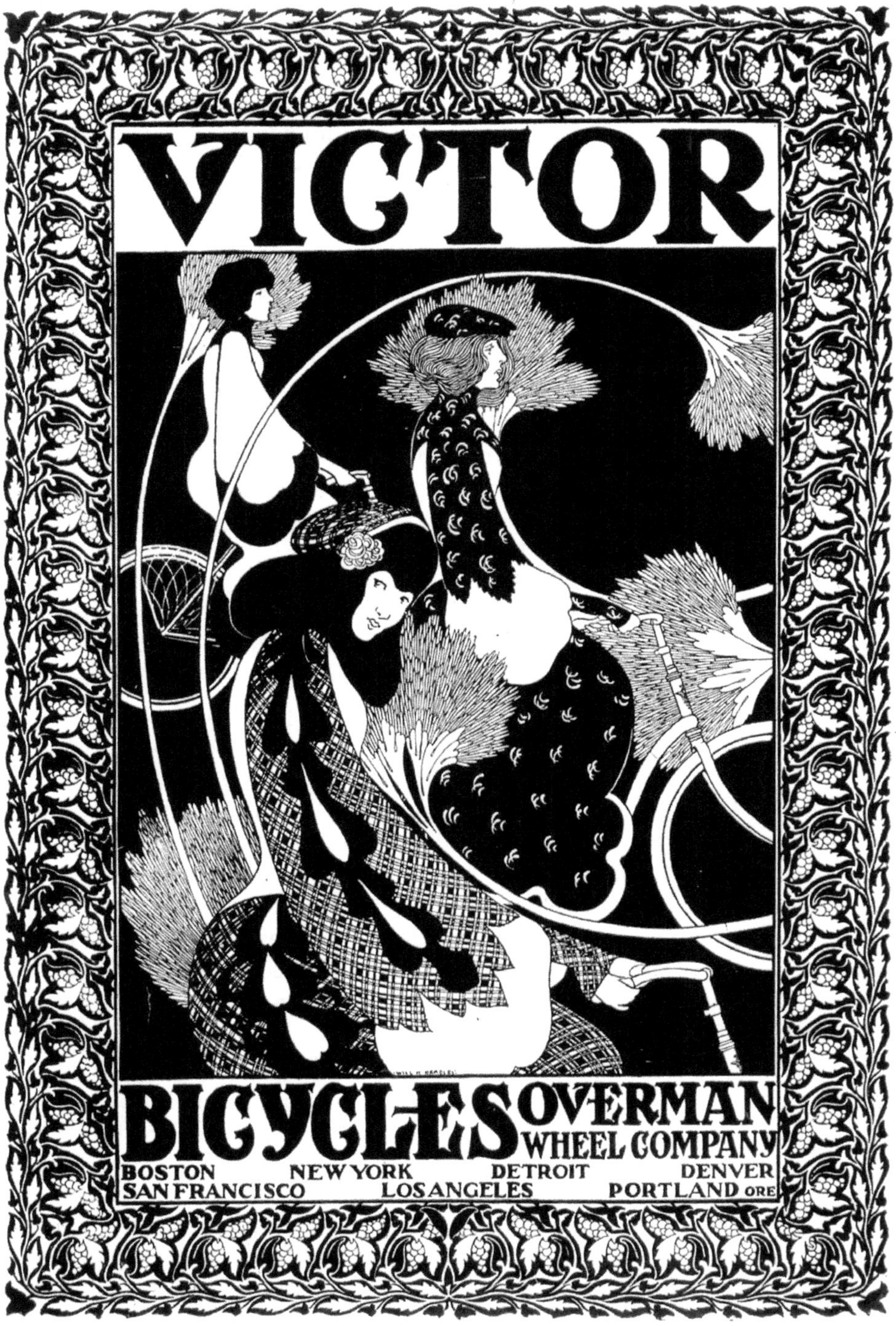

Figure 29. Overman Wheel Company catalog, Victor bicycles, 1896. Intense competition among bicycle companies prompted similarly intensive advertising strategies, extending to the elaborate design of catalogs. Courtesy the Lyman and Merrie Wood Museum of Springfield History, Springfield, MA.

business and calling Pope's tactics "wholesale oppression." Those complicated patent imbroglios erupted into litigation involving Pope, Overman, and the country's third major bicycle manufacturer during this period, the Gormully and Jeffery firm. In February 1886, Pope attached all the property of Overman's business in Chicopee, including the bicycles and parts being fabricated at the Ames Company mills, halting production for Ames as well as Overman. Although the litigants settled their dispute in June of that year, after considerable cost to each, the personal enmity that had begun when Overman trespassed in Hartford became permanently etched.[5]

Overman's production remained in Chicopee Center only until 1887, the year he moved to nearby Chicopee Falls, where he first leased and then purchased the factory of the Massachusetts Screw Company. He soon demolished most of that plant, and in 1888 retained the architectural and engineering firm of D.H. Tower and A.B. Tower of Holyoke to design a five-story brick factory in its place, completed by 1889. Long before Overman's commission, David Tower and his younger brother Ashley had developed a very successful practice specializing in the design of paper mills, and Ashley, who had served as city engineer in Holyoke, would later form a partnership with Joseph Wallace in New York City. Overman must have been pleased with the results because the following year he erected a second factory, in turn followed by a third, equally commanding structure in 1892; builders D.G. Canty and M.E. Cummings guided much of that construction, none of which survives. Whether through foresight, or just as likely backward glances at Pope's contemporaneous acquisition and expansion of the Weed Sewing Machine works, Overman had positioned his company well to meet the growing demand for safety bicycles. Moreover, his obsessive concern for quality and his determination to manufacture most of the parts for Victor bicycles helped to elevate his company's reputation, even among his detractors.[6]

Overman's departure from Chicopee left a substantial void at the Ames plant, and the company turned to the manufacture of other bicycles or bicycle parts, including King high-wheel safety bicycles in 1886 or 1887, using patents granted to the Rev. Homer King, founder of the King Wheel Company in New York City; New Mail bicycles in 1887 for dealer William

Figure 30. Overman Wheel Company works at Chicopee Falls, designed by Holyoke architects David Tower and Ashley Tower in three phases, 1889, 1890, and 1892. None of the buildings has survived. *Scientific American* 64 (May 1891).

Read & Son in Boston; Eagle bicycles for the Eagle Bicycle Manufacturing Company in Stamford, Connecticut, in 1889; Sylph bicycles for Rouse, Hazard and Company in Peoria, Illinois; and Credenda bicycles for the A.G. Spalding and Brothers concern. The firm also produced several models with the Ames insignia. Although the company diversified and began manufacturing sewing machines, financial difficulties continued and forced the sale of all but the Ames Sword Company in 1898.[7]

As the bicycle boom resounded, Overman profited from the capacity of his new factories. However, sharp competition quickly developed, and with a watchful eye on Pope, who late in 1889 had established the Hartford Cycle Company to produce a less expensive model, Overman in 1890 formed a seemingly strategic, long-term partnership with Spalding, part-owner of the successful sporting goods concern in Chicago. Spalding, who became vice-president of Overman's company, agreed to serve as the firm's western sales agent and to acquire a substantial percentage of Overman's annual production of Victor bicycles, offering protection against price discounts and paying a hefty share of advertising expenses. As part of the arrangement, Overman engaged the Lamb Knitting Machine Company (little more than a block away in Chicopee Falls) to produce lower-priced bicycles—the Credenda—for Spalding, who intended to market them to children as well as adults.[8]

Probably from the outset of that agreement, or at least soon after, Spalding recognized the benefit of shifting both his company's skate manufactory in Newark and its gymnasium factory in Philadelphia to Chicopee, thus consolidating diversified production year-round at a single location. With those long-term objectives in mind, Spalding began to acquire a controlling interest in the knitting machine concern and in October 1893, publicized reorganization of the business as the Lamb Manufacturing Company. Spalding also had realized that manufacturing his own bicycles would be more profitable than selling Victors, and by the time of his announcement (which mentioned plans for a full line of safety bicycles that eventually included a "Spalding Special" for $125), Spalding already had resigned from Overman's company. Exactly when Overman noticed the competition emerging practically next-door is unclear, but at the end of the 1893 season, Spalding complained about being overstocked with unsold Victors, most likely because he had focused on marketing the less-expensive Credendas produced by Lamb. Not wanting to sell the previous year's Victor models in 1894, he sought to return the bicycles to Overman at a discounted price, but the latter refused.

If Overman had been slow to assess his predicament, Spalding's strategy soon became apparent. He opted to disregard the contract and matter-of-factly offered the unsold bicycles to dealers at marginal prices, undermining the prospects for Overman's sales in 1894; he also refused to accept new models, leaving Overman without a western agent. Adding insult to injury, Overman's foreman, E.P. Edmans, accepted a job with the new rival. With few other options available, Overman initiated a lawsuit in April 1894, but one that the company never resolved successfully. A few days later, in a vain gesture of pique, Overman announced a new department for manufacturing sporting goods, including Victor baseballs, and advertised them as locally made.[9]

Overman's stubborn nature also led him astray in other ways. Although he readily pointed to the success of racers who used his bicycles, he refused to support a professional racing team, noting that "Victor riders, fast or slow, pay for their machines." His impressive works in Chicopee Falls carried considerable debt, a factor of increasing importance as prices and markets for bicycles began to fluctuate

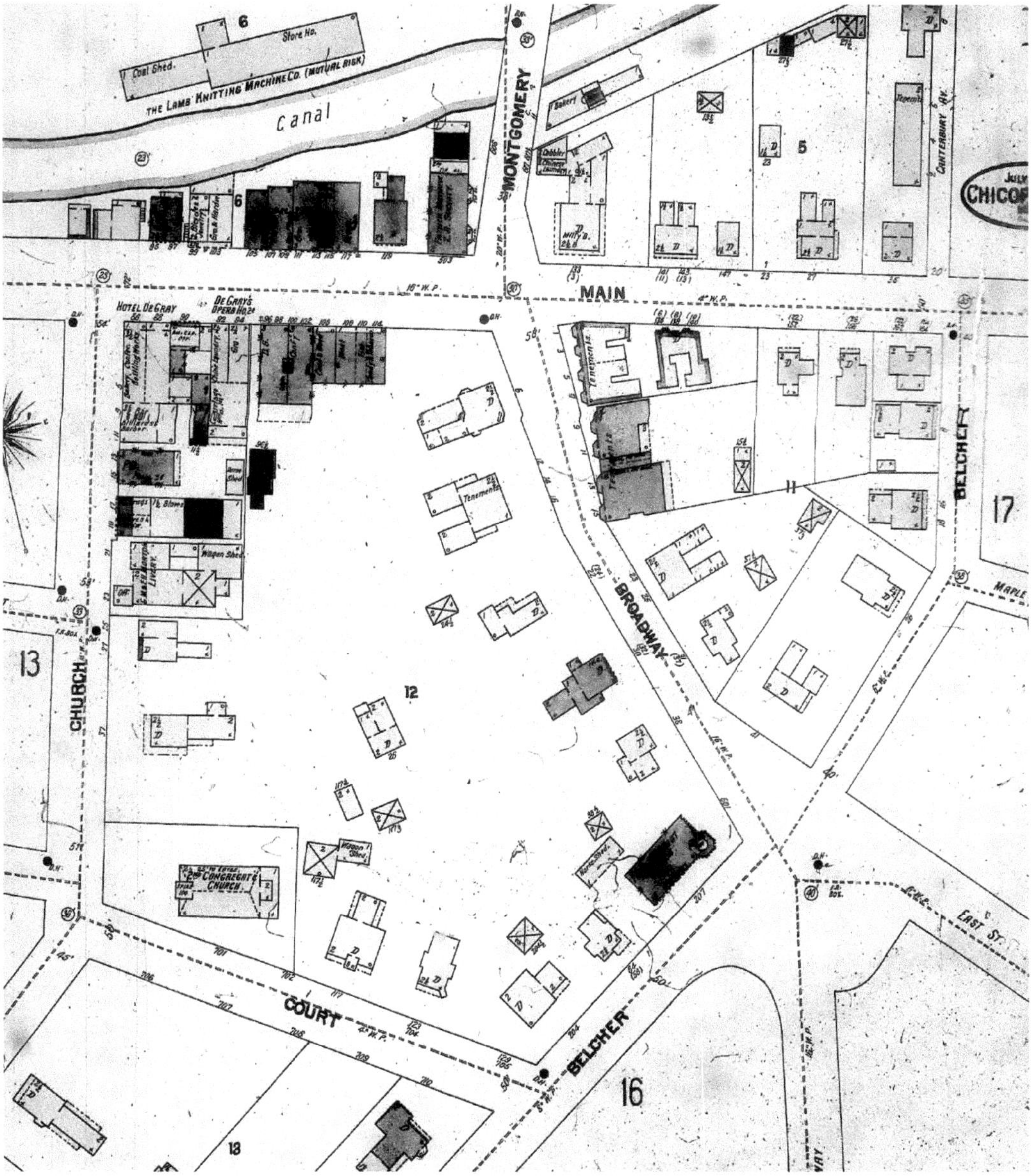

Figure 31. The Lamb Knitting Machine Company works, where Overman began producing Credenda bicycles for Albert Spalding, were located along a power canal about two blocks from the Overman factory, the latter just south of the intersection of Belcher and Broadway as shown on the Sanborn map. The factory has not survived. Sanborn Map Company, Insurance Maps of Chicopee, Hampden County, Massachusetts (July 1902), Plate 14, Library of Congress, Geography and Map Division.

wildly, but he adamantly refused to lower the Victor's $100 tag, despite substantial reductions by his competitors; labor strife also hampered production. Moreover, Overman's access to dealers in western states had been weakened severely, not just by the litigation with Spalding but also by the Lamb company's investment to secure western agents for Credenda bicycles early in 1894 (an undertaking also led by a former Overman employee), which ultimately yielded returns for Overman's rival. Even more troublesome, emerging fractures in the industry foretold the financial manipulations by Spalding, Pope, saddle-maker Arthur Garford, and others that would lead to formation of the American Bicycle Company (ABC) monopoly in the summer of 1899, a consortium that absorbed the Lamb Manufacturing Company but excluded Overman.[10]

Late in December 1897, Overman's company could pay neither its wages nor debt obligations, and he assigned the firm's assets to a trustee for the benefit of creditors. Although the plant reopened less than a week later under supervision of the trustee and a creditors' committee, and struggled back to productivity in advance of the 1898 and 1899 seasons, the outlook grew increasingly bleak. In June 1899—little more than a month before the ABC's public declaration—the company cut the price of Victor bicycles from $50 to $28; work that summer focused on remains from the previous season rather than new production—an ominous sign; in August the company closed all branch stores; and in October the firm's name was missing from a group of independent companies that formed the Cycle Trades' Protective Association to challenge the patents owned by the ABC monopoly. To the surprise of few, late that year the trustee offered the plant for sale, creditors having been paid fifty cents for each dollar of investment to that point. Simultaneously, the trustee also filed a successful petition to abate property taxes for 1898 and 1899, tactically contending that the works and its machinery had been overvalued—an argument bolstered by the ungenerous amounts being offered for the factory. In February 1900, the J. Stevens Arms and Tool Company from Chicopee acquired the plant and a year later reintroduced the Victor wheel, albeit briefly.[11]

Figure 32. A.G. Spalding and Brothers Company catalog for 1898. In 1893, Albert Spalding acquired a controlling interest in the Lamb Knitting Machine Company and began producing Spalding bicycles as well as less expensive Credenda models at the Chicopee Falls factory. Courtesy Lyman and Merrie Wood Museum of Springfield History, Springfield, MA.

Owners of the Lamb Manufacturing Company also sustained substantial losses when ABC failed in 1902, ending the large-scale manufacture of bicycles in Chicopee Falls and scattering the former knitting company's various divisions elsewhere. As in many other cities where bicycle companies failed, skilled machinists and other workers suffered, as did the city's general economy.[12]

Meanwhile, Overman resurrected his experiments with automobiles, which had begun in 1895 with a gasoline-powered motor, but in March of 1899 Overman demonstrated a steam-powered version, also called the Victor. After successfully exhibiting the car in Paris and securing financial backing from investors in New York, Overman established his new business as a New Jersey corporation in May 1900. Two months later, he returned to the starting point of his bicycle venture in Chicopee Center and leased space in the old Ames works, eventually painting a large white sign, "Overman Automobile Company," which extended nearly the full length of one mill building.[13]

Production of the car began during the early months of 1901, and residents of Chicopee greeted Overman's return warmly, anticipating that he might soon acquire the entire factory complex. The company also developed an experimental gasoline-powered car. However, whispers about the company's future began to circulate the following year, and in October 1902 Overman announced plans to relocate in Bridgeport, Connecticut, merging his business with that of the Locomobile Company. He placed his sixteen-room, Springfield mansion on the market for roughly one-half its $125,000 construction cost, departed for Europe for an extended period to promote the company, and eventually settled at his country residence in Westmoreland, New Hampshire, living there until his death in 1930 at age eighty.[14]

Although Spalding had retired in 1901, his company continued to manufacture sporting goods in a section of the Lamb factory for a short period, and the firm expanded opportunistically into Overman's former plant in the fall of 1902. Yet that space also proved inadequate, and early in 1904 the company left Chicopee Falls after purchasing the Ames complex in Chicopee Center, continuing production there for many decades and never taking the trouble to remove the oversized Overman name from the building's façade. To an ever-smaller number of knowing citizens, the letters emblazed defiance, but one gradually fading in clarity until 1985, and then forgotten altogether. That year, the mill's owners converted the complex into housing units, erased the sign, and christened the project "Ames Privilege" in reference to the grants of waterpower and land acquired more than 150 years before.[15]

4

Iver Johnson Arms and Cycle Works

Fitchburg, Massachusetts

Both Albert Overman and Iver Johnson began manufacturing bicycles during the high wheel era; both produced bicycles of exceptional quality; both of their companies became engaged in disputes about patents; and both men relied on the adaptability of standard mill construction to house the production of bicycles. Johnson's former factory complex, erected by the Walter Heywood Chair Company in 1870 and acquired by Johnson in 1891, is located on River Street in Fitchburg, and has remained in use for commercial and light industrial purposes until very recently when new owners have developed plans to convert the complex to residential apartments or condominiums.[1]

However, the similarities between Overman and Johnson end there. Unlike Overman, or for that matter Pope, Spalding,

Figure 33. In 1891, Iver Johnson purchased the Walter Heywood Chair Company factory complex, built in 1870 in Fitchburg, Massachusetts. Fitchburg brick masons Wetherbee & Derby and stone masons Samuel A. Wheeler & Son constructed the buildings, and the chair company's carpenters completed the interior finishing. Until very recently, the works continued to serve commercial and light industrial uses, but plans are underway to convert the complex to residential apartments and condominiums. Courtesy Fitchburg Historical Society.

and the heads of many other bicycle concerns, Johnson possessed uncommon mechanical ingenuity, and he spent a sizable portion of his life at shop benches, tinkering not just with designs for numerous products, but also with the labor-saving machines that fabricated his many patented and unpatented creations—the latter often hidden from inquisitive eyes. That innate inventiveness became the foundation for a business ultimately diversified enough to weather the bicycle industry's economic turbulences.[2]

Unfortunately, Johnson's gifts did not extend to physical health, and he died in 1895 at age fifty-four. However, his widow, Mary Elizabeth (Speirs) Johnson, and eldest son, Frederic Iver Johnson, drew from their own wells of resourcefulness and began managing the business. Although conflict between mother and son eventually developed, company ownership remained with family members for almost six decades, and the firm continued to manufacture bicycles until the Second World War, briefly renewing production under different ownership in 1974. Thus, the company became one of the country's very few concerns to manufacture bicycles continuously for more than half a century—one of fewer still originating during the nineteenth century, and among that select group, one of very few traceable to the high-wheel era. Moreover, the company's substantial history expands the context for bicycle manufacturing illustrated by Overman's business, particularly the complex web of connectivity spun by company owners and patent holders. As well, Johnson's surviving factory complex is well documented and illuminates the bicycle-manufacturing process far more clearly than the Ames Mills in Chicopee.[3]

Origins

Iver Johnson, born in 1841 in Nordfjord, Norway, revealed mechanical aptitude at an early age and left home to work as a gunsmith's apprentice in Bergen, eventually emigrating to America in 1863. By 1871, he had established a partnership with another gunsmith, Martin Bye, in Worcester, Massachusetts, doing business as Johnson, Bye and Company, and in 1875 the partners purchased an industrial loft on the northerly side of Central Street (today Martin Luther King Boulevard), where they expanded their line of products to include police equipment, fireworks pistols, carpenters' tools, ice and roller skates, children's scooters, toys, and fluting irons for clothing.[4]

Destined to expand, Johnson acquired Bye's interest in 1883, renamed his firm "Iver Johnson and Company," and between 1885 and 1887 added bicycles to his production line—the short-lived Springfield Roadster, a high-wheel safety bicycle driven with levers rather than pedals. Joseph L. Yost and Joseph B. McCune, two sewing-machine tradesmen from Springfield, Massachusetts, patented the components for that bicycle in 1886 and formed the Springfield Bicycle Manufacturing Company that same year, designating Johnson's Worcester building as the company's works and opening an office in Boston. However, in 1888 the firm moved to Highlandville, a village in suburban Needham, and Johnson's dealings with the business soon ended.[5]

However, by the late 1880s, Johnson also had begun to produce bicycles for the John P. Lovell Arms Company in Boston—the Lovell Diamond safety. Lovell, born in East Braintree, Massachusetts, in 1820 and a generation older than Johnson, also became a gunsmith's apprentice at an early age, and through hard work parlayed that trade into a successful arms and sporting goods business, occupying a five-story building in Boston by 1874, located in the Dock Square district.

Common experience as gunsmith novitiates likely explains the genesis of the Lovell-Johnson affiliation. The two negotiated an agreement as supplier and agent, and soon developed close personal as well as business ties. By 1876, the birth year of Johnson's second son, John Lovell Johnson, those attachments were clearly strong. John Lovell retired in 1883, the same year that Johnson purchased Martin Bye's partnership share, suggesting that by then Johnson and Lovell had established mutually secure arrangements for their respective businesses. Johnson's close association with Lovell also extended to one of the latter's sons, Benjamin S. Lovell, who described Johnson's Worcester shop as the Lovell factory, and who, as Johnson's contemporary and president of the subsidiary Lovell Arms and Cycle Company, became principally involved in the production of Lovell bicycles, assisting with selection of the Fitchburg factory in June 1891.[6]

By 1890, Johnson already had begun considering a change from the cramped quarters in Worcester, and although several factors probably influenced his decision, the amount of space required for Lovell's growing bicycle business became a principal concern. In the fall of 1890, Fitchburg businessman Elijah M. Dickenson had purchased the five-acre Heywood plant at auction for $60,000, hoping to attract a new industry to their city. Walter Heywood had died in 1880 and his business declined, but that auction price fell far short of the $250,000 to $300,000 cost of construction reported in newspapers in 1870. Johnson asked for neither pecuniary assistance nor tax abatements from the Fitchburg community, and earlier had declined subscriptions of $15,000 to relocate in nearby Hudson. In doing so, he ignored a common practice among industry owners, and one willingly exploited by the heads of many bicycle companies—further distinguishing him from his cycling competitors.

The Iver Johnson Works

The impressive Fitchburg factory complex, erected with brick, stone, and slate after a fire destroyed its predecessor, included three main buildings (pragmatically called One, Two and Three, front to back), each two stories and 300 feet long; an engine house with steam engine fabricated by the Putnam Machine Company in Fitchburg; a French Second-Empire style office with mansard roof and attached warehouse; and various sheds, stables and outbuildings. Expansive enough to accommodate 300 workers, the buildings stood largely completed by the early months of 1871, a credit to Fitchburg brick masons Wetherbee & Derby and stone masons Samuel A. Wheeler & Son; the chair company's carpenters completed most of the interior finishing. Spur tracks of the nearby Fitchburg Railroad served the works, and concern about fireproofing led to the slate shingles on building roofs and to the installation of Halls sprinkling systems in the main buildings and private hydrants on site. Johnson renamed the complex, added a forge shop with bridge; a small addition to Building Three for the setting and drying of enamel; and Walworth automatic sprinklers in Building One, where bicycle assembly took place on the second floor, at least initially. By 1894, he also had installed a new steam engine and two dynamos for electric lighting.[7]

Several distinctive features of the Johnson works add to our understanding of standard mill construction. One is the traditional pitch of the gable roofs, which is inconsistent with the very low-pitched or flat roofs mandated by factory mutual insurance companies. Opposition to the latter types of roofs in northern climates, where concerns about shedding water and snow were paramount, sometimes managed to overcome the dictates of insurance companies. Moreover, although the protection against fire offered by slate roofs pleased insurers, the shingles required a substantial slope to shed water properly, and they also added considerable weight, requiring a very rigid truss frame

Figure 34. Building One, Iver Johnson Arms and Cycle Works, used for bicycle production. The decorative brick corbelling, cornice dentils, and pendills that break the severity of regimental brick walls are functional as well as ornamental, extending the width of eaves and thus helping to shed water away from the building but also adding depth to the wall head that carries the weight and stresses of the roof frame and its heavy slate shingles, the latter a protection against fire. The synthesis of structural function and architectural embellishment is also visible at the corner and intermediate piers that increase wall depth at crucial junctures on these long, narrow buildings—length governed by the limits of overhead mill shafting to distribute power over long distances, and width constrained by the need for natural light. Yet the piers' recessed panels just below the cornices also add visual appeal, as do the segmentally arched window lintels that establish rhythmic effect. Photo by the author.

for support. Not surprisingly, builders clung tenaciously to proven methods of construction.

Also very visible are the buildings' architectural embellishments in the form of brick pendills, corbelling, and cornice dentils that break the severity of brick walls. Yet much of this brickwork is functional as well as ornamental, extending the width of eaves and thus helping to shed water away from the building but also adding breadth to the wall head that carries the weight and stresses of the roof frame and cladding. This synthesis of utility and decoration is also apparent elsewhere on the building. For instance, corner and intermediate piers are structurally functional because they increase wall depth at essential junctures on these long buildings. Yet the piers' recessed panels just below the cornices also add visual emphasis. Windows with segmental arches as lintels improve the fenestration's rhythmic effect, as do the prominent windowsills of stone. The pairs of arched windows in gable peaks also add to the buildings' overall architectural appeal, and even minor features contribute, including the small windowsill brackets, which were omitted from rear facades.[8]

Such efforts to improve the appearance of factories underscore the different approaches to the design of standard mill construction by engineers, architects, builders, insurance companies, and owners. Although not indifferent to proper proportion, engineers emphasized an exterior form that announced functional utility—an aesthetic doctrine rooted in the intrinsic beauty of efficient design. Architects countered by observing that efficient design need not equate with unsightliness, and they sought to express the utilitarian character of industrial buildings in stylistic terms, drawing attention to important structural elements or emphasizing prominent features such as entrances, towers, and separate office buildings.

Yet owners sometimes found themselves betwixt and between. For some, whose factories became emblems of ascendancy, handsome edifices heightened pride of ownership and community standing; others, however, saw no purchase in the expenditure of funds for architectural sake. To the relief of just about everyone, brick embroidery could relieve the monotony of stark walls without excessive cost, and both architects and builders found creative ways to employ that very simple building material to satisfy owners' wishes or accounting ledgers, a dexterity amply illustrated by the Fitchburg factory. By no means did skilled brick or stone masons

Figure 35. Overhead mill shafting in Johnson's milling shops distributed power to machinery via wheels, pulleys, and belts. By the time of this photograph, about 1925, electric motors turned that shafting, minimizing the inefficiencies and torsional stresses occurring when a single power source governed the long, heavy, revolving shafts. The incandescent lighting also supplemented natural lighting, but at an additional cost, and the webs of fast-moving, noisy belts remained hazardous until each machine could be fitted with individual electric motors, a system called unit drive. Iver Johnson Arms and Cycle Works booklet, undated, courtesy Fitchburg Historical Society.

require the guiding hands of architects to produce work of originality, but the very bold stylistic features that Iver Johnson could not have overlooked in 1891, particularly those on the office building, suggest the contribution of an architect, yet to be identified.[9]

The Fitchburg works are also noteworthy for illustrating the versatility of standard mill construction and its facile adaptability to different types of manufacturing. Such diversification remained crucial for industries such as bicycles due to seasonal lulls, fluctuating markets, or advances in production. That Iver Johnson's company successfully converted the Fitchburg works to the manufacture of numerous products for more than fifty years is ample testimony to the innate versatility of standard mill construction.

Company Expansion

Johnson's business quickly grew to fill the spacious Fitchburg buildings, and although the business remained a sole proprietorship, Johnson incorporated a separate business in February 1893, the Iver Johnson Sporting Goods Company, to enter the retail cycling trade with his eldest son, Frederic. Two years later, he clinched an agreement with Sidney J. Francis, the owner of a bicycle and sporting goods business in Fitchburg, to reorganize Johnson's fledgling company with Johnson as president, Fred Johnson as vice-president, and Francis as both treasurer and store manager. The shop became a retail outlet for Johnson's manufactured articles, and symbolically unified two of the area's cycling clubs represented by Francis, a bicycle agent since the high-wheel era and long-standing member of the Rollstone Cycle Club, and Fred Johnson, captain of the Fitchburg Cycle Club.[10]

Equally important, the agreement established Johnson's firm as one of the region's largest sporting goods concerns, in direct competition with the Lovell business in both the manufacturing and retail sectors, and in February 1895 the new company announced plans to offer Spalding, Victor, and Waverly models in addition to Lovell bicycles. Although formal announcements by the Lovell firm did not circulate until the fall of 1895, earlier that year that company had purchased a factory in South Portland, Maine, stating their intention to use that location to increase production of Diamond and Excel bicycles, and the company soon reorganized under Maine law.[11]

Sadly, in August 1895 Johnson succumbed to tuberculosis, leaving his widow and twenty-four-year-old Frederic to manage the business under a trust, with Mary Johnson as executrix and trustee. Almost immediately after his father's death, the Lovell firm severed its connections with Frederic and Mary Johnson, exposing the fractures that had been widening during the preceding years. Belying his youth and inexperience, Fred Johnson, an aspiring racer, filled that breach by introducing a new bicycle and giving the wheel his father's name; he also marketed a second, less expensive model—the Fitchburg. Little more than a month later, January 1896, he stepped onto the floor of Madison Square Garden as one of the youngest company managers to exhibit at the annual bicycle-show extravaganza.[12]

Determined to fill the considerable gap left by Lovell's departure, Johnson won a loyal clientele by soliciting new customers with a persuasive appeal: "This is not a new cycle, but an old established one that has borne our name as manufacturer upon the nameplate since 1890." For approximately a dozen years following his father's death, Fred Johnson functioned as general manager of the business and, aided by a cadre of skilled employees, steadily expanded the company—soon joined by his younger brothers, John Lovell and Walter Olof. Johnson eventually secured a patent for the bicycle's very recognizable truss frame, and in 1901, he secured another patent, one for an improved crank hangar with detachable barrel, allowing the ball cups and crank bearings to be fitted to the barrel separately from frame assembly, thus protecting those parts from excessive heat during frame brazing. In addition, Johnson adroitly steered the company away from the American Bicycle Company's tentacles and became a principal organizer and first president of the Cycle Trades' Protective Association. Commendably, he sponsored a racing team led by Major Taylor, the country's African American cycling champion—a principled decision that proved to be profitable, as well.[13]

Plaudits for the company's great success in bicycle manufacturing after Iver Johnson's death are clouded by the familial conflict that arose between mother and son over control of the company, but much of the credit belongs to Fred Johnson. His position as the firm's general manager, and as vice-president, general manager and shareholder of the Iver Johnson Sporting Goods Company, explicitly placed him at the core of the firm's bicycle production during that difficult, transitional period, as did his experience in club activities and racing. The machinists trained by his father also played critical roles.[14]

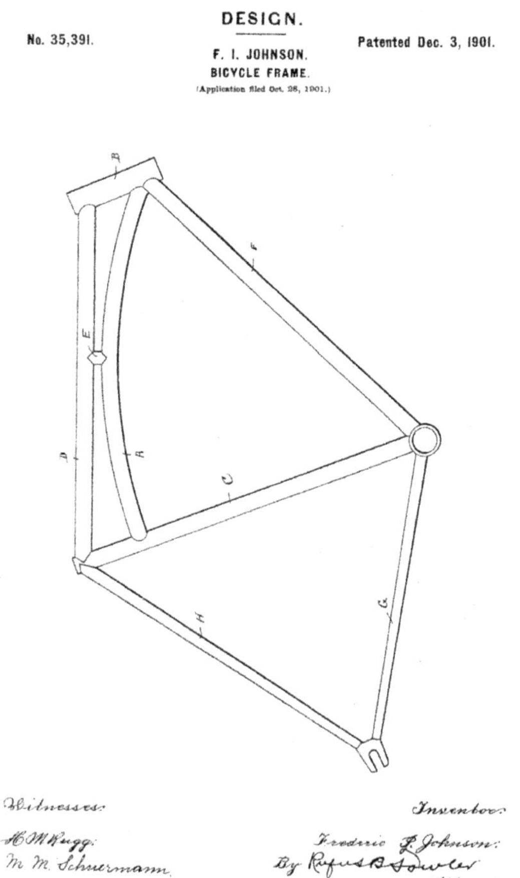

Figure 36. Frederic Johnson patented a distinctive truss frame, which became a well-known company moniker. United States Patent Office.

Industrial and Commercial Growth

With production of the Iver Johnson bicycle in 1896, the break with the Lovell firm became irreversible, and expansion during the 1896 and 1897 seasons led directly to the opening of a retail bicycle store at 200 Boylston Street in Boston in June 1897, managed by J.M. Savage and J.P. Land, the latter a member of the Press Cycle Club; the company also constructed a large addition to their plant in October of that same year. Several months later, they announced plans to offer a complete line of ten different chain-driven wheels for the 1898 season at prices ranging from $85 to $40—a racer, light roadster, roadster, ladies' models, and two tandems (all with the Iver Johnson moniker) and two Fitchburg models—and well as a more expensive chainless prototype. During the spring of 1898 the company also moved its Boston store to 406–408 Washington Street, sharpening competition with the Lovell store nearby. In addition to bicycles, the shop offered a complete range of athletic goods including cameras for touring cyclists.[15]

Separately, but also indicative of the firm's prosperity, in 1898 the company constructed the Iver Johnson Building, a commanding, five-story block in downtown Fitchburg, and the new home of the Iver Johnson Sporting Goods Company. Designed by Worcester architects Albert Barker and Walter Nourse (who also designed a factory for the Trinity Cycle Manufacturing Company that same year), with assistance from Fitchburg engineer George Raymond, the building offered commercial space on the ground floor, offices on the second floor, and apartment suites on the third, fourth, and fifth floors, with both public and private dining halls also placed on the upper story. Located at the corner of Main and Putnam Streets until destroyed by fire in 2011, the building proclaimed the convenience of apartment-house living in cities, with easy access to churches, depots, theaters, street railways, and shops. The Johnson family—mother, three sons and daughter—lived for many years in the building, which became known as the Johnsonia Hotel. By 1910, however, its use as a hotel had declined, and Walter Johnson eventually sold the property in 1922.[16]

All the while, the destinies of the Johnson and Lovell companies remained coupled. In mid-July 1897, John P. Lovell suffered a stroke and died later that month. Not long before, the Lovell firm had sued Johnson's company unsuccessfully, claiming patent infringement relating to the

Figure 37. The Iver Johnson Building in downtown Fitchburg offered commercial space on the ground floor, offices on the second floor, and apartment suites on the third, fourth, and fifth floors. Designed in 1897 by Worcester architects Albert Barker and Walter Nourse with assistance from Fitchburg engineer George Raymond, the building housed the Iver Johnson Sporting Goods Company and was later renamed the Johnsonia. Fire destroyed the building in 2011. Author's postcard.

design of single-barreled guns. By then, however, the Lovell company faced more serious troubles. An employee of the company's principal lender, the Globe National Bank, quietly had begun managing the Lovell business to recover undisclosed loans exceeding $600,000 made by the bank's president, Charles H. Cole. Late in 1899 the bank failed, auditors discovered the outstanding debts owed by the Lovell concern, Cole admitted numerous instances of mishandling bank funds, turned over the Lovell notes and most of his personal assets before fleeing to California, where he was arrested. In January 1900, the Lovell factory in South Portland closed, and the bank's directors began liquidating the company's assets. Adding a note of finality, Ben Lovell, who served as treasurer of the parent company as well as president of the subsidiary cycle company, died the following month.[17]

The reasons for the rift between the two companies were probably multifaceted, but ruptures in the Lovell firm's financial standing likely began before 1895 and may have been at the root of that separation. However, the Lovell firm's failure also spelled opportunity for Fred Johnson, and in March 1900, his sporting goods concern purchased the remaining stock, fixtures, good will, and store lease of the Lovell business on Washington Street, moving to that location in April and posting a signboard: "Iver Johnson Sporting Goods Co.—Successors to John P. Lovell Arms Co."[18]

Led by Fred Johnson, the firm's phenomenal rise continued despite collapse of the bicycle craze, with firearms assuming a large percentage of their business, primarily revolvers and shotguns. However, the company also introduced a long-lasting line of juvenile bicycles in 1908 and experimented with motorcycle production for a ten-year period beginning in 1912. Having outgrown the Boston shop by 1908, the company commissioned a new, eight-story commercial block that year, on a ground lease practically next door at the corner of Cornhill and Washington Street, intending to offer a daylight department store devoted to all types of sporting activities.

Architect Clinton J. Warren, a native of Massachusetts who in 1880 joined the Chicago partnership of Daniel Burnham and John Welborn Root, but who later returned to Boston, designed the skeletal, steel-frame structure, cladding the building with brick and terra cotta but giving greatest emphasis to large, Chicago-style windows. Warren's design borrows from Root and other Chicago architects who gave architectural expression to the underlying steel structure of tall buildings—innovations that made the great height of commercial blocks possible—but also unveiled the latent beauty of skyscrapers. The building is divided into three well-defined parts: a two-story base; an uninterrupted column of middle stories, with piers revealing the building's underlying frame but also accentuating verticality; and the crowning capital, richly decorated with terra cotta. Those compositional innovations derive from Chicago architect Louis Sullivan, as do the enormous display windows dominating the building's first two stories, features not possible with load-bearing masonry and thus obliquely revealing the building's internal frame. Warren also specified that the foundation, sub-basement, and frame of the initial structure be able to support two additional floors.[19]

Newspaper accounts hailed the building as one of the world's largest sporting goods establishments, but in the context of cycling history the building stood apart for its architectural significance. By 1919 the firm needed still more space and leased its old store on Washington Street, erecting a passageway between the two structures. A year later, the company acquired full title to the new building, which unfortunately succumbed to demolition in 1979.[20]

Figure 38. Failure of the John P. Lovell Arms Company offered opportunity for the Iver Johnson firm, and in 1908 the family erected a commercial building at the corner of Cornhill and Washington Street in Boston. Architect Clinton J. Warren, formerly with the architectural firm of Burnham and Root in Chicago, designed the building and employed a skeletal steel frame that stood in three divisions: a two-story base with large display windows; a column of six stories (later eight) with brick-clad spandrel shelves; and a decorative capital or cornice. Its large windows also borrowed from the Chicago School of tall buildings and flooded the department store's interior with daylight. The landmark joined the Johnsonia as two of the country's most important commercial buildings erected by a bicycle manufacturer but was demolished during the late 1960s. Author's document.

Reorganization

Meanwhile, the simmering disputes between mother and son over control of the company had erupted into litigation. Much of the conflict can be traced to the elder Johnson's will, which placed the residue of his estate, including the factory, land, machinery, stock in trade, and accounts, into a trust for the support and education of his four children, including a daughter, Mary L. Johnson, and for his widow, Mary Elizabeth Johnson, during the remainder of her life, or until she remarried. By appointing his widow as trustee, the will gave tacit control of the company to her, and disposition of the company's income, whether to be held in trust for the children and distributed, or hers unfettered other than obligations to support her children, became a principal point of contention. Fred Johnson demanded an accounting in 1908, and Mary Johnson soon revoked her son's authority as general manager, barred him from access to the factory, and replaced him with his younger brothers.[21]

On December 31, 1895, the estate's appraisers valued the concern at $431,657, a figure that served as the trust corpus. However, between 1895 and 1908, revenue from the business alone surpassed $3,176,500, and that figure did not include income from interest, dividends, and rentals that totaled nearly $400,000 in additional funds. Nor did it include the value of numerous patents or the company's good will. For his role in that growth, Fred Johnson received a salary of $780 per year between 1895 and 1898, and from 1898 to 1908, $4,000 per year. His yearly allowances under the trust arrangement averaged about $420, but those stipends dropped substantially after 1899 and to as little as $30 in 1902.[22]

A Worcester County probate judge agreed with Fred Iverson, ruling in October 1911 that income from the trust should be received and held by Mary Johnson in trust for herself and for her four children in equal shares, and subject to the requirements of accounting. However, the Massachusetts Supreme Court reversed that decree in 1913, siding with Mary Johnson and hardening estrangements that were never resolved. When she died little more than two years later, in October 1915, Mary Johnson disinherited her eldest son, leaving him $1,000 and bequeathing the residue of her estate, approximately $3,000,000, to his three siblings to share equally. Nevertheless, he may have salvaged a measure of economic standing because his mother's death also led to dissolution of the trust created by his father, with its principal shared equally by the four children. In addition, he reached an agreement with his brothers and sister in January 1916 not to contest his mother's will in return for the purchase of all his interest in his father's business. He also remained as a director and shareholder of the sporting goods concern, but strained relationships with his siblings may have taken a toll, and he died four years later at age forty-nine.[23]

In the context of cycling history, the principal outcome of these conflicts occurred in March 1916, when the three siblings incorporated their father's company as the Iver Johnson Arms and Cycle Works, equally dividing 6,000 shares calculated at $100 par value, for a capitalization of $600,000. As the company's president for the ensuing two decades, John Lovell Johnson maintained the firm's high standing as a manufacturer of well-made bicycles and firearms, and in the fall of that year he reassured the company's cycling clientele by announcing that prices on all but three of the company's seventeen models to be offered in 1917 would not change from the previous year. Walter Johnson, who as a young man had exhibited some of his father's mechanical ingenuity, stepped instead into the role of company treasurer, and Mary L. (Johnson) Otto became a company director.[24]

John Lovell Johnson Era

By the time John Lovell Johnson, at age 40, assumed control of his father's business, the concern had attained an international reputation for the quality of its revolvers and Champion guns, but he continued to experiment with efficient organization of the factory and its manufacturing processes, so critical to the company's diverse productions. The world-wide reputation of its firearms may have benefited bicycle sales, and although the bicycle boom had long-since ended, and cycling as a sport had declined, the company nevertheless maintained modest production levels. Soon after reorganizing the firm, Johnson announced plans to ship a large order of bicycles to China and Hawaii, and orders from other countries continued to arrive during the remainder of the year—despite the growing international conflict. European orders also helped to sustain the company's small motorcycle business during these difficult years.[25]

Described by his colleagues as affable and kind, if not over-exuberant, Johnson had attended Worcester Polytechnic Institute before leaving to work for the family business, and in 1896 participated in bicycle races. Yet he devoted much of his time to state and local politics, and the five scrapbooks of newspaper clippings he assembled during his career suggest that politics dominated his outlook. That he carefully requested his mother's permission to pursue political office is suggestive of both Johnson's and his mother's dispositions—and may also hint at the source of strife occurring between his mother and elder brother.[26]

Johnson's keen personal interest in politics confirms that a substantial share of the credit for the company's continued success rests with the firm's skilled and inventive machinists. By the time of Lovell Johnson's tenure, many of them had worked for the company for as long as five decades, or represented successive generations traceable to the firm's origins in Worcester. Among these individuals were John Berg, who began working for Iver Johnson when the partnership was founded in 1871, and remained until 1915; Gus Ellstrom, the long-time foreman and later factory manager with forty-five years to his credit; Ewald Ramgren, general superintendent; and numerous foremen with loyalties exceeding forty years, including Edward Joyce, Patrick Hackett, C.E. Arline, W.D. Preston, Gustav Anderson, and John Corneli.[27]

Johnson acknowledged his deference to the experience and expertise of these men and expressed belief that sound organizations should provide steady employment with reasonable working hours under pleasant conditions. Admirably, the firm remained open during the economic slump following World War I, further cementing loyalties among department heads—as did annual outings at Johnson's marshland camp near Fitchburg. There, he established a refuge for migrating birds, safe from sportsmen, and after constructing a dam with gate and spillway to control the level of a spring-fed pond, he planted wild rice and celery.[28]

Numerous challenges marked Johnson's tenure as company head. In 1919, for instance, striking workers formed an independent shop union, demanding eight-hour working days with the same salary earned for ten-hour shifts; a half-holiday on Saturdays; and pay and one-half for overtime. An estimated 300 workers vacated the plant in mid–June and voted to join the American Federation of Labor, which negotiated a settlement later that summer. Dwindling demand for bicycles after the War also proved troublesome, and by 1921 the company had reduced its output by 50 percent from the previous year, albeit not as severely as some competitors. Yet Johnson remained cautious about lowering prices on the company's bicycles, reasoning that dealers forestalled purchases in anticipation of additional price cuts. Rather, the company sought to gauge yearly demand accurately prior to the purchase of raw materials, and to rely on gun production to counter the uncertainty in bicycle markets. With a similarly cautious outlook, Johnson ended motorcycle production in 1923, predicting that automobiles would soon dominate overland travel and would alter the balance of competition among the country's manufacturers of wheeled vehicles.[29]

Selectively, Johnson continued to diversify the company's wheeled products, approving the introduction of velocipedes in 1922 (children's tricycles in three sizes and two colors—red or blue with white head and nickel fork), followed by the company's trademark Juniorcycles in 1926. That year, the company's forty-first in bicycle manufacturing, demand for bicycles began to increase and the firm offered five new models available in several new finishes. Production of sidewalk pedal scooters followed in 1931, and that same year the company purchased the Wonder Manufacturing Company in Middletown, Ohio, a successful fabricator of baby walkers. The firm also established a Canadian factory at Coburg, Ontario.[30]

Johnson's strategy reflected a desire to offer wheeled vehicles to people of all

Figure 39. During his first decade as company president, John Lovell Johnson circulated a company booklet with extensive photographs of shop work. Undated, but circa 1925, the publication is among the best visual documentations of bicycle manufacturing in America during this period. In the assembly room, workers completed the manufacturing process by hand, each according to specifications provided by the order. Benches lined window walls to maximize the benefit of natural light. Courtesy Fitchburg Historical Society.

ages, from cradle to grave as he put it, and he encouraged dealers to stock as many such products as possible, thus building an interest in bicycles among children at an early age. He also embarked on an advertising campaign that offered bicycles as prizes for newspaper subscription contests in New England and Middle-Atlantic states. Johnson's foresight paid dividends, because by the mid–1930s Hollywood movie stars had begun riding bicycles, hastening a national revival in cycling, but one that soon emphasized European-style, light weight, serviceable bicycles for adults—without the numerous and weighty accessories that encumbered American bicycles for children.[31]

Unfortunately, Johnson did not live to see the upshots of rejuvenation in American cycling that had begun to develop during this period. Early in November 1935, at age fifty-nine, he perished from a heart attack while at his summer home. His younger brother Walter, then fifty-six and a resident of Newton, immediately replaced him and continued to manufacture bicycles until World War II when, at the government's request, the fabrication of all cycle models ended, leaving only the company's baby walkers in production. Following the war, the company confined its manufacturing to single-barrel shotguns, target revolvers, boys' rifles, and the baby walkers. Walter Johnson remained president of the company until his death in 1953 at age seventy-four.[32]

5

Pope Manufacturing Company

Hartford, Connecticut

Scarcely a trace of the rivalry that once entangled the three Alberts (Overman, Pope, and Spalding) is to be found at the sites of their former industrial works, although Pope's eventual dominance in his contests with Overman remains evident in Hartford where fragments of his manufacturing empire survive. In addition, the contributions of Overman and Spalding remain visible in the well-preserved mills of the Ames Manufacturing Company in Chicopee Center. In Hartford, a single factory extension—the center wing—is the sole remnant of a vast complex of buildings that once housed the production of the Columbia ordinary. The brick outline of a vanished gable roof suggests the original dimensions of that wing, but whether Pope's predecessor in title, the Weed Sewing Machine Company, widened or rebuilt that wing either before or after 1878, the year Pope first commissioned the firm to build Columbia bicycles, is not known. Nevertheless, the building's current width was in place by 1886, and Pope enlarged the building in 1890 or 1891 by adding another story. The three-story structure that survives joins the Ames mill

Figure 40. Lithograph of the factories owned by the Pope Manufacturing Company in Hartford, Connecticut, produced by Kyes & Woodbury, Worcester, Massachusetts; G.H. Buck and Company, New York City, printers. Undated but 1892 or 1893. The Columbia Tube Mill, designed by George Keller in 1893, is located at left, formerly at the corner of Laurel and Park Streets, several blocks from Pope's Capitol Avenue complex. Of the buildings shown, only the center wing and west wing survive. Author's document.

and the Gormully and Jeffery factory as the country's three most tangible reminders of high-wheel manufactories in our built environment.

Hartford's Bicycle Industry Beautiful

Although the story of Albert Pope's role as one of cycling history's outsized figures is widely told, his contributions to the history of industrial architecture, industrial housing, urban design, and park planning are also notable, and thus the significance of the company's surviving buildings in Hartford enlarges the scope of this study. The exquisite lithograph of the Pope Manufacturing Company works, undated but completed in 1892 or 1893 by the firm of Kyes and Woodbury in Worcester, Massachusetts, provides a stunning vantage point for considering these broader topics. The large image depicts four different factory complexes dispersed across an urban expanse known as Frog Hollow, albeit each in accessible proximity, and arranges them in a distorted composite view that requires clarification. In addition, Pope continued to expand his industrial works between 1893 and 1897, and thus the lithograph provides only a partial view.

The Capitol Avenue works, the company's nucleus and the domain of Columbia bicycles, dominates the center of the lithograph on the northerly side of Capitol Avenue. Two large wings in that complex—the center wing with entrance drive and office doors, and a companion west wing built in 1893—face the street, and those two wings are the only buildings shown on the lithograph that survive today in the Capitol Avenue complex. However, almost entirely excluded from view are surviving blocks of handsome company-built housing located on Columbia and Putnam Streets, directly opposite the complex, completed between 1888 and 1889.

Far in the background, surreptitiously diminished in scale and importance, is the plant of the subsidiary Hartford Cycle Company completed in 1892, which produced less expensive Hartford bicycles. Pope concealed his ownership, fearing that potential purchasers of Columbia bicycles instead would select the cheaper models. Yet the factory, which has not survived, stood about three short blocks west of the center wing at what is today the southeast corner of Capitol Avenue and Woodbine Street, and much closer to the Capitol Avenue complex than any of the other buildings shown.

The lithograph also places the Columbia Tube Mill, designed in 1893 by George Keller but demolished in 1965, to the immediate left of the Capitol Avenue complex. However, that building stood one block west and two long blocks south of the Hartford Cycle Company factory, at what is today the northwest corner of Laurel and Park Streets. The lithograph also depicts the plant of the Hartford Rubber Works, acquired by Pope in 1892 and enlarged that same year, directly behind the Columbia Tube Mill. Instead, the rubber plant occupied land at the southwest corner of Park Street and Bartholomew Avenue in the city's Parkville district, two long blocks west of the tube plant and more distant from the center wing than any of the other factories or offices. Nothing of the rubber works depicted on the lithograph survives, although two 1895 additions designed by George Keller remain, as does a 1903 building.

By skillfully altering the setting, the artists successfully portrayed the factories in a burnished, commanding light that clearly reflects Pope's own view of his central role in the bicycle industry. Thus, the image is partly lavish advertisement, indicative of Pope's devotion to publicity, but also consistent with the practice among many industry owners. Yet the image also informs. Pope's expansion in Hartford coincided with a growing civic-mindedness among many of the country's industrial leaders, an outlook emboldened by the grand vision for American cities projected by architects of the World's Columbian Exposition of 1893 in Chicago. Typically, that vision is revealed through lustrous renderings showing axial vistas, monumental neo-classical buildings, spacious plazas, tree-lined boulevards, and formal parks. Historians have credited the industrial benefactors who, distrustful of corrupt city governments, channeled their wealth into civic organizations that paid for improvements during the City Beautiful movement. Often overlooked, though, are efforts by industry to improve its own public facades, a response to the noise, soot, congestion, and dismal tenements that had tarnished urban environments and the image of industry itself, in turn spurring calls for municipal reform.

Considered in that context, the Hartford lithograph surpasses mere advertisement and reveals a visualization for a grand urban industrial district to join the public seats promoted by City Beautiful—and an artist's impressions worthy of comparison to the radiant views of American cities inspired by the Chicago fair. Allegiance to that vision by Pope and by those who either did his bidding or influenced him, notably George Day and George Keller, resulted in the transformation of marsh-filled wastelands in the vicinity of the Park River in the city's southwesterly sector. Commitments to those ideals become evident on several fronts: Day's formal participation in the exposition as one of Connecticut's appointed delegates; Day's and Pope's arrival in Chicago for the fair's official dedication in the fall of 1892; the closely timed commission for the lithograph; design of subsequent improvements to the Capitol Avenue complex; plans for additional housing on nearby Park Terrace; the dedication of land for a pleasure ground (today Pope Park) designed by the Olmsted brothers in 1897 and linking the company's dispersed factory complexes; and the enduring vestiges of those features, offering a glimpse of that vision to those who are willing to look beyond urban decline. The progressive, inventive spirit of the bicycle industry reinforced that outlook, as well. Just a few blocks away, its gilded dome visible, the Connecticut State Capitol and its complex of buildings provided daily reminders of civic prospects.

Center Wing

The Hartford atlas of 1869 reveals the location of what would become the center wing in Pope's Capitol Avenue complex, a street-facing extension of the Sharps Rifle Manufacturing Company works on Rifle Avenue, which became Capitol Avenue. The factory occupied by the Weed Sewing Machine Company stands on the northerly side of the Park River, part of a complex of industrial buildings belonging to the Pratt and Whitney Company. By the spring of 1878, at the start the bicycle era, the former already had moved across the river into the buildings owned by the rifle concern, and in 1880 the Weed firm began to enlarge that complex.[1]

By 1881, the Weed Company had acquired full title to the land and buildings on both sides of Capitol Avenue, and two articles published that year, one in *Bicycling World* and the other in *Frank Leslie's Popular Monthly*, include identical wood-engraved illustrations of the complex, revealing the center wing as a two-story structure with gable roof, cupolas, and skylights. Both articles confirm that the buildings shown in the illustration are occupied largely by the bicycle works and explain that the street entry opens to the company's front offices and in

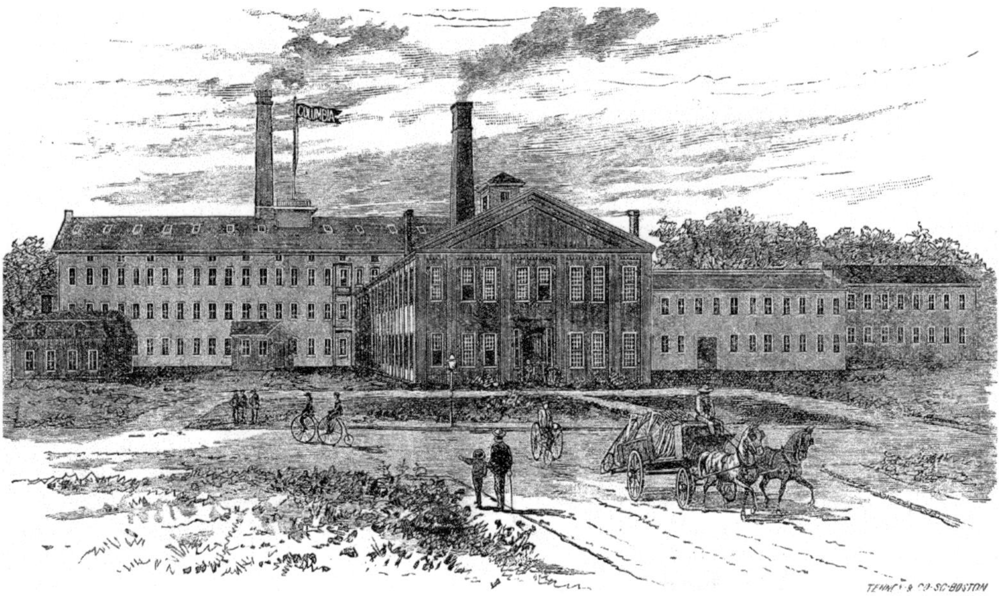

Figure 41. Weed Sewing Machine Company works (*L.A.W. Bulletin*, February 26, 1886).

turn leads to the designing, drafting, and model rooms. From there, a corridor leads to the forge and factory nucleus. Both articles also illustrate the factory's milling and assembly rooms.[2]

By the mid–1880s, Pope had dispelled any doubts among the Weed owners about the bright prospects for bicycle manufacturing. A Sanborn Map and Publishing Company plan of 1885 places a machine shop on the first floor of the center wing, with storage on the second. The main factory houses machine shops on the first, second, and third stories; tricycle fitting on the third story; storage in the attic; and a cleaning room for castings in a one-story extension at the building's easterly end; automatic sprinklers protect the attic of the primary building, but not the center wing. A group of buildings to the east of the main factory are used for electro plating, Japan enameling, varnishing, fitting, and shipping.[3]

Wood-engraved illustrations from two articles published in the *L.A.W. Bulletin*, the first in 1886 and the second in 1888, and an undated photograph taken no later than 1889 or 1890, add clarity. Both wood-engravings show the center wing's street-facing entrance, and the photograph from about the same time (see Introduction) confirms skylights, cupolas, facade piers, and an unusual double-pitch to the gable roof. A panoramic photograph from 1909 provides a rare view of the center wing's Capitol Avenue façade, confirming the building's width as it appeared in the 1886 and 1888 engravings.[4]

During the spring of 1890, Pope acquired ownership of the Weed Company, which became a subsidiary of the Pope Manufacturing Company, then a Maine corporation. Improvements to the site followed immediately and included enlarging the center wing to three stories, giving prominence to the front entrance facing Capitol Avenue, and reorganizing the interior. Illustrations of the center-wing published in *Wheel and Cycling Trade Review* in January 1891, place offices and a drafting room on the first and second floors, respectively; a milling and drilling room on the first floor; model room and machine shop on the second floor; and general machine

Figure 42. Weed Sewing Machine Company high-wheel ordinary assembly room. ***Frank Leslie's Popular Monthly*** **12 (November 1881).**

work on the third floor. The main block houses stocks and supplies in the basement; inspecting and packing rooms on the first floor; general machine work on the second and third floors; and storage in the attic. Behind the large factory is the felloe and punch press room, engine room, boiler room with pattern rooms on the second and third floors, and forge shop. At the rear of the complex, left to right, are buildings for brazing, case hardening and tempering, blacksmithing, machine work and polishing, tires, stock, assembly, inspection, and wheel-setting. The saddle and nickel-plating departments are combined in a single building, and an annex to the main block is devoted to nickel-buffing.[5]

West Wing and Expansion

Construction of the three-story west wing followed in the summer of 1891, heralding the company's emerging public facade. Newspaper articles about the west wing project proclaim slow-burning construction recommended by the Association of Manufacturers Mutual Fire Insurance Companies, and accounts also describe the building's features, including lockers and lavatories in the basement adequate for 800 employees; bicycle storage and a time-keeper's office on the first floor; general work on the second floor; and storage on the third floor, with plans for a dining hall as well. The company served as its own general contractor, retaining carpenter Peter Taylor and mason William F. O'Neill as superintendents.[6]

Improvements to the Capitol Avenue complex continued from 1891 to 1893, including construction of duplicate fire-proof buildings for storage, located to the east of the center wing and with maple floorboards set in concrete for the first-floors, and boiler-plate (literally) floors on the second stories. The

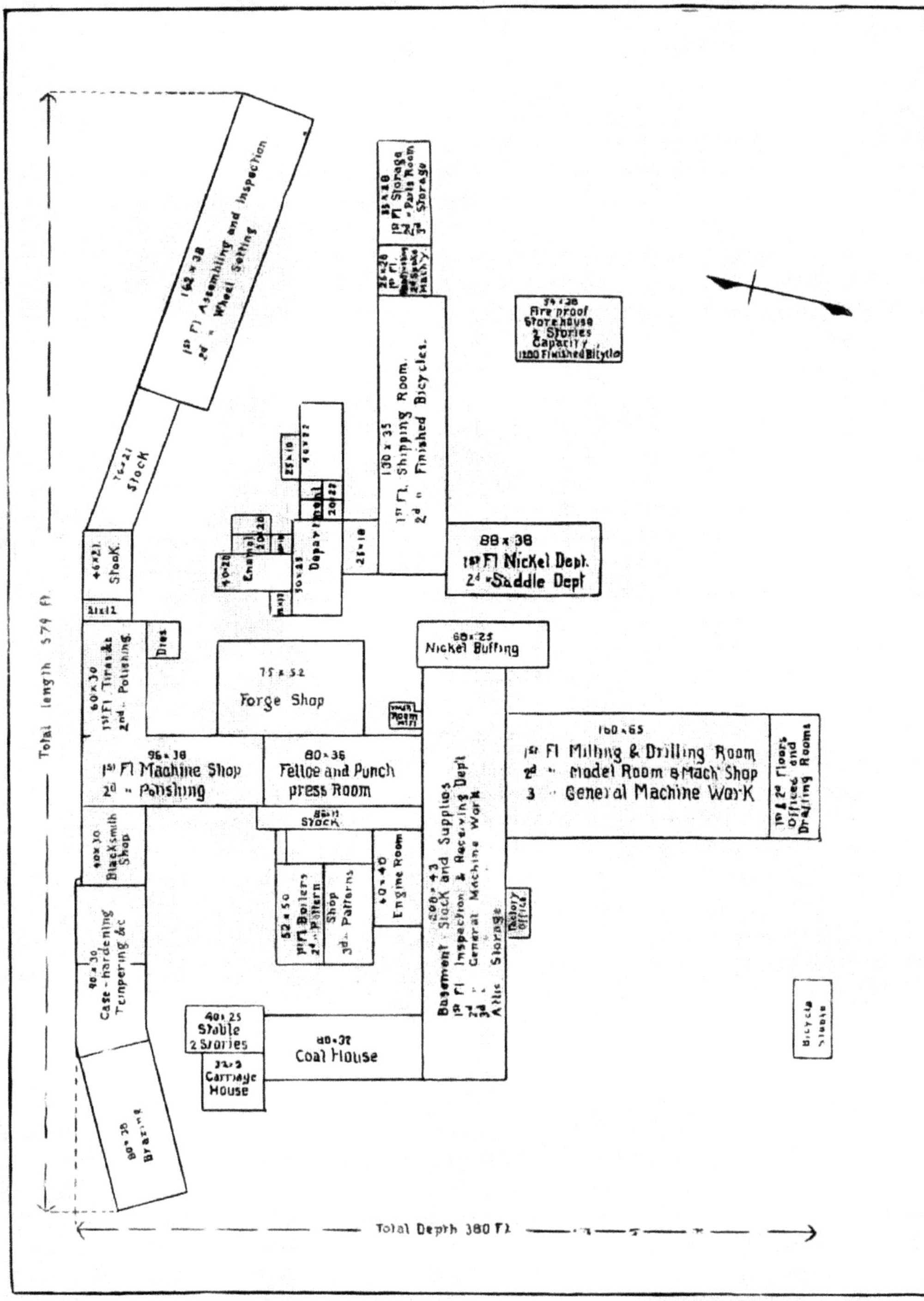

Figure 43. During the spring of 1890, the Pope Manufacturing Company acquired the Weed Sewing Machine Company, added a third story to the center wing, began enlarging the factory complex, and reorganized departments. *Wheel and Cycling Trade Review* 6 (January 30, 1891).

company also encircled the works with a five-foot high, wrought-iron fence fabricated in Cleveland, Ohio. In 1893, workers erected a small building to test different strengths of steel used in Columbia's frames, and completed the large east wing that fall. The testing house stood between the center and west wings, and the three-story east wing added 50,000 square feet of floor space near the main factory, with a fireproof basement devoted to enameling and protected by asphalt floor and brick-arched ceiling sprung from the flanges of steel beams. Shipping rooms and offices occupied the first floor; frame-setting the second; and wheel-setting the third, with vats and ovens housed in adjoining buildings.[7]

World's Columbian Exposition

Expansion of the Capitol Avenue complex coincided very closely with plans in Chicago to commemorate the 400-year anniversary of the landing of Columbus in the New World. Pope's selection of the name Columbia in 1878 reveals, if not personal attentiveness to the country's origins, at least an awareness of the public's growing ardor for national identity following the Centennial Exposition in

COLUMBIA BICYCLES, POPE MFG. CO., HARTFORD, CONN.

Figure 44. During the fall of 1892, both Albert Pope and George Day attended the World's Columbian Exposition, traveling to Chicago for the official dedication ceremonies as invited guests of Connecticut's delegation on the "Connecticut Special" train. Day also served as treasurer of the Connecticut Board of World's Fair Managers and as one of four members of the board's publications committee. Both Day and Pope carried the fair's vision of City Beautiful back to Hartford, where—with architect George Keller's assistance—the company built more housing, fashioned a dignified industrial façade along Capitol Avenue, and joined the company's dispersed factories with a public park designed by John Charles Olmsted and Frederick Law Olmsted, Jr. Courtesy Harriet Beecher Stowe Center, Hartford, CT.

Philadelphia just two years before—and the marketing potential created by that enthusiasm![8]

However, George Day established much closer connections between the glittering view of American cities presented at the Chicago fair and the commanding industrial façade emerging along Hartford's Capitol Avenue when, in March 1892, he attained appointment to the Connecticut Board of World's Fair Managers, serving eventually as its treasurer and as a member of the building committee for the Connecticut House. Equally important, Day became one of four members of the board's publications committee, which in 1898 circulated its report in a lengthy bound volume that included impressionistic sketches of the fair by visitors from the state. The very first of those letters, offered by Judge Simeon E. Baldwin and titled "A Dream of Beauty," acknowledged the original intent of the fair's organizers, specifically the desire to show the progress of human invention. Yet Baldwin joined throngs of visitors who regarded the setting as the great attraction, noting:

> Nothing could have been finer than the architectural and topographical setting of the Columbian Exposition. Whatever else of scenes once visited may be forgotten, no one who saw Jackson Park in 1893 will ever cease to remember that dream of beauty which rose from the shore of Lake Michigan to dazzle every eye that beheld it, with its resplendent, yet solemn, majesty.[9]

The committee's selection of that theme as a chapter introduction could not have been happenstance. Nor could either Day or Pope have overlooked that vision of beauty when they (together with George Pope, Albert's cousin) arrived in Chicago in October 1892 for the official dedication exercises, the latter two men having traveled as invited guests of the state's delegation on the "Connecticut Special," a train joined by ten palace cars decorated with bunting. Likely, too, all three men returned to Hartford with that visualization of an Elysian city very much in mind.[10]

George Keller's Corporate Palazzo

The fantastic popularity of safety bicycles boosted the company's profits markedly, in turn spurring the continued enlargement of the Capitol Avenue complex. However, mounting demand for bicycles also strained the firm's ability to manage its increasingly complex production and distribution systems from offices in Boston, and in the spring of 1894, Pope announced plans to move the company headquarters to Hartford. Pope remained in Boston, commuting by train and leaving supervision of day-to-day operations to George Day, by then the company's vice president. The dignified new corporate headquarters built that year, together with the south wing erected in 1896, both according to designs by George Keller, fulfilled the vision shared by Day, Keller, and Pope for a stately corporate facade along Capitol Avenue, one to demonstrate that beauty and utility could be combined. Editors of the *Hartford Courant* agreed, suggesting that even architectural critic John Ruskin would soften his hardened disdain for industry and factories.[11]

Keller emerged as a central figure in the industrial expansion taking place. Born in Cork, Ireland, in 1842, he discovered art at an early age in his father's wallpaper business and, following arrival in New York City in 1853, channeled most of his educational energies toward design. Lacking resources for formal architectural study, he found work as a draftsman for a succession of architects, including James Renwick and Peter B. Wight, the latter becoming a friend of long-standing. Wight's admiration for the polychromatic Venetian Gothic, extolled by Ruskin, greatly influenced Keller's art.[12]

During the Civil War, Keller found work in Brooklyn's Navy Yard, where he added knowledge of construction methods to his informal education. He eventually accepted a position as resident designer for Hartford builder James G. Batterson, who used Keller's drawings to enter the design competition for the Connecticut State Capitol. Although Renwick won the commission, Batterson secured the construction contract, and Keller gained familiarity with the city's growing industrial district nearby. Batterson also controlled a quarry and marble company, and Keller began designing monuments, a practice that ultimately gave him national recognition and led to an association with sculptor Caspar Buberl. Facing limited prospects in Batterson's employ, Keller opened his own office in 1872, and fashioned a self-determined career spanning seven of Hartford's decades.[13]

Keller's biographer, David Ransom, places Keller among talented local or regional practitioners in America, who interpreted the country's broad architectural trends successfully, helping to transform provincial cities into more sophisticated urban environments. Ransom might have added that the rise of industry and invention, together with the wealth it created, offered unusual opportunities for these architects, and that the progressive idealism infusing many such industries, bicycles among them, heightened those prospects and stimulated creativity. The collaborative, forward-looking outlook shared by Pope, Day, and Keller illuminates this important but often overlooked aspect of American architectural history.[14]

Keller designed public buildings, churches, factories, bridges and residences, but his most famous commissions are the triumphal Soldier's and Sailor's Memorial Arch in Hartford, dedicated in 1886, and the Garfield Memorial in Cleveland, which opened on Memorial Day in 1890. Both secured his reputation, undoubtedly cementing admiration from Pope and Day, and both reveal his affinity for architectural romanticism during that period. However, by the time Keller designed Pope's corporate headquarters, architectural favor had shifted to a neo-classicism celebrated by the Chicago Exposition. Although Keller may have been susceptible to trends, offering what he believed clients would favor as fashionable, his affiliation with Pope and Day was secure, and he needed no stratagems to gain favor. Rather, his selection of a neo-classical design for the office represented a reasoned choice for the building's context, revealing in Keller an eclecticism fundamental to standards of competency demanded by the architectural profession.[15]

Ironically, Keller probably never attended the Columbian Exposition. He was among the five architects invited by Connecticut's Board of World's Fair Managers to submit design proposals for the Connecticut House, and did so, but the building committee instead selected Warren Briggs from Bridgeport, and Keller was not one of those who traveled to Chicago with Connecticut's delegation in the fall of 1892, despite his association with Day.[16]

Nevertheless, the neo-classical corporate palazzo fronting Capitol Avenue became Keller's most accomplished work for Pope and Day, and the building also deserves to be counted among the architect's most important commissions. Whether due to the austere character of the surrounding brick factories, or to Keller's desire to challenge on his own terms the shift toward neo-classicism, or to Albert Pope's wish to recall his company's Boston office (which survives), Keller's building responded superbly to its context, fitting comfortably with its surroundings but not at the expense of individuality; adding formality and discipline to an industrial facade of organic origins, but not at the expense of creativity; and offering rich, contrasting color and texture

Figure 45. Pope, Day, and Keller continued to advance the aims of City Beautiful on behalf of the bicycle industry, and when Pope moved his company from Boston to Hartford in 1894, George Keller designed new headquarters on Capitol Avenue. He also designed the east wing and south wing in 1896, and a front appendage to the west wing in 1897, that appendage serving as a substation for the United States Postal Service. The matching designs of the west and south wing's street facades framed the industrial complex along Capitol Avenue and accentuated Keller's corporate palazzo, set well back from the street and fronted by ample lawns and ornamental plantings, all within view of the Connecticut State House. Courtesy Harriet Beecher Stowe Center, Hartford, CT.

to the setting, but not at the expense of practicality. That the building has not survived is a great loss, both to the city and to the industry that produced it.

Keller placed the three-story office to the east of the center wing, screening shops and the tall east wing from view along Capitol Avenue. The Renaissance-inspired design employed cream-colored brick trimmed in molded brick and terra-cotta of similar tint, and although the light color contrasted sharply with the surrounding factories of red brick, emphasizing the building's administrative function, the shared use of brick avoided complete detachment of the building from its milieu. Keller's arrangement of the upper two stories proved obedient to curricular rules, and he employed tall arches in groups of three to organize the front elevation, establishing three distinct bays with the center bay slightly recessed, all resting on a well-defined, one-story rusticated base. Prominent, two-story pilasters supported each of the nine arches, and Keller nearly doubled the width of the pilasters that framed each of the three bays on the front elevation.[17]

Keller managed to insert several devices to enrich the design, notably a selective use of polychrome visible in the red sandstone foundation, trim above the arches and at the cornice, and lunettes decorated with

Figure 46. Although Albert Pope moved the company's headquarters to Hartford, he continued to use the former offices and showroom on Columbus Street in Boston. A fire destroyed the building in 1896, but Pope promptly retained Boston architects Peabody and Stearns to design and supervise rebuilding of the structure and it survives today as one of the country's most important commercial buildings related to bicycle manufacturing. The building currently houses residential units. Photo by the author.

bull's eye rondels of brown tinted glass above each arch. He also applied a liberal measure of brick and terra-cotta embroidery to all facades, most noticeably the spandrel walls and cornice, the latter embellished by medallions, thus amplifying the building's executive character. A one-story portico with flat roof capped by a balustrade sheltered the center-bay front entrance, accessible via a massive oak door, and the portico's single set of polished, red-granite Ionic columns added more color, responding to more romantic modes nearby.[18]

The building's interior placed separate offices for the advertising and bookkeeping departments on the first floor; rooms for clerical and junior staff, the second; and offices for Day and Pope, the third, accompanied by an apartment for Pope, a dining room, library, and lecture room; oak wainscoting by Roche and Sons from Bucyrus, Ohio, graced all three floors. Keller devised fire-resistant construction with interior partition walls of brick, or metal lath fastened to channel iron and coated with King's Windsor cement; similarly protected truss floor systems installed by the Berlin Iron Bridge Company eliminated the need for intermediate vertical posts. The Donnelly Brick and Terra Cotta Company from Berlin, Connecticut, supplied the masonry; telephone utilities reached the building underground; and carpenter Peter Taylor and mason William F. O'Neill superintended. Construction began in July 1894, at about the same time that the company built a wooden, circular bicycle track on the roof of the west wing, thirteen laps to the mile—possibly to entice the sixty Boston employees who relocated to Hartford later that year.[19]

Columbia Street, Parkside Terrace, and Pope Park

Keller, Day and Pope also collaborated in the planning, design, and construction of worker housing to secure a dependable force of skilled labor, but also to complement their shared vision for the Frog Hollow district. In 1888, the Weed company conveyed enough land to the city to dedicate a one-block access road extending from the southerly side of Capitol Avenue, and hired Keller to design twenty-four residential units, twelve on each side of the road—christened Columbia Street. In 1890, the firm conveyed the completed project, together with single houses built by the company on nearby Putnam Street, to the newly-chartered Hartford Real Estate Improvement Company, whose six founders were Katherine Beach Day, Josephine Beach, Jane L. Howard (a relative of Connecticut's Lieutenant Governor, James L. Howard, who later became president of the real estate concern), Homer Blanchard (president of the Weed company from 1876 to 1886), attorney William Waldo Hyde, and George Day. Although organized for the purpose of buying and selling real estate, the company set an altruistic course guided by its civic-minded women shareholders.[20]

Keller's design for the housing units underscored his facile eclecticism but more importantly revealed his natural fondness for the romantic trends in England's domestic architecture from this period, which drew inspiration from country houses of the seventeenth and early eighteenth-centuries, particularly vernacular traditions, but interpreted them in creative ways. Those designs developed into what would be described as Queen Anne buildings in both England and America, but the style developed quite differently in the two countries. Keller's units reveal a creative assortment of forms and materials: stubby corner towers with conical roofs; broad façade gables clad in wood shingles; well-defined entrance porches with steeply-pitched gable or hipped roofs; window bays; broad dormers with banks of horizontal windows; and prominent chimney stacks. Those features are richly varied and distinguish each unit, despite the

Figure 47. In 1888, Hartford architect George Keller designed twenty-four residential units for company workers, twelve on each side of Columbia Street, which intersected with Capitol Avenue. The houses received such acclaim that in 1894 Pope retained Keller to design a third row of twelve rowhouses on Parkside Terrace, one block west of Columbia Street and facing a proposed park. All the rowhouses survive. Courtesy Harriet Beecher Stowe Center, Hartford, CT.

interior plans being nearly identical. At the same time, Keller artfully unified the exteriors into a cohesive composition by studious repetition of key features and careful selection of materials, primarily brick, wood shingles, slate, and limited amounts of stone. The houses received such acclaim that even Keller admitted surprise.[21]

The success of the Columbia Street rowhouses precipitated plans for a more substantial workers village on roughly eighty acres of land southerly of Park Street and known as the Bartholomew Farm, which Pope purchased individually during the fall of 1892 and then transferred to his company in December of that year, after returning from Chicago. Plans for industrial communities were common in New England during the nineteenth century, and Pope or Day could have been inspired by any of numerous examples, the closest of which was practically within view—Samuel Colt's armory and workers housing along the Connecticut River, a short distance southeast of Frog Hollow. However, planned development of the Bartholomew

Figure 48 (*opposite*). In 1894, Pope commissioned Olmsted, Olmsted and Eliot to design a park that replaced plans for a large workers village. The 1898 plan by John Charles Olmsted and Frederick Law Olmsted, Jr., is a picturesque pleasure ground, and despite its small size, about ninety-three acres, Pope Park included landscape features common to much larger parks by the Olmsteds. The park provided places for repose as well as active forms of recreation, including tennis courts at the foot of Columbia Street, adjacent to Keller's townhouses. Equally important, the park linked the Capitol Avenue complex with the company's dispersed factories, including George Keller's Columbia Tube Mill, located at the corner of Park and Laurel Streets. National Park Service, Frederick Law Olmsted National Historic Site.

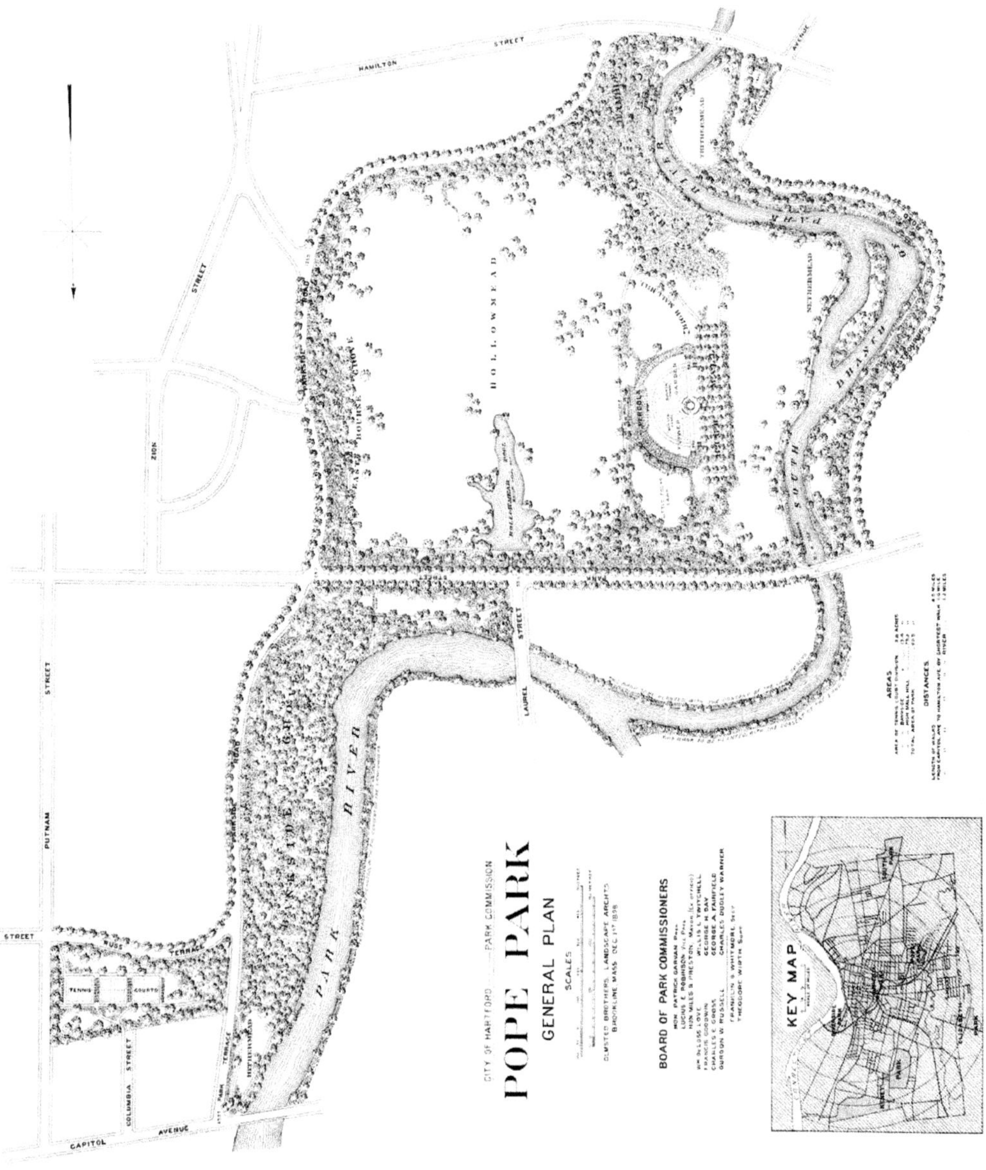
CITY OF HARTFORD — PARK COMMISSION
POPE PARK
GENERAL PLAN
BOARD OF PARK COMMISSIONERS
KEY MAP
AREAS
DISTANCES
HAMILTON STREET
ZION STREET
PUTNAM STREET
CAPITOL AVENUE
COLUMBIA STREET
LAUREL STREET
PARK RIVER
SOUTH BRANCH PARK RIVER
HOLLOWMEAD
TENNIS COURTS

Farm coincided so precisely with the trip to the Chicago Exposition in October 1892 that the latter likely influenced Pope's and Day's shared vision for a workers village. The company's rapid growth also reinforced Pope's belief that the continued success of his business depended upon the welfare and orderly lives of employees, policies reinforced by the company's Mutual Benefit Association.[22]

Day began negotiating with city officials, hoping for financial commitments to extend streets and provide other necessities, explaining that the company could reduce the costs of construction by 25 percent if cottages were built in groups using the Columbia Street model. As discussions evolved, landscape plans called for carving up the farm into 416 building lots. However, negotiations stalled over the city's unwillingness to invest in infrastructure, and in November 1894 Pope and Day instead offered to donate the farm and adjoining land to Hartford for a park, with the condition that the city open access roads, acquire a parcel of land linking the donated property to Columbia and Putnam Streets, and invest in utilities without assessments to Pope or his company.[23]

Pope's individual motivations represented a balance of vision, philanthropy, and common business sense. In addition to giving his employees opportunities for restful scenery and recreational activities, the park's access roads also improved connections between the Capitol Avenue complex, the Columbia Tube Mill and the Hartford Rubber Works, both on Park Street, and the soon-to-be site of the Pope Tube Company factory on Bartholomew Avenue. The company's continuing expansion, combined with the move to Hartford in 1894, had added urgency to those considerations and, while officials studied the proposal, Pope and Day strategically helped the city visualize the setting by retaining Keller that same year to design a third row of twelve rowhouses on Parkside Terrace, one block west of Columbia Street and facing the proposed park. Keller revisited his plans for the earlier project, modified a few features, oversaw construction during the spring and summer of 1895, and then retained one of those units as his fee for the commission, residing there for several decades.[24]

Although George Day likely steered Pope's company toward altruistic considerations, questions remain concerning the origins of the park idea, and the Chicago Exposition once again looms large in Pope and Day's vision for Frog Hollow. As early as 1894, Pope may have begun consulting with the Olmsted firm regarding plans for the park. Frederick Law Olmsted, one of the principal designers of the Chicago Exposition, traveled to Chicago in October 1892 to supervise the planting for his wooded island, the fair's lone picturesque landscape, and Pope and Day might easily have conversed with Olmsted during the formal dedication ceremonies that month. Pope and Olmsted, too, would have been familiar with each other's respective accomplishments and activities in Boston and its suburbs. However, Olmsted became incapacitated soon after the fair, and Pope likely worked with John Charles Olmsted to develop the preliminary plans that were presented to the city in November 1894.[25]

With this added picturesque element, the vision for Industry Beautiful shared by Pope and Day acquired an important new dimension—a place for repose. The final plan for Pope Park is dated December 1898 and is the work of John Olmsted and Frederick Law Olmsted, Jr., by then practicing as the Olmsted Brothers. The pair remained true to the elder Olmsted's regard for parks as places for quiet contemplation of scenery, and despite the park's small size, about ninety-three acres, the two designers skillfully integrated a range of landscape features common to much larger parks. These included an open meadow, Hollowmead;

a lakelet, Hollowmead Pool; a single formal element, High Mall; a more rugged sector, Hillside Ramble; a park-like setting with open understory called Bank Side Grove; and several intimate glades: Nethermead, Hithermead, and Thithermead. The Park River, with a small island in the park's southwesterly corner, established a westerly edge for much of the park, and easterly of Park Terrace the park included tennis courts that became accessible from Columbia and Putnam Streets.[26]

South Wing and Expansion

Back on Capitol Avenue, in 1896 the three-story south wing added more than 65,000 square feet at right angles to the east wing, with a narrow lawn fronting the street. Adhering to the plan for a dignified public facade, Keller placed a prominent appendage at the building's public-front, giving the street elevation additional height and width—the former achieved with a cornice parapet, and adding decorative brick on spandrel walls and cornices. He also organized that extension's three principal elevations using full-height piers to divide those facades into bays. A large showroom dominated the wing's first floor, leading to a shipping room behind; a tire pumping station strategically located outside the showroom entrance lured riders inside. Clerical offices for advertising and printing occupied the second floor, and rooms for repairs the third, with storage of printing material in the basement.[27]

In 1897, the company added a nearly identical appendage to the west wing and leased the building's first floor to the United States Postal Service as Station A for an extended period at a nominal rent. By that time, Hartford's growing industrial district employed roughly 6,000 workers, who lacked convenient access to the city's main post office. The building's upper floors provided offices for drafting, designing, and modeling. Although newspaper descriptions of the project do not identify an architect, the similarities in design to the appendage on the south wing require that credit be awarded to Keller, if not explicitly then by emulation. That year, too, the company added an eighty-foot-long bicycle stable for its workers.[28]

Keller's decorative appendages served as bookends for the industrial campus that Pope and Day created along Capitol Avenue, and photographs from the early twentieth century depict a well-balanced ensemble of three-story buildings fronted by immaculate lawns with ornamental plantings, a tree-lined street bordered by sidewalks, and orderly workers housing opposite. Although iron railings and gates no longer sequestered the company from its urban environs in those images, the fence continued to mark the complex's easterly and westerly edges—a slender boundary separating the bicycle from its outshone industrial neighbors.

Consolidation by the American Bicycle Company

Well before the close of the 1897 season, fractures in the bicycle industry already had begun to widen, the result of over-production and fluctuating demand. By then several manufacturers, including Charles F. Smith of the Indiana Bicycle Company in Indianapolis (Waverly bicycles), Arthur Garford of the Garford Manufacturing Company in Elyria, Ohio (Garford saddles), R. Lindsay Coleman of the Western Wheel Works in Chicago (Crescent bicycles), and Robert S. Crawford of the Crawford Manufacturing Company in Hagerstown, Maryland (Crawford bicycles), had explored strategies for creating a bicycle trust, but without success. Although Garford continued the quest, Albert Spalding emerged as the lynchpin for the conglomerate American Bicycle Company, which formed in the spring of 1899 as a New Jersey corporation with the stated goal of stabilizing the industry by monopolizing production and thus limiting competition. Spalding and Pope, already united by their mutual dislike of Albert Overman, reached an accord after an intermediary, lumber baron Charles R. Flint, offered financial assistance in exchange for protection of his rubber investments. That pact precipitated founding of the bicycle combine, and Pope sold the Capitol Avenue complex to the newly-formed ABC in August of that year. Spalding served briefly as president before retiring, replaced early in 1900 by Coleman, with Garford as treasurer and Pope as board chairman.[29]

In 1900, too, the Sanborn-Perris Map Company inspected the Columbia works, describing a few more details of the manufacturing process. The second floor of the center wing housed die sinking as well as model and machine work; the west wing offered reading and recreation rooms in addition to bicycle storage on the first floor, with machine shops on the third. The east wing basement provided space for the spoke and celluloid departments, truing had been added to the first floor, and assembly occurred on both the second and third floors. That year, too, Pope confirmed changes to the east and west wings to accommodate the production of Spalding bicycles, and pattern specialists crafted models for the Columbia, Hartford, and Spalding bicycles in three separate departments.[30]

Lacking predictable income, heavily burdened by debt, beset by inflated values of the companies it had acquired, shackled by long-held grudges over ancient patent disputes involving Pope and western manufacturers, divided internally by a faction more interested in automobile technology than bicycles, and quickly challenged by the Cycle Trades' Protective Association, ABC would have faced daunting trials even if the bicycle industry had not been edging toward a precipice. Gloom pervaded the 1900 and 1901 seasons as the company closed factories, sold plants and equipment, and created subsidiary units in a futile attempt to stem losses. Controlled by directors loyal to Coleman and western interests, the company paid only scant attention to the Columbia works in Hartford, and the farsighted plans shared by Day, Keller and Pope to beautify the city's industrial district faded far into the background.[31]

At the end of the 1901 season, the bicycle industry showed no signs of reversing its downward spiral, and in December the struggling conglomerate split its business into two principal concerns: the American Cycle Manufacturing Company and the International Motor Company. Joseph Bromley, beholden to Coleman, headed the former from offices in Chicago, and George Pope served as president of the latter. The parent ABC then transferred the Capitol Avenue complex to the bicycle division, officially designating the works as the American Cycle Manufacturing Company—Columbia Factory and staffing it with managers and foremen appointed by Bromley. Unfortunately, that strategy proved to be far too little and much too late, and early in September 1902, after the ABC defaulted on its interest payments to bondholders, the company entered receivership. Pope, Coleman, and court representative John A. Miller served as receivers; all but the sales department of the Capitol Avenue complex closed, putting nearly 150 employees out of work; and the New York City department also shut its doors.[32]

Pope Manufacturing Company, the New Jersey Corporation

Yet Pope had not forsaken the Columbia works in Hartford. As one of the company's principal bond holders, he remained in a position of strength

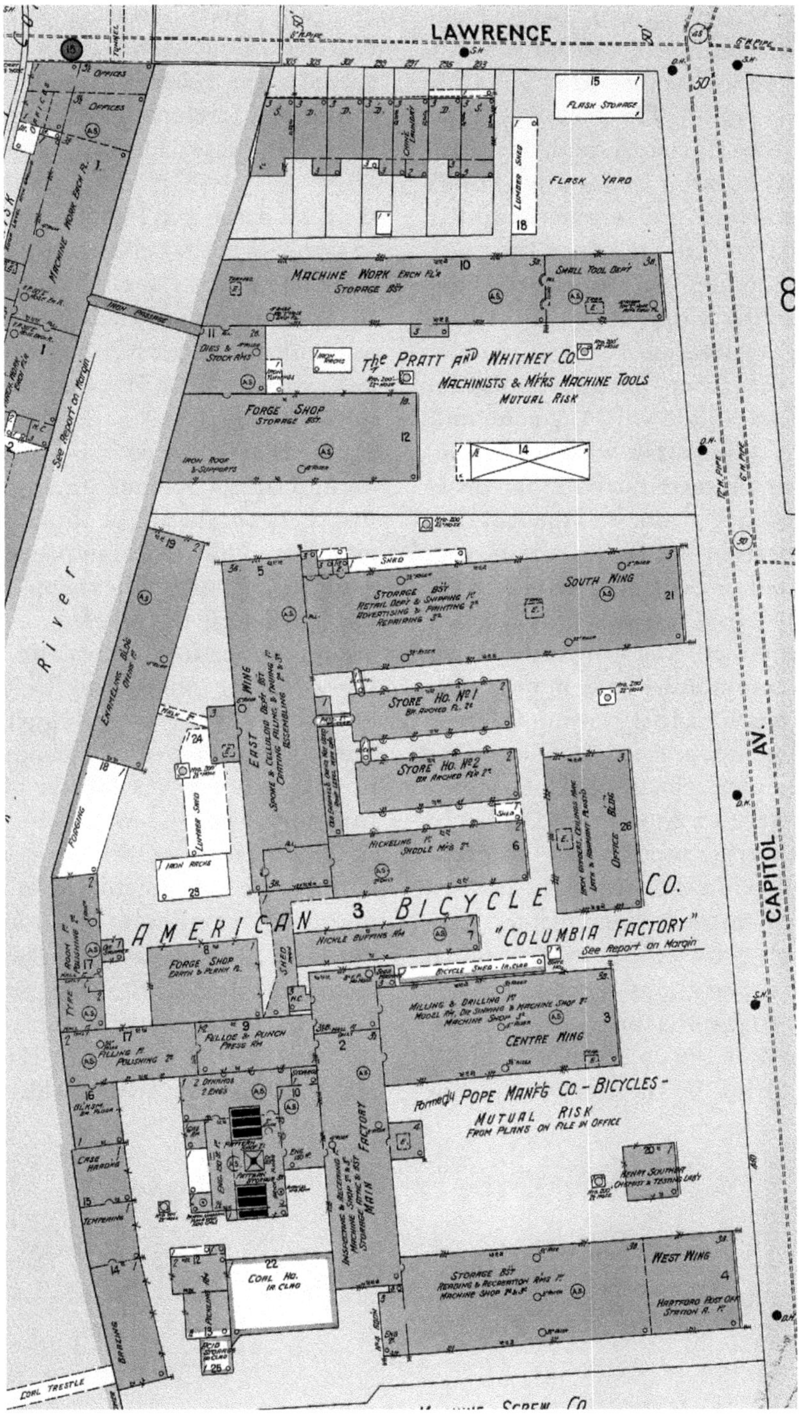

Figure 49. Pope, Day, and Keller continued to expand the complex, all the while advancing the aims of City Beautiful on behalf of the bicycle industry. Keller designed the east and south wings in 1896, and a front appendage to the west wing in 1897, the latter serving as a substation for the United States Postal Service. Sanborn-Perris Map Company, Insurance Maps of Hartford, Vol. 2 (1900): Plate 83, showing the Capitol Avenue complex soon after acquisition by the American Bicycle Company in 1899. Library of Congress, Geography and Map Division.

and had secretly bolstered that leverage by accumulating a substantial share of stock, immediately presenting a plan to rescue the company. The presiding judge assented, the Hartford plant quickly reopened (but soon headed by Pope's former managers and foremen), and in August 1903 the ABC returned the Capitol Avenue complex to a reorganized Pope Manufacturing Company, this time a New Jersey corporation.[33]

However, when grand visions for urban milieu collide with the economic imperatives of industry, whether the latter is real or perceived, troubling consequences are likely to follow. If the ABC had been ill-conceived and the goals of its owners conflicted or even devious, the bicycle industry's core problem of dwindling demand remained, and growing fascination with automobiles and motorcycles explained much of that waning interest. To his credit, Pope grasped the value of the bicycle as a simple, efficient means of going from one place to another and believed correctly that the industry would eventually stabilize. In the meantime, he used advertising to target different sectors of the market, hoping to secure at least marginal loyalty from wary, opportunistic dealers. That strategy also provided a logical way to organize the company's far-flung bicycle factories. By the start of the new company's first full season, 1904, Columbia bicycles produced in Hartford once again served as the industry's standard, but were joined by Cleveland bicycles fabricated in Westfield, Massachusetts, both part of the firm's Eastern Division. Rambler, Crescent, Monarch and Imperial models made in factories in the Chicago area, part of the company's Western Division, occupied a middle price-range; and Crawford bicycles assembled in Hagerstown, Maryland (also part of the Eastern Division), offered economy versions.[34]

However, the course of development along Capitol Avenue during the ensuing years would not be dictated by bicycles. Economic historian Bruce Epperson gauges that automobiles supplied the true motivation for the takeover by Pope, his attempt to secure a dominant position in that fledgling industry just as he had with bicycles. Within a very short time following the takeover, Pope consolidated or sold many of the former bicycle factories of the ABC, including those producing bicycles, and soon commanded automobile manufacturing at four sites, giving his name to four different models, three of them gas-powered: the luxurious Pope-Toledo; the moderately-priced Pope-Hartford, a touring car; an economical Pope-Tribune built in Hagerstown; and the Pope-Waverly, an electric vehicle

Figure 50. The matching designs of the west and south wings' street facades framed the industrial complex along Capitol Avenue and accentuated Keller's corporate palazzo, fronted by ample lawns and ornamental plantings, all within view of the Connecticut State House. The panoramic view is dated 1909 and is a rare view of the entire corporate façade (including the testing building) conceived and planned by Albert Pope, George Day, and George Keller following the World's Columbian Exposition. Pope died in 1909, and by then the company had been in decline for several years. Library of Congress, Photograph Division.

produced at the former Indiana Bicycle Company plant in Indianapolis. Pope also made motorcycles at some of those factories, and during the summer of 1905 the company began moving all bicycle production to the Westfield plant, which produced various models including the Hartford, Tribune, Rambler, Cleveland, Crescent, Monarch, Imperial, and several others, at least until 1907. He then converted the Capitol Avenue works to the manufacture of the Pope-Hartford and to commercial trucks, once more taking for granted the adaptability of standard mill construction.[35]

Pope Manufacturing Company, the Connecticut Corporation

Nevertheless, by this time American industry faced complex financial and technological changes—shifts that also encompassed the design of production systems and factory buildings by engineers and architects. Pope's automobile venture stayed afloat for little more than three years, and then succumbed to receivership following a crippling, seven-month strike at the Toledo plant in the summer of 1907. In 1908, a newly reorganized Pope Manufacturing Company, this time a Connecticut corporation, secured ownership of two principal assets: the Capitol Avenue complex and the plant in Westfield, where the firm produced both motorcycles and bicycles. However, by then Pope had become incapacitated by poor health, and he died in the summer of 1909 at age sixty-six, two years after the company's declaration of insolvency.[36]

Between 1908 and 1912, the Pope family—George Pope; Albert's brother Arthur W. Pope; and Albert's two sons, Albert Linder Pope and Harold Linder Pope—held the reorganized company together, resuming the manufacture of automobiles and trucks at the Capitol Avenue complex and at the company's second tube factory on Bartholomew Avenue, by then called the Western Works. The Westfield plant churned out bicycles, motorcycles, and automobile bodies. In a burst of optimism early in 1912, the company began building a new motor-car plant, a four-story edifice squeezed between Capitol Avenue and the center wing, extending along the edge of the sidewalk almost to the west wing, and swallowing the testing building. The Hartford architectural firm of Ford, Buck and Sheldon designed the factory (which survives), and a Meriden construction firm, the H. Wales-Lines Company, completed the building in December of that year, adding 70,000 square feet to the complex. The project also led to the relocation of Post Office Station A, and to the use of that space by the Pope concern.[37]

From one perspective, the building's skeletal frame of reinforced-concrete with flat-slab floors demonstrated a modern alternative to standard mill construction, achieving a completely fire-proof building and maximizing admission of natural light through large steel-sash window-walls unobstructed by floor beams, thus making the factory's added width practical. To their credit, the architects nodded to the surrounding buildings by applying brick veneer to the exterior piers and spandrel walls, softening the harsh appearance of raw concrete in the process. At the same time, they left the spandrel shelves exposed in an honest expression of structure, resorting to an architectural solution that would become widely used for factories.[38]

To accommodate the design of production systems, the architects or their engineers minimized vertical obstructions in the floor plan, spacing mushroom-head columns at twenty-three feet across the more-than-seventy-foot width, and twenty-five feet along the floor length. An inclined driveway led to the lowest floor, permitting cars to exit the building under power, and an exhaust system ventilated the building from the basement.

Figure 51. In 1912, the fourth Pope Manufacturing Company, then a Massachusetts corporation, erected a four-story factory to manufacture automobiles. The scale and orientation of the skeletal-frame, reinforced-concrete structure destroyed much of the orderly urban-industrial design created by Pope, Day, and Keller along Capitol Avenue. The project also required demolition of the testing building, erased the front elevation of the center wing, diminished the stature of the company's office palazzo, likely contributing to the eventual demolition of Keller's master work, and dramatically altered the streetscape. Today, the factory abuts the surviving west wing and its front block, the latter built as a post office and designed by Keller. The center wing survives behind the automobile factory and is one of possibly three or four surviving buildings in America where the production of high-wheel bicycles occurred. Photo by the author.

Undeniably, the factory is in many ways a significant example of industrial architecture during an important period of evolving design.[39]

From another perspective, however, the building thoroughly disrupted the plans for Industry Beautiful that Pope, Day, and Keller had so carefully orchestrated along Capitol Avenue. Apart from its abundant brick, the motor-car plant turned a cold shoulder to its architectural context in terms of height, massing, spatial relationships, and architectural detail. The center wing and its entrance walk, for decades the plant's principal facade, disappeared behind the new building, and Keller's 1896 corporate palazzo assumed a much-diminished stature, its dignified setback and front lawn serving instead to hide the building from public view along the avenue's westerly approach. In addition, the book-end blocks fronting the west and south wings no longer bore any visual connection to one another, and the plan for an urban industrial campus vanished altogether, replaced by a four-story wall of brick, concrete, and glass rising at the street's edge.

Pope Manufacturing Company, the Massachusetts Corporation

Nor did the building rescue the company from downfall, and events soon exposed the project to be one of financial desperation. Proposing to launch production of a less costly car, curiously priced at $2,250 (Ford's Model T in 1908 sold for $825), the company financed construction of the plant by issuing two-year bonds in the amount of $1,000,000, paying 6 percent interest; newspaper accounts later placed the cost of construction at $130,000. However, in December 1912, even before the building had been completed, the company reorganized a third and final time, on this occasion a Massachusetts corporation, and before the year's end conveyed the Capitol Avenue complex to the reorganized business. Little more than a month later, February 1913, the newly-formed company filed for bankruptcy and soon moved its corporate offices from Keller's elegant building into the former Post Office Station A, a metaphor for the company's demise.[40]

In December 1913, George Pope and two court-appointed receivers completed an appraisal of the company's assets, placing the value of land at the Capitol Avenue complex at $84,750, and buildings at $634,375; equipment, machinery, small and special tools, patterns for automobile parts, and furniture in the corporate headquarters added $544,799 to the total. Early in January 1915, a court-ordered receiver's deed transferred the land and twenty-four buildings comprising the old Columbia factory complex to the Pratt and Whitney Company for the sum of $300,000. The new owners continued to use the buildings until the late 1950s, but then sold the complex to the Aetna Life Insurance Company, which demolished most of the structures. Today, the center and west wings, the building initially built as Post Office Station A, and the motor-car plant are owned by the State of Connecticut and provide office space.[41]

Hartford Rubber Works

Apart from the homes he designed on Columbia Street and Parkside Terrace, and the street-front appendage to the west wing (Post Office Station A), the sole remaining examples of George Keller's industrial architecture for Pope and Day are the 1895 office and adjoining factory for the Hartford Rubber Works, together with

Figure 52. The Pope Manufacturing Company absorbed the Hartford Rubber Works to produce tires for Columbia and Hartford bicycles. Among the buildings shown, only the three-story factory and its front office building designed by George Keller, both with distinctive stepped-parapet gables, remain standing at the corner of Park Street and Bartholomew Avenue. "Hartford Rubber Works," *McClure's Magazine* 8 (April 1897).

his contributions to the design of the 1896 Pope Tube Company works.

Tires gradually became one of Pope's four principal branches of manufacturing in Hartford; bicycles, automobiles, and steel tubes represented the other three. During the first decade of their bicycle manufacturing enterprise, Pope and Day relied satisfactorily on a local manufacturer of molded rubber products, merchant John W. Gray, who in 1881 had established rubber works in a single building, which housed a few rolling mills and mixing machines driven by a small steam engine. Adapting rubber manufacture to the specific demands of bicycles required experimentation, and focus turned to the quality of rubber and to the methods of vulcanizing or hardening rubber in cylindrical form. Gray, Pope and Day collaborated successfully to produce the solid rubber tires that could be fitted to the wheels of Columbia bicycles, both high-wheel ordinaries and early safety models. With a dependable market assured, Gray's business expanded rapidly, and he incorporated the Hartford Rubber Works Company in 1888, the same year that a Scottish veterinary surgeon living in Belfast Ireland, John Boyd Dunlop, patented a pneumatic tubular tire that transformed the bicycle industry. When coupled with pneumatic tires, safety bicycles achieved a spectacular improvement in performance, and bicycles suitable primarily for athletic young men instead became international vehicles for transportation and recreation.[42]

Dunlop's tire employed two separate tubes, an inner inflated tube and an outer protective covering, and the business that he and financier, Harvey Du Cros established managed to monopolize production due to their control of patents for mounting tires onto rims using wire strands or beads. Unlike some designs requiring cement to secure tires to rims, the wire strands allowed temporary removal of the outer covering to permit repairs to the inner tubes.[43]

Dunlop and Du Cros did not immediately license their double-tube pneumatic tire to American bicycle firms, which were slow to develop practical alternatives. Experimental types called "cushion tires" with hollow cores proved barely serviceable during the early 1890s. Gray, Pope and Day struggled to devise a practical design for tires, and produced versions of all three types: pneumatic, cushion, and solid. Gray died in 1892 with perfection of a pneumatic tire not yet achieved, and Pope opted to purchase a controlling interest in the company, becoming the major shareholder as well as principal customer and occupying the president's chair; George Day initially served as treasurer, soon replaced by Lewis D. Parker, who became general manager and eventually president.[44]

The Kyes and Woodbury lithograph depicts the rubber works complex soon after Pope's acquisition and includes at least two buildings erected during that transitional summer of 1892, one identified only as a brick extension on the southerly end of the plant, and the other an addition to the boiler-house. With or without those adjuncts, the image reveals the extent to which Gray had expanded the business in concert with the manufacture of Columbia and Hartford bicycles, the latter commencing in 1890. However, the lithograph precedes Keller's 1895 buildings.[45]

The summer prior to Pope's acquisition of the rubber works, he and Day had traveled to Europe to study pneumatic tires, and despite the visible superiority of Dunlop's double-tube design, especially for the repair of punctures, Pope favored the simplicity of single-tube tires. However, Pope also purchased patents belonging to an American inventor from Cranston Rhode Island, Pardon W. Tillinghast, whose tire closely resembled the published but unpatented design for a single-tube tire by an Englishman, I.W.

Boothroyd. Pope's engineers then tackled the problem of punctures by devising a repair kit reliant on an inverted, mushroom-shaped plug to be inserted through the tire wall from inside the tube; large cuts required shop repair with renewed vulcanizing—or preferably a new tire. Similar plugs successfully held valve stems in place, leaving just one more troublesome problem: locating punctures or leaks.[46]

Pope's commitment to single-tube pneumatic tires, despite being difficult to repair, set him apart from most of the bicycle industry in 1892, but he justified the decision because his tire was both durable and well-suited for the wooden rims used on so many bicycles. The description "single tube" belies the tire's three separate layers vulcanized into a single surface: an inner tube of rubber that held the air; two layers of encasing fabric giving strength to the tire; and an outer cover or wearing surface, also two layers, which protected the inner fabric from abrasion and moisture. Workers completed the manufacturing process by vulcanizing the entire fabrication in individual iron molds. For the outer cover, company managers had difficulty finding a fabric with weaves resilient enough to avoid tearing, which precipitated damage to the inner layers, but not so resilient as to reduce strength and durability. After many experiments, Pope's craftsmen found the correct balance in specified weaves of Georgia's expensive Sea Island cotton, closely woven but at the same time soft and strong.[47]

Pope also claimed that the tire was faster, and by 1896 other manufacturers were following his example. However, by that time he had hedged his commitment to single-tube tires and had purchased licenses to manufacture the superior double-tube tires as well, including both the Dunlop and Gormully and Jeffery versions, the latter manufactured by the G and J Tire Company in Indianapolis and sold through the B.F. Goodrich Tire Company.[48]

Thus, in 1895 when Keller obtained a commission to design two brick additions to the rubber works, Pope's tire-manufacturing process had stabilized. The larger, three-story building housed the storage of materials and finished products, as well as space for departments that had outgrown the existing plant; the two-story front appendage with elevated basement, arched entrance with decorative brickwork, and semi-circular fanlight above the recessed door, provided office space. Keller provided distinctive stepped gables with oculi windows beneath the gable peaks, adding a visible insignia to Pope's expanding industrial works in Parkville. At about the same time, the company also added a three-story office block establishing a primary entrance and focal point facing Bartholomew Avenue. Keller probably designed that edifice as well, but he introduced an ample measure of architectural embellishment, giving formality to a small segment of the sprawling complex.[49]

Pope owned the company for only seven years, and in 1899 the Hartford Rubber Works became part of ABC. However, Charles Flint demanded control of the Hartford firm, and in November 1899 the struggling ABC sold that unit to Flint's conglomerate Rubber Goods Manufacturing Company. The business retained its corporate structure and name—the Hartford Rubber Works Company—and Lewis Parker eventually added to his responsibilities, heading five of the consortium's businesses. Under his capable management, the Hartford firm prospered and, in the summer of 1903, erected a three-story brick factory reliant on standard mill construction, but with a prominent if stubby central tower capped on its four corners by truncated finials. Located on the easterly side of Bartholomew Avenue, the building stood completed the summer Pope returned to Hartford after collapse of the ABC, and

Figure 53. George Keller's design for the factory and offices of the Hartford Rubber Works included oculi windows as well as stepped-parapet gables, and when the Pope Tube Company erected its works a short distance away on Bartholomew Avenue, builders of the factory used similar windows and a modified version of end-gable parapets. The insignia visually helped to unify the dispersed factories of Albert Pope's bicycle and automobile empire. Photo by the author.

briefly served bicycle manufacturing under the reorganized Pope concern.[50]

At this point, the story of Hartford's rubber industry begins to diverge from the context of the city's bicycle production, which ended after 1905, and turns instead toward the manufacture of tires for automobiles. The Rubber Goods Manufacturing Company soon became enmeshed in its own internal struggles, and by the following spring, reports began circulating concerning a merger with an older rubber consortium formed in 1892, the United States Rubber Company, which eventually absorbed the Hartford Rubber Works. The latter continued to operate the plant, investing more than three million dollars between 1919 and 1921 to erect four new reinforced-concrete buildings on the easterly side of Bartholomew Avenue and southerly side of Park Street. However, during the summer of 1929 the company closed the plant and moved its tire-manufacturing operation to Detroit, leasing the Hartford buildings to various businesses until 1945, when a syndicate of three real estate companies purchased the entire works, by then comprising ten buildings.[51]

Today, several of the later factories on the easterly side of Bartholomew Avenue survive, but Keller's two buildings and the 1903 plant are all that remain of the Hartford Rubber Works complex as it existed during the Pope era of bicycle manufacturing in Hartford. Keller's buildings also are among the few surviving buildings once owned, albeit very briefly, by the doomed ABC.

6

Pope Tube Company

Hartford, Connecticut

In the far southwesterly reaches of Albert Pope's industrious vision for Hartford, at the corner of Bartholomew Avenue and Hamilton Street in the city's Parkville district, the 1896 Pope Tube Company factory stands as one of the city's five surviving industrial buildings related to bicycle manufacturing, joining the center wing, the west wing and its post office appendage, George Keller's 1896 additions to the Hartford Rubber Works, and the 1903 factory on Bartholomew Avenue. By contrast, during the late 1890s at least fifty buildings contributed to that ambit, with Pope Park easily accessible to all; today, too, the park is much diminished, and both physically and visually severed from Bartholomew Avenue.

Both the Pope Tube Company factory and its predecessor, Keller's 1893 Columbia Tube Works, are significant in the context of nineteenth-century bicycle manufacturing because Pope contributed to three related aspects of tube manufacturing: the testing of steel used for bicycle frames, forks, and handlebars; the methods used for manufacturing seamless tubing, specifically both cold-drawing and cupping processes; and the quest for vertical integration in the bicycle industry. Both factories also contribute to the broader historical context of seamless steel tube fabrication in America, an important chapter in the history of steel manufacturing and one tied closely to bicycles. Equally significant, the surviving tube factory is an early example of industrial architecture that unifies the design of both building and manufacturing systems into a single, integrated process, anticipating trends not yet widely exploited by engineers and architects as a field of specialized practice.

Just as Albert Pope had sought to monopolize the manufacture of bicycles through ownership of patents, he also maneuvered to secure a dominant position in the production of tubing. Challenged by a host of obstacles, Pope orchestrated three notable results: a landmark example of industrial architecture in Hartford; acceptance by the steel industry of fifty-carbon steel as the precise balance of strength and light weight suitable for numerous industries, including bicycles; and the use of nickel-steel for superior strength.[1]

Tube Fabrication Technology

Long before bicyclists pedaled into view, inventors had sought seamless tubes of both ferrous and non-ferrous metals. Methods of tube production, with or without seams, varied widely but shared certain characteristics, primarily a lengthy, labor-intensive, and costly process, with results not always satisfactory in gauge, strength under stress, and overall quality. Each of those concerns became critically important as the bicycle industry

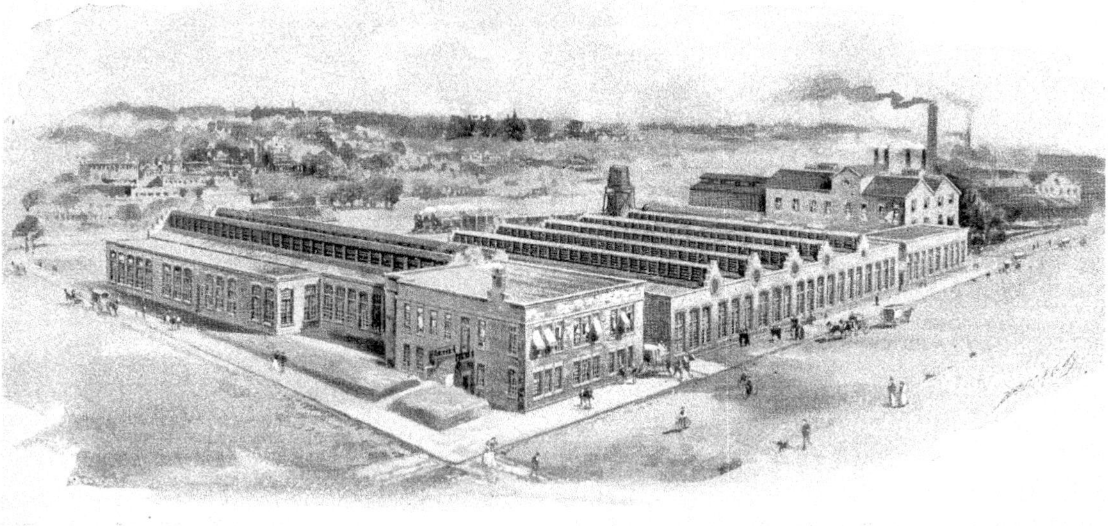

Figure 54. The Pope Tube Company works on Bartholomew Avenue in Hartford. Renowned mechanical engineer Erasmus D. Leavitt, aided by Asa M. Mattice, designed the plant's inner workings and power systems, and Mattice turned to structural engineers at the Berlin Iron Bridge Company to design the roof structure. The monitors' stepped gables and oculi windows were George Keller's contribution, and Henry A. Wolcott, a contractor from West Hartford, supervised construction. Pope Tube Company Catalog (1896), author's document.

flourished, and during the early 1890s American bicycle manufacturers challenged European dominance of tube manufacture, launching America's seamless tube industry in the process. Those efforts also led directly to the two factories Pope built to produce tubes, adding to our understanding of each building.

Generally, manufacturers produced welded tubes from flats strips of metal called skelps, pressing or rolling them into cylindrical form with butt or lap edges fused by welding; or, created lock-jointed or clinched tubes by rolling or pressing skelps with dies, the former with edges turned inward and coupled, the latter having interlocking serrated edges, with the seams of both types then brazed. Companies favoring seamless tubes instead purchased short billets of iron or steel, hollowed them by drilling or punching end to end, and then lengthened and refined the gauge of the billets with a series of cold or heated draws using mandrels to govern interior diameters, followed by annealing after each draw to restore metallurgical integrity. Workers also lengthened heated hollow billets by passing them through successive rolling mills of various designs. Resorting to a more tedious process called cupping, machinists converted a blank disc into a cup-like shape through successive die presses, severed the bottom edge, and then elongated the hollowed cup using either cold or hot drawing methods, or by rolling.[2]

However, bicycles arrived amid a revolutionary discovery in the manufacture of seamless tubes, an invention called rotary piercing and patented in 1885 and 1886 by two German engineers, Max and Reinhard Mannesmann. Inadvertently, the two brothers discovered that by placing a set of rotating discs or barrel-shaped rolls at a skewed angle against a solid, heated round, one disc or roll on each side to create axial rotation of the round, the simultaneous pressure on both sides of the rotating round created a soft internal cavity. As the round passed through those cross rolls, which pulled the round forward, a stationary mandrel pierced the cavity and smoothed the interior surface from end to end. In a single, rapid, one-step pass, the process not only converted a solid round into a fully hollow seamless tube but also configured the tube's internal diameter, external circumference, and gauge of the metal, reducing the time of fabrication by an astonishing margin. Metal displaced from the core also increased the tube's length. By 1890 the Mannesmanns had achieved a European monopoly, just as the safety bicycle's fantastic prospects had become apparent, and their mills also marketed successfully to the American bicycle industry during the late 1880s and early to mid 1890s.[3]

If not purchased from the Mannesmanns during that period, seamless tubular steel for many American bicycles originated with hollow billets produced in Sweden and elongated in English factories reliant on cold or hot-drawing, hot rolling, or a combination of the two. The complexity and cost of fabricating seamless tubes placed American bicycle manufacturers in positions of vulnerability as demand for tubes (and for tubes of greater length) increased and as competition intensified. In addition, light frames (particularly in the racing sector), required calculable strength, as did the introduction of pneumatic tires by 1890, which increased speeds and created corresponding stresses on frames.[4]

American Advances

As early as 1882, Albert Pope had studied English methods of manufacturing cold-drawn weldless tubing for the backbone frames of high-wheel bicycles. At the cost of considerable weight, adequate strength of those tubular frames could be attained through heavy gauge, and American bicycle manufacturers remained content to import tubing, or to purchase imported tubes directly from Pope. However, the arrival of safety bicycles forced changes in outlook, and contemporaneously with his company's acquisition and enlargement of the Capitol Avenue complex in 1890, Pope turned his attention to the manufacture of tubing, traveling to Europe in the summer of 1891 to investigate both tube-manufacturing and the production of pneumatic tires.[5]

Lozier-Yost Seamless Tube Works. However, two other enterprising Americans, Henry Lozier and Joseph Yost, were several steps ahead of Pope. Lozier, a sewing machine agent in Cleveland, added a line of safety bicycles to his catalog in 1887, and in the summer of 1889 joined with Joseph Yost, who had ended his association with Joseph McCune and the Springfield Bicycle Manufacturing Company in January of that year, to form the Lozier and Yost Bicycle Manufacturing Company in Toledo. Both men foresaw the need for an American tube mill and traveled to England and Ireland for seven weeks in 1890, with plans to purchase tubing and observe the industry. In January 1891, the two partners formed the Lozier-Yost Seamless Tube Works as an Ohio corporation, with Albert Pope as a major shareholder, but chose to locate the concern in Shelby in north-central Ohio, changing the name by mid-summer to the Shelby Steel Tube Company—a token gratuity to the citizens of Shelby who paid approximately $50,000 in stock subscriptions to attract the business.[6]

The Shelby Steel Tube Company. The firm began production that same summer using machinery and a process licensed by an English firm, Hudson and Gay, that converted imported, pierced, hollow billets into seamless tubes through the slow, hand-operated process of heated rolling rather than cold-drawing, requiring a dozen or more passes through a two-high rolling mill. In addition to Lozier, Yost, and Pope, founding shareholders included industrialist William E. Miller from Elyria, Ohio, and David L. Cockley from Shelby, the latter serving as the company's first president. From those beginnings, America's seamless tube industry expanded at a pace nearly equal to that of bicycle manufacturing, and between 1891 and 1897 a sequence of events created the context in which Pope's tube factories in Hartford are best understood.[7]

Columbia Tube Works

In an amicable agreement reached in December 1891, Lozier acquired Yost's interest in their bicycle company and then reorganized the concern as the Lozier Manufacturing Company, which began producing Cleveland bicycles at the Toledo plant, with tubes supplied by his Shelby firm. In Hartford, following his study of European tube-manufacturing practices in 1891, Pope implemented plans to produce his own tubing, and during the summer of 1893 completed construction of the Columbia Tube Mill, located at the corner of Laurel and Park Streets. As depicted on the Kyes and Woodbury lithograph, the building exemplifies standard mill construction and offers convincing evidence that factory owners, builders, engineers, and architects did not just adapt that type of building to different uses as needs arose, but instead sought that versatility from the outset of the design process.[8]

Pope faced a long list of uncertainties about tube manufacturing, including the complex and costly methods of fabrication; the revolutionary but closely guarded invention by the Mannesmann brothers; lack of knowledge about the proper strength of tubes used for bicycle frames; the vagaries of American iron and steel manufacturing; and the new tube works underway in Shelby. In response, he chose to erect a building that would be suitable for other manufacturing purposes if for any reason the company no longer needed to produce its own tubes. The dignified head-house, crowned by tower with clock, is also consistent with the quest for versatility—a visually appealing front office attributed to architect George Keller and demonstrating the architect's eclectic repertoire. The building's heavy massing and tower, particularly the latter, reveal the influence of Henry Hobson Richardson's Romanesque, but the design also borrows from a German architectural mode, *Rundbogenstil*, which represented a synthesis of classical and medieval traditions in that country and became fashionable during the middle of the nineteenth century. The form acquired the moniker Round-Arched style for industrial and commercial buildings in America, reflecting a belief that such buildings should express utility and function but with a measure of architectural effect to avoid the monotony of severe brick or stone.[9]

Pope began producing seamless tubes that summer, using the cold-drawn process, and he also erected the small building fronting Capitol Avenue, between the center and west wings, to test the strength of his tubing (see Chapter 5). However, he retained his interest in the Shelby concern, where both he and George Day became directors. Nor did he overlook the potential for collaboration with the Mannesmann firm, with the goal of producing tubes for steam engine boilers as well as bicycles. At least by the summer of 1894 Pope had reached a tentative agreement to establish a separate business, the Pope-Mannesmann Company, requiring construction of a new factory in

Hartford, at his expense, with equipment and expertise to be supplied by the German firm.[10]

Ellwood Weldless Tube Company. Lozier, too, remained dissatisfied with the status quo, partly because of conflict that had developed with William Miller over control of the Shelby business, and he devised a shrewd strategy to thwart Miller. During that same summer of 1894, Lozier began negotiations with a Swiss engineer, Ralph C. Stiefel, who had worked at the Mannesmann company's plant at Landore in Wales. The Mannesmann's rotary piercing created a rope-like twist of metal fibers on the exterior of the tube due to the increased speed of rotation along the axis of the round when it passed through the discs or rolls, and their patent claimed that this twisting added strength to the tube. Subsequent testing proved that claim to be incorrect, and Stiefel conceived a design that eliminated the twisting and torsional strain—a plan that he divulged to Lozier.[11]

Sensing opportunity, Lozier sold his stake in the Shelby business in the fall of 1894, and with Stiefel acquired a controlling interest in the Ellwood Shafting and Tube Company of Ellwood City, Pennsylvania, northwest of Pittsburgh near Beaver Falls. He changed the name of the business to the Ellwood Weldless Tube Company and appointed Stiefel plant manager. Together, Lozier and Stiefel successfully circumvented the Mannesmann invention with Stiefel's own rotary-piercing American and British patents, the former secured in December 1895, after contentious litigation by the Germans. When in June 1895 Lozier and Stiefel first began production, the Ellwood company liberated America's dependence on Europe for hollow billets, reducing the cost of tube production by nearly one third. In doing so, the Ellwood concern became the Shelby firm's reviled competitor.[12]

Confronted by this turn of events, the Mannesmann company withdrew from its agreement with Pope, leaving him to his own solutions. However, with tube production already underway in Hartford by 1893, Pope either could import hollow billets from Europe or purchase tubes at lower cost from Lozier once the latter's production began, leaving Pope free to test the strength of steel and to design an efficient system for elongating tubes. Ultimately content with securing reliable quality and quantity of tubular steel, and having little need for the Shelby product, Pope sold his shares to Miller in 1894, and the latter became president of the Ohio company in the fall of 1896.[13]

Greenville Tube Company. Lozier wasted no time exploiting the tactical advantages afforded by the Stiefel patent, and he began supplying hollow pierced billets to the growing number of American tube mills, whether derived from American or European steel. Nor did he give Miller a moment's respite. In the spring of 1896, Lozier and Stiefel expanded production by opening a second factory, the Greenville Tube Company, in Greenville, Pennsylvania, situated north of Beaver Falls on the Shenango River. As before, Lozier inveigled funds from local citizens in exchange for locating the plant in Greenville, but this time most of the $45,000 inducement amounted to an outright grant to the company rather than subscriptions for stock.[14]

A year later, the spring of 1897, Lozier found another way to confound Miller by urging tariff protection under the Dingley Tariff Law, then being reassessed by President McKinley's new administration. Pointing to the government's goal of protecting infant industries, Lozier argued that imports of certain types of unfinished materials (such as the solid blooms or billets purchased by Ellwood) should face a lower tariff than other partially-finished products (for example, the hollow pierced

(No Model.) 2 Sheets—Sheet 2.

R. C. STIEFEL.

MECHANISM FOR MAKING TUBES FROM METALLIC INGOTS.

No. 551,340. Patented Dec. 10, 1895.

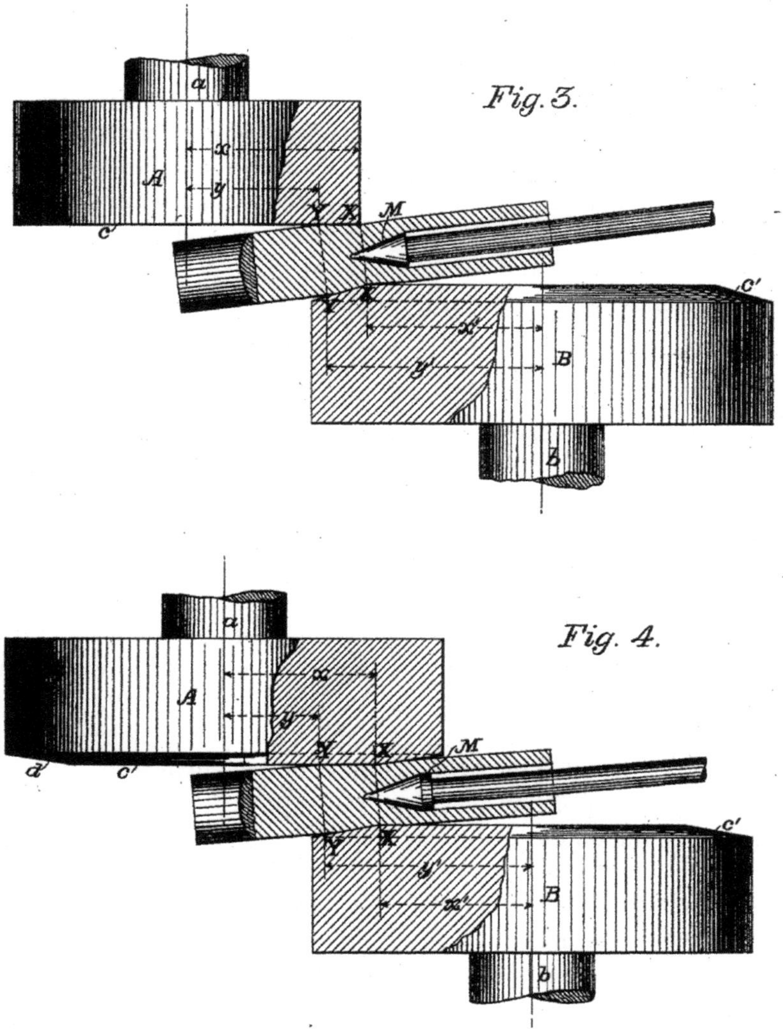

WITNESSES:
L. G. Hopper.
Ike Isaacs.

INVENTOR,
Ralph C. Stiefel.
BY Wm A. Skinkle
ATTORNEY.

Figure 55. Swiss engineer Ralph C. Stiefel improved a revolutionary process for fabricating tubes called rotary piercing, invented by German engineers Max and Reinhard Mannesmann. Stiefel and Henry Lozier acquired the Ellwood Shafting and Tube Company of Ellwood City, Pennsylvania, and began manufacturing seamless tubes using rotary piercing, successfully circumventing the Mannesmann patents despite vigorous litigation by the latter. United States Patent Office.

billets imported by Shelby). Miller turned successfully to Ohio's congressional delegation to sidestep the snare, but barely in time to confront another maneuver by Lozier that same spring.

Tubes (America) Limited. Seeking to maximize profit from the Stiefel patent, which had been widely accepted in England and France, Lozier orchestrated an American-European tube syndicate called Tubes (America) Limited, an English corporation to be headquartered in Cleveland with Lozier as president and Stiefel as general superintendent and mechanical engineer. Lozier and his vice president Henry Hartman persuaded English investors, among them industrialists William and Arthur Pilkington, to acquire options to purchase the Ellwood and Greenville plants as well as a third company, the American Weldless Tube Company in Toledo. The consortium published a prospectus early in July 1897, announcing that an agreement had been reached to license use of the Stiefel patent for a period of five years.[15]

Shelby Steel Tube Company Reorganized. Alarmed, Miller traveled to Europe and announced plans by the Shelby firm to open trade with England and to undercut the price of European tubes being sold to bicycle manufacturers by substantial margins. English investors became skittish, trading of the syndicate's stock halted, and by the fall of 1897, Lozier's scheme had collapsed. Confronted by deadlock, the two men reached an understanding that profit rested in union rather than rivalry, and in October 1897 six American tube manufacturers (including the Ellwood, Greenville, and Toledo concerns) merged under the umbrella of a reorganized Shelby Steel Tube Company ("The" omitted), a Pennsylvania corporation.[16]

At least three developments important to the bicycle industry and to Pope's enterprise in Hartford emerged from that unfolding context. Miller, as president of Shelby, placed the company on course for securing a monopoly in the production of seamless tubes in America; Lozier amassed a small fortune from the sale of the Ellwood and Greenville plants, but also reclaimed his seat on the Shelby board of directors, where he monitored the availability of tubes for his own bicycle manufacturing interests; and Pope remained true to his plans, well underway by 1895, to produce high-quality tubes for Columbia bicycles, conforming to the standards set by his experimental testing of tubular steel, and on a scale requiring construction of an exemplary factory, a substitute for the factory planned with the Mannesmann firm and a successor to the Columbia Tube Works.

Although still facing the prospect of purchasing hollow steel billets, Pope likely reasoned that he could counter those costs by perfecting a system for elongating tubes of precise strength; by fabricating reliably strong tubes for other markets, including steam boilers; and by investing in an exceptionally efficient factory that fused building design with production systems. Totting up, he continued to believe that by paying tribute to quality the costs would fall into place. Although the Shelby concern had acquired the Stiefel patent, refining the dimensions of tubes for various uses remained a substantial part of the manufacturing process. In addition, Miller continued to expand the Shelby firm by absorbing other companies, solidifying its monopoly but also creating inefficiencies that added to the cost of producing each tube.[17]

Experiments at Columbia Tube Works

With both the Columbia Tube Mill plant on Laurel Street and the testing building on Capitol Avenue in operation by the summer of 1893, Pope and Day began experiments to test both the strength of tubular steel and the most efficient methods for elongating that steel through cold-drawing, with several important results. Initially, the company's engineers devised methods of testing with few guiding precedents, thus underscoring the progressive, trial-and-error nature of their endeavors. Moreover, the steel industry soon credited Pope with having been among the first to demonstrate that high-carbon steel possesses an optimum combination of strength and lightness. As well, the collective knowledge acquired by company engineers from that testing became integral to the sophisticated design of the landmark tube factory built in 1896 on Bartholomew Avenue. Secondarily, although Pope seldom missed an opportunity to advertise—and certainly not the promotional bonanza offered by his princely investment in testing—the company's research amounted to much more than a marketing venture, placing Pope's claims that Columbia bicycles set an industry standard in a more genuine light.

Department of Destruction. The testing required expertise in engineering and metallurgical science, and two important figures, Navy Lieutenant Harold Haydon Eames and engineer Henry Souther, joined the company's ranks of employees. Eames, born in Shanghai, China, and a graduate of the United States Naval Academy,

Figure 56. The Pope Manufacturing Company's testing building on Capitol Avenue housed an Emery Hydraulic Testing Machine. Pope's engineers demonstrated that carbon content of 0.50 percent, or fifty-carbon steel, offered maximum endurance under vibratory strains but with sufficient elasticity to resist heavy shocks. Based on those experiments, the country's steel manufacturers credited the bicycle industry as the first to recognize the value of higher carbon content to achieve optimum strength and lightness. *Iron Age* 59 (January 14, 1897).

became manager of the tube works, and Souther, a chemical-engineering graduate from MIT, headed the testing unit dubbed the Department of Destruction, where he conducted chemical analysis of steel specimens and also operated an array of costly machines designed to break the tubes that Eames produced. Together, the two units comprised a fully equipped, chemical and physical laboratory for testing steel—the only example of its kind among bicycle manufacturers; the only such laboratory in the country specifically testing tubes; and one of very few such testing programs outside the steel industry.[18]

Experiments to test the strength of tubular steel relied upon several different machines designed for specific purposes. At center stage in the testing building, the company's Emery Hydraulic Testing Machine could exert up to 100,000 pounds of pressure in either compression or tension, but the apparatus also could create and measure stresses of only a few ounces. The device transferred stresses to a scale housed in a free-standing cabinet, and then weighed the stresses independently of any friction caused by the forces being exerted on the tube. Fabricated by William Sellers and Company of Philadelphia, Pope's model cost a hefty $10,000 but was a much smaller version of a very large weighing machine invented in 1879 by a Connecticut firm, the A.H. Emery Company, and commissioned by the federal government for use in the Watertown Arsenal near Boston, where comparisons of iron and steel had begun.[19]

A second apparatus resembling a large lathe tested torsional and bending-moment stresses by introducing axial rotation of tubes and then loading the center of the tube with weight equivalent to that of a rider, thus flexing the tube in opposite directions at each revolution. The results demonstrated remarkable variations in the strength of tubes, with some tubes failing after 5,000 revolutions and others after 3,000,000 turns over a period of weeks. A third device, a frame testing machine, stressed assembled frames to destruction by applying compression forces between two points on the frame—the bottom bracket and the saddle post socket—until distortion occurred, thus exposing the weakest point of the frame. A fourth machine called a dynamometer, developed by J. Burkitt Webb of the Stevens Institute of Technology in Hoboken, New Jersey, measured the extent to which stresses absorbed by different parts of the bicycle frame varied according to different conditions such as speed, level roads, or hills. The results isolated the weakness or superiority of one part of the frame over another.[20]

Fifty-Carbon Steel. Tubular frames must absorb tension, compression, and bending stresses simultaneously on several parts of the tube's section, and the company's most important discoveries from testing concerned the level of carbon content in steel. Bicycle frames typically succumbed to two very different types of strains: vibrations occurring during ordinary use; and the effects of heavy shocks or bending, as in a collision with another object. The latter demanded sufficient elasticity in the metal to absorb the shocks without fracturing, but the former required sufficient strength to avoid eventual rupture from fatigue, which causes the steel to lose strength and become brittle. Carbon adds strength to steel, thus countering the long-term effects of vibration, but also makes the steel more brittle, rendering the metal vulnerable to fracture from heavy shock or bending. Eames and Souther together demonstrated that carbon content of 0.50 percent, or fifty-carbon steel, offered maximum endurance under vibratory strains and sufficient elasticity to resist heavy shocks. Nickel-steel alloy yielded an even stronger metal, countering concerns about brittle characteristics, and could be used at the points of greatest stress on frames.

Although a difference of one-quarter of 1 percent carbon content may seem small, that margin is far from negligible when considering the engineered factor of safety, defined as the calculated strength of a machine or structure beyond its intended loads. A boiler, for example, easily might be designed to a factor of six times its expected capacity, and justly so. However, bicycles presented a conundrum for engineers because the quest for faster speeds demanded lighter frames; lighter frames sacrificed structural strength; and faster speeds increased stresses on frames. Eames highlighted those challenges in a letter published in *Iron Age*, observing that the factor of safety for bicycles was exceptionally low, about one and one-quarter times expected strains. Thus, when the company's tests showed that

Figure 57. In addition to testing the strength of steel tubing in the company's Department of Destruction, engineers Harold Haydon and Henry Souther operated other machines designed to test different bicycle parts. One apparatus, a frame testing machine, stressed assembled frames to destruction by applying compression forces between the bottom bracket and the saddle post socket—until distortion occurred, thus exposing the weakest point of the frame. *Iron Age* 59 (January 14, 1897).

fifty-carbon steel lasted eight times as long as twenty-five-point carbon steel, the value extended not just to longevity but also to safety.[21]

Approval by Steel Industry. The importance of Pope's testing program extended well beyond bicycle production and captured the attention of America's steel industry. Explicit recognition of the testing in Hartford came from John Fritz, an exceptionally talented ironmaster and one of very few men able to chronicle the many trials of the Bessemer steel-making process in America, from its inception to the close of the nineteenth century. Fritz superintended two of America's pioneering steel manufacturers: the Cambria Iron Works in Johnstown, Pennsylvania, in 1854, and the Bethlehem Iron Company, which in 1899 became the Bethlehem Steel Company. He worked with Alexander Holley to design a Bessemer converting plant for the Pennsylvania Steel Company near Harrisburg in 1867, among the country's first, and at Bethlehem, Fritz designed the plant's foundry and heavy forging equipment.[22]

Fritz's tribute to Pope's engineers was neither casual nor solicited. He had grounded much of his work at both Johnstown and Bethlehem in experimental tinkering, and thus the empirical testing in Hartford, underway the year Fritz retired from Bethlehem, may have stirred his interest. In 1896, as retiring president of the American Society of Mechanical Engineers, he complied with a request to present a paper recounting the country's history of iron and steelmaking, but he then shifted the discussion to advances in machine design made possible by perfections in steel strengthened by nickel, oil tempering, and proper amounts of carbon. He then explained that recent tests of forged shafts used in steam engines and fabricated with varying levels of nickel and carbon revealed that a shaft of nickel-steel could achieve the same strength as one of puddled wrought iron (with low carbon content) but at one-quarter of the weight. He then congratulated the bicycle industry "as the first to recognize the value of the development in the manufacture of steel, in the direction of higher carbon, with all its salient advantages, with regard to combining strength with lightness."[23]

Production Testing. Testing at the Columbia Tube Works had addressed other areas of production as well, including the operation of drawing machines; amount of reduction possible for each draw of a tube; temperature of the annealing ovens as measured by pyrometers; length of time required for annealing; and the number of draws required to achieve proper tubular strength. If some variances proved to be small, those differences nevertheless translated into larger benefits as the quality of tubes advanced from one stage to the next, and the company gained a proprietary advantage from its testing and fabrication experience. As demand for the company's tubes increased after 1893, Pope or Day installed more draw benches in response. Yet only a factory carefully designed to meet the specific demands of tube manufacturing could achieve Pope's quest for cost efficiencies, and plans for that building were underway by 1895 on land he had acquired from the Bartholomew estate.[24]

Pope Tube Company Factory

Pope's steep investment in testing machinery, expensive fifty-carbon and nickel-steel, routine sampling of steel orders to assure uniformity of carbon content, and lengthy process of tube-drawing and annealing, had created costs disproportionately high to the overall expense of manufacturing Columbia bicycles. To recoup those expenditures, Pope embarked on a strategy for manufacturing tubes in which the engineering of building, machinery, power systems, furnaces, circulation of materials, interior space, lighting, and ventilation became a single, integrated work of design—the physical plant just one of numerous engineered components contributing to a cohesive industrial process, orchestrated to achieve a calculated return on investment: design and profit incorporated.

Pope, Day, Eames, Souther and other company engineers or machinists approached the task of designing the new factory with extraordinary thoroughness, drawing from their experience at the Columbia Tube Works and requiring an expansive open interior on a single floor to allow the continuous movement of heavy materials back and forth between draw benches and annealing ovens, unobstructed by vertical supports. A sophisticated design for the roof structure thus became essential, with three principal requirements: maximize clear spans of the roof's structural framing to minimize the need for interior vertical posts; incorporate sufficient loading capacity into that structural system to carry overhead traveling hoists; and provide for roof lighting and ventilation.

Consulting Team. Pope and Day assembled an exceptional team of consultants to assist with design, including mechanical engineers Erasmus D. Leavitt and Asa M. Mattice, as well as structural engineers from the Berlin Iron Bridge Company. Leavitt, a prominent resident of Cambridgeport near the campus of MIT and a founding member of the American Society of Mechanical Engineers, began designing steam engines for Navy vessels prior to the Civil War and taught steam engineering at Annapolis. He embarked upon a consulting career soon after the War had ended and quickly established international renown for his designs of multiple-expansion steam engines. Mattice, who graduated from the Naval Academy at the top of his class in 1874, also taught engineering at Annapolis and in 1887 became an assistant to the Navy's Engineer in Chief (later Admiral) George W. Wallace during a period of modernization for the Navy's ships, including the introduction of expansion steam engines, water-tube boilers, and armor plating. He left the Navy in 1889 and moved to the Boston area, where he became an aid to Leavitt, and together they developed specifications for the boilers, pumping engines, and hydraulic systems to power Pope's tube factory, with Leavitt acting as lead consulting engineer for the entire plant. Henry A. Wolcott, a contractor from West Hartford experienced in factory construction, supervised much of the work.[25]

Journalists also attributed design of the factory's roof to Mattice, but much of the credit belongs instead to the Berlin Iron Bridge Company, New England's most important manufacturer of metal truss bridges. Located in East Berlin, Connecticut, the company began business in 1868 as the Corrugated Metal Company, a fabricator of iron roofing, but soon acquired patents for lenticular trusses, established a successful bridge division, changed its name in 1883, and gained fame for its graceful iron bridges with curving upper and lower chords and decorative portals.

However, the firm also applied its considerable expertise in structural engineering to the design of roof framing for many industrial clients, and by the early 1890s had begun erecting entire buildings with iron framing, offering ample width, light, and strength. The company's own shops, enlarged in 1891, easily could have served as a model for Pope's tube-factory engineers, displaying a skeletal frame of iron enclosed by curtain walls of glass and sheltering a vast, one-story interior of open space uninterrupted by vertical columns; iron trusses supported the roof load but also carried the traveling cranes essential for moving heavy iron or steel fabrications. By 1898, too, the company had completed a three-story shop of steel, glass, and brick spandrel walls for the Veeder Company (see Chapter 1), which manufactured cyclometers for bicycles at a factory complex in Hartford, almost within sight of Pope's works. Although Mattice may have collaborated with the Berlin firm in designing the roof, possibly its unusual saddle-roof monitors (which leaked badly) and their orientation in relation to the draw benches and annealing ovens, the structural solutions for spans of continuous trusses and plate girders essential to achieving a well-lighted, capacious interior belonged to the East Berlin firm. Moreover, most of the building's structural parts, whether rolled beams or built-up girders, conformed to standard sizes, thus avoiding the added costs for custom fabrications and pointing reliably to an expertise rooted in truss design.[26]

Building Design. As depicted in the plan published in 1897, the tube plant is ell-shaped, with the largest block fronting Bartholomew Avenue and housing a tall, one-story open shop with concrete floor for the hydraulic draw benches and annealing ovens. That room (237 by 161 feet) is ceiled by five saddle monitors extending across the shop, front to back. Continuous Warren trusses ten feet in depth support the ridge of each monitor and in turn are supported by three box-girder posts spaced at intervals of approximately forty feet, also front to back. The five rows of trusses, each with three supporting posts, also are spaced at approximately forty feet across the shop's length, creating five rows of three posts—all evenly spaced. Each truss is further supported by three continuous plate girders joined to each truss at the latter's points of connection with vertical posts. Intermediate continuous plate girders also extend across the shop's full length. Together, the girders and trusses carry channel beams that in turn carry trolley hoists and mill shafting.[27]

Thus, only fifteen vertical posts are required to ceil an enormous space of more than 38,100 square feet. By comparison, a factory conforming to standard mill construction (300 by 60 feet) with floor beams spaced at ten-foot intervals and a central row of supporting posts, would require twenty-nine posts to ceil 18,000 square feet, or roughly twice the number of posts for less than half the space; and many such mills used two supporting posts for each floor beam. Exterior bearing walls of brick with tall window openings, segmentally-arched transoms, and steel sash carry only perimeter loads, and stepped gables, each with a single oculus light, both conceal the saddle monitors and provide architectural effect for the street facade.[28]

The distinctive gables and oculi windows are repeated on the power plant and are the architectural contribution of George Keller, whether by commission, collaboration, or the compliment of imitation. During the same summer that Pope began constructing the tube factory, 1895, Keller designed the three-story factory and two-story office for the Hartford Rubber Works complex, adjoining the tube plant to the north, and each of those connected buildings displays similar stepped gables and oculi windows, unifying Pope's spreading industrial works in Hartford's Parkville district.[29]

The one-story ell fronting Hamilton

Figure 58 (*opposite*). The most spacious room of the Pope Tube Company works housed draw benches and annealing furnaces. The Berlin Iron Bridge Company's structural engineers ceiled an open space of more than 38,000 square feet with only fifteen vertical posts spaced at forty-foot intervals, minimizing obstructions to the constant movement of tubes from draw benches to annealing ovens, and back. The monitor roofs were aligned to provide adequate roof lighting above both the draw benches and annealing ovens. *Iron Age* 59 (January 7, 1897).

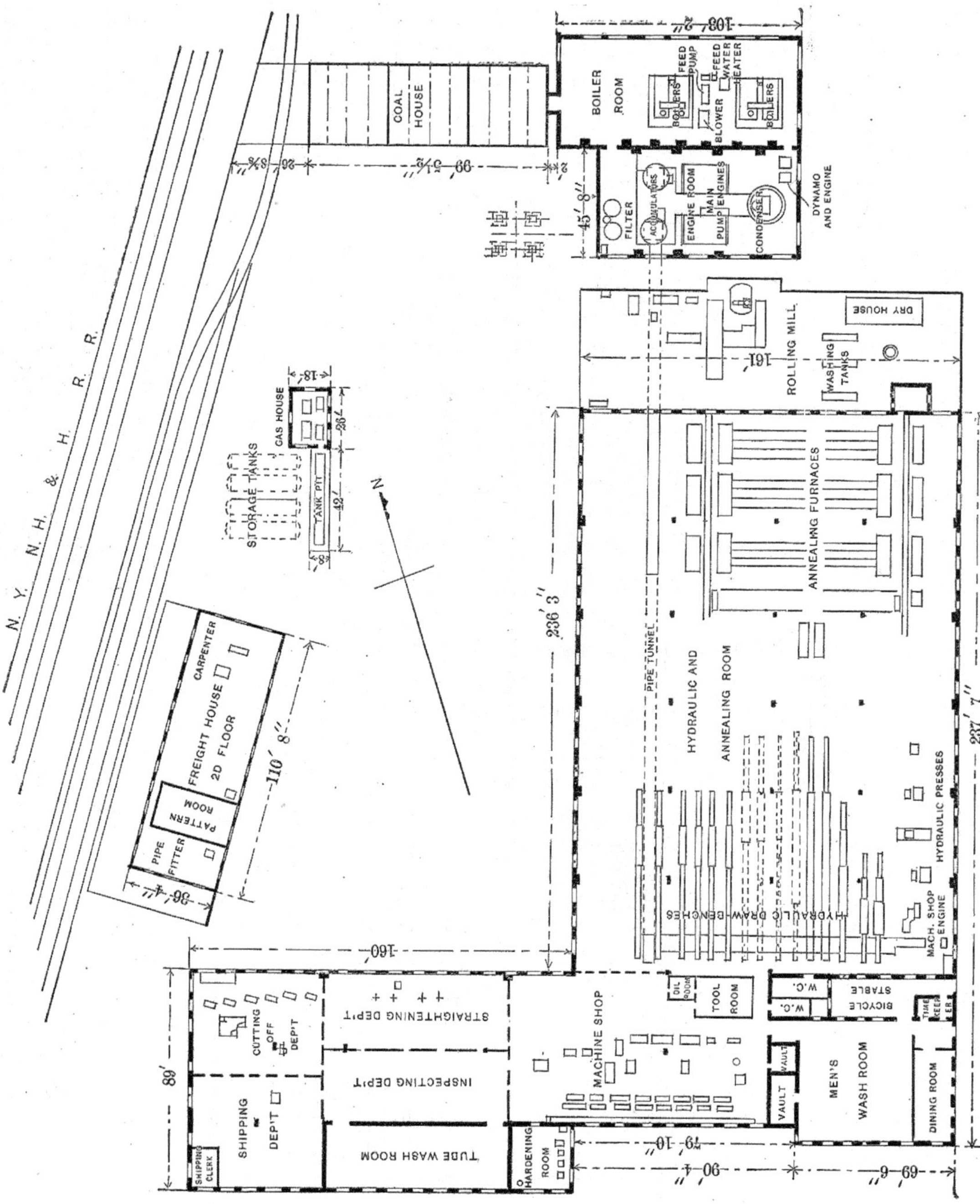
N. Y. N. H. & H. R. R.
COAL HOUSE
BOILER ROOM
FEED PUMP
FEED WATER HEATER
BOILERS
BLOWER
BOILERS
108' 2"
99' 5½"
26' 8¾"
FILTER
ACCUMULATORS
ENGINE ROOM
MAIN PUMP ENGINES
CONDENSER
DYNAMO AND ENGINE
45' 8"
DRY HOUSE
ROLLING MILL
161'
WASHING TANKS
GAS HOUSE
18'
26'
STORAGE TANKS
TANK PIT
42'
8'
N
ANNEALING FURNACES
PIPE TUNNEL
HYDRAULIC AND ANNEALING ROOM
236' 3"
237' 7"
HYDRAULIC PRESSES
HYDRAULIC DRAW BENCHES
MACH. SHOP ENGINE
FREIGHT HOUSE 2D FLOOR
CARPENTER
PATTERN ROOM
PIPE FITTER
110' 8"
36' 4"
160'
CUTTING OFF DEP'T
STRAIGHTENING DEP'T
INSPECTING DEP'T
TUBE WASH ROOM
SHIPPING DEP'T
SHIPPING CLERK
89'
HARDENING ROOM
MACHINE SHOP
OIL ROOM
TOOL ROOM
W.C.
W.C.
BICYCLE STABLE
TIME KEEPER
VAULT
VAULT
MEN'S WASH ROOM
DINING ROOM
79' 10"
90' 4"
69' 6"

Figure 59. Continuous Warren trusses, ten feet in depth, support each monitor roof and in turn are supported by continuous girders at each post. Other continuous girders are carried by the trusses and in turn carry traveling hoists. Hydraulic power pulled and pushed tubes through a series of dies at fourteen lengthy draw benches with oil troughs. Rather than add the weight of power shafts to the roof structure, Leavitt and Mattice melded building and power distribution by designing a tunnel linking the power plant with draw benches, where hydraulic pipes rose to a trench just below floor level. Thus, the building's design became an integral part of power distribution, not simply a structural frame to which mill shafting could be attached. *Iron Age* 59 (January 7, 1897).

Street is also capped by a saddle monitor but is devoted to multiple purposes, including a large machine shop as well as smaller, individual shops for straightening, washing, inspecting, hardening, cutting, and shipping tubes. The plant increases to two stories at the juncture of the ell and main block—the corner of Bartholomew Avenue and Hamilton Street—with the first floor quartering a very large washroom for workers, dining room, and bicycle stable; general offices and drafting rooms occupy the second floor. The plan also shows a forty-five-foot extension along the northerly end of the hydraulic and annealing room, housing washing tanks and a rolling mill, but the company delayed erecting that wood-frame structure until 1899.[30]

Power Plant. The complex melding of building, power generation, and distribution of that power to machinery is similarly sophisticated, and both the engine and boiler rooms of the power plant still stand. Leavitt created the specifications for two complete hydraulic systems, each powered by a vertical triple-expansion pumping engine designed by German engineer Johann Stumpf and fabricated by the Chicago firm of Fraser and Chalmers, generating 1200 pounds of median pressure but capable of achieving 2000 pounds. Pipes linked all draw benches and presses to both engines, making each of the two systems interchangeable and capable of functioning jointly or individually, generating different pressure at different times or for different purposes, thus economizing power and anticipating failure in one system. From the outset, Pope had adopted a "spare no expense" approach, reasoning that superior machines would recover high initial costs over time, and Leavitt and Stumpf repaid Pope's faith in quality by reducing required steam pressure and promising a substantial savings in coal and parts repair.[31]

Draw benches operated intermittently, causing fluctuating demands for power, and Leavitt coupled each of the pumping engines to enormous tanks called accumulators and weighted with water, one for each engine, to store surplus energy when draw benches idled, or to supply added pressure at times of increased demand. Water level could be adjusted quickly to achieve desired hydraulic pressure without stopping the power plant, and the tanks enveloped enormous cylinders containing columns of water connected to the hydraulic system. The accumulators allowed pumping engines to function smoothly, thus freeing pipes from added stress, and saving energy, fuel, wear and tear on parts, and ultimately costs. Leavitt and Mattice also synchronized engine speed with the level of pressure being exerted by the accumulators; if engine speed slowed substantially, the engines were bypassed and accumulators supplied the required pressure. Although hydraulic forces governed movement of the accumulators, the engineers placed the tanks in tension with heavy springs to guard against shocks to the system from sudden motion. Pope's tendency to crow makes it difficult to assess the level of engineering inventiveness at work, but the editors of *Iron Age*, who published a three-part series about the project, called it the most economical hydraulic power pumping plant in the world, and their opinions are likely credible.[32]

In addition to the pumping engines

Figure 60. Pope Tube Company powerhouse. Leavitt and Mattice designed two complete hydraulic systems, each powered by a triple-expansion pumping engine housed in this building. George Keller's distinctive stepped gables and oculi windows visually linked the Pope Tube Company factory and its powerhouse with the adjacent Hartford Rubber Works on Bartholomew Avenue. Photo by the author.

and accumulators, the engine plant housed a dynamo and steam engine to power the plant's electrical system; a water-filtering plant reliant on electrically powered stirrers; and a condenser to absorb steam expended from the pumping, electric light, and shop engines. Exhausted steam from the pumping engines also fed a fuel-saving water heater in the adjacent boiler room, or could be split between the water heater and the overhead heating pipes for the entire works, supplied primarily by steam exhausted from the shop steam engine. A three-story tower adjacent to the engine room stored water in three separate tanks, each level serving different aspects of the power system and fed by an artesian well.[33]

Automated Coal Conveyance. In the boiler room and adjoining coal bunker, the latter no longer standing, Leavitt and Mattice introduced nearly complete automation governing the movement of coal to water-tube boilers, designed by Leavitt and fabricated by the Lake Erie Engineering Company. Much of that mechanization depended on a mechanical stoker patented in 1893 by mining engineer Eckley B. Coxe, whose family business, Coxe Brothers and Company, established shops near Hazleton in Pennsylvania's anthracite region. Coxe's traveling grate allowed small particles of previously discarded anthracite coal, described as buckwheat, to create continuous and uniform combustion without mixing with fresh fuel, eliminating clinkers in the process and cooling before being consigned to waste storage. A steam engine drove the traveling grates and powered a blower that forced the boiler draft, helping to maintain steam pressure at a constant level regardless of power demands and reducing the height of the requisite chimney.[34]

The boiler room and automated coal-conveying system, the latter constructed by the Steel Cable Engineering Company of Boston, required the attendance of only a single worker. Although full automation and use of particle-anthracite represented substantial savings in both labor and fuel, the fixed costs of coal for the plant, including transportation, negated some of the engineered efficiencies because coal in Ohio and western Pennsylvania remained less expensive. Still, the plant's steel-sided coal pockets were large enough to store large quantities of coal, pending seasonal reductions in prices.[35]

Integration of Building and Production Systems. The irregular shape of the five-acre lot and access to railroad spurs created limitations for the physical orientation of the tube works, and for arrangement of its internal parts—particularly the draw benches. Those constraints caused the most serious obstacles to efficient distribution of hydraulic power, and the engineers conceded that the engine house and boiler room were located on the wrong side of the factory, much too far from benches and presses. However, rather than add the weight of pipes to the roof structure, dimming natural light and interfering with traveling hoists, Leavitt and Mattice instead elected to fuse building and power distribution in the form of a tunnel extending from the engine house to the draw benches, where pipes rose to a trench just below floor level, simplifying linkages to numerous machines. The lengthy tunnel contained all hydraulic, steam, heat, drain, and electrical conduits, and engineers designed the corridor to be large enough to accommodate any work required for the high pressure pipes. Thus, the physical building literally became a component of power distribution, not simply a structural frame to which mill shafting was attached.[36]

Tube Production

Late in June 1896, as completion of the building neared, Pope formed a new corporation, the Pope Tube Company, infused the business with $500,000 of capital subscribed in 4,960 shares of stock in Pope's name and the remaining shares in George Day, George Pope, Arthur Pattison, and Harold Eames, each ten shares; Eames served as the plant's inaugural manager and Fidel Bubser superintended the plant. Pope then moved machinery from the old Columbia Tube Works and commenced production of tubes during the fall of that year. Fourteen lengthy draw benches with oil troughs occupied the entire end of the plant's main room, where hydraulic power pulled and pushed tubes through a series of dies, with the outer diameter of the tube governed by the dimensions of the die, and the resulting thickness of the tube controlled by the space between die and the tube's mandrel head. Tongs gripped the tube's tapered ends and pulled, while the triblet rod and its mandrel head, inserted through the tube from the opposite end, centered the tube against the die and maintained a consistent separation between die and mandrel head. Avoiding waste in production depended on careful adjustments to that separation; too thick, and tubes required repetitive draws; too thin, and tubes ruptured under pressure of the draw. Pistons pulling the tubes were enclosed in protective cylinders of pipe, and workers controlled the draw benches by hand-operated wheels located at the center of the benches, adjacent to the die holder.[37]

From the outset, the company also fabricated tubes of nickel-steel using the cupping method. The process required stamping circular discs from plates of 5 percent nickel alloy obtained from the Bethlehem works, followed by rounding those blank discs repetitively with hydraulic draw-presses. Once sufficiently elongated (to a length of about one or two feet) and its rounded edges sheared, the embryonic tube moved to the draw benches, where as many as twelve draws—the draws followed by annealing—could make the manufacture of nickel-steel tubes a lengthy, three-week process. Experiments by Eames and Souther had shown that a strong alloy of 5 percent nickel still allowed the bending or flanging of parts during bicycle assembly, and use of that precise alloy exclusively for Columbia bicycles separated Pope from other bicycle manufacturers using a lower ratio of nickel.[38]

No matter the type of tube, each cold draw strained and hardened the steel, requiring annealing and gradual cooling to soften the metal and stabilize its molecular structure. Sets of furnaces, fired by gas to generate uniform heat, dominated the opposite end of the plant's main room, and each furnace faced a brick muffle or cooling oven, with opposing furnace and oven doors separated by a narrow alley with rail tracks. Workers loaded the drawn tubes into cylindrical steel containers called retorts with threaded end-caps, each retort roughly a dozen feet long and capable of holding more than one hundred tubes. Small rail carts transported the cylinders into position in front of the furnaces, and crews then charged the furnaces by trundling the air-tight retorts through low, horizontal door openings. Annealing typically lasted forty-five minutes, and workers then transferred the retorts to the cooling ovens. Once cooled and rolled onto carts, retorts then traveled via mechanized hoists, returning to the draw-bench sector where workers removed the tubes and resumed the drawing process.[39]

Although Pope had failed to obtain rights to use rotary piercing from the Mannesmann concern, he nevertheless gained protection for his tube manufacturing venture by acquiring an exclusive American license for the annealing process, invented by mechanical engineer and Hartford resident, Horace K. Jones, a Vermont native and holder of more than one hundred patents. In 1896, at age fifty-eight, Jones patented a non-oxidizing process for annealing metals by using pressure to separate metal from combustion, thus avoiding scaling and other imperfections and eliminating the tedious pickling in troughs full of acid. Tubes improved in both quality and uniformity, and withstood brazing and filing more effectively, allowing Pope to guarantee tolerances measured in thousandths of an inch. Both American and European bicycle manufacturers seemed to accept Pope's claims of quality, and his new tube company began producing tubes of fifty-carbon steel for the cycle trade at large, advertised through a company catalog issued in 1896 with price lists and specification tables.[40]

During the summer of 1896, the company predicted an annual production capacity of 1,000,000 feet per month for the coming year, although by 1898 that figure had dropped to 10,000,000 feet; generally, tube diameters remained in the range of two inches or smaller. Whether nor not Eames and his successors, Robert Parker and Charles Sponsel, obtained pierced steel from American plants is not clear, but steady shipments of hollow billets or ingots continued to arrive in bundles from English ports at Swansea and Hull, and from Hamburg in Germany throughout most of 1897. However, imports declined in 1898 and probably ended altogether in 1899.[41]

Industry Consolidation

In the context of industrial architectural history, the Pope Tube Company factory is exemplary for its rational integration of building and specialized manufacturing processes, exhibiting advanced structural and mechanical engineering in every detail of its design. In 1911, when Henry Grattan Tyrell published *A Treatise on the Design and Construction of Mill Buildings*, he theorized that industrial buildings represented one of the largest investments in economic production and should be carefully designed for specific needs to minimize costs. In Hartford, Pope had put that theory into practice nearly fifteen years earlier.[42]

Yet in that same context, the Hartford plant is also exemplary because it demonstrates a crucial oversight on the part of engineers and architects who dismissed standard mill construction as generic shells and functionally inefficient. That oversight is rooted in the failure to consider what many factory owners understood intuitively, namely the ever-changing disposition of American industry and the difficulty of adapting factories designed for specific purposes to other types of manufacturing. Tyrrell's dictum that companies carrying on profitable businesses in out-of-date plants would fall behind competitively, offers little assurance that the harsh economic forces engendered by competition, often resulting in industry consolidation, would not cause modern buildings to fall out of date just as quickly as the buildings they replaced.[43]

Once again, Pope's vision for Hartford's Industry Beautiful collided with overpowering economic forces. Late in May 1899, the same month that the American Bicycle Company conglomerate formed, the Shelby Steel Tube Company announced another step toward monopolizing seamless tube production by acquiring both the Pope Tube Company and the Albany Manufacturing Company in Albany, Indiana, the country's last two bicycle manufacturers engaged in the production of tubes. With patronage from the ABC secure, Shelby temporarily closed Hartford's tube works in January 1900, and began considering ways to expand the plant's range of production. However, later that year the United States Steel Corporation absorbed both Shelby and the National Tube Company, thus capturing trade from the bicycle industry and monopolizing tube production. In the spring of 1901, orders arrived to shut the Hartford plant permanently, and removal of draw benches and machinery commenced.[44]

The four-year-old tube plant on Bartholomew Avenue, designed by the country's most inventive engineers at the exceptional cost of $500,000 including machinery, stood idle for almost a decade until the third Pope Manufacturing Company repurchased it in 1909, primarily to gain access to 500 feet of rail spur. The company paid $75,000 for the property, spent $30,000 adapting it to automobile repair work and to the assembly of commercial and public service wagons, renamed it the Western Works, and appointed Harold L. Pope as manager. By that time, however, journalists already had begun calling the plant "the Old Tube Works," and when company president George Pope appealed the city's tax assessment of $130,000 for the property, he explained that the plant was difficult to value because it had been built for a special purpose and could not be adapted to other lines of manufacturing. He gathered a coterie of discouraged would-be buyers who offered similar testimony, and a judge agreed, reducing the assessment to $75,000.[45]

However, the reprieve lasted only a short time. Following the company's declaration of bankruptcy in February 1913, receiver George Pope vacated the Western Works and offered the building for sale that summer. At a court hearing two empty years later, Thomas F. Garvan outbid representatives of the Hartford Rubber Works and acquired the plant for his family's paper company, P. Garvan Incorporated, for $80,000; bidding had started at $61,000. By May 1915, Garvan's firm had completed its move into the plant, leaving offices the company had occupied on Hartford's State Street since 1864. The Garvan firm continued to own the factory until the 1970s, its workers likely unaware of the sophisticated engineering that sheltered the storage of textile waste and paper bales.[46]

Versatility of Columbia Tube Works

Sharpening the irony that enveloped the Pope Tube Company plant for most of the twentieth century, the older Columbia Tube Mill on nearby Laurel Street remained in nearly continuous use after the Bartholomew Avenue plant superseded it, evolving into an enormous complex of buildings reliant on standard mill construction. By 1896, the Hartford Typewriter Company had begun renting a substantial portion of the main factory, and Pope had created a passageway between that block and a one-story building to house his newly created Motor Carriage Department. There, he provided a laboratory for experiments with motorized vehicles (both gasoline and electric), under the supervision of Eames and his brother-in-law, inventor Hiram Percy Maxim, who became chief engineer of that motor department soon after his arrival in Hartford in 1895.[47]

In an elaborate pooling of patents in the spring of 1899 (as complex in execution as it is tedious to explain), Pope established a new concern, the Columbia Automobile Company, owned equally by the Pope Manufacturing Company and by the Electric Storage Battery Company, the latter a subsidiary of a third concern, the Electric Vehicle Company (EVC), an existing holding company controlled by a group of financiers including Warren C. Whitney and John Jacob Astor. The EVC and the Columbia Automobile Company then formed the Columbia and Electric Vehicle Company (CEVC), sharing ownership equally.

Figure 61. Columbia Tube Mill, designed by George Keller in 1893, as it appeared on the lithograph by Kyes & Woodbury, Worcester, Massachusetts, also in 1893. Formerly located at the corner of Laurel and Park Streets, several blocks from Pope's Capitol Avenue complex. Author's document.

Parent EVC intended to create transportation businesses in numerous cities, which would then acquire vehicles produced by CEVC and lease those vehicles to prospective users. George Day (as president), Harold Eames (as vice-president, secretary, and manager), and Maxim (as chief engineer) transferred their talents to CEVC, declaring their shared allegiances to motor cars rather than bicycles. Pope conveyed the Laurel Street factory to CEVC, and that summer he increased the height of the main factory to four stories and erected a four-story addition called the north wing; he also built a lengthy, three-story appendage to the Motor Carriage Department. Late that year too, CEVC acquired the former plant of the Hartford Cycle Company, by then part of the American Bicycle Company, and bicycle production moved to the Capitol Avenue complex.[48]

During the summer of 1900, the EVC acquired Pope's remaining interest in the Columbia Automobile Company and thus absorbed CEVC, becoming sole owner of the Laurel Street and Hartford Cycle plants in the process. Day and Maxim assumed comparable roles for the EVC but in December 1900, Eames resigned in opposition to the EVC's over-extended mergers and acquisitions. Maxim followed him a few months later but returned in 1903, remaining until 1907. Day also departed in 1903 to become general manager of the Association of Licensed Automobile Manufacturers, whose members were licensees of the patents owned by EVC, including the ill-fated 1879 patent held by George

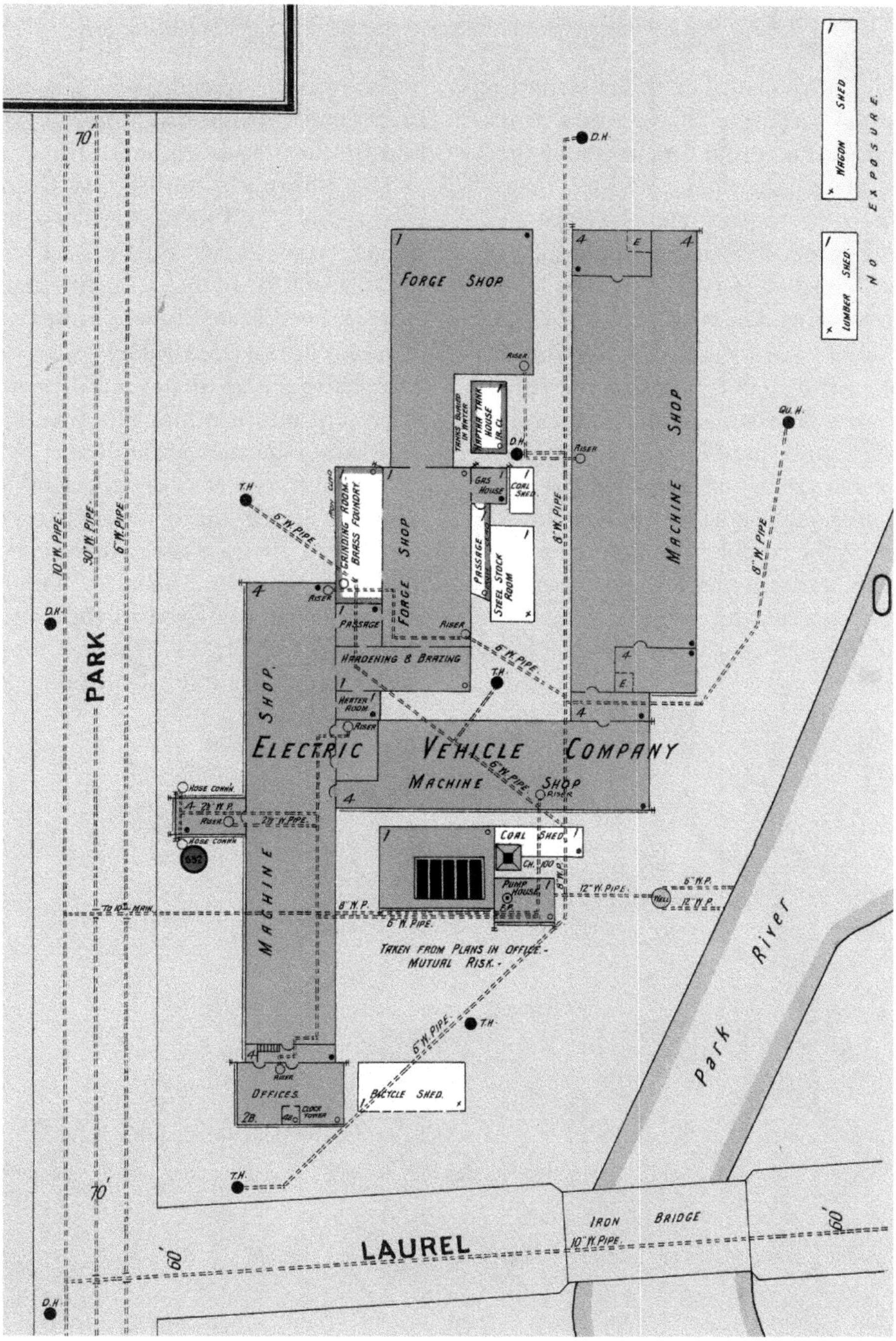

Figure 62. Former Columbia Tube Works. When Albert Pope transferred tube manufacturing to the factory on Bartholomew Avenue, he converted George Keller's old Columbia Tube Mill to the manufacture of motor vehicles, orchestrating a complex cadre of owners who formed the Columbia and Electric Vehicle Company. The enlarged complex continued to house automobile production until patent litigation brought assembly to a halt in 1912. Tool manufacturer Billings and Spencer purchased the complex in 1914 and continued to use the factory until 1965, when the buildings were demolished. Sanborn-Perris Map Company, Insurance Maps of Hartford, Connecticut (1900), Vol. 2, Plate 126. Library of Congress, Geography and Map Division.

Selden for a road vehicle powered by a gasoline motor.[49]

Amid this shaky financial structure, the factory on Laurel Street stood its traditional ground, providing workable space for the manufacture of both electric and gasoline-powered vehicles. In 1905, EVC added a large, four-story appendage of standard-mill construction, probably the northwest wing depicted on the city's 1909 atlas, to be used for a repair department and blacksmith shop, and in the spring of 1906 the company publicized its catalog of large and small touring automobiles. However, financial and mechanical problems continued to surface, and on November 1, 1907, the company defaulted on bond payments, entering receivership a month later. Three weeks after the declaration of default, George Day succumbed to heart failure.[50]

Despite these impediments, the prospects for royalties from the Selden and other patents owned by EVC remained bright enough in the summer of 1909 for bondholders to reorganize the concern as the Columbia Motor Car Company of Hartford, and in September a federal judge rewarded that optimism by ruling in favor of EVC in its patent infringement suit against Ford Motor Company and others, commenced many years before. That ruling, and its potential menace to other automobile manufacturers, captured the attention of Benjamin Briscoe, president of the Maxwell-Briscoe Motor Company, with factories in Tarrytown, New York; Providence, Rhode Island; and New Castle, Indiana. The Maxwell concern belonged to the conglomerate United States Motor Company, which purchased the Columbia Motor

Figure 63. Although substantially altered and unrecognized for its contributions to architectural and engineering heritage, the Pope Tube Company factory represents the bicycle industry's most sophisticated example of industrial architecture that unifies building plan, structure, and manufacturing functions into an integrated design process. Photo by the author.

Car Company and its Laurel Street factory early in 1910. At about the same time, however, a federal appeals court declared the Selden patent invalid, and collapse of the Association of Licensed Automobile Manufacturers followed. By the summer of 1912, the United States Motor Company had failed, and a court-ordered sale of its assets ensued, resulting in a brief ownership of the factory by the Maxwell-Briscoe concern, but culminating with the purchase of the entire Columbia Tube Works factory in July 1914 by the Billings and Spencer Company, by then a long-established manufacturer of tools and drop forgings.[51]

Adding his own strand of irony to this web of developments, Charles Billings had worked with George Fairfield to fabricate sewing machine tables for the Weed Sewing Machine Company many years before, and then had benefited from the prosperous years of bicycle production in Hartford after forming his partnership with Christopher Spencer. That company's continued success had outpaced the capacity of its factory at the corner of Russ and Lawrence Streets, two blocks from Pope's Capitol Avenue complex, and the space available at the Columbia site offered ample room for expansion. With little hesitation, the company invested $100,000 in alterations, including consolidating what had been two separate forging departments in the Columbia plant into a single open floor and adding a steel roof.[52]

Billings and Spencer remained in the building for half-a-century, finally closing its tool and forging divisions in 1962 after the Connecticut Highway Department acquired two acres of the company's land for the East-West urban highway project (today Interstate 84), thus limiting space for expansion. New owners demolished the factory complex in August 1965, replacing it with a Stop and Shop and Bradlees food and department store.[53]

Despite its curious use as a warehouse for storing paper products, or just as likely because of it, the Pope Tube Company plant on Bartholomew Avenue has survived, withstanding the onslaught of years and the relentless urban decline that surrounds it, and contributing another layer of irony to the story of Hartford's bicycle industry.

7

Lozier Manufacturing Company

Toledo, Ohio, and Thompsonville, Connecticut, and Westfield, Massachusetts

The irony that entwines the Pope Tube Company plant and the Columbia Tube Works in Hartford calls attention to one of the principal developments in American industrial architecture at the turn of the twentieth century, specifically the shift from versatile standard mill construction to factories designed and

Figure 64. The Lozier Manufacturing Company works on West Central Avenue in Toledo, Ohio, where Henry Lozier produced Cleveland bicycles. In 1889, Joseph Yost and Henry Lozier formed the Lozier and Yost Manufacturing Company and began producing Giant safety bicycles at this site in a factory erected in 1884 by the Jewel Manufacturing Company to make sewing machines. Lozier soon acquired Yost's interest and rapidly expanded the works, retaining Toledo architects Norval B. Bacon and Thomas F. Huber to design several additions. A fire on the day before Thanksgiving in 1894 destroyed most of the factory, but Lozier turned again to Bacon and Huber to rebuild the plant during the winter of 1894–1895. The artist's illustration of the rebuilt works shown here, heightened in perspective, appeared in the company's 1897 catalog and exemplifies the common practice among company owners to use factories to promotional advantage—the insignia of industrial prowess. None of the buildings in the complex survives. Courtesy Lyman and Merrie Wood Museum of Springfield History, Springfield, MA.

engineered to achieve maximum production efficiency by integrating building and manufacturing processes into a coherent, unified plan. However, many bicycle works confirmed a continued dependence on standard mill construction at the close of the nineteenth century, and reliance on its versatility through much of the twentieth century, with owners introducing creative systems to achieve efficient production.

In Toledo (Ohio), Thompsonville (Connecticut), and Westfield (Massachusetts), Henry Lozier relied on just such a strategy to build a bicycle empire. Among the industrial works at those three sites, the works in Westfield, now demolished, held significance as one of the country's most thoroughly documented examples of a late nineteenth-century factory complex and its evolving production systems designed specifically to manufacture bicycles. That record benefits from a series of drawings prepared by the Factory Insurance Association during the period between 1919 and 1937, and by a descriptive tour of the factory prepared in 1952 by Westfield engineer Harold Maschin, commemorating the seventy-fifth anniversary of Columbia bicycles.

Lozier and Yost Bicycle Manufacturing Company

When, during the summer of 1889, Joseph Yost and Henry Lozier formed the Lozier and Yost Bicycle Manufacturing Company to produce moderately-priced Giant safety bicycles, with Lozier as president, Yost was by far the more experienced of the two at building bicycles, and he assumed the role of general manager and treasurer. Selecting a venue familiar to many bicycle manufacturers, the partners acquired a factory built in 1884 by the Jewel Manufacturing Company to produce sewing machines. Purchased at a sheriff's auction for $33,334, a price that included machinery and mill shafting as well as substantial acreage, the building lacked only trip-hammers essential for forging. The three-story edifice with flat roof fronted Central Avenue, adjacent to the Lake Shore and Michigan Southern Railroad corridor. A small, one-story portico sheltered the principal entrance at the base of a central, projecting pavilion, in turn topped by a decorative tower with mansard roof; arched window lintels, cornice brackets, and brick corbelling added architectural embroidery. A two-story, one-hundred-foot ell extended from the rear elevation, housing the power plant at its far end, and the works included a separate, nearly square outbuilding containing a pattern room and carpenter's shop.[1]

Both Yost and Lozier either were clairvoyant about the impending popularity of safety bicycles, or likely had watched closely as the enterprises owned by Pope, Overman, and R. Philip Gormully with his partner Thomas Jeffery prospered, and between August 3, 1889, the date of purchase, and December 1891, the month that Lozier secured complete ownership of the works, Yost expanded the factory's capacity to meet an annual quota of 12,000 bicycles, most of which were delivered to Lozier's Cleveland business, which became the company's sales division. Yost possessed a rare blend of mechanical ingenuity, marketing savvy, and administrative aplomb, and the task of adapting the building to the efficient production of bicycles fell to him, aided by assistant manager and Civil War veteran Colonel William H. Raynor. The company commissioned contractors to increase the ell's height to three stories; construct secondary buildings for storage of materials; introduce an inventive system of drip-piping to lubricate machine tooling without wasteful loss of oil (see Chapter 2); and installed an oil-fueled power plant, which so impressed George Day that he adopted a similar system for the Hartford works. Yost probably introduced electric incandescent lighting

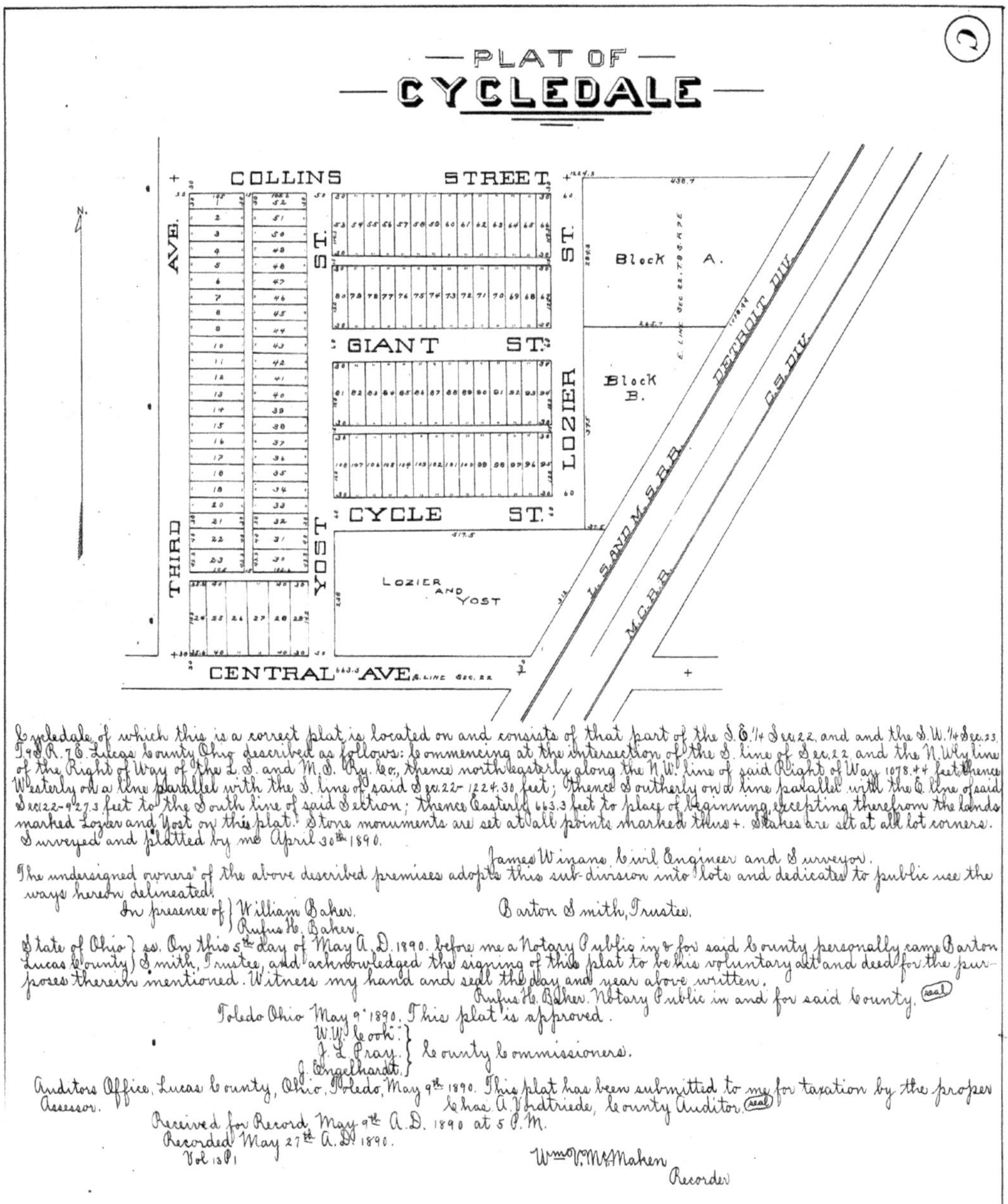

Figure 65. Lozier and Yost also worked with a group of real estate investors who developed a plan for worker housing, titled Cycledale and platted in April 1890 by engineer and surveyor James Winans. Subsequent enlargement of the factory complex swallowed most of that land, and the plat was later vacated in 1912. Lucas County Recorder's Office.

during this period, as well. The company also collaborated with a group of real estate investors to develop the adjoining land for workers housing, calling the subdivision Cycledale, with streets named Cycle, Giant, Yost, and Lozier.[2]

Yost's industrious juggling sapped his health, and he sold his share of the Toledo plant to Lozier profitably, before departing for California to recuperate. However, he soon returned to Toledo, establishing a new bicycle business during the summer of

1892, the Yost Manufacturing Company, to produce Falcon bicycles. With contractor W.H. Long from Auburndale, Yost adapted an unusually wide, seventy-six foot, two-story, wire-nail factory with sweeping gable roof, a building expansive enough to fabricate all necessary parts other than tires and saddles. He rearranged the distinctive factory extensively and installed several sophisticated machines, including one to produce chains, one to cut cones and bushings from forged steel, and another to fabricate sprocket wheels. Also located along the Lake Shore and Michigan Southern Railroad corridor, at what became known as Yost Station, the complex stood a little more than two miles southwesterly of Lozier's Central Avenue works. By 1895, too, Yost had created another firm, the Maumee Cycle Company (Tally-Ho and Volant bicycles), and Samuel Snell had developed a sprawling plant adjacent to the Yost factory to produce bicycle fittings.[3]

Although the accounts of Yost's and Snell's respective businesses diverge from the history of Lozier's evolving works, as do the stories of at least seven other bicycle manufacturers in Toledo by 1895, the existence of those firms is germane because they demonstrate the extraordinarily rapid growth of the bicycle industry, as well as the competition accompanying that growth, local and regional as well as national. Both aspects strongly influenced decisions regarding factory selection or design and the organization of manufacturing processes.[4]

Cleveland Bicycles—Toledo Works

If lacking mechanical ingenuity, Lozier managed to counter that limitation with ambition, marketing dexterity, intuitive business timing, and sharp practices with local officials. Once having acquired the Toledo factory, he promoted Cleveland bicycle as a marque of quality and began expanding the works on Central Avenue, retaining the Toledo architectural firm of Bacon and Huber to design a large, three-story addition of standard-mill-construction. Completed during the fall of 1892, the forty-foot-wide building lengthened the factory's primary facade by 100 feet and displayed similar architectural embellishment as well as a projecting pavilion with entrance portico.[5]

As did George Keller, partners Norval B. Bacon and Thomas F. Huber embraced the romantic styles of that period and, similar to Keller, were swayed by the work of Henry Hobson Richardson. Bacon, brother-in-law to President Grover Cleveland, was born in Hamilton, New York, in 1838 and studied at various schools in central New York including Hamilton Academy prior to becoming a teacher at age nineteen. Subsequently, he trained under the tutelage of portrait painter Albert J. Purdy in Ithaca, followed by the study of architecture in Utica and Boston between 1868 and 1873, before establishing his Toledo practice. Ohio-born Huber joined Bacon as an architectural student in 1882 and eventually became a partner. Huber drew inspiration from the Chicago School and Lewis Sullivan for some of his commercial blocks, including the Spitzer Building where the firm established offices in 1896.[6]

As did Keller, too, Bacon and Huber demonstrated eclectic proficiency, and although Bacon often reveled in the exuberant romanticism of the late nineteenth century, the partners drew from diverse historical references, neo-classical as well as romantic, while designing many of Toledo's important commercial, civic, industrial, and residential buildings. In doing so, they helped to shape the city in much the same way that Keller molded Hartford during the same period. If points of departure exist among Keller, Bacon, or Huber, they rest on Keller's ability to interpret architectural references with greater clarity or coherence, and in Huber's explorations of the Chicago School.[7]

Early in 1893, Lozier reorganized his Toledo business as the Lozier Manufacturing Company. In addition to Lozier as president, officers of the company included George A. Burwell, vice president and superintendent; Henry Lozier, Jr., secretary; and Charles J. Moore, formerly with the Ames Manufacturing Company in Chicopee, as treasurer and general manager. The company added three acres of land from the trustees of Cycledale and began enlarging the factory complex with a three-story building, longer than the original factory together with its 1892 addition. The new plant fronted Yost Street at right angles to Central Avenue and formed an interior courtyard, where four or five new buildings achieved various stages of completion during the spring and summer of 1893: boiler and engine plant for steam power; warehouse and shipping room; blacksmith shop; and tool building. In its enlarged capacity, the plant could house an estimated 1000 employees.[8]

Cleveland Bicycles—Toledo Works Rebuilt

Thus, by 1894 the Lozier works had expanded to suit the company's growing needs. However, during the early evening of November 28, 1894, the day before Thanksgiving, much of the plant burned to the ground as fire-fighters watched, unable to tap sufficient pressure from the city's two accessible hydrants for water to reach the flames. The fire consumed all the main shops fronting Central Avenue and Yost Street, together with the stock room, enameling room, and rubbing room; the engine house, boiler room and coal sheds were destroyed, as well. The company valued the plant at $500,000, but held insurance coverage of only $350,000. In addition, 472 workers found themselves unemployed.[9]

The episode placed the often-guarded dance between industry owners and municipal officials into sharp focus. Toledo's Chamber of Commerce immediately convened to address the prospect of losing Lozier's business, and quickly vowed support for improving the city's inadequate water supply and for paving surrounding streets. Lozier took a strong lead, twirling from sincere ("I don't want to leave Toledo, but I may not be my own master in the matter"); to coy (reporting telegrams from other manufacturing towns inviting relocation, one of which included a bonus of $100,000); to calculating (a request that the city exempt the company from taxes for ten years); to demanding ("We positively will not rebuild unless we are guaranteed good pavements and an ample water supply"); to an ultimatum announcing that he would depart for new locales if temporary quarters were not provided by the following day at no cost to his company. After explaining that tax exemption could not be granted lawfully, local businesses dipped into their treasuries and agreed to share rental costs, and a special committee organized by the Chamber of Commerce began visiting available factories. On December 20, Lozier ended the suspense by announcing that he would remain in Toledo and rebuild.[10]

Lozier and Yost had expanded the factory during a period of growth, using traditional methods of design and construction, but they also had organized the buildings, machinery, and other improvements into a well-integrated, efficient production system, and after the fire Lozier lamented the loss of "the special machinery and hundred-and-one improvements" introduced during the preceding years. Lozier pledged to complete the new building with every modern convenience available for bicycle manufacture, and his conversion to electrical power to drive machinery fulfilled at least part of that promise. The principal changes to the complex included relocation of the brazing and enameling departments to a new, one-story building with monitor roofs, enclosing a quadrangle and at a safer distance from the principal shops but awkwardly distant from the assembling rooms. In addition, Lozier and Moore erected new buildings for offices, crating, and the rubber department. To protect production systems, Lozier installed sprinklers served by a newly-dug pond, and he rejected an open-floor plan, preferring instead to separate rooms and to avoid open connections between the rooms. Selecting timber because it reached structural failure more slowly than unprotected iron or steel during a fire, a characteristic verified by factory mutual insurance companies, the firm ordered twelve-by-fourteen-inch pine for floor beams and vertical posts.[11]

Bacon and Huber compensated for loss of the prominent tower by designing matching pavilions symmetrically placed along the Central Avenue elevation, each with identical entrance porticos and segmentally-arched crown parapets. Windows with slightly-arching lintels marched uniformly across the facade, a horizontal rhythm emphasized by the slightly projecting first-story base capped by a stringcourse that visually supported and unified

Figure 66. Lozier eventually sold his bicycle empire to the American Bicycle Company in 1899, and this undated photograph shows the complex just before or soon after that transfer. Following collapse of the ABC, the reorganized Pope Manufacturing Company adapted the building to the production of Pope-Toledo motor cars, but in 1907 John North Willys purchased the plant and began manufacturing Willys-Overland and Willys Jeep automobiles. Motor vehicle production continued at the much-expanded complex throughout the twentieth century and into the early years of the twenty-first century. Photograph courtesy Toledo Lucas County Public Library.

the upper two stories. Although decorative, the brick corbelling on the reconstructed buildings was more restrained than that on the original buildings, evident on the surviving blacksmith shop and shipping house.[12]

While wringing what they could from the city and its fearful business community, Lozier and Moore began to look more closely at the actual loss to the plant, and quietly circulated reassuring communiqués to a few select dealers, explaining that circumstances were much better than initially believed, and predicting that all orders for Cleveland wheels would be met by early February. Inspectors determined that the tool room and its machinery were unharmed, including special tools for 1895 models as well as several thousand wheels, and men began working in that building early in December. The blacksmith, forging, and brazing shops also had been spared, as had a brick storehouse with 462 bicycles from 1894, which remained in packing crates ready to ship. Lozier's decision to remain in Toledo likely hinged on several factors, including assurances about the short length of time required to rebuild the principal shops; the impracticality of abandoning the surviving buildings and housing subdivision; and the competitive advantages of Toledo as a point of distribution to mid-western and western states. The city's financial encouragements, although beneficial, may have been secondary. In any case, most of the plant had been rebuilt within an astounding sixty days, insurance companies cancelled $232,000 of the costs, and the company had begun turning out 500 bicycles a week in April.[13]

Cleveland Bicycles—Thompsonville and Toronto Junction Works

Toledo's overtures notwithstanding, the full explanation for the company's decision to rebuild is hidden among the goals of expansion that the Loziers, Moore, and Burwell already were pursuing, plans probably withheld from Toledo's business leaders. One immediate objective concerned establishing a New England division to compete more effectively with manufacturers in that region; a second goal involved avoiding the 35 percent duty on bicycles distributed in Canada. Lozier attended to the first by building a plant in the village of Thompsonville, Connecticut, located just north of Hartford in Enfield. He solved the second problem by acquiring and enlarging a factory in Toronto. Thus, keeping an established plant in reliable production at a single, geographically advantageous location such as Toledo became critically important as Lozier's plans for expansion unfolded during the spring and summer of 1895.[14]

Possibly as the result of the fire, the company had begun using an existing factory in Hartford to fabricate hub cones and screw parts. Early in June, however, Moore and Burwell traveled to Connecticut to locate a building large enough to establish a New England branch, visiting about a dozen towns including New Haven, Bridgeport, and Manchester. They finally selected Thompsonville, where at the urging of the town's Board of Trade, the Hartford Carpet Company agreed to sell Lozier a parcel of land, slightly more than two acres, at the northeast corner of School and Commerce Streets, adjacent to the tracks of the New York, New Haven and Hartford Railroad. Helping to close the deal, trusting local citizens paid $20,000 in subscriptions for the privilege of securing Lozier's business, with promises by the latter to employ 200 workers. Lozier again directed Bacon and Huber to design the factory, and the Toledo architects in turn relied on a Hartford consultant, R.M. Lincoln, to prepare specifications.[15]

Early in July, Moore signed a $17,000 construction contract with two bidders

Figure 67. Henry Lozier's factory in Thompsonville, Connecticut, erected during the summer and fall of 1895. Designed by Toledo architects Bacon and Huber, with structural specifications prepared by Hartford consultant R.M. Lincoln, the building stood at the northeast corner of School and Commerce Streets. Carpenter F.E. Hosmer and mason Watson Tyron, both from nearby Windsor, won the bidding to build the works. Cleveland Bicycle Catalog, 1897. Courtesy Lyman and Merrie Wood Museum of Springfield History, Springfield, MA.

from Windsor, Connecticut—carpenter F.E. Hosmer and mason Watson Tryon—for a three-story machine shop of standard mill construction, using the template of 200 feet long by forty feet wide, with instructions to lengthen the plant with another shop of identical dimensions if required. The architects placed imposing entrance pavilions along School Street, similar to those on the Toledo factory, but also added an octagonal tower at each of the building's front corners, although only one was built. To accommodate machinery of varying sizes, Lincoln specified ceiling-heights of fifteen, fourteen, and thirteen-and-one-half feet, first story to third, respectively; required timber floor beams planed and chamfered to reduce vulnerability to fire; extended those floor beams the building's full width (likely with intermediate posts); and called for floor planks of planed spruce topped by maple floorboards. The contract also required a boiler house and established a completion date of August 15. Lozier delegated oversight of construction to Moore, and transfer of the land occurred in February 1896, with the deed containing a single covenant that the factory never be used to manufacture textiles. Moore soon transferred responsibility for the plant to R.P. Judson and later to Charles P. Ball, and the Board of Trade may have been pleased with its trophy for at least a few months. However, in mid–June, the company laid off 200 machinists until September, leaving a force of fifty employees working two-week stints, followed by two-week furloughs.[16]

By July or August of the previous summer, 1895, Lozier also had acquired a former sewing machine factory on Weston Street in Toronto Junction, today part of Toronto proper. Illustrations of the works following adaptation by Lozier show separate, two- and three-story plants placed at right angles to one another, forming an interior yard framed in turn by substantial one-story buildings with monitor roofs, the latter presumably housing forging and brazing departments as well as enameling ovens. Lozier appointed his brother-in-law, Edwin R. Thomas, as manager of the plant, and appealed to the loyalty of Canadians by advertising that all parts of the bicycles, other than tubes, were produced in that country.[17]

Cleveland Bicycles—Westfield Works

Lozier's pas-de-deux with Toledo's Chamber of Commerce resumed during the spring of 1896, little more than a year after the Toledo works had been rebuilt, when rumors began circulating about a compact between the company and the town of Westfield, Massachusetts, where the Board of Trade had offered to raise $75,000 as an incentive for Lozier to relocate. In July, Westfield newspapers gleefully reported that an agreement had been reached, that most of the funds had been pledged, and that the company had promised to erect a large new plant. To entice subscribers, Westfield resident James Noble, Jr., promised to donate funds to the Noble Hospital, matching any amount contributed to the fund above $62,500. Plans progressed rapidly, beginning in July with acquisition of roughly eleven acres owned by Noble. The signing of a construction contract followed in early August, with the goal of commencing bicycle production by December—in time for the 1897 season. Contractor George Blodgett of Westfield won the bidding contest, and two months later sold a house to Charles Moore, who became general manager. W.L. Gleason moved from Toledo to become superintendent of the plant.[18]

By the end of December, the factory's first principal buildings stood ready for use, with roofs and windows in place, and journalists compared the company's mocking-bird whistle to Gabriel's trumpet. However, production fell behind schedule and shipments of wheels did not occur until March, when Charles Moore explained to residents that work had started too late in the season to begin on the grand scale that assuredly would follow. Fortunately for Toledo residents, the company did not abandon bicycle manufacturing in Ohio, an intention Lozier may not have disclosed to Westfield's Board of Trade.[19]

Financial incentives such as those offered by Westfield and Thompsonville varied widely. Outright purchase of subscriptions could mean simply shares of stock owned by individuals, with little security other than the company's contractual obligations to invest in a new factory. Contracts might also require businesses to employ an average number of workers per day over a period of years, with assorted methods of enforcing those promises. Lozier's agreement with Westfield's Board of Trade, for example, stipulated that the company would equip the building for the average employment of 500 workers over a period of five years, and placed subscriptions into a Lozier Fund controlled by the board. Wisely, the board specified that trustees retain the deed of conveyance until contract terms had been satisfied, and the agreement also stipulated that funds would be transferred to the company in installments as work on the buildings advanced. Trade boards might also encumber deeds of conveyance or require that obligations be specified in a debt instrument such as a promissory note or bond, which then could be secured with a mortgage on the land, buildings, fixtures, or trade fixtures; both strategies, however, could present problems if companies sought additional financing from a different source.[20]

Significance. In the context of factory design, the Westfield works are significant because they offer further evidence that Yost, Lozier, Burwell, Moore and Raynor, had fashioned a very tested production system that could be transplanted from one place to another. Notably, the Westfield works borrowed heavily from the Toledo plant and created the beginnings of a quadrangular complex similar to that developed in Ohio. The large machine shop comprising the complex's front elevation extended 400 feet, long enough to allow the construction of extensions built at right angles if desired, and the interior

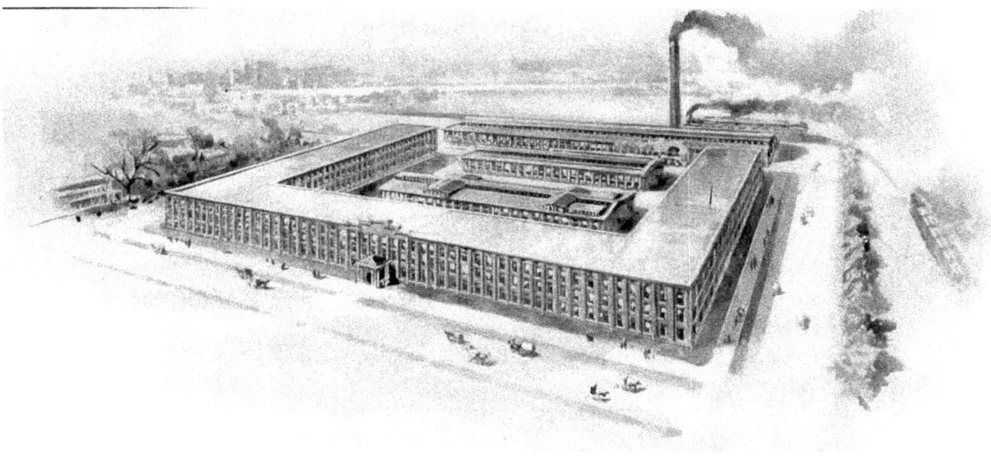

Figure 68. After Henry Lozier received financial assistance from the Toledo Chamber of Commerce to rebuild his factory following the 1894 fire, and after securing $20,000 from the Thompsonville Board of Trade in 1895 to build a factory in that city, he persuaded the Board of Trade in Westfield, Massachusetts, to contribute $75,000 to his third American factory. Contractor George Blodgett from Westfield oversaw construction, and in November 1896 city engineers surveyed the buildings and water mains, sketching the locations (front or northerly to back) of the three-story machine shop, a one-story brazing and enameling plant, a one-story plating and polishing building, and the engine house with boiler room, chimney stack, and separate room for punch presses. Production began early in 1897, and that year the company catalog promoted this exaggerated illustration of the new works. In 1901, after moving Toledo's bicycle production to Westfield, the American Bicycle Company added a three-story, easterly wing, probably the only new building related to bicycle manufacture erected by ABC. Westfield's Board of Trade contributed $15,000 toward construction, and the R.L. Fosburgh and Son Construction Company from Pittsfield built the addition. Courtesy Lyman and Merrie Wood Museum of Springfield History, Springfield, MA.

buildings were compact enough to accommodate such extensions.

In addition, drawings and plans of the complex prepared by inspectors of the Factory Insurance Association have survived, providing valuable information about interior arrangements and machinery installed during the twentieth century. Lozier's blueprint extended even to plans for workers housing by a real estate trust, the Cycle Heights Company, established initially by shareholders from nearby Springfield, but including Charles Moore. Residents referred to the subdivision colloquially as both Cycle Heights and Lozierville, with homes along Cleveland, Toledo, and Lozier Avenues and the factory itself facing Cycle Street. As in Thompsonville, the New York, New Haven, and Hartford Railroad provided spur service.[21]

Equally significant, the Westfield works continued to demonstrate the versatility of standard-mill-construction throughout most of the twentieth century, accommodating the production of bicycles until the early 1990s despite a succession of challenges, including exploitive owners, economic upheavals, war, and advances in machine technology. In the process, the complex became the country's only factory erected during the nineteenth century specifically for the manufacture of bicycles and used continuously for that purpose (war years included) for almost a century, surpassing cycling's tenure at Iver Johnson's factory in Fitchburg by several decades.

Design. By November 1896, construction had advanced far enough for city engineers to survey the site, locate

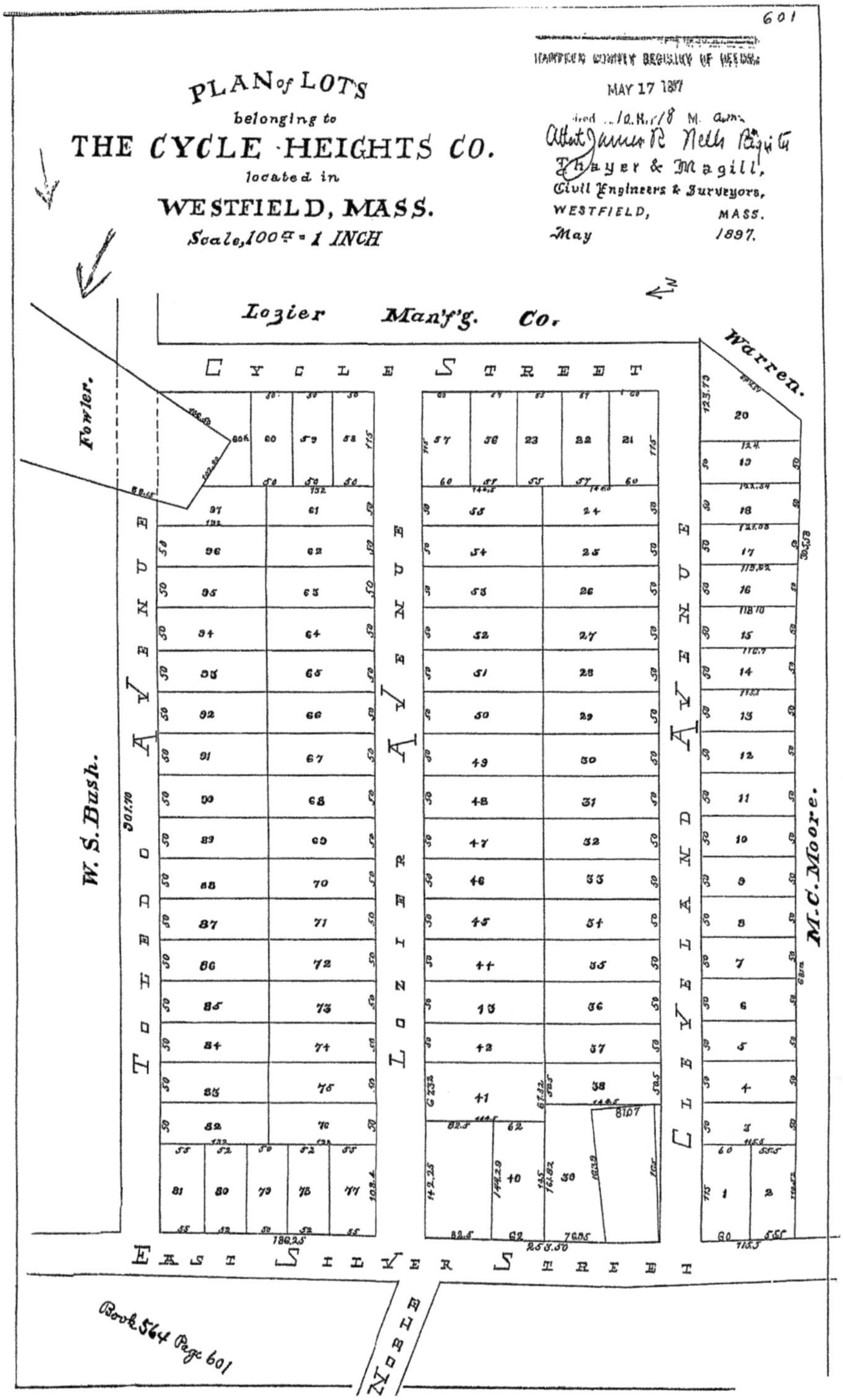

Figure 69. As he had in Toledo, Henry Lozier collaborated with local real estate investors to build housing for workers, and the Cycle Heights Company also repeated some of the street names used in Toledo, notably Lozier Avenue and Cycle Street. Westfield civil engineers and surveyors Thayer and Magill prepared the subdivision plat, and several of the first houses were built along Cleveland Avenue. Courtesy Hampden County Registry of Deeds.

buildings and water mains, and show the complex in two-dimensional plan. Although the city's surveys are minimal, Westfield's journalists marveled at the "big Lozier bicycle shops" nearing completion by January 1897. Those first drawings identify, front to back, the three-story machine shop; a one-story brazing and enameling plant; a one-story plating and polishing building; and the engine house with boiler room, chimney stack, and separate room for punch presses. The city's drawings are important because they reveal the rapid progress of construction and because they corroborate the dimensions and relationships of the original brick buildings, several of which were later modified or enlarged. The complex did not quite achieve its full quadrangular form until the reorganized Pope Manufacturing Company acquired the works from the defunct American Bicycle Company and erected two sizable shops, but Lozier probably had considered plans for the opposite easterly wing during the summer of 1898; ABC finally erected that wing in 1901. The first meticulous drawings by the Factory Insurance Association, prepared in 1919, depict the works as developed by Lozier, ABC and Pope, and all the major buildings shown on those drawings were in place by 1906.[22]

The principal plant, identified by the city's 1896 plans as "Main Factory" and by the insurance drawings as Building No. 1, consisted of two connected blocks, each 200 feet long, and insurance drawings from 1919 and 1921 show a dividing entrance corridor with stairwell and fire walls; the stock room occupied the third story, lathes the second, and a machine shop the first floor. Eventually, the westerly block also housed a belt room on the first floor, offices on the second, and drafting room on the third; the easterly block provided space for general shop work and possibly assembly. The drawings also specify the manner of construction: plank floors rested on timber floor beams, in turn held aloft by timber posts; exterior brick piers supported those floor beams and reduced the load bearing requirements of spandrel walls with windows of moderate size; open floor joists conformed to industry standards for slow-burning construction; and wood trusses carried the roofs.

Insurance drawings show enlargement of the brazing and enameling plant to accommodate Japan ovens for enameling, a heat-treating room, and a store house for rough stock—the latter two added between 1919 and 1921. Slate-clad roofs secured the buildings against fire from adjacent shops, and monitor roofs provided ventilation and interior light, but corrugated-iron roofing may have been used for some of the structures. The nickel-plating and polishing building initially housed the heat-treating room and later included an adjoining tumbling shed built before 1919. The boiler house eventually included a blacksmith shop with monitor roof and a testing room.[23]

Design Modifications. As in Toledo, the company's Westfield factory presented a uniform and commanding front façade. Yet the Westfield building is far more austere and lacked not only the formal pavilions and entrance porticos that distinguished the Toledo plant, but nearly eliminated entrances on that primary facade altogether, other than a modest central doorway and sheltering, one-story porch kept closed during winter months. Instead, the company placed the primary entrance on the opposite elevation facing the factory yard and behind a small building containing washrooms for workers, in turn flanked on both sides by bicycle sheds built before 1919 for employees who pedaled to work; a single entrance opened at the shop's westerly end.[24]

Administrative Office. Viewed from Cycle Street, the building's long, horizontal bearing is countered by the vertical height of piers, which rise nearly to the top of the cornice where the recessed spandrel walls are brought forward with a flourish of brick corbelling. Other than that functional corbelling, granite windowsills, and slightly arching window lintels, only a stepped-parapet crowning the cornice above the building's six central bays softened the factory's austerity, and then only to provide a recessed panel to display the company's name.

The Spartan character of the plant is allayed by the residential character of the surviving office building standing outside the quadrangular complex and offering a very visible transition between the residences planned for Cycle Heights and the industrial complex. Constructed during the early months of 1899 as a one-story building with prominent dormers and bay windows, the office was enlarged to two stories in 1915, and the stylized, Art Deco keystone panel above the narrow doorway is later still, sometime after 1933 but before 1948. In addition to providing a welcoming entrance to the works, the building hid views of the shops and sheds that once stood directly behind the office. By 1921, a small, one-story gate house with slate roof marked the workers' entry to the complex near the office.[25]

Manufacturing Process. The Westfield complex refined the compartmentalized manufacturing process employed in Toledo in several ways. Lozier and Moore consolidated the power plant and heavy machinery into a single, substantial building at the rear of the works, rather than inserting just the power plant into an ell extension as in Toledo. In addition, the brazing and enameling departments moved closer to the principal machine shop (Building No. 1), and the tooling department also may have moved into that shop, drawing all three departments into closer proximity to the final assembly and finishing process. Rail service extended along the complex's full length.[26]

Consolidation by American Bicycle Company

Charles Moore's reassurances to Westfield residents in March 1897, seeming to confirm plans for expanded production at the factory, concealed a growing awareness by Lozier that overproduction already existed during the 1896 season. If Lozier and Moore truly harbored ideas for continued expansion of the Westfield works, those intentions may have been forestalled by declining bicycle prices, which led to consolidation of the industry by ABC. Those circumstances muddled the relationship between the company and the Westfield Board of Trade, also linking expansion of the Westfield plant to the fate of the Thompsonville factory.[27]

At Thompsonville, workers had been producing small parts for bicycles, and the company had experimented creditably with a group of women workers, who proved to be dependable, created a civilizing influence in the shops, were adept at detail work, and offered a cost savings in hourly wages—the last benefit ultimately leading to grumbling by the union of polishers. That body of men hid its true concern behind complaints that the work was too dirty and unhealthy for women. However, as demand for bicycles declined, Lozier had difficulty satisfying the contractual quota of employees for the Westfield works, and by the summer of 1898 he had decided to transfer the Thompsonville operation to Massachusetts; not, however, before seeking concessions from Westfield's Board of Trade—a brazen request to annul the contract, transfer the deed, and furnish funding for a new addition in return for improving the prospects for workers in Westfield and augmenting the city's tax list.[28]

By relinquishing ownership and control of the Thompsonville factory, members of Thompsonville's Board of Trade had been naive in their dealings with Lozier, who remained free to relocate his business elsewhere. Lozier, though, probably underestimated the resolve of Westfield's board, which declined his requests and refused to relinquish the deed. The city also denied the company's petition to abate taxes, assessed at $54,000 for the building and $10,000 for machinery. Negotiations continued into the spring of 1899, when news of the impending bicycle trust likely softened the outlook of trade board members. The company's strong exports to Germany also may have swayed board members. Talks culminated with a new contract specifying relocation of the Thompsonville machinery to Westfield by the summer of 1899, reducing the average quota of workers employed to 400, and planning the construction of a new addition. Although acquisition of both the Thompsonville and Westfield works by ABC intervened, and delays in implementing the transfer ensued, ABC eventually honored the agreement in 1901.[29]

By the time ABC formed during the spring of 1899, Lozier likely had realized that companies joining the consortium were overvalued, and he shrewdly requested mostly cash ($1,000,000) in addition to stock in the new company, as compensation for selling his three American plants to the trust: Toledo, Thompsonville and Westfield, together with his Cleveland-based sales company. For another profitable sum, he then sold the Toronto works to Canada's emerging bicycle conglomerate, the Canadian Cycle and Motor Company, and after converting most of his investments in tube manufacturing into cash as well, sought new horizons—by then a very wealthy man. Not so prudently, he joined Albert Pope and R. Lindsay Coleman, all three serving as directors of ABC, who provided substantial loans to the company to put the trust on a solid surface during its first tumultuous year.[30]

Unfortunately, although both the Cleveland and Columbia models maintained a standard of high quality, the syndicate's weak financial structure and heavy debt made investment in new buildings unrealistic. Predictably, ABC closed the Thompsonville plant, moving all production and machinery to Westfield during the spring of 1900. Incensed residents faulted members of Thompsonville's trade board for not striking a better bargain with Lozier by requiring that the company remain for a longer period and withholding the deed until that condition had been satisfied.[31]

In Westfield, where the deed continued to be held in trust, the trade board's foresight paid dividends in the form of a large, three-story wing completed during the fall of 1901, and possibly the only building related to bicycle manufacture erected by ABC. Shown as Building No. 7 on the insurance drawings of 1919, the wing enclosed the quadrangle's easterly elevation and exploited the benefits of gravity, housing bicycle assembly on the third floor, inspecting and crating rooms on the second, and frame and polishing departments on the first floor. The trade board contributed $15,000 toward construction; stipulated that the company continue the business for three years and not sell the property for four years; prepared a deed conveying the property to ABC but then retained that deed; and secured the contract with a mortgage on the property. A large firm from Pittsfield, the R.L. Fosburgh and Son Construction Company, won a bidding competition advertised simply as "brick work, mill construction floors and roof, and iron work," with dimensions and other details available separately. The brevity of those specifications also underscores the broad familiarity with standard mill construction at the time.[32]

Pope Manufacturing Company—The New Jersey Corporation

Other than that large wing, the Westfield works remained mostly unchanged during the period of ownership by ABC and its bicycle spin-off, the American Cycle Manufacturing Company, from the summer of 1899 to the fall of 1903, when the reorganized Pope Manufacturing Company acquired the plant. Despite the ABC's financial sieves, production at the Westfield plant remained consistent during the 1901 season, averaging 250 to 300 finished bicycles each day, sustained in part by exports. However, the sales office moved to New York City that fall; Charles Moore departed, replaced by Brayton S. Lewis from Milwaukee, who represented Western interests; and labor rolls dropped. Late the following summer, George Russell from Erie, Pennsylvania, replaced Lewis as manager, and his Tribune bicycles accompanied him. Long-time superintendent Gleason resigned the following spring, 1903, and Captain Jarvis P. Kelly, a mechanic who had worked for the Overman Wheel Company in Chicopee, for the Warwick Cycle Manufacturing Company in nearby Springfield, and for Lozier and ABC at the Thompsonville plant, moved to Westfield, replacing Gleason. Lozier's death soon after in 1903 marked a close to this interstitial period. Amid those upheavals, the trade board's cautious agreement kept ABC from rashly closing the plant.[33]

Once having secured the factories in Toledo, Westfield, and Thompsonville, Pope devoted most of the 1904 season to reorganization of his scattered bicycle and automobile divisions. However, by 1905 the company had moved almost all bicycle production to Westfield, and the factory complex entered a brief period of expansion, beginning with contracts for two large shops during the spring of 1906, awarded to the Berlin Construction Company, successor to Pope's trusted builder, the Berlin Iron Bridge Company, and depicted respectively as Buildings No. 8 and No. 9 on the factory insurance drawings of 1919.[34]

Building 9 established the quadrangle's westerly façade, providing space for finished stock, with a small annex for tires. Whether the testing department adjoining the blacksmith shop, as well as the small experimental laboratory adjacent to the carpenter's shop, can be attributed to Lozier and Moore, to ABC, or to Pope after 1903, is not known. Beyond the complex's westerly perimeter, a one-story frame building housed a mail room, drafting room, and space for storage. A series of small, one-story shops or sheds clustered near the rail spur included a garage; the carpenter's shop; wood chip shed; and shed for scrap and pipe stock, all in place by 1912.[35]

During the period between 1905 and 1912, the Westfield works, known locally as the "The Pope," continued to fabricate prominent marques including Columbia, Cleveland, Rambler, Tribune, and Crescent bicycles. However, the company produced many other models for various commercial enterprises, reflecting the shift in markets from adults to children and from recreation to utility—a means of transport for workers, messengers, and delivery services. By 1906, under the management of Edward E. Hinsman, Westfield workers also had begun producing bicycle saddles and acetylene lamps; by 1909, bodies for Pope-Hartford automobiles; and, toward the close of that period, motorcycles.[36]

Westfield Manufacturing Company

When, late in 1912, the Pope Manufacturing Company reorganized for a third time, becoming a Massachusetts Corporation, and then failed for a second and final time early in 1913, the Westfield works remained in receivership until 1915, the year George Pope sold the plant to a new concern, the Westfield Manufacturing Company, chartered by long-time

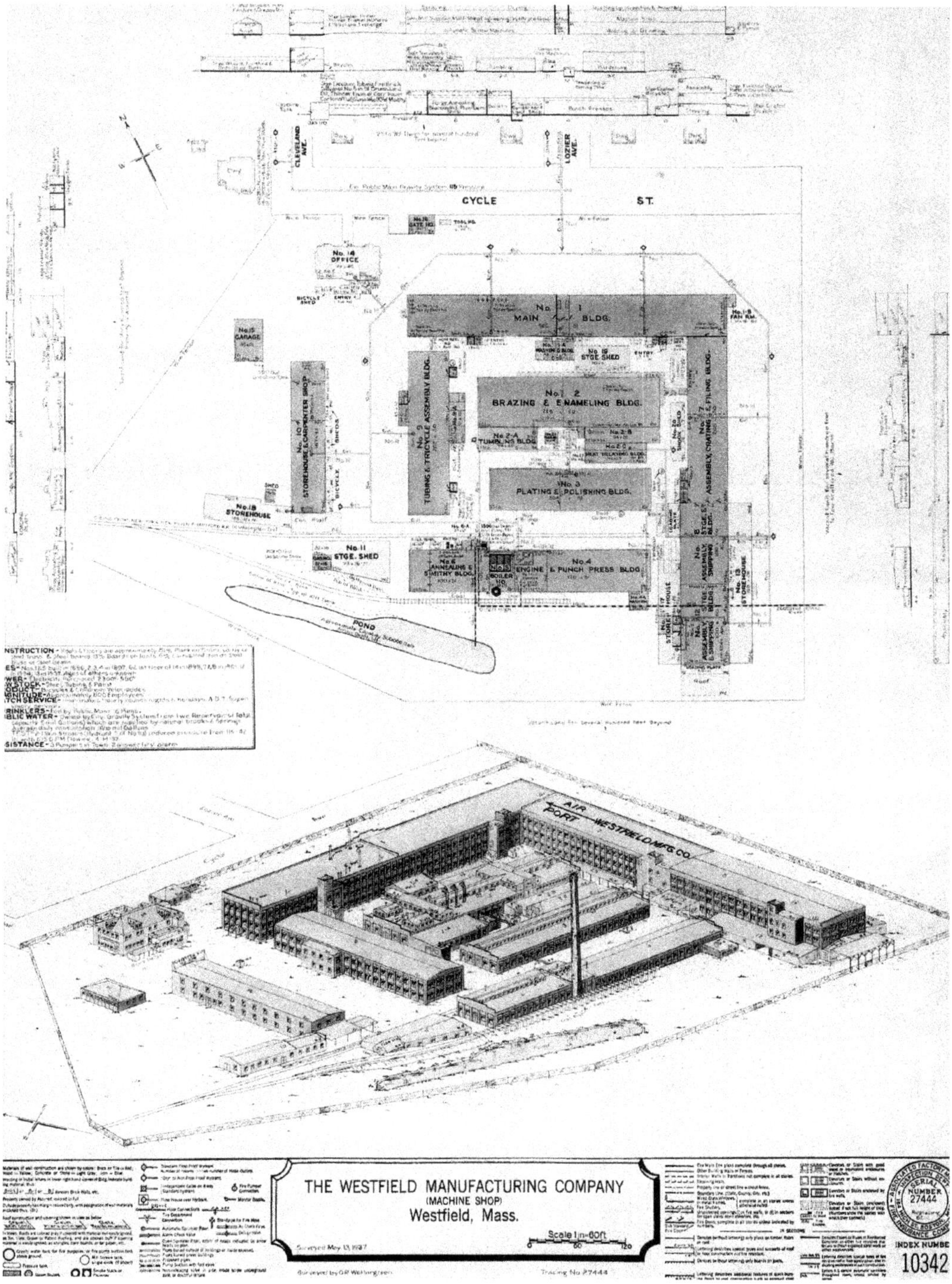

Figure 70. Factory Insurance Association, "The Westfield Manufacturing Company, Machine Shop, Westfield, Mass.," initially surveyed December 5, 1919, revised October 11, 1921, and again on May 13, 1937, shown here. Surveyed by O.R. Wellergreen. Most of the buildings shown were in place by 1921, and the series of insurance maps produced for the company and its successors are among the best documentations of bicycle manufacturing and its production systems during the period before and after World War II. Courtesy Columbia Manufacturing Company, Westfield.

THE CLIPPER Name-plate has long been known as a mark of "satisfaction guaranteed." The new CLIPPER Juvenile Models are worthy of their name, all features of construction and equipment having been selected for lasting service and to uphold the reputation of the CLIPPER makers. CLIPPERS are low in price but high in quality.

Guarantee

These Bicycles are warranted in accordance with the universal guarantee adopted by the Bicycle Manufacturers' Association as follows: We agree with each purchaser of these bicycles to repair or replace, without charge, within one year from date of sale by us, any part which in our opinion shows defect due to material used or imperfect construction, provided it is returned to us *transportation charges prepaid*. This agreement does not cover the cost of repairing bicycles when damaged by accident, misuse, or neglect. Tires, saddles, pedals, rims, handlebars, coaster brakes, chains, or any other finished parts manufactured by others than ourselves, *are not guaranteed* by us, and any claims must be taken up with their respective manufacturers. A bicycle is built to carry one rider. Riding "double," as sometimes dangerously practiced, automatically CANCELS THIS GUARANTEE.

Westfield Manufacturing Company

WESTFIELD, MASSACHUSETTS

Pioneers and Still Supreme

CLIPPER Juvenile Bicycles Make Happy, Healthy Boys and Girls

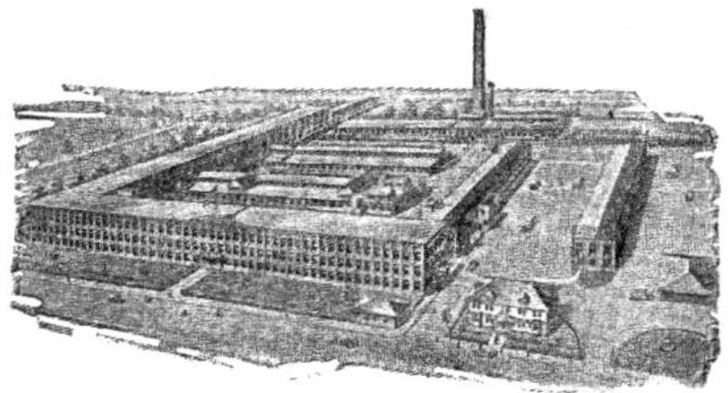

The Home of the *Clipper* Bicycle

Attractive, Sturdy, Splendidly Built and Equipped

secretary of the Pope firm, Wilbur Walker, who served as president. Walker's brother Charles (formerly a vice-president of the Pope concern who had departed that company under dark financial clouds) rejoined his brother in the new business as vice president, and Stephen C. Millett (a senior partner in the well-established Wall Street banking firm Millett, Roe and Hagen) became treasurer. The Walkers hired two other former Pope employees, John Fogarty and Norman Russell Clarke, to manage plant operations while the Walkers remained in Hartford—Fogarty as general manager and secretary, and Clarke as assistant manager. In 1925, Fogarty replaced Charles as vice-president, Clarke became secretary, former sales manager Leon D. Harden became assistant secretary, and Frank W. Pratt served as plant superintendent during at least part of that period.[37]

By 1915, production levels for the bicycle industry had stabilized, but the nature of the business also had begun to change as influence shifted to specialty manufacturers of standardized components. During World War I, the Westfield factory profited from contracts with the government for the Columbia military bicycle and for ordnance. The company added new machinery during those years and may have begun increasing the size of several buildings in anticipation of new business following the war. Evidence of completed improvements surfaced between 1919 and 1921 when, following introduction of the Columbia bicycle for children, insurance drawings show that the company enlarged or replaced several of the buildings.[38]

Profitability and expansion continued during the 1920s, although industry-wide standardization led to a simplification of styles and models at the Westfield works. The company continued to market the Columbia, Cleveland, and Rambler marques, added a Pope model, and promoted a line of juvenile bicycles under the Clipper badge. To counter the increasingly seasonal nature of production, which also included tricycles and scooters, the company diversified in 1925 by establishing a subsidiary concern, the Columbia Wheel Company, to make a composition product known as Rub-Wood. In 1928, the firm reached new levels of output and the following season introduced a popular chromium finish with a blue tint, applied over nickel plating. As the decade closed, residents of Lozierville could boast that nearly half the country's annual bicycle production originated in Westfield. Less promising, in 1928 the company also declared a 100 percent stock dividend, channeling most of the firm's revenue to principal shareholders. Then, early in October 1929, directors inflated the company's capitalization, selling shares to trusting buyers including Fogarty and Clarke, and two years later declared unearned dividends. Not surprisingly, the business succumbed to the exploitations of its principal owners during the Depression and entered receivership in 1932. Fogarty had quietly resigned the year before, most of his investment lost.[39]

Torrington Company

Following a court-approved sale in December 1933, the Westfield Manufacturing Company became a subsidiary of the Torrington Company, located in the city of that name not far west of Hartford. Edward H. Broadwell, the court-appointed

Figure 71 (*opposite*). In addition to the Cleveland Motobike for juniors, the Westfield Manufacturing Company offered juvenile bicycles with the monikers Empire and Clipper. The catalog is undated but probably circulated during the mid–1920s. Courtesy Lyman and Merrie Wood Museum of Springfield History, Springfield, MA.

MODEL CL 55—18" Frame, 26" Wheels
Also supplied in 16" Frame, 24" Wheels (MODEL CL 33)

MODEL CL 55T—18" Frame, 26" Wheels
Also supplied in 16" Frame, 24" Wheels (MODEL CL 33T)

MODEL CL 66—18" Frame, 26" Wheels
Also supplied in 16" Frame, 24" Wheels (MODEL CL 44)

Figure 72. Catalog for Clipper junior bicycles, circa 1925. The company sold identical or otherwise very similar bicycles using the Empire name. Courtesy Lyman and Merrie Wood Museum of Springfield History, Springfield, MA.

receiver, served as president; Clarke became vice president and general manager; Fogarty's son Charles became sales manager; and in 1933 Norman A. Clarke, Russell's son, began working for the company as an apprentice draftsman. Founded in 1866 as the Excelsior Needle Company, the Connecticut firm had gained prosperity from the manufacture of sewing machine needles, but had diversified with other light, machine-manufactured products during the 1890s, including spokes and nipples for bicycle wheels produced by a subsidiary, the Torrington Swaging Company, and eventually pedals and friction-free ball bearings. Company owners Achille F. Migeon and Charles Alvord also acquired a controlling interest in the Eagle Bicycle Manufacturing Company, which had moved to Torrington in 1891.[40]

In 1933, the Factory Insurance Association revised its drawings of the Westfield works, confirming reorganized production systems to improve efficiency. By that time, too, the company had installed an electric welding machine on the first floor of Building No. 9 to manufacture tubes, replacing a cumbersome, five-step oxy-acetylene process. Punch presses and various machinery for children's velocipede manufacturing occupied other parts of that floor, with dip-plating, drying, and assembly taking place the second floor.[41]

Under Broadwell's and Clarke's management, the Westfield business slowly but steadily returned to profitability during the difficult Depression years. However, Torrington's directors just as steadily tapped the subsidiary firm's revenue to fuel the parent company's substantial quest for growth. Production reached 1000 bicycles per day by 1935, and employees shared in that success by forming a Bicycle Workers Union, winning a pay raise and a forty-hour work week during the spring of 1937, several months before Clarke replaced Broadwell as president. Engineer Harold F. Maschin also began his lengthy tenure for the company during the 1930s, initially as a draftsman but later developing patented designs for bicycle kickstands and stabilizers. With the onset of World War II, Westfield again built bicycles for the military, with authorization to sell limited quotas and models to civilians, and the company also devoted much of its production to other military uses, including bomb components.[42]

Building Capacity

At least two decades before the war, the Westfield works had exceeded the employment capacity envisioned by Lozier and Moore in 1899, the year of consolidation by ABC—space for roughly 800 to 900 employees. Yet during the war employment reached 1400 with three shifts working around the clock, demonstrating another aspect of versatility inherent in these substantial buildings. Modest additions between 1933 and 1948, the year the Factory Insurance Association revised its plans once again, enlarged the plant only marginally, and the company built very few structures other than storage facilities during the ensuing five decades. Thus, building capacity remained fixed for most of the twentieth century.[43]

However, that capacity bore a very direct relationship to decisions about production, which proved to be anything but static as businesses (such as Sears, Roebuck and Company; Montgomery Ward; Western Auto Supply Company; and other mass-merchandisers, wholesale jobbers, or retailers) began purchasing components directly from parts manufacturers to control prices, and then turned to bicycle manufacturers to build frames and assemble inexpensive finished products under retailers' names. Westfield's owners responded by fabricating many of their own parts, yet decisions about which parts to produce depended heavily on numerous factors, including building capacity. Thus, constant adjustments to buildings in response to ever-changing conditions remained fundamental to efficient production. No less essential, versatility of factory space became a crucial part of that adaptive effort.[44]

Fogarty and Clarke well understood those important relationships long before acquisition by Torrington, and company managers explained to journalists that the company paid close attention to the orderly and sequential performance of manufacturing processes. Eschewing acquisition of most parts, other than saddles, tires, brakes, and chains, the firm focused on the refinement of heavy-duty machinery and on internal improvements as the favored paths to better production, rather than simply increasing floor space.[45]

The 1948 insurance drawings confirm the plant's minimal expansion during the preceding fifteen years—mostly increased storage space. However, the drawings also document the rearrangement of internal systems, including the acetylene welding and soldering units and several other departments. Also moved were the spraying booths; drying units; and the prime-coat, washing, and bonderizing departments (the latter a method of coating and etching metal to improve paint adherence).[46]

Factory Tour

Following the war, building capacity and versatility, together with the Columbia name, served as reliable constants as new and increasingly complex challenges confronted America's bicycle industry, precipitating a renewed emphasis on efficient manufacturing processes and automation. In 1952, commemorating the seventy-fifth anniversary of Columbia bicycles, Harold Maschin prepared a short history of the company including a sequential tour of the bicycle works. Maschin keyed each step of the manufacturing process to the buildings in the complex, thus providing a rare, comprehensive look at the interior of a bicycle factory.

Receiving. Maschin began the tour in Building No. 10, where all incoming supplies, materials, and shipments passed through a first-floor receiving room for recording; the second floor of that building housed records and general storage, as did the adjoining Building No 18 and its Quonset hut.[47]

Tubing. Tube production occupied the ground floor of Building No. 9, which housed the plant's single most expensive machine—a tubing mill manufactured by the American Electric Fusion Co. and installed during the early 1930s, with progressively-sized roller dies that transformed a flat strip of steel or skelp into coils and then electrically welded the seams into finished tubing at a rate of seventy-two feet per minute, each bicycle averaging eighteen feet of tubing. That same room also housed machines for cutting, bending, swaging (a process for shaping or tapering metal using dies, required for parts such as front forks or for tube ends at joints), and polishing the tubes. The company turned to tube manufacturers to acquire the heavier gauge tubing required for headsets and crank hangers, and workers drilled that tubing at the points of connection with frame members.[48]

Machining, Tool Room, Engineering. On the ground floor of the westerly half of Building No. 1, the company's New Britain-Gridley automatic screw machines fabricated shells and cones for front hubs from solid bar steel. Special-purpose Rhemberg machines bored holes and ball-cup seats in the heavier head-set and hanger tubes, and a Cincinnati centerless grinder then polished these various pieces. On the second floor, the engineering office and tool room provided space where engineers and machinists designed and fashioned many of the jigs and special equipment used throughout the plant.

Frame Room. Assembly of tubes and parts into frames occurred on the ground floor of the adjoining half of Building No. 1, utilizing a process of silver-brazing, with brazing material flowing into the joints by capillary action. Workers also joined some frames with acetylene welding, dip brazing, or spot welding, depending on the model. Company engineers and machinists designed and fabricated the brazing fixtures, which were automatically timed for brazing periods, the latter calculated precisely by the engineering department. Frames then moved to the ground floor of Building No. 7, where automatic pickling baths containing a mild acid compound, Deoxodine, removed brazing flux, rust, and scale from the frames; formerly, workers hand-dipped the frames in cypress tanks containing the bath.

Small Machining. By the time of Maschin's tour, the machining of small parts and various boring, drilling, and milling operations had moved to the upper floor of Building No. 7.

Press Room and Crank Department. The press and stamping room, Building No. 4, contained approximately thirty-five presses of various types and sizes for parts such as fenders, wheel rims, and chain guards; the largest presses stamped sprockets. The converted blacksmith shop, Building No. 6, housed special-purpose machines that forged cranks to close measurement tolerances.

Plating, Polishing and Tumbling. In Building No. 3, the company offered three types of plating: zinc, nickel, and chrome—the last used for bright parts. Zinc plating utilized a combination of hand-dipping and barrel dipping, the latter with baskets developed by company engineers for smaller pieces, but both nickel and chrome plating required automatic machines—that for chrome introduced in 1950 and replacing hand dipping. Before plating could take place, metal parts moved through the polishing room, and returned to that room for buffing after completion of the plating process. Alternatively, small parts could be brightened in rotating drums located in the tumbling room, an addition to Building No. 2, using either sand burnishing-balls or soap flakes.

Heat Treating. Electrically-operated furnaces in a separate addition to Building No. 2 hardened or tempered metal parts subject to stress such as cranks. That same room also housed oil-fired furnaces where front forks could be dip-brazed in molten brass.

Dip Painting and Phosphate Coating. The company used both dipping and spraying processes for painting. The former, less expensive, took place in Building No. 2, as did a five-step process of phosphate coating, a paint conditioner applied prior to enameling to improve adherence of the paint and to inhibit rust. Machines applied the coating as parts traveled on a conveyor passing through various baths and driers.

Enameling and Striping. Maschin's tour provided an intriguing description of the enameling process, which had moved to the third floor of the westerly half of Building No. 1 by 1948. Painters spray-painted base coats in metal rooms called "waterfall spray booths" that prevented vaporized paint from entering the air exhaust system. After spraying, workers then baked the parts in drying ovens heated to temperatures of 335 degrees. Once dried and hardened, paint could be decorated using either a spray or a silk-screen process. Decorations applied with spray paint received a finishing coat of quick-drying lacquer; silk-screened decorations required a second baking. Parts then moved to the third floor's opposite end for hand-striping by skilled workers, who applied gold leaf or other colors; special lightweight frames received as much as twenty feet of striping. Other frames received applications of varnish-type or water-type transfers and decalcomanias.

Tagging and Preliminary Assembly. The early stages of assembly also began on the third floor of the easterly half of Building No. 1, in the tagging department where employees coordinated the painting and assembly of bicycles to assure that the correct fenders and chain guards reached the assembly process with the correct frames. Workers attached nameplates, small hardware, and specification tags with serial numbers to the frames, which then moved to the adjacent wheel room, where staff used machines to assemble or lace spokes, nipples, rims, brakes, and hubs into completed wheels, and to tighten and true the wheels by placing spokes under equal tension; wheels then moved to the assembly room on the third floor of Building Nos. 7, 8 and 12.

Assembly. Bicycle historians have long debated the contributions of the bicycle to the development of assembly-line production, with few conclusive results, and Maschin's 1952 tour sheds little light on bicycle assembly methods employed during the late nineteenth century. Nevertheless, his description makes clear that the company relied on an assembly-line process utilizing a conveyor, with bicycles positioned about five feet apart, beginning with attachment of the crank and sprocket to the frame. Farther down the line, the attachment of rear fender, wheel, and chain guard followed in that order before inspectors conducted preliminary tests. Assembly of fork, front wheel, and front fender followed, as did the attachment of special features such as gas tank facsimiles or carriers, each in turn. A second inspection came next, accompanied by application of model numbers and decals, before the conveyor transferred finished bicycles to the crating room for packing, located on the second floor of Building No. 7.

Crating, Packing and Shipping. Workers organized completed bicycles according to wheel size and packed them in cartons with equipment boxes for handlebars, pedals, lamps, saddles, and other parts. Cartons then moved through an automatic machine that glued and sealed the carton flaps, before transferring the cartons to an elevator leading to the ground-floor shipping rooms in Building Nos. 8 and 12. There, workers added routing information to cartons and recorded the shipments. The second floors of Building Nos. 8 and 12 also housed storage of orders for customer repairs, service, and parts purchased from other manufacturers.

Columbia Manufacturing Company

For the remainder of the twentieth century, owners of the Westfield works continued to improve machinery but made few changes to the factory complex, other than a small building built in 1952 to house the manufacture of tubular school furniture, an effort to diversify during a period of weakness in America's bicycle industry. Instead, the company's history becomes one of frequent challenges and several changes in ownership. In *Peddling Bicycles to America*, Bruce Epperson tells that story well, relying on timely and adroitly-conceived interviews with Norman A Clarke, who succeeded his father as president in 1955. Those accounts offer an important, first-hand view of bicycle manufacturing and its administrative challenges during the period between 1933 and 1974, when Clarke finally retired.[49]

Epperson's chronicle is thorough, and need only be outlined here, beginning with the flood of English Raleigh bicycles following the War—our government's attempt to bolster England's devasted post-war economy but ruinous for the American bicycle industry; the Torrington Company's sale of the business in 1960 to Clarke and a group of investors, who adopted a new name: Columbia Manufacturing Company; the importing of Shimano parts from Japan a year later,

Clarke's initiative that other members of the Bicycle Manufacturers Association copied almost immediately; the development of the country's first ten-speed adult bicycles in 1960; the difficulty of raising capital to improve the factory, resulting in sale of the company in 1969 to the Modern Tool and Design Company, a manufacturer of lawn mowers based in Cleveland; labor strikes; peak production during the boom of 1970s; bankruptcy of Columbia in 1987; followed by sale of the business to company employees; and finally the abandonment of bicycle manufacturing in 1991.[50]

Columbia Epilogue

Ultimately, the versatility and adaptability that contributed to the longevity of the bicycle works orchestrated by Henry Lozier in Toledo, Thompsonville, and Westfield also contributed to the demise of those buildings, the result of constant, heavy use and economic imperatives. Today, the loss of these important industrial buildings underscores the uncertain future of the scarce examples of bicycle history in our built environment. Thompsonville's factory, the first to sever association with the bicycle industry, was also the first to go.

In Toledo, automotive history began dominating Lozier's factory complex after ABC transferred the buildings to its International Motor Car Company subsidiary late in 1901. The reorganized Pope Manufacturing Company continued automobile production in 1903, but failure of that second Pope concern in 1907 set the stage for acquisition of the Toledo plant by John North Willys, whose Willys-Overland Motor Company and its successors produced many popular automobiles, including the Willys-Overland

Figure 73. The last surviving remnant of the original Central Avenue factory in Toledo succumbed to demolition in 2015, six years after the date of this photograph and by then regarded as an eyesore. Photo by the author.

Figure 74. The Westfield Manufacturing Company entered receivership in 1932 and a year later became a subsidiary of the Torrington Company, manufacturer of machine-tooled products and various bicycle parts. Bicycle production continued after the Torrington concern sold the works to investors led by Norman Clarke, who had managed the company for the Torrington group and who formed the Columbia Manufacturing Company in 1960. Bicycle production continued until 1991, the company then owned by its employees. Unfortunately, industrial waste left by military production and by plating processes resulted in an order from the Environmental Protection Agency to clean the contaminated soil. Removing the buildings offered the least costly method of compliance, and demolition of the entire historic complex commenced in July 2008. Demolition of the much-altered administrative office building occurred in 2022. Photo by the author.

and general-purpose military vehicles (GP), eventually known as the Willys Jeep. The economic challenges confronting the bicycle industry proved to be a quiet prelude to those faced by the automotive industry throughout the twentieth century, and in 2015 the lone surviving building from the Lozier era, one of the two blocks facing Central Avenue and built in 1895 following the fire, succumbed to wrecking crews, the factory by then regarded as an eyesore.[51]

In Westfield, the industrial waste left by military production and plating processes resulted in an order from the Environmental Protection Agency to clean the contaminated soil. Removing the buildings offered the least costly and least cumbersome method of meeting that order, and demolition of the entire historic complex commenced in July 2008. When the tall chimney stack, emblazoned with the name "Pope Manufacturing Company," fell to earth, our country's most visible reminder of cycling's nineteenth-century origins vanished.

8

Crawford Manufacturing Company

Hagerstown, Maryland

Robert S. Crawford joins Henry Lozier, Albert Pope, and several other cycling impresarios who, if not inclined toward invention, nevertheless recognized the mechanical ingenuity inherent in bicycle design and applied financial acumen to convert that insight into profit, in the process rising to the upper tiers of a mercurial industry—albeit for medium-priced bicycles in Crawford's case, an adroit strategy of market segmentation. Just as Lozier and Pope methodically enlarged their respective manufacturing domains, a means to meet demand as well as command market share, so too did Crawford steadily expand his factory in Hagerstown, Maryland, into a sprawling industrial complex, remnants of which survive. As did Pope and George Day in Hartford, Crawford also understood the value of providing adequate housing for workers, and his company arranged for the purchase of hundreds of building lots outright and made them available to employees at reasonable costs, partly avoiding the type of speculative ventures surrounding Lozier's factories in both Toledo and Westfield. Ultimately, as did Lozier and Pope, Crawford joined the nucleus of select companies forming the American Bicycle Company.

As a young man, American-born Crawford sought adventure at sea and left his Gettysburg home to work for Scotland's Anchor Line steamship company, where he gained knowledge of marine and mechanical engineering on passages between Glasgow and New York. Sustained by travel abroad, Crawford became affiliated with a bicycle company in Glasgow, adding to his knowhow, and after returning to America formed a partnership with Henry Calver in 1888—Crawford and Company—to build bicycles. Working from a modest machine shop on E Street NW in Washington, D.C., Crawford put his familiarity with European trends in cycling design to good use and focused exclusively on safety bicycles at a time when some American companies continued to market high wheels.[1]

Crawford shrewdly filled a gap in the bicycle trade by concentrating on juvenile models, producing Gazelle safeties with tubular-steel drop frames for girls and boys ages eight to sixteen; cross bars could be added for the latter. By the start of the 1890 season, he had accumulated orders from numerous retailers in major cities, and he attached price-tags of $35 and $40 that year. He also began manufacturing Gazelles for women that summer and for men later that same year, intending to provide well-built models in a medium price range beginning at $50. By comparison, top Columbia, Victor, and Warwick Perfection safeties sold for $135 that season; the Lovell Diamond safety built by Iver Johnson sold

Figure 75. In 1890, Robert Crawford began negotiating with the Hagerstown Manufacturing, Mining, and Land Improvement Company for a site to relocate his small concern, which produced Gazelle juvenile bicycles in Washington, D.C. Aided by subscriptions from Maryland investors, Crawford completed construction of a factory that year and continued to expand the works until 1898, the year he completed this portion of the complex, with a central, three-story entrance tower decorated by crenelations and arched atrium to create a formal public façade for a one of Hagerstown's very profitable ventures. As did so many other bicycle factories, the Hagerstown works subsequently housed automobile production, including the Pope-Tribune gasoline-powered model, but later Dagmar motor cars produced by the M.P. Möller Motor Car Company, which also manufactured taxi cabs for several firms, including the Checker Taxi Company in Chicago. Photo by the author.

for $85; and Lozier and Yost offered a Giant safety for $85 and a Little Giant for children for $35. That season, too, Pope marketed the less expensive Hartford for $100, and Albert Overman retained the Lamb Knitting Machine Company to produce the Credenda for Albert Spaulding, priced at $90 for the 1891 season. In addition, Crawford may have reinforced his marketing niche by locating south of the Mason-Dixon line—one of very few bicycle manufacturers to do so.[2]

Hagerstown Works

Results from that spring's production rewarded Crawford's foresight, and long before the 1890 season ended, he had begun looking for a suitable site for a new factory of adequate size. Late in August, after discussions with investors from Chambersburg, Pennsylvania, Crawford and Calver instead reached an agreement with the Hagerstown Manufacturing, Mining, and Land Improvement Company for property in that firm's platted addition on Mechanic Street in the city's southerly sector, adjacent to tracks of the Baltimore and Ohio Railroad's Washington County Branch and located in part of the city known as Corbett's Addition. The land company's plat created numerous blocks of narrow residential lots but also several large plots designated as free sites for manufacturers, most of which Crawford's expanding works eventually consumed, stretching between Maple Avenue to the south and Howard Street to the north.[3]

Initial reports that month described the proposed factory as a two-and-one-half-story structure with attic for storage, a separate office, and a detached boiler house. Hagerstown entrepreneur S. Milford Schindel played a pivotal role in securing financial incentives for Crawford and Caliver, who acquired title to slightly less than an acre of land in March 1891. Schindel then replaced Calver and in May 1891, Crawford, Schindel, and several Hagerstown investors including Edward W. Mealey, George F. Updegraff, James B. Lambie, and William Byer formed the Crawford Manufacturing Company, with capital stock of $50,000. Crawford occupied the president's chair, and Mealey, a lawyer and banker, served as treasurer, although A.R. Van Mater soon became secretary and treasurer; Updegraff had served as captain of the Hagerstown Bicycle Club during the high-wheel era. Conveyance of the property to the newly-formed corporation followed in June for the price of $30,000, apportioned into 366 shares of stock worth $27,000, representing slightly more than half the corporation's capitalization, and $3,000 in cash. Thus, Crawford converted his initial investment in the partnership with Calver and what minimal price he may have paid for the land into value sufficient to control the corporation, taking modest profits in the process.[4]

All the while, construction of the Mechanic Street plant had advanced to completion by early November 1890, including installation of machinery for seventy workers. Crawford thus placed the factory into service more than four months prior to acquisition of the land, the corporate charter, and transfer of the property to the company, suggesting that he had agreed to move his business to Hagerstown provided Schindel's investors supplied or reimbursed construction costs, possibly in the form of subscriptions similar to Henry Lozier's agreements with the Westfield and Thompsonville trade boards. In its initial form, the brick factory represented standard mill construction (but with gable roof and attic), and housed machine tools and a buffing department on the first floor; nickel plating, assembly, and wheel building on the second level, accessible via a freight elevator at the northerly end; and an office on the first floor of a two-story tower with a wood-frame entrance porch; the tower's upper floor provided storage space. The adjoining boiler house stood directly behind the plant, with enameling stoves on the second floor and an attached, one-story tool room.[5]

1891 Additions. In April 1891, two months prior to conveyance of the factory to Crawford's company, journalists reported that plans to enlarge the building already were underway to meet increased demand. Completed by mid-summer, that addition took shape as a two-story brick structure behind the boiler house and sheltered a blacksmith shop and forge on the first floor; painting and packing departments on the second; and an attached, one-story, coal bunker with access to the railroad. Later that fall, the company installed separate gas-production plants for illumination and for stoves used to heat enameling ovens, and erected a small, one-story brick enameling shop with adjoining stove room; however, a much larger enameling shop replaced that latter building three years later. By the spring of 1892, the company also had erected a one-story, brick buffing house connected to that department in the main plant.[6]

Crawford produced approximately 2,500 bicycles during the 1891 season, generating impressive profits. With contract orders in the offing and expecting to double both production and employment rolls during 1892, he traveled to Europe in

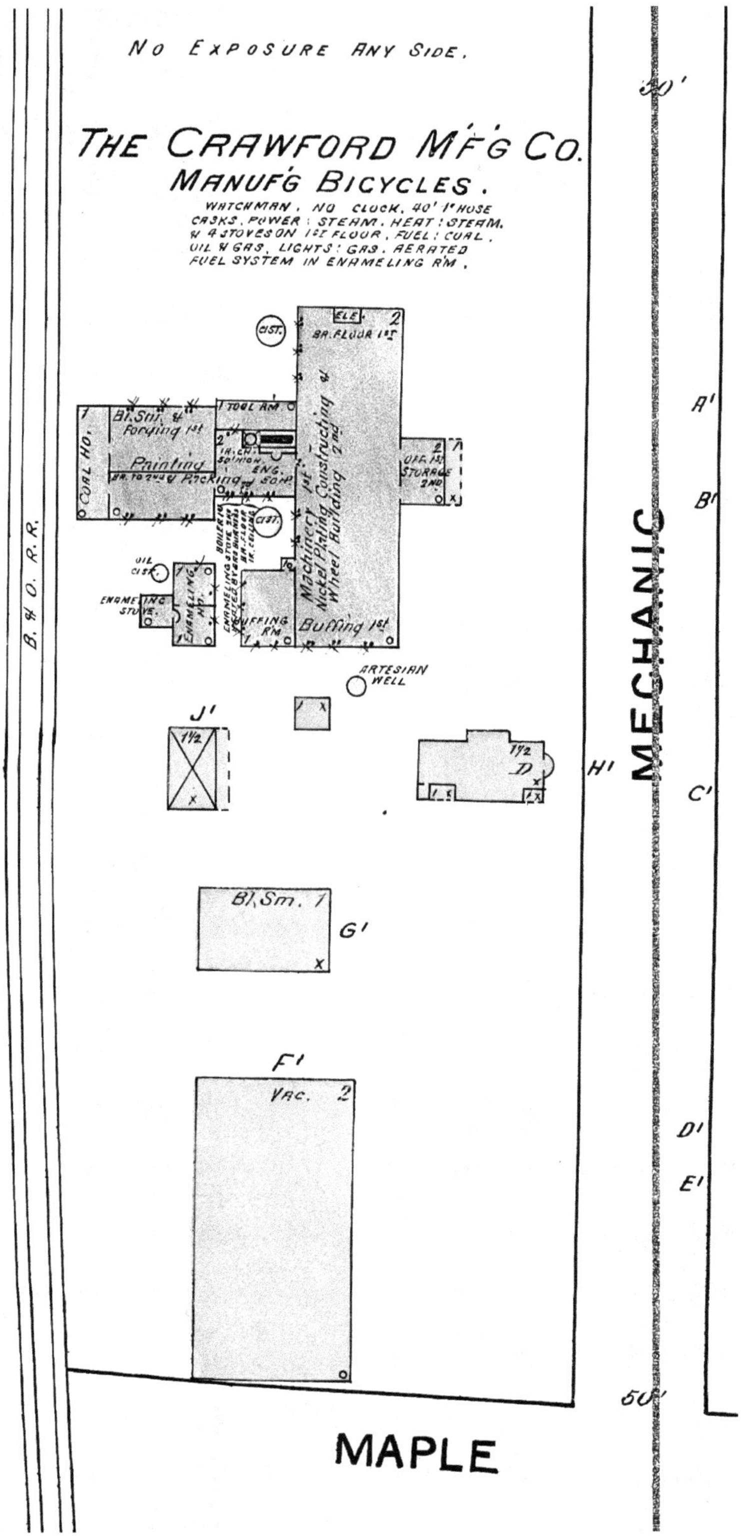

Figure 76. The Crawford works, Sanborn-Perris Map Company, Hagerstown, Maryland, Washington County (May 1892): Plate 20. Library of Congress, Geography and Map Division.

October to purchase raw materials, investing $6,000. He also began plans to design a high-grade wheel, setting his sights on the enticing profit margins achieved in that sector of the industry. He also made plans to develop several styles of bicycles for various jobbers. Plans for expanding the factory complex also ensued, and between 1892 and 1897 Crawford created one of the industry's best examples of organic factory evolution reflecting the rise of bicycles—the built environment becoming a telling mirror of an important cultural phenomenon and its rapid growth year by year. Moreover, most of the new buildings or additions led to refinement of production in one form or another. Labor-saving organization of production systems developed in distinct ways because unlike Lozier's quadrangular factory complexes in Toledo and Westfield, Crawford's works stretched in narrow linear form, constrained by the railroad to the west and by Mechanic Street to the east.[7]

1892 Additions. During the spring of 1892, the company explored several alternatives for a major enlargement to accommodate the separate production of both high and medium-priced models. Early in July, Crawford announced plans to increase capitalization to $100,000, and the land company offered twenty-seven building lots to Crawford's investors as security for additional subscriptions. Although the Hagerstown land venture was a profit-making concern and thus differed from the boards of trade whose members negotiated with Henry Lozier in Westfield and Thompsonville, or lacked the altruistic outlook that guided the Hartford Real Estate Improvement Company, the interests of bicycle company, real estate venture, and city aligned in similar fashion in all four places. By making land available to Crawford at little or no cost, and by finding investors to underwrite construction of the factory, the land company created a market for its undeveloped residential lots, and its land values rose; city tax revenues increased, and local businesses benefited. In addition to gleaning the windfall of funds generated by local investment, the bicycle company secured a workforce nearby.[8]

In return for Crawford's mid–July agreement to enlarge the factory, pave Mechanic Street with a macadam surface, and build a boardwalk from the factory to Potomac Street in Corbett's Addition, the land company conveyed a large chunk of its free sites north of the original conveyance to Crawford and southerly of Howard Street, roughly four acres and quadrupling the company's land. Later that month, the company invested $12,000 to construct two large wings on that land, adding 12,000 square feet of space and doubling the factory's existing size. The 1897 Sanborn-Perris Insurance Company map shows a two-and-one-half-story brick wing adjoining the main block to the north and housing continuations of the latter's departments: automatic screw machine room on the first floor; wheel room on the second; and storage on the third floor, or attic, with additional space for storage on the first floor, probably for raw materials and finished parts, which also filled (then or later) a connected, three-story brick ell. A second ell extended from that wing toward Mechanic Street, with a room for drill presses on the first floor; continuation of the wheel room on the second floor; varnishing (likely for wooden wheels) on the third floor; and a small, attached, one-story room for storing fire hoses.[9]

Work on the buildings continued for the remainder of the year and, upon completion, offered capacity for producing 8,000 bicycles annually. However, sorting out the production systems for both medium and high-priced models is difficult because enlargement of the factory occurred so steadily between 1892 and 1897, the years the Sanborn-Perris Map Company furnished plans for the complex.

Reporters who inspected the factory in the spring of 1893 observed that work moved continuously from department to department without retracing any steps, and the Sanborn maps confirm that machine tooling of parts stretched continuously from the first floor of the original factory into at least three of its northerly extensions. Those same reporters also noted that production from raw materials to finished bicycle required 250 different manufacturing steps. Production systems also seem to have been aided by gravity, with heavy raw materials stored on the first floor and converted into parts in the machine tool departments at that same level. Parts, easily handled, then moved vertically into assembly rooms on the second floor, and from there finished or partly-finished bicycles moved into storage in the more confined attic floor areas; elevators facilitated transport from floor to floor. The company eventually added another one-story brick building for storage, facing Mechanic Street. Coincidentally or not, by 1897 a brick-manufacturing concern had established its works adjacent to the factory, on the railroad's opposite side.[10]

Figure 77. Crawford Manufacturing Company, Catalog, circa 1897. Robert Crawford adroitly exploited market segmentation by specializing in juvenile bicycles and medium-priced bicycles of good quality for adults, rather than emphasizing novel components that commanded higher prices. That strategy proved beneficial when increasing competition forced manufacturers to reduce price tags after 1897, leading to accusations of artificial rates. Crawford also foresaw consolidation of the bicycle industry and may have proposed formation of a bicycle trust as early as 1897. Library of Congress.

Despite ongoing construction, the company still managed to produce about 4,000 bicycles in 1892, including a line of Gotham safeties sold through Manhattan firearms and sporting-goods retailer, Schoverling, Daly and Gales. However, Crawford's building campaign paused during the 1893 season, giving the company time to consolidate gains and to bolster distribution networks. By then, the company offered at least eight different models, ranging in price from $25 for children's wheels to $125 for the premium roadster. In July, the company retained Lionel B. Whymper to manage sales and production, offering him a large block of the company's stock to lure him away from the Schoverling firm, where he had developed a successful cycle trade. Crawford then opened an agency in New York City that fall, eventually occupying a showroom in an eye-catching stone building on Chambers Street in the city's Downtown cycle district, and soon placed the very capable Whymper in charge of the company's entire eastern business, hoping to increase the results of 1893 production, 4,500 bicycles, to 7,000 in 1894.[11]

1894 Additions. At the 1894 season's start, Francis Prial, editor of *Wheel and Cycling Trade Review*, took stock of an industry scarcely able to keep pace with the bicycle's accelerating popularity. Observing that Pope, Overman, and R. Philip Gormully commanded positions as the "Big Three," Prial also pointed to a second prominent trio, who dominated the market for lower-priced wheels: R. Lindsay Coleman of the Western Wheel Works and Arthur Featherstone, owner of Featherstone and Company, both in Chicago, and Charles F. Smith of the Indiana Bicycle Company in Indianapolis. As well, Prial might have chosen that moment to draw comparisons between the two sectors more sharply (thus giving his readers a glimpse of the industry's future pricing contests), had the durability of parts fabricated by the stamping methods employed at Coleman's firm and elsewhere been more widely accepted at the time. In any case, Prial predicted that each of the two sectors soon would be joined by fourth parties, respectively, Henry Lozier and Robert Crawford.[12]

Prial described Crawford's steady rise as quiet but persistent. Had he known Crawford a little better, he also might have described him as impetuous, a trait that Crawford admitted could cause trouble at times, as when he allowed a Republican candidate for Congress to tour the factory during the 1894 fall election but denied that same privilege to the Democratic nominee. Yet Crawford was also capable of converting spontaneity into generosity, much to the benefit of his employees, who in 1895 received bonuses distributed from $10,000 of company profits that year; day workers received a raise of 10 percent. Prial called attention to Crawford's liberal investment in his workers, proclaiming optimistically that the cycle trade needed no assistance from union delegates.[13]

Crawford's impetuous nature likely propelled the building campaign, as well. Construction resumed in the fall 1894 after the company paid $1,200 for land south of the original tract, giving the company title to all the land between Howard Street on the north and Maple Street on the south. With more room to grow, Crawford erected a one-story, brick enameling shop with a battery of three, gas-fired enameling ovens, each with a sixty-foot chimney stack.[14]

Expansion also took other directions, and late in 1894 Crawford's company paid $6000 to acquire the Hagerstown plant of the Surbridge Manufacturing Company, built in 1892 to produce bicycles and consisting of a two-story, brick factory; a brick powerhouse; and a frame finishing and blacksmith shop. Milford Schindel, eager for a chance to repeat his success with Crawford's business, convinced the Standard Manufacturing Company to expand from Martinsburg, West Virginia, and its owners then formed the Surbridge concern, capitalized at $50,000, and acquired property on Spruce Street in the land improvement company's platted No. 2 Addition, two blocks west of Crawford's factory. However, Crawford had more in mind than simply eliminating nearby competition, and early in 1895 he incorporated the Crawford Wheel and Gear Company to manufacture buggies, wagons, and sulkies with ball-bearing axles, pneumatic tires, and tubular running gear, promptly moving the new business into the Surbridge works. Joining him were a brother, George Crawford; another family member, William H. Crawford; Whymper; and investors Charles T. McCue and Charles H. Carlisle, with McCue selected to manage the concern. Crawford proclaimed the ball-bearing axle to be positively dust and waterproof and promoted the design as suitable for a variety of vehicles.[15]

1895 Additions. Crawford met or exceeded production goals for 1894, and by the early spring of 1895, with enough orders booked to keep the firm's 600 workers busy day and night until August, the company began constructing several buildings, including a large brick addition that more than doubled the existing factory and established floor space of more than three and one-half acres. He also enlarged the recently-built enameling shop, adding three more ovens and chimney stacks; erected a wood-frame forge shop with drop hammer; installed a 200 horsepower, Eclipse Corliss steam engine; and increased the number of boilers from two to four. Mill shafting distributed power in various buildings, with separate main shafts and department lines. The system required several external overhead power shafts, including one between the polishing works and the forge shop, and some of those may have used rope drive. The one-story, brick building housing the polishing department may have been erected at this time, too, because Crawford introduced a model system for sand-blasting that summer. The company also added a towering chimney stack, with two flues for the boilers; one for ventilating the blacksmith shop; and one for dust from the polishing machines. Executive staff moved to the elegantly-appointed second floor of a large, two-story brick wing at the northeast corner of the works, directly above the tooling room; employees gained basement washrooms and lockers, additional elevators, and a carriage house to stable horses.[16]

The 1895 expansion also included extensive plans for fire protection, primarily Grinell glass-seat sprinklers installed throughout nearly all buildings, but also the use of metal and slate roofing. Seeking membership in one of the factory mutual fire insurance companies, Crawford increased the existing supply of water in elevated tanks by building a large underground cistern, accessible by the city's fire department. By that time, the complex included six hose-houses with sets of city fire-hydrants in each house. Anticipating employment rosters of 1,000 once the expansion had been completed, Crawford took steps to secure a nearby work force by obtaining 400 building lots from Hagerstown's land company, offering them to employees at favorable terms—a supplement to the sharing of profits with workers later that summer. He also persuaded the owners of one of the city's street railways to provide connections to the factory.[17]

In mid-summer 1895, while this major expansion unfolded, Crawford began thinking about the 1896 season. Giving free rein to his impetuous temperament, he leased a private rail car, supplied it with sample models, and traveled about the country, booking orders for the coming year. The company offered eight wheels for that 1896 season, the lightest road wheel at twenty-two pounds and the heaviest at twenty-four, with prices for those models ranging from $90 to $100. Dust-proof and maintenance-free axle bearings, lubricated and sealed at the factory, may have been the company's principal contribution to bicycle technology, but the firm also offered a novel design for pedals, credited to R.L. Hill and George Gruenewald. Although by that time the company's higher-priced models had captured cyclists' attention, Crawford did not abandon either medium-priced designs or juvenile bicycles, and in 1896 the company offered four models in that last category.[18]

If the expansion of 1895 spilled into 1896, construction had mostly ended by summer and remained dormant until 1898. Meanwhile, in August 1896 the company took time to reshuffle corporate offices. Unlike so many bicycle manufacturers doing business during the 1890s, organized on the anticipated value of a patented design and often pitting inventor against investor, Crawford maintained tight control over the business as company president, providing much-needed continuity as the country's inventories of unsold bicycles swelled and pricing competition intensified. As the firm's new vice president, Charles Carlisle provided what mechanical or inventive skills Crawford may have lacked, and Carlisle may have exercised oversight of the plant's internal workings. George D. Crawford served as secretary and A.R. Van Mater as treasurer, with Whymper, Edward Mealey, and Norman McPherson joining those officers to fill directors' seats. Crawford's officers and directors also assumed atypical tasks, namely guarding against Crawford's political outbursts. Once again, the company's president found himself in difficulties when, in October 1896, he threatened to cancel a large order of bicycles if William Jennings Bryan were elected president—generating considerable outcry in Baltimore papers.[19]

All the while, Crawford continued to elevate both his company and his own position within the cycling industry, exploiting what may have been his most natural talent—promotion. He became a large shareholder and director of the National Cycle Board of Trade and eventually part of its membership committee, joining Arthur Garford. He also embarked on a campaign to avoid jobbing houses by enlarging the firm's agency network, penetrating the challenging New England region by opening a store on Congress Street in Boston in November 1897, and the following year selecting the firm of McCallister and Van Mater in Philadelphia, with a store and repair shop on Arch Street, to serve as distribution agents in southeastern Pennsylvania and southern New Jersey. Edward Mealey replaced Van Mater as treasurer in the fall of 1897, the latter joining William McCallister in their new venture but remaining a director of Crawford's business.[20]

Although the Sanborn-Perris Map Company plan of 1897 offers a very clear picture of the remarkable expansion occurring at the Hagerstown works between 1892 and 1897, visualizing the organizational, sequential flow of production inside the buildings becomes difficult because departments are dispersed. In addition, the plans don't reveal how Crawford organized production for different models within discrete departments. In Hagerstown, that becomes important because the company emphasized smaller juvenile bicycles, but also because Crawford began manufacturing other types of vehicles and produced some parts for those vehicles at the bicycle factory.[21]

Complexities of production aside, price upheavals during the 1897 season reached almost every corner of the industry. Fortunately, the Hagerstown concern had specialized in the manufacture of sturdy, medium-priced bicycles from the start, aiming for all-around quality at that level rather than fleeting success based upon

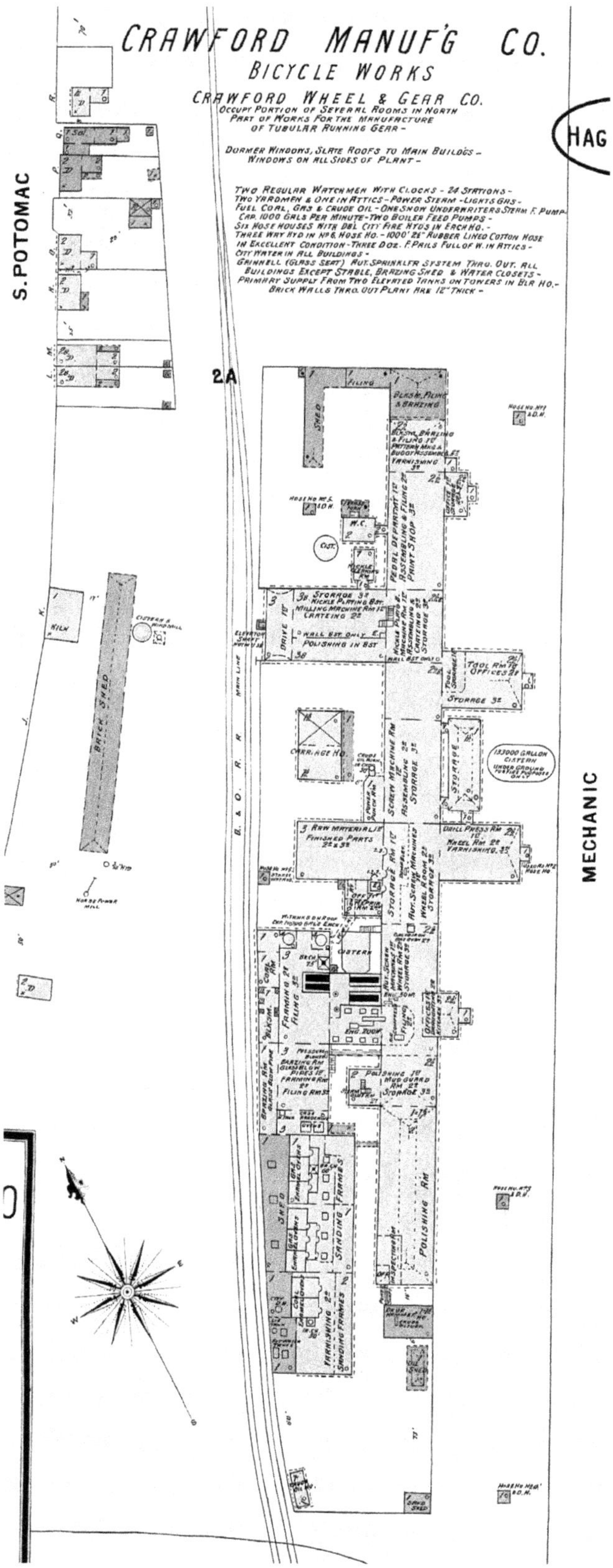

novel features. Crawford pointed to those circumstances to avoid accusations of artificial rates and to justify maintaining existing prices of $50 for medium-grade wheels. In addition, the company dodged growing conflict about chainless bicycles, refusing to join forces with Coleman's Western Wheel Works and fight Albert Pope's patents for bevel-gears used in the chainless design. Instead, Crawford and Whymper opted to offer a chainless wheel for $75, strategically under license from Pope. Rumors about an embryonic trust among makers of medium-priced wheels also began to circulate during the late fall of 1897, with Crawford's name mentioned conspicuously. Although he dismissed the speculation, subsequent accounts concerning formation of the American Bicycle Company conglomerate two years later referred to previous efforts and pointed to several individuals, including Crawford.[22]

1898 Additions. Despite the industry's unpredictable direction by the late 1890s, Crawford continued to expand the factory complex, which closed temporarily in July 1898 to enable new construction—probably a long, narrow, two-and-one half

Figure 78. Sanborn-Perris Map Company, Insurance Maps of Hagerstown, Maryland, Washington County (September 1897), Plate 25. The plan illustrates Crawford's phenomenal growth between 1892 and 1897, a demonstration of equally remarkable growth occurring in the bicycle industry during those years. Library of Congress, Geography and Map Division.

story unit fronting Mechanic Street near its intersection with First Street. The new building provided more space for offices, storage, and tool room, and its central, four-story entrance tower embellished by crenelated architectural detail provided a more formal public façade for a company that unexpectedly had become one of Hagerstown's most profitable ventures. An open, ground-level atrium framed by arched passageways accentuated that principal entrance. In addition, sometime between 1898 and 1904 the company built a one-story, brick testing house at the complex's northerly end.[23]

American Bicycle Company Consolidation

At the start of the 1899 season, Crawford's company offered sixteen models, with prices of the most popular adult bicycles ranging between $25 and $75, the differences in price governed principally by size and weight; by the three-piece or the more expensive two-piece crank hangers; and by chainless drives. By that time, however, Crawford had turned his attention to larger concerns. Late in February1898, he had joined a majority the National Board of Cycle Trade's shareholders who voted to dissolve that body, a tacit admission that the organization had been unable to thwart the glut of inexpensive bicycles overwhelming the industry. For Crawford and other manufacturers of medium-priced bicycles, consolidation represented the best hope of controlling the trade. Thus, when Albert Spalding finally managed to convene the industry's figureheads during a lengthy sojourn at New York's Waldorf Astoria Hotel in March 1899, Crawford was among the select group who first gave purchase options to Spalding—the cream of the trade as Francis Prial described them: Pope, Gormully, Coleman, Lozier, A.D. Meiselbach in Milwaukee, and Crawford. Prial interviewed Spalding, who acknowledged that among the twenty or so owners who had tried to form a trust during the preceding years, Crawford had come nearest to success.[24]

Crawford returned to New York in June for the trust's organizational forum, finding time between meetings at the hotel to take afternoon drives in Central Park—and possibly to reflect upon what seemed to be hard-won personal success at the time, or to contemplate his new role as a director of the American Bicycle Company. Editors of *Cycle Age and Trade Review* estimated Crawford's annual production capacity to be 35,000, but Prial declined to attach company names to the *Wheel and Cycling Trade Review*'s assessments, which may have been slightly lower for Crawford. Regardless, the latter journal acknowledged that Crawford's success had resulted from his ability to organize and expand the Hagerstown factory in an extraordinarily capable manner.[25]

In August, the Maryland company conveyed its plant and several residential lots to ABC, but excluded the Crawford Wheel and Gear Company factory built by the Surbridge Manufacturing Company. At the trust's meeting of directors in September, Crawford received added responsibilities as chairman of the committee appointed to oversee sales of bicycles to the jobbing trade, joined by Meiselbach and J.A. Carter of the Geneva Cycle Company in Geneva, Ohio; Coleman, Gormully, and J.W. Spalding composed the committee on sales to dealers. Crawford's group acknowledged the challenging prospect of setting prices for about thirty-five bicycle models, many of which had sold for similar prices but had varied greatly in quality—hardly the type of admission to inspire confidence among impatient jobbers.[26]

The trust's directors met again in January 1900, most members expressing general satisfaction about the company's affairs. However, optimism around the board table belied the uncertainties facing employees of the companies joining the trust. Months before, rumors had begun to circulate about plant closures and layoffs for both managers and department workers, but Crawford's prominent role in the consolidation, combined with oversight of the jobbers committee, may have placed the Hagerstown workers in a better position than most—illuminating just one aspect of the industry's enormously complex upheaval. Charles Carlisle moved into the head office at the Hagerstown factory, but speculation followed Crawford's every step. Early in December, journalists reported that he planned to sell all his real estate in Hagerstown and move to New York City, and a week later the sales department of the trust's Lamb group of bicycles (the Lamb Manufacturing Company in Chicopee Falls reorganized by Spalding before it became part of ABC), moved into the Crawford company's store on Chambers Street. Those marques, including the Spalding, Ames and Frost, Crawford, and Nyack, represented the trust's early organization of mid-priced models, with responsibility for eastern sales given to one of the city's venerable, high-wheel–era cyclists, Albert Barkman.[27]

As the new bicycle season approached, Crawford may have found himself at loose ends, with little clarity, and just as likely little satisfaction regarding his role in the trust. Looking elsewhere for opportunity during the spring of 1900, he joined with Hagerstown investors Alexander Mason and Charles Shaw to form a land company, and the trio acquired timber and coal reserves in Kentucky. All the while, he remained a director of both ABC and the Crawford Manufacturing Company subsidiary of ABC, giving him enough sway to guide decisions concerning the Hagerstown works. His influence became apparent in August when ABC agreed to withdraw Crawford models from sales agencies and to market the factory's entire output directly from Hagerstown under the supervision of Whymper, aiming primarily at jobbers and assuring continuous production—at least according to predictions. A year later, September 1901, the subsidiary shuffled administrative positions, electing Edward Mealey president and Harry S. Wise secretary, with Whymper, C.W. Dickerson (formerly with the Sterling Cycle Works in Kenosha, Wisconsin), Edward E. Hinsman (who later managed the Westfield works), George Pope, and Crawford serving as directors.[28]

Production of bicycles at the Hagerstown plant undoubtedly suffered as the industry continued its steep descent, although Crawford's influence and Whymper's abilities allowed Hagerstown workers to fare better than employees of many other companies swallowed by ABC. When the parent ABC split into two divisions at the end of the 1901 season, the Hagerstown works became part of the doomed American Cycle Manufacturing Company unit. In August 1903, the reorganized Pope Manufacturing Company acquired the Hagerstown works along with most of the other remaining assets of ABC and its subsidiaries. Crawford's earlier alliance with Pope concerning chainless bicycles continued to pay dividends for Hagerstown workers because Pope produced Crawford models as an economy bicycle, as well as Fay juvenile wheels. The Crawford model eventually joined production at the works in Westfield, Massachusetts. Pope adopted a similar strategy for automobile manufacturing in Hagerstown, with production of Pope-Tribune gasoline models—a modern car at a moderate price. In 1904, Pope's circular, *The Pope Manufacturing Company: What It Is, What It Was*, described the plant as having 252,000 square feet and capacity for 1,200 workers.[29]

By that time, Crawford had begun building automobiles in family stables near the corner of Summit and Surrey Avenues. With organ manufacturer Mathias P. Möller, Hagerstown mayor Henry Holzapfel, Jr., and local investor George Nelson, the Crawford brothers formed a new corporation in 1902, the Crawford Automobile Company, and produced limited numbers of hand-built Crawford models in a factory that the brothers soon erected at the site. Holzapfel, educated as a horticulturalist, served as secretary and treasurer, and a fourth associate, William F. Bickle, joined the business as plant superintendent. The brothers had begun experimenting with automobiles many years before and had developed a trial electric vehicle in 1895, testing it in a Chicago race. Robert embraced this new venture energetically and in 1906 he shipped two of the company's touring models to Buffalo for entry in the Glidden Race, a 1090-mile adventure from Lake Erie to Breton Woods in New Hampshire via Montreal. Crawford arrived in Buffalo in time to drive one of the cars, and William Danzer from Hagerstown piloted the second.[30]

Ultimately, Danish-born Möller would join Robert Crawford as the two most important figures in the history of Crawford's bicycle factory. Möller arrived in this country in 1872 as a sixteen-year-old apprentice cabinet maker, and he settled in Pennsylvania where he learned to design and build pipe organs. In 1877, he moved to Greencastle, located southwest of Harrisburg and not far from the Maryland border, and there formed a partnership, Möller, Brenisholtz and Company, to manufacture both reed and pipe organs. Hagerstown investors lured him to their city in 1881, and through hard work and enterprise he steadily expanded to become one of the country's largest organ manufacturers.[31]

Production of Crawford automobiles at the Summit Avenue site putted along for several years but offered none of the exhilarating returns that had characterized the early period of Crawford's bicycle business. By 1908 enthusiasm for the venture had waned for several investors, the Crawfords among them, and Möller acquired a controlling interest. He then expanded from hand-built to assembly production (with most parts fabricated elsewhere), built a few Crawford trucks, and introduced a six-cylinder motor for cars in 1912, a power unit that became standard after 1916.[32]

All the while, Pope's automobile venture, with factories in Indianapolis, Toledo, Hartford and Hagerstown, flickered on and off for several years and then succumbed to receivership in 1907, followed by reorganization as the third Pope Manufacturing Company (the Connecticut corporation). With that shift, the company sold the Hagerstown factory to the Montross Metal Casket Company for $57,500, the latter probably enticed by the stamping and press machines. However, Sanborn Map Company plans from 1910 show the factory complex functioning well below its capacity, with very limited use of the second floor and attic spaces. In 1914, the Montross concern sold the plant to the New York and Hagerstown Metal Stamping Company, which reorganized as the Maryland Pressed Steel Company, in turn absorbed by the Poole Engineering and Machine Company of Baltimore, all within the span of a few years. During World War I, the factory housed munition production, but following that conflict Maryland Pressed Steel fabricated parts for a biplane and wire wheels for automobiles. However, by 1922 the factory stood vacant and a local real estate business, R.J. Funkhouser and Company, acquired the plant.[33]

Ironically, by 1918 the city had changed the name of Mechanic Street to Pope Avenue, likely in appreciation for Albert Pope's decision to rescue the factory from the ruins of ABC and to maintain production of Pope-Tribune automobiles between 1904 and 1907. Although Pope's role in the history of American bicycle manufacturing is a central one, the street dedication in Hagerstown does little to recognize the factory's origins and remarkable expansion under the guidance of Robert Crawford between

1891 and 1899, or to the latter's contribution to bicycle history.[34]

In any case, by the time Raymond Funkhouser acquired the old bicycle works, Möller had exhausted available space at the Crawford Automobile Company's Surry Avenue factory. Although production had declined during the War years, sales had begun to revive, and in 1922 Möller introduced a luxury sports roadster that would turn a corner for the company's fortunes. Christened the Dagmar, the middle name of Möller's daughter and the name of a legendary Danish monarch, the car sold for $3,500 and became a surprising success. At about the same time, Möller won a contract from a Manhattan company to manufacture 300 taxi cabs, pushing the need for greater production capacity to a critical stage.

In 1923, Möller purchased the Pope Avenue plant and a year later renamed the business the M.P. Möller Motor Car Company, ending production of Crawford automobiles shortly after. In 1926, he incorporated the company with capitalization of $1,000,000, and then transferred the bicycle factory complex to the new corporation. Between 1923 and 1928, he secured profitable contracts with several taxi companies including the Astor Cab Sales Company in New York and the Luxor Cab Manufacturing Corporation, the latter moving into the third floor of Möller's factory to assemble its Luxor cabs. Both businesses were controlled by New Yorker Allie S. Freed, a principal figure in the country's taxi industry, who worked closely with Möller and who also controlled a delivery van business, the Elysée Motors Corporation, that relied on Möller's assembly system to produce the Elysée in various models. A third concern, the Tri-State Taxi Sales Company, ordered cabs for several concerns, among them the Checker Taxi Company in Chicago. Production of Dagmars continued until about 1927, and in several different models, but when Freed consolidated his several businesses into the Paramount Cab Manufacturing Corporation that year and added a deluxe model, the Paramount, to the Hagerstown catalog, he powered Möller's company into the upper tiers of the country's taxi industry. At its peak during the late 1920s, Möller's factory workers built 125 taxis each week, as well as delivery vans, trucks, and station wagons, and gave Crawford's bicycle factory its second most productive era.

Orders for taxis continued to arrive from Freed during the early 1930s, including the very decorative Five-Boro Paramounts named for New York's five boroughs, and the company also continued to receive orders from Chicago. However, by 1931 Freed's Paramount business had begun to lose money, and although orders still trickled in from New York, Washington, and Baltimore, taxi production in Hagerstown had mostly ended by 1934. Möller died in 1937, and his company dissolved soon after. At auction in November 1939, Raymond Funkhouser repurchased the factory and began adapting it to various new industries. Although today the complex is much altered from its days as a bicycle factory, buildings from the Crawford era have survived, including the 1898 entrance tower, now truncated but with crenelations intact.

9

Eagle Bicycle Manufacturing Company

Stamford and Torrington, Connecticut

If nineteenth-century industrialists routinely favored enlarging factories to suit growing and varying needs, rather than reconsidering factory design, the owners of several bicycle companies defied that general practice. The Pope Tube Company plant is an exceptionally good illustration, but other noteworthy examples exist, including the Eagle Bicycle Manufacturing Company plant in Torrington, completed

Figure 79. In Torrington, Connecticut, Waterbury architect Theodore Peck designed this factory for the Eagle Bicycle Manufacturing Company in 1895. Located on Northwood Street, and still standing but without its tower, the complex combined traditional standard mill construction with a large, one-story, open-floor, machine room capped by saw-tooth roofs to provide natural light for workers. Photo by the author.

during the early months of 1896. Resorting to a blend of convention and innovation, the company combined standard mill construction with a sprawling, one-story machine room capped by a saw-tooth roof—a work-area offering the type of floor space Horace Arnold recommended in his 1896 articles for *Engineering Magazine.*

Eagle Bicycles

Although not a factory where workers produced high-wheel bicycles, the Eagle plant in Torrington joins the Iver Johnson works in Fitchburg as one of very few surviving industrial buildings erected or owned by bicycle firms founded during the high-wheel era. The genesis of Eagle bicycles traces to an 1887 patent issued to thirty-year-old engineer Leonard B. Gaylor from Stamford, Connecticut, who joined the roster of inventors seeking to liberate high-wheel ordinary riders from the perils of headers. Gaylor's design for a high-wheel safety, similar to Star bicycles manufactured by the H.B. Smith Machine Company, aligned the main or driving wheel behind the small wheel. Rather than the pivoting treadle levers used on the Star bicycle, Gaylor instead selected standard crank pedals. Observing that such pedals exerted driving power primarily between the forward half and third of the wheel, Gaylor reasoned that use of treadle levers thus became unnecessary, making his bicycle cheaper to build, lighter, faster, and more durable than Star bicycles.[1]

To assure stability of his machine, he placed the saddle on a bow-shaped spring, permitting forward or backward adjustments to the seat's position. By placing the saddle slightly in front of the vertical axis of the large wheel, riders positioned their weight advantageously, directly over the

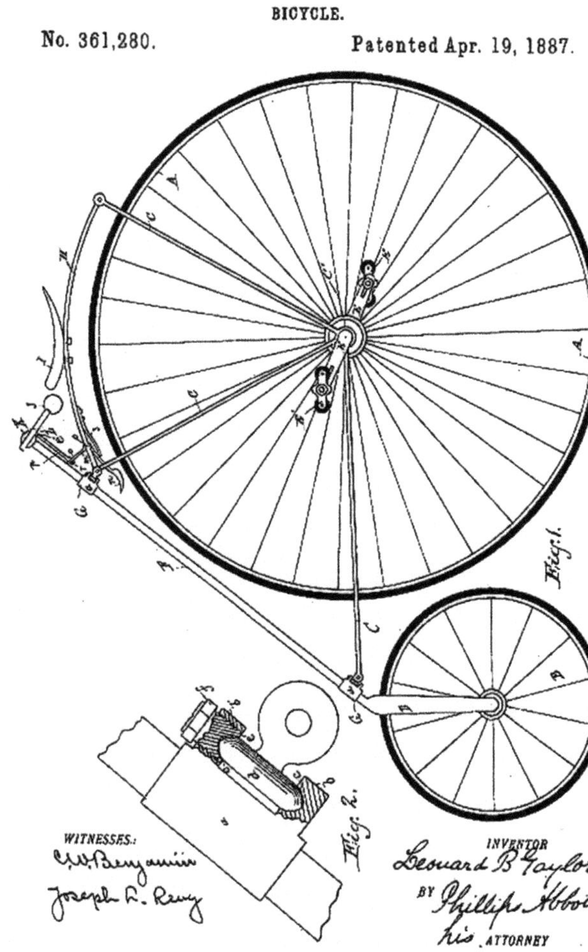

Figure 80. Leonard Gaylor's 1887 patent for a high-wheel safety bicycle with small front steering wheel and large, rear driving wheel with pedals attached to crank arms. By 1890, high-wheel bicycles were fast becoming obsolete and in 1891, Gaylor turned his attention to the design of safety bicycles with two wheels of equal size and rear-wheel chain drive. United States Patent Office.

pedals, without fear of the front wheel lifting unexpectedly and tipping the bicycle backward, called a "backer" and as bad or worse than a header. To climb, riders could adjust the saddle to a position behind that vertical axis but lean forward, thus gaining greater leverage. Gaylor also gave the small wheel maneuverability via a steering rod that oscillated in relation to the main frame, creating independence between steering and the lateral pull of pedal strokes on the drive wheel (an idiosyncrasy of some high-wheel safety bicycles), and adding weight to the bicycle's front.[2]

The company created to convert Gaylor's patents into profit also provides a useful counterpoint to the overextended grasps for lucre that befell some bicycle manufacturers. Instead, the founders of the Eagle concern represented a small and prudent group of investors who sought to market a workable design, one of the few high-wheel safeties that could match the speed and efficiency of high-wheel ordinaries, and who emphasized building a sound business. Recorded minutes of meetings for both directors and shareholders have survived, offering valuable insight into the early stages of a newly-founded bicycle company and revealing debate about factors such as adequate capitalization; the quest for economical types of industrial space; and the potential value of merger to gain access to machine-manufactured parts. In addition to explaining much about the bicycle's phenomenal popularity during the 1890s, the company's records chronicle weighty deliberations about whether to join the American Bicycle Company conglomerate, illuminating the difficult choices faced by a small but well-managed business at that critical juncture.[3]

Stamford Factory

Gaylor, aided by his father, banker Charles Gaylor, gathered a group of prominent Stamford businessmen and investors who chartered articles of association for the Eagle company in March 1888, with capital stock of $50,000. The firm's board of directors included the head of Stamford's board of trade, Charles Lounsbury, as president; Leonard Gaylor, vice-president and superintendent; and Edward S. Walsh, secretary and treasurer. Walsh, Gaylor, and Leonard Gaylor's cousin, Charles E. Gaylor, also were members of the Stamford Wheel Club. Edwin L. Scofield, an attorney, state legislator, and Stamford's second mayor, joined dentist Dr. Isaac F. Wardwell and businessman Walton Ferguson as board members and shareholders; the elder Charles Gaylor occupied a board seat as well.[4]

The company purchased Gaylor's 1887 patent, supplemented by a second patent issued to him in August 1890, and the company's financial statement prepared in September 1890 listed assets in the amount of $20,000 for patents, amounting to 40 percent of the company's value. Ironically, by then the design protected by those patents already teetered toward obsolescence, and the firm's advertisements in December candidly acknowledged those prospects, urging wheelmen to return to the high wheel—with its easy gliding motion never to be equaled by safety bicycles with wheels of equal size. To credit the company's directors fairly, other manufacturers (Albert Pope among them) also clung to the high wheel's allure during these transitional years, and Stamford's investors recognized that the bicycle was in its infant stages as an invention.[5]

Financially cautious from the outset, the company leased a retail shop in the Bell Block on Atlantic Street in Stamford, and by March 1889 had commissioned the Ames Manufacturing Company in Chicopee to fabricate 900 completed bicycles for the approaching seasons. Frank Weaver, a member of the New Haven Bicycle Club, likely selected one of those bicycles for his transcontinental journey, New Haven to San Francisco, begun in April 1890 and offering an advertising bonanza for the young company. By the close of the that season, December 1890, Gaylor anticipated having 400 regular wheels on hand for the coming spring, but he also recommended offering 250 light roadsters and fifty bicycles for boys. Beginning a few months later, in April 1891, Nelson Bradt from Johnstown, New York, pedaled a second Eagle bicycle out of New York City and across the country, arriving in San Francisco in July with similarly beneficial publicity.[6]

Early in September of the previous year, 1890, board members had begun debating whether buying parts directly from manufacturers and assembling the bicycles in Stamford would be preferable, and Gaylor's favorable report concerning cost savings led to a second debate—whether to lease or build factory space. In October 1890, the board acknowledged the benefits of owning a building but remained wary of acquiring real estate given the company's untested financial standing; instead, directors appointed a special committee with authority to secure an acceptable lease. However, the following month that body recommended rejecting all rental offers and instead advised the board to build a small factory. In pointed contrast to Henry Lozier's brazen style, the company purchased a modest lot on the west side of Garden Street for $1,000. After retaining local architect Gage H. Inslee to draft plans for a frame building with corrugated iron roof, the board paid carpenter Noah Hoyt to build the structure for $3,950, but without subsidy from the city's trade board.[7]

During the 1891 season, Gaylor turned his attention to tooling patterns for a new safety bicycle, but the company also struggled to find machined parts in Stamford. Opportunity arrived in the person of Charles Alvord, part owner of the Excelsior Needle Company in Torrington, who had begun riding an Eagle bicycle that summer. Alvord and the firm's president, Achille F. Migeon, proposed to move the bicycle business to Torrington, offering to invest sufficient funds to increase the company's capital to $100,000 and to lease Excelsior's Field Street factory. Walsh, Lounsbury, and the Gaylors formed a negotiating committee, and by mid-October the two concerns had reached agreement.[8]

Field Street Factory, Torrington

After depreciating the Stamford group's stock, probably to reflect the decreasing value of Gaylord's patents, Migeon, Alvord and other Torrington investors subscribed to sufficient shares to control the board of directors, with much of that investment credited to Migeon. The company moved into a well-equipped factory with steam power, electric lighting, and rail service—barely in time to begin production for the 1892 season. Equally important, the firm gained easy access to foundries and component manufacturers including the Torrington Swaging Company, maker of Torrington spokes and also owned by Migeon and Alvord. In January 1892, directors of the reorganized Eagle concern elected Migeon president, Leonard Gaylor vice president and superintendent, and Walsh secretary and treasurer; both Gaylors retained seats on the board of directors, as did Scofield and Walsh, but Lounsbury ended his association with the business. The company also retained its small factory in Stamford, which has not survived.[9]

In March 1892, as employees numbered nearly one hundred and working days stretched to fourteen hours, Gaylor guided local journalists on a factory tour, possibly assisted by his foreman, William van Wagoner, both a racer and a mechanic. Although the firm continued to sell a modest number of high-wheel bicycles, the company already had shifted its full energies to safety bicycle production. Weldless tubing arrived from the Shelby Steel Tube Company, and Gaylor turned to various sources to obtain drop forgings, which required boring and careful milling with newly-acquired, advanced machine tools. Gaylor and van Wagoner fitted Eagle bicycles with both Tillinghast and Thomas pneumatic tires, as well as cushion tires of solid gum rubber; buyers could select saddles according to personal preferences.[10]

Having secured a well-equipped and well-situated factory prior to the 1892 season, and benefiting from several years of marketing experience, the company joined a select list of firms poised to take full advantage of the bicycle's sudden surge in popularity. Gaylor and Walsh immediately pressed those advantages, focusing on ever-lighter models fitted with aluminum rims and intended for road use—thirty pounds for 1893 models and, in 1894, the twenty-two-pound Bald Eagle, suitable for both racing and road use at the princely sum of $150.00. The firm also adapted the technology developed by Migeon and Alvord for the manufacture of spokes and applied cold swaging of tubes to reinforce frame joints. At the ends of each tube cut to length for frame assembly, workers inserted shorter, three-inch-long tubes, slightly smaller in section, and then compressed and consolidated the two in a swaging machine that tapered and reduced the dimensions of the tube ends; brazing of each joint followed.[11]

Company directors remained cautious about increasing production capacity at the start of the 1894 season, possibly because Gaylor had resigned from the firm by then to become vice president of the newly-chartered Black Manufacturing Company in Erie, Pennsylvania, the home of Tribune bicycles. Explanations for Gaylor's departure are not known, but with no potential profits from the high-wheel patent, his prospects may have dimmed; or, having had an opportunity to manage the company he created, Gaylor may have yearned for a more commanding role in the bicycle industry and chafed under the conservative control of Migeon and Alvord. In any event, Charles S. Dikeman, as secretary and general manager, and Elisha Turner, as vice president, replaced Gaylor, but Walsh remained as treasurer. Two Torrington businessmen, J.C. Turner and Thomas W. Bryant, became active members of the board, and Joseph Dikeman, a brother, joined the company as an employee, as did another relation, William Dikeman.[12]

Although not the only bicycle manufacturer to experiment with aluminum during this early period, the Eagle concern successfully adapted the metal to wheel rims for both detachable pneumatic tires with tubes, controlled by the Dunlop company, and for tubeless tires cemented to the rims, particularly the desirable G & J tire; the company also fashioned a second aluminum rim for clincher tires. In 1893, Dikeman patented a reinforcing clip to join scarfed or overlapping rim ends at their weakest point—the hole for the valve stem—thus converting that section into the strongest part of the rim. At the time, J.E. Dauchy headed the rim department and in 1894 devised a method for fusing aluminum rim ends, before resigning to seek fortune elsewhere, and the company continued to use Dikeman's clip as the bicycle's popularity swelled in 1895. To meet orders during this period, the Field Street factory operated both day and night with two shifts, and at a special meeting in July the board of directors voted to construct a new plant, located on land about two blocks away and donated to the company by Migeon. Directors also approved plans for the new factory by Waterbury architect Theodore B. Peck, and by the end of the month had signed a construction contract with local builder C.D. Janssen, anticipating that the plant would be ready by the beginning of November.[13]

Norwood Street Factory—Torrington

Theodore Peck is another of the many proficient regional architects whose work during this period reflected national architectural trends, but also revealed the influence of other similarly-placed professionals whose commissions encompassed a great variety of residential, commercial and industrial projects. Born in Bristol, Connecticut, in 1856, Peck attended Cornell University and trained in the office of Robert Wakeman Hill, a successful Waterbury architect tutored, in turn, by prominent New Haven architect Henry Austin. Hill schooled numerous Waterbury architects, bolstering an exchange of ideas and creative outlook among a coterie of regionalists. Peck designed buildings in various Connecticut cities including Waterbury and Bristol as well as Torrington.[14]

As did George Keller in Hartford, and Norval Bacon and Thomas Huber in Toledo, Peck improved the appearance of industrial cities where clients sought his skills; and as did Keller, Bacon, and Huber, Peck catered to clients' wishes by embracing stylistic eclecticism, shifting confidently from romantic modes such as Queen Anne for residential designs, to Richardsonian Romanesque for civic buildings, and to Neo-Classical renderings for banks. Although he lacked the opportunity in Torrington to unify an expansive industrial ensemble such as that achieved by Keller in Hartford, Peck nevertheless elevated the visual quality of the factories he did design. Moreover, Peck may have gained considerably more understanding about factory planning than Keller because he became directly involved with the inner workings of the Torrington plant and produced a design that responded to the specific demands of the company's manufacturing methods, ranging from 400 to 500 steps depending on the bicycle model.[15]

Peck's plans for the factory consolidated various parts of the manufacturing process into a compact, cohesively-organized arrangement of discrete but connected units, capable of producing 20,000 to 25,000 bicycles each year. To create a public façade, Peck designed a two-story block of standard mill construction, providing space for two principal offices at the westerly end of the first floor; packing and shipping occupied the remainder of that floor, and storage the second; center posts supported floor and roof beams for the open areas. Unlike the decorous Ionic portico that Keller designed for Pope's Renaissance headquarters in Hartford, Peck and his corporate clients remained content with an inconspicuous, single-bay porch with shed roof supported by turned

Figure 81 (*opposite*). Plan No. 1. Theodore Peck's elevation drawings of the Northwood Street factory in Torrington. The architect articulated the discrete parts of the manufacturing process as clearly defined units, but he also organized those units into a cohesive ensemble, further unifying segments of the composition with rhythmic bands of arches and demonstrating his fluency with American Round-Arch style for industry. Taking advantage of the site's sloping terrain, Peck placed a second shop for heavy machinery beneath a portion of the principal machine room and installed the engine room at the northerly end of that ground-level shop, where steam power drove mill shafting in the machine room directly above and minimized the distance required for power distribution. The engine room also housed a steam-powered dynamo to produce electric lighting and current for the electro-plating equipment and polishing machines in that ground-level shop. Although Peck's original plans do not show the prominent elevator tower, he added that feature as part of the final design. Collection of the Torrington Historical Society, Torrington, CT.

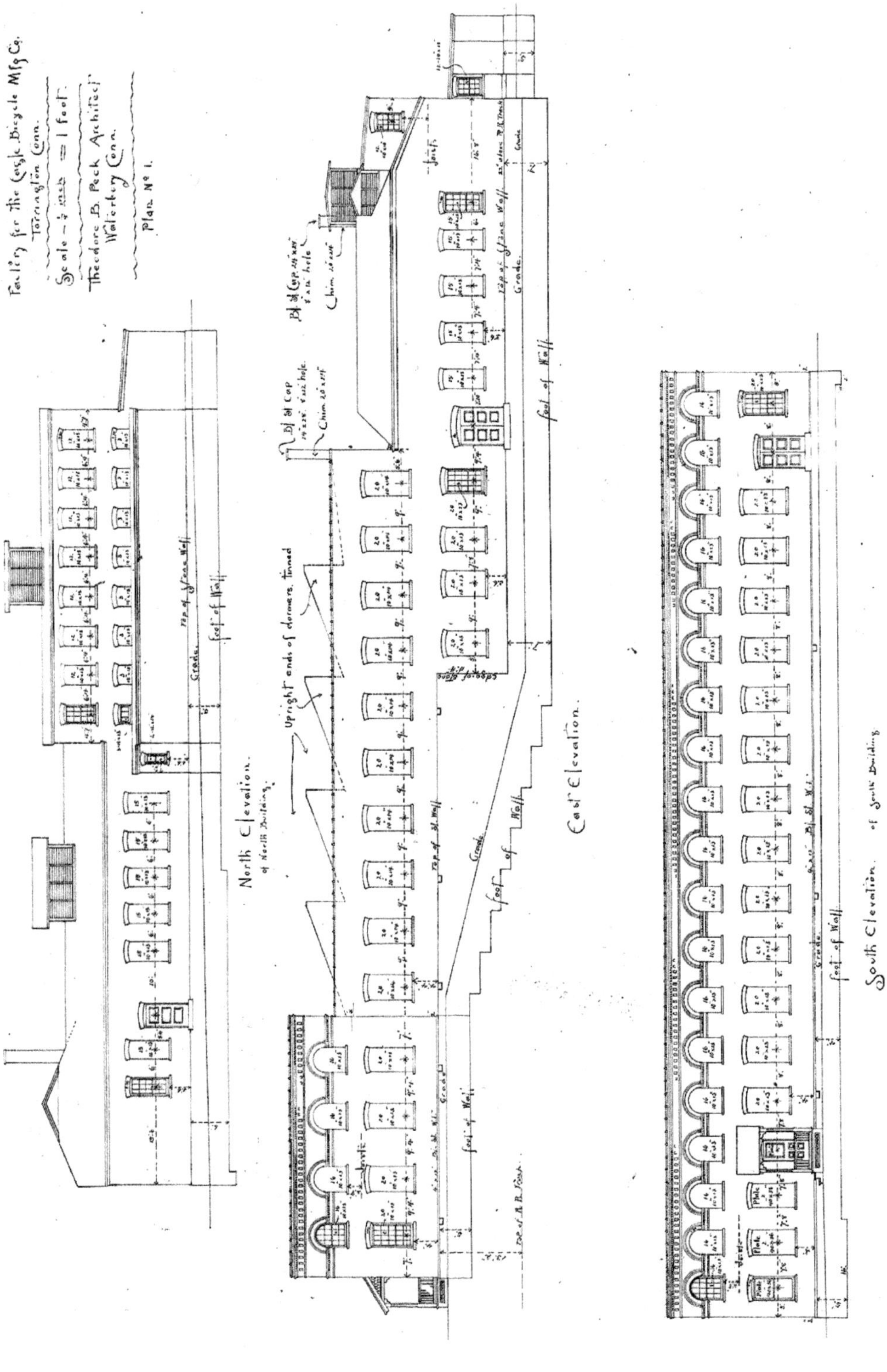
Factory for the Eagle Bicycle Mfg Co.
Torrington Conn.
Theodore B. Peck Architect
Waterbury Conn.
Plan No 1.
North Elevation.
East Elevation.
South Elevation.

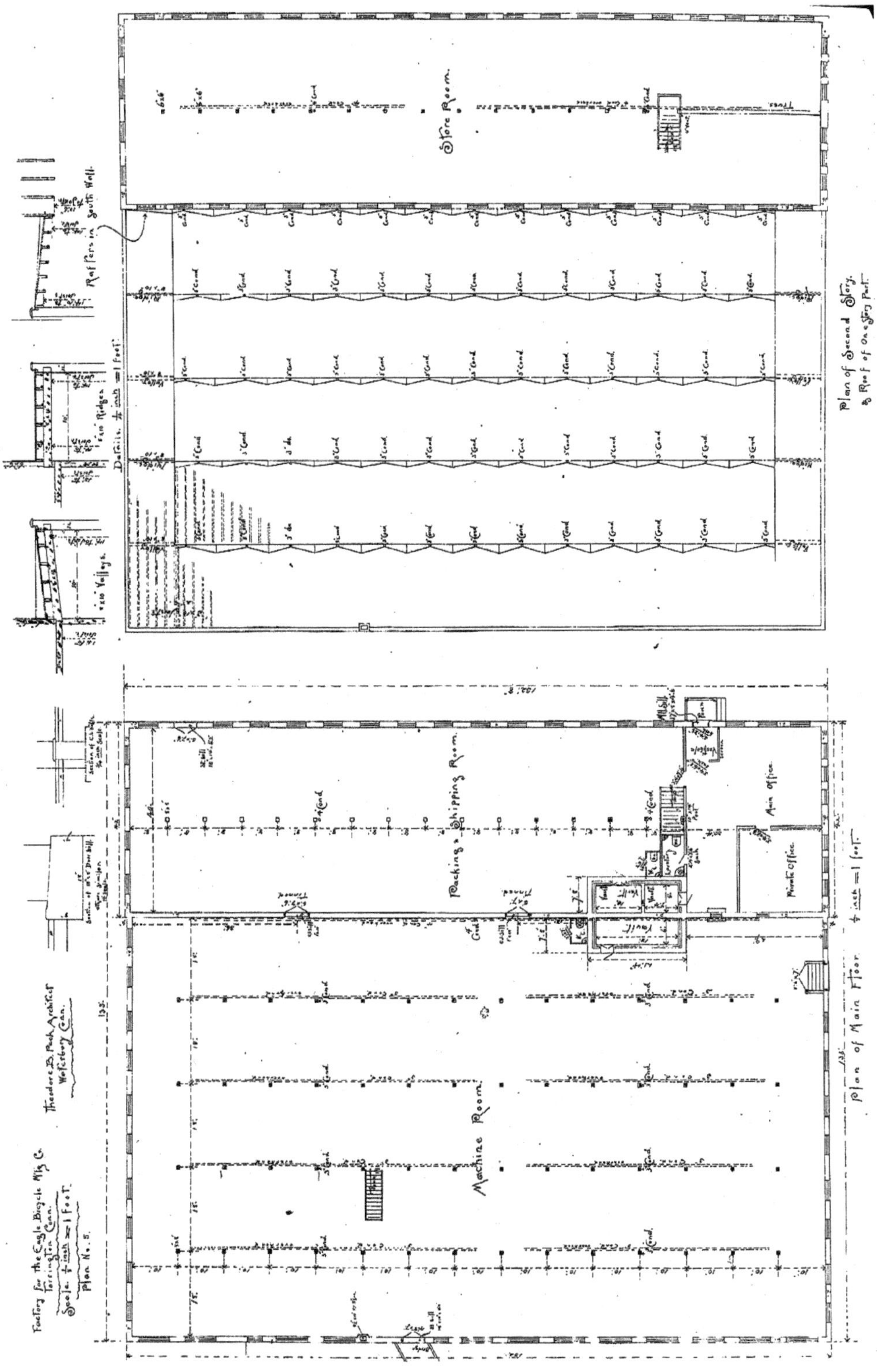
Store Room
Packing & Shipping Room
Main Office
Private Office
Machine Room
Plan of Second Story & Roof of One Story Part
Plan of Main Floor
Theodore B. Peck Architect
Waterbury Conn.
Plan No. 5

posts and brackets, easily mistaken for a secondary entrance.[16]

Peck placed the factory's most imaginative feature, an expansive, one-story machine room (152 by 91 feet), at the back of that principal building, but with limited points of entry. More than twice as wide as the front building, the shop provided space where the flow of materials and parts could be organized efficiently in a single room, with ten-foot interior columns supporting the roof—four rows in all, each with fourteen columns and each row spaced at eighteen-foot intervals. Load-bearing brick walls carried mostly their own weight, and daylight flooded the room's central area via overhead, saw-tooth skylights, by then accepted features on American factories. Peck and company managers must have used care to calculate the square footage (13,800) of that single room, and likely would have preferred to reduce the number of columns (56) to provide more versatile open space, unobstructed by vertical supports that impeded circulation of materials, arrangement of machinery, and distribution of power. By comparison, the Pope Tube Company plant achieved nearly three times the square footage with one-quarter of the columns, and with substantially more lighting—albeit with a leaking roof. Nevertheless, the machine room at the Eagle factory represented a considerable improvement over much more confined spaces with limited natural light.[17]

Using the site's sloping terrain to advantage, Peck created a ground-level shop beneath the northerly four bays of the machine room and placed the engine room at the easterly end of that shop, where a steam engine manufactured by C.H. Brown and Company in Fitchburg transferred power to the mill shafting suspended from the machine shop's ceiling directly above, thus minimizing the distance of power distribution, increasing efficiency, and reducing costs. The engine room also housed an eddy dynamo driven by a steam engine built by the Ames Iron Works in Oswego, New York, serving both arc and incandescent electric lighting and producing the current required for electro-plating and polishing, also conducted in that ground-level shop. A tall one-story boiler room extended the engine room into the corner of a second, closely-spaced building used for brazing and enameling, separated from the machine room to assure clean working conditions but connected by a short pedestrian bridge. Ten brazing furnaces and a battery of enameling ovens filled that unit, its westerly half rising to two stories. Gas furnaces fabricated by the American Gas Furnace Company in Elizabeth, New Jersey, heated black enamel to 350 degrees, colored enamels to lower temperatures. Small outbuildings including a bicycle shed for employees completed the complex.[18]

From one vantage point, the company's selection of steam power rather than electricity to drive the factory's overhead line shafting lacked innovation. Yet that decision may be a revealing one, pointing to 1895 as a pivotal year during a transitional period in American industry when reliance on the two power systems began to overlap. Doubtless, the company's experienced owners would not have made that choice without careful deliberation, and the choice may have hinged on the use of existing shafting. In addition,

Figure 82 (*opposite*). Plan No. 5. The one-story machine room (left) provided 13,800 square feet of working space with more than twice the width of the floors in the adjoining two-story building. Four rows of interior columns ten feet tall were required to support the roof structure, each row with fourteen columns and each row spaced at eighteen-foot intervals. Peck's detailed instructions for framing the roof skylights, window sash, tin-plate roofing, and drainage systems illustrate important, evolving advances in factory design during the late nineteenth century. Collection of the Torrington Historical Society, Torrington, CT.

the company did rely on electricity to power the electro-plating and polishing machines. Nevertheless, two other bicycle companies, the Keating Wheel Company in Middletown and the Trinity Cycle Manufacturing Company plant in Keene, New Hampshire, installed electric motors to power heavy shafting in their new factories, erected in 1896 and 1897 respectively, as did Henry Lozier in his rebuilt works early in 1895.[19]

Architecturally, the Torrington factory's most imposing feature is a four-story tower to house an elevator and its machinery, suitable for moving raw materials or finished bicycles to and from storage on the second floor of the front building. Peck's drawings do not show the structure, but instead assign floor space in that sector of the first floor to three vaults: one opening to the main office; another to the packing and shipping room; and a third to the machine room. However, an artist's illustration of the newly-completed plant appearing in *Scientific American* in January 1896 **(See Fig. 16 on page 25.)**, confirmed the tower as part of the original construction. If Peck initially had overlooked the necessity of an elevator, he nevertheless unified the tower with the factory's main building by a series of rhythmic brick arches with dark trim, visually supported by flat, two-story pilasters on both the tower and the building's Northwood Street facade. He also placed identical arches above all second-story windows on the remaining elevations of that main building. Peck's design displayed both his fluency with American Round-Arched style and the capacity of that mode to temper the austerity of industrial brick. Unfortunately, parsimonious

Figure 83. Although Theodore Peck employed bands of arches to unify elevations of the factory's two-story block, the company's owners elected to confine that embellishment to the corner of the building that housed company offices and to the tower. Although most of the original factory survives, owners recently chose to remove the tower rather than repair it. Photo by the author.

company owners confined Peck's arches to the tower and to the corner offices, and only a decorative cornice provided a measure of overall unity.[20]

The company's expectations about occupancy in November 1895 proved to be optimistic, possibly thwarted by conflict that developed with two subcontractors. However, by mid–February 1896 the company had nearly completed the move, and Joseph Dikeman, by then plant superintendent, conducted journalists on a tour of the new factory that month, announcing that the business would offer nine models for the coming season, two of which were tandems. The following month William Dikeman supervised the Eagle exhibits at the Torrington Bicycle Show, where manufacturers placed more than fifty wheels on display. At a directors meeting in August, Charles Dikeman reported a successful year of sales, and his financial report covering the fiscal year ending June 30, 1896, showed a surplus of more than $78,000, although that figure included the value of the new plant and its land, together assessed at $40,000. Pleased with those results, directors voted to sell Dikeman twenty shares of the company's treasury stock at par value.[21]

Later that year, journalists interviewed a member of the firm anonymously and queried whether the price of high-grade Eagle models would decline in 1897, given the rivalry already bubbling over. Answering slowly, and acknowledging his reply to be a strong statement, the respondent nevertheless remained certain that $100 would always be the price of first-class bicycles. If justification for that opinion rested on the company's continuing acquisition of improved materials and machinery, necessitating both capital investment and skilled labor, the statement accurately reflected a trend among many bicycle manufacturers. Yet competition quickly proved overwhelming, and when Albert Pope cut prices of his company's top model from $100 to $75 effective July 1, 1897, tremors circulated throughout the industry. Not long before, trade board member Joseph Yost had reduced the price of Falcon bicycles from $75 to $45, specifically in response to the flood of cheap wheels. By the time the 1898 season had begun, the Eagle company offered its best bicycle for $50 and a reliable, up-to-date version for $35, with juvenile bicycles selling at $30.[22]

Whether due to Migeon's and Alvord's long-experience in the machine tool industry, or to their frugality, or to the absence of debt other than a Stamford mortgage, or to the high quality of Eagle bicycles, or to the managerial skills and marketing gambits of Charles Dikeman, the company withstood the industry's financial struggles and showed a surplus of more than $110,000 after the 1897 season. Surplus exceeding $99,000 followed in 1898, with revenue greater than the previous year but reduced by the cost of additional machinery and new buildings, probably a new carpenter shop, shipping room, and warehouse; undeterred, directors voted a 10 percent dividend on August 1, 1898. Dikeman, by then in his mid-thirties and commanding in both frame and personality, may have been a persuasive strategist because in January 1898 the directors of the ill-fated National Board of Trade of Cycle Manufacturers, among them George Day, Arthur Garford, R. Philip Gormully, R.L. Coleman, and Robert S. Crawford, had selected Dikeman to be their president; Coleman and Day served as first and second vice-presidents, respectively.[23]

Dikeman's role as head of the National Board of Trade placed the Torrington company among the inner circle of bicycle manufacturers, who experimented with an assortment of abortive tactics to control production and stabilize prices. For example, in a report to the trade board in January 1898, concluding his year-long tenure as president, Arthur Garford underscored members' unanimous support for the board's resolution to boycott bicycle exhibitions, proclaiming them to be a waste of money and time. Unable to resist touting the boycott's professed success, Garford obliquely revealed the ploy's true purpose—to prevent non-members from organizing financially successful shows. In Torrington, Dikeman set his own radical course toward stable prices, declaring rashly that "price never creates a demand for anything," and arguing that workingmen were buying most of the bicycles being sold and were willing to pay a fair price for good value. However, he hedged his bets and engaged an unnamed company to produce a cheaper model. The company also advertised its refusal to use materials dumped on the market by bankrupt concerns. Debate aside, the firm's annual report for fiscal year 1899 seemed to verify his strategies, showing a surplus of $118,628.00.[24]

Dikeman's trade board presidency lasted the full year, but only because a vote to dissolve the moribund body failed in December due to shareholder apathy. Ironically, by the time the requisite number of ballots trickled into the board's offices in January 1899, trade shows in Chicago and New York were set to open. Failure of the trade group exposed the industry's deep divisions, the consequence of a great many factors including rapid growth. However, by then efforts to organize the American Bicycle Company conglomerate were well underway. Dikeman's ties to directors of the defunct trade board also positioned the Eagle company advantageously as industry consolidation loomed.[25]

American Bicycle Company Negotiations

During the trust's planning stages, Albert Spalding and Arthur Garford had assembled a select list of companies to form the consortium's nuclei, and they also had gathered estimates of annual production capacity for each. Not surprisingly, key selections exemplified large and successful businesses, among them the firms founded by Pope, Lozier, Gormully, Coleman and Crawford. Yet when a June issue of *Cycle Age and Trade Review* published Spalding's preliminary roster of nineteen manufacturers identified as ABC companies (a list that included the Eagle firm), the tally showed a wide range of annual production capacity, from 6,000 to 135,000 bicycles, indicating that organizers also had favored certain smaller businesses, likely because they were on solid financial footing, or because company owners or managers were astute. The Eagle concern, with estimated annual production of 12,000 bicycles, wealthy owners, and a Rooseveltian manager in Dikeman, as one reporter described him, met all those criteria. Consequently, Dikeman was among the four or five men assigned to chair committees at the ABC's organizational meeting at the Waldorf-Astoria Hotel in June 1899. Garford replaced Pope as head of the organizational committee; C.W. Dickerson from the Sterling Cycle Works oversaw domestic sales; Henry Lozier foreign sales; and Dikeman manufacturing. After the gathering adjourned, Spalding issued an official press release giving the public its first glimpse of the fledgling trust's proposed composition, some thirty-five bicycle manufacturers as well as various other firms producing tires, saddles, wood rims, chains, and other fittings.[26]

Spalding's announcement concluded more than two years of speculation about formation of a bicycle trust, but as editors of the industry's trade journals scrambled to assess those developments, negotiations with a substantial number of companies continued, including the Eagle concern. Late in May, the Eagle firm's shareholders had met to consider Spalding's initial offer of $350,000 for the company, which they considered to be a fair price. However, the offer included several unsatisfactory provisions, and a motion to revise the contract and to require payment in cash carried unanimously. Later that summer, Spalding prepared a counter-offer of $385,000, split into three types of payment: $105,000 cash, $105,000 in ABC preferred stock, and $175,000 in common stock.[27]

The company's directors and shareholders reconvened in separate meetings early in August 1899 to consider the new proposal, which also included stipulations that shareholders of the company not compete with ABC in the manufacture or sale of bicycles for fifteen years, and that Charles Dikeman specifically not engage in the manufacture and sale of bicycle parts or sundries for three years. At the directors meeting on August 8, Dikeman spoke at length, summarizing the challenges the company would face should it remain outside the bicycle trust: obtaining supplies such as tubing, tires, and saddles; or competing with the price of ABC's bicycles; or defending claims of patent infringement. In that eventuality, too, he recommended that the firm increase its capital and enlarge the plant, better to face an anticipated increase in competition. The directors then considered a letter that Dikeman had addressed to Migeon, explaining that the restrictions against competition would be onerous to Dikeman individually, in the event of acquisition by ABC, and requesting that the firm compensate him for that loss in income. Directors agreed and voted to convey $37,500 in ABC common stock to Dikeman should shareholders vote to sell on the morrow.[28]

After calling the shareholder meeting to order, Migeon yielded the chairman's role to Isaac Wardwell, foretelling the meeting's outcome. Understandably, Migeon, Alvord and other shareholders of the Torrington Company, the parent organization of the Excelsior Needle Company and its subsidiary, the Torrington Swaging Company (later renamed the Standard Spoke and Nipple Company), voiced opposition to the terms prohibiting competition, which the company's attorney interpreted broadly enough to include the manufacture of bicycle parts. Elisha Turner and J.C. Turner, owners of hardware firm Turner and Seymour Manufacturing Company, which produced certain types of chains, probably had similar objections. Together, Migeon, Charles and George Alvord, Bryant, and the Turners controlled about 45 percent of the company's shares, and whether Dikeman favored the sale to ABC or not, he owned only 16 percent of the concern, not enough when added to the shares held by the Stamford faction to achieve a majority—assuming the latter preferred to sell. The meeting concluded with a request that the contract be revised to exclude shareholders of the Torrington Company from those conditions, a provision that Spalding subsequently rejected. When, toward the close of August, news of the Eagle company's eleventh-hour withdrawal from ABC reached the pages of cycling's journals, Dikeman explained tactfully that the matter was one of shareholder interest.[29]

Aftermath

As a well-managed, independent business headed by experienced owners, the Eagle company adds clarity to our picture of the bicycle industry during the years following organization of the trust. Unlike many businesses that frantically sought to capture a share of the bicycle boom, accumulating debt rapidly, the Eagle's owners remained on solid financial footing, making it easier to adjust to changing conditions. However, unlike the Iver Johnson firm, the company lacked other well-established products capable of generating consistent revenue; nor did the company join the Cycle Trades Protective Association, possibly because of Dikeman's close ties to ABC's organizers.

Thus, the principal challenges were those described by Dikeman to his directors and shareholders at the August meetings, coupled with the difficulty of gauging demand accurately enough to avoid purchasing an excess of materials and parts. Dikeman's concern about the costs of defending patent infringement claims proved to be prescient, and in December 1899 the ABC began thorny litigation against the Torrington group and several other companies for infringement of the Smith bottom bracket patent of 1888, which the Eagle's owners regarded as invalid.[30]

Dikeman's difficult position also illuminates complexities faced by other company owners or managers who, lacking clairvoyance, weighed the prospects of joining ABC or remaining apart. On the one hand, his close association with ABC's founders probably justified an expectation of employment in the trust's upper echelons, a measure of security in the event ABC acquired the Torrington factory and then decided to close it. In addition, the guaranteed dividend of ABC stock awarded by the Eagle company's directors may have been an added incentive to sell. However, both Dikeman and his brother had begun experimenting with designs for bicycle frames and frame fittings, and in 1900 and 1901 the pair secured a series of seven patents, which the company unveiled in November 1900 when it offered a mechanically jointed frame—called a take-down model—based on the Dikemans' inventions. The frame, joined at the seat-post cluster, could be taken apart and reassembled easily, facilitating cleaning and repair. Although the design reveals the company's emphasis on sophisticated machine tooling, whether the model's principal value rested in marketing the Eagle as distinct from other bicycles, or instead showed true innovation, is unclear. Nor is it clear whether the Dikemans could expect a better return on their investment by remaining apart from ABC, illustrating just one of many conundrums caused by the consolidation. In August 1901, too, the Miller Manufacturing Company, maker of bicycle arc lamps, appointed Charles Dikeman as trustee, suggesting that his interest in that company had been established prior to the prohibitions dictated by Spalding.[31]

Between 1900 and 1904, the company adjusted in several ways: acquiring an adjoining factory formerly used for nail manufacture; retaining its sales office in Boston; diversifying by manufacturing gasoline motors for marine launches and then motorcycles; and reducing the price of the Dikemans' quad-stay roadster to $40. However, other events intervened: Charles Alvord died in 1901, and Edward Walsh resigned early in January 1902, the last director with ties to the company's Stamford origins. In November 1902, a month after the failure of ABC, Dikeman, Pope, and other industry survivors returned to the scene of negotiations three years before, the Waldorf-Astoria Hotel, to establish the Bicycle Manufacturers Association, which set minimum prices for bicycles to curb the growing influence of jobbers. However, early in 1903 a reorganized National Cycle Trade Association controlled by jobbers countered those efforts, and the two organizations eventually achieved promotional equilibrium. Unfortunately, Migeon's death in January 1903 must have forced remaining directors to reassess the company's prospects, and a week later they voted to sell the Stamford factory. Dikeman, who may have lost an important ally in Migeon, sold his interest and resigned in August 1903. George Hammann succeeded Dikeman as secretary and general manager, with John Alvord as president and George Alvord and James Alldis filling the remaining offices.[32]

The company issued a catalog for its 1904 season, offering five models priced between $25 and $40, and continued to sell bicycles as the 1905 season approached. However, in July 1905, a federal judge in

Buffalo sustained the Smith patent three months before its expiration date, potentially affecting every bicycle built after December 1893 (six years prior to the start of litigation) and adding to the industry's woes. Less than two months after the court decision, and two weeks before Albert Pope, as successor to ABC, launched thirty separate lawsuits against manufacturers and jobbers to enforce the decree, the company sold the Torrington factory to the Progressive Manufacturing Company. Led by John Alvord and Hammann, the new company turned to hardware production—primarily rivets, bolts and screws, but also gasoline engines. A month later the Alvords, Alldis and Hammann, acting as directors of the Eagle firm, voted to dissolve the bicycle business and wind up all company affairs, thus escaping Pope's reach.[33]

The Progressive Manufacturing Company continued to use the factory until 1960, when it sold the works to Pheoll Manufacturing Company, an upper Midwest business that produced fasteners but ceased operation in 2003. Although the factory survives, mostly unused, owners recently demolished the tower's upper tier as a less-costly alternative to completing structural repairs.

10

Keating Wheel Company

Holyoke, Massachusetts, and Middletown, Connecticut

The Eagle Bicycle Manufacturing Company and the Keating Wheel Company invite comparison in notable ways, with parallels that are striking and pregnant with irony. Both companies were founded by wheelmen drawn to high-wheel bicycles; both firms originated with patents for safety bicycles (albeit very different versions), and with quests by the inventive owners of those patents to convert ingenuity to profit; both firms secured financial support from local investors; both built a reputation for fabricating high-quality, lightweight bicycles; both achieved economic advantages by strategically relocating their respective factories; both introduced important modifications to standard mill construction for the design of those factories; both negotiated with the American Bicycle Company trust, and in the end each remained apart from that consortium; and each company adds clarity to our picture of the industry at the periphery of the country's dominant bicycle manufacturers. Yet crucial distinctions separate the two businesses at every one of those junctures, leading to very different outcomes and to a more complete view of the bicycle industry's rapid growth and precipitous decline during the last decade the nineteenth century.[1]

Robert M. Keating, born in 1862 to Irish immigrants, lived in Springfield, Massachusetts, for much of his life. Unlike Leonard Gaylor, whose father was a banker, Keating's improvident parent died in 1875, leaving his large family in peril financially. Forced to find and fund his own way, Robert apprenticed with a local machine shop, Richard and Dole, and there honed his innate mechanical ability. High-wheel bicycles arrived in Springfield at an opportune moment in Keating's life, and the city's cycling stars shone brightly after the Springfield Bicycle Club formed in 1881. Two years later, club founder Henry Ducker began publishing the *Springfield Wheelman's Gazette*, a widely-circulating cycling journal and forum for promoting the city's cycling tournaments at Hampden Park—public extravaganzas that Keating could not have overlooked. However, unlike Gaylor, Keating was slow to join his city's club, possibly due to the steep membership fee.[2]

Bicycle manufacturers also took notice of events in Springfield during the 1880s, and although a complete record of Keating's employment is not known, he gained valuable experience working for firms that had begun building bicycles in the vicinity, whether the Ames Manufacturing Company in adjoining Chicopee Center; or Albert Overman's works, initially within the Ames complex but by 1887 in Chicopee Falls. In Springfield, too, George Warwick founded the Warwick Cycle Manufacturing Company in 1888 and soon after appointed Keating superintendent. Thus,

Figure 84. In Middletown, Connecticut, bicycle manufacturer Robert M. Keating and building contractor Casper Ranger collaborated in the design and construction of one of the country's first factories built expressly for automobiles as well as bicycles. Completed in 1896, the building is thus significant for its contributions to the evolution of one of the twentieth century's most important types of industrial buildings. As built, the factory extended one thousand feet in length but only fifty feet in width, and the building is accessible via three shallow entrance pavilions separated at even intervals, each pavilion housing sets of stairs but also serving structural functions by adding stability to the excessively long, load-bearing walls. Photo by the author.

by the close of that decade Keating had gained considerable insight about the profitability of bicycle design and manufacturing. More importantly, he had discovered in bicycles a gratifying outlet for his inventiveness as a mechanical engineer.[3]

Keating's exceptional mechanical skills likely surpassed those of Gaylor, evident from the first bicycle patents awarded to each. Although the ingenuity of Gaylor's 1887 and 1890 patents for the Eagle bicycle should not be discounted, he generally adapted existing crank-drive technology to the Star bicycle, carefully positioning the seat and adding a steering rod. By contrast, Keating's two models of velocipedes described in very detailed patents, issued in February and April 1890, offered several novel features for safety bicycles with two wheels of equal size and rear-wheel chain drive. For the first model he engineered a gearing mechanism built into the crank axle and engaged by a clutch with linkages extending to the handlebars. He also provided an adjustable frame, allowing women riders to lower the position of a telescoping brace connecting the seat post with the frame backbone. In addition, he added spring levers to the handle-bar post to reduce vibrations amplified by hard tires, and modified handle-bar grips to avoid injury to hands in the event of a fall. For the second model, he added substantial spring-loaded levers to both the front and rear forks and also to the cross-member supporting the seat post, describing the oddly-shaped assemblage as a diamond-braced frame. He also

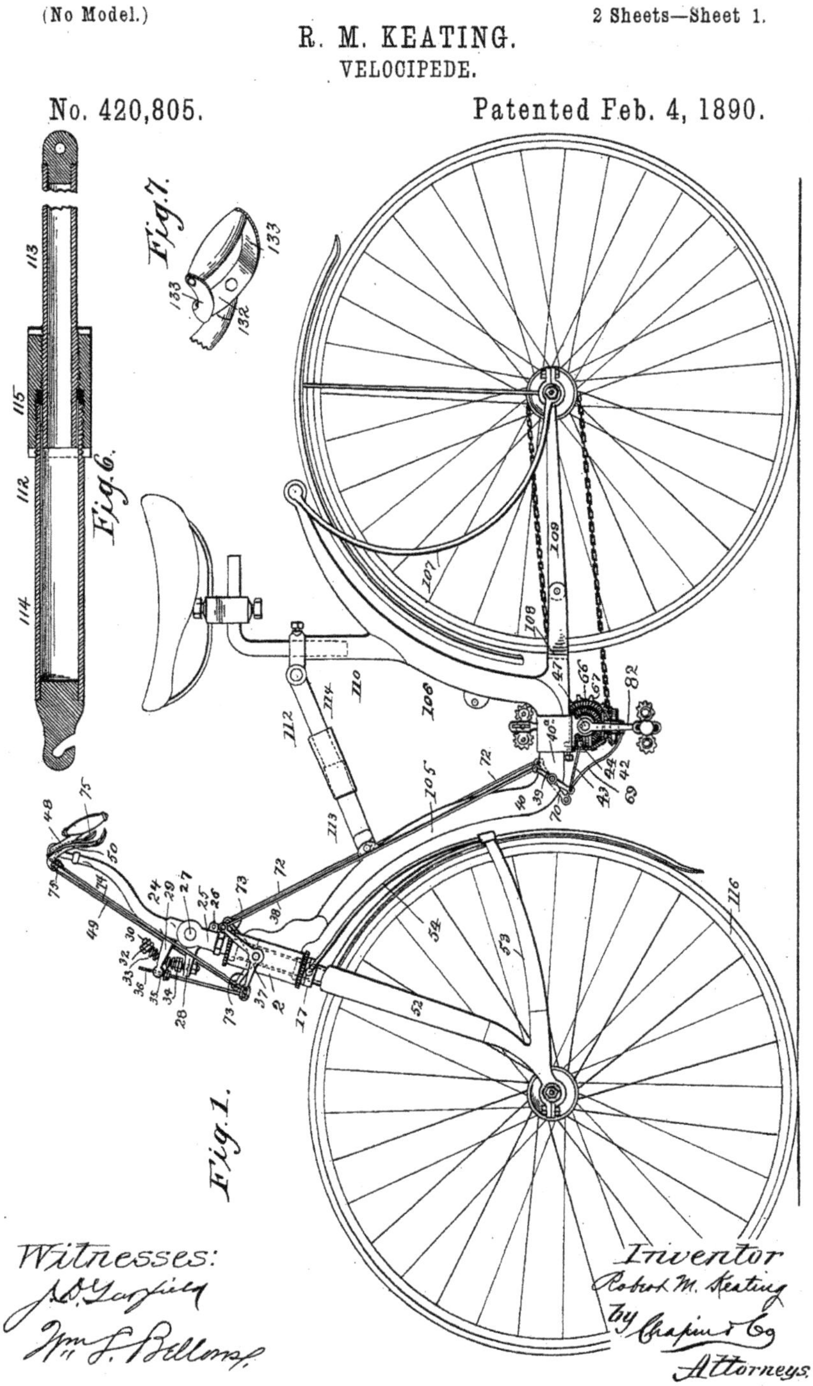

Figure 85. Robert Keating secured two patents for safety bicycles in 1890. The first, issued in February, employed a gear sprocket attached to the crank axle and engaged by a clutch with linkages to the handlebars. Women could modify the frame by adjusting a telescoping drop bar connecting the seat post with the frame backbone. He also added spring levers to the handlebar post to reduce the vibrations caused by hard rubber tires. Courtesy United States Patent Office.

devised a complex rear-wheel brake with a brake-ring fixed to the rear hub and connected by linkages to a plunging rod partially concealed within the head tube, in turn controlled by a braking lever on the handlebars.[4]

Granted, some of the features on Keating's first ventures into bicycle design may not have passed the test of practicality, especially the frame with flexible upper arm, and other originators soon developed more workable versions of safety bicycles. So, too, did Keating when he designed a true diamond frame in 1894, marked by a center post curved at its bottom-bracket joint, a feature he described as a frame stiffener; it also allowed a slightly longer chain. Yet Keating's patents reveal a depth of proficiency that distinguishes his designs from Gaylor's conceptions. Separately, the spring mechanisms he employed on both models suggest that he was familiar with the Victor safety and its flexible front fork, unveiled by Albert Overman in 1887 but far less complex than Keating's design; such a familiarity also may hint that he worked for either the Ames company or for Overman. Moreover, he likely acquired first-hand knowledge of patent disputes when, in 1886, Albert Pope attached all the property of Overman's business in Chicopee. In any case, Keating clearly understood the crucial value of patents, securing more than four dozen during his life to protect a great variety of inventions.[5]

Keating's biographer, R.K. Keating, has described the man as a consummate tinkerer, prone to spending more time on the shop floor than confronting administrative tasks. Keating's penchant for tinkering invites comparison to Iver Johnson as well as Gaylor, and clearly separates him from owners such as Overman, Pope and Lozier. That tendency also surfaces as a crucial factor at each stage of his company's development, initially with bicycles but later with motorcycles and automobiles. Absent financial resources of his own, Keating's patents offered the likeliest path to success, and his dogged adherence to that path eventually separated his company from the Eagle concern and led to very different outcomes.[6]

Westfield Factory

By the late 1880s Keating felt confident enough to start his own company. By chance, willing investors resided in nearby Westfield, where in 1887 a group of civic and cycle-minded individuals, meeting in the parlors of the Wheelmen's Association, had formed the Westfield Business Men's Association to attract new firms to the city. In 1890, the group began soliciting stock subscriptions to establish a bicycle manufacturing concern, raised $10,000, and chartered the Keating Wheel Company in September of that year, with journalist and printing-company owner, Joseph D. Cadle, as president, F.H. Sackett as clerk and treasurer, and Keating as superintendent. James Noble, Jr., who years later would be instrumental in luring Henry Lozier to Westfield, became one of seven directors, Keating among them. The fledgling company leased a small space in a factory on Elm Street, began employing ten to twenty workers during the spring of 1891, and produced seventy-five Superior bicycles that season, offering the sprung-saddle frame and a cushion tire that Keating had patented. The company also added $5,000 to its capital account during those early months.[7]

Thus, at age twenty-seven, Keating ventured into the shaky realm occupied by inventor and investor, where no amount of mechanical tinkering could calibrate financial equilibrium. In Gaylor's instance, stability had been achieved at the outset through his father's business connections and Gaylor's own friendships. For Keating, inexperienced as a business partner, the steps required to guide a new enterprise toward solid footing were risky ones. Yet there is little to indicate that the Westfield investors harbored exploitive intent. Instead, the earnest character of their organization and the desire to improve the town's economy by providing employment opportunities, together with a common interest in bicycles, suggests that the company may have been well founded and with an optimistic outlook comparable to that among Gaylor's founding partners.

Fortuitously, Keating's shop opened just as safety bicycles had begun to garner public enthusiasm, and his Superior model generated substantial regional demand, certainly a confidence-booster for a budding entrepreneur. However, Keating's desire to meet that demand lured him irresistibly toward rapid expansion—a novitiate quest for capital that would place financial equilibrium beyond his reach for most of the remaining decade.

Holyoke Factory

Even as shop workers in Westfield labored to meet orders for the 1891 season, Keating began negotiations with three Holyoke financiers, Marciene Whitcomb, Ernest C. Clarke, and Edwin Netherwood, who had approached Keating with inducements to move the company to their city. The offer included a substantial increase in capitalization together with a promise to build a large new factory with greatly expanded capacity. Alarmed, Westfield investors tried to forestall the move by increasing local contributions, but to no avail as Whitcomb led a subscription campaign in Holyoke, raising more than $46,000. A newly-formed Keating Manufacturing Company secured a corporate charter in July 1891, with capitalization of $200,000, and then orchestrated acquisition of the Westfield business by purchasing shares of the latter above par. The charting block of Holyoke shareholders included Whitcomb, Clarke, Netherwood, George W. Collins, and Herbert M. Farr, each owning ten shares at $100 par value; Keating and his attorney, Allen Webster, each held one share. Keating's patents appeared undervalued at $100, at least compared to Gaylor's patents valued at 40 percent of the company's capitalization; yet within two years Keating had accumulated 1,000 shares, representing either compensation for employment, patent royalties, or corporate restructuring.[8]

Initially, Clarke, Keating and Allen served as the only three directors, with Clarke as president and Keating treasurer. However, the company's financial and administrative structure quickly changed, becoming complex on several fronts. Although Whitcomb remained the owner of the factory, leasing it to the company, a small group of controlling shareholders led by Whitcomb also loaned funds to the company and obtained chattel mortgages on machinery, materials, and completed stock as collateral, making those men creditors as well as owners and setting the stage for eventual conflict. Adding to this complexity, Whitcomb, Farr, Clark and Netherwood shuffled the company's administrative assignments several times during the company's formative period, relegating Keating to the position of managing shop superintendent but with Netherwood switching from president in July 1891 to assistant manager in December, hinting at discord. A younger brother, John Keating, began working for the company at about this time and eventually would supervise the plant following a subsequent move to Middletown, Connecticut; Joseph Quirk, a brother-in-law, also would join the business.[9]

During 1891, the company continued to build bicycles in Westfield as plans for constructing the Holyoke factory progressed. Early in August of that year, Whitcomb retained a well-respected

Holyoke builder, Casper Ranger, to erect a four-story, brick factory with roughly 48,000 square feet of standard mill construction with capacity to manufacture 6,000 to 8,000 bicycles annually. Whitcomb specified that the bearing walls be adequate to support the construction of additional stories at some point in the future, and Ranger also minimized the number of mid-span posts to avoid obstructing the floor plan, possibly at Keating's suggestion. Ranger turned to the Landers Brothers firm in Holyoke for masonry work and predicted occupancy by mid–October, with estimated costs of $35,000. However, the four-story building—an addition to an existing mill already owned by Whitcomb adjacent to a power canal—remained unfinished until the early months of 1892.[10]

Nevertheless, journalists received tours in December and January, beginning at the principal entrance facing Dwight Street (the factory's second floor), with administrative offices adjacent to display windows. The offices fronted the primary machine room, which housed four rows of small machinery including turret lathes, automatic screw machines, and a large, ball-head adjusting cone machine, which converted brass rods into screws for fastening spokes to the rims of wheels. Separate departments for the fabrication of wheel rims and mud guards, and for pattern

Figure 86. Keating's first company, chartered in September 1890 as the Keating Wheel Company, leased space in a small factory in Westfield, Massachusetts, and produced Keating's Superior model. Less than a year later, investors from Holyoke lured Keating from Westfield and formed the Keating Manufacturing Company in July 1891, which then acquired its predecessor. By August, financier Marciene Whitcomb, a shareholder of the new company, had begun construction of a four-story factory that increased the length of Whitcomb's existing mill along a power canal in Holyoke, and leased the new building to the bicycle company. Whitcomb retained Holyoke contractor Casper Ranger to design and build the factory, which was ready for occupancy by the early months of 1892. Formerly located on Dwight Street, the factory provided 48,000 square feet of space with capacity to manufacture 6,000 to 8,000 bicycles annually. Courtesy Lyman and Merrie Wood Museum of Springfield History, Springfield, MA.

making, occupied the rear portion of that large machine floor. Forges, brazing furnaces, tube fabrication, and a stock room dominated the lower level, as did a grinding machine for precision tooling. The third floor provided space for additional machinery and for assembly, but Keating eventually segregated a portion of that area for enameling and nickel-plating; he also placed enameling ovens on that floor. Initially, Keating used the fourth floor as a riding school but later moved wheel and frame assembly onto that level, joined by inspection. Lathe manufacturing specialists Benjamin and Vernon Prentice from Worcester, doing business as the Prentice Brothers Company, furnished machinery, as did the Pratt and Whitney Company.[11]

The factory's narrow lot stretched between the power canal to the east and tracks of the Holyoke and Westfield Railroad to the west. To the company's seeming benefit, Whitcomb owned water rights generated by the power canal, and he transferred that power to the factory's mill shafting via cable, eliminating the need for central steam power. Whitcomb also installed a dynamo to generate electrical power for lighting and electro-plating, but whether water or steam turned that dynamo is not known. Unfortunately, some of the financial benefits accruing from that power source were nullified by frustrating closures of the factory when repairs to the canal became necessary, creating troublesome delays in production. In any case, the Holyoke plant may have been the country's only works built specifically for bicycles and powered primarily by water; regrettably, the building has not survived.[12]

The Keating Manufacturing Company occupied Whitcomb's factory pursuant to a five-year lease, and thus at the same precise moment—the start of the 1892 season—both Keating and Gaylor became engaged in the production of safety bicycles in expansive factories owned by the controlling shareholders of their respective companies. When viewed strictly from the vantage point of production, Keating's mechanical training, experience in bicycle manufacturing, and head-start in the design of safety bicycles gave his company potential advantage over the Eagle concern. However, the financial footings of each firm contrasted markedly, and during the 1892 and 1893 seasons those differences became evident when both Gaylor and Keating faced conflict with company owners.

In Torrington, Gaylor's move to Erie resolved that conflict, the firm's financial structure remained sound, and the company enjoyed steady production. In Holyoke, Keating's company not only succumbed to internal bickering but became overextended as well. During the late summer of 1892, the company reorganized dramatically, amending its charter by reinstating the name Keating Wheel Company, increasing capital stock to $250,000, adding two positions to the board of directors, and electing Keating, Farr, George Bosworth, Wilbert T. Dean, and A.W. Esleeck to fill those seats. Farr occupied the office of president, Keating that of vice president, and Bosworth treasurer, with Keating the manager in charge of shop work; Keating also relinquished some of his shares to secure the reorganization. At that point, Whitcomb, Clark and Netherwood ceded day-to-day control of the company to Farr, Bosworth, and Keating.[13]

By the fall of 1893, however, the company's debt obligations—two promissory notes in denominations of $38,000—had become overdue, and Whitcomb's faction of shareholders elected to foreclose through a sheriff's auction. The company's ledger revealed assets of $165,958 and liabilities of $65,747, but with $44,000 in cash available to cancel much of that debt. More importantly, the creditors seeking foreclosure (the list included Whitcomb, Bosworth, and Farr) held only one third of the company's capital stock outstanding, putting small shareholders at risk of losing their investment. Armed with support from those minor shareholders and with a salvageable balance sheet, Keating's lawyer persuaded a court to enjoin the sale pending efforts to obtain new financial backers.[14]

Tracing the sources of those financial troubles becomes difficult, but Whitcomb, who had no experience in the bicycle industry, may have approached the venture with expectations of immediate profit rather than a willingness to reinvest proceeds for future growth. He also seems to have been opportunistic in his attempts to gain control of the company's assets by sheriff's auction, likely at a discount, and forcing Keating out of the picture in the process—tactics that surface with surprising frequency during the boom era of bicycle production. Keating may have given too much attention to rapid expansion, possibly neglecting the challenging tasks of meeting demand realistically, ordering materials in timely fashion, securing a dependable labor, developing efficient production, and creating effective advertising and sales networks. Even had he addressed those concerns adequately, the business was too heavily burdened by debt to overcome the inevitable stresses faced by a newly-formed company.[15]

Springfield resident Charles D. Rood, one of the founders of the Hamilton Watch Company, rescued Keating from calamity in October 1893. Rood had amassed a modest fortune in the jewelry and watch business, but he also had begun investing in the bicycle industry, securing control of the Warwick Cycle Company in the fall of 1892 but remaining in that role for less than a year. With capital in hand, he then forged reorganization of Keating's business by securing 500 of Keating's shares, 570 shares of treasury stock, and 22 percent of stock held by other shareholders. He occupied the offices of both president and treasurer, forced Keating and Netherwood to resign from the board that Rood also headed, but then retained Keating as plant superintendent. Any sense of relief that Keating may have felt must have been tempered by the high price of the salvage: Rood demanded the first 10 percent of the company's profits with no more than $5,000 of those profits counted as credit, and Keating drew only enough salary to pay for living expenses, assigning the rest to company debt. Rood, too, became a principal creditor of the company as it struggled to meet the costs of operations; harshly, Rood often required Keating to guarantee that credit personally.[16]

Although Whitcomb and his cohorts twice scheduled sheriff's auctions in January 1894, Rood managed to deflect those maneuvers, giving the company a welcome if precarious period of financial stability for three seasons, 1894 to 1896, and well-timed to take advantage of the country's exploding demand for bicycles. He appointed William Osgood to oversee sales, opened branch offices in several cities, and exhibited at important shows in New York, Philadelphia, and Chicago. Rood also challenged the city's assessed value of the factory to reduce the taxes ($6,000) paid by the company under Whitcomb's lease agreement. Left free to tinker, Keating filled the company's catalogs with new models including a nineteen-pound Model K suitable for racing as well as road use, and a remarkably light seventeen-pound Special Racer; he also turned his attention to inventive designs for women's bicycles. The diamond frame with seat-post curve at the bottom bracket became the company's moniker, and Keating patented the design in 1896 after a wait of almost eighteen months. Between December 1893 and September 1896, he also patented a tire, crank shaft assemblies, ball-bearing race, wheel hub, and adjustable handlebar. Accord between Keating and Rood seems to have improved as well, evident from Keating's election as vice president, treasurer, and board member at the annual shareholders' meeting in August 1895.[17]

By that time, Keating bicycles had won acclaim, and his declarations of strength, durability and light weight ring true. Success placed the company in the thick of competition with many other well-made wheels offered by moderately-sized firms, for example the Iver Johnson and the Eagle models, but also models by major manufacturers such as Pope, Lozier, and Overman. Nevertheless, assessing the superiority of one marque over another can be difficult due to the promotional nature of reviews in cycling journals. In addition, although Keating racing models enjoyed success on the track, so many variables dictated results at the finish line that assigning credit principally to the machine becomes capricious at best; in addition, records set one month often fell the next. Nor did Keating's ingenuity, evident in his frequent patent applications, necessarily elevate his bicycles over others during an era when mechanical invention never ceased; much the same can be said about Leonard Gaylor, Charles and Joseph Dikeman, and George Warwick. Moreover, as competition in the bicycle industry intensified, and as buyers came to expect new models each year, patented features became essential to distinguish one company's wheel from another's; patents, too, were a means for inventors to exercise control over corporate affairs.

Proclamations of strength and durability, which echoed from one manufacturer to the next, are a little easier to verify because they depended heavily on the quality and gauge of metal used in frames, the manner of fabricating tubing, the methods of joining frame members, and the forging or tooling of crucial parts such as hubs, cranks, and crank-shaft brackets. Rather than hinging on mechanical ingenuity, such factors instead depended on investments in machine tools that reduced labor costs and, as competition increased, on the availability of materials or parts. Keating's shift from rolled, to spirally-welded, to seamless tubes is consistent with allegiance to quality, but also corresponded to an industry-wide shift by the mid–1890s, at least among major manufacturers. And, if his company's hallmark, the curving seat-post at the bottom bracket, truly stiffened the frame, so too did Iver Johnson's truss frame, but in a much more convincing manner—albeit adding weight.[18]

Yet at least three important aspects confirm Robert Keating's unusual abilities as well as his commitment to the production of superior bicycles. One factor concerned his quest to lower the weight of the company's wheels, although exactly how he achieved that objective is not entirely clear. Keating's friendship with diminutive racing champion, William "Willie" Windle, may have spurred that effort when Windle commissioned Keating to design a special light-weight racer. A second factor involved Keating's plans to produce motorized carriages, contemplated at least as early as 1895, even though his bicycle venture had only just begun to reach level ground financially. Additional evidence emerged when industry savant Arthur Garford invested in Keating's company that same year, also purchasing Keating bicycles for himself and for members of his family—a far more convincing testament to Keating wheels than promotional writing in trade journals. As a major investor, Garford played a principal role in the next phase of Keating's expansion, the move to Middletown and plans for manufacturing motor carriages as well as bicycles.[19]

Middletown Factory

Toward the close of the company's 1895 season, its ledgers showed narrow margins. By that time, Keating already had begun looking ahead to the 1896 season, with the goal of producing 20,000 wheels. However, Whitcomb's Holyoke lease, set to expire during the fall of 1896, provided insufficient space for Keating's plans to expand, and conflict with Whitcomb had surfaced again. Thus, Keating began to look elsewhere and entertained overtures from several Connecticut communities. In October 1895, and gazing in the direction of Holyoke, voters in Middletown offered a ten-year moratorium on property taxes for any new industry locating in the town before January 1, 1897. The Middletown Board of Trade had orchestrated that gambit, and Keating the tinkerer negotiated a plum financial subsidy that even Henry Lozier must have admired.[20]

In addition to the tax abatement, the agreement required the city to loan the company $100,000 to build a new factory, receiving in return a promise to repay in the form of corporate bonds, redeemable at 4 percent interest and secured by a mortgage on the plant or by chattel mortgages on machinery. The pact, announced in March 1896, anticipated employment of 400 workers and obligated the company to purchase land for the factory as well as to supervise construction of the works. Prior to the compact, the trade board prudently asked a group of conservative local businessmen to assess the company's financial standing, resulting in a reassuring proclamation of sound fiscal prospects. Local banks agreed to underwrite municipal bonds to help raise money, and banks also agreed to provide additional credit to Keating's company.[21]

In June, the company paid $6,500 to acquire more than twenty-eight acres of boggy meadow abutting the branch lines of the New York, New Haven and Hartford Railroad. After a competitive bidding process, Keating turned once again to Casper Ranger's company to build the factory, with an expected construction period of four months. For the next eighteen months, Keating juggled production in the Holyoke factory for the 1896 season and most of the 1897 season; oversaw design and construction of the Middletown factory; organized transport of the machinery and mill-shafting to the new plant as operations in Holyoke ceased; launched production at Middletown; cajoled Garwood, Rood, and local banks into providing cash needed to keep plants in two locations functioning; and tallied notes coming due. Although Keating deserves enormous credit for his Herculean efforts, none of those feats helped to balance the company's teetering ledgers.[22]

Predictably, Casper Ranger's construction estimates were optimistic, but changes to the factory's design saved time, and the building shell stood ready for occupancy by the end of December 1896, pending installation of the mill shafting and machinery being moved from Holyoke. Ranger joins Charles McClallan from Springfield as one of New England's very important builders. Born in Alsace-Lorraine, Ranger emigrated to this country as a young boy and learned the carpentry trade in Holyoke. In 1877, he created his own business and later chartered the Casper Ranger Lumber Company and the Casper Ranger Construction Company; he also acquired the Hampshire brickyards in nearby South Hadley. His companies built an extraordinary number of Holyoke's mills, as well as numerous industrial and institutional buildings in surrounding towns including the Smith College library, most of the campus of Mt. Holyoke College, and buildings for the Massachusetts Agricultural College at Amherst. Aided by his three sons (William, Joseph, and James), Ranger steadily expanded throughout New England and into New York, eventually employing as many as two thousand workers.[23]

The two-story factory that Keating and Ranger designed in tandem without oversight by the architectural or engineering professions is unique in plan among bicycle works, but the building is also important in the larger context of industrial architecture because its design represents a resourceful adaptation of a traditional structural type—standard mill construction—to serve a specific manufacturing process in an efficient manner. Moreover, ample evidence confirms that Keating also intended the factory to house automobile and motorcycle production, making the plant one of the country's first works erected for those purposes.[24]

To distribute power through the factory's thousand-foot length—a great hall seemingly made endless by the building's fifty-foot width—Keating and Ranger turned to electrical power to drive overhead mill shafting, thus improving the production process and eliminating several redundancies. Although not alone in its use of electricity during this period, the factory is nevertheless an excellent example of a building designed during a transitional phase of grouped electrical power before the advent of more advanced unit drive; the building also hints at the freedom in factory design that electrical power would hasten during the ensuing decades. Secondarily, the building also demonstrates the careful balance achieved between window size and load-bearing walls by one of New England's most experienced builders of industrial works.

Building Plan. As conceived in plan, nearly one-hundred feet in width, the building's principal spaces are the elongated first and second floors, devoted to parts manufacture and assembly, respectively. Main entrances to the factory are in three, shallow, two-story pavilions separated at even intervals along the building's southwesterly elevation, each pavilion housing sets of stairs but also serving a structural function by adding stability to the excessively long, load-bearing wall; a fourth set of stairs stands externally at the building's southeasterly gable end. Plans for a separate, two-story office, isolated at the northeasterly corner of the site, proved to be too ambitious and were abandoned. Instead, Keating settled for placing the front office at the northwesterly end of the factory's second story.[25]

To accommodate the orderly flow of work, Keating planned five separate, one-story shops (each 100 by 50 feet) projecting as ells at right angles to the northeasterly elevation of the factory, each shop with a monitor roof and clerestory windows. Plans show the wall of the enameling shop forming a continuous plane with that of the main block at the factory's southeasterly corner, and the nickel-plating, polishing, and brazing shops are each spaced fifty feet apart, from southeast to northwest, respectively. The fifth ell, a blacksmith shop for forging and case hardening, projects from the main block slightly northwest of the latter's mid-point, and a sixth, two-story extension (200 by 50 feet) housing repairs on the first floor and storage on the second, extends in perpendicular alignment opposite the most northwesterly entrance pavilion. Thus, the elongated corridors on two floors and their subsidiary shops reveal Keating's vision for an ideal fabrication and assembly system, with shops located precisely to aid the flow of production. Separately, a two-story power plant with monitor roof is located opposite the enameling and plating shops at the southeasterly corner of the complex, completing the works.[26]

Unfortunately, construction costs mounted and the factory, as built, did not conform to Keating's conception, considerably reducing the anticipated 150,000 square feet of production space by nearly halving the proposed width. The company also scrapped plans for the long repair and storage ell, eventually replacing it with a small store house built late in 1898 for vehicle production; the polishing shop also succumbed to cost-cutting, and both the enameling and plating shops measure only about sixty and fifty feet in length,

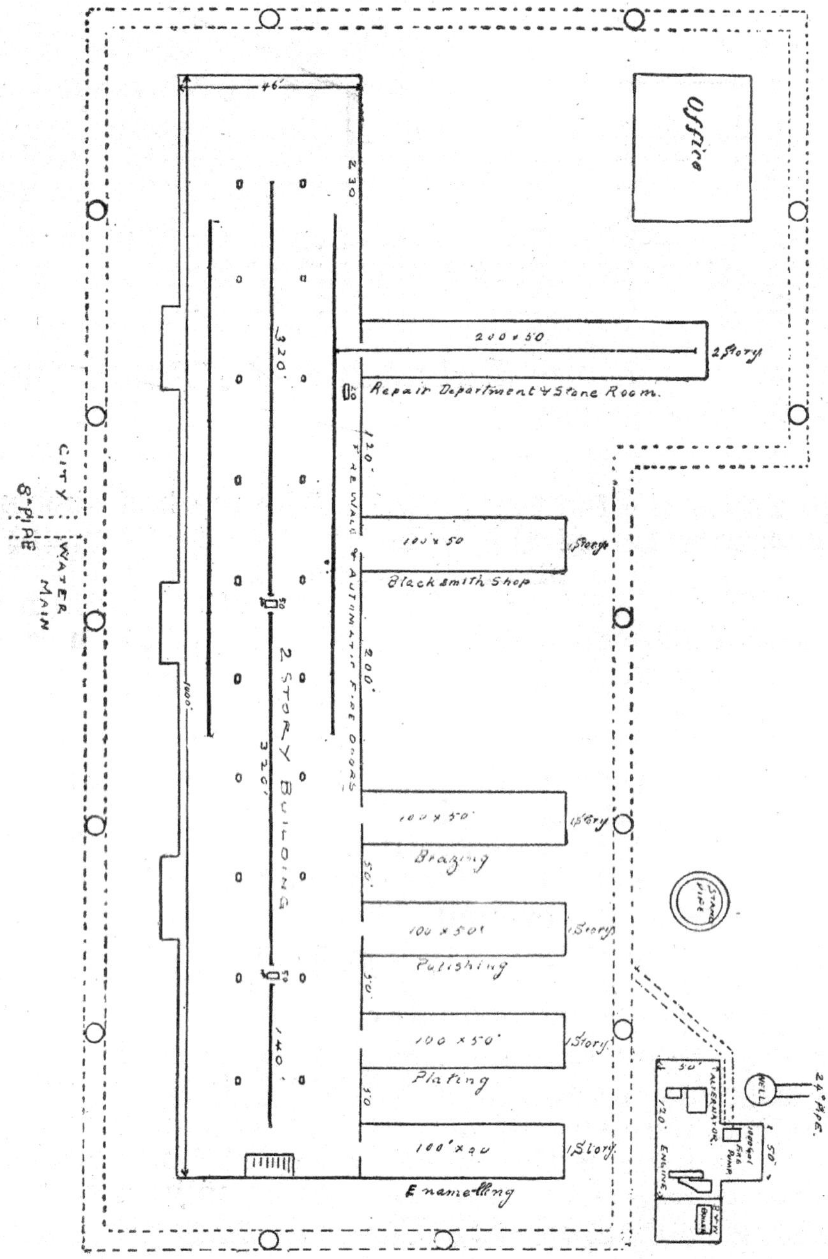

Figure 87. In 1896, Keating moved his company to Middletown, Connecticut, where the town and local investors offered a ten-year moratorium on property taxes and a loan of $100,000 to build a new factory. As conceived, the building's design is unique among that era's bicycle works, with its principal space a one-thousand-foot corridor nearly one-hundred feet wide and devoted to manufacturing on the first floor and to assembly on the second. To accommodate production, Keating designed five separate, one-story subsidiary buildings projecting at right angles from the primary corridor, each shop with a monitor roof and clerestory windows. The elongated corridor and its connected shops thus reveal Keating's vision for an ideal fabrication and assembly system for automobiles as well as bicycles. *Wheel and Cycling Trade Review* 18 (February 12, 1897).

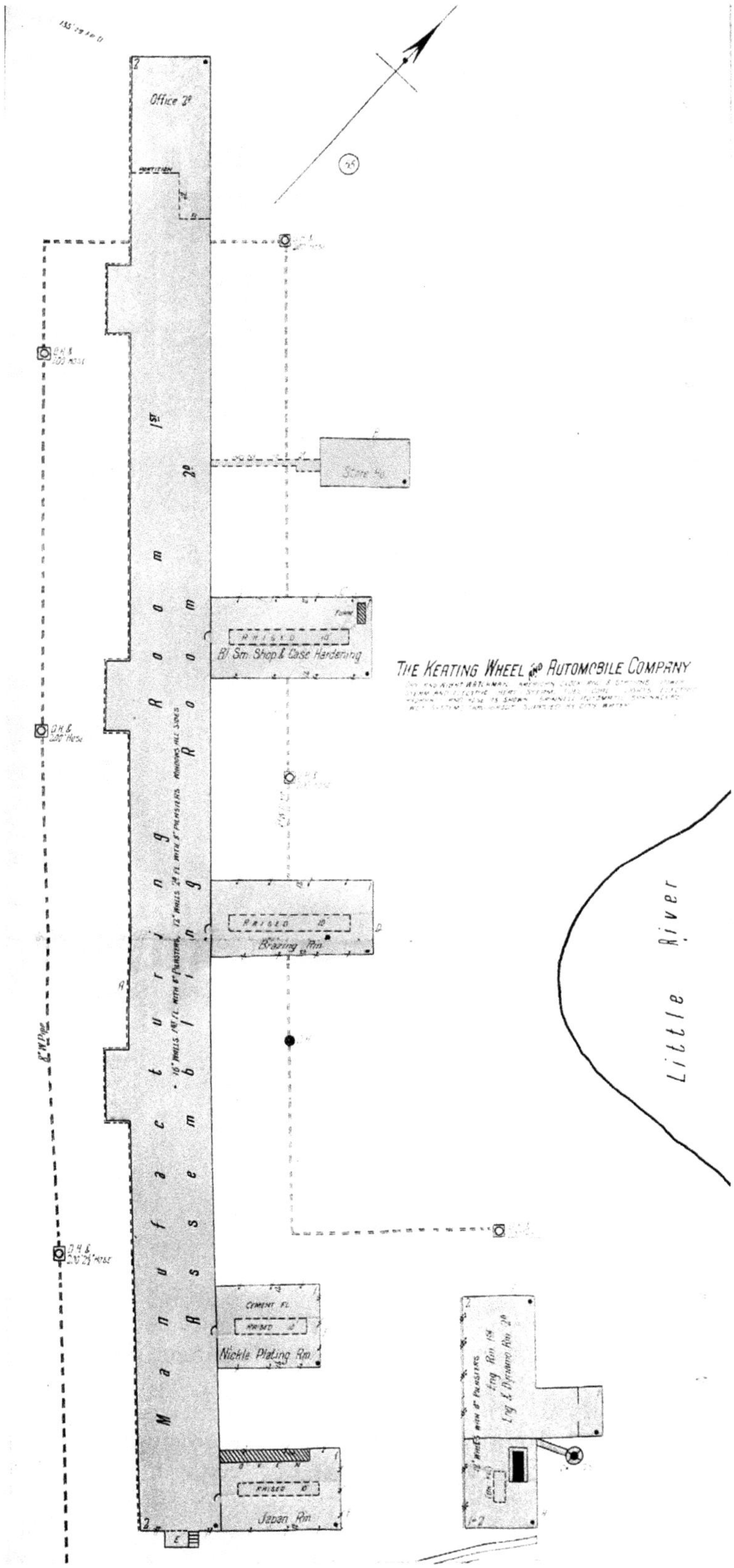
The Keating Wheel and Automobile Company
Manufacturing Room
Assembling Room
Bl Sm. Shop & Case Hardening
Brazing Rm
Nickle Plating Rm
Japan Rm
Store Ho.
Little River

respectively. To his credit, Ranger managed to reduce costs by securing a rail spur leading through the center of the building, facilitating the unloading of foundation stone by derricks; once masons had completed the foundation, railroad workers moved the track to the edge of the factory complex. Ranger also obtained sand for mortar from a nearby island in the Connecticut River, ferrying it by barge on the Little River tributary (today the Mattabesset River) adjoining the site and saving time and money.[27]

Electrical Power. Once Keating decided to design lengthy manufacturing and assembly spaces with minimal interruptions to the flow of work, he faced crucial choices regarding the distribution of power. By installing an intermediate system that relied on electric motors to drive the mill shafting that had been moved from the Holyoke factory, Keating avoided the high cost of coupling an electric motor to each machine. His electrical engineers divided the first floor's central mill shaft (800 feet long) into three sections, with two, fifty horse-power, General Electric motors separating those sections, each motor suspended from the first-floor ceiling and with two pulleys at each end, thus capable of driving four independent shafts. Electric motors also permitted the selective operation of machinery

Figure 89. Keating's plan for long production corridors to facilitate the flow of work placed new demands on the distribution of power throughout the factory, and he and Ranger turned to electricity to drive overhead mill shafting, which had been moved from Holyoke. The factory thus represents a transitional phase of electrical power in industry before the advent of more advanced unit drive, requiring costly retrofitting of machine tools with electric motors, or the purchase of new machines. The factory's two-story power plant with monitor roof housed a steam engine designed by Noble Tuckerman Greene and built by the Providence Steam Engine Company to drive a General Electric generator together with a separate dynamo for electric lighting. *The Electrical Engineer* 23 (February 10, 1897).

Figure 88 (*opposite*). Keating's new Middletown factory stood ready for occupancy by the end of December 1896, and although the building's width and shop extensions were reduced in size and number for reasons of cost, the factory represents a resourceful adaptation of a very traditional type of structure, standard mill construction, to fit a very specific manufacturing process but without oversight by either the architectural or engineering professions. Sanborn-Perris Map Company, Insurance Maps of Middletown, Connecticut (1901): Plate 2. Library of Congress, Geography and Map Division.

placed in proximity and powered by secondary shafts, thus avoiding the cost of operating long central shafts able to power as much machinery as needed at any given moment. Although published plans do not show power distribution in all plant areas, engineers installed at least two secondary shafts on the first floor, also driven by fifty-horsepower General Electric motors, as well as secondary shafts powered by smaller motors in the ancillary shops.[28]

The factory's substantial power plant housed a Greene cross-compound condensing steam engine (500 horsepower), designed by Noble Tuckerman Greene and built by the Providence Steam Engine Company. The engine drove a General Electric three-phase generator (250 kilowatts) with an exciter turned by a pulley on the generator shaft to precipitate the electro-magnetic field; plans also called for a second generator of similar capacity, together with a separate dynamo to power electric lighting. Babcock and Wilcox boilers, sequestered from the generators by a brick wall, produced the steam, and the power plant initially fed two circuits leading to the main factory.[29]

Building Structure. Although electric lighting extended hours of operation, natural lighting cost much less, and thus window dimension and placement high above floor level remained important, as did the relationship of window

Figure 90. Keating's Middletown factory reveals the challenge of maximizing window size in buildings with load-bearing walls. Only fading light reaches the center of the shop floor's moderate fifty-foot width, and bright light adequate for bench work is limited to the window walls. The electric lighting installed by Keating and Ranger supplemented natural light, but at greater cost. Photo by the author.

size to the load-bearing capacity of walls. The Middletown factory is a traditional load-bearing structure with exterior wall piers supporting interior floor beams held secure by floor-beam anchors extending through the walls and fastened to exterior pier-surfaces by decorative plates. Piers and floor beams are spaced at ten-foot intervals, and pairs of vertical posts frame a central corridor in the manufacturing sector and shops, a feature that Keating may have specified to facilitate the movement of materials, finished parts, and people; single posts would have been adequate to support the fifty-foot span of floor beams. Alternatively, Ranger may have recommended the additional support in the event Keating planned to increase the building height or to add heavy machinery to upper floors.

The exterior wall piers reduced the load requirements of spandrel walls and thus permitted larger window openings, comprising about 50 percent of the total wall area between pier centers. Wood sash are configured in divisions of four, with paired rectangular units below smaller square units, all with small panes of glass (see Chapter 1). Thus, casing, rails, stiles, mullions and muntins reduce the amount of light reaching the interior, but light penetration is adequate for the building's moderate width, and the sash beneath shallow, arching lintels give the building a very disciplined and orderly facade.

Production at Middletown

Although Ranger had concluded construction by the end of 1896, delays in leaving Holyoke were inevitable given the crucial timing of production prior to the start of that year's bicycle season. Machinery and additional mill shafting finally began arriving in Middletown during the spring of 1897, but installation depended on the arrangement of machinery, some of it leased from Pratt and Whitney but slow to arrive. The move progressed in stages throughout the summer before the factory became fully operational in October 1897. Ominously, just as Keating applied finishing touches to the Middletown factory, several New England bicycle companies failed, including Overman; Warwick; the Everett Cycle Company in Boston; and the short-lived Worcester Cycle Company, which had moved much of its production from Worcester to Middletown in 1896, creating a separate business, the Middletown Cycle Company.[30]

During the transitional 1896 and 1897 seasons, Keating's financial structure wobbled from one month to the next. The cost of the move ($35,000), coupled with the firm's narrow margins would have been bad enough given the industry's impending decline, but internal struggles for control of the business persisted. Garford, who viewed Keating's company as part of a larger plan to consolidate the industry, willingly provided loans and conspired with Keating to deceive Rood and weaken the latter's control; he also encouraged Keating to secure credit from local banks by misrepresenting available stock as collateral. Rood, deeply invested in the company, recognized that his position as a shareholder and creditor had become secondary to that of Middletown's bond holders, whose investment was secured by a mortgage on the factory. Naively, but with few alternatives, he welcomed Garford's cash dispensary and requested that the company provide him with a second mortgage on its factory and assets. As he had with Whitcomb, Keating regarded Rood's demands as a personal attack and an attempt to gain control of the business; he also questioned Rood's honesty. Whether, instead, Rood simply had reached a point of alarm at the company's shaky ledgers is difficult to assess, but Keating's assurances to Garford that the business remained sound lack credibility.[31]

Garford, aware of the company's vulnerabilities, encouraged Keating to negotiate with a new set of financial backers led by former Connecticut governor Owen V. Coffin from Middletown, joined by prominent members of the community's banking, insurance, and manufacturing sectors. As had Rood, Garford also asked for security, but in the form of an assignment of accounts receivable. In June 1898, barely six months after the start of production in the new factory, Coffin, Garford, Rood and Keating reached a financial accord that placed control of the company's assets with a new set of Middletown financiers and left both Rood and Garford in the position of shareholders and creditors, albeit secured by collateral agreements with the company. Rood and Garford also entered into a two-party collateral agreement, the former guaranteeing that funds from notes coming due, held by Rood, signed by Keating and endorsed by Garford, would free corresponding collateral; Rood also held collateral in the form of company notes to Keating in lieu of compensation. Once again, the company dodged disaster by reorganizing, and at the annual shareholders meeting meeting in October, 1898, voters increased the number of seats on the board of directors from five to seven, occupied by Coffin, Rood, Keating, Maxwell Crampton, William Burrows, Joseph Merriam, and George Coles, the last three all from Middletown. Directors then elected Coffin as president, Keating as vice president and general manager, and Crampton treasurer and assistant clerk.[32]

Miraculously, the company managed to sell bicycles—some 9,306 in 1897. Meanwhile, Keating continued to tinker and applied for three patents in 1897: a sprocket chain with reduced friction; a successful bicycle for ladies with reinforced open frame; and a back-pedaling brake. As he looked toward the 1898 season, still struggling with the industry-wide problem of pricing unsold 1897 bicycles, Keating continued to expand the company catalog. In contrast to the Eagle company, which offered its best 1898 model for $50, Keating's top bicycle sold for $75, with a ladies' version priced at $50. Unfortunately, sales dropped to 7,837 in 1898, with about 43 percent of those representing leftover 1897 models.[33]

All the while, the head of the company's sales department, Manfred Goss, sent a flurry of letters to Garford in Ohio, complaining about Keating's inability to manage the company, describing him as "unfit by nature, education and experience." Arthur Patrick, a relative of Garford who worked in Middletown as Garford's agent in place, mailed weekly communications about the firm's confidential affairs, expressing equally harsh opinions of both Keating and his brother. Goss and Patrick eventually lost their jobs, and relations between Garford and Keating deteriorated still further. The year closed with an announcement in November that the company would diversify by manufacturing wagons with pneumatic tires, making use of Keating's hub and wheel patents and hinting at Keating's veiled focus that fall.[34]

American Bicycle Company Negotiations

Optimism is not easily extinguished. Although today, looking back to the late 1890s, the outcome of the public's declining demand for bicycles might have been foreseeable, many industry observers predicted stability, if not a full reversal of trends, and Keating likely belonged among the optimists. Shunning the fad of chainless models, which added pounds, and reminding wheelmen and wheelwomen that the company had always emphasized durability and light weight, Keating stayed the course for the company's 1899 models: the Keating Special for $75; Light Roadster Models 90 and 91 for $50;

and Light Roadster Models 80 and 81 for $40; all ranging from twenty-one to twenty-two pounds. Dealer discounts varied from 30 to 45 percent, plus an additional 5 percent for cash paid within ten days. Yet Keating also competed with the glut of cheaply-made bicycles and that year introduced the Mattabesset for $35, tacitly accepting the industry-wide trend toward buying from parts makers. He also began selling to jobbers and department stores—signaling a clear willingness to negotiate quality but specifying the Keating name not be used.[35]

Early in 1899 when organizers of the American Bicycle Company invited bicycle makers to submit financial statements, Keating complied, joining sixty-three other independent firms identified by *Cycle Age and Trade Review*; editors listed more than eighty companies that had not responded. Keating claimed production that year would reach 17,000 bicycles, but with capacity to produce 90,000 without expanding facilities—wildly glorified figures. Ironically, if Keating's representatives attended the ABC's organizational meeting at the Waldorf-Astoria Hotel in June, they likely met with the manufacturing committee headed by Charles Dikeman.[36]

Similar to ABC's negotiations with the Eagle firm, discussions with Keating's company involved conflicts for both parties, adding to the puzzles surrounding formation of the consortium. Garford, who assisted Spalding by selecting candidates for the trust, knew of Keating's exaggerated production estimates because Arthur Patrick had given Garford a list of every bicycle sold by the company in each state in 1897 and 1898. Moreover, Keating's vexing relationship with Garford must have been a factor, although at one point ABC may have considered hiring Keating to manage the Middletown plant. Yet from a personal perspective, both Rood and Garford undoubtedly relished an opportunity to escape the company's financial web, and they likely encouraged acquisition. As well, Spalding and Garford probably regarded the newly-built Middletown works favorably, ideal for its capacity, machinery, electrical power, and low production costs. However, ABC's goal of geographically dispersed bicycle production may have been satisfied in New England by the plants owned by Pope and Lozier in Hartford and Westfield, respectively. Separately, residents of Middletown who were astute enough to see dark clouds on the bicycle's horizon may have been reluctant to cede control of a local business to a national conglomerate.[37]

Surprisingly, the Middletown works became a deciding factor, but not for reasons anticipated by Garford, Spalding, or Rood; and not, as had occurred in Torrington, because company owners bristled at ABC's prohibitions against competition. In January 1899, not long after Keating's announcement about wagon production, the company revealed plans to license a gasoline engine patented by inventor Charles Alsop and to adapt it for wagons and carriages. Late in May, soon after ABC filed its articles of incorporation, the Keating directors met to consider increasing the company's capitalization to $1,000,000 with the help of New York City financiers, intending to manufacture both electric and gasoline automobiles. The company then followed with a public announcement of those plans early in July, not long after closing the plant pending the outcome of negotiations with ABC, or so journalists presumed.[38]

If the Middletown owners of the Keating Company sought advantage by inflating the value of their company to include the production of automobiles, all the while expecting to be absorbed by ABC, they overestimated the trust's financial strength and failed to consider that the owners of many of the companies being acquired by ABC had proffered similarly inflated valuations. Or, if the owners remained convinced about the bright prospects for automobile manufacturing in Middletown and sought a quick start in that embryonic industry unfettered by ABC, they underestimated the complexity and cost of production as well as the competition. Or, if they approached that new venture cautiously, perhaps swayed by Keating's mechanical ability and reliant on the factory's versatility, they failed to consider the incessant drive for expansion that had guided Keating's oversight of the company from its Westfield days, and his ever-present financial shadows. Whether rooted in the pursuit of wealth, or in the prize of mechanical invention, or both, Keating's quest led the company away from the fold of industry consolidation represented by ABC—such as it was at the time—and instead toward continued control over the factory, but for automobiles rather than bicycles. That quest also placed fiscal equilibrium well beyond the company's reach once again.

Automobile and Motorcycle Production

In September shareholders answered any lingering questions about whether the company would become part of ABC when they voted to reorganize by increasing the company's capital to $5,000,000 represented by 50,000 shares at $100 par value, and to change the firm's name to the Keating Wheel and Automobile Company, with Keating as president. Less than a month later, Keating reported receipt of $3,000,000 in subscriptions from Boston and New York City investors and revealed that an experimental vehicle neared completion. Simultaneously, the company announced that all models of Keating bicycles produced in 1900 would be identical to 1899 models, thus avoiding retooling costs and anticipating the sale of leftover 1899 bicycles as 1900 models. Keating made that clear in correspondence with Garford, expressing a desire to remove the bicycle business from the factory altogether.[39]

Early in November, on factory grounds, Keating demonstrated a successful test of the company's first motor vehicle, pronouncing the delivery wagon ready to ship to Siegel-Cooper and Company, a department store in New York City's Flatiron District. To the surprise of some observers, electricity supplied the motive power—enough to transport the small, six-speed lorry forty-five miles on ordinary roads, but even more on well-paved city streets. Charging the batteries required less than an hour, and operating costs reduced those of horse-power carriers by 40 percent. Lighter than comparable horse-drawn wagons by half-a-ton, and capable of carrying loads of 1,500 pounds, the rear-wheel-drive vehicle rolled on solid rubber tires and borrowed from trolley technology by mounting the double motors on the axle using a spring suspension to keep the cogs engaged during use. Keating also disclosed plans for an electric wagon of the phaeton type as well as a delivery wagon powered by a gasoline engine, the latter vehicle still in experimental stages but without the heavy Alsop motor.[40]

Remarkably, in fewer than six months the company's chief product had changed from bicycles to automobiles, accompanied by proclamations of much better profit margins. Unfortunately, no motor vehicle could keep pace with the company's speedily-deteriorating finances and overdue interest payments on bonds. In February 1900, the company's reorganization committee tried to forestall collapse by offering an alternative to the reorganization plan from September, still in limbo without bondholder agreement. Adding to those troubles, tax assessors reassessed the property at fair market value ($165,000), then challenged the town's agreement for a nominal listing and sued to enforce the new assessment. Unpaid taxes began to accumulate pending outcome of the dispute.[41]

Despite desperate maneuvering by Keating, Garford, Rood, Coffin, Burrows, and Merriam, instability continued throughout the spring and early summer of 1900. Garford crafted a plan to replace the company with one of his own conception (ultimately an automobile and cycle parts company), and to remove Keating in the process, but he accomplished little more than isolating both Rood and himself from Keating's Middletown backers. On July 2, 1900, a court order placed the business in receivership and appointed Frederick A. Betts, former state insurance commissioner and a political ally of Owen Coffin, to oversee the company's affairs. The parties optimistically tabulated assets at $700,000 and liabilities approaching $500,000.[42]

At that moment, a line of conflict long in the making finally became a permanent schism, that between the bondholders and other creditors from Middletown led by Coffin, generally on Keating's side, and the two creditors from afar, Garford and Rood. Early in November, the court's appraisers placed the company's value at $147,898, with factory, tools, fixtures, shafting, machinery, and office furniture representing roughly $132,956 of that figure. In March, the court allowed creditors' claims totaling $285,250, with Keating granted $90,496 for royalties and interest; Garford $20,610 (all through his saddle company); and Rood $171,602. Those three claims composed 99 percent of all claims by creditors, who stood in line behind the secured bondholders from Middletown, who had funneled more than $325,000 into company coffers, with Owen Coffin's Middlesex Mutual Assurance company by far the largest investor other than Rood.[43]

Betts kept the business functioning to protect bondholders, and the court gave him permission to borrow $25,000 to assemble unfinished bicycles and to seize completed bicycles held as collateral, but also recommending payment of interest due to bondholders to avoid foreclosure of the factory mortgage. Keating, no longer in control, remained free to tinker in his factory, and he continued experimenting with a gasoline-powered motor of his own design, one light enough for a recreational automobile but also adaptable to bicycle frames. By the end of December 1900, he had filed applications for more than six patents related to the design of motorcycles, all eventually awarded. Keating thus joined the vanguard of motorcycle designers who sought a rational approach for coupling motor and frame into an integrated machine, balancing strength, durability, weight, power, the placement of the motor and its brackets, length of wheelbase, and position of the rider.[44]

Additional significance attaches to the Middletown works because Keating successfully developed and tested a motorcycle prototype during the closing months of 1900, leading to a collaboration with Betts and a brief period of motorcycle production at the factory, opened to the public in April 1901 to display Keating's two-horsepower models to buyers. Betts entertained visions of salvaging the company, but Keating seems to have focused on the factory instead, and he assigned all the patents to a new business, the R.M. Keating Motor Company, chartered with a capitalization of $500,000 early in April 1901, shortly before he made an unsuccessful bid to buy the plant that spring. Keating's biographer offers an important historical note, explaining that Keating's motorcycle preceded that of George Hendee and racer Oscar Hedstrom, whose partnership resulted in development of the renowned Indian motorcycle.

Eisenhuth Horseless Vehicle Company

While owners of the Eagle Bicycle Manufacturing Company in Torrington were adjusting to the industry's upheavals, the Keating works in Middletown remained a magnet for tumult, but unrelated to bicycles and with Keating himself fading into the background. Turmoil resulted from an ill-conceived decision by Betts in June 1901, with court approval, to sell the factory to a buyer of dubious financial record, John Eisenhuth, owner of the Eisenhuth Horseless Vehicle Company. Bondholders immediately objected to terms of the sale, bickering continued, and a New York financier, Isaac E. Gates, salvaged the sale by guaranteeing bonds to be issued by Eisenhuth's company. Gates pledged to invest in the company and its factory, but with a stipulation that the revised tax assessment be returned to a nominal amount, and Eisenhuth finally obtained a deed to the works in December 1901.[45]

Predictably, conversion of the Keating company bonds did not advance according to plan, and without adequate capital Eisenhuth could not begin automobile production. The jumbled assembly of bicycles ended in the Middletown factory during 1902, and the plant remained underutilized for much of that year. Directors of the Keating Wheel and Automobile Company dissolved the business, and Betts' final report showed a modest profit of $12,191 during his management (July 1900 to December 1902), with only $17,000 remaining to meet claims by creditors. Garford absorbed the losses through his company, but Rood was less fortunate, returning to his watch business to rebuild his fortune and then lose it again in the communications industry; Coffin entered bankruptcy in 1903. Pinpointing the cause of the company's demise becomes difficult because so many aspects influenced the outcome, and Keating's company was far from alone in failing. Yet Garford may have isolated a key factor in one of his many letters, more objective than most. Acknowledging Keating's large ability as a mechanic, Garford observed that Keating seemed unable to engage in manufacturing at a profit when competition remained close, noting that his methods were careless and extravagant, and his capacity as a manager well below par.[46]

Keating, relegated to the status of an Eisenhuth employee, became plant manager, but he also used part of the factory for his new motorcycle company and filed four more patent applications during 1902. Eisenhuth finally began automobile production in 1903, following a merger with the Graham-Fox Motor Car Company, located in East Hampton, Connecticut. The company's owners, David Graham and Frank Fox, had developed a gasoline motor, and the Eisenhuth Compound automobile enjoyed brief success during 1904. However, Eisenhuth and Fox clashed over the use of Fox's patents, and Gates removed Eisenhuth before reorganizing the business in 1905, changing its name to the E.H.V Company to erase any association with Eisenhuth. However, by the end of that year the company was mired in debt, and by the close of 1906 had been forced into receivership. In March 1907, the factory and its fittings, valued by the court appraiser at $75,000, sold at public auction for $21,000 to an attorney representing a New York investor: Isaac Gates. Middletown's bondholders, who reluctantly had agreed to convert their securities into preferred stock in Eisenhuth's company, soon learned that the business had no other assets, ending their tortuous venture that began with the Middletown Board of Trade's invitation to Keating at the height of the bicycle boom.[47]

Aftermath

In 1909, Gates, in turn, sold the works to a new business, the Noiseless Typewriter Company, ending the factory's contributions to transportation history but also marking the start of a new chapter that gradually erased the building's origins from public memory. The typewriter company landed in receivership in 1914, the factory sold again at public auction, but the new buyer, former Keating Company board member and investor Joseph Merriam, reorganized the company and diversified. Moderate success followed and the business merged with the Remington Typewriter Company in 1924, eventually becoming part of the office-equipment conglomerate Remington-Rand.[48]

Keating's involvement with the Eisenhuth company ended late in 1903, and Keating's biographer reports that in 1904 Keating moved his motor and motorcycle business to a small shop near the empty Worcester Cycle Company building in Middletown, installing machinery that he obtained as part of a settlement with Eisenhuth. However, his marine and vehicle motor business languished, and during the summer of 1906 he entered bankruptcy, returning to Springfield penniless. A long period of dormancy followed, but by 1913 his inventive nature reemerged and he began a second career with a series of patents for plumbing devices, establishing the Springfield Valve Company in 1914. In addition, he pursued successful claims against both the Hendee Manufacturing Company and the Harley-Davidson Motor Company for patent infringement, the latter boldly identifying the Keating patents on its frame. The out-of-court settlements for both lawsuits provided capital for his new valve company, which became successful and achieved the financial equilibrium that had eluded him throughout the bicycle era. During the early 1920s, he renamed the business the Robert M. Keating Company, with plans for new and improved versions of the valve he had designed. Unfortunately, poor health intervened, and he succumbed to cancer in 1922, at age fifty-nine.[49]

11

Warwick Cycle Manufacturing Company

Springfield, Massachusetts

While Leonard Gaylor and Robert Keating were still in the early stages of securing patents for bicycle designs, a third entrepreneur, Englishman George Thomas Warwick, already had established a creditable list of bicycle inventions, both in England and America. His father's successful English firm, Thomas Warwick

Figure 91. The Warwick Cycle Company factory, designed by Springfield architects B. Hammet Seabury and Francis R. Richmond in 1891, joined a very small number of new factories designed specifically for the manufacture of bicycles at the start of the safety-bicycle era. Most of the structural innovations are credited to Richmond, who began specializing in the design of industrial buildings. Formerly located at the corner of Heywood Avenue and Warwick Avenue, the factory was demolished less than a decade ago. Only the former powerhouse and forge shop survive. Photo by the author.

and Sons in Birmingham, manufactured parts for high-wheel bicycles, famously the all-important backbones and wheel rims, and the younger Warwick journeyed to America during the mid–1880s with ideas about perfecting a bicycle for the American market. The eponymous company he founded in March 1888, the same month and year that Gaylor chartered his Stamford corporation and slightly more than two years before Keating opened his shop in Westfield, helped to burnish Springfield's aura as a city for cyclists.

The Warwick Cycle Manufacturing Company, the Eagle Bicycle Manufacturing Company, and the Keating Wheel Company are of a kind in many ways. All three exhibited familiar patterns of development: the sprout from roots in mechanical ingenuity; the thorny relationships between inventor and local investors; the bloom of high-quality bicycles—each Warwick bicycle bearing the stamp: "Built on Honor"; and the rise of impressive new factories. The owners of all three also negotiated the rapidly-developing transition from high-wheel to safety bicycles, organizing just in time to capitalize on public fervor for the latter. All three were similarly sized, and all three battled for a share of a market dominated by larger companies, adding to our understanding of the bicycle industry's dynamic middle-ground during the boom period of the 1890s. All three also contributed to the complex web of human connectivity that characterized the industry during that same period, particularly in the New England region.

Other aspects also invite comparison. As did so many bicycle companies, the Warwick concern exploited the willingness of trade boards, civic improvement

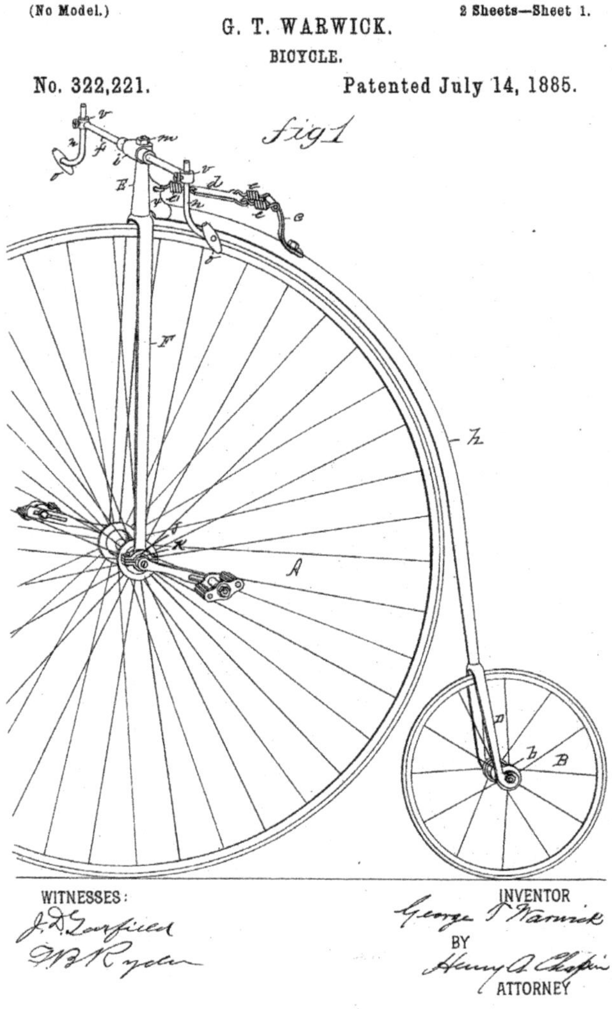

Figure 92. The second of three patents issued to George Warwick in 1885 protected his improved design for adjustable ball bearing casings at the hubs and axles of both large and small wheels, and he also designed adjustable handlebars. His first American patent strengthened sheet-metal wheel rims by creating an overlap on the rim's lower surface. His wheel also used tangent spokes that could be replaced without removing the tire, and his third patent protected the die used to shape those rims. Several other Warwick patents focused on perfecting components of high wheel and safety bicycles. United States Patent Office.

associations, and local investors to offer financial incentives. As did both Gaylor and Keating, George Warwick found himself at odds with those financiers and, as did Gaylor, resigned from the firm he founded after a brief period, leaving the company without the spark of inventiveness so vital to creating a distinctive marque, such as that fashioned by Keating. However, unlike the Eagle company's benefactors in Torrington, Springfield's well-heeled, investors-turned-owners possessed neither mechanical ingenuity nor close ties to the cycling industry's complex inner-workings. Although New England had no shortage of experienced machinists, and although the Warwick company owners were successful businessmen, they lacked the crucial insight needed to anticipate the industry's rapidly shifting heading. Whether due to that limitation alone, or likely coupled with other factors, the company stumbled from year to year, enduring six reorganizations and seven different presidents during the period between 1888 and 1895, and two years later succumbed to insolvency forced by one of the concern's principal investors, rubber-industry baron Joseph Banigan from Providence, Rhode Island. As a result, the firm never entered the fray surrounding formation of the American Bicycle Company trust.

Perfection Bicycles

When George Warwick arrived in this country, already an experienced machinist and cyclist, he voiced admiration for the *American System* of manufacturing. By 1884 he had established residency in Springfield, site of the United States Arsenal and a cradle of precision machine tools. His father's firm already owned the patents for numerous bicycle parts, several of which were used by Americans including Albert Overman and distributor William Reed in Boston, who sold New Mail bicycles fabricated at the Ames factory in Chicopee, and Warwick very quickly began applying for American patents. His inventions reveal a thread of consistency, that of an intention to refine both the engineering and the methods of manufacturing high wheel bicycles, a means to achieve perfection in design—as the moniker of the company's first model suggests. His earliest American patent, awarded in April 1885 but issued in England two years before, advanced the design of hollow, sheet-metal wheel-rims with a strengthening overlap on the lower surface of the rim, together with tangent spokes that could be replaced without removing the tire. In July of that same year, he secured an omnibus patent demonstrating improvements for adjustable ball-bearing casings at the hubs and axles of both large and small wheels; and for saddle supports and adjustable handlebars. Three months later, Warwick collected a third patent for a die to shape the rims described by the April document.[1]

In June 1888, Warwick displayed a prototype of the Perfection high-wheel bicycle during a Friday evening wheel parade in Springfield, and a local journalist described the bicycle's many refinements in design: a backbone strengthened at the head and beneath the saddle; a steel and rubber spring (the former absorbing tension and the latter vibration) within the fork frame above the hub, as well as rubber springs at various joints; a plunger brake easily applied without releasing the handle-bar grips; non-elastic tires guaranteed to stay on rims; dust caps on both the headset and pedals; and various other small improvements.[2]

Exactly when and where Warwick first occupied shop space in Springfield is unclear, but presumably he needed access to machinery to develop his patent applications. In any case, by 1887 or 1888 he had become acquainted with Diodate L. Swan, probably through one of Swan's sons,

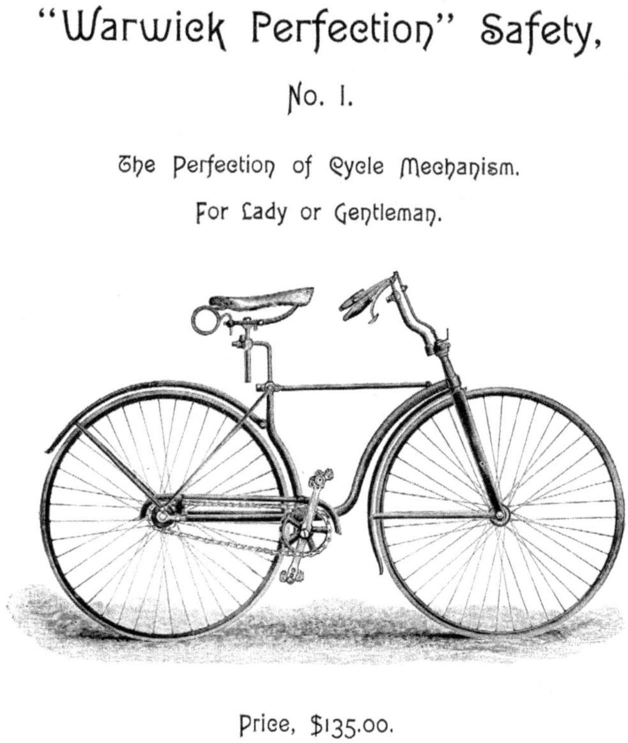

Figure 93. Although Warwick was reluctant to abandon the company's high wheel bicycles, he developed designs for both single and tandem safety bicycles, the former convertible for use by either men or women and priced at $135 in the company's 1890 catalog. Courtesy Hagley Museum and Library.

Frederick R. Swan, who joined the Springfield Bicycle Club in 1885. D.L. Swan had created a very successful real estate business before acquiring ownership of the New England Card and Paper Company, where his sons joined him. To Warwick's benefit, Swan owned a large brick factory fronting a two-block length of Hanover Street in Springfield's southerly district near the banks of the Connecticut River. In addition to housing Swan's card business, the plant also provided shops for a pistol manufacturer and a screw company.[3]

Warwick's new firm, chartered as a Maine corporation, leased portions of at least two floors in that factory, roughly 3000 square feet on each floor, and ordered specialized machine tools from Pratt and Whitney and other companies with the goal of starting production by May 1888, with fifty workers. Four stockholders—Warwick, Frederick Swan and his brother-in-law, banker George K. Tapley, and F.A. Nickerson (also a member of the city's bicycle club)—each held a single share at par value of $100, with total capitalization of $100,000 and the remaining 996 treasury shares unissued. The charter named Warwick and Tapley as president and treasurer, respectively, with Fred Swan joining the pair to fill the company's three director seats. Paid-in capital soon increased to $60,000 and the lease agreement with Swan expanded to 15,000 square feet. By June of that year, Swan's two other sons, Frank N. Swan and Wilbur M. Swan, had joined the board of directors.[4]

During the fall of 1888, Warwick conducted tours of the plant for journalists from both *Bicycling World* and *Wheel and Cycling Trade Review*, all the while touting the inventiveness of the company's high-wheel bicycle, in his words original from the top of the handlebar to the low edge of the rim; he also unveiled designs for a safety bicycle with anti-vibration bearings. That fall, too, he applied successfully for another patent relating to wheel ball-bearings and front-fork suspension, and by that time he may have begun plans for a tandem safety (convertible to a single), which he described in a patent application filed the following spring, April 1889, and eventually awarded in August 1890. Thus, Warwick was not so immersed in the design of high-wheel bicycles that he overlooked the impending shift toward safety bicycles. However, his preoccupation with perfecting the engineering of both types may have distracted him from the mundane aspects of operating a business—a lapse that seems to have shadowed the company from its inception.[5]

Unfortunately, production during the 1889 season faltered, and reports suggest several problems. Although the English firm's sturdy reputation likely stimulated interest in Warwick's new American high-wheel bicycle, sentiment already had shifted to safety bicycles in some sectors, possibly affecting demand. In addition, Swan's factory lacked an adequate foundry, and Warwick arranged a lease agreement with the Springfield Foundry Company, located on Liberty Street in the city's northeasterly sector, hardly convenient to production. Moreover, even if Swan's building had offered more space, Warwick lacked sufficient capital to expand or to add more machine tools. The firm also received financial inducements to relocate to an unnamed western city, complicating company affairs. In response, Warwick quickly adopted American business tactics and informed the Springfield Improvement Association that his company would move unless the city could provide economic incentives and improved facilities.[6]

Reorganization 1889

A cadre of prominent and civic-minded investors with familial and business ties responded by fully capitalizing the company at $100,000 (or nearly so), and by October 1889 the firm had completed its first reorganization. The new owners included Edward S. Brewer (successor to his family's hardware business); Nathan D. Bill and George A. Russell (owners of the National Papeterie Company); Andrew B. Wallace (owner of the city's large department store chain, Forbes and Wallace, and father-in-law of Nathan Bill); publishers Herbert Myrick and George S. Graves (eventual owners of the Phelps Publishing Company); George Dutton (brother-in-law of Nathan Bill); George Bleloch (machinist and founder of the National Needle Company in Springfield, and also a substantial shareholder of the Excelsior Needle Company in Torrington); and George D. Chamberlain (a bookkeeper and auditor). Warwick stayed put as president, Brewer became vice president, and Chamberlain treasurer and business manager; those three together with Bill, Bleloch, Myrick, Russell, and Wallace served as directors, although Bleloch died in 1891; and the Swans, Tapley and Warwick remained shareholders. Wallace, Brewer, Bill and Tapley all were members of the Springfield Board of Trade, and Wallace and Myrick served on the Springfield Improvement Association. In addition, Brewer, Bill, Chamberlain, and Myrick all had joined the Springfield Bicycle Club by 1892 (as had Warwick), and Chamberlain actively supported the good roads movement.[7]

A month later, November 1889, Warwick acknowledged the courtesies paid to the company by the trade during that difficult year, vowing to demonstrate worthiness of their credit during the coming 1890 season, when focus would turn to the Perfection safety model, capable of conversion for use by either men or women.[8]

Robert Keating's stint at the Hanover Street factory during this period becomes an intriguing part the story, not just for Warwick's business but for Keating's company, as well. Although very little is known about their working relationship during that brief tenure, several inferences seem plausible. Warwick's training as a machinist and proclivity for invention, coupled with his emphasis on bicycle design as a single, integrated work of engineering suggest that he became a mentor for Keating. That Keating served as superintendent of one or more of Warwick's production divisions reinforces that assumption, as well as confirming the latter's recognition of Keating's abilities.[9]

Equally important, an inspection

of Keating's early patent applications for safety bicycles from October and December 1889, presumably submitted while he was still working for Warwick, reveals the latter's influence on Keating's inventive outlook. Warwick's focus on cushion springs and advanced braking devices is clearly visible on both Keating patents, which introduced sprung forks, seat-post springs, and drive-train braking, all of which represented more complex versions of the devices utilized by Warwick. Keating's earlier patent also introduced an adjustable frame capable of accommodating either men or women. Even the name of Keating's first safety model, Superior, hints at Warwick's pursuit of refinement in overall bicycle design.[10]

For both Warwick and Keating, whether those refinements today pass the test of practicality is probably less important than the spark of curiosity that seems to have driven both men. Conceivably, each found the quest for invention to be a form of refuge from the uncertainties of investment and the vagaries of investor, and that pursuit may have become overriding, inevitably shaping the course of the companies each man founded.

In March 1890, with increased capital available and focus narrowed exclusively to the Perfection safety, Warwick confirmed that production capacity would be doubled, necessitating additions to the roll of ninety workers and increases in payroll, which ranged between $50,000 and $60,000. The company also increased floor space to 26,000 square feet and began installing new machinery. As the season advanced, the company's daily production rose to a dozen bicycles, eventually reaching 1200 for the year. However, earlier that spring company officials had acknowledged the need to construct a new factory on a different site to meet growing demand. In July, the firm began looking for a suitable location and increased capital to $150,000.[11]

Reorganization 1890

During the fall of 1890, the company reshuffled its management a second time. Keating had departed by September, and after assessing inventory the following month, directors named Brewer president and shuttled Warwick to the newly-created office of mechanical engineer, where he could attend to patent applications. To govern production, the directors hired a general manager, Joel H. Hendrick, appointing him vice-president and placing him on the board of directors. In addition to his familiarity with machine-tools used in arms manufacturing, Hendrick also contributed administrative experience. To replace Bleloch, Warwick's directors added a ninth member to the board, George R. Bidwell from New York City, owner of a large sales agency, repair shop, and riding school in Manhattan's Bidwell Building. In 1882, Bidwell had helped to found that city's Citizens Bicycle Club and had served as state consul for the New York State Division of the League of American Wheelmen, before becoming one of the league's vice presidents early in 1890. By the spring of that year, too, Bidwell had begun selling Warwick Perfection bicycles, along with Columbia, Victor, and Eagle models at top-of-the-line prices, together with more modestly-ranked St. Nicholas wheels.[12]

In late fall 1890, the company estimated production of 2500 wheels for the 1891 season, and announced plans to introduce a new model, the Warwick Diamond Safety. Yet that target fell far short of the owners' expectations to keep pace with competition and to achieve a calculated return on their investment, the latter hampered by debt obligations. Frustrations with Warwick, not publicly voiced at the time, explains much of the reorganization, but whether those concerns grew from his inability to manage production, or to his natural preference for invention and his neglect of other tasks is unclear. For instance, the directors may have doubted Warwick's ability to oversee plans for a new factory, an essential step toward increasing production capacity. Likely, too, concern for the latter loomed large after directors learned of Keating's negotiations with Holyoke investors and the offer of a large new plant in that nearby city—tidings circulated in newspapers during the spring of 1891. All the while, directors also recognized the need to establish closer ties to the cycling industry and thus improve the company's marketing reach, leading to Bidwell's appointment and to the hiring of a new sales agent, A. Kennedy-Childe.[13]

Surprisingly, the 1890 season seemed to close on a bright note in November when, following a competition, the United States Postal Service announced that postal carriers in Washington, D.C., would use Warwick bicycles supplied with front pouches. That city's asphalt streets made collection by bicycle practical, and a similar contract from Columbus, Ohio, followed soon after. The firm attributed those successes to Warwick's patented design for repairable spokes. However, that same month directors also announced that par value of company's stock had been diluted from $100 to $60.[14]

Warwick Avenue Factory

In May 1891, Brewer and his directors resolved to increase production by purchasing land for a new factory. Situated in the city's sparsely developed northeasterly district, six or seven blocks east of the Springfield Foundry Company works and not far north of the United States Arsenal grounds, the property bordered tracks of the Boston and Albany Railroad to the south, with access to Liberty Street to the north. The parcel also abutted land owned by Nathan Bill's father, Gurdon Bill, who donated a small corner of his lot to simplify the boundary alignment but who also specified that the company complete construction of the factory within a year at a cost not less than $40,000. The company commissioned Springfield architect B. Hammett Seabury to design the factory, and in mid–July signed a general construction contract with a local building firm, E.W. Shattuck and Company, anticipating completion by early November. Work started immediately and when completed early in 1892, the factory's three-story main block displayed dimensions that would become common to the bicycle industry (325 feet by 50 feet), with capacity to produce 10,000 bicycles annually. However, the building's structure, and distinctive elevations belonged more to Seabury's former architectural partner, Francis R. Richmond, who modified the plans, and to local masonry sub-contractors, D.W. Mellen and W.D. McKenzie.[15]

Just as the mechanical ingenuities of Gaylor, Keating and Warwick invite comparison, the buildings erected by their respective companies encourage consideration as a group, despite the very recent loss of the Warwick plant to demolition. Each is significant in the context of bicycle manufacturing, but for different reasons. Unlike both the Eagle and second Keating plants, the Warwick factory explored little new ground in the evolution of industrial architecture, although the company's selection of electric lighting warrants mention. Instead, the factory's date and its reliance on standard mill construction marked the plant as a template for the design of new bicycle factories at the onset of the bicycle boom in an industry on the cusp of rapid expansion. Granted, the factory served as a form of passive shelter, its overall square-footage dictated by the number of machines, tools, and workers required to achieve production quotas. However, the factory plans also demonstrated the collaborative contributions of architect, mechanical engineer, builder, brick masons, and company owners

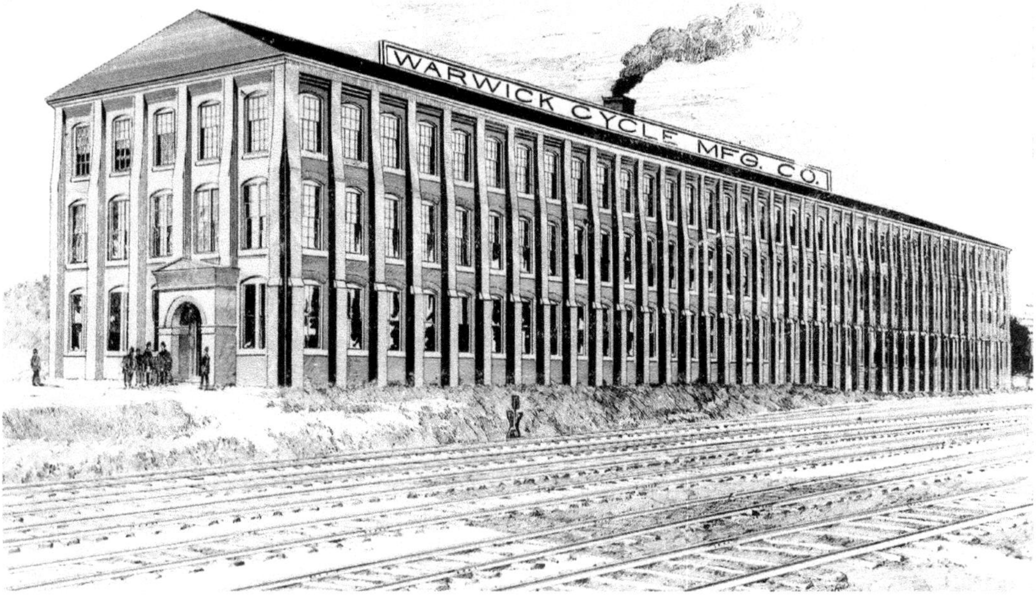

Figure 94. Design of the Warwick Company's factory represented a collaboration among architects, mechanical engineers, builders, and company owners who sought departmental organization for bicycle production. The building's length (325 feet), width (50 feet), and three-story height provided capacity to produce an estimated 10,000 bicycles annually, and the designers of many later factories would adopt similar dimensions for bicycle production.

With no plans for heavy machinery on the third floor, initially intended to provide space for a riding school, the depth of second-story piers could be reduced, and architect Francis Richmond introduced a gradual taper, flattening the piers still more on the third story. His design also accentuated the regimental rows of windows, reducing material costs in the bargain, and his truncated hipped roofs added architectural effect, as did the muscular, pedimented entrance pavilion with portal arch. George S. Graves, Co., *Progressive Springfield* (1916).

who understood the importance of departmental organization.

Among factories newly built by bicycle companies during the 1880s and 1890s, a number preceded the Warwick works, for example Albert Overman's expansive complex in Chicopee Falls (1889, 1890 and 1892). True as well, the Keating factory in Holyoke stood ready for occupancy at the same time as the Warwick plant (January 1892). However, both the Chicopee and Holyoke works can be distinguished from the Springfield factory. Overman already had established his company as one of the country's largest bicycle manufacturers, and he sought to solidify that standing with imposing works to rival Pope's industrial complex in Hartford, where the new west wing stood completed in 1891. In Holyoke, Keating's four-story factory became an addition to an existing mill, constrained in function by excessive vertical circulation and by reliance on waterpower, and constrained in size and capacity by the limited site, which precluded subsidiary buildings. In addition, although the mill's owner, Marciene Whitcomb, and his builder, Casper Ranger, had little understanding of the bicycle industry, they possessed an abundance of knowledge about mill systems, and they likely influenced many aspects of the building's design in the rush to win a new industry for Holyoke.

Building Design. As a template for new bicycle factories, the Warwick plant is significant for its precise delineation of the company's numerous departments, their size, the integration of departmental divisions, circulation, production flow, and distribution of power. Seabury's drawings, published in the *Springfield Republican* in May 1891, show a four-story structure with a wide stringcourse of brick separating the first and second floors. With little but empty land to the north, he turned the building's front elevation to face the railroad, for all who traveled by rail to see, and decorated the pitched roof with a pair of short towers capped by pyramidal roofs. Conceivably, he intended those towers to house machinery for elevators, but visual effect is just as likely an explanation.[16]

Seabury's plans placed all the departments and principal halls along the building's full length, all carefully measured beginning with the general offices on the ground floor at the factory's westerly end, with a hall separating those offices from the main machine room; followed in turn by the stock room and then the fitting and filing room at the factory's easterly end. On the second floor, the main office and its adjoining hall matched those spaces directly below, followed by the separate assembling, polishing, and inspecting rooms; the wheel room; the plating and buffing room; and the enameling room; with four brick Japan ovens snugly positioned against an exterior wall and lined with iron plate. The third story, free from mid-span posts according to Seabury's plans, provided enough room for a riding school, with an adjoining retiring room for riders directly above the offices on the first and second floors; a storage room consumed the remainder of that floor.[17]

Those first plans also called for a subsidiary, two-story ell at the factory's rear westerly end and designated as a carpenter's shop and repair shop on the first floor, with shipping department on the second floor reliant on an inclined runway leading to ground level and access to a rail spur and to an adjoining street. At the rear of the easterly end, a one-story ell with monitor roof provided sufficient space for the rim department, the blacksmith shop, and the power plant. Chamberlain also proposed constructing a small building for social or dining purposes, with a smoking lounge for the noon hour.[18]

A month after Seabury's drawings circulated, the company retained Richmond, who limited the building's height to three stories and lopped off fifteen feet of length, adding a basement beneath the factory's easterly half for coal storage. Presumably intent on decreasing costs, he jettisoned the towers, reworked the easterly ell, and eliminated the westerly ell altogether, establishing the factory's principal, single-bay entrance at the southerly corner of the building's westerly end. He also redesigned Seabury's entrance portico, formerly centered on the westerly ell, and replaced it with a muscular, one-story, projecting pavilion capped by a low-pitched gable roof supported, in turn, by a wide band of brick corbelling above a sheltering arch with brick voussoir. In addition, Richmond pulled the building's pitched roof back into a shallow hip at each end, adding accent to those very visible elevations.[19]

Functionally, the arrangement of departments and interior circulation changed only marginally, mostly on the third floor where the easterly half provided enough space for the carpenter shop and the crating divisions (both of which moved from the aborted westerly ell), as well as a tire-fitting department with small ovens. As built, the third floor included center posts with substantial struts to support the roof's rafters. The riding school ambitiously planned for that floor's westerly half managed to survive the cost-cutting, but the large open space soon succumbed to storage, and its water closet may not have been installed. In a corner of the large machine room on the first floor, Richmond found space for the repair shop, also housed initially in the westerly ell.[20]

For the auxiliary units, Richmond may have considered dividing the easterly ell into three one-story buildings, beginning (from west to east) with a blacksmith and forge shop; a brazing and rim shop; and a powerhouse with boiler room and engine room separated by a brick fire wall. However, a reliable Sanborn-Perris Map Company insurance map from 1896 shows the blacksmith and rim shops as separate units in a single, one-story structure the equivalent of two stories in height and capped by monitor roof. The powerhouse, with its brick chimney and a large adjoining washroom, stood as a separate unit with monitor roof. Access to all annex rooms could be gained from the main block's ground floor, which housed two freight elevators in its easterly half.[21]

The forge shop housed hardening ovens on the ground floor and a resourceful layout for elevated Japan enameling ovens extending outward from the exterior wall of the main block but opening to the factory's second floor. Initially coal-fired, the ovens rested on piers rising from the forge shop below, with fireboxes placed four feet beneath the factory's second-story floor surface and accessible to workers who fed and cleaned the units from the upper deck of the forge shop. Company officials expressed pride in that inventive system, which marked a change to Seabury's original plans, but whether credit belongs primarily to Richmond,

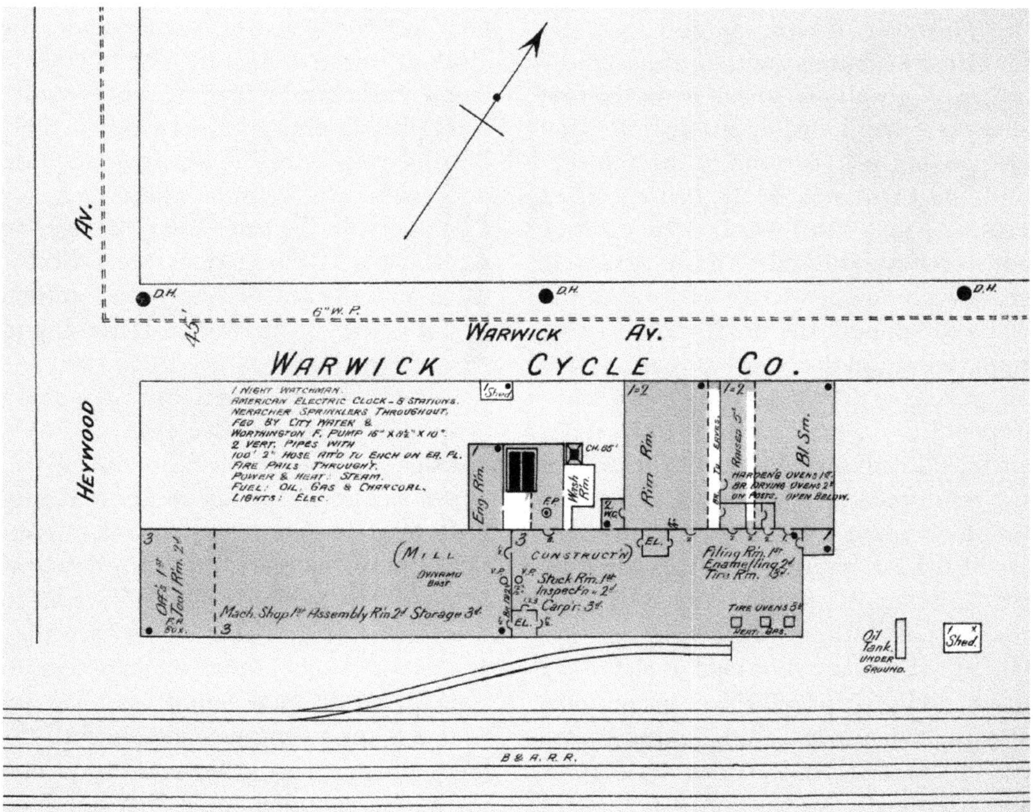

Figure 95. The factory's subsidiary buildings included blacksmith and rim shops as separate units in a single, one-story structure the equivalent of two stories in height and capped by monitor roof. The powerhouse, with its brick chimney and a large adjoining washroom, stood as a separate unit with monitor roof. Both the blacksmith and rim shops survive, as does the powerhouse; an adjacent, two-story shop with similarly tapered piers, possibly designed by Francis Richmond as well, was constructed by a subsequent owner. Sanborn-Perris Map Company, Insurance Map of Springfield, Massachusetts (1896), Plate 82. Library of Congress, Geography and Map Division.

Warwick, or masonry contractors, the feature nevertheless illustrates an imaginative solution resulting from a collaborative approach to design.[22]

Functionally and structurally, both Seabury and Richmond sought to maximize admission of natural light, and Seabury's first plans called for five-foot-wide window openings spaced at three-foot intervals, which placed floor beams on piers with center-points eight feet apart. Ultimately, the total amount of glass surface and its height relative to floor level determined the most efficient balance between structural strength and natural light, and visitors to the Warwick factory consistently applauded the well-lit interior.[23]

However, Richmond substantially modified Seabury's structural design by buttressing wall piers heavily on the first story and then reducing the depth of that buttressing proportionally for the second and third stories; he also specified pressed brick—uniform in size, density, and strength. In addition, he extended granite windowsills across entire spandrel walls to support the brick window surrounds, but whether those sills also rested on sections of the piers, giving further support to the spandrel walls, is unclear. At any rate, Richmond may have believed that the reinforced piers eliminated the need for floor-beam anchors. As did designers of the Fitchburg factory acquired by Iver Johnson, Richmond added mass to the walls beneath the eaves to bolster support for the heavy roof load of slate, and to extend the drip line. He, or his masons, also added brick corbelling to underscore the transition from wall surface to eaves and used a similar but more decorative treatment above the recessed third-story windows.

Architecturally, the distinctive taper of wall piers, punctuated by rows of deeply recessed windows in the spandrel walls on the first story, gave the building a dynamic architectural effect that embodied Richmond's most creative contribution to the design. His solution suggests that he understood the challenge architects faced when trying to soften the austerity of lengthy, unadorned brick walls, and that he also understood the practice of expressing structure as one manner of confronting that challenge. That he found a creative method to improve the building's structural capacity and at the same time distinguish its elevations visually by adding strong vertical elements is a credit to his skills as an architect.

The logic of his structural device is evident, that of adding material mass to the ground-floor piers to increase the strength of the walls and to reinforce the floor-beam pockets at the second floor; he also underscored the transition in taper at that key juncture by capping the first-story piers with slanting granite blocks, possibly hinting at the location of the floor-beam pockets within. With no plans for heavy machinery on the third floor, the need to reinforce the second-story piers diminished, and the buttressing decreased in a smooth taper on that floor, flattening to an even thickness on the third story. As the taper of the piers decreased, the depth of window recess also decreased and windows gained greater visibility on the two upper stories, resulting in an emerging horizontal rhythm in tension with the vertical rise of the piers; brick window lintels with shallow arches added accent to that rhythm. That Richmond also specified pressed brick set in tinted mortar seems to confirm his desire to emphasize this vertical and horizontal tension, and even the minor change from gable to hip at the end elevations complemented that dynamic quality. Seabury and Richmond apparently agreed that flat roofs were unsuitable in northern climates, notwithstanding the dictates of factory mutual insurance companies.[24]

Francis R. Richmond. Richmond can be counted among the corps of regionally-influential architects who specifically sought commissions from factory owners, and thus his work with the Warwick company marks a key collaboration between architect and bicycle manufacturer in the quest to establish ideal factory plans. That the Springfield factory was among America's earliest new factories to represent that collaborative effort adds to its historic significance and underscores the gravity of its recent loss.

Born in Shelburne Falls, Massachusetts, in 1851 and later residing in Amherst, Richmond joined the carpentry trade with his father and, after settling in Springfield in 1870, began working for architect Eugene C. Gardner, who subsequently practiced with his son, George Gardner, and another partner, George Pyne, as Gardner, Pyne and Gardner. The elder Gardner, author of numerous architectural pattern books and a disciple of English architectural critic John Ruskin, became Springfield's most prolific architect during the post–Civil War era when romantic eclecticism flourished. Gardner moved easily among fashionable styles for the firm's many civic, commercial, residential, and industrial commissions, one of which included the surviving, four-story clubhouse for the Springfield Bicycle Club, erected on Worthington Street facing Stearns Park just as construction of the Warwick factory began. Coincidence or not, drawings of both building proposals circulated in the *Springfield Republican* on the same day in May 1891.[25]

Gardner heavily influenced Richmond's career, and when the latter eventually formed a partnership with Hammett Seabury, their designs for churches, schools, fire stations, and commercial buildings reflected a like-mindedness regarding architectural eclecticism, working in neo-classical as well as romantic modes. However, Richmond steadily gravitated toward industrial works, and following dissolution of his partnership with Seabury early in 1890, Richmond opened his own office and advertised proficiency in the design of heavy construction. In August 1891, when Springfield hosted the annual convention of the country's fire chiefs, Richmond was one of several presenters who offered papers on topics related to building construction and defects in buildings described as fire-proof construction. His contribution, titled "Strength of Material" and all but naming the Warwick factory, described the design for typical mill construction, three stories in height and fifty feet wide, with center posts and twenty-five-foot floor beams eight feet between center points. Richmond recommended southern yellow pine for framing and provided dimensions for floor beams (16 by 12 inches); first story posts (10 by 10 inches) to carry loads of 100 pounds per square foot (or round posts 11 inches in diameter); second-story posts (9 by 9 inches); rafter posts (8 by 8 inches); and brick piers (24 by 20 inches).[26]

Separately, Richmond also addressed the topic of iron as a substitute for wood in mill construction, for many decades a matter of concern to owners, insurance companies, and fire officials alike. Vulnerable to intense heat and subject to hidden imperfections originating with the fabrication process, particularly in cast form, iron had remained suspect as an industrial building material. However, by the early 1890s iron and steel manufacturers had improved standards of quality, and although Richmond acknowledged that wood resisted heat longer than iron, he assured his audience that round, wrought-iron columns (6 inches in diameter with a 5/8-inch shell, or cast-iron columns free from defects, 6 inches in diameter with a 5/8-inch shell) were comparable in load capacity to his first-story posts.[27]

Cycling's trade journals and a city compendium, *Progressive Springfield*, monitored the factory's construction, supplementing details about the building's design and machinery. With mechanical equipment newly purchased or moved from the Hanover Street works, the company utilized machine tools manufactured by Pratt and Whitney, the Ames Manufacturing Company, Brown and Sharpe, and the Garvin Machine Company. Safety devices included a sprinkling system and a network of electric emergency signals leading to the engine room where power could be shut off immediately. Springfield manufacturer, the R.F. Hawkins Iron Works, fabricated the boilers for the engine built by the Providence Steam Engine Company, and possibly the boiler for the unusual hot-water heating system installed by the H.Q.N. Evans Construction Company of New York City.[28]

After the company elected to abandon the westerly wing, Richmond rearranged the first-floor offices, creating a large general office for bookkeeper, clerk, and stenographer accessible directly from the principal entrance on the factory's westerly elevation. Two smaller offices of equal size—the first for the president and the second for the vice-president, secretary, and directors—opened into the general offices. Warwick, as mechanical engineer, planned to share the second-floor offices with draftsmen and the company's general sales agent.[29]

Reorganization 1891

Production of bicycles at the Hanover Street factory continued while construction of the new works advanced during the summer and fall of 1891. The company dodged disaster late in October when a portion of the old factory occupied by the New England Card and Paper Company burned, with the cycle shops saved only by a thin firewall of brick. For company owners, the narrow escape added to the firm's internal woes that culminated with George Warwick's resignation about three weeks later. Edward Brewer, as president, had not taken an active part in financial management of the business, delegating that role to George Chamberlain but also creating a void in authority that allowed conflict to fester, particularly between Warwick and Chamberlain, with Hendrick an ally of the latter. Brewer, believing that company officials should be engaged actively in the business, resigned, and although he remained a director, the board appointed Chamberlain president and treasurer, with Hendrick as vice president and secretary. After announcing his retirement, Warwick tactfully explained to reporters that the company he founded remained sound, but he also warned that without Brewer's guidance the balance of power rested too much in the hands of a single individual. The following day, Chamberlain was far less charitable in his comments to reporters, confiding that board members had long been dissatisfied with Warwick. Chamberlain also announced that the plant superintendent, Captain J.P. Kelly, would replace Warwick as mechanical engineer, Kelly thus succeeding the man who had hired him in 1888. To consolidate the changes, the company planned to reorganize as a Massachusetts corporation and voted to increase capitalization to $200,000, but without naming any new investors.[30]

Chamberlain, at age thirty-three, became the company's third president in four years. Born in Troy, New York, to parents whose ancestors arrived from Hingham, England in 1638, he lived for a period in Stockbridge and Chicopee before his family moved to Springfield in 1876. Prior to becoming treasurer and business manager for the Warwick company, he had worked as a bookkeeper for a publishing house, paymaster at the United States Arsenal, and traveling auditor for the Connecticut River Railroad; he also had completed studies at the Stebbins Collegiate Institute, later called Springfield Collegiate

Institute. If his age and business experience showed scant preparation for heading a fledgling bicycle company, Chamberlain nevertheless had overseen day-to-day affairs under Brewer's tutelage for two years and had earned the confidence of board members. He was also an avid cyclist and a few years later would embark on an adventurous journey by bicycle through the Berkshire Mountains with friends.[31]

All the while, the company devoted the ensuing months to moving into the new factory and to publicizing their new Perfection safety model for 1892, which hedged against mounting demand for pneumatic tires by offering three options: cushion tires; the Thomas pneumatic tire; and the air cushion tire, which combined the advantages of the first two but remained temporarily usable in the event of a puncture. To gauge popularity for pneumatics, Chamberlain polled sales agents, who calculated shortsightedly that only 60 percent of buyers favored the tire, prompting the company's guarded strategy. The new model, which the company briefly considered calling either the Pilgrim or the Puritan, also revealed several minor improvements, including a slightly longer diamond frame to move the saddle farther away from the handlebars; a strengthened and simplified drive chain; and adjustable pedals. However, the front-wheel plunger brake remained one of the model's recognizable features.[32]

If the company's new factory and expanded production capacity fostered optimism for the coming cycling season, patent quarrels with Warwick, Albert Pope, and Albert Overman clouded that bright outlook. In March 1892, the company's directors obtained an injunction against Warwick restraining him from exploiting or assigning any of the patent rights that the company had acquired after Springfield investors took control of the business. Warwick expressed surprise at the litigation but assumed it was an attempt to discourage him from competing. Yet he also disclosed that he had secured several new patents since departing, including one of curious design for a strong but light safety-bicycle frame developed by an English inventor, Samuel Vale. Warwick also confided that he had received several offers to establish a new business and had been negotiating with a syndicate of investors in Toledo to build a new plant.[33]

Along another skirmish line, the company received better news late in May 1892, when a federal judge in Hartford dismissed a protracted suit by Albert Pope for infringement of an 1888 patent acquired from Englishman George Illston relating to detachable handlebars and to adjustable seats, features that Warwick had adapted for the latter's American bicycles. However, not until February 1893 would a federal judge in Boston dismiss a similar infringement claim by Overman.[34]

Warwick continued to live in Springfield, pursuing his considerable inventive talents. In September 1893, he joined a gathering of bicycle manufacturers and tradesmen in Springfield, among them Joseph Yost and Samuel Snell from Toledo, to consider formation of a society of manufacturers. The following fall, he formed a partnership with a New Jersey dentist, Dr. Charles S. Stockton, to manufacture bicycle parts and sundries, including hubs, chains, and pedals. Stockton provided the financing and factory, Warwick the inventive outlook and patents, and the Warwick and Stockton Company moved into Stockton's plant (no longer standing) at the corner of New Jersey Railroad Avenue and Hamilton Street in Newark. However, disagreements again developed, leading to litigation that concluded this time in Warwick's favor, awarding him half the company's profits. All the while, he focused on developing and securing patents for numerous specialized tools, including machines to produce metallic spokes; screw blanks; and rims for automobile steering wheels. In 1902, he also patented a coaster brake for bicycles.[35]

Reorganization 1892

Meanwhile, Warwick's former company had attracted a new investor from Springfield, Charles Rood, who replaced Chamberlain as president and treasurer in September 1892. Chamberlain willingly retired from the company and relinquished his position on the board of directors to Rood, but also agreed to remain for several weeks to assist with the transition. Whether due to exhaustion or poor health, Chamberlain announced plans for a much-needed rest, and at a testimonial gathering the company's directors praised his diligent efforts.[36]

With Rood's investment, the company approached its goal of $200,000 capitalization and outwardly appeared to be on sound financial footing. Yet directors remained guarded about production numbers and financial standing, and any infusion of capital from Rood may have been used to control unit costs without forsaking economic opportunity as the market for safety bicycles with pneumatic tires accelerated. Competition to meet that demand increased, and directors must have kept a close watch on the Overman and Keating shops nearby. Although financial controversy seemed to swirl around Keating's company throughout its history, newspaper accounts nevertheless offered a much better picture of those problems than those of the Warwick concern, described by journalists as very conservative.[37]

The earliest public indicators that the firm faced financial distress did not circulate until May 1893, when the company announced a drastic reduction in bicycle prices—much to the industry's consternation—applicable to all unsold 1893 models, lowered from $150 to a jaw-dropping $85, and to $65 for its leftover 1892 models. The company limited the sale's duration and required cash, but offered a one year guarantee for all pneumatic tires. George Hendee, who had retired from racing by then, agreed to market the discounted bicycles locally from his Springfield shop, where he had been selling Waverly bicycles manufactured by the Indiana Bicycle Company. Once having converted overstock to cash, the Warwick firm expected to start anew and return to fair prices using industry standards for their 1894 models.[38]

The company's price reductions at the selling season's peak are curious, not just because the decision sheds light on the company's internal workings, but also because it reveals that fractures already had begun to appear in some sectors of the industry by that early date. Increasing demand for safety bicycles, rapidly occurring advances in bicycle design, invention of specialized machine tools, aggressive marketing techniques, complex and vulnerable distribution networks, and ever-mounting competition all forced equally prompt adaptations by manufacturers as the predictable costs and methods of production honed during the high-wheel era succumbed to scrutiny. Neither in substance nor time did responses to those troublesome challenges occur evenly across the industry, as the Warwick example illustrates. Close by in Hartford, Albert Pope did not reduce the price of Columbia bicycles from $125 to $100 until the fall of 1894, and demand had still not crested by then. Whether or not Warwick's managers can be faulted for their inexperience as bicycle manufacturers, the challenges occurring throughout the trade were formidable even for industry leaders.

Reorganization 1893

Company directors viewed events in a different light, identifying the problem as neglect by management, and that same month, May 1893, announced their decision to remove Rood after only nine months, neglecting to anticipate that he would take control of the Keating business and become a competitor that fall. Nathan Bill filled the role of president and manager temporarily, and Joel Hendrick succeeded him that summer while directors searched for someone to head daily operations. After George Hendee declined the firm's offer in July, directors began negotiating with Alpha O. Very, head of the A.O. Very Cycle Company of Boston, a large sales agency. Late that month, Very accepted the position of treasurer and manager, obtained shares of stock, took a seat at the board of directors' table, and agreed to relocate to Springfield, relinquishing day-to-day control of his Boston agency to a son, Frederick A. Very.[39]

The elder Very, who had founded a Boston business to market sewing machines, began selling bicycles in 1889, becoming an agent that year for the Union Cycle Company, the Lozier and Yost Bicycle Manufacturing Company, and the Warwick concern. By 1892, he had added Liberty, Sylph, and Eclipse bicycles to his showroom, along with lower-priced Ben Hur and Reindeer wheels, and had developed a solid business relationship with Kennedy-Childe. Very also arrived in Springfield as an inventor, having patented designs for sewing-machine needles as well as adjustable handlebars for bicycles, assigning the latter to his new employer in September 1894, after becoming the company's fifth or sixth general manager in five years.[40]

Although Hendrick's tenure as the Warwick president was also brief, he nevertheless reinforced the complex web connecting the firearms and bicycle industries. Prior to the Civil War, he had worked in Chicopee Falls for the Massachusetts Arms Company, founded in 1850 by Joshua Stevens, James T. Ames, Timothy Carter, and others to produce pistols under patents granted to B. Tyler Henry and Daniel Wesson, both of whom had worked for the Robbins and Lawrence Company or its successors, as had Christian Sharps. After serving in the Civil War, Hendrick began working in Springfield for Wesson and his partner Horace Smith, who had formed their own firm, Smith and Wesson. That connectivity also extended to numerous factories. The Massachusetts Arms Company acquired land for its works in Chicopee Falls from the Ames Manufacturing Company, but later sold that plant to the Lamb Knitting Machine Manufacturing Company, in turn absorbed by Albert Spalding's business and adapted to the manufacture of bicycles in competition with Albert Overman. Joshua Stevens eventually formed another company, the J. Stevens Arms and Tool Company, which acquired Overman's works after that latter company failed, and briefly turned to the manufacture of bicycles.[41]

At long last, during the closing months of 1893, the Warwick company seemed to leap forward, winning commendations from the editors of cycling's trade journals. In December, the firm announced plans to offer eight models during 1894, with prices ranging from $100 to $150 and weights between twenty-one and twenty-six pounds. Men and women could choose between two ranks of models, one priced at $100 and the other $115, the latter with several options including either wood or steel rims for men, wood rims for women, Very's adjustable handlebars, and rear-wheel disc brakes that could be applied from either the front or rear of the bicycle. The company priced three models at $125, two for men and one for women, the former with a forty-eight-inch wheel-base and weighing twenty-five pounds, and the latter advertised as the lightest wheel for women on the market at twenty-six pounds; the Warwick racer with vermillion rims cost $150 and weighed nineteen pounds. In addition, the company installed a department for wood rims on the factory's third floor.[42]

In March, anticipating the start of the 1894 cycling season, Very's Boston firm opened a branch store on Springfield's Worthington Street, and that cycling center became the Warwick company's retail headquarters—but also offering Raleigh and Eclipse bicycles. The following month, the body corporate finally found its way from Maine to Massachusetts and became fully capitalized at $200,000, aided by a temporary loan from the Springfield Safe Deposit and Trust Company in an undisclosed amount and secured by a temporary mortgage on the land and factory.[43]

A comparatively stable and profitable outlook dominated the 1894 and 1895 seasons, although Kelly resigned in March 1894 and Hendrick accepted an appointment as Springfield's city marshal in December of that year, yielding the president's chair to George A. Russell, the latter becoming the company's seventh president in six years. As partners, Russell and Nathan Bill had acquired the National Papeterie Company, but Bill eventually sold his interest to the former. The striving Russell also presided over two other local companies; invested heavily in two cutlery businesses; served as a director of the Second National Bank of Springfield; and occupied a director's chair for two regional paper companies.[44]

Very brought with him substantial financial backing by Providence multi-millionaire Joseph Banigan, who became the company's principal creditor with loans initially amounting to $180,000. Having cash in hand, a factory with increased annual capacity (Very optimistically estimated 40,000 bicycles), and an employment register of 250 workers at peak times, the company was well placed to take advantage of the cresting mania for safety bicycles. In January 1895, the company announced seven models for the coming 1895 season, with prices ranging from $80 to $125. At the close of that season Very reported a handsome profit on sales of 6,000 bicycles and an undisclosed number of orders unfilled. He then declared a 6 percent dividend, and with other directors voted to shrink the board from nine members to five: Russell, Very, Wallace, Brewer and Nathan Bill, with Russell and Very the major shareholders.[45]

Insolvency, 1897

The 1896 season began on an upbeat note with pending orders of 10,000 bicycles and a marketing campaign promoting bright vermillion rims on several of the Perfection models—red rims visible everywhere according to the company's advertisements. Very introduced only minor changes to the previous year's models, possibly hedging against rumors of declining demand, but prices remained high at the season's outset, with top models (including the racer) reduced modestly to $100. Although worries about bicycle sales continued to circulate, the 1896 season nevertheless passed quietly (if not profitably) for the company, with Russell and Very earning respective annual salaries of $2,000 and $5,000 by the close of that year. Very then turned his attention to 1897 models, again offered with few changes other than one-piece cranks and a wide range of sprocket sizes. Early in February, the New England Cycle Show opened in Boston, and the Warwick business again presented its top model for $100, available in vermillion, black, dark green, or royal blue. That season also passed quietly, but the silence had become an ominous one.[46]

Following the annual shareholder meeting late in October 1897, when Very's report as treasurer revealed the season's poor results, Joseph Banigan instructed his accountant, Alfred S. Clarke, to audit the company's ledgers, and when due dates for two notes totaling $150,000 lapsed in November, Banigan promptly attached the company's assets. Banigan's about-face came as a complete surprise to Russell, who at one point hadn't convened a directors' meeting in more than a year and paid scant attention to the company's daily operations. Whether feigned or not, Very also proclaimed astonishment despite his awareness that Clarke had learned about loans made by the Warwick business to Very's sales agency, which teetered on the edge of insolvency, and also about the manufacturer's paltry sales during 1897 and outstanding debt to local banks. A few days later, Very traveled to Worcester to plead with Banigan's attorney, without success, and barely two weeks elapsed before Very assigned both his Boston business and a second firm in Wellsville New York, doing business as Very and Osborne, to a receiver. Early in February 1898, the Warwick company filed for bankruptcy and was judged insolvent later that month. At about the same time, an accounting disclosed that the liabilities of Very's Boston business exceeded $42,000, and Frederick Very promptly filed for personal bankruptcy.[47]

All the while, other creditors of the Warwick concern formed a queue, Charles Rood among them, and by March 1898 the company's debts surpassed $210,000, including loans of $20,000 by Russell's Second National Bank of Springfield, whose president, Gurdon Bill, owned shares of stock in the Warwick company where his son served as a director, and by the Pynchon National Bank in Springfield for an identical amount; property taxes remained unpaid, as well. Assets included the factory, existing inventory, parts, materials, and accounts that together exceeded the company's debt by at least a respectable figure, possibly as much as $40,000; the company also owned at least some of the valuable machinery, but several of the creditors such as Pratt and Whitney and the Cleveland Machine Screw Company may have held chattel mortgages or instead leased the machinery.[48]

Banigan's election to force the company into insolvency, despite favorable aspects to the firm's balance sheet, may have resulted from several factors—poor timing among them—but the decision nevertheless made him a central figure in Springfield's corner of the bicycle industry. Banigan's story truly is one of rags to riches, accompanied by long memory, and began when his destitute family emigrated from Ireland to escape the potato famine and settled in Providence, Rhode Island, in 1847, when he was eight years old. He began full time employment a year later, becoming a child of industry in a region where Yankee capitalists regarded the indigent and illiterate Irish Catholics with disdain. In 1864, after years toiling in the machine tool and jewelry industries, he set a new course and at age twenty-five formed the Woonsocket Rubber Company. There, as Banigan's biographer Scott Molloy explains, he built an empire in footwear through tireless work, encyclopedic knowledge of the industry, sharp business practices, a willingness to employ Irish workers at reasonable wages, staunch Catholicism, and unstinting philanthropy. When in 1893 Charles Flint orchestrated formation of the United States Rubber Company trust, more than half a decade before he provided the financial lynchpin needed to create the American Bicycle Company monopoly, Banigan sold his business to the rubber cartel for the astonishing sum of $9,200,000, becoming the company's controlling stockholder and inaugural president.[49]

Logically, Banigan's willingness to underwrite the Warwick company following its 1893 reorganization may have been prompted by a desire to diversify his considerable fortune, and prospects for the bicycle industry certainly were tempting. However, conflict with Flint and with other owners of the rubber cartel soon developed, leading to Banigan's resignation in 1896 and to litigation to recover back wages. Compounding those challenges, cancer forced Banigan to confront his own mortality, and during the early days of 1898 when the Warwick company edged toward failure, Banigan's focus came to rest elsewhere. Nevertheless, he offered to reinstate the financing provided the company's owners raised $75,000 of new capital and applied $25,000 of that amount to his outstanding debt. By the end of January, Russell and his associates had managed to collect $50,000, but Russell became ill and the negotiations stalled.[50]

The choice for Warwick's owners thus became a stark one—whether to invest more deeply in the company, increase debt, and gamble on the bicycle's future, or instead to assign the company's assets to a receiver for distribution to creditors and then dissolve, limiting their personal losses. After a series of shareholder meetings during the early months of 1898, including a half-hearted attempt to convince skeptical creditors to accept less than full payment, Russell and other owners voted to dissolve. On March 16, the Hampden County Court of Insolvency conveyed the firm's property to two assignees, Alfred Clarke and Joel Hendrick, the latter agreeing to serve after Banigan's attorney and several creditors objected to Russell's appointment, arguing that his neglect had contributed to the firm's losses. Clarke and Hendrick began selling the company's property and by August had found a buyer for the assembled bicycles, A.H. Tennis of New York. On July 28 the company announced it would close indefinitely in mid–August, and on that same July day Banigan succumbed to illness at age fifty-nine.[51]

Clarke and Hendrick set a high price for the factory and machinery, $100,000, and began negotiating with several interested parties, including George Chamberlain, who found support from unnamed New York investors and submitted an offer late in October, hoping to start a new bicycle company managed by Springfield workers having experience in the industry. However, Clarke and Hendrick rejected the offer, and as the months slipped by the unattractive prospect of selling the plant at auction seemed inevitable. All the while, Russell, Very and Tennis had been scheming quietly, and in February 1899 they announced a newly-formed business called the Warwick Cycle Company, disclosing the purchase of a small portion of the factory's machinery together with the name and good will of the insolvent company. Although the factory had closed, Very had been developing a bevel-gear, chainless bicycle using dies and modeling owned by the old company, and the new partners planned to offer both chainless and chain-driven versions under the moniker New Warwick, just in time for the 1899 season and priced at $75 and $50 respectively. With Russell as president, Very as treasurer and general manager, and Tennis as sales agent, the company moved into Russell's National Papeterie Company factory, aiming for small-scale manufacturing. Whether Tennis had negotiated with Clarke and Hendrick on behalf of the partnership without revealing his agreement with Russell and Very is not clear, but Tennis's prompt purchase of the completed bicycles may not have been guileless.[52]

Not quite a year later, November 1899, Daniel B. Wesson of Springfield, president of the Cheney-Bigelow Wire Works, concluded negotiations with Clarke and Hendrick and purchased the factory for his wire company, paying $45,000 for the building, power systems, mill shafting, enameling ovens, scales, shop benches, and other fixtures; the deed made no reference to machinery. After that agreement, dividends to creditors climbed to slightly more than 27 percent of the outstanding debt.[53]

Meanwhile, litigation ensued—and on several fronts. Clarke tenaciously sought to recover assets on behalf of Banigan's estate, and he and Hendrick successfully sued the Second National Bank of Springfield for fraudulent receipt of $10,000 paid to the bank by Warwick's treasurer in November 1897, giving preference to the bank's loans over debts owed to other creditors at a time when both the Warwick company directors and bank officials knew the firm to be insolvent. In testimony, the bank's president, Gurdon Bill, acknowledged that he had attended the bicycle company's annual shareholder meeting that fall with his son, Nathan Bill, and had heard the treasurer's glum report, followed soon after by Banigan's vow to audit the company's records. In a separate action, but without Hendrick, Clarke also sued Russell, Very, Nathan Bill, Edward Brewer, and Andrew Wallace, who as officers and directors of the company negligently had allowed the firm's liabilities to exceed its capitalization by almost $60,000. He then attached assets owned by the defendants in the amount of $80,000. For their part, Very and Russell sued Clarke for unpaid salaries as officers of the company. Much of the litigation moved up and down the Massachusetts court system for several years, with parts of it reaching the state Supreme Court. When the insolvency court approved the final accounting in February 1902, creditors received about 35 percent of outstanding debts—most of the increase due to the recovery of $9,239 from the Second National Bank.[54]

During the pendency of his appeal for back wages, eventually successful, Very turned his attention to the manufacture of automobiles as well as bicycles at Russell's factory, and he and Russell changed the name of the business to the Warwick Automobile and Cycle Company. By 1901, the firm was ready to market the New Warwick, a gasoline powered model using a French internal-combustion motor developed and licensed by Marquis Jules-Abert de Dion and his partner Georges Bouton. Very contributed the designs for the running gear and traction control as well as a muffler, the latter patented in 1901, and he subsequently patented several other automobile-related devices, among them a starting mechanism and a vehicle body. The company also offered both chainless and chain-driven bicycles for the 1901 season, with prices ranging from $75 to $35.[55]

Wesson continued to use the Warwick Avenue factory for a period of years, adding a separate building for weaving and stretching, as well as a sales office, and by 1911 had also leased the third floor to the Natick Underwear Company. Other owners exploited the factory's versatility throughout the twentieth century and early years of this century.

Aftermath

The manner of the Warwick company's dissolution also invites comparison to the Eagle and Keating firms. Specifically, the company's abrupt failure illuminates an important but shadowed corner of American bicycle history occupied by local investors who, either as earnest members of city boards of trade or simply opportunists, acquired controlling interests in fledgling companies and sped forward on the strength of an extraordinary invention. Whether civic-minded or not, they soon found themselves straining to keep pace with the industry's phenomenally rapid growth, or to adjust to its equally swift decline. Even granting that such owners commanded expertise in corporate management, held a healthy regard for balanced ledgers, and harbored the best of intentions (and Warwick's captains seem to have satisfied those criteria), the industry changed so dramatically from year to year during the decade of the 1890s that sterling business qualifications were not enough. Intimate knowledge of an increasingly complex and competitive trade also became necessary, including the ever-evolving design of bicycles; shifting demand; dependable access to raw materials, especially tubing; the extraordinary advances in specialized machine tools; efficient production systems; marketing strategies; and labyrinthine distribution networks vulnerable to manipulation by sales agents. Among the Springfield company's succession of managers before 1894, only George Chamberlain may have grasped the extent of those challenges, and he also may have been one of the first to suspect that George Warwick lacked the navigational interest or skills needed to guide the company profitably.

By contrast, if the founders of the Eagle concern also found themselves in unfamiliar territory, they confronted those limitations by merging with Torrington's business owners, who added bicycles to their orbit of companies turning out machine-tooled products. The gap between the manufacture of bicycles and the production of sewing-machine needles, spokes, and other bicycle parts in Torrington was not so great as the distance between bicycles and the manufacture of paper products or general publishing in Springfield, and owners of the Connecticut concern were in a far better position to monitor the bicycle industry's incessant shifts. If contrasts between the two companies remained veiled at the height of the bicycle boom, the industry's implacable decline soon made those differences starkly evident. Unlike the Warwick firm's sudden collapse forced by a single creditor, Torrington's owners avoided crippling debt and simply continued to build bicycles until profitability ended, converting their business to a related manufacturing sector at that point.

Moreover, invention played such a critical role in the bicycle's evolution during this period, and in so many ways, that those companies with the capacity to encourage innovation held an advantage, not only the prospects for marketing improved designs to outshine rivals, but also attracting talented machinists. And, as competition in the industry escalated, the quest for resourceful personnel intensified. Keating, for all his lack of financial acumen, nevertheless fostered a progressive outlook that provided continuity for his company, an attribute that the Springfield concern lacked after George Warwick resigned. Whatever Warwick may have been unable or unwilling to provide as corporate head, his talents as an inventor were clear, and whether different owners with a better understanding of the bicycle industry could have used his skills more strategically is a fair question.

Consistency in management became important in other ways, as well, and the company's difficulty in finding capable managers ultimately led to the hiring of Alpha Very, who allowed the lure of future profits to cloud decisions about the company's mountain of debt to a single creditor. True, Very may have followed practices common to the industry at the time, but not every company adhered to that trend, and unlike the owners of the Eagle concern, Bill, Hendrick, and Russell either were too far removed from the industry's complexities to provide useful insight, or just too inattentive—the latter likely so in Russell's case.

Granted, a complete picture of the firm's financial history is lacking because, unlike the Eagle concern, records of meetings of the shareholders and directors have not surfaced. In addition, the company seemed determined to withhold its production figures and financial standing from journalists, in stark contrast to the edifying drama that followed Keating's business from Westfield to Holyoke to Middletown; Keating's voluminous archive of correspondence with Arthur Garford also added clarity to the firm's financial tumult. Still, the schedule of assets and liabilities made public during the Warwick company's insolvency proceedings tells much of the story.

A fourth company, the Trinity Cycle Manufacturing Company in Keene, New Hampshire, enlarges this context of small or mid-sized bicycle manufacturers financed by local investors who, as did Warwick's owners, failed to anticipate the industry's sudden decline. Ironically, Keene's investors celebrated the founding of their company during the same month, November 1897, that Banigan's attachment foretold the Warwick firm's demise.

12

Wheel Works in Worcester and Keene

Worcester, Massachusetts, and Keene, New Hampshire

Worcester, located roughly midway between Boston and the clustered Connecticut River cities of Springfield, Chicopee, and Holyoke, developed into one of Massachusetts' principal industrial centers by encouraging trade with Providence via the Blackstone Canal and the Providence and Worcester Railroad, the latter partly usurping the corridor made profitable by the former. Worcester's various iron and steel works attracted numerous foundries and metal-working industries, including at least five bicycle manufacturers. When he began fabricating frames and parts for Yost and McCune's Springfield Roadster in 1885 or 1886, Iver Johnson likely became the city's first bicycle maker, and his Central Street shops also housed production of diamond frame safety-bicycles for John P. Lovell before Johnson moved to Fitchburg and continued production there. Johnson's brother-in-law, John C. Speirs, joined the trade in 1892, followed in 1895 by three other concerns, all of them short-lived: the Worcester Cycle Company, the Decker Cycle Company, and the Windle Cycle Company.[1]

Among buildings owned or occupied by those five firms, only the factory built by Speirs on Nebraska Street, today adapted to apartments, and the 1879 Salisbury Factory Building at 25 Union Street, an industrial loft leased by the Decker company for little more than a year, survive. The Worcester concern, which acquired the defunct Worcester Steel Works on Bloomingdale Road, long-since demolished, merged with the Middletown Cycle Company in Connecticut in 1896 and failed a year later. The Windle firm, which occupied shops (also gone) near the corner of Mann and Chandler Streets, succumbed in 1896 through no fault of its founder, racing champion Willie W. Windle, other than misplaced trust in the solvency of his financial backer. Investors from New Hampshire and a new owner, Frank T. Fowler, rechristened Windle's wheel the "Trinity" and moved the company to Keene, where a new factory stood ready for occupancy in November 1897, even as many bicycle companies had begun closing their doors—the Warwick concern prominently so.[2]

Windle was not the only champion cyclist to give Worcester a lofty place in cycling history. When Louis "Birdie" Munger, also a talented racer, sold his interest in the Munger Cycle Manufacturing Company in Indianapolis and moved east in the fall of 1895 to manage the Worcester Cycle Company, he took with him a sixteen-year-old Black American understudy, Marshall Walter Taylor, who in 1899 would become the American

Figure 96. After Iver Johnson moved from Worcester to Fitchburg in 1891, his brother-in-law, John C. Speirs, established a wood-frame machine shop and foundry at the southeasterly corner of Nebraska and Winona Streets, not far from the city's commercial center. In 1892, he obtained financial assistance from Worcester industrialist Horace H. Bigelow and formed the Speirs Manufacturing Company to produce bicycles and bicycle parts in a factory built by the company that year opposite the foundry. Courtesy Lyman and Merrie Wood Museum of Springfield History, Springfield, MA.

sprint champion and also world champion, breaking numerous world records in the process. In Worcester, Major Taylor, as he is best known, found opportunities to compete in a vigorous cycling city where racial hostility was not as overt as in Indianapolis. He joined the all–Black Albion Cycle Club, one of at least ten local bicycle clubs, and began the 1896 racing season with a sixth-place finish in the *Worcester Telegram* Trophy Race, a ten-mile road circuit through city streets and an extravaganza observed by tens of thousands of spectators. That race and its course are historically significant to cycling because Taylor and other members of the Albion Club competed on integrated terms with White cyclists, giving Taylor an early opportunity to measure his abilities against those of the country's best racers.[3]

Speirs Manufacturing Company

John Cherry Speirs, born in 1858 to a large Worcester family with eight children, developed into a machinist of inventive disposition and a businessman of considerable resilience. Some of his early tutelage may have come from Iver Johnson, who in 1868 married Speirs' older sister, Mary Elizabeth Speirs. Although little is known about Speirs' education or his relationship with Johnson, the latter's good reputation and family connections benefited Speirs on several occasions, and the two men became linked in business matters, whether by plan or circumstance.

When Johnson moved from Worcester to Fitchburg during the summer of 1891, Speirs already had begun to fill the void Johnson left by establishing his own business that spring, the John C. Speirs Company, with a wood-frame machine shop and foundry at the southeasterly corner of Nebraska and Winona Streets (the latter is Envelope Terrace today). Soon after, January 1892, Speirs and a group of investors also organized the Speirs Manufacturing Company for the purpose of producing bicycles and other mechanical devices. Financial backing for the venture, capitalized at $75,000, came from Horace H. Bigelow, a wealthy shoe manufacturer, inventor, real estate developer, and owner of the Worcester and Shrewsbury Railroad, who also had sold the Central Street factory to Iver Johnson and Martin Bye in 1875. Bigelow became president; Irving E. Bigelow, a son, treasurer; and Eben F. Thompson, company clerk. Speirs managed factory production, all the while continuing to oversee work in his foundry.[4]

Construction of the three-story, brick bicycle factory along Nebraska Street advanced during the summer of 1892 and, upon completion, typified standard mill construction, although wall piers are more closely spaced than on many factories from that era. Tall window openings fill the entire spandrel walls, and windows on the first two stories are capped by segmentally-arched lintels sprung with three header-courses of brick; granite lintels placed directly beneath the cornice crown the third story windows. A heavy granite-slab stringcourse provides a sill for the elevated first floor, rising above a high water-table, and divides the first story from basement piers and flanking rectangular windows directly below that granite course. Stubby, quarter-round brackets mounted on the wall piers support the cornice and the flat roof's overhang, and protruding floor-beam anchor bolts are tightened against the wall piers with circular plates on the front and rear elevations. The factory complex also included an attached boiler room and a separate, one story, brick building for brazing. Speirs then filled the factory with machinery acquired from the Bullard Repeating Arms Company in Springfield, founded by James Bullard, long the superintendent of the Springfield Sewing Machine Company, thus adding another strand to the complex web joining manufacturers of arms, sewing machines, and bicycles.[5]

The company offered a safety model for $90 that first year and followed soon after with production of a tandem. Speirs also adopted Johnson's practice of fabricating bicycle parts for other companies,

Figure 97. The company's catalog for 1896 offered a variety of parts as well as several bicycle models finished in black enamel with nickel-plated bright parts. Courtesy Connecticut Valley Historical Museum.

notably hubs and pedals, and he diversified by producing sporting goods, supplying the Lovell Arms and Cycle Company's branch store in Worcester. Following Johnson's death in 1895, Speirs assisted Benjamin Lovell by equipping and managing the company's new factory in Portland, Maine, and in return Lovell promised to buy bicycles manufactured by Speirs. That contract likely aggravated the growing fractures between the Lovell and Johnson concerns, and may have strained Speirs' relationship with the Johnsons as well. Ironically, though, just as Lovell's disagreements with Frederic Johnson ended in litigation, so too did Lovell's contract with Speirs, who sued unsuccessfully for $15,000 in services and machinery supplied to the Lovell factory. Separately, Speirs' desire to manufacture bicycle components may have included partially finished parts, and in 1896 he executed a year-long contract to produce forgings for the Union Drop Forge Company, the latter agreeing to supply materials; enforcement of that contract also landed in court but more profitably for Speirs.[6]

Even before Johnson's death, Speirs had begun tinkering with the design of bicycle components, and in March 1895 he secured a patent for an adjustable bicycle saddle with springs. He also patented improvements to adjustable wrenches that same month, assigning rights to his corporation and securing a supply contract with the Pope Manufacturing Company. Encouraged by the bicycle industry's

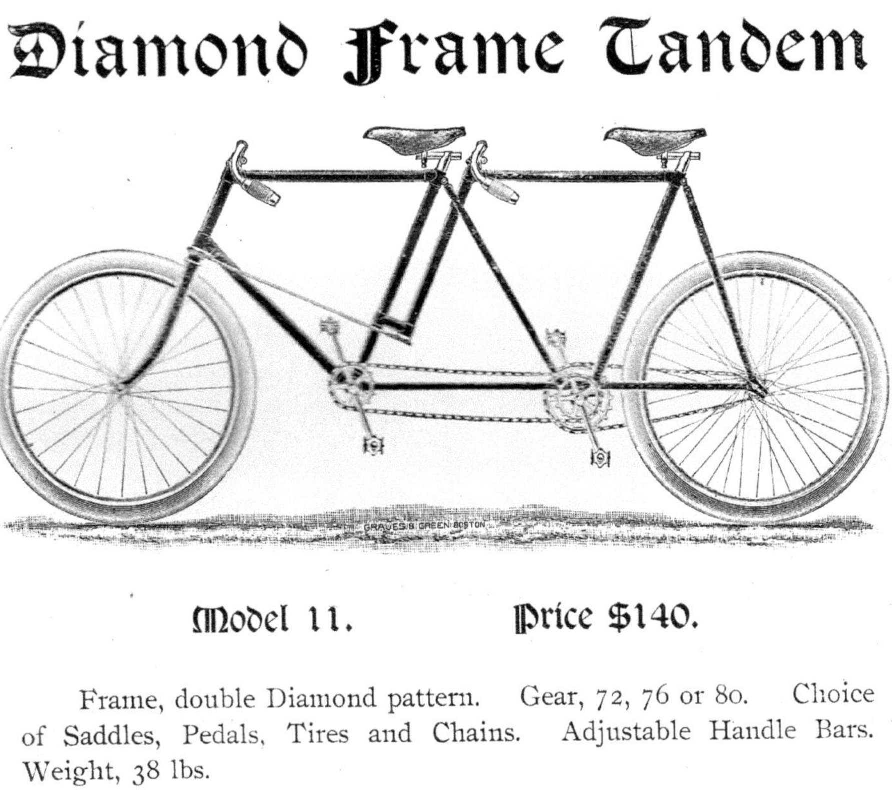

Figure 98. The 1896 catalog offered roadster models for men and women, priced competitively at $100 and $85, respectively, and a tandem bicycle with oddly designed double diamond frames connected indirectly at the front seat post and rear headset. Courtesy Lyman and Merrie Wood Museum of Springfield History, Springfield, MA.

success, Speirs and Bigelow enlarged the factory during the summer of 1897, adding more than 100 feet to its length at a cost of $8,000. The design is identical to that of the main block and creates an impressive, uniform façade along Nebraska Street.[7]

However, Speirs' optimism proved to be fleeting, and less than a year later, April 1898, he filed a voluntary petition for insolvency, applicable to his foundry and machine shop business, with liabilities of $90,000 and assets of only $33,000. The long list of creditors included banks, steel and iron suppliers, machine manufacturers, and another maker of bicycle parts and accessories, the Elastic Tip Company of Boston, claiming the single largest debt of almost $24,000; the list also included a $12,000 loan from a family member, likely another older sister, Jane. Speirs conveyed all his property to two trustees, and less than a month later, the Speirs Manufacturing Company assigned all its property to trustees for the benefit of the company's creditors, who unfortunately stood in line behind investors holding bonds issued in the amount of $50,000 and secured by a mortgage against the property.[8]

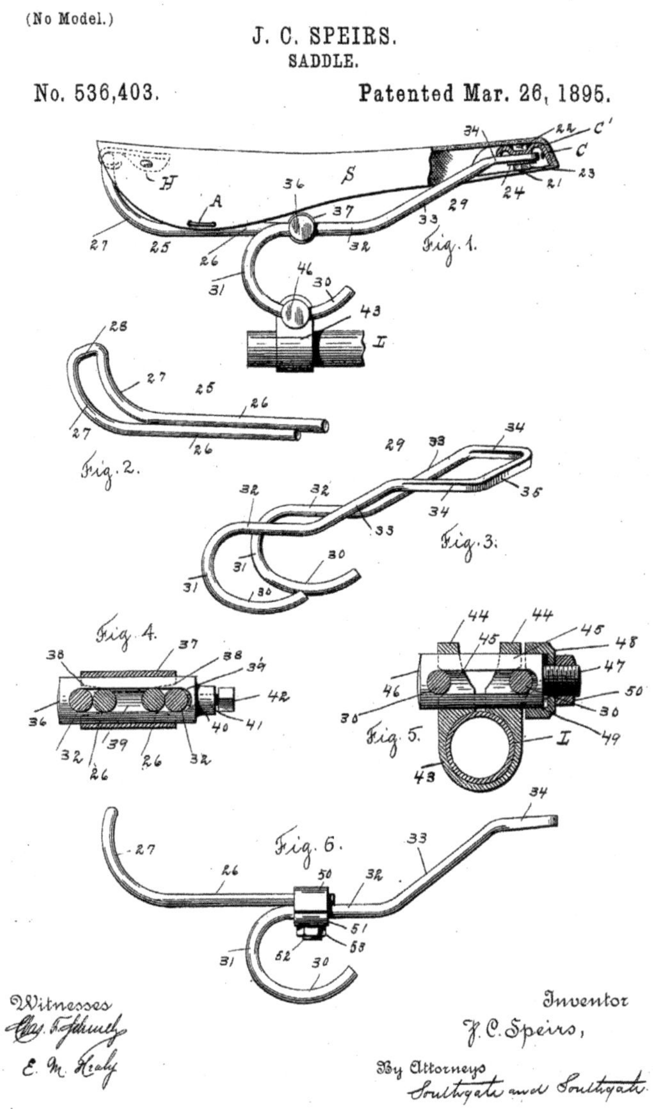

Figure 99. John Speirs secured patents for an impressive number of inventions, many of them related to motor carriages. He won two of his earliest patents in 1895, one for an adjustable bicycle saddle and the other for an adjustable wrench, the latter leading to a contract to supply the Pope Manufacturing Company with wrenches for bicycle tool kits. United States Patent Office.

In February 1899, Horace Bigelow rescued his corporation by investing $70,000 to acquire the factory and its fixtures. He then promptly reconveyed the property to the company, and between 1899 and 1901 the firm resumed the manufacture of specialized bicycle parts including frames, posts, cones, cups, pedals, hubs, and wheel rims, as well as offering to build bicycles to the order of any purchaser. During that same period, the company began fabricating hubs, wheel rims, stampings, and screw machine work for motor carriages, suggesting that the company also had resumed some form of contractual agreement with Speirs, who in August 1899 conveyed his foundry and machine shop to the Locomobile Company of America.[9]

Despite his financial collapse, John Speirs joins Iver Johnson as Worcester's two most important contributors to bicycle manufacturing. That remains true despite Speirs being overshadowed at the time by the Worcester and Windle concerns, each of which existed for little more than a year but generated much greater publicity because of their association, respectively, with well-known racers Birdie Munger and Willie Windle. With its well-publicized store in Worcester, too, the Lovell concern was far more visible, even though Iver Johnson fabricated that company's bicycles until construction of the former's plant in Portland, Maine, in 1895. Explanation for lack of recognition given to Speirs may have rested on his awareness that success as a parts supplier hinged on maintaining neutrality (if not anonymity) among competing bicycle builders. In addition, Speirs seems to have had a knack for keeping journalists at bay, a policy he may have learned from Johnson, and construction of the Nebraska Street factory progressed very quietly, in sharp contrast to the comprehensive news accounts and descriptions of newly erected bicycle factories in other cities.

Another factor also may have dictated the company's course of development, namely Speirs' fascination with motorized vehicles. Even at the height of the bicycle craze, 1895, Speirs began working with a partner to develop an electric vehicle, and he continued to experiment with the design of various components for automobiles. Between 1900 and 1904 he secured

Figure 100. In 1897, Speirs extended the length of the factory by more than one hundred feet, but by then the bicycle industry's decline had gathered momentum, and he filed for bankruptcy the following year. Worcester financier Horace Bigelow rescued the company and continued to build specialized bicycle parts as well as parts for motor carriages until 1901, when biscuit manufacturer Cartwright Borden Company purchased the factory. Today the versatile, well-preserved building is called the Biscuit Lofts. Photo by the author.

patents for numerous inventions including a small steam engine, hydrocarbon burner, tube sheet for boilers, engine frame, and a universal joint. He assigned several of those patents to the Locomobile Company, located in Bridgeport Connecticut, where he eventually managed the company's factory. However, he assigned the 1904 patent for a universal joint, developed with partner Harry E. Dey, to the Autocar Company based in Ardmore, a Philadelphia suburb where Speirs served as plant manager for a company that eventually specialized in heavy commercial vehicles and survives today. He later filled a similar role for the American Motors Corporation, the origins of which can be traced to Thomas Jeffery's purchase of the Sterling Cycle Works in Kenosha, Wisconsin (see Chapter 1), where he began building Rambler automobiles rather than bicycles.[10]

Much later, 1920, Speirs became founder and president of the National Chain Motor Service Corporation, created to provide a nationwide chain of high-grade motor service shops. In that company's prospectus, Speirs offered an impressive resume but omitted any reference to his bicycle days; eventually, he retired to Ardmore. Back in Worcester in 1901, Horace Bigelow sold his factory to biscuit makers, the Cartwright Borden Company, which evolved into the New England Biscuit Company—underscoring the breadth of versatility for standard mill construction. Today, the factory is known colloquially as the Biscuit Lofts.[11]

Decker Cycle Company

If Worcester's other bicycle manufacturers merely overshadowed the contributions of Iver Johnson and John Speirs, Decker bicycles remained practically invisible. In the spring of 1894, Worcester machinist and inventor William Lloyd Decker applied for a patent to protect his design for a crank-shaft and front sprocket with eccentrics placed forward of the crank shaft and two sets of compound levers or arms to turn the crank shaft, one short and fixed to the crank-shaft and the other longer with sliding connections. Power could be applied to either lever arm, thus providing the equivalent of a very large gear on the front sprocket if desired. With financial support by a wealthy lumber company owner from Worcester, William H. Sawyer, Decker incorporated the Decker Cycle Company, and after the United States Patent Office accepted his novel design a year later, he assigned the patent to his company in September 1895, which by then occupied the upper floors of an industrial loft.[12]

Previously that spring, April 1895, Decker had applied for another patent refining the design of his crank and pedal to allow riders to adjust the pedals along a slotted crank arm to achieve either concentric or eccentric revolutions, thus either increasing leverage during the downstroke and correspondingly decreasing leverage on the upstroke, or reversing that leverage. In September 1895, he sought a third patent for a chain-adjustment device, and in March 1896 he applied for a patent for an adjustable clamp to support saddles. Patent officials granted all three applications between November 1896 and August 1897, but by that time Decker's business had collapsed. Conclusively, in August 1896, a day before the company faced a foreclosure sale, a fire swept through the floors occupied by his shops, destroying machinery and stock.[13]

The pattern of inventor seeking investor to launch a new bicycle business, resulting in the construction of new factories, occurred frequently during the 1890s. However, Decker's business links the bicycle industry with late nineteenth-century refinements for another building type fundamental to manufacturing: industrial lofts. As American commerce and industry expanded during the middle of the nineteenth century, multi-story urban buildings providing commercial store space at ground level and several rentable floors above for light manufacturing offered a practical way to accommodate industrial work on a measured scale—often the next step for promising inventors who had begun experimenting in neighborhood shops. In dense commercial districts, concern for adequate light, vertical circulation of materials, working space that minimized columns, distribution of power, floor load capacity, and resistance to fire all remained challenges to the design of lofts, many of them long and narrow and filling city lots front to rear. As improvements in the efficiency of steam engines after the Civil War led to smaller and less costly engines, industrial lofts became a viable form of real estate investment, with the two, industry and loft building, mutually dependent. Lofts also evolved into a very efficient form, providing versatile space suitable for diverse work activities.

In Worcester, Stephen Salisbury II and Stephen Salisbury III, scions of one of the city's wealthy families, built a series of industrial lofts in the vicinity of Lincoln Square, a short distance north of the city's central business district, precipitating a trend in the city's growth. Decker's company filled the upper floors of a five-story brick loft at 25 Union Street, built by the Salisburys in 1879. An exterior elevator served all five floors, and a one-story engine house and two-story boiler plant provided power to the building.

Following the fire, Decker assigned his saddle clamp patent to John Abner Mead, a physician from Rutland Vermont, who became that city's mayor in 1893 and then governor in 1910. Mead later became president of the Howe Scale Company in Rutland, which manufactured bicycles for a brief period during the late 1890s, and Decker may have relocated there.[14]

Windle Cycle Company and Trinity Cycle Manufacturing Company

On the evening of November 12, 1897, the Monadnock Cycle Club and the New Hampshire Good Roads Association staged a grand celebration to dedicate a just-finished factory—the Charles A. Jones Block—for the city of Keene's newest industry, the Trinity Cycle Manufacturing Company. Celebrants convened on the factory's third floor where seating to accommodate 350 people quickly filled, leaving standing room only for another 150 enthusiasts. The festivities opened with John Philip Sousa's rousing new quickstep, "Stars and Stripes Forever," followed by dancing to the music of a fourteen-piece orchestra. Newspaper accounts described the event as the largest ball in the city's history, reflecting the aura of optimism that surrounded the bicycle's bonanza years. Keene investors had moved quickly to snatch a share of that prosperity and were poised to compete for the 1898 season. Brimming with confidence, merry makers danced into the early morning, blissfully unaware of the fractures already surfacing in the country's bicycle industry.[15]

Windle Cycle Company. The story of Keene's factory began in Worcester during the summer of 1895 with local cycling hero, Willie Windle, who grew up on a family farm in nearby West Millbury. In July that year, the twenty-five-year-old Windle announced plans to manufacture bicycles based on a prototype he developed after retiring from championship racing in 1893. The white enameled model that he unveiled to a select group of reporters had been built by another successful racer, Peter J. Berlo, using Windle's designs and drawings.[16]

Worcester offered familiar terrain to Windle and became a logical place for his new bicycle business. As a youth he had ridden a high-wheel ordinary into the city from West Millbury to attend school, and he first competed on a harness racing track at the city's fairgrounds. Although his new business faced local competition from Munger and Speirs, he benefited from popularity generated by his racing career. In addition, he maintained a close friendship with Robert Keating, whose ventures in starting a new company would have been encouraging for Windle.[17]

Optimistic about business prospects, Windle obtained financial support from a business partner who chose to remain anonymous to the public. By early August 1895, Windle had negotiated a five-year lease in a recently-built, two-story, frame mill with an adjoining, one-story power house and shed. The building provided sufficient space to manufacture an estimated five thousand bicycles yearly, and Windle planned to begin production by September. He assumed the role of superintendent and hired Charles R. Moules as general manager and sales agent.[18]

Unfortunately for Windle, the silence of his partner, a textile manufacturer from Millbury, Fred A. Lapham, failed to shield the latter's insolvency, and the ensuing events that fall and winter reveal the challenges of entering the booming bicycle industry. In January 1896, Lapham's creditors, John Speirs among them, forced an assignment of his assets to trustees, temporarily ending Windle's connection with the six-month old business. In addition to the bicycle company, Lapham's property included a woolen mill in Millbury, and early in April the trustees conveyed both assets to two investors from Keene, New Hampshire—Alfred T. Batchelder, a lawyer, financier, president of a manufacturing firm, and former Keene mayor, and Elisha F. Lane, the president of a local bank and owner of commercial buildings on Keene's Main Street. The new owners asked Windle to manage the bicycle factory until July.[19]

That spring Batchelder and Lane retained a Worcester architectural firm, Fuller, Delano and Frost, to design a three-story factory in Keene. One of Lapham's creditors, however, challenged the sale, and Lapham was judged insolvent in court proceedings in April. Windle testified about the terms of his one-year partnership with Lapham, the latter supplying $20,000 and receiving an annual return of 6 percent, plus 60 percent of profits; Windle collected a salary of $84 per month. Although the extraordinary earnings generated by the bicycle industry during this era attracted many investors, the undercapitalized partnership agreement with Lapham illustrates a common problem caused by financial backers seeking substantial returns on investment rather than company growth.[20]

Frank T. Fowler Manufacturing Company. The trustees' sale survived challenge, and the Windle Cycle Company endured a precarious existence during the next six months while Batchelder and Lane sought a buyer capable of managing the bicycle business. On November 19 the front pages of Worcester newspapers heralded the arrival of a thirty-year-old Chicagoan, Frank T. Fowler, as the Windle firm's new owner. Founder of the Fowler Cycle Manufacturing Company, the Chicago boomer was a charter member and vice president of the Chicago Racing Wheelmen Club, devoted entirely to road and track racing. Although not a successful racer himself, Fowler had ridden in club events, including Chicago's famed Pullman Road Race, and the bicycle he designed offered a distinctive truss frame that had gained a creditable reputation among racers—enough to support a branch office in Boston. Although Fowler had sold his fledgling firm in January 1896 under a cloud of conflict, the same month that Windle's company failed, the former's qualifications looked good enough for Keene's investors.[21]

If Batchelder and Lane inquired, Fowler probably cited disagreements with his financial partners as explanation for severing his stake in the Chicago business. Although he had remained as company manager, that arrangement soon deteriorated into litigation in October 1896. By then, Fowler had begun to look for other opportunities, and late that month he agreed to purchase Birdie Munger's company in Indianapolis, which had been assigned to a receiver in June that year. Fowler planned to move the Munger concern to Chicago and to compete with his former business, but two weeks into November, Fowler and the receiver failed to agree on a final price and the sale dissolved. More likely, Fowler had already learned about the Windle concern and had assessed it as a better opportunity. A week later he quickly reached an agreement with Batchelder and Lane, vowing to make the business profitable, and began enlarging the Windle factory, convincing several of his former employees to join him.[22]

During their brief control of the Windle concern, Batchelder and Lane understood the need for experienced management in an industry unfamiliar to them. Yet both were able businessmen, probably aware of the extraordinary profits being generated by bicycle manufacturers,

Figure 101. In November 1896, Chicagoan Frank T. Fowler purchased the Windle Cycle Company of Worcester, Massachusetts, and formed the Frank T. Fowler Manufacturing Company. Undisclosed to the Worcester community, the purchase agreement included an option clause requiring Fowler to move the business to Keene, New Hampshire, if two of that city's investors, Alfred Batchelder and Elisha Lane, secured sufficient public funds to build a new factory by the end of 1896. Batchelder and Lane succeeded in raising $40,000, and in January 1897, the trio changed the name of the business to the Trinity Cycle Manufacturing Company, and in June of that year Fowler negotiated an agreement with Keene businessman Charles A. Jones to build a factory three blocks from Keene's Central Square and lease it to the company for ten years. Keene's City Council also agreed to forego property taxes for ten years. Worcester architect Walter Nourse designed the building. Courtesy Historical Society of Cheshire County, NH.

and sensed an opportunity. Unknown to Worcester journalists, sale of the Windle company contained an option clause requiring Fowler to move the business to Keene if funds sufficient to build a new factory, $40,000, were secured by December 8, 1896. Batchelder and other Keene businessmen succeeded in selling subscriptions to the new company, despite attempts by Worcester residents and by Fowler himself to purchase the option. In addition, the company's local investors convinced the Keene City Council to forego property taxes for ten years. On December 12, the Frank T. Fowler Manufacturing Company (similarly named but a different entity than the Chicago concern) obtained a charter as a New Hampshire corporation, with Fowler, Batchelder, and several local mill-owners as shareholders.[23]

Fowler traveled to Keene that week and began planning a new factory, hoping for occupancy by July 1, 1897. The company convened its inaugural stockholders' meeting, electing Fowler president and selecting the name "Trinity" for its bicycles, which would be assembled in the Worcester factory during the spring. They also discussed desirable features for the new factory, principally in terms of dimensions sufficient to accommodate 750 employees.[24]

Trinity Cycle Manufacturing Company. The rapid pace of events in November and December 1896 slowed during the first six months of the following year as Fowler turned his attention to the Worcester shop. In January 1897, directors changed the corporate name to Trinity Cycle Manufacturing Company; and increased capital stock from $100,000 to $140,000. Fowler made key staff appointments; commissioned the design and printing of a catalog for the 1897 season; and began advertising in a newsletter format he had used successfully at Chicago bicycle shows, substituting a new title, *The Trinity Chimes* in the masthead. He also made several additional trips to Keene that spring to view possible sites for the new plant. During a June visit he met Charles A. Jones, owner of a city block near Keene's Central Square not far from Jones's own carriage business. The following day, June 18, Jones agreed to construct a factory, retaining ownership but leasing exclusively to Fowler's company for ten years.[25]

Charles A. Jones Block. Fowler retained his own architect, Worcester's Walter Nourse, to develop plans and specifications for the factory, although he and Jones completed most of the design themselves during the twenty-four hours it took to reach an agreement. As they conceived the building, it would be a three-story, L-shaped, brick block with principal facades on three streets. The elevation facing Church Street would provide space for a store, with offices on the second floor above; the longest elevation (165 feet) fronted Wells Street; and employees would enter from shop doors on the Railroad Street façade. A sprinkler system would be installed, and a second, smaller, fireproof building with metal roof would be used for brazing and enameling. George A. Gordon bid successfully to oversee the building's construction; G.F. Ball supplied the brick; Charles E. Woods won the contract to build the walls; ground-breaking began by July 20; and bricklaying started August 23.[26]

Conceived specifically for the manufacture of bicycles by the Trinity company, the factory's design represents a collaborative effort by Nourse, Jones, and Fowler and is cycling's best-preserved example of an industrial loft—well documented by the city's local newspaper, the *Keene Evening Sentinel*. Plans balance the competing requirements of structural strength and maximum light by consolidating brick bearing walls into rows of piers spaced to support floor beams, and the regiments of piers add to the building's visual order—especially important for an industrial building located within view of the city's Central Square. Gordon and Wood used granite for windowsills but capped windows with segmental brick arches and added decorative brick corbelling below the cornice and below the third-story windows. Above wide entrances for doorways and loading docks, the design called for steel beam or plate girder spans. Nourse centered floor beams of Georgia pine (14 by 10 inches) at eight-foot intervals, and pinned three-inch, tongue-and-groove floorboards to those beams. Builders also spiked the ground floor planking to stringers soaked in creosote and covered by tarred paper with a coating of hot tar.[27]

The anticipated arrival of the bicycle business in town provided incentive for the Keene Gas Light Company to expand, and less than a week after Jones and Fowler publicized their agreement, the light company announced the construction of a new plant to supply electrical power and light to the factory. Editors of the *Keene Sentinel* applauded arrival of the new bicycle business and chronicled the speed with which the building was assembled. By early October, Woods's crew had finished the brickwork, but they discovered that one of the piers had settled slightly, causing minor delays because a steel span required replacement. By the end of that month, however, the factory stood ready for occupancy. Between mid–October and early November workers erected the second building, a two-story brick block, nearly square, to be partly occupied by the cycle business. The company's production system also started to take shape during October and early November when machinery from the Worcester factory began arriving. By late November, company employees had started handwork on the frames for 1898 models, and machinery began operating in mid–December.[28]

Fowler had invested in traditional overhead mill shafting to distribute mechanical power at the Worcester plant, and it made economic sense to reuse it. In the Keene factory, however, electrical motors turned the shafting, marking an advance over steam. Separate, ten-horsepower motors controlled the shafting in each of two areas: the tool-making department and the brazing room; a single thirty-horsepower motor governed the shafting in the lower-floor machine shop; and three motors operated on the third floor. Polishers, buffers, and nickel-plate workers toiled upstairs, either on the second or third floors—the latter free of partitions. Steam heat circulated through overhead coils suspended by chains, and the company installed both incandescent and electric-arc lights. Esty automatic sprinklers offered protection against fire; and separate gas furnaces served the brazing and enameling units housed in the adjacent building.[29]

Fowler's Financial Finagling. By this time Keene's sprint to secure a place in the bicycle industry had taken a surprising turn. At the company's annual shareholders' meeting in late September 1897, Batchelder informed the company that debts owed by Fowler to Chicago concerns had forced his retirement from the Keene business. Batchelder agreed to cover those debts in exchange for Fowler's interest in the Trinity firm, thus removing any exposure to Fowler's creditors but also leaving the plant without an experienced hand in the manufacture of bicycles. In addition, Fowler had established a poor record of production at the Worcester shop for both Windle and Trinity models, thus squandering critical sales opportunities when bicycles required replacement parts.[30]

Unfortunately, the murky financial picture that emerged was fairly common for the period and occasionally tarnished the public's image of the bicycle industry as a shining example of American ingenuity. Had Batchelder and Lane investigated Fowler's record more carefully, they would have discovered a troubling pattern. In 1891 at the age of twenty-five, he had joined the Moffat Cycle Company in Chicago, founded that year by George D. Moffat from New Orleans. Fowler

Figure 102. Church Street façade, Charles A. Jones Block, Keene, New Hampshire. Designed specifically to accommodate the manufacture of bicycles, the factory is one of cycling history's best-preserved examples of an industrial loft. The factory's architect designed space for a retail bicycle shop on this elevation, with the company's offices above, and workers also erected a small adjacent building to house the enameling shop. Contractor George A. Gordan oversaw construction, and mason Charles E. Woods built the brick walls. Groundbreaking occurred on July 20, 1897; bricklaying began on August 23; and the factory stood ready for occupancy by late October of that year. Photo by the author.

served as secretary and treasurer, and his father-in-law, Mark Hill, helped finance the venture. However, Hill very soon obtained judgments against Moffat, forcing the firm into insolvency, and he then bought the company's assets at auction in August 1892, for a small percentage of the inventory and accounts receivable; Fowler quickly purchased all the fixtures in the retail store for a nominal sum, and reporters for cycling's trade journals harshly criticized both Hill and Fowler.[31]

By November of that year a newly formed Hill Cycle Manufacturing Company, successor to Moffat's concern, introduced the Fowler safety bicycle. Hill assigned supervision of the firm to Fowler, who at age twenty-seven became one of the industry's youngest general managers. The following summer, 1893, Moffat sued the Hill family and Fowler, claiming a conspiracy to destroy his business, but he never managed to regain control of his company. Less than a year later, April 1894, Fowler left the Hill concern, perhaps weary of his father-in-law, but Hill died about two weeks later and Fowler resumed management of the business until establishing his own company late in 1894 or in 1895, aided financially by his mother-in-law. Then, in January 1896, editors of the *Wheel and Cycling Trade Review* reported the sale of Fowler's interest in his firm for the sum of $200,000. The aborted acquisition of the Munger firm and the hasty purchase of the Windle concern followed.[32]

Fowler's explanation to Batchelder about his reasons for returning to Chicago may have been partly true. Late in October 1897, the Fowler Cycle Manufacturing Company in Chicago failed and assigned all its assets to a trustee. Conceivably, Fowler had remained financially obligated as part of the terms of agreement regarding the sale of his Chicago business, exposing him to the company's creditors. Yet nothing that transpired after Fowler's return to Chicago suggests that those debts, if they existed, presented a quandary. Instead, the most plausible explanation is that Fowler once again intended to purchase an insolvent company at minimal cost, a profitable strategy he had adopted previously in Chicago and Worcester. Any doubts about Fowler's intentions regarding either the failed Chicago company or the Trinity concern vanish when, early in January 1898, he appeared at a court-conducted auction sale and, for the sum of $25,000 paid in cash, repurchased the company he had sold two years before for $200,000, a concern that the court still valued between $100,000 and $186,000.[33]

Those events in Chicago place the earlier transactions in Worcester and Keene in a clearer light. From the outset Fowler almost certainly intended to build value quickly in the Windle concern and then take profits. When viewed in that manner, the assets raised by Keene investors to charter a new company and to erect a factory, a 62 percent increase in space, became a windfall to Fowler, thus explaining the absence of any serious dispute about the move from Worcester to Keene. The city's property tax waiver, granted on the assumption that the bicycle company would be erecting its own factory, also illuminates the financial contriving. In June 1897, when Fowler returned to the council with a request that the tax abatement be transferred to the property owned by Charles Jones, his request was met with cynicism by several members. Yet Fowler explained that under the terms of the lease with Jones, the bicycle company would be required to pay property taxes, and thus the situation remained identical to the earlier understanding.[34]

Some council members expressed doubts about the need for Fowler to solicit public investment in the company if his past business had been so successful and suggested that the company post a bond guaranteeing profits and employment. Fowler reminded the council that he had tried to buy the option from Batchelder and Lane and would have been content to stay in Worcester. Under the circumstances, however, the sincerity of that claim seems unlikely. In the end, the council relented to the ten-year abatement, but specified that it be applied only to those parts of the factory used by the bicycle concern. And, the new firm climbed in book value, at least enough to convince Batchelder to buy Fowler's interest.[35]

Trinity Bicycles. With the new bicycle factory rapidly taking shape, but nobody to build bicycles, Batchelder turned to Reynold Janney to serve as superintendent. Janney, a Quaker from Martinsville, Ohio, who had established his own small business, the Janney Bicycle Company, proved to be both mechanically gifted and capable. He began a career as a high-school teacher in Chillicothe, Ohio, and later received an appointment as a mathematics and astronomy professor at nearby Wilmington College. Tempted by manufacturing and mechanical engineering, he eventually moved to Westborough, Massachusetts, and there began designing bicycle parts, including pedals and dust-proof ball-bearing casings used on both pedals and hubs, obtaining several patents in the process. He continued to invent after relocating to Keene and remained with the Trinity concern throughout its short history.[36]

By all available evidence, the company's New Hampshire owners built bicycles that competed in quality and price with those produced by industry leaders. True, Fowler's apparent intention to build company value quickly, coupled with production problems at the Worcester plant in 1897, cast at least some doubt on the quality of the first Trinity bicycles. True, as well, although the company's catalog for 1897, clearly Fowler's contribution, offered very detailed descriptions of components and stressed manufacturing technology, those circulars must be considered as advertisements. In addition, as new entrants to a competitive industry, the company would have been intent upon investing no more than necessary to begin production and generate revenue, leaving matters of expansion to the future. Yet Trinity's owners likely priced every part available from specialty manufacturers and used a number of components produced elsewhere, assuring competitive quality. These included spokes from the Excelsior Needle Company in Torrington, Connecticut; laminated wood rims assembled by the Boston Wood Rim Company in Bedford, Massachusetts, and favored by many American bicycle companies for their elasticity and lightness; tires, mostly single tube, from several different manufacturers including the Hartford Rubber Works; and Perry-Humber chains produced in Birmingham, England. The company probably purchased ball bearings and handlebars from parts suppliers as well.

Trinity bicycles entered the market just in time to join the country's debate about the merits of chainless bicycles driven by a beveled-gear and shaft mechanism that would eventually prove less efficient than chain drive. Janney argued adamantly in favor of chain drive, principally for its adaptability to any misalignment of working parts, and in February 1898 editors of the monthly journal *Outing*, which evaluated yearly models, included a lengthy statement from Trinity's designers, citing it as a very clear explanation about the merits of chain drive.[37]

Among the bicycle's many components, Trinity advertised the use of cold-drawn steel in its tubing, probably acquired from the Pope concern in Hartford. However, other means of fabricating seamless tubing had gained wider use, and the company probably selected from available supplies at times of scarcity during the production season. As did most other bicycle companies, Trinity offered several different models at varying prices, and the grades and gauges of tubing may have varied among those models.[38]

To increase the strength of frame

connections for its racing and roadster models, priced respectively at $125.00 and $100.00 at the start of the 1897 season, as well as to minimize brazing at the joints, the company used swaged tubes. The company also used internal drop-forged lugs in flush frame connections and at principal points of strain, rejecting the less-expensive, stamped sheet-metal components and extensive brazing being introduced on cheaper bicycles, improving the appearance of frames in the process. The company also used nickel plating on forks, providing a contrast to the black, maroon, imperial blue, olive green, or canary yellow enamel offered on the 1897 roadster, which weighed about twenty-five pounds; the racer for that year, at nineteen pounds, arrived only in imperial blue with maroon and orange side stripes.[39]

Several distinguishing features on Trinity bicycles suggest thoughtful efforts to improve standard designs, seemingly to facilitate cleaning or repairs. For example, the bored-steel rear hub is notable for its spoke flanges that accommodated straight-headed spokes, eliminating the bent-angle spokes used on many bicycles and permitting spoke replacement without removal of the wheel. After 1897 the company also promoted Janney's dust-proof designs for bearing cups and cones. The assembly of crank hangar, cranks, and crank axle is also notable. Each single crank and half-axle were drop-forged as a single piece and then joined together in the middle of the crank hanger by a lap joint within a threaded steel sleeve, the ends of which form the bearing cones. A very similar, patented design had been introduced on Pope's Columbia models in 1895, using a V-joint. Ease of disassembly for cleaning or repair appears to have been the design objective, eliminating the use of force to extract the cranks and sparing damage to the ball bearings in the process; a key inserted from the bottom of the hanger held the sleeve in place during removal of cranks and axle-halves. Toward that same end company machinists also fitted each crank hanger with ball bearing retainers to prevent loss of the bearings when the cranks and axle halves were removed. For purely aesthetic distinction, Trinity's designers fashioned a forged front sprocket with a five-point star and perimeter rim pierced by a ring of decorative circles, reducing weight as well as adding visual appeal.[40]

By the late 1890s, technological advances in bicycle design had slowed from their frenetic pace over the preceding years and manufacturers had begun to specialize in standardized parts, thus leveling the overall cost of building bicycles across the industry. To some extent, these economic developments aided smaller companies attempting to secure dependable local or regional markets, and owners of the Trinity concern may have calculated that New Hampshire dealers would be loyal to their Keene business. Among the very few other concerns or shops competing for that loyalty, a small firm in Nashua, the Corson Cycle Manufacturing Company, likely posed little challenge.[41]

Steep Descent. Impressive new building aside, Keene's investors had unwittingly entered the bicycle industry at precisely the moment when declining public interest collided head on with overproduction fueled by years of clamoring demand. Yet judging from available accounts, the owners and managers of the Trinity firm anticipated the 1898 production season about as judiciously as anyone could expect, given their inexperience and considering the circumstances that were just then becoming apparent. Keeping pace with the rest of the industry, prices of the Trinity racer and roadster shown in the company's 1897 catalog dropped at the outset of the 1898 season. Miraculously, modest-sized orders continued to arrive, and the company also managed to secure a generous supply of tubing. Work at the factory remained steady during the first four months of 1898, with production increasing from fifteen to twenty bicycles per day in February to thirty per day in March and forty in April, requiring overtime. At the peak of production that spring, the company employed 150 workers.[42]

From the outset, Fowler had intended for Trinity to compete in Chicago, and its Keene owners wisely continued to engage that market as a hedge against regional competition, employing an agent, Charles Larson, who reported successful sales in western states that season. The company also expressed special pride in two tandem bicycles, one with nickel plating and the other in blue and white enamel, and the firm displayed both at a local shop before delivery. Although newspaper accounts of factory activity dwindle after the 1898 production season, that circumstance may reflect a lack of newsworthiness concerning daily quotas rather than declining sales. If the company began to face economic difficulties, the *Keene Sentinel* remained silent.[43]

A similar absence of articles about the factory during the early months of 1899 cannot be dismissed so easily. The company's catalog for that year offered the Trinity Special (models G and H for men and women, respectively) at $65.00, and the racer (Model I) for the same price. Two versions of a roadster (models J and K for men and women, respectively) sold for $50.00, with similar models (L and M) offered to the trade at $35.00. When invitations to submit purchase options to organizers of the American Bicycle Company trust circulated that spring, Trinity's owners probably complied, and editors of *Cycle Age and Trade Review* estimated annual production at 4,000 bicycles. However, negotiations never advanced very far, and although orders continued to arrive that summer, and bicycles continued to be

THE TRINITY TANDEM
(Diamond Frame)

Figure 103. The Trinity company commissioned the design and printing of a catalog for the 1897 season, adopting a newsletter format that Frank Fowler had used successfully at Chicago bicycle shows but substituting a new title, The Trinity *Chimes,* in the masthead. That season, the company offered several models, including a roadster and racer as well as a tandem, two of which—one in nickel and the other in blue and white enamel, stood on display in a local hardware shop before being shipped to buyers. Unlike the Speirs tandem, the Trinity model uses a pair of continuous cross tubes. Trinity Catalog (1897). Courtesy Hagley Museum and Library.

built, by October Trinity's owners faced an uncertain future. If a bright spot could be found that year in Keene, it may have been the perfection of an interchangeable wheel hub by Reynold Janney and company machinist Edward Little. The patented hub could be applied to any ordinary form of carriage or wagon axle to provide the wheel bearings essential for pneumatic tires, but without the cost of replacing axles. Little and Janney produced the hub at the Trinity shop as a separate business.[44]

Company owners seem to have confronted the industry's bleak prospects capably, and in December they hired three agents to scour the country for next year's orders. The firm also encouraged Janney to continue experimenting with automobiles, and on July 4, 1900, Janney introduced a new runabout built to his design, similar to a Corning road wagon but with a light, stiff frame of bicycle tubing and driven by a gasoline-fired steam engine placed beneath the foot board, with the boiler located below the carriage. A simple lever served as a steering mechanism. The road test that day wasn't trouble free, but Janney's inventive design nevertheless attracted attention, and early in 1901 Trinity's owners transferred the company to the Steamobile Company of America, organized as a Delaware corporation, which absorbed Trinity's factory lease, machinery, and patents. Little more than a year later, however, the reorganized concern sold its Keene assets to the Standard Roller Bearing Company of Philadelphia, which soon closed the shop.[45]

Postscript. Although the story of Trinity bicycles had ended by 1901, the people who played central roles in the company's origins and evolution managed to adapt, as did its factory building. Janney's mechanical curiosity continued to guide his career in creative ways, and he served as superintendent of the Steamobile Company before moving to Bridgeport and probably meeting John Speirs at the Locomobile Company. Later, he began working as an engineer for the Waterbury Tool Company in New Britain, Connecticut, and while there he invented a hydraulic speed gear used on armaments, leading to a gold medal from the Franklin Institute for his contribution to mechanical arts.[46]

Frank T. Fowler continued to sell Fowler bicycles, reducing the size of the firm he had founded, sold, and then reacquired; diversified by adding a mail order business; served as president of the Illinois Cycling Club; and entered politics, winning an election as a city alderman. He also acquired a stable of trotters, dabbled in harness racing, and traveled to Boston to purchase a sloop that he then sailed back to Chicago. He also reintroduced the newsletter format of advertising, brazenly calling his catalog *The Fowler Truth.*[47]

For a time, Willie Windle continued to ponder organizing another bicycle company, but possibly concerned about earlier financial pitfalls, he embarked instead on a career in banking, becoming a bank president at age sixty. He made his home in West Millbury, not far from his family's farm.[48]

Alfred Batchelder and other shareholders in the Trinity firm who subscribed to the bright future of bicycles may have recovered at least some of their investment following transfer to the Steamobile Company of America. Keene's taxpayers, however, earned a poor return on the city's short-lived tax waiver, and factory machinists and workers turned elsewhere for employment. To the credit of its architect and builders, the Charles A. Jones Block provided factory space over many decades for a succession of diverse industries and businesses, initially the Brattleboro Overall Company but eventually a series of automobile dealers and repair shops, precisely as it was designed to do. Today, the building is well preserved and provides housing and commercial space.

13

Emblem Manufacturing Company

Angola, New York

In 1897, just as Robert Keating, John Speirs, and Frank Fowler all put finishing touches, respectively, on their new bicycle factories, and as troubling alarms sounded in several sectors of the bicycle industry, inventive engineers coincidentally began demonstrating the great potential of concrete and reinforced concrete for industrial buildings, offering what America's factory mutual insurance companies had been seeking for most of the nineteenth century: a structure generally immune to fire. That year, an English-born engineer living in California, Ernest Ransome, designed a factory for the Pacific Coast Borax Company in Bayonne, New Jersey, using a combination of load-bearing walls of concrete block and an interior cage of reinforced concrete. For a 1903 addition to that plant, Ransome advanced to a full, skeletal-frame structure of reinforced-concrete.[1]

Between 1887 and 1902, another inventor, Harmon Palmer, secured a series of patents perfecting a portable, automated machine to mold hollow, rock-faced blocks of concrete, launching an entire industry in the process. In 1906, workers of the Emblem Manufacturing Company in Angola, New York, employed that type of machine to fabricate concrete blocks on site for their new bicycle factory, which combined load-bearing walls with a partial skeletal-frame of reinforced concrete and nudged and nudged the bicycle industry's contributions to nineteenth-century industrial architecture into the twentieth century. Although the American Bicycle Company had begun closing rather than building factories by the time of Ransome's and Palmer's innovations, the glint of progressive outlook that once enlivened bicycle manufacturing but had since shifted to automobiles, still flickered in a few machine shops where production of two-wheeled transport continued. The Emblem company joined the depleted ranks of American manufacturers continuing to build bicycles until World War II, surviving as a supplier for Sears and Roebuck and other large retailers.[2]

Angola Factory

The village of Angola, located in the town of Evans, borders Lake Erie in western New York, roughly twenty miles south of Buffalo, all part of Erie County. The story of the Emblem Manufacturing Company's contribution to cycling history is notable, partly because its factory is among the industry's first to employ concrete construction, and partly because the building likely represents New York's last surviving factory built specifically to produce bicycles—when once more than a dozen companies fabricated bicycles in Buffalo alone. Equally important, the company's origins depart from the familiar pattern of shaky partnerships formed by inventors and local

Figure 104. The Emblem Manufacturing Company factory defines an important period in Angola's town history and is prominently visible from the village center. In addition, the building represents New York's last surviving factory built expressly for the manufacture of bicycles and is also one of America's last new bicycle factories erected during the declining years of the country's seminal bicycle era. Long unused, deteriorating, threatened by demolition, and damaged by a recent fire, the building has nevertheless garnered reviving interest and plans for rehabilitation are being considered. Photo by the author.

investors and are owed instead to a group of employees unwilling to accept their employer's bankruptcy. Creditably, the group boldly formed the Emblem company in 1904, when the industry's scant surviving businesses struggled to remain viable. Moreover, the company's successful, four-decade history began, literally, in a backyard building belonging to one of the company's founders, but soon developed into Angola's principal employer. The business grew to define the character of that small village—physically and economically but also culturally with both the factory and its bicycles becoming ever-present features in the community, a relationship symbolized by the very visible racing track and baseball field built by the company adjacent to its factory. The company also awarded a bicycles as annual prizes for honor students.[3]

Origins. The company's story began in 1895 in a sector of Evans known as Idlewood but later renamed Lakewood, where a group of investors formed the Queen City Cycle Company and erected a large, flimsily-built, wood-frame factory to house the manufacture of Erie bicycles. In 1898, several of the company's owners sold their interests to a newly-organized concern, the Day Bicycle Company, which produced Day bicycles until bankruptcy in 1903 forced the business to close and to sell its factory, which was disassembled to salvage its lumber. Several of the Day company's former employees, among them William Heil, Otto Waibel, Albert Shepker, and John C. Glass pooled their resources, acquired machinery from the defunct concern, and began building bicycles in a carriage house behind Heil's home in Lakewood.[4]

William Schack, who had been a prominent racer and club cyclist in Buffalo during the 1880s and 1890s, and who had opened a small shop along a section of Buffalo's Main Street known as Bicycle

Row, began selling bicycles as an agent for several different companies, and he likely turned to the Queen City and Day concerns to produce bicycles using his own monikers, the Emblem and the Schack, which he began selling in 1894. As part of that agreement, he also may have invested in those successive companies or possibly achieved a position as a sales agent. Following bankruptcy of the Day firm, he joined with Heil and other former employees to incorporate as the Emblem Manufacturing Company in 1904, capitalized with $40,000. Schack also was well acquainted with George Pierce, Buffalo's most successful bicycle manufacturer, and may have acquired additional materials or machinery from Pierce at the time, enough when combined with the value of his own business to exchange those assets for a sufficient block of Emblem stock to claim seats as president and treasurer of the new company, with Heil as vice president. Harry F. Scomark from Washington, D.C., and John Sykes from Trenton joined Schack, Heil, and Glass on the board of directors. Schack guided the company as general manager during the ensuing four difficult decades and emerged as one of the industry's important but overlooked figures.[5]

The business required larger space to house its accumulated machinery and moved to Angola in 1904, enticed by a local subscription campaign that may have contributed to the company's lease of a brick building on South Main Street, the 1872 Tifft Block (no longer standing), within view of the village center across the tracks of the Lake Shore and Michigan Southern

Figure 105. In Evans, New York, former employees of the Queen City Cycle Company and its successor, the Day Bicycle Company, both defunct, pooled their resources and joined with a prominent cyclist and shop owner from Buffalo, William Schack, to form the Emblem Manufacturing Company in 1904. The fledgling company leased space in the Tifft Block on Main Street in the small village of Angola, also located in the town of Evans. Courtesy Town of Evans Historical Society.

Railway, part of the New York Central's Water Level Route between Buffalo and Chicago. With production steady, including shipments of bicycles to Japan, and a lease set to expire on July 1, 1906, the company began negotiating with village trustees, offering to build a new factory in return for donation of a suitable site for the building—very reasonable terms when compared to the demands made by Henry Lozier, for example. The trustees complied, subject to the condition that the company erect a factory of not less than 14,000 square feet within one year or pay a penalty of $600; officials also offered residents who had not contributed funds to the earlier campaign a chance at redemption.[6]

No one wasted any time. By February 1906, the village had brokered an exchange for a one-acre parcel located a stone's throw northerly of the company's shops, accessible via LaSalle Street. That spring, carloads of sand and Portland cement, the latter from the Penn-Allen Cement Company in Allentown, Pennsylvania, began arriving to mold the blocks, and by mid–May a local builder, Elbridge Bundy, had completed work on the foundation and had begun casting the rusticated concrete blocks. By early June, workers had poured the floor surface at ground level and were erecting side walls, and by the end of July they had completed half of the third story walls. The company began to move during September's third week, and the land transfer took place before month's end. In all, the construction phase lasted fewer than eight months. As completed in 1906, the factory stood three stories, and

Figure 106. In addition to the Emblem model, the company eventually manufactured bicycles for several mass retailers, Sears and Roebuck among them, and used several monikers, including Pierce and Elgin. One of the frames displayed in this shop floor (left) is similar to that patented by Frederic Johnson for the Iver Johnson Arms and Cycle Works. Courtesy Town of Evans Historical Society.

its adjoining powerhouse with boiler room just one story. No less remarkable than the speed of construction is the company's decision to design the building and oversee project construction, further distinguishing the plant from its bicycle-industry siblings.[7]

Much of the responsibility for construction devolved to John Glass, who served as the plant's superintendent; he also may have been a key figure in decisions to enlarge the factory. Although the precise sequence of events is not fully clear, the company constructed a three-story ell during the spring of 1910 and later that same year decided to increase the height of that wing to four stories. Two years later, the company removed the water cistern standing above the original factory and added a fourth story to that arm of the works, as well.[8]

Hollow Concrete Block. The company's selection of hollow concrete block as a building material placed the firm amid a then-modern trend in construction that by 1906 had proliferated, but only a few years before barely had existed. Harmon Palmer had continued to improve the cast iron machine protected by his 1887 patent, and in 1899, by then having relocated from Chattanooga to Chicago, he added adjustable face plates and cores to solve the difficulty of removing the fresh block from the mold before setting. In 1901, he followed that invention with a patented design for buildings with walls of interlocking concrete-blocks, and in 1902 with patented improvements to the 1899 machine, providing a means to mold blocks of varying sizes.[9]

Largely due to Palmer's efforts, the period between 1899 and 1902 marked

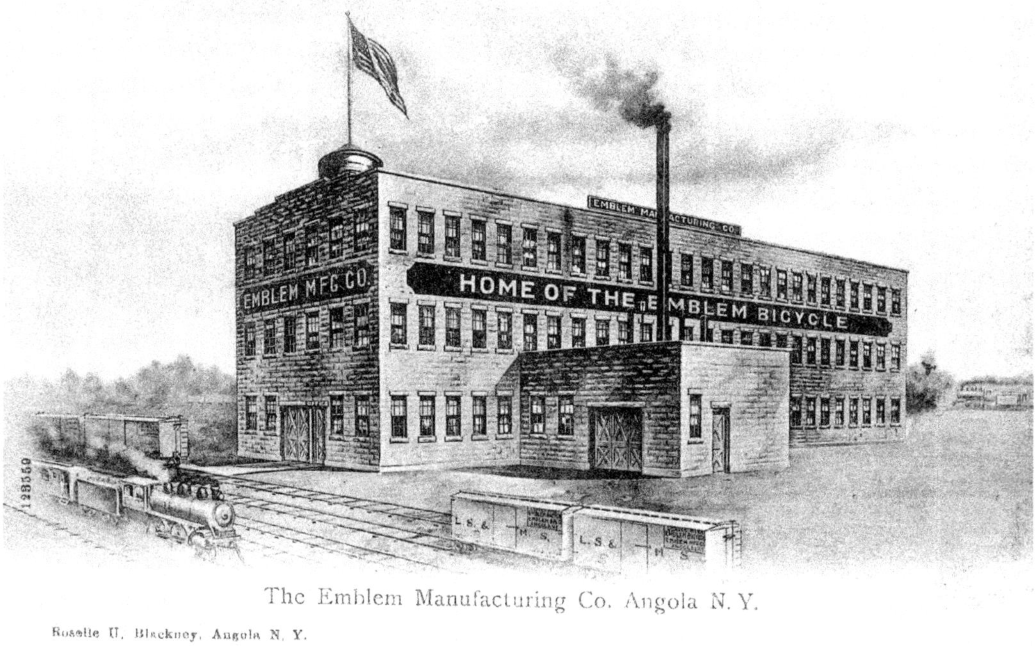

Figure 107. In 1906, the Emblem company's owners agreed with Angola's village trustees to build a new factory, provided the community donated land for the project. Company workers assisted with construction by mastering the machines used to form the rock-faced, hollow concrete blocks from raw materials delivered to the site. Work began that spring and bicycle production commenced that fall, in time for the 1907 season. Author's document.

the genesis of the country's hollow concrete-block industry, but other developments contributed as well, including advances in the formulas used for the manufacture of Portland cement, which coincided with improved understanding about the material's structural properties. New uses caused growing demand for the product that in turn justified investment in the industry's expansion. As a result, cement became more readily available; the building process quickly became well understood and required only minimally skilled labor; materials such as sand and aggregates could be obtained easily and inexpensively; and competition among manufacturers of machines similar to Palmer's intensified despite his patents, keeping prices in check. In 1906, a prominent engineer and Cornell University chemistry professor, Spencer B. Newberry, estimated that more than a thousand American companies or individuals had begun manufacturing hollow concrete block. Writing for the journal *Concrete and Constructional Engineering*, Newberry observed that most machines represented repetitions of a fundamental design and varied only in mechanical details.. That estimate may have included the Newberry family's Cleveland business, the Sandusky Portland Cement Company, which later became the well-known Medusa Portland Cement Company and profited from a formula for cement developed by Newberry and his brother, William.[10]

Thus, hollow concrete block construction seemed perfectly matched for the Emblem company's cost-conscious owners determined to erect a more substantial factory than the cockup at Lakewood. Newberry observed that most machine-makers had adopted standard dimensions for the blocks: thirty-two inches long and nine inches high, with widths offered in eight, ten, and twelve-inch dimensions. Those at the Angola plant are thirty-one and one-half inches, by eight and one-half inches, by twelve inches, with the half-inch discrepancies possibly explained by shrinkage, which could be affected by composition of the concrete; blocks used for the upper walls may be less than twelve inches in width. Whether Glass purchased Palmer's machine or another company's version is not known, but workers generally could form 150 blocks in ten hours. Depending on composition of the concrete and proper forming, blocks could absorb 2000 pounds of compression stress after a four-week curing period.[11]

For the Emblem factory, though, the strength of the concrete block is less important for building height than for the capacity of the walls to accommodate window openings. Wall piers are noticeably absent from the factory, and windows are domestic in scale and very closely spaced—a total of twenty-six per-floor over the building's original length (120 feet). By contrast, the architect of the Trinity loft in Keene calculated twenty windows per-floor on the factory's longest, Wells Street façade (165 feet); and builders of the Speirs factory in Worcester installed twenty-one windows along the initial Nebraska Street elevation (156 feet); for both factories, too, wall piers separated each window, adding moderate shadow as well as increasing the cost of materials and labor. Granted, such comparisons are incomplete absent consideration of window size, and windows on both the Trinity and Speirs factories are slightly larger than those on the Emblem plant. Nevertheless, the greater number of closely-spaced windows on the Emblem factory gave that building an advantage, and if additional windows increased costs, some or all of that extra cost may have been recovered by using domestically-scaled windows.[12]

Transitional, short-lived hollow-concrete block construction for industrial buildings soon surrendered to skeletal-frame assembly with expansive window walls that improved light admission dramatically, rendering the types of windows used in Angola, Keene, Worcester and elsewhere obsolete. Yet Schack and other company owners still deserve credit for paying close attention to the load capacity of hollow concrete block and the relationship of that capacity to window size and total admission of natural light.

Floor Framing System. The Emblem factory is similarly transitional in the design of its interior floor framing, which combines both steel and concrete. That interior structure incorporates several principal elements: a row of concrete columns standing at the floor-span's mid-point and spaced at five-foot intervals, center to center; a central, longitudinal girder of reinforced concrete extending the building's full length and supported by the columns; rolled I-beams thinly encased in concrete and serving as floor beams, which rest on the exterior load-bearing walls and central longitudinal girder; and a floor slab reinforced by steel mesh. The longitudinal girder is reinforced with steel, but its form—whether encompassing reinforcing rod, one or more steel I-beams, or a single plate-girder encased in concrete—is not clear; the manner of reinforcing in the columns is also unclear, although they are almost certainly tied together vertically from floor to floor.

That structural system is transitional in the sense that at least part of the assembly process resembled traditional standard mill construction because the floor beams rest individually on the exterior load bearing walls and central longitudinal girder. As a result, the building lacks the more advanced methods for designing and integrating columns, floor beams, girders and floor slabs into the type of unified, monolithic structure that signifies true skeletal frame design in reinforced concrete, a method of construction that Ernest Ransome had demonstrated in 1903. In addition, the columns are very closely spaced, even more so than in traditional standard-mill construction, thus increasing rather than decreasing the number of vertical obstructions to the organization of manufacturing processes—another of the important advantages offered by true skeletal-frame buildings. Moreover, although the steel used for floor beams and for the longitudinal girder is encased in concrete and thus shielded from heat caused by fire, the extent of that protection may depend on the size of steel used in relation to the depth of concrete sleeves. As well, workers added a fourth floor with steel columns, beams, and plate girders, and thus the building is not entirely fireproof; the roof is also framed and ceiled in wood.

Architectural Effect. Intentionally or not, Schack, Heil, Glass and whoever else participated in the Emblem factory's design gave the building a distinctive architectural quality most clearly visible in the rugged, quarry-faced block exterior and the rhythmic, shoulder-to-shoulder cadence of the domestically-scaled windows. As well, the company selected smooth-faced concrete block for the wall surface between the second and third stories to accommodate a sign band and included a stepped parapet on the building's front or northwesterly elevation facing the railroad. Both features announced the business to passersby traveling by train, and workers added a more truncated version of the parapet when topping-off the fourth story addition. The company's offices also faced the railroad, as did a wide set of adjacent doors that opened to a rail spur accessible via an elevated drive at the second-story level.

In overall composition, the building thus represents a vernacular version of transitional standard mill construction, concrete-block bearing walls, and reinforced-concrete skeletal frame interior, a characteristic reinforced by the direct involvement of company owners and employees in the building's design, construction, and fitting. Records of that

Figure 108. Bicycles became Angola's principal industry, and both the factory and Emblem wheels became very visible features in the town. Tracks of the Lake Shore and Michigan Southern Railway separated the plant with its bicycle racetrack and baseball fields from the village center, directly opposite. Courtesy Town of Evans Historical Society.

process are limited, and explanations for the company's choice of material are speculative, but William Schact, who continued to live in Buffalo, was likely aware of George Pierce's new automobile factory also under construction in 1906, a sprawling complex of reinforced concrete buildings but far more advanced in design and the work of architect Albert Kahn and the Boston architectural firm of Lockwood, Greene and Company. Or, the company may simply have been looking for an economical alternative with the added benefit of a fireproof building, and although Schack or Glass hired building contractors such as Bundy, they also selected employees to assist with various aspects of construction such as foundation excavation, plumbing, gas lighting (converted to electricity after 1916), and heating; employees also helped to move machinery and stock into the new building when completed. Manufacturers of the machines marketed to produce hollow concrete block advertised that the blocks could be formed easily by the do-it-yourself-minded public, and Emblem's owners expanded those claims on behalf of the bicycle industry.[13]

The building also offers a sharp contrast to the trend in industrial architecture, already underway by 1906, toward the specialized design of factories by architects or engineers to achieve maximum production efficiency by integrating building and manufacturing processes into a coherent, unified plan. The 1897 factory by the Pope Tube Company is the bicycle industry's most sophisticated example of that trend but is also one in which the Hartford company's engineers and employees became engaged in the design process, if not in the physical construction. And, if the factories in Hartford and Angola occupy opposite ends of architecture's industrial spectrum, the two buildings nevertheless demonstrate that company owners understood the crucial relationships between factory design and manufacturing processes.

Production. With a new factory to assure consistent production capacity, the Emblem company managed to establish a small but secure niche in the bicycle trade during the years before and after World War I, filling breaches created by the industry's collapse and venturing into motorcycle production after 1907—also called the Emblem. When the Pierce Cycle Company failed and began lengthy bankruptcy proceedings in 1910, Schack eventually absorbed the firm's assets and began manufacturing bicycles with the Pierce marque, pushing employment rolls into the hundreds and justifying construction of the four-story wing and fourth-floor addition to the original factory, giving the works 70,000 square feet. After World War I, Schact ended motorcycle production to devote full attention to bicycles, and Sears and Roebuck Company developed into one of the company's major customers, selecting the Elgin badge for its Japan market; Schack also secured contracts with other mass retailers or jobbers, building bicycles with several different monikers. That clientele generated prosperity for the company during the 1920s, despite the trend toward specialization in parts that permitted mass retailers to demand lower prices from those companies still assembling finished products.[14]

Schack's enduring oversight as general manager explains how one small bicycle company survived when many others failed, and although overshadowed by figures such as Horace Huffman or Ignaz Schwinn and his son Frank W. Schwinn, Schact nevertheless deserves recognition similar to that accorded to Norman R. Clarke and his son, Norman A. Clarke, who guided bicycle production at the Westfield Manufacturing Company and its successor Columbia Manufacturing Company for so many decades. From his early successes as a local racer during the 1880s, as owner of his small shop in Buffalo during the 1890s, and as president of the Emblem concern from 1903 until the onset of World War II, Schack mastered the trade, and he employed effective strategies to confront many of the industry's trials. All the while, he played an active role in trade organizations, holding elected positions for the Bicycle Manufacturers Association of America and the Cycle Trades of America, responsibilities that led to lobbying to protect duties on imported bicycles.[15]

From the start, the Emblem company countered modest capitalization with minimal debt, and Schact negotiated a reasonable subsidy from Angola's elected trustees, repaying the town many times over. He wisely selected then-modern building materials to design and build a fireproof factory, relying on employees to assist with work. Ever-cost conscious, he continued to rely on steam power and overhead mill shafting long after electricity arrived in Angola in 1916, postponing the expensive conversion until practicality intervened; however, he did install a sprinkling system in 1917. As well, he adroitly absorbed the Pierce Cycle Company, capturing a bonanza of good will earned by the exceptional quality of bicycles built by George Pierce, and journalists occasionally referred to the factory as the Emblem-Pierce works. He also won competitive contracts with several major retailers. Yet Schact also continued to produce most of the parts needed for bicycles other than saddles, tires, and pedals—resisting the industry trend and probably weakening profit margins as a result—but improving control over production.[16]

Although the early years of the Depression took a toll on the company's profits, lowering employment rolls to as few as forty, Schack still managed to navigate those difficult years, diversifying by building vending machines and sidestepping offers of acquisition by the DuPont consortium. During the mid–1930s, by then in his early eighties, he also guided the company's quiet renewal, shipping large orders of ladies' wheels to California where motion picture celebrities had reawakened public interest in bicycles. Employment climbed to more than one hundred and the factory once again approached production capacity. Only when Sears and Roebuck cancelled its contract with the company after the outbreak of World War II, did the firm finally succumb.[17]

Following closure of the plant, a line of new owners engaged in various manufacturing enterprises including chain hoists used by ships and railroad cars; engine parts; and stainless-steel products. During the late 1950s and 1960s, the plant provided storage space for plate steel and other materials including wooden pallets and plastic drums. By 1970, the plant was empty and unused, eventually opening to the weather and suffering continuing deterioration. Property taxes are long unpaid, and Erie County government has long sought an opportunity to demolish the building.

14

Davis Sewing Machine Company

Dayton, Ohio

Bicycle companies often profited from the sewing machine industry, either because the factories and machine tools designed for sewing machine production could be adapted easily to bicycles, or because bicycles offered a means for existing sewing-machine manufacturers to diversify and expand. A few examples, notably the Davis Sewing Machine Company in Dayton, Ohio, demonstrated both, and that company's former factory on Davis Avenue is the country's best surviving example of the symbiotic ties between the two industries. In addition, the company's Dayton marque became one of the country's very popular bicycles after 1895, a creditable feat given the intense competition by then. No less significant, the firm continued to produce bicycles at that factory until the early 1920s, avoiding the American Bicycle Company trust, diversifying, but also manufacturing military bicycles for Russian, American and French troops during World War I—similar to the adjustments adopted by the Iver Johnson firm in Fitchburg. Although the fluctuating post-war economy forced liquidation of the Davis firm in 1923, a newly formed Huffman Manufacturing Company emerged from that failure and subsequently revived bicycle production in 1934. That successor company occupied a non-descript, one-story, 60,000 square-foot plant (still standing) on Gilbert Street, a site that had been absorbed by the Davis company's sprawling industrial complex, and there produced various marques to meet growing enthusiasm for bicycles during the 1930s. Following World War II, the company introduced its successful Huffy bicycle and to meet increasing demand moved in 1955 to a new factory in Celina, Ohio, about seventy miles north of Dayton, where the firm eventually became America's largest bicycle manufacturer.

Dayton Factory

The Davis Sewing Machine Company, which formed in 1868 to produce a superior type of sewing machine with a vertical shuttle invented by Job Davis, became a thriving business in Watertown, New York. Seeking better access to Midwest markets, the company found a willing suitor in Dayton's Board of Trade led by George P. Huffman, whose landed family had been seeking opportunities for real estate development in Dayton's easterly environs. Negotiations culminated in December 1888 with a promise extracted from the trade board to provide a site for the factory and $50,000 in local subscriptions. During the spring of 1889, Huffman and other Dayton financiers formed a real estate firm, the National Improvement Company, which took title to large tracts of land platted by William Huffman, the family's patriarch, and later that year sold a single lot, roughly six acres, to the Davis concern for $150,000. By that time, William Huffman and George Huffman had become controlling shareholders and directors of the sewing machine concern, with the younger Huffman, at age twenty-seven, serving as president. The company already had retained Watertown architects John Hose and David Kieff to design the factory, doubling the size of its Watertown works. In July 1889, the company set the cornerstone for its new factory at an event attended by Governor Joseph Foraker, and the rapidly-built works stood ready for occupancy by mid–January 1890.[1]

Similarities between the two industries also extended to reliance on standard mill construction for the design of new factories, and the plans by Hose and Kieff called for three principal buildings, all in brick: a very long, 500-foot, two-story main block with quarry-faced stone foundation and elevated basement, adjoined by two, two-story wings extending at right angles; a tall, one-story foundry with monitor roof; and a two-story office with tower. As completed, the complex generally adhered to that plan, although directors postponed construction of the office building. In addition, the company added a boiler house to the wing used as a power plant, vented with a seventy-five-foot chimney stack; erected a separate one-story building with monitor roof to house annealing ovens; and built a large storage shed. The shop for annealing ovens and the adjacent storage house stood in close proximity to a spur line linking the factory to the Pittsburgh, Cincinnati, Chicago and St. Louis Railroad, known as the Panhandle Route because it passed through West Virginia's Panhandle.[2]

Figure 109. The Davis Sewing Machine Company formed in 1868 and developed a thriving business from its headquarters in Watertown, New York, before moving to Dayton, Ohio, in 1889. The Dayton Board of Trade raised $50,000 in local subscriptions, and the company purchased land from members of the Huffman family, who became controlling shareholders of the firm. Watertown architects John Hose and David Kieff designed the new factory, completed during the early months of 1890. Bicycle production began in 1892, and by the time of this photograph, c. 1910, the factory had been much enlarged. From the Collection of Dayton History.

Although today extensively enlarged, the factory's principal block relies on load-bearing piers to support floor beams internally; the original plans eliminated mid-span supporting posts on the first floor, used as a machine shop, but later insurance maps show two rows of posts on all floors. Window openings in the intervening spandrel walls are capped with segmentally arched lintels, and paired wooden sash have nine-over-nine pane configurations on the first floor, but nine-over-six on the second floor; lintels above the basement windows are granite block. By 1906, the company successfully had added a third story with windows matching those on the second story, confirming the accuracy of the original plans regarding the structural capacity of spandrel walls in relation to the size of window openings. Builders of the Davis factory also added brick corbelling to mark the transition between spandrel walls and cornice, and decorative corbelling may have embellished the building as well; if so, the third-floor addition erased those details. Gable roofs with small, shed-roof dormers originally capped the main block and its wings.[3]

Dayton Bicycles. With construction of its new factory underway by July 1889, the company exhibited its machines at the World's Exposition in Paris that summer and fall, giving valuable recognition to Dayton's new business and assuring profitability in the sewing machine industry for many years. By 1892, George Huffman also had begun building bicycles, initially for various jobbers, but in August 1895 he announced plans to design the firm's own model—the Dayton, in carmen livery. That same month, the company reorganized as an Ohio Corporation, with William Huffman, George Huffman, Frank T. Huffman, John Stoddard, Eugene J. Barney, and Levi A. Johnson as incorporators; Johnson, secretary and general manager, had moved with the company from Watertown. With capitalization established at $600,000 and 10 percent subscribed in the form of 6,000 shares at $100 par value, the newly established corporation acquired the Dayton works for $452,500 represented by 4,525 shares of stock. That summer, the company added a third, similarly long wing to the complex, devoting its three stories exclusively to bicycle production, with filing and brazing in the basement; machine tooling and wheel-fabrication on the first floor; plating and buffing on the second floor; and assembly on the third floor, all accessible via two elevators.[4]

With bicycle production well established, the Davis company joined several other bicycle manufacturers who engaged in urban planning in cities such as Westfield, Hagerstown, Hartford and Toledo, but far surpassing those undertakings in terms of the sheer scope of real estate development. When the Davis concern left Watertown for Dayton, so too did many employees, and the Huffmans initially estimated a demand for 250 houses. In 1889 and 1890 alone, William Huffman and the family's National Improvement Company recorded at least ten platted subdivisions, creating more than 870 small building lots, most of them between thirty-five and forty feet in width, squeezed into blocks divided by narrow alleys, in turn framed by grids of streets. As the Davis company expanded, that pattern of monotonous development spread outward, so very typical of urban growth in America. To their credit, the Huffmans did provide sites for a church and elementary school, contributing to the construction of those buildings, and planned a few large homes with the hope attracting more affluent residents. Nevertheless, architectural models or urban amenities such as parks and parkways are missing; absent, too, is the type of idealized vision for urban industrial environments evident in the contributions of Albert Pope, George Day, and George Keller in Hartford.[5]

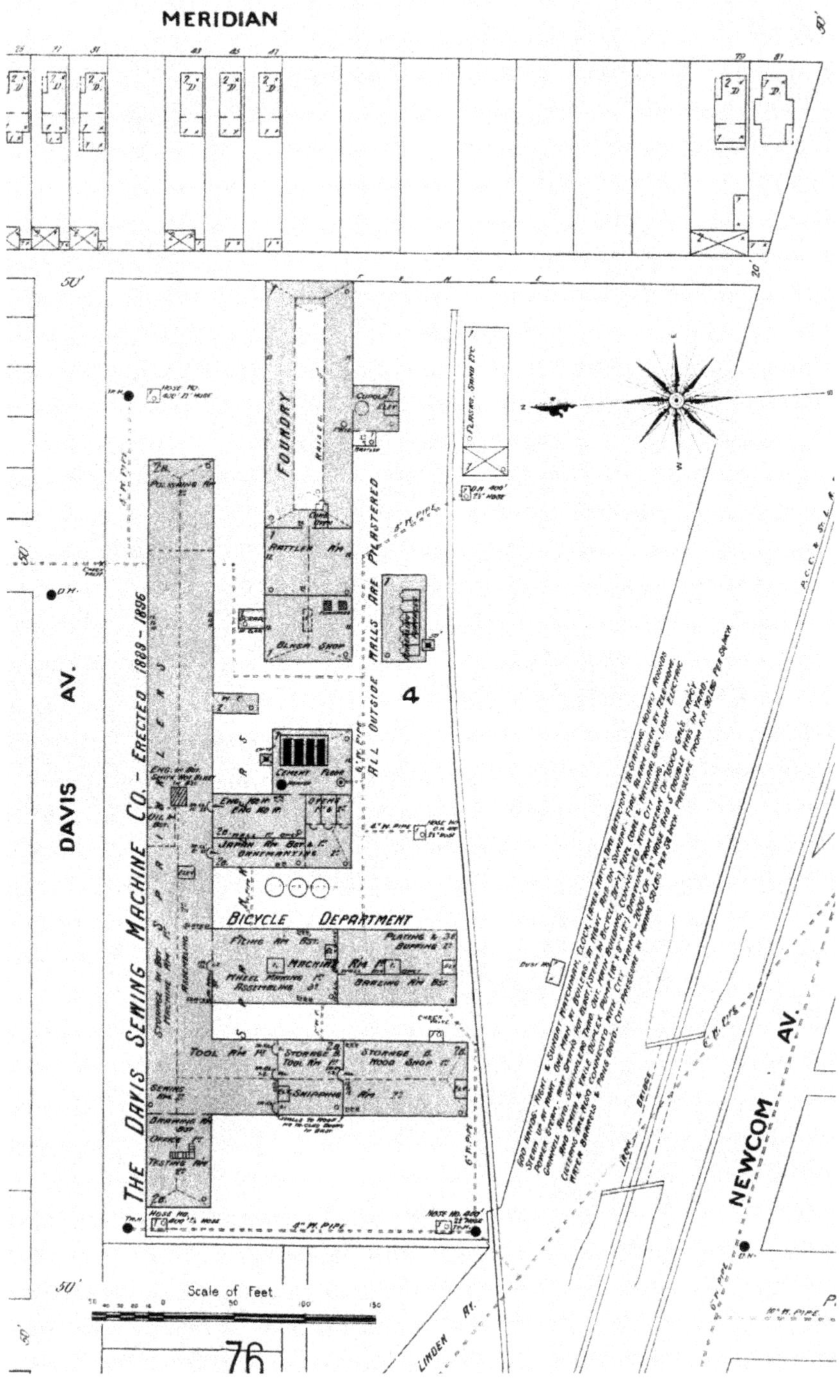

Figure 110. As completed in 1890, the factory included a very long, two-story block with two, two-story wings, one of which was used as a power plant with an attached boiler house; the complex also included a one-story foundry and a shop to house annealing ovens. By 1897, the company had completed the office addition fronting Linden Avenue, intended to be part of the original design; had extended the westerly wing; and had added a third wing for bicycle production. Sanborn-Perris Map Company, Insurance Maps of Dayton, Ohio, Vol. 2 (1897–1898): Plate 77. Library of Congress, Geography and Map Division.

Figure 111. Dayton commuters who worked for the National Cash Register Company could inflate their tires at a compressed-air station provided by their company. From the Collection of Dayton History.

George Huffman timed the company's investment in two-wheeled transportation very well, and by 1897 the firm had joined the country's upper ranks of bicycle manufacturers. However, that year he suffered a fatal heart attack and his brother, Colonel Frank T. Huffman, replaced him as president. During that season and the next, the company steadily expanded, confident that if warnings of overproduction in the bicycle industry proved to be accurate, sales of sewing machines offered a reliable cushion. The company also followed trends in bicycle design, offering a chainless model. During the spring of 1899, the company likely received an invitation to join the American Bicycle Company Trust, and editors of *Cycle Age and Trade Review* estimated annual production at 10,000 bicycles, with capacity for 12,000. However, no merger occurred, and the following year Frank Huffman led a campaign to expand the company's factory complex, acquiring eight additional lots at the corner of Davis and Linden Avenues, where in 1901 or 1902 he erected a commanding front office as well as substantially more factory space. In 1903, the business also doubled its capitalization to $1,200,000, issued in 6,000 shares of preferred stock.[6]

Office Design. The company's discretely neo-classical office establishes an architectural focal point for the industrial complex, just as George Keller's office palazzo became a centerpiece for the Pope Manufacturing Company's works in Hartford. The Dayton office is a tall, three-story, square brick block, with its added height achieved by an elevated basement and by a crowning parapet that encircles the roof above the cornice, forming a solid brick railing with panels. Structural wall piers, standing on a stone stringcourse shelf that caps the elevated basement, become pilasters with flat, corbelled-brick capitals that seem to pierce the cornice, reemerging as piers to support the parapet. A prominent public entrance, accessible via a long flight of steps, corresponds in height to the basement stringcourse and is sheltered by a one-story, single-bay pavilion, also capped by a parapet railing. The original paired entrance doors, framed beneath an elliptical arch in brick but sprung from stone blocks and with decorative keystone, once opened below an elliptical fanlight. Large, rectangular windows with stone sills but no brick lintels fill nearly the entire spandrel walls, which are almost certainly carried by iron or steel spandrel girders above the window openings, supported in turn by wall piers internally. Rows of small, corbelled, brick arches decorate the entablature beneath the cornice. A three-story block combining various functions extends directly behind the office, linking the latter to the main block of the original factory, which was probably increased to three stories at the same time, or in any case by 1906. Contemporaneously, the company added a

Figure 112. The Davis Sewing Machine Company did not join the American Bicycle Company trust and instead became active in the Cycle Trades Protective Association. Although bicycle and sewing machine manufacturing revived during World War I, a New York bond firm, Blair and Company, purchased the business in 1915, intending to manufacture machine tools. By 1918, the factory complex had more than doubled in size, extending along both Davis and Linden Avenues. Bicycle production continued in the old factory until 1922 or 1923, shortly before the New York firm dissolved. In 2009, the year of this photograph, the factory remained underutilized. Photo by the author.

series of three-story shops bordering Linden Avenue and the rail spur, creating an interior mill-yard.[7]

Outside the ABC Trust. Having avoided ABC's lure, and able to garner what limited benefits the Cycle Trades' Protective Association might offer, the firm joined those ranks of manufacturers who managed to build bicycles during the first two decades of the twentieth century. Declining demand and the shift to children's bicycles represented two challenges and, as demand eventually stabilized, changes to manufacturing processes posed a third, primarily the standardization of parts to satisfy mass merchandisers. Frank Huffman responded to these quandaries by continuing to sell sewing machines and by adding motorcycles and washing machines to the company catalog. In 1908, Horace M. Huffman, the son of George P. Huffman and a recent college graduate, joined the company, rising to sales manager for bicycles four years later.[8]

During this period Frank Huffman continued to enlarge the factory complex and to improve production efficiency—an economic imperative. The company converted the long, original 1889 wing to bicycle production and moved the rim department into a one-story, brick, single-room shop built adjacent to the bicycle wing. In that latter wing, staff added a dipping room for electro-plating on the first floor and additional bench work on the second floor; they also added a small shop for steel scrap adjacent to the brazing department in the basement. In 1910, the company built a new, three-story wing for bicycle frame production, relying on a fireproof structure of reinforced-concrete and placing heat treating and grinding on the first floor, polishing on the second, and the frame department and annealing ovens on the third floor.[9]

Sales of the company's products, including both bicycles and sewing machines, declined prior to World War I, but production capacity nevertheless attracted a New York bond firm, Blair and Company, which acquired all the firm's common stock in 1915 and planned to produce drill presses, screw machines, and drop forgings. Frank Huffman remained as president and the company reorganized as a Delaware corporation. During this period, too, the company acquired the rights to produce other models including Yale, Snell and National bicycles, tapping lucrative market-sectors; the firm also built an enormous new foundry. With the arrival of World War I, sales of sewing machines, bicycles, and munitions for the military revived the company temporarily. Soon after that conflict, one of the company's engineers, Elmer M. Lewis, invented a successful process for manufacturing frames and forks that led to several patents, issued in 1921. Nevertheless, losses mounted, and the New York owners replaced Frank Huffman with a new president, C.A. Hawkins, but with little success. The company entered receivership in May 1923, voted to liquidate, and agreed to transfer the existing inventory of bicycles and sewing machines to Horace Huffman, as payment for his services as trustee. The transfer also included the Gilbert Street building, which had been used for munitions. Bicycle production in the old factory ended in 1922 or 1923 and did not begin in the Gilbert Street plant until the 1935 season. However, that later year marks the second phase of adaptive use of the Davis Sewing Machine Company's works for bicycle manufacturing.[10]

Gilbert Street Munitions Factory. Beginning in 1924, Horace Huffman scrabbled together a business from the scant remains of his father's once-prosperous company. Ensconced in the low, single-story, former munitions factory, Huffman began by selling remaining inventory as well as repair parts for bicycles, sewing machines, and washing machines. He then added the manufacture of blow torches and oil measuring devices with spouts and

Figure 113. When Blair and Company dissolved in 1923, Horace Huffman acquired its inventory of bicycles and bicycle parts, as well as the company's Gilbert Street factory, used to produce munitions during World War 1. Huffman began selling repair parts, expanded into the manufacture of automotive service equipment, incorporated the Huffman Manufacturing Company in 1928, and returned to bicycle production in 1934. In 1935, he became the sole supplier of bicycles to Firestone Tire and Rubber Company, and a year later his eldest son, Horace M. Huffman, Jr. joined the business. In 1949 the younger Huffman introduced the very successful Huffy bicycle in this nondescript building. The company later constructed a new factory in Celina, Ohio. From the Collection of Dayton History.

spill-proof tops. With his brother, George P. Huffman, Jr., and several cousins, he incorporated the Huffman Manufacturing Company in 1928, expanding his automotive service-equipment business but plotting all the while to return to bicycles and working two jobs to stay afloat. Then, in 1934 during the depths of the Depression and staring down a financial abyss, he announced plans to manufacture bicycles in small numbers, first securing a loan from a local bank with a home mortgage and soon after adding his life insurance policy as collateral for another loan. Mustering a determination excelled only by his timing and salesmanship, Huffman reentered the industry just as interest in bicycles had begun to grow among both adults and children. In 1935, with capital provided by his brother-in-law and major shareholder, John W. Clements, Huffman landed a crucial contract as sole supplier of mass-merchandiser Firestone Tire and Rubber Company, and a year later his eldest son, Horace M. Huffman, Jr. (Huff), joined the business. Thus began one of cycling history's most intriguing success stories, and in the unlikeliest of buildings—a stark contrast to the architectural insignia of industry next door.[11]

Erected quickly to accommodate wartime production and clad in faux-brick compositional siding, the wood-framed factory is unremarkable in both structural design and appearance. However, it did offer Huffman at least one principal advantage because production could be consolidated onto a single floor. To the extent feasible, rows of large, paired, operable sash windows filled the walls, providing natural light at least along the interior's perimeter, and three small monitor roofs added modest light to the central interior; electricity furnished the rest. However, the building lacked a sufficiently advanced structural system to provide more efficient saw-tooth roof lighting or to minimize vertical supports, and the numerous interior posts created obstacles to efficient organization of production systems. Small, pyramidal rises in the roof funneled water toward drain spouts, at least some of which opened on the building's exterior.

Before Huffman acquired the building, the interior space had been divided into three departments of roughly equal size: one unit for inspection and stock and two machine shops. The stock room continued to serve that function, joined by the shipping department, and Huffman added a paint spray booth to the middle unit; the company also built a small, wood-frame building on Davis Avenue to house bicycles ready for delivery and installed a conveyor leading into that building. Automatic sprinkling provided protection against fire.[12]

The bicycles Huffman reintroduced were similar to the popular moto-bikes designed many years before as imitation motorcycles for juveniles, with tanks mounted on the frame's horizontal tube—at the expense of greater cost and weight. However, he also added fashionable balloon tires with white sidewalls, spring-cushioned ride, and a host of deluxe accessories such as horns, fender-mounted head and taillights powered by batteries, speedometers, and luggage racks—borrowing tactics from automobile manufacturers. By 1937, his company offered twenty-two different models, headlined by the Dayton but also joined by marques from earlier years, including the Dixie-Flyer, Snell, and National. In addition, the years between 1928 and 1935 had given Huffman an opportunity to update machinery, and the company began designing new models such as the Safety Streamline with a sloping, double rear fork, in livery of sea-mist green with black and yellow trim.[13]

Assembly-Line Production. Year-to-year profits fluctuated during this early period of growth, with important accounts won or lost depending on profit margins. To improve production efficiency in the factory's constrained space, the younger Huffman designed an assembly line system after studying a Buick factory in Flint, Michigan, completing installation during the early months of 1941. With an assembly line conveyor to speed production, the company responded more quickly to seasonal orders, and output increased dramatically that year. Private-sector orders ended during the war years, but Huffman and the Westfield Manufacturing Company became two of the country's firms awarded contracts to build military and military-worker bicycles—the civilian transport model with standardized design and interchangeable parts.[14]

Huffy Convertibles. Horace Huffman, Jr., replaced his father as president in 1942, but his father died three years later, leaving the younger Huffman to face a wide range of post-war challenges, including drastic shifts in economic cycles; the need to strengthen management personnel; shortages of materials; weaknesses in work efficiency; and the changing technology of bicycle design. Early in 1946, he hired Frederick Smith, a young military officer with a business background and placed him in charge of materials procurement, the first non-family member of the company's management team. Huffman also implemented work-simplification strategies, for his suppliers as well as for his own business, and embarked on innovative marketing campaigns. In 1949, the company also diversified by inaugurating an electric lawnmower business. A year later, Huffman introduced the enormously successful Huffy Convertible, a single bicycle to replace tricycle, sidewalk bike, and juvenile bike—fixed with starter training wheels that could be converted later to other uses.[15]

The limitations of the old munitions factory had become painfully obvious during this period, and in 1951 the company moved its service-station equipment business to an existing factory in Delphos, Ohio, not quite ninety miles north of Dayton. By that time, too, American bicycle companies had begun to feel the effects of competition from English manufacturers, who had been subsidized by post-war American relief efforts and by reduced tariffs. In response, Huffman and Smith, by then executive vice president, forged an agreement with the English company, T.I. Raleigh, Limited, to produce a line of Huffman lightweight bicycles. Demand for bicycles in America climbed during the early 1950s, and in 1953 Huffman secretly began to develop production plans for an ideal new factory with greater production capacity. By 1955, the company was ready to move into the Celina plant, with 100,000 square feet, and that same year Huffman introduced the novel Huffy Radiobike, with a radio built into its tank.[16]

Huffy Corporation. The story of the munitions factory and its role in bicycle history mostly ends here, although Huffman moved the company's executive offices into the second floor of the old Davis Sewing Machine Company works, where the customer service and parts departments once had been located. The history of the company, though, unfolds in several more chapters dominated by phenomenal growth continuing through the 1980s, including acquisition of plants in California and other parts of the country; a licensing agreement to build American bicycles under the Raleigh name; new offices and a technology center in Miamisburg, Ohio, where the company developed bicycles for professional racing; increased diversification; and continued expansion of the Celina factory.[17]

In 1961, Horace Huffman, Jr., became chairman of the Board of Directors and Fred Smith moved into the president's chair; Robert Huffman, Horace's brother, also had joined the company as vice president. In 1966, the company's stock became publicly traded, and in 1972 the firm reorganized its management: Huffman retired from active involvement with the business; Smith replaced him as Chairman of the Board, and a new president, Stuart Northrop, assumed control. By the end of the 1975 season, the company had become the country's largest bicycle manufacturer. Two years later, the company consolidated its various divisions under the umbrella Huffy Corporation, and by 1979 the company had built thirty-million bicycles, donating that much-awaited model to the Smithsonian Institution. By 1986, both Huffman and Smith had entered full retirement, and a year later the company reached its fifty-million bicycle milestone. But just as the bicycle boom from a century earlier had befallen dramatic economic and social shifts, so too did the Huffy Corporation succumb to the vagaries of international trade and price-dictates by American mass-retailers, contributing to the company's bankruptcy in 2004. Spared from that day, Horace Huffman, Jr., suffered a heart attack in December 1996. Today, the firm's offices are located in Dayton, but manufacturing takes place in other countries.[18]

15

Ride and Park

Today, debate about obstacles impeding the bicycle's route to a safe and rightful place as a supremely practical, healthy, environmentally sound, spirit-lifting, or otherwise enjoyable form of transportation—universally accepted—are often little more than retrospectives of challenges faced by late nineteenth-century cyclists, who routinely devised creative responses to many of those impediments. Moreover, many of their solutions are as viable today as then. Not surprisingly, conflicts with other forms of transportation and pedestrians were and are ever-confounding in those discussions, and calls during the 1890s for entirely separate roads for bicyclists—wheelways by another name—remain a tempting reverie to which today's cyclists return again and again. And, if cycling's enthusiasts of the 1890s glossed over some of the hindrances to collective reliance on bicycles—the physical exertion required to travel long distances or climb hills, or the lack of protection from precipitation, wind, and cold—the futuristic velomobiles, Etrikes, and electrically assisted bicycles of today offer heartening possibilities.

Cyclists of the 1890s also confronted a problem that grew large during that period, and today has loomed ever more pressing in urban areas where bicycle commuters travel to work in multitudes. Corporate boards and city planners alike have struggled to find suitable places to park those bicycles, keeping office hallways and sidewalks free from wheels, frames, cables, chains, and various locking devices. The predicament has become acute in Japan, the Netherlands, Belgium, and other countries where reliance on bicycles is prevalent. In the context of industrial complexes, wheelmen and wheelwomen of the 1890s met that quandary by encouraging company owners to design a new architectural type: the bicycle house. High-style examples justify that moniker, but many others were more rudimentary versions off-handedly described as sheds. Although bicycle manufacturers needed little convincing to accommodate their own workers in this manner, some of the most impressive buildings belonged to other progressive sectors of industry. Providing simple protection from the elements posed few structural challenges, but efficient use of interior space to maximize capacity, coupled with the need for well-defined entrances, exits, and corridors to manage hectic late-arrivals in the morning or rapid departures in the late afternoon, called for more serious study, and structural devices invented to secure bicycles in place became essential features for those shelters. The resulting industrial buildings represent a distinctive melding of architectural form and engineered fixtures.[1]

Some progressive companies also provided clubhouses for wheelmen, a manner of sponsorship for cyclists who competed in races and carried company colors in one form or another. Alternatively, such buildings provided starting points for country rides or gathering places for evening social

Figure 114. Men's (left) and women's bicycle houses at the National Cash Register Company factory in Dayton, Ohio, in an 1897 photograph. The shelters, built before 1896 as company stables, fronted Stewart Street and faced the company's factory, erected in 1888. Architect Charles I. Williams designed that factory but later formed a partnership with Frank Mills Andrews, practicing as Williams and Andrews, and that firm (or Williams acting alone) probably designed the bicycle houses. Landscape architects Olmsted, Olmsted and Eliot, principally John Charles Olmsted, designed the pergola and ornamental landscaping. From the Collection of Dayton History.

events and were intended to encourage worker loyalty. Bicycle clubhouses afforded to company employees mostly lacked the architectural ornament and interior appointments common to quarters occupied by exclusive bicycle clubs in large cities, investments intended to attract new members. More modest demeanor notwithstanding, company clubhouses occasionally employed architectural details to reveal the purpose of these buildings, for example high-wheel bicycles in tooled wood as substitutes for other wall-surface decorations.

Company Bicycle Houses, Sheds and Clubhouses

National Cash Register Company. For appealing design, few bicycle houses can compare to those built in Dayton, Ohio, by the National Cash Register Company, shelters attributable to the architectural firm of Williams and Andrews, in collaboration with landscape architects Olmsted, Olmsted and Eliot, chiefly John Charles Olmsted. Founded in 1884 by brothers John H. Patterson and Frank J. Patterson, respectively president and vice president, the Dayton concern erected its first factory in 1888, selecting farmland owned by the Pattersons in a down-trodden suburb described colloquially as Slidertown. Designed by Charles I. Williams prior to his partnership with Frank Mills Andrews and completed in sixty-four days, the two-and-one-half story plant of standard mill construction, extended along Stewart Street, with taller blocks at each end, punctuated by projecting towers. The factory signaled the beginning of what would become a transformative period for the company and its environs, measured by increasing profitability and expansion of the works over ever-larger acreage. The company's progressive system of cooperative labor paid meticulous attention to the well-being of its employees (physical, mental, moral, social, and financial)—a method of productivity that Patterson described as welfare work. The company also converted the factory site and its surrounding neighborhood into a model industrial works and workers community, with gardens and ornamental landscaping that commended the name South Park.[2]

The company implemented so many innovative policies and programs to benefit its employees that the novel design of the bicycle houses might easily be overlooked. That long list included, in part, a committee system of supervision to replace superintendents; a week's vacation at full salary; ten hours pay for nine and one-half hours work; short recreational periods devoted to calisthenics; bathing facilities available before or after work; a relief association for ill employees; an awards program for best suggestions to improve the company; subsidized lunches served in a comfortable dining hall; a library; clean, well-ventilated interiors; and a color scheme (light yellow) to reduce eye-strain.[3]

Exercise by bicycle fit easily into the company's philosophy of welfare work, leading to plans for two sets of sheltering houses, one for men on Rubicon Street and the other around a corner on Stewart Street for men and women, each adjacent to the factory complex. The Stewart Street shelters served initially as stables and were built before 1896, probably during the early 1890s. The Rubicon Street buildings stood ready for use in 1896 or 1897, and each shelter contributed in a small way to Patterson's comprehensive campaign to enlarge and beautify the company's industrial grounds following the World's Columbian Exposition in 1893, which he visited. By then, the company's business had trebled, and just as George Day and Albert Pope returned from Chicago with grand ideas for their industrial works in Hartford, so too did Patterson pursue similar visions for his rapidly growing firm in Dayton, albeit advancing the contributions of American industry to the City Beautiful movement on a more all-encompassing scale.[4]

During this period, Williams formed a partnership with architect and engineer Frank Mills Andrews, a graduate of Cornell University who had worked with William Le Baron Jenney and William Bryce Mundie in Chicago, assisting with that firm's commissions at the exposition, where he met Patterson. The firm of Williams and Andrews became the company's principal architects during this period of expansion, but only until December 1898, when the partnership dissolved and Andrews continued to design for Patterson.[5]

Attribution of the bicycle house designs to the firm of Williams and Andrews rests mostly on the cohesive use of building materials and color, principally the dark-stained, novelty clapboard siding, which heightened shadow, and corrugated metal applied to the hipped roofs; in addition, the architects would have provided structural drawings. However, Patterson also retained Olmsted, Olmsted and Eliot to develop landscape plans for factory lawns and gardens, and presumably John Charles Olmsted could have collaborated in any schematic drawings for the simple buildings on Rubicon Street. Patterson and Olmsted exchanged correspondence in 1895, followed by the firm's first plans for the company in January 1896, including a planting list that year. The 1896 plan includes the existing stables, with pencil notations indicating the planned conversion to bicycle houses, but the Rubicon Street houses and wheelman's clubhouse are not shown; Olmsted also visited the company's site in 1898.[6]

Although he would not have designed the other, similarly-clad, wood-frame industrial buildings on the factory

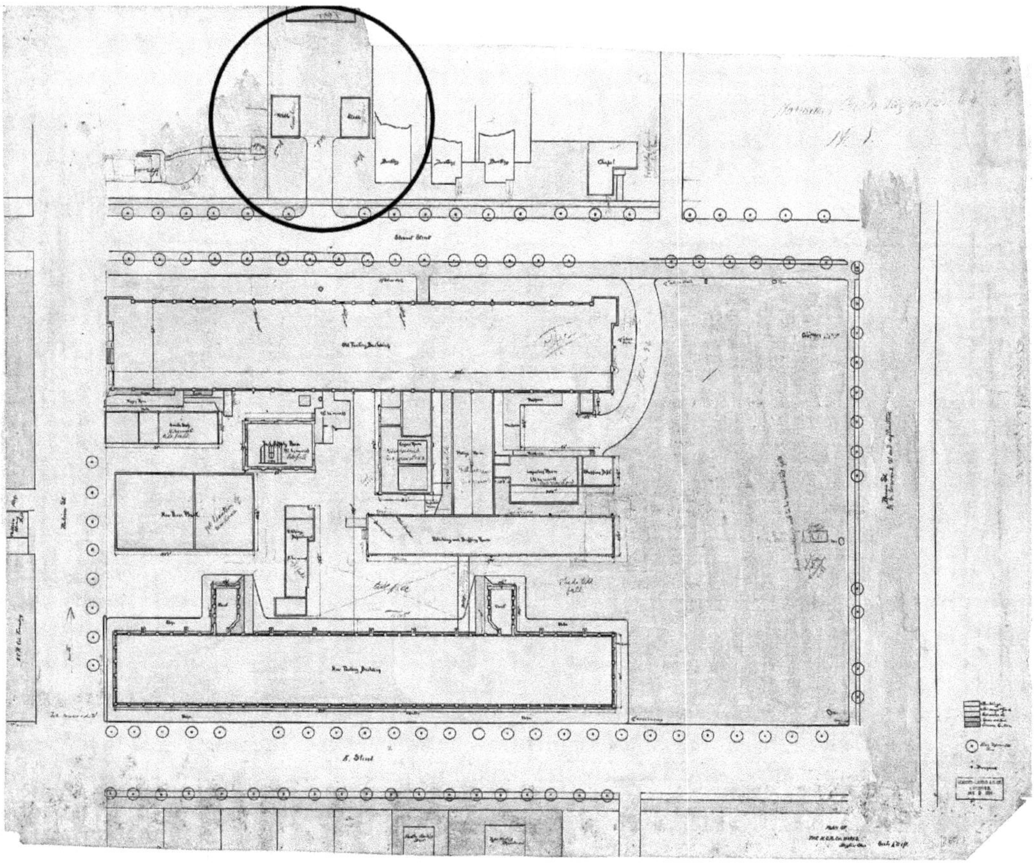

Figure 115. Plan of National Cash Register Company's Works, January 9, 1896, by Olmsted, Olmsted and Eliot, Plan No. 280–1. The Stewart Street bicycle houses are shown as stables with penciled notations indicating conversion to bicycles. Plans for the arching pergola are also noted in pencil. National Park Service, Frederick Law Olmsted National Historic Site.

grounds, Olmsted's active involvement in the project clearly influenced plans for both the Stewart Street and Rubicon Street bicycle houses. His hand is most evident in the arching, vine-covered, lattice pergola with shingle-clad roof at the entrance to the Stewart Street buildings, forming a portal above the drive that led beyond the houses to the company's stables, where Patterson summoned company officers for early morning exercise. In addition, the ornamental, curving planting beds in front of those same bicycle houses strengthened the overall design, and in the process likely inspired increased attention to the design of the Rubicon Street houses, most evident in the lattice-framed passageway behind the latter houses, as well as the matching sign boards that closely link all three buildings.[7]

A fourth shelter for bicycles, probably similar to those on Rubicon Street, stood behind the men's pavilion on Stewart Street by 1897, and although Patterson sought to curtail distinctions among white and blue-collar labor in the workplace, men of higher corporate standing may have been assigned to those houses due to the proximity of the women's shelters. By limiting the workday for women to eight hours, the company indirectly avoided congestion among bicycle riders; women arrived at eight o'clock, one hour later than men, and left fifteen minutes earlier.

Figure 116. By 1900, the date of this photograph (top), the Olmsted firm's landscaping plan and pergola had given the bicycle houses a picturesque appearance. The small shed in the foreground sheltered fire hoses, and a large water tank stood behind the men's house. By 1919, the Stewart Street houses had been enlarged to include space for motorcycles. From the Collection of Dayton History.

Figure 117. In 1896 or 1897, the National Cash Register Company also built bicycle houses and a watchman's house on Rubicon Street, around the corner from the Stewart Street houses and adjacent to the company's club house for wheelmen (right). The photograph is dated 1897. From the Collection of Dayton History.

The company also provided a station with compressed-air valves where riders could inflate tires. A small house for fire hoses fronted the women's pavilion, and a water tank stood directly behind.[8]

By 1919, the stables at the Stewart Street complex had been converted to bicycle and motorcycle storage, and additional sheds built, possibly to replace those on Rubicon Street when the company erected a new factory on the site in 1899 or 1900. Unfortunately, none of the buildings has survived and little is known about the design of interior mechanisms to hold bicycles. Nevertheless, photographs show that the Stewart Street houses provided two levels of storage, and the clubhouse photograph shows a metal bicycle rack similar to racks patented in 1899 and 1900, one by W.H. Humphrey and the other by H.L. Wilcox.[9]

Even less is known about the company's clubhouse for wheelmen, located adjacent to the bicycle sheds on Rubicon Street. When the company moved to South Park in 1888, modestly-sized, wood-frame houses stood in scattered locations in the surrounding blocks near the factory, and private builders erected new houses as the roster of company employees multiplied. However, the company also built an assortment of residential structures for its own purposes, and the one-story wheelman's clubhouse probably falls into that category. Although some of the architectural ornament would have been common

Figure 118. National Cash Register Company's clubhouse for wheelmen, abutting the Rubicon Street bicycle sheds. The wall poster announces that Dayton's 1898 racing season is underway, and the bicycle stand depicted may have been similar to those placed in the adjacent sheds. From the Collection of Dayton History.

for any residential structure, eaves brackets on the porch for example, the decorative gable-peak and the sculptural woodcarvings on the window lintels are more distinctive, as are the crests mounted on the walls. Thus, attribution may once again belong to Williams and Andrews, and the building's date probably corresponds to that of the Rubicon Street shelters, 1896 or 1897.[10]

Yet clear credit also belongs to the Olmsted firm, just as it does for the bicycle houses. Patterson's plans for landscape improvements extended well beyond factory grounds and included neighborhood houses, where by 1900 John Olmsted and Frederick Law Olmsted, Jr., practicing as the Olmsted Brothers, had provided detailed planting recommendations for house lots, including vine covered fences to improve privacy; shrubbery or perennial plantations to screen fences and outbuildings; fruit and forest trees for shade and varied backgrounds or skyline; and fenced vegetable gardens. If the company followed the Olmsteds' advice, the trellis separating the clubhouse from its adjoining lot is adorned with Virginia Creeper.[11]

Comstock, Cheney and Company. The bicycle sheds erected in Ivoryton, Connecticut, by Comstock, Cheney and Company are far more typical of the shelters provided by manufacturers for commuting wheelmen and wheelwomen. Located in the town of Essex, not far from the mouth of the Connecticut River, the village of Ivoryton is one of New England's numerous factory towns, planned and dominated by single industries—some with tarnished legacies. Established shortly before the Civil War by partners Samuel M. Comstock and George A. Cheney, the company engaged in the ivory trade with East Africa to produce combs, piano

Figure 119. Brothers Robert and Archibald Cheney, owners of Comstock, Cheney and Company in Ivoryton, Connecticut, provided employees with bicycle sheds of simple but efficient design. The wide-open bays accommodated arrivals and departures without difficulty, and low racks elevated the handlebars of alternating bicycles to maximize capacity in the buildings. Decorative eaves brackets added modest architectural detail to the otherwise ordinary structures. Courtesy Ivoryton Library Association.

and organ keys, billiard balls, and various other products. At one end of that trade, exploitation of human, non-human, and ecological resources left devastatingly permanent scars; at the other, the company built homes and dormitories for workers as well as public buildings such as a company hall for plays and concerts (today a playhouse), or subsidized the cost of still others including the town library, which survives as a village centerpiece.[12]

Bicycles had arrived by the time brothers Robert and Archibald Comstock inherited the business, and both men were active members of the Ivoryton Wheel Club, organized in 1892. Both also understood that bicycles were good for business, creating a more mobile and thus more expansive work force, and the two bicycle sheds furnished by the company encouraged that mode of transportation. As designed, the shelters were elongated, open bay structures with slightly-raised floor boards and capped by shingle-clad gable roofs with short hips at each end. Sturdily built with heavy posts that framed the open bays, the sheds also revealed modest architectural detail in the shape of decorative brackets at the eaves. Within each shed, the company installed racks that elevated the handlebars of alternating bicycles, thus increasing overall capacity. The wide, open bays addressed the challenge of crowding during arrivals and departures in a simple, inexpensive manner. Ironically, the design for the shelters may have originated with the company's elongated bleaching houses, nearly identical to the bicycle sheds in shape and roof configuration.[13]

Figure 120. The Cheney brothers also were active cyclists, and the company erected a house for the Ivoryton Wheel Club, which formed in 1892. Located on Main Street near the village center, the building displayed a variety of architectural embroidery, including a wooden emblem of a high-wheel ordinary bicycle mounted on a panel in the building's gable peak. The club later added a bowling alley behind the house and added a wing on the building's opposite side, lengthening the porch in the process. Courtesy Ivoryton Library Association.

As cycling enthusiasts, the Comstock brothers brooked no stint in the building of the two-story clubhouse, which is substantially larger and architecturally more ambitious than its counterpart endowed by the Patterson brothers in Dayton. Located on Main Street at the village center, a short walk from the cutting factory, the house included a parlor and library on the first floor of the two-story, gable-front structure, and a billiards room in a one-story wing. A spacious front porch with very low-pitched or flat roof supported by lathe-turned posts with scroll brackets, in turn carrying a spindle valance, visually unified the building's two units, as did the spindle balustrade above the porch and wing. The porch also offered ample space for social gatherings, and when the club later added a second wing on the building's opposite site, righting the imbalance, members also extended the porch to shelter the entire street façade. Modest architectural details included alternating bands of clapboard and patterned shingles, eaves brackets, and decorative window-pane configurations, revealing the influence of America's Queen Anne style, so popular during the 1890s. However, the wooden model of a high-wheel bicycle crowning the gable peak, together with the prominent sign band above the porch, announced the building's function and suggest that the builder was also a cycling enthusiast. Club rides to nearby towns were standard fare, and members later built a bowling alley behind the clubhouse.[14]

Bicycle Racks. Although the devices employed to support bicycles in both the Dayton houses and Ivoryton sheds are not visible in the photographs, both

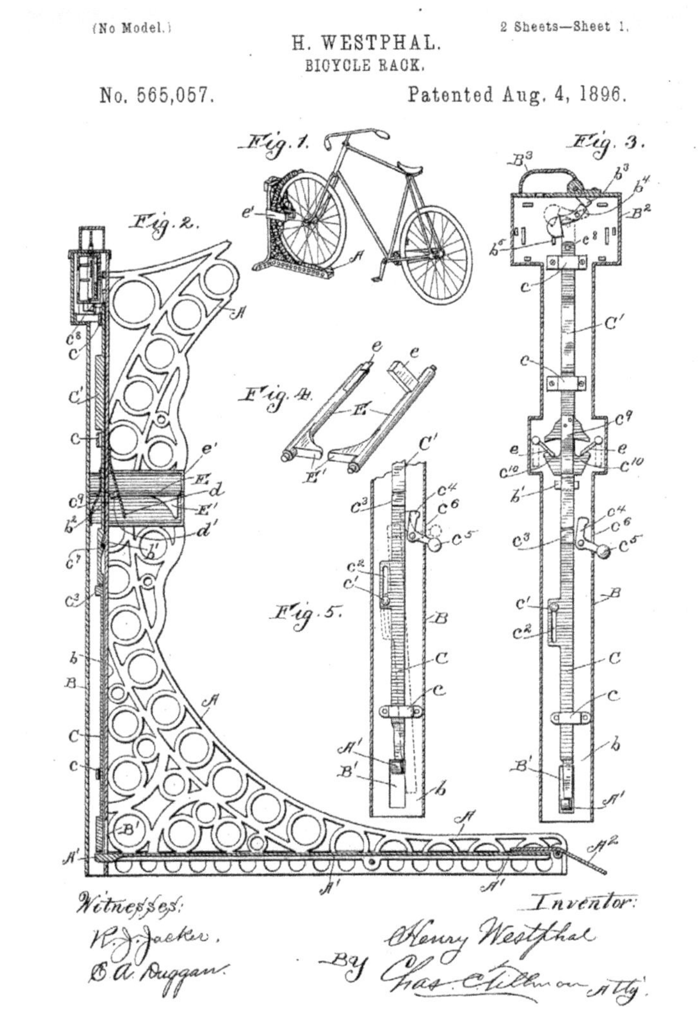

Figure 121. Securing bicycles in standing positions to maximize available space in bicycle houses required supporting devices, and the bicycle industry's astounding record of patented inventions extended to bicycle stands and racks. Company owners could choose from numerous designs, ranging from the very simple, such as that patented by W.J. Smart in 1896, to more ornate examples including that patented by Henry Westphal, shown here, that same year. United States Patent Office.

companies faced no shortage of options. Not surprisingly, as with just above every aspect of the bicycle industry, inventors created and patented numerous designs for bicycle racks, most of which were developed during the height of the bicycle craze and range from very minimal to complex. Among the simplest of early examples, that patented by Walter J. Smart of South Orange, New Jersey, in June 1896, relied on a single, looping bar of metal bent twice at right angles to create vertical arms and slightly arched at the arms' two lower ends, which passed through the sockets of a floor-mounted base with contoured surface to accept a wheel. Short intended his device to provide support without the use of clamps that could mar the finish of bicycles and required time-consuming adjustment. His design also consumed little space, but the thin arms were susceptible to damage. Little more than a month later, August 1896, Henry Westphal from Chicago secured a patent for a far more durable and ornamental rack, with latches that could be closed with lock and key; Westphal also secured a second patent that year for a much-simplified version, using a short arm capable of being attached to a wall or post.[15]

The following summer, Howard Brundage from Newburgh, New York, patented a bicycle rack similar to the most common types of racks in use today, intending his invention to be simple, inexpensive to construct, durable, and designed to accommodate bicycles with wheels and tires of different sizes by tapering the center of each spindle. Earlier that spring, April 1897, the George Hirschmans, father and son, of Morristown, New Jersey, had patented a similar device but with hinged base-blocks capable of securing a larger number of bicycles. By 1899, Henry L. Wilcox from Great Barrington, Massachusetts, had added angle reinforcements to prevent the weight of multiple bicycles from tipping the rack, intending the device to be constructed of either wood or metal. As with both the Brundage and Hirschman designs, Wilcox's racks could be folded and thus transported. Nor did inventors overlook the value of transporting bicycles by trolley during this period, and in 1898 Thomas Coleman Du Pont of Johnstown, Pennsylvania, devised a bicycle carrier to be mounted on the rear of railway cars in a manner that allowed bicycles to be secured or removed easily but did not impede the movement of passengers.[16]

Accessibility. The design of supporting devices represented only one part of the problem of sheltering bicycles; easy access presented additional difficulties, and in 1898, German architect and engineer Carl Bernhard, who traveled and worked in America, won first prize in a design competition sponsored by the Prussian Society of Engineers for a bicycle storage house. Describing the challenge as one of interest to factory owners as well as station masters on suburban railroads, the competition criteria specified a low building that occupied minimal area but accommodated 200 bicycles capable of being stored and removed with a minimum of confusion or loss of time. Bernhard designed a simple, two-story structure with a partially-below-grade first story and a slightly extended second story to facilitate each floor's system of ingress and egress.[17]

Bicycles stood in place with the help of parallel floor strips creating a channel, with end posts supported by short struts framing a single rack. On the basement level, floor strips formed three rows, one abutting each long side and one occupying the center of that room, creating passageways on both sides of the central row, where Barnard staggered the floor strips to maximize use of space. On the upper floor, two rows of staggered, symmetrically-placed racks established three passageways. Each of the five passageways led to or from individual entrance and exit doors, and flights of steps dictated the different uses of those

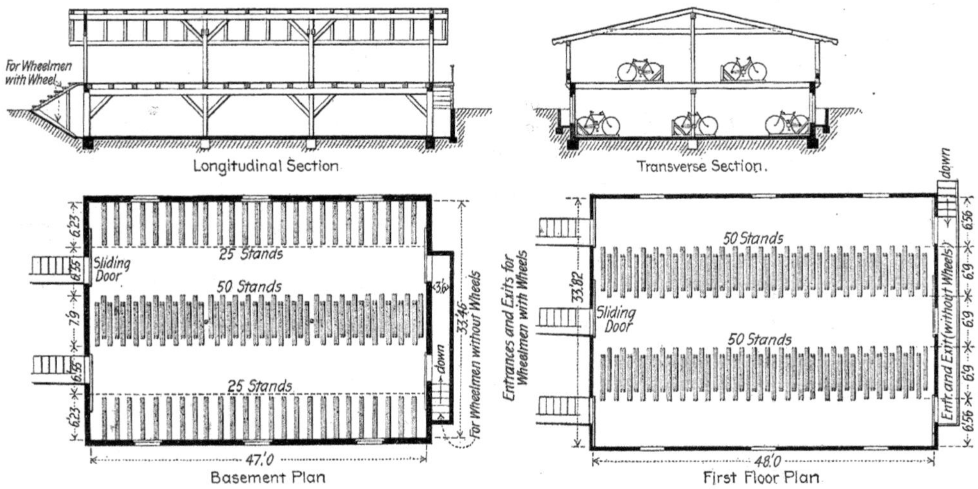

Figure 122. Securing bicycles in an upright position and arranging stands to maximize capacity represented two manageable challenges for companies, but designing systems that allowed workers to arrive and depart with a minimum of confusion or loss of time could be more troublesome. In 1898, German architect and engineer Carl Bernhard, who traveled in America, won first prize in a design competition sponsored by the Prussian Society of Engineers for a bicycle storage house. Bernard established five separate passageways that led to or from individual entrance and exit doors, and flights of steps dictated the different uses of those doors. At one end of the building, cyclists with bicycles used short flights of steps (with abutting inclines for bicycles) to enter or leave either floor; on the building's opposite end, doors on both floors abutted platforms extending across the building's full width, each platform accessible via a single flight of steps for pedestrians. Barnard's design provided space for 100 bicycles on each floor, and wheels stood in place with the help of parallel floor strips, staggered to accommodate handlebars. *Engineering News* 39 (March 31, 1898).

doors. At one end of the building, cyclists carrying bicycles used short flights of steps with abutting inclines to enter or leave either floor; on the building's opposite end, doors on both floors abutted platforms extending across the building's full width for cyclists on foot, each platform accessible via a single flight of steps. Barnard's design provided space for 100 bicycles on each floor.[18]

Editors of *Engineering News* published in New York suggested that the design held potential as a paying venture in parks and along boulevards of major cities, but a few months later the Westcott-Jewell Company of Seneca Falls, New York, offered the journal's editors an American version of bicycle storage, enabling three-times as many bicycles in the same floor space as Barnard's plan, without compromising accessibility. The Westcott-Jewell system employed sets of three parallel channel arms occupying forty inches of linear distance, with the center arm elevated slightly to prevent the handlebars of the center bicycle from becoming tangled with those of the adjacent bicycles. In double-tier form, the rack could hold six bicycles in the same linear distance, and with a double row in a sufficiently wide room, twelve bicycles. The company had installed its devices successfully at New York's first Grand Central Station and several hotels, and the concern also manufactured bicycle racks for mounting on electrified trolley cars, front and back.[19]

Post Bicycle-Boom. The precipitous decline of bicycle-riding among adults after 1900, and subsequent transformation of cycling to an activity for children, did not occur uniformly in all sectors of American society, nor in all regions. If bicycles were no longer fashionable for urbane riders, workers nevertheless continued to wheel from home to work and back—at midday for meals as well as during morning and late afternoon hours. Lingering use surfaced in various places and in different contexts, but especially in parts of New York State where county side path commissions continued to fund repairs to side paths traveled by factory workers as the twentieth century's first decade ended. Moreover, if Henry Ford's Model T gradually put automobiles within economic reach of many Americans after 1908, World War I exposed critical flaws in the country's transportation networks, particularly the inability of trolley and interurban routes to serve essential factories and shipyards, as well as the inadequate service, haphazard schedules, rising fares, and vulnerability to strikes for those that did.

Bicycles solved many of those problems, and immediately after the war the Bicycle Manufacturers Association sought to capitalize on the bicycle's proven value to the country's war industries by encouraging manufacturers to purchase bicycles for their employees and to offer repayment by installments. Headed by Joseph Goodman, former editor of *Bicycling World*, the association published a short booklet in 1919, titled *The Bicycle: Admittedly the Lowest Cost Means of Transportation Between Two Given Points.* Unambiguously targeting industry,

Figure 123. Soon after public announcements of Carl Barnhard's prize, the Westcott-Jewell Company of Seneca Falls, New York, proclaimed that its storage design enabled three times as many bicycles in the same floor space as Barnard's plan, without compromising accessibility. The Westcott-Jewell system employed sets of three parallel channel arms, with the center arm elevated slightly to prevent the handlebars of the center bicycle from becoming tangled with those of adjacent bicycles. In double-tier form, the rack could hold six bicycles, and with a double row in an adequately wide room, twelve bicycles. The company installed its devices successfully at New York's first Grand Central Station, and the concern also manufactured bicycle racks for mounting on electrified trolley cars, front and back. *Engineering News* (May 5, 1898).

Figure 124. During World War I, bicycles provided an efficient means of commuting for workers employed at factories and shipyards. After the war, Joseph Goodman, secretary of the Bicycle Manufacturers Association, encouraged companies to give loans to employees to buy bicycles and invited company owners to send photographs of bicycle shelters. Images in the resulting publication also reveal creative methods for supporting bicycles, including overhead hangers shown at the Underwood Typewriter Company in Hartford (former factory of the Hartford Cycle Company). Bicycle Manufacturers Association, *The Bicycle: Admittedly the Lowest Cost Means of Transportation Between Two Given Points* (1919).

Goodman listed the bicycle's advantages to employers: reduction of illness by avoiding crowded trolley cars; healthful exercise; moderate cost; minimal maintenance; timely arrivals; and strengthened morale among workers.[20]

Goodman also observed that bicycles were easy to park, and he anticipated the need to persuade company owners about the value of parking facilities by soliciting support from various manufacturers, who responded with letters and photographs that provide the best documentation of bicycle houses and sheds erected during the 1890s and early years of the twentieth century, or in any case prior to World War I, as well as several creative devices to hold bicycles in place. Coincidence or not, Goodman's booklet leads with a reply from Charles Rice, factory manager for the Underwood Typewriter Company in Hartford, which by then occupied the factory built during 1891 and 1892 for Albert Pope's Hartford Cycle Company at the southeasterly corner of Capitol Avenue and Woodbine Street, a complex much expanded by 1919. There, workers hung bicycles on hooks of alternating lengths, secured in longitudinal arms that were suspended, in turn, from massive floor beams.[21]

The Pierce-Arrow Motor Car Company in Buffalo, also with ties to bicycle manufacturing, provided space for 800 wheels and used a suspension system as well, but with tall frames—some of which were freestanding. Several concerns

Figure 125. In Middletown, Ohio, the American Rolling Mills Company erected shelters with stands for 1,000 bicycles, estimating that at least 1,600 workers commuted by bicycle during the company's three shifts. The racks are low arms mounted on the floor, and the buildings' design suggests an architect's hand. Bicycle Manufacturers Association, *The Bicycle: Admittedly the Lowest Cost Means of Transportation Between Two Given Points* (1919).

in Springfield, Massachusetts, including Smith and Wesson, the United States Armory, the Boston and Albany Railroad Company, and the Gilbert and Barker Company, built open-bay structures with metal roofs and low frames to hold bicycles in place, not much different than those patented by Brundage and the Hirschmans. In Ohio, the Dayton Steel Foundry Company erected a similarly mundane structure but with two levels, as did that city's Domestic Engineering Company.[22]

However, a few companies may have hired architects to prepare designs, and those erected by the American Rolling Mills Company in Middletown, Ohio, rival the houses built by the National Cash Register Company. The firm built four elongated structures with metal-clad gable roofs and fully open sides, but the buildings conclude with gable-end walls, each pierced by oversized window openings, extended in height by parapet eaves, and crowned by a chimney cap. Centered along the front house is a pavilion with cross-gable façade similar to those on the gable ends but with a large, arched window that appears to be glazed, thus enclosing what may have been a utility room. The houses shelter floor-mounted bicycle supports, but with arms raised horizontally to accept wheels, rather than vertically. Those and other bicycle houses can be added to the long list of contributions to industrial architecture precipitated by the manufacture of bicycles.

Appendix: Other Bicycle Factories in the East and Midwest

Length of the preceding chapters precludes full consideration of roughly a dozen other surviving factories devoted to the manufacture of bicycles during the late nineteenth century, many of them adapted to that use and then converted to other purposes following collapse of the bicycle boom. Hopefully the documentation of these additional works will encourage historians to seek out other surviving examples located in or beyond the boundaries of this study.

New Jersey

Liberty Cycle Company—Rockaway Works. Located on Stickle Avenue in Rockaway, New Jersey, and built in 1889–1890 by the Rockaway Manufacturing Company Consolidated, chartered in 1885 as the Rockaway Manufacturing Company by two Philadelphia investors, John H. Palmer and Richard W. Dorphley, and a third local shareholder, William H. Davis, to import, export, and manufacture bicycles, tricycles, and machine tools for bicycles. In 1889, with funding from local investors Byron K. Stickle and George W. Stickle, and New York financier Frederick Stimson, the company merged with the Acme Buttonhole Manufacturing Company, Ltd., and erected the factory. The firm produced bicycles by contract, including a brief agreement with Harry Rouse and Charles Duryea to build Sylph bicycles. In 1889, Scottish machinist Robert Perkins became superintendent of the Rockaway works, which began producing Meteor bicycles for a New York importer, Banker and Campbell Company, and Referee bicycles for a Philadelphia concern, Bretz, Curtis and Company. In 1892, the firm began manufacturing its own Liberty bicycles, and in December 1894 the business reorganized as the Liberty Cycle Company, aided by a New York retail agency, Wilson, Myers and Company. As demand for bicycles increased, straining the limited space at the Rockaway works, controlling shareholders moved production to Bridgeport, Connecticut, in 1895, creating conflict among shareholders and leading to receivership in 1896, followed by a split of ownership. Production of Liberty bicycles remained in Bridgeport (the factory does not survive), and a new business, Cycle Components Company, owned principally by Perkins and George Stickle acquired the Rockaway factory and began producing chains, pedals, and other parts until about 1898. By 1900 Perkins had formed his own bicycle business, the Perkins Cycle Company, and continued to use the factory briefly. The works eventually provided space for the Rockaway Automobile Company, which ended production before 1911.

Zimmerman Manufacturing Company. A wood frame factory located where Elm, Conover, and Hudson Streets converge in Freehold, New Jersey, and built before 1886 for textile-related businesses. After becoming world champion at Chicago in August 1893, and announcing his decision to turn professional, Albert Augustus Zimmerman—along with his brother-in-law Joseph McDermott, George S. MacDonald (manager of the American Raleigh Company), and Martin Peters (a fourth investor from Philadelphia)—chartered the Zimmerman Manufacturing Company in April 1894, and were soon joined by W.W. Walford, owner of the Nimrod Cycle Company in Bristol, England, who succeeded MacDonald. The company purchased the factory in 1895 and began building bicycles with the Zimmy moniker that season, with parts manufactured in Bristol and assembled in Freehold that first year. By the spring of 1896, Englishman George Bailey had become superintendent of the Freehold plant, while Zimmerman promoted his bicycle by becoming an international phenomenon on the racing circuit, acquiring considerable wealth in the process. Conflict with Walford developed, and in 1897 Zimmerman used his fortune to rescue the company, reorganizing as the A.A. Zimmerman Manufacturing Company. Financial problems continued, however, and in the fall of that year William S. Burtis, Zimmerman's friend and partner in a retail sporting goods business, purchased the factory and its machinery with the help of local investors, reorganizing as the A.A. Zimmerman Cycle Company. For a few years, Zimmerman continued to travel, race, and promote his bicycles, but profitability at the Freehold factory remained elusive, and the company became insolvent once again. The factory sold at a sheriff's sale in 1900 for $10.00, and Zimmerman retired from cycling in 1903, turning instead to hotel management in Point Pleasant, where he remained for many years. The factory returned to textile use and has provided space for various commercial and industrial uses ever since.

H.B. Smith Machine Company. In 1889, inventor George W. Pressey from Hammonton, New Jersey, patented a design for a high-wheel bicycle that promised greater safety by placing the small wheel in front of the large wheel and employed ratchet levers rather than pedal cranks, the former requiring an up-and-down leg motion that also placed the rider's driving weight slightly forward of the center of gravity to keep the small wheel grounded. To manufacture the bicycle, Pressey turned to another inventor, Hezekiah Bradley Smith, who had patented machine tools for the woodworking industry and who, following the Civil War, had acquired the industrial village of Shreveville in Burlington County, New Jersey, renaming it Smithville in 1878 and forming the H.B. Smith Machine Company. Following its introduction in 1881 and its success on the racing circuit with Arthur Zimmerman, the American Star bicycle produced by Pressey, Smith, and the latter's machinists contributed to the bicycle's evolving technology during the high-wheel era, creating ties to the wood-working tool industry rather than the arms and sewing-machine industries. Production continued into the safety bicycle era, to about 1892, but the bicycle's novelty had faded by then. The Pressey-Smith joint venture also shaped the latter's company town, and although most of the shops once devoted to industrial use have not survived or stand protected as ruins, other parts of the community are well preserved, and today Smith's industrial village is the Historic Smithville Park, owned by Burlington County and managed as part of its park system—one of very few such historic sites devoted to interpretation of cycling history in America.

Pennsylvania

Relay Manufacturing Company. Constructed in stages as a wool-hat factory and comprising a complex of buildings and factory yard on the westerly side of Maple Street between Chestnut and Spruce Streets in a neighborhood of row houses in Reading, Pennsylvania. Parts of the complex probably date to 1871, and thus are among the country's oldest surviving buildings to house bicycle production, which began with acquisition of the works by the Relay Manufacturing Company in 1895. John R. Miller, a manufacturer of wool hats, and machinist J. George Ziegler formed that business in 1892 and began producing Relay bicycles and saddles in a small shop on Cherry Street. In 1894, Ziegler patented a slotted rear-wheel fork that allowed wheels to be removed for repair without parting the chain, and the following year the company introduced several distinctive designs for three-wheeled delivery carriers, necessitating the larger building and reorganization of the business. In 1896, Ziegler patented a design for pressed, sheet-metal fittings with coupling sleeves that reinforced frame joints, turning to a stamping process that New England's bicycle manufacturers were slow to adopt and providing a marketing opportunity for the 1897 season. In 1899, the firm granted ABC an option to purchase the factory, but the latter declined and in 1900 Relay quietly sold the factory and dissolved. By 1904, the Pennsylvania Knitting Mills Company had adapted the factory to textile production.

Reading Cycle Manufacturing Company. Constructed in 1890 as a two-and-one-half story, load-bearing-brick car barn for the

Reading City Passenger Railway Company and located at Exeter and Tenth Streets. Reading hat-company owner Henry C. England, cycle-shop owner, mechanic, and frame designer Charles Dundore, and other investors organized the Reading Cycle Manufacturing Company in 1896 and acquired the building that year, retaining builder Henry Price to modify the structure. The company began producing Vindex, Grand Vindex, and Simplex bicycles under an agreement with the National Sewing Machine Company based in Illinois, which marketed various products using the Vindex name. In 1898, Dundore departed and England began manufacturing chainless bicycles as well as bicycle parts, leasing the factory in 1899 to the Reading Chainless Gear Company, which acquired rights to chainless drive systems patented by Oliver H. Gentry and assigned to the Vindex Toy Company. By that time, England had turned to automobile production and late in 1899 changed his company's name to the Reading Automobile and Gear Company. A year later, Charles Duryea moved to Reading from Springfield, Massachusetts, where he and his brother Frank had developed one of the country's first gasoline-powered motor cars. In Reading, Duryea, Herbert M. Sternbergh and Henry Millholland formed the Duryea Power Company in 1901, and between 1902 and 1907 produced three-wheeled, three-cylinder Duryea vehicles, followed by four-wheeled Phateon models, using space in the 10th Street factory during part of that period. By 1902, England had changed his company's name to the Relay Motor Car Company. A business fabricating steel alloys for special purposes currently uses the building.

Keystone Match and Machine Company. Constructed in 1894 as a two-story, brick factory of standard mill construction to manufacture matches and located between Lafayette and Walnut Streets in Lebanon, Pennsylvania, home to architect Edward C. Euston who designed the building. In 1893, machinist and inventor John G. Xander patented a bicycle frame called "Neversink" and assigned a one-half interest in the patent to James C. Reber, who with Xander and James T. Reber formed the Acme Manufacturing Company to produce Stormer bicycles. Xander and the Rebers severed their business ties in 1896, and Xander purchased the Keystone Match and Machine Company works in 1897, retaining Reading architect Abner A. Richter to design a substantial two-story addition along Walnut Street, where he produced Xander and Penryn bicycles for several seasons. Xander's company remained outside the ABC conglomerate and began building steam-powered automobiles, but productivity declined and Xander returned to Reading in 1900, creating the Xander Machine and Supply Company. The Lebanon factory sold at auction in 1904 to Lebanon resident Milton H. Schnader, who partnered with New York inventor Colcord Upton to build Upton Motorcars for several years. A reorganized Lebanon Motor Works assumed control of the business from 1905 to 1907, when production ended. Over the decades the factory has been adapted for use by the Hershey Company, a textile manufacturer, and Jubilee Ministries—a fellowship of Anabaptist Churches LMC (Lancaster Mennonite Conference), its current owner.

Ohio

Winton Bicycle Company. Constructed in 1892 by the Cleveland Standard Lighting Company as a three-story factory of standard mill construction for the manufacture of vapor cook stoves and ovens, and located on Perkins Avenue in Cleveland, home to architect Fenimore C. Bate who designed the building. Armed with several patents for safety bicycles, Scottish inventor Alexander Winton, who had formed the Winton Bicycle Company in 1890, attracted the interest of the lighting company's owners, who acquired a controlling interest in Winton's firm in 1892 and provided space to manufacture bicycles that year. In 1893, the company retained Bate to design several large additions to the factory complex, completing the work by 1895. However, by 1894 Winton had begun experimenting with automobiles and in March 1897 formed the Winton Motor Carriage Company, using a different site. He also formed the Winton Engine Company, which he then sold to General Motors. The Standard Lighting Company continued to build bicycles until profitability ended and the company turned its attention to other products.

Union Manufacturing Company. Constructed in phases between 1864 and 1882 at the corner of Hamilton and Bismarck Streets in Toledo, Ohio, for the manufacture of sewing machines and wood products. During the early 1890s, William Peter, the patriarch of a wealthy family of German descent, acquired the factory and with his son, Alvin Peter, and another relative, Frederick A. Peter, expanded production to include milling machinery and, by the spring of 1895, Viking, Norseman, and Hero bicycles. The company represented a conspicuous sector of the bicycle industry at the height of its craze, that of firms owned by local investors who, having experience in manufacturing, borrowed the advancing technology of bicycle design and exploited public demand. The Peters steered away from novel components that attracted cycling's elite and instead remained content to build dependable bicycles for the rank and file at reasonable prices—forging a solid reputation among retailers in the process. The company also secured contracts in Australia, New Zealand, England, Sweden, Russia, and South Africa. Following a successful 1897 season, Alvin Peter and several other investors incorporated the Viking Bicycle and Motor Company, and in 1899 became one of only three Toledo bicycle manufacturers to join the ABC trust, leaving more than a dozen other companies or parts makers in the city outside the conglomerate. The trust moved production of Viking bicycles to the former Lozier works, and by 1904 the Hamilton Street factory belonged to the Toledo Furniture and Manufacturing Company.

Indiana

Henley Machine Tool Works. Constructed in 1884 by Quaker Micajah Henley for the manufacture of roller skates, and located on Sixteenth Street in Richmond, Indiana. Over his lifetime, Henley secured roughly two dozen patents, many of them for roller skates but others for a great variety of machines, including lawn mowers, pulley lathes, and a portable device for weaving pickets into wire fences. Henley and his father, a building contractor, oversaw design and construction of the four-story factory, which borrows from standard mill construction but also exemplifies regional building traditions, especially the unusual window proportions, wide enough to hold paired sash, as well as the height of spandrel walls between windows, which decrease as building height increases. In 1885, he doubled the plant's size, becoming the country's leading manufacturer of roller skates. He was also among Richmond's first to own a high-wheel bicycle and by1884 had established a sales agency for Columbia bicycles. In June 1895, he announced plans to produce bicycles and promoted his eponymous moniker by supplying a team of racers, who competed at the Richmond Driving Park on the National Road. As demand for bicycles decreased after 1897, he accepted limited profits but also avoided heavy losses and continued to diversify, producing bicycles, lawnmowers, and roller skates in seasonal succession, respectively, with other products such as machine tools and natural gas meters. Henley remained content to offer carefully built bicycles of quality, albeit unexceptional in design, and ignored an invitation to join ABC. He continued to produce bicycles until 1904, and despite the bicycle industry's collapse by then, Henley and his factory remained perfectly matched in adaptability until he retired in 1921.

Diamond Chain and Manufacturing Company. A four-story factory of skeletal-frame, reinforced-concrete construction built in 1918 at the intersection of West Street and Kentucky Avenue in Indianapolis, Indiana. The original works included a one-story plant, also reinforced concrete but in the form of a production shed, and in 1928 Indianapolis architects Bishop, Knowlton, and Carson designed an Art Deco office addition. The company traces its origins to the Indianapolis Chain and Stamping Company, formed in December 1890 by Arthur C. Newby, Edward C. Fletcher, and Glenn Howe, sole owners soon joined by Charles E. Test. Newby, as president, promoted the company as the country's only (and later the first) manufacturer of chains designed exclusively for bicycles, and Fletcher and Test added mechanical ingenuity, securing patents for their originations. In 1895, the company built a new factory at the corner of Georgia and Mississippi Streets (no longer standing) and soon dominated the American chain market, commanding acquisition by the ABC trust in 1899. Led by Lucius "Lew" Wainwright, the American Bicycle Company Chain Factory became part of the ABC's subsidiary Automobile and Cycle Parts Company, later the Federal Manufacturing Company, and production became more diverse to meet the growing demands of motorized vehicles. Chain production remained profitable, partially stemming ABC's losses as bicycle sales plummeted, and after ABC failed in 1902, Wainwright and local investors formed the Diamond Chain and Manufacturing Company in 1905 and acquired the Georgia Street factory. Production increased so steadily that within a decade the company had outgrown the 1895 factory, leading to construction of the existing works in 1918. The company is likely the last surviving business to have been part of ABC, but its factory is now closed and threatened with demolition pending plans to build a soccer stadium.

Chapter Notes

The following abbreviations are used for the cycling journals cited extensively throughout this work.

American Cyclist	*AC*
American Wheelman	*AW*
Bicycling World	*BW*
Bicycling World and L.A.W. Bulletin	*BWLAWB*
*Bicycling World and Motorcycle Review**	*BWMR*
L.A.W. Bulletin	*LAWB*
Wheel and Cycling Trade Review	*WCTR*

**Bicycling World and Motocycle Review* changed its name to *Bicycling World and Motorcycle Review* in September, 1906.

Introduction

1. "The Cycle Industry as Disclosed by the Census," *BW* 45 (June 5, 1902): 280–281; and "The Chicago Cycle Show," *American Machinist* 19 (January 30, 1896): 128–129. See also Bruce D. Epperson, *Peddling Bicycles to America: The Rise of an Industry* (Jefferson, NC: McFarland, 2010), 159–162. Charles Hetzel, a member of the Wheelmen organization (thewheelmen.org), has compiled a list of bicycle manufacturers and brands numbering 3,366 from 1890 to 1918. Although many manufacturers marketed numerous models, or sold to various retail concerns which then used their own trademarks, this accounting nevertheless proclaims the astonishing popularity of bicycles at their peak during the mid–1890s. Those who have explored local history have supported those tabulations, among them Carl Burgwardt, *Buffalo's Bicycles: Reflections on Buffalo's Colossal and Overlooked Bicycle Heritage* (Orchard Park, NY: Pedaling History Bicycle Museum, 2001). Some companies briefly added bicycle manufacturing to well-established production lines.

2. In Chicago, the factory first used by Arnold, Schwinn and Company in 1895 still stands at the corner of Lake and Peoria Streets, but the company moved to a new factory in West Chicago well before World War I. Following the 1871 fire in that city, Adolph Schoeninger rebuilt his Western Toy Company factory on Wells Street between Schiller and Sigel Streets, later changed the company name to Western Wheel Works, and constructed a new factory on West Schiller Street at the close of the high-wheel era. For origins the Gormully and Jeffery factory complex, see "Gormully & Jeffery," *WCTR* 4 (August 30, 1889): 5; "Drop Forgings," *WCTR* 5 (February 28, 1890): 19; "Trade Items," *WCTR* 8 (September 25, 1891): 139; "The Stars and Stripes…," *WCTR* 13 (March 2, 1894): 22; and "New Factories," *The Cycle* 1 (July 23, 1886): 291. See also Gormully and Jeffery, *Catalog* (1884), Chicago Historical Society.

3. Hugh Dolnar (né Horace Arnold), "Bicycle Tools-1" and "Bicycle Tools-16," *American Machinist* 18 (October 3, 1895): 781 and (February 13, 1896): 182, respectively.

Chapter 1

1. C.J.H. Woodbury, *The Fire Protection of Mills and Construction of Mill Floors; Containing Texts of Full Size Wood Mill Columns* (New York: John Wiley & Sons, 1882).

2. Betsy Hunter Bradley, *The Works: The Industrial Architecture of the United States* (New York: Oxford University Press, 1999), 136.

3. Frank Kidder, *Architects' and Builders' Handbook* (New York: John Wiley & Sons, 1882), 484–456; and 1931 ed., 320–21 and 854–898.

4. For "Modern Mill Building," see Boston Manufacturers Mutual Fire Insurance Co., *Report No. V, Slow Burning or Mill Construction* (Boston: published by the author, 1902, 1904, and 1908). For the Eclipse factory, see "We Make Progress" (July 3, 1895), 7; and "Eclipse Bicycle" (July 6, 1895), 7, both in *Elmira Daily Gazette*; the architects were Pierce and Bickford. See also "A Great Industry at Elmira," *BW* 31 (September 27, 1895), 761. See also Warranty Deed from the Elmira Industrial Association to Eclipse Bicycle Company, recorded July 2, 1895, in Volume 106, Page 538, Chemung County Registry of Deeds (Elmira). See also Sanborn-Perris Map Co., Ltd., "Elmira, New York" (1898), Plate 3. William C. Allington was the builder and Abel Hodgkins the brick mason.

5. Portions of this section are taken from two previous articles by the author, "Bicycle Factory Remnants: The Heritage of 19th and 20th Century Cycling," in *Cycle History 20. Proceedings of the 20th International Cycling History Conference, Freehold, New Jersey, USA (July 30 to August 1, 2009)*, Gary W. Sanderson, ed. (Cheltenham, England: Quorum Print Ltd. for the John Pinkerton Memorial Publishing Fund, 2010), 206–218; and "Wheels of Fortune: The Bicycle Boom, Trinity Cycle, and its Keene Factory," in *Historical New Hampshire* 67 (Fall–Winter 2013), 52–81.

6. Lindy Biggs, *The Rational Factory: Architecture, Technology, and Work in America's Age of Mass Production* (Baltimore: Johns Hopkins University Press, 1996), 1–3.

7. Bradley, *The Works*, viii–ix.

8. Horace Arnold, "Modern Machine Shop Economics," *Engineering Magazine* 11, Part 2 (May 1896): 263–298, at 268–269 and 288; and "This Plant is Five Hundred Feet Long," *WCTR* 15 (July 12, 1895): 31. Arnold's series about automated tools for the bicycle industry, published using the pen name Hugh Dolnar, begins as "Bicycle Tools-1," *American Machinist* 18 (October 3, 1895): 781, and ends with "Cycle Tools-31," *American Machinist* 19 (September 24, 1896): 894; his biographical sketch can be found in *Engineering Magazine* 9 (1895): unnumbered pages after that issue's index, page 12. Arnold recommended that machine shops of any configuration be designed to permit extension as business increased.

9. Dolnar, ne Horace Arnold, "Bicycle Tools-7" and "Bicycle Tools-18," *American Machinist* 18 (November 28, 1895): 941–942, and 19 (February 27, 1896): 231–232, respectively.

10. "Rebuilding the Lozier Factory," *WCTR* 14 (December 18, 1894): 52.

11. "The Remarkable Rise of the New Lozier Factory," *WCTR* 15 Supplement (March 8, 1895): 49.

12. Biggs, *Rational Factory*, 25.

Chapter 2

1. In "Bridging the American System and Mass Production: Albert Pope's System of Bicycle Manufacture," *Tools and Technology: Newsletter of the American Precision Museum* (Summer 1997): n.p., author Glen Norcliffe provides a lucid context for considering the contributions of bicycle manufacturing to American industry.

2. Patent 240,898 titled "Fly-Wheel and Bearing for Sewing Machine Stands," dated May 3, 1881, issued to George Fairfield.

3. Robert Perkins, "A Marvel of Mechanical Engineering," *Engineering Magazine* 9 (May 1895): 281–301. For Perkin's biographical sketch, see *Engineering Magazine* 9 (1895): unnumbered pages following that issue's index, page 14.

4. Guy Hubbard, comp., "Geneaology of the Machine Industries of Windsor, Vermont" (1922). Large wall chart available at the American Precision Museum, Windsor, Vermont.

5. Hubbard, "Genealogy." See also Patent 5,763 titled "Breech-Loading Fire-Arm," dated September 12, 1848, and issued to Christian Sharps. Between February and July 1852, the company acquired the land via a series of deeds from the heirs of Cornelius Butler, among them John, Abby, and Betsy Beach, Elisha Colt, Henry French, and William Imlay. See, for example, Warranty Deed from Elisha Colt, Samuel W. Collins, and Sarah H. Collins recorded March 1, 1852, in Volume 82, page 408; the company also conveyed a mortgage to Samuel Robbins and others, recorded in Volume 84, page 310, both in Hartford City and Town Clerk.

6. Hubbard, "Genealogy." See also Quitclaim Deed from Edward M. Archibald to the Weed Sewing Machine Company, dated May 29, 1869, recorded in Volume 130, page 105; Warranty Deed from the Sharps Rifle Manufacturing Company to the Weed Sewing Machine Company, recorded April 4, 1874, in Volume 152, page 472; Quitclaim Deed from the Charter Oaks Life Insurance Company to the Weed Sewing Machine Company, recorded January 26, 1881, in Book 184, page 308; Warranty Deed from Richard S. Laurence to Weed Sewing Machine Company, recorded May 11, 1882, in Book 188, page 52; and Quitclaim Deed from the Weed Sewing Machine Company, to Pope Manufacturing Company, a Maine corporation, recorded January 10, 1891, in Book 218, page 153; all in Hartford City and Town Clerk.

Land records provide no evidence of a leasehold agreement for the factory between 1866 and 1874, but the Weed concern may have rented space during that period. The Sharps concern did sell property to the Weed firm at another location (College Street) in March 1871, and also leased additional space at that location (possibly a retail store) three months later. See Warranty Deed dated March 1871, recorded in Volume 135, page 522, and Lease dated June 28, 1871, recorded in Volume 137, page 233, both in Hartford City and Town Clerk.

7. Hubbard, "Genealogy." For the Hartford Machine Screw Company, see Sanborn Map and Publishing Company, "Hartford, Connecticut" (1885): Plate 12.

8. David Hounshell, *From the American System to Mass Production: 1800 to 1932* (Baltimore: Johns Hopkins University Press, 1984), 194–207; and

Hugh Dolnar, né Horace Arnold, "Bicycle Tools-26," *American Machinist* 19 (June 25, 1896): 617–619. See also "Bicycle-Making," *Frank Leslie's Popular Monthly* 12 (November 1881): 641–644.

9. Norcliffe, "Bridging the American System."

10. Epperson, *Peddling Bicycles*, 235–238.

11. *Ibid.*

12. In "The First Commercial High Wheel Bicycle Made in America," *The Wheelmen* 82 (May 2013): 2–7, Lorne Shields has documented the manufacture of bicycles by Charles James Wall and brothers John and Melville Poland in Boston, as early as 1875. For patents, see James T. Allen, *Digest of Cycles or Velocipedes with Attachments Patented in the United States from 1789 to 1892* and *Patents and References: Lists of United States Patents for Cycles or Velocipedes, 1789 to 1893, Supplement* (Washington, D.C.: U.S. Patent Office, 1894); and Ross Hill, "Patents, Licenses, Contacts, and Litigation of the Pope Manufacturing Company During the Nineteenth Century," in *Cycle History 20. Proceedings of the 20th International Cycling History Conference, Freehold, New Jersey, USA (July 30 to August 1, 2009)*, Gary W. Sanderson, ed. (Cheltenham, England: Quorum Print Ltd. for the John Pinkerton Memorial Publishing Fund, 2010): 188–194.

13. In *WCTR*, see "This Plant Is Five Hundred Feet Long," 15 (July 12, 1895): 31; and "A Ramble Through the Sterling Works," 22 (December 1, 1898): 30. See also Horace Arnold, "Modern Machine Shop Economics," *Engineering Magazine* 11, Part 2 (May 1896): 263–298, at 268–269 and 288.

14. "Ideal Cycle Factory," *WCTR* 15 (April 26, 1895): 25.

15. *Ibid.*

16. *Ibid.*

17. "Manufacturing Cost," *CATR* 20 (February 10, 1898): 532.

18. Dolnar, "Bicycle Tools-1," *American Machinist* 18 (October 3, 1895): 781; the numbered series ends with "Cycle Tools-31," *American Machinist* 19 (September 24, 1896): 894, but articles published in subsequent issues (October 1, 1896, and November 19, 1896) are probably attributable to Arnold. See also Arnold, "Modern Machine Shop Economics," *Engineering Magazine* 11, Part 2 (May 1896): 263–298, at 268–269 and 288. For Arnold's biographical sketch, see *Engineering Magazine* 9 (1895): unnumbered pages following that issue's index, page 12.

19. Dolnar, "Bicycle Tools-1" and "Bicycle Tools-16," *American Machinist* 18 (October 3, 1895): 781, and (February 13, 1896): 182, respectively. See also "A New Bicycle Ball-Case Grinder," *American Machinist* 19 (September 10, 1896): 847; although not named, Arnold is presumably the author. See also advertisements by the Billings and Spencer Company in Hartford, the W.P. Davis Machine Company in Rochester, and the Garvin Machine Company in Philadelphia, all in *American Machinist* 18 (December 19, 1895): 1020.

20. Dolnar, "Bicycle Tools-18," *American Machinist* 19 (February 27, 1896): 231–232. At a minimum, Arnold inspected the following factories: Sterling Cycle Company (Sterling bicycles) Kenosha, Wisconsin; Perkins & Co., Grand Rapids, Michigan; Monarch Cycle Company (Monarch bicycles), Chicago; Gormully and Jeffrey Manufacturing Company (Rambler bicycles), Chicago; Western Wheel Works (Crescent bicycles), Chicago; St. Nicholas Manufacturing Company (St. Nicholas bicycles), Chicago; Stover Bicycle Manufacturing Co. (Iroquois bicycles), Freeport, Illinois; Indiana Bicycle Company (Waverly bicycles), Indianapolis; Plymouth Novelty Manufacturing Co. (wooden rims), Plymouth, Indiana; Lozier Manufacturing Company (Cleveland bicycles), Toledo and Thompsonville, Connecticut; Yost Manufacturing Company (Falcon bicycles); Toledo; Pope Manufacturing Company (Columbia bicycles), Hartford; Hartford Manufacturing Company (Hartford bicycles), Hartford; Liberty Cycle Company (Liberty bicycles), Rockaway, New Jersey and Bridgeport, Connecticut; Warwick Cycle Manufacturing Company (Warwick bicycles), Springfield, Massachusetts; and Overman Wheel Works (Victor bicycles), Chicopee, Massachusetts.

21. Dolnar, "Bicycle Tools 12," *American Machinist* 19 (January 9, 1896): 50–52.

22. Perkins, "A Marvel of Mechanical Achievement."

23. "Ideal Cycle Factory," *WCTR* 15 (April 26, 1895): 25. See also "American Industries-No. 35," *Scientific American* 42 (March 20, 1880): 181; "A Great American Manufacture," *BW* 2 (April 1881): 326–331; and "Bicycle Making," *Frank Leslie's Popular Monthly* 12 (November 1881): 641–644.

24. "American Industries-No. 35," *Scientific American* 42 (March 20, 1880): 181; "A Great American Manufacture," *BW* 2 (April 1881): 326–331; "Bicycle-Making," *Frank Leslie's Popular Monthly* 12 (November 1881): 641–644; "Ninth Annual Greeting, Pope Manufacturing Company," *LAWB* 2 (February 26, 1886): 134–162; and "The Columbia Bicycle Factory," *LAWB* (February 3, 1888): 54.

25. "American Industries-No. 35," *Scientific American* 42 (March 20, 1880): 181; and "A Great American Manufacture," *BW* 2 (April 1881): 326–331. See also Patent 250,289, titled "Die for Forging Rear Forks of Bicycles," dated November 29, 1881; Patent 250,981, titled "Die for Forging Bicycle-Head Blanks," dated December 13, 1881; and "Patent 250,902, titled "Die for Joining Fellies for Bicycle Wheels," dated December 13, 1881; all issued to Henry T. Russell and all assigned to the Pope Manufacturing Company. See also Perkins, "A Marvel of Mechanical Achievement"; "History of the Iver Johnson's Arms and Cycle Works," a typewritten manuscript, undated and unsigned, c. 1950; and an untitled list of products manufactured by the firm from the date of its inception, also typewritten and undated, but circa 1933, available at the Fitchburg Historical Society.

26. Hounshell, *American System*, 200–202; Norcliffe, "Bridging the American System"; and "A Great American Manufacture," *BW* 2 (April 1881): 326–331.

27. "Ideal Cycle Factory," *WCTR* 15 (April 26, 1895): 25; "Arnold, Bicycle Tools—19," *American Machinist* 19 (March 5, 1896): 252–256.

28. Dolnar, "Bicycle Tools—12," *American Machinist* 19 (January 9, 1896): 50–53.

29. "American Industries-No. 35," *Scientific American* 42 (March 20, 1880): 181; "A Great American Manufacture," *BW* 2 (April 1881): 326-331; "Bicycle Making," *Frank Leslie's Popular Monthly* 12 (November 1881): 641–644; and "The Factory of the Pope Manufacturing Company," *WCTR* 6 (January 30, 1891): 602–603.

30. Dolnar, "Bicycle Tools—19 and 20," *American Machinist* 19 (March 5, 1896): 252–255; and (March 12, 1896): 275–276, respectively.

31. "William W. Tucker," *Hartford Courant* (July 8, 1901): 7.

32. Dolnar, "Bicycle Tools—22," *American Machinist* 19 (April 2, 1896): 348–350.

33. Dolnar, "Bicycle Tools—19 and 23," *American Machinist* 19 (March 5, 1896): 252–255; and (May 7, 1896): 474–476, respectively.

34. Dolnar, "Bicycle Tools—19, 24, and 25," *American Machinist* 19 (March 5, 1896): 252–255; (May 14, 1896): 495–497; and (May 21, 1896): 517–519, respectively.

35. "Bicycle Making," *Frank Leslie's Popular Monthly* 12 (November 1881): 641–644; Patent 352,365, titled "Die for Making Rolled Forgings," dated November 9, 1886; Patent 358,629, titled "Die for Making Rolled Forgings," dated March 1, 1887; Patent 449,965, titled "Ball Bearing," dated April 7, 1891; and Patent 466,444, titled "Ball Bearing," dated January 5, 1892; all issued to George F. Simonds. See also Patent 672,525 titled "Rolling Machine," dated April 23, 1901, issued to Gulow A. Gulowsen and assigned to the Simonds Rolling Machine Company. See also Dolnar, "Bicycle Tools—26," *American Machinist* 19 (June 25, 1896): 617–619; and "A New Bicycle Ball-Case Grinder," *American Machinist* 19 (September 10, 1896): 847; although not named, Arnold is presumably the author of that second article. See also Robert Kanigel, *The One Best Way: Frederick Winslow Taylor and the Enigma of Efficiency* (New York: Viking Press, 1997): 287–288; Tony Hadland and Hans-Erhard Lessing, *Bicycle Design: An Illustrated History* (Cambridge: MIT Press, 2014): 101–102; Epperson, *Peddling Bicycles*, 124–128 and note 95, Chapter 7; and "Ninth Annual Greeting, Pope Manufacturing Company," *LAWB* 2 (February 26, 1886): 134–162.

36. "Pedal-Bearing Drilling and Facing Machine—Drill Press for Bicycle Pedals," *American Machinist* 19 (October 1, 1896): 929–930; although not named, Arnold is presumably the author. See also Hadland and Lessing, *Bicycle Design*, 298–301.

37. Dolnar, "Bicycle Tools—30," *American Machinist* 19 (September 17, 1896): 871–873; and Arnold, "The Milling Machine," *Engineering Magazine* 9 (April 1895): 65–72.

38. Dolnar, "Bicycle Tools—31," *American Machinist* 19 (September 24, 1896): 894–896. See also "Chain Block Drilling and Reaming Machine," *Iron Age* 53 (June 14, 1894): 1125; and Hadland and Lessing, *Bicycle Design*, 148–151.

39. "Ideal Cycle Factory," *WCTR* 15 (April 26, 1895): 25; "Cycle Chain-Riveting Machine," *American Machinist* 19 (January 30, 1896): 127–128; and Dolnar, "Bicycle Tools—31," *American Machinist* 19 (September 24, 1896): 894–896.

40. "American Industries-No. 35," *Scientific American* 42 (March 20, 1880): 181; "A Great American Manufacture," *BW* 2 (April 1881): 326-331; "Bicycle Making," *Frank Leslie's Popular Monthly* 12 (November 1881): 641–644; and Pope Manufacturing Company, "Ninth Annual Greeting," *LAWB* 2 (February 26, 1886): 134–138. The company continued to improve the steering head for its high-wheel bicycles, but see Patent 250,917, titled "Steering-Head for Bicycles," dated December 13, 1881, issued to Horace B. Hicks and assigned to the Pope Manufacturing Company.

41. Dolnar, "Bicycle Tools—29," *American Machinist* 19 (August 6, 1896): 736–739; and "Bicycle Brazing," *American Machinist* 19 (November 19, 1896): 1077–1081.

42. Cleveland Moffett, "The Marvels of Bicycle Making," *McClure's Magazine*, Part 3: "A Visit to the Works of the Pope Manufacturing Company," Vol. 8 (April 1897): 33–50 (also titled "A Visit to the Columbia Bicycle Works"). The Pope Manufacturing Company printed a condensed version of Moffett's articles in pamphlet form under the title "How a Bicycle is Made. One of America's Great Industries," but without date; available at the Connecticut Historical Society. The article published in *McClure's* gives Columbia frames thirty brazed joints, but the reprinted pamphlet revises that number to twenty; see pages 8–9. See also Dolnar, "Bicycle Tools—29," *American Machinist* 19 (August 6, 1896): 736–739; Dolnar, "Bicycle Brazing," *American Machinist* 19 (November 19, 1896): 1077–1081; and Hounshell, *American System*, 205–206.

43. Dolnar, "Bicycle Tools—29," *American Machinist* 19 (August 6, 1896): 736–739; and "Bicycle Brazing," *American Machinist* 19 (November 19, 1896): 1077–1081. See also Moffett, "How a Bicycle is Made," 8–9.

44. Dolnar, "Bicycle Tools—29," *American Machinist* 19 (August 6, 1896): 736–739; and Moffett, "How a Bicycle is Made," 8–9.

45. Dolnar, "Bicycle Tools—29," *American Machinist* 19 (August 6, 1896): 736–739; and "Bicycle Tools—30," *American Machinist* 19 (September 17, 1896): 871–873. See also Hounshell, *American System*, 205–206; and Epperson, *Peddling Bicycles*, 121–123 and notes 71 and 72, Chapter 7.

46. Hadland and Lessing, *Bicycle Design*. See also Nick Clayton, "Who Invented the Penny-Farthing," *Cycle History 7. Proceedings of the 7th International Cycling History Conference*, Rob Van der Plas, ed. (San Francisco: Cycle Publishing, Van der Plas Publications, 1997): 36–38.

47. Hadland and Lessing, *Bicycle Design*, 93–95. See also Dolnar, "Bicycle Tools—16," *American Machinist* 19 (February 13, 1896): 182–184.

48. Dolnar, "Bicycle Tools—12," *American Machinist* 19 (January 9, 1896): 50–52; and "Bicycle Tools—16," *American Machinist* 19 (February 13, 1896): 182–184.

49. Dolnar, "Bicycle Tools—6," *American*

Machinist 19 (November 14, 1895): 909–910; and "Bicycle Tools—7," *American Machinist* 19 (November 21, 1895): 924–925. See also Pope Manufacturing Company, "Ninth Annual Greeting," *LAWB* 2 (February 26, 1886): 140.

50. Dolnar, "Bicycle Tools—6," *American Machinist* 18 (November 14, 1895): 909–910; "Bicycle Tools—7," *American Machinist* 18 (November 21, 1895): 924–925; and "Bicycle Tools—8," *American Machinist* 19 (December 5, 1895): 963–964. See also "Making a Bicycle," *Iron Age* 48 (1891): 1070–1071.

51. Dolnar, "Bicycle Tools—11," *American Machinist* 19 (January 2, 1896): 1–2; "Bicycle Tools—12," *American Machinist* 19 (January 9, 1896): 51–52; "Bicycle Tools—14," *American Machinist* 19 (January 23, 1896): 104–105; and "Bicycle Tools—21," *American Machinist* 19 (March 26, 1896): 325–326.

52. Dolnar, "Bicycle Tools—11," *American Machinist* 19 (January 2, 1896): 1–2.

53. Dolnar, "Bicycle Tools—12," *American Machinist* 19 (January 9, 1896): 51–52; and "Bicycle Tools—14," *American Machinist* 19 (January 23, 1896): 104–105.

54. Dolnar, "Bicycle Tools—21," *American Machinist* 19 (March 26, 1896): 325–326.

55. Dolnar, "Bicycle Tools—18," *American Machinist* (February 27, 1896): 231–233; and "New Bicycle Ball-Case Grinder," *American Machinist* 19 (September 10, 1896): 847; although not named, Arnold is presumably the author of that second article.

Chapter 3

1. In the *Springfield Republican*, see "The Legislature" (February 1, 1877): 4; "Hampden County" (April 21, 1877): 6; "Hampden County" (September 16, 1878): 6; "Death of Charles McClallan" (June 23, 1879): 5; "Death of William C. McClallan" (September 16, 1888): 5; and "The Late McClallan" (September 17, 1888): 4. See also *Springfield City Directory and Business Advertiser, Combined With Directories of New West Springfield, Chicopee and Chicopee Falls, 1877-1878* (Springfield: Clark W. Bryan & Co., 1877), 436.

2. Kidder and Parker, *Architects' and Builders' Handbook*, 18th ed. (1931): 911–912.

3. Orra L. Stone, *History of Massachusetts Industries: Their Inception, Growth and Success*, Vol. 1 (Boston: S.J. Clarke, 1930), 629–633.

4. In *BW*, see "We received...," 4 (April 7, 1882): 258; "Personal" 5 (July 21, 1882): 446; "Currente Calamo" 8 (November 23, 1883): 27; and "Currente Calamo" 9 (October 10, 1884): 383, 391. In *Springfield Republican*, see "The Victor Bicycle" (February 5, 1885): 3; "Sporting Gossip of the Week" (January 2, 1887): 7; "Local Notice" (May 27, 1887): 6; "Chicopee" (September 8, 1889): 7; and "Unable to Meet Its Notes" (December 28, 1897): 3. See also "Anything and Everything," *Canadian Wheelman* 1 (February, 1884): 43; "News Notes," *Springfield Wheelmen's Gazette* 2 (February, 1885): 157; "Touring Department," *LAWB* 4 (January 28, 1887): 76; "The Story of the Bicycle: The Overman Wheel Company," *Progressive Springfield* 1 (May 1891): 207–209; and "Victor Bicycles," *Scientific American* 64 (May 1891): 271, 278. In "The Master of Chicopee Falls," *WCTR* 14 (December 21, 1894): 25, editor Francis Prial offers insightful observations about Overman, including the print of Napoleon in Overman's office; and in "Overman Opinions," *WCTR* 16 (October 18, 1895): 29, the author is granted a personal interview with Mr. Overman. See also "The Overman Wheel Company Articles of Organization," dated February 3 [*sic*], 1882, recorded February 2, 1882, in Vol. 16, page 389, Connecticut Secretary of State. For Overman's patent acquisitions, see Patent 241,395 titled "Velocipede," dated May 10, 1881, issued to James A. McKenzie; and Patent 242,212 titled "Tricycle," dated May 31, 1881, issued to James A. McKenzie and assigned to the Overman Wheel Company.

5. "Looking After Its Rights," *LAWB* 2 (February 26, 1886): 169; and "End of the Bicycle War," *Springfield Republican* (June 27, 1886): 5. For Hodges and Overman, see Karl Kron, *Ten Thousand Miles on a Bicycle* (New York: Karl Kron, 1887): 662; and "Litigation," *BW* 7 (March 12, 1886): 323–330, which reprinted the case pleadings.

6. In *Springfield Republican*, see "Chicopee" (September 8, 1887): 4; "Holyoke" (April 19, 1888): 6; and "Affairs in the Local Courts. Experts on the Overman Plant" (May 26, 1900): 14. In *BWLAWB* (combined issue), see "The Overman Wheel Company," 20 (March 7, 1890): 420; and "Factories in Chicopee Falls. Mill No. 3, 1892," 25 (12-16-1892): 222, and Supplement i. See also "The Overman Wheel Company's New Factory," *WCTR* 5 (June 13, 1890): 466; and "Overman Wheel Company's New Factory, Chicopee Falls," *WCTR* 5 (June 27, 1890): 530. See also "Mr. Ashley B. Tower...," *American Architect and Building News* 73 (July 20, 1901): 18; "David H. Tower Dead," *New York Times* (December 23, 1907): 9; *Holyoke City Directory Including South Hadley Falls, 1890* (Holyoke, MA: Transcript Publishing Co., 1890), xiv and 327; and Julius Wilcox, "Revery of a Veteran. Recollections of Some of the Men and Things of Long Ago," *BWMR* 42 (January 10, 1901): 381.

7. In *Springfield Republican*, see "Chicopee" (April 7, 1887): 5; "Chicopee" (December 12, 1894): 6; "Spalding Wheels for 1895" (December 18, 1894): 7; and "Chicopee" (October 4, 1894): 6. See also *Minutes, Board of Directors, Eagle Bicycle Manufacturing Company* (March 16, 1889): 40, a bound volume available at the Torrington Historical Society; "Exhibits in Detail," *WCTR* 16 (January 24, 1896): 87; and Carl Wiedman, "High Wheel Safeties. Mechanical Concepts," *Wheelmen* 36 (May 1990): 9–10.

8. In *Springfield Republican*, see "Hampden County" (February 13, 1890): 6; "Chicopee" (October 9, 1890): 6; and "Business with the Lamb Company" (October 11, 1890): 6. See also "The Hartford Cycle Co.," *WCTR* 4 (January 3, 1890): 363; and "Hartford Cycle Company's New Home," *WCTR* 8 (December 4, 1891): Supplement iii. See also "Mr. A.G. Spalding....," *BWLAWB* 20 (February 21, 1890): 369.

9. In *Springfield Republican*, see "New Bicycle Works at Chicopee" (October 10, 1893): 6; "Chicopee" (March 15, 1894): 6; "The Overman-Spalding Suit" (April 3, 1894): 7; "Spalding Wheels for 1895" (December 18, 1894): 7; "To Manufacture Sporting Goods" (March 16, 1898): 8; "Birth of a New Football Game" (April 7, 1894): 4; "Superior Sporting Goods" (September 14, 1894): 8; and "Southern League Adopts Victor Ball" (February 24, 1903): 3. See also "A.G. Spalding & Bros. Factory," *WCTR* 16 (January 10, 1896): 96; and "Overman Wheel Co. Assigns," *CATR* 20 (December 30, 1897): 246. See also Theodore M. Szetela, *History of Chicopee* (Chicopee: Szetela and Rich Publishing Co., 1948), 111–119; and Epperson, *Peddling Bicycles*, 157–158. In 1898, a foreman in Overman's shops, Charles B. Whitney, formed a new company and purchased the sporting goods business. Spalding, too, seemed capable of holding a grudge because he vigorously opposed Whitney's successful contract with the Southern League, a minor league division, to use Victor baseballs.

10. In *Springfield Republican*, see "Springfield" (January 18, 1894): 6; and "The Labor Trouble at the Falls" (June 2, 1901): 4. See also "Dame Rumor...," *WCTR* 15 (August 2, 1895): 21.

11. In *Springfield Republican*, see "Unable to Meet Notes" (December 28, 1897): 3; "Overman Company to Reform" (June 8, 1899): 4; "To Pay Second Installment" (August 5, 1899): 4; "Chicopee" (August 12, 1899): 8; "The Victor Spinroller Wheel" (October 24, 1899): 7; "Overman Company Petition to Abate Taxes" (January 3, 1900): 3; "Sale of the Overman Plant" (February 6, 1900): 4; "Overman Property Overvalued" (December 28, 1900): 3; "Statement by A.H. Overman" (November 17, 1900): 4; and "Victor Wheel to be Sold Again" (January 11, 1901): 4. See also "Overman Goes On," *WCTR* 20 (January 7, 1898): 23; "Overman Outlook Brightens," *WCTR* 22 (August 18, 1898): 9; "Floats. American Bicycle Company," *WCTR* 23 (July 20, 1899): 7–8; "Overman Changes," *WCTR* 24 (August 24, 1899): 8; and "Independent Makers Organize," *WCTR* 24 (November 9, 1899): 13. See also "Overman Wheel Company Assigns," *CATR* 20 (December 30, 1897): 246.

12. "Falls Loses Another Industry," *Springfield Republican* (March 10, 1901): 4.

13. In *Springfield Republican*, see "Remarkable Automatic Devices" (March 12, 1899): 2; "Overman Automobile Company" (May 10, 1900): 3; and "Has Leased the Ames Plant" (July 11, 1900): 3.

14. In *Springfield Republican*, see "The Victor Automobile" (November 18, 1900): 5; "Chicopee" (February 22, 1901): 8; "More Space for Automobile Company" (April 2, 1901): 8; "Mr. Overman To Sell His Residence" (December 5, 1901): 8; "To Absorb Overman Company" (January 15, 1902): 4; "Big Gasoline Automobile at the Overman Works" (March 18, 1902): 8; "$60,000 Less Than Cost" (April 29, 1902): 5; "Finishes First Riker Machine" (May 21, 1902): 8; "Overman Company Going" (October 9, 1902): 7; and "A.H. Overman Dies; Headed Cycle Concern" (August 14, 1930): 7. See also "Mr. Overman's Horseless Carriage," *WCTR* 16 (November 8, 1895): 62.

15. In *Springfield Republican*, see "Spalding Company Enlarges" (October 23, 1902): 8; and "Ames Building Formally Transferred" (January 21, 1904): 10. See also Vina E. Spence, "The Manufacturing Industries of the City of Chicopee, Massachusetts," M.A. Thesis, Clark University (1930), 146–150; Henry Filar, "Developers Turn 19th Century Plant Into Apartment," *Springfield Morning Union* (June 4, 1985): 12-H. Among various privileges granted to the Ames Company in deeds of conveyance, see Quitclaim Deed from the Springfield Canal Company to the Ames Company, recorded May 1, 1837, in Book 100, page 94, Hampden County Registry of Deeds. Little or nothing of the Lamb Manufacturing Company plant survives.

Chapter 4

1. Deed from Elijah M. Dickinson to Iver Johnson, recorded November 7, 1891, in Vol. 50, Page 589, Worcester County Registry of Deeds, Fitchburg Division.

2. "History of the Iver Johnson's Arms and Cycle Works," a typewritten manuscript, undated and unsigned, c. 1950 (presumably prepared by a family member); and an untitled list of products manufactured by the firm from the date of its inception, also typewritten and undated, but circa 1933. Both are available at the Fitchburg Historical Society.

3. Deed from Elijah M. Dickinson to Iver Johnson; and "History of the Iver Johnson's Arms and Cycle Works." Copies of various corporate filings at the office of the Massachusetts Secretary of State are also available at the Fitchburg Historical Society, and these include a certificate issued to Iver Johnson's Arms and Cycle Works, dated March 29, 1916, and a Stamp of Dissolution dated April 12, 1961; a certificate issued to Iver Johnson Cycle Works, Inc., dated September 23, 1974; and a certificate of name change to Iver Johnson's Cycle Works, Inc., dated January 8, 1975. See also "Mechanical Genius of the Johnsons," *WCTR* 24 (February 8, 1900): 22.

4. Warranty Deed from Horace H. Bigelow, Trustee of Bigelow Hilling Machine Association, to Iver Johnson and Martin Bye, recorded March 17, 1875, in Vol. 947, Page 58, Worcester County Registry of Deeds (Worcester Division).

5. Warranty Deed from Martin Bye to Iver Johnson, recorded May 17, 1883, in Vol. 1149, Page 37, Worcester County Registry of Deeds (Worcester Division). See also "History of the Iver Johnson's Arms and Cycle Works"; "On Iver Johnson History," and an untitled list of products. See also "Iver Johnson. August 6, 1895. Successful Business Career in Worcester and Fitchburg," a typewritten obituary, presumably prepared by a family member, which states Johnson's date of birth as February 14, 1811. All three documents are available at the Fitchburg Historical Society. See also "Notice," *Worcester Daily Spy* (May 21, 1883): 2; "Iver Johnson,"

Worcester Daily Spy (August 4, 1895): 1; and "Have Parted Company," *WCTR* 16 (October 25, 1895): 40.

Carl Wiedman, "High Wheel Safeties. Mechanical Concepts," *Wheelmen* 36 (May 1990): 11–12. General production of the Springfield Roadster may not have begun until 1887 although the bicycle may have been introduced as early as 1885. For the Springfield Bicycle Manufacturing Company, see Articles of Incorporation dated February 18, 1886, recorded March 4, 1886, in Massachusetts Charter Book 6, page 2485. See also "Yost-Dewey," *WCTR* 13 (June 22, 1894): Supplement. After moving to the Highlandville plant (no longer standing), the company produced a short-lived version of the Springfield Roadster, a true safety bicycle called the Volant. Formal dissolution of the company is recorded in 1892, but its activities probably ceased in 1889, the year it sold the plant to McCune's newly formed concern, the Union Cycle Manufacturing Company. That company briefly continued to supply the Springfield company's bicycles and bicycle parts, but soon began producing the Union Bicycle. See "Union Cycle Mfg. Co.," *WCTR* 4 (December 6, 1889): 286; and "Union Cycle Company's Factory," *WCTR* 4 (January 24, 1890): 425.

6. "Fire at Boston," *Boston Globe* (December 20, 1882): 1 (Lovell Building); "Lovell Diamond Safety," *BWLAB* 20 (March 14, 1890): 447. See also "Fitchburg Windfall," *Worcester Daily Spy* (June 9, 1891): 6; "City News," *Worcester Daily Spy* (June 16, 1891): 2; and "A Change of Ownership," *Worcester Daily Spy* (January 26, 1893): 2. See also "John P. Lovell," *Iron Age* 60 (August 5, 1897): 34. John Lovell Johnson was called Lovell Johnson, distinguishing him from John P. Lovell, another of Lovell's sons called John W. Lovell, and a grandson, John P. Lovell, II. Articles of Incorporation for the Lovell Arms and Cycle Company were dated January 31, 1893, and recorded on February 18, 1893, in Charter Book 31, page 5310, Massachusetts Secretary of State, with Benjamin S. Lovell as president and Henry L. Lovell as treasurer.

7. "The New Heywood Chair Shop," *Fitchburg Sentinel* (August 6, 1870): 3; "Heywood Chair Company," *Fitchburg Weekly Sentinel* (August 13, 1870): 3; "Building Improvements," *Fitchburg Sentinel* (December 17, 1870): 2; "Walter Heywood Chair Co.'s Works," *Fitchburg Weekly Sentinel* (May 27, 1871): 2; Sanborn Map and Publishing Company, *Insurance Maps of Fitchburg, Massachusetts* (November 1887), Plate 16; and Sanborn-Perris Map Company, *Fitchburg, Massachusetts* (March 1892), Plate 18; and "Fitchburg. Prosperous Concern," *Worcester Daily Spy* (December 14, 1894): 5.

8. Kidder and Parker, *Architects' and Builders' Handbook*, 18th ed. (1931): 911–912.

9. In *The Works*, 201–237, Betsy Hunter Bradley's discussion of the role of architects and engineers in the design of industrial buildings is excellent.

10. Corporate Charter, Iver Johnson Sporting Goods Company, dated February 19, 1893, capitalized with 100 shares of stock at par value of $100; see Certificate of Payment of Capital, dated February 20, 1895, recorded February 23, 1895, in the Massachusetts Department of Corporations and Taxation. See also "Another New Firm," *Fitchburg Weekly Sentinel* (February 2, 1895); "Trade Talk," *WCTR* 15 (March 1, 1895): 54; and "A New Partnership," *Worcester Daily Spy* (February 17, 1895): 9. See also "First and Final Account of Mary Elizabeth Johnson, Executrix," Estate of Iver Johnson, Worcester County Probate Court, Case No. 18669, March 18, 1896. The estate included fifty-five shares of stock in the Iver Johnson Sporting Goods Company, par value $100.

11. "Trade Changes," *WCTR* (September 6, 1895): 52; and "Have Parted Company," *WCTR* 16 (October 25, 1895): 40. For the location of the Lovell Cycle and Ether Motor Co. plant, see Sanborn-Perris Insurance Map Co., *Insurance Maps of Portland Maine* (1896): Plate 61.

12. "Cycles and Cycle Makers," *New York Times* (January 25, 1896): 6; "Iver Johnson," *Worcester Daily Spy* (August 4, 1895): 1; and "The Lovell Failure," *WCTR* 24 (December 28, 1899): 13–14.

13. "Cycles and Cycle Makers," *New York Times* (January 25, 1896): 6; "Independent Makers to Fight A.B.C. Patents," *WCTR* 24 (October 19, 1899): 10; and "New Bicycle Combine," *Hartford Courant* (November 15, 1899): 5. See also Patent Design 35,391, Serial No. 80,349, titled "Design for a Bicycle Frame," dated December 3, 1901; and Patent 670,957, titled "Crank-Hanger for Bicycles," dated April 2, 1901; both issued to Frederic Johnson. Documents in the Worcester County Probate Court, Estate of Iver Johnson, Case No. 18669, indicate that Fred Johnson served as general manager of the concern until about 1908. See specifically "Amended Answer of the Respondent, Fred I. Johnson," undated but c. 1910. See also Andrew Ritchie, *Major Taylor: The Extraordinary Career of a Champion Bicycle Racer* (Baltimore: Johns Hopkins University Press, 1988), 150–151.

14. "Surplus Goes to the Widow," *Boston Globe* (June 20, 1913): 4.

15. "History of the Iver Johnson's Arms and Cycle Works," and an untitled list of products manufactured by the firm. See also "Mechanical Genius of the Johnsons," *WCTR* 24 (February 8, 1900): 22; "Have Parted Company," *WCTR* 16 (October 25, 1895): 40; "Wheels for 1898," *Fitchburg Daily Sentinel* (January 10, 1898): 6; "High Grade Wheels," *Boston Globe* (June 23, 1897): 2; "New Bicycle Store," *Boston Globe* (April 5, 1898): 9; and "Iver Johnson Strike Settled," *Boston Daily Globe* (October 29, 1898): 2.

16. "And Still It Grows," *WCTR* 20 (October 15, 1897): 15; Iver Johnson Company, *The Iver Johnson Building, Fitchburg, Massachusetts* (Fitchburg, MA: Iver Johnson Company, c. 1898), a nineteen-page printed booklet available at the Fitchburg Historical Society; "Gov. Walsh Drew Johnson Will," *Boston Globe* (January 2, 1916): 24; and "Iver Johnson Building Bought by T.F. Keith for $205,000," *Fitchburg Daily Sentinel* (January 30, 1922): 1.

17. John P. Lovell," *Iron Age* 60 (August 5,1897): 34; *Lovell vs. Johnson*, 82 *Federal Reporter* 206 (1897); and 91 *Federal Reporter* 160 (1898). In

WCTR, see also "The Lovell Failure," 24 (December 28, 1899): 13; "Sweeping Victory for Iver Johnson," 24 (January 5, 1899): 21; and "Lovell Factory is Closed," 24 (January 4, 1900): 20.

18. "Johnson Speaks of Lovell," *WCTR* 25 (February 22, 1900): 30; "Iver Johnson Company Buys Lovell Stock," *WCTR* 25 (March 15, 1900): 28; "Iver-Johnson's Purchase," *Boston Globe* (March 15, 1900): 8; "All Sporting Goods Here," *Boston Daily Globe* (December 18, 1900): 7; and "Marvelous Collection of Iver Johnson Company's Store, *Boston Daily Globe* (December 22, 1908): 7.

19. "Real Estate Matters," *Boston Evening Transcript* (September 24, 1907): 5; "To Be Ready June 1," *Boston Globe* (February 13, 1908): 2; and "Real Estate Matters," *Boston Evening Transcript* (September 24, 1907): 5. Ownership of the land remained in the Thorndike estate, and its representatives may have retained Warren. See also Carl W. Condit, *The Chicago School of Architecture: A History of Commercial and Public Building in the Chicago Area, 1875 to 1925* (Chicago: University of Chicago Press, 1964), 127–142.

20. "History of the Iver Johnson's Arms and Cycle Works," and an untitled list of products manufactured by the firm. See also "The Iver Johnson Motorcycle," *Motorcycling* (April 27, 1911), Scrapbook 4; "To Be Ready June 1," *Boston Globe* (February 13, 1908): 2; "In New Building," *Boston Globe* (June 3, 1908): 2; "Iver Johnson Again on Original Site," *Boston Daily Globe* (June 11, 1919): 3; and "Iver Johnson Co. Buys Building," *Boston Daily Globe* (April 21, 1920): 3.

21. "Surplus Goes to the Widow," *Boston Globe* (June 20, 1913): 4. See also "Petition of Wife Heard," *Worcester Telegram* (May 9, 1911), John Lovell Johnson Scrapbook 4. Newspaper clippings are organized chronologically in each of Johnson's five scrapbooks but without page numbers for the articles; the scrapbooks pages are also not numbered. All are available at the Fitchburg Historical Society. See also "Amended Answer of the Respondent, Fred I. Johnson," Worcester County Probate Court, Case No. 18669.

22. "Amended Answer of the Respondent, Fred I. Johnson," Worcester County Probate Court, Case No. 18669. See also "Widow Claims Care of Income," *Boston Globe* (March 16, 1912): 5. See also "Petition of Wife Heard," *Worcester Telegram* (May 9, 1911), John Lovell Johnson Scrapbook, Book 4, Fitchburg Historical Society.

23. "Petition and Decree in Equity, Mary Elizabeth Johnson, Executrix and Trustee Under the Will of Iver Johnson, vs. Mary Elizabeth Johnson, et al," Worcester County Probate Court, Case No. 18669; Decree dated October 19, 1911, recorded in Vol. 743, pages 96–112; and "Final Decree After Rescript," Mary Elizabeth Johnson, Executrix and Trustee, vs. Mary Elizabeth Johnson, et al, Supreme Judicial Court, Commonwealth of Massachusetts, filed October 22, 1913, recorded in Vol. 782, page 337. See also "Surplus Goes to the Widow," *Boston Globe* (June 20, 1913): 4; "Will Disposing of $3,000,000 Filed," *Boston Globe* (October 19, 1915): 10; "Gov. Walsh Drew Johnson Will," *Boston Globe* (January 2, 1916): 24. See also "Johnson Will Case Settled Out of Court," *Fitchburg Daily News* (January 19, 1916), and "Johnson Will Contest Ends," *Boston Globe* (January 19, 1916), both in John Lovell Johnson Scrapbook 4.

The settlement agreement with his siblings appears not to have included Fred Johnson's shares of the sporting goods company, the capitalization of which had been increased in 1898, 1900, and 1912, and he remained a director of that company until his death in 1920. See "Frederic Iver Johnson Dies at Fitchburg Home," *Boston Daily Globe* (December 10, 1920): 16. The five scrapbooks of newspaper accounts compiled by John Lovell Johnson contain only a single entry regarding Fred Johnson: his obituary in the *Boston Globe*. See also records of the Massachusetts Department of Corporations and Taxation, Iver Johnson Sporting Goods Company, available at the Fitchburg Historical Society.

24. "Certificates of Incorporation for Johnsonia, Inc. and Iver Johnson Arms and Cycle Works," *Fitchburg Daily Sentinel* (August 3, 1916) and *Sporting Goods Sales Journal* (April 19, 1916); both in John Lovell Johnson Scrapbook 5. See also "Mechanical Genius of the Johnsons," *WCTR* 24 (February 8, 1900): 22.

25. "Iver Johnson Arms and Cycle Works," *Fitchburg Daily Sentinel's Magazine* (1917); "500 Bicycles Going to China and Hawaii," *Fitchburg Daily News* (May 10, 1916); "Send Bikes to Orient," *Worcester Daily Telegram* (May 10, 1916); "Iver Johnson Arms and Cycle Works," *The Franco-American Journal* (March 30, 1917); "Deliveries the Chief Difficulty," *Sporting Goods Sales Journal* (April 1917); all in John Lovell Johnson Scrapbook 5.

26. In John Lovell Johnson Scrapbooks, see *Worcester Telegram* (May 10, 1896), Scrapbook 1 for bicycle race; for permission from Mary Johnson, see *Boston Post* (October 17, 1915), Scrapbook 4. See also "Candidate for Senator," *Fitchburg Daily News* (November 4, 1907); and "Republican Candidate for Senator," *Winchendon Courier* (October 31, 1907), Scrapbook 2.

27. "Iver Johnson's Forty-Year Record," *Hardware and House Furnishings Journal* (June 1922); "Iver Johnson Employees Entertained," *The Sporting Goods Dealer* (1927); both in John Lovell Johnson Scrapbook 5.

28. "Iver Johnson's Forty-Year Record," *Hardware and House Furnishings Journal* (June 1922); "Iver Johnson Employees Entertained," *The Sporting Goods Dealer* (1927); both in John Lovell Johnson Scrapbook 5. See also "Privately Owned Wild Game Refuge," *National Sportsman* (May 1922); and "J. Lovell Johnson Has Private Game Preserve," *Sporting Goods Dealer* (June 1922); both in Scrapbook 5.

29. "Iver Johnson Men Walk Out," *Fitchburg News* (June 13, 1919); "Johnson Plant Employees Strike," *Fitchburg Sentinel* (June 13, 1919); "New Union Not With the Reds," *Fitchburg News* (June 1919); "Steps to Settle Iver Johnson Strike," *Fitchburg News* (June 1919); "Mayor Refuses His Good Office," *Fitchburg News* (June 1919); "J. Lovell

Johnson Hits Straight from the Shoulder," *Motorcycling and Bicycling* (August 24, 1921); all in John Lovell Johnson Scrapbook 5.

30. "Great Bicycle Demand in 1926," *Motorcycle and Bicyclist* (January 1926), John Lovell Johnson Scrapbook 5; and "History of the Iver Johnson's Arms and Cycle Works."

31. J. Lovell Johnson, "Dealers Should Handle Juveniles," *American Motorcyclist and Bicyclist* (January 1932); and "Visitor Tells of Bike Craze" (July 20, 1934), unnamed newspaper, Ogden, Utah; both in Scrapbook 5.

32. "J. Lovell Johnson," *American Motorcyclist and Bicyclist* (December 1935); and "Death Takes Iver Johnson Plant's Head," *Worcester Telegram* (November 10, 1935); both in John Lovell Johnson Scrapbook 5. See also "History of the Iver Johnson's Arms and Cycle Works."

Chapter 5

1. *Atlas of Hartford City and County* (Hartford: Seth E. Marsh, C.E., and H.G. Loomis, 1869): Plate 24; "Weed Sewing Machine Company Enlarges Facilities," *Hartford Courant* (March 1, 1880), 2; *Hartford Courant* (April 21, 1899), 3; *Atlas of Hartford, Connecticut* (Philadelphia: G.M. Hopkins, C.E., 1880): Plates D and N; and various secondary sources, including Epperson, *Peddling* Bicycles, 30–33.

2. Quitclaim Deed from Edward M. Archibald to Weed Sewing Machine Company, recorded May 29, 1869 in Vol. 130, page 105; Warranty Deed from the Sharpe Rifle Manufacturing Company, to the Weed Sewing Machine Company, recorded April 4, 1874, in Vol. 152, page 472; Quitclaim Deed from Charter Oak Life Insurance Company and Talmadge Baker, Trustee, to the Weed Sewing Machine Company, recorded January 26, 1881, in Vol. 184, page 308; and Warranty Deed from Richard S. Laurence to the Weed Sewing Machine Company, recorded May 11, 1882, in Vol. 188, page 52; all in the Hartford City and Town Clerk. See also "A Great American Manufacture," *BW* 1 (April 1881), 326–331; and "Bicycle Making," *Frank Leslie's Popular Monthly* 12 (November 1881), pages 641–645.

3. Sanborn Map and Publishing Company, *Map of Hartford, Connecticut* (1885): Plate 12.

4. Haines Photo Company, Conneaut, OH, *Pope Manufacturing Company No. 2* (1909). Library of Congress, Prints and Photographs Division, Panoramic Photographs, Gelatin Silver, 9.5 by 43 inches; Control Number 2007662033.

5. Quitclaim Deed from the Weed Sewing Machine Company to Pope Manufacturing Company (Maine Corporation), recorded January 7, 1891, in Vol. 218, page 153, Hartford City and Town Clerk. See also *Hartford Courant* (November 11, 1889): 1; "A Big Deal," *Hartford Courant* (April 21, 1890): 1; and "Pope Manufacturing Company," *WCTR* 6 (January 30, 1891): 602.

6. "To Make More Bicycles," *Hartford Courant* (July 10, 1891): 1.

7. Moffett, "The Marvels of Bicycle Making," *McClure's Magazine*, Vols. 8 (November 1896 to April 1897) and 9 (May 1897 to October 1897). See also "Another Bicycle Building," *Hartford Courant* (June 27, 1893): 3; and "Enlargement of the Pope Factory," *BWLAWB* 26 (July 7, 1893): 387.

8. Publications Committee, Connecticut Board of World's Fair Managers, *Connecticut at the World's Fair. Report of the Commissioners From Connecticut of the Columbian Exhibition of 1893 at Chicago. Also Report of the Work of the Board of Lady Managers* (Hartford, CT: Case, Lockwood and Brainard Company, 1898): 10–11.

9. Publications Committee, *Connecticut at the World's Fair*, 21–28; 44–45; and 59–60.

10. Publications Committee, *Connecticut at the World's Fair*, 34–36; 105; and 127.

11. "New Building at Pope's," *Hartford Courant* (May 26, 1894): 4. See also Judith Stoddart, *Ruskin's Culture Wars* (Charlottesville: University Press of Virginia, 1998).

12. John Ruskin, *The Stones of Venice*, Vol. 2 (New York: John W. Lovell Company, 1872 edition): 279.

13. Keller's *Reminiscences* are held at the Stowe-Day Foundation in Hartford. See also David F. Ransom's work, *George Keller, Architect* (Hartford: Hartford Architecture Conservancy and The Stowe-Day Foundation, 1978), which includes an introduction by art and architecture historian Barry Hannegan.

14. Ransom, *George Keller*, 13–17, and 43–44.

15. *Ibid.*

16. Publications Committee, *Connecticut at the World's Fair*, 44–45. Keller's wife traveled to Scotland during the summer of 1893, and extensive correspondence between the two establishes that Keller spent most of that period in Hartford. I found no correspondence indicating that he had traveled to Chicago during that summer. See George Keller family correspondence, MS101847, Connecticut Historical Society.

17. In *Hartford Courant*, see "New Building at Pope's" (May 26, 1894): 4; "Pope's Clerical Force" (December 24, 1894): 6; "Model Modern Office" (December 28, 1894): 4; and "Columbia Bicycles. Factories of the Pope Manufacturing Company" (July 13, 1895): 28. See also "The New Hartford Offices of the Pope Manufacturing Company," *BW* 29 (June 1, 1894): 17. The *Atlas of Surveys, City of Hartford, Connecticut* (1896), Plate 5 shows an enlarged nickel department building, as does the Sanborn-Perris Map Company, *Insurance Map of Hartford* (1900): Plate 83. The atlas is available in the Maps Department, Office of the Hartford City Engineer.

18. "Model Modern Office," *Hartford Courant* (December 28, 1894): 4.

19. In *Hartford Courant*, see "New Building at Pope's" (May 26, 1894): 4; "Pope's Clerical Force" (December 24, 1894): 6; and "Model Modern Office" (December 28, 1894): 4. See also "The New Hartford Offices of the Pope Manufacturing Company," *BW* 29 (June 1, 1894): 17; and "A Roof Garden Cycle Track," *BW* (July 13, 1894), 241.

20. National Fire Insurance Company of Hartford, Connecticut, *A Quarter Century's Fire Underwriting. 1871–1896* (New York: De Vinne Press, 1897): 135. State of Maine, *Certificate of Organization of a Corporation, Hartford Real Estate Improvement Company*, dated May 24, 1890, recorded May 27, 1890, in Vol. 14, page 579, Maine Office of the Secretary of State. See also "Board of Trade," *Hartford Courant* (May 24, 1893): 2.

21. Ransom, *George Keller*, 179–181.

22. In *Hartford Courant*, see "Board of Trade" (May 24, 1893): 2; "An Encroaching Veranda" (August 10, 1893): 3; and "New Pope Building Opened" (November 13, 1896): 5. See also Deed from Albert Pope to Pope Manufacturing Company, recorded January 25, 1893, in Vol. 226, page 451; and Deed from George M. Bartholomew Estate to Pope Manufacturing Co., recorded June 6, 1894, in Vol. 233, page 375; both in Hartford City and Town Clerk.

23. In *Hartford Courant*, see "Board of Trade" (May 24, 1893): 2; and "A Noble Gift" (November 16, 1894): 1.

24. In *Hartford Courant*, see "A Noble Gift" (November 16, 1894): 1; and "Block of Twelve Houses" (March 29, 1895): 3.

25. Witold Rybczynski, *A Clearing in the Distance* (New York: Simon & Schuster, 1999): 391–92; "A Noble Gift," *Hartford Courant* (November 16, 1894): 1.

26. Olmsted Brothers, *Pope Park* (December 1, 1898). National Park Service, Frederick Law Olmsted National Historic Site.

27. In *Hartford Courant*, see "Pope's New Building" (June 4, 1896): 5; and "Notes" (June 11, 1898): 14. See also *Atlas of Surveys, City of Hartford, Connecticut* (1896), Plate 5, which identifies the south wing as part of the east wing.

28. In *Hartford Courant*, see "Permits to Build" (January 9, 1897): 5; "Branch Post Office" (June 29, 1897): 1; "Station A Ready" (November 30, 1897): 6; and "Board of Trade Annual" (January 12, 1898): 12. The Post Office is shown on the Sanborn-Perris Map Company, *Insurance Map of Hartford* (1900): Plate 83, and the *Hartford City Atlas* of 1909. See also Lease from Pope Manufacturing Company, lessor, to United States of America, lessee, dated April 6, 1904, recorded May 17, 1904 in Vol. 299, page 661, Hartford City and Town Clerk.

29. Epperson, *Peddling Bicycles*, 162–165, and 171–178. See also Warranty Deed from Pope Manufacturing Company to American Bicycle Company, recorded September 28, 1899, in Vol. 267, page 716, Hartford City and Town Clerk. Properties of the Hartford Rubber Works and the Hartford Cycle Company were also conveyed to the American Bicycle Company, but the Pope Tube Company remained independent of the bicycle trust. In the *Hartford Courant*, see also "Big Real Estate Deal" (September 29, 1899): 14; and "Bicycle Combine" (May 13, 1899): 1.

30. Sanborn-Perris Map Company, *Map of Hartford* (1900), Plate 83; and "Spalding Bicycles," *Hartford Courant* (June 18, 1900): 12.

31. Epperson, *Peddling Bicycles*, 8, and 171–178; and "Failed Colossus: Albert A. Pope and the Pope Manufacturing Company, 1874 to 1900," *Cycle History 9. Proceedings, 9th International Cycling History Conference, Ottawa, Canada* (August 1998), Glen Norcliffe and Rob Van der Plas, eds. (San Francisco: Van der Plas Publications, 1998): 93–108.

32. In *Hartford Courant*, see "American Bicycle Company" (December 21, 1901): 2; "Columbia Bicycle Factory" (December 27, 1901): 3; "Bicycle Combine" (September 4, 1902): 4; "Bicycle Works Closed" (September 29, 1902): 7; and "Hartford in 1902" (December 31, 1902): 14. See also Warranty Deed from American Bicycle Company, a New Jersey corporation, to American Cycle Manufacturing Company, a New Jersey corporation, recorded December 26, 1901, in Vol. 284, page 590, Hartford City and Town Clerk.

33. Receiver's Deed from R. Lindsay Coleman, Albert A. Pope and Arthur L. Shipman, as receivers of American Cycle Manufacturing Company, to American Cycle Manufacturing Company, a New Jersey corporation, recorded September 12, 1903, in Vol. 295, page 701; Warranty Deed from American Cycle Manufacturing Company, a New Jersey Corporation to Pope Manufacturing Company, a New Jersey corporation, recorded December 9, 1903, in Vol. 299, page 218; and Receiver's Deed from R. Lindsay Coleman, Albert A. Pope, and Arthur L. Shipman, receivers of American Bicycle Company, a New Jersey corporation, to Pope Manufacturing Company, a New Jersey corporation, recorded December 2, 1903, in Vol. 299, page 185; all in the Hartford City and Town Clerk. In *Hartford Courant*, see also "Receivers Transfer Property" (September 14, 1903): 4; and "Columbia Plant Transferred" (December 10, 1903): 18.

34. Pope Manufacturing Company, *What It Is, What It Was* (Hartford: Pope Manufacturing Company, 1904); pamphlet available at the Connecticut Historical Society. See also Epperson, *Peddling Bicycles*, 189–194.

35. "Change at Pope Works," *Hartford Courant* (June 6, 1905): 1. See Epperson, "The Monopoly Machine: The Lallement Patent and the Attempted Monopolization of the American Bicycle Industry, 1880–1886," in *Cycle History 15. Proceedings, 15th International Cycling History Conference, Vienna, Austria* (September 2004), Rob Van der Plas, ed. (San Francisco: Van der Plas Publications, 2004): 102–120. See also Pope Manufacturing Company, *An Industrial Achievement* (Hartford: Pope Manufacturing Company, 1907); the extent to which the Westfield plant continued to produce bicycles under many different names during the period before and after 1907 is not clear.

36. Receiver's Deed from Egbert T. Tamblyn, Albert L. Pope, and George A. Yule, receivers of Pope Manufacturing Company, a New Jersey corporation, to the Pope Manufacturing Company, a Connecticut corporation, recorded December 28, 1908, in Vol. 335, page 626, Hartford City and Town Clerk. See also Epperson, *Peddling Bicycles*, 198–206.

37. In *Hartford Courant*, see "Pope Company's Report" (September 24, 1910): 6; "Pope

Manufacturing Co. to Build New Factory" (March 14, 1912): 7; "Factory and Garage" (July 25, 1912): 16; and "Erection of Two Fine Buildings" (December 21, 1912): 24.

38. "Erection of Two Fine Buildings," *Hartford Courant* (December 21, 1912): 24.

39. *Ibid.*

40. In *Hartford Courant*, see "Pope Manufacturing Co. to Build New Factory" (March 14, 1912): 7; "Factory and Garage" (July 25, 1912): 16; "Erection of Two Fine Buildings" (December 21, 1912): 24; "Wheels to Turn in Pope Factory Within a Month" (January 4, 1915): 6; and "The Pope Manufacturing Company" (March 13, 2013): 20. See also Quitclaim Deed from the Pope Manufacturing Company, a Connecticut corporation, to the Pope Manufacturing Company, a Massachusetts corporation, recorded January 10, 1913, in Vol. 381, page 634, Hartford City and Town Clerk.

41. In *Hartford Courant*, see "Property of Pope Company Appraised" (December 19, 1913): 20; "Looks Like Sale of Pope Plant" (December 22, 1914): 19; "Offer is Made to Buy Pope Plant" (December 23, 1914): 5; and "Pope Plant Goes to Pratt and Whitney" (January 1, 1915): 12. See also Receiver's Deed from George Pope, receiver of the Pope Manufacturing Company, a Massachusetts corporation, to Pratt and Whitney Company, recorded January 11, 1915, in Vol. 410 page 12, Hartford City and Town Clerk.

42. Moffett, "The Marvels of Bicycle Making," *McClure's Magazine*, Part 1: "A Visit to the Hartford Rubber Works," 1–16. For the corporate name, see Warranty Deed from the Hartford Rubber Works Company, a Connecticut corporation, to the American Bicycle Company, recorded September 28, 1899, in Vol. 267, page 718, Hartford City and Town Clerk. In *Hartford Courant*, see also "May Be Shake-Up in Rubber Works" (June 6, 1904): 1; and "Work Is Started for Rubber Co." (October 17, 1919): 6.

43. Moffett, "The Marvels of Bicycle Making," Part 1.

44. In *Hartford Courant*, see "Obituary. John W. Gray" (June 2, 1892): 4; "Colonel Pope Controls" (August 29, 1892): 1; and "Parker Out of Rubber Co." (June 8, 1904): 1. Pope continued to offer Columbia high-wheel bicycles during the early 1890s, probably accounting for the continued manufacture of hard rubber tires.

45. "Colonel Pope Controls," *Hartford Courant* (August 29, 1892): 1.

46. Moffett, "The Marvels of Bicycle Making," Part 1. See also Patent No. 467,502, titled "Pneumatic Tire for Bicycles," dated January 26, 1892, issued to John W. Gray. For a more thorough discussion about the technology of bicycle tires during this period, see Epperson, *Peddling Bicycles*, 118–121, 221; the company also devised an ill-fated repair system requiring injection of viscous rubber.

47. "The Cycle Tire Factory at Hartford," *BWLAWB* 26 (July 14, 1893): 383; Moffett, "The Marvels of Bicycle Making," Part 1; and "Rubber Goods Company," *Hartford Courant* (November 10, 1902): 3.

48. Moffett, "The Marvels of Bicycle Making," Part 1. See also Patent No. 670,866, titled "Pneumatic Tire," dated March 26, 1901; and Patent No. 723,945, titled "Pneumatic Tire," dated March 31, 1903; both issued to Pardon W. Tillinghast.

49. "New Pope Buildings," *Hartford Courant* (July 6, 1895): 3; *Atlas of Surveys, City of Hartford, Connecticut* (1896): Plate 17; and Epperson, *Peddling Bicycles*, 221.

50. Warranty Deed from the Hartford Rubber Works Company, a Connecticut corporation, to the American Bicycle Company, recorded September 28, 1899, in Vol. 267, page 718, Hartford City and Town Clerk. In the *Hartford Courant*, see "Price of Rubber Works" (December 25, 1899): 16; "Rubber Goods Company" (November 10, 1902): 3; "Rubber Works Buys Land" (September 2, 1901): 8; and "Building Permits Issued" (July 11, 1903): 18. See also "Hartford Building as Addition," *BW* (August 8, 1903): 561; and Epperson, *Pedaling Bicycles*, 174–176.

51. In *Hartford Courant*, see "Attachment of $200,000" (October 15, 1903): 8; "Parker Out of Rubber Co." (June 8, 1904): 1; "Rubber Goods Merger" (May 16, 1905): 18; "Business and Stocks" (February 11, 1907): 9; "Rubber Goods Had Prosperous Year" (April 12, 1907): 5; "To Abandon Rubber Shop Here Aug. 28" (August 20, 1929): 1; "Box Company Occupies Rubber Works Building" (June 10, 1931): 9; "Shoor Brothers Lease Space in Rubber Works" (July 17, 1931): 15; "Rubber Plant Is Purchased By Syndicate" (September 6, 1945): 1; and "Rubber Properties Sold to Three Corporations" (December 19, 1945): 7.

Chapter 6

1. The complicated history of those ventures is well-documented in J. Perc Boore's enduring work, *The Seamless Story* (Los Angeles: Commonwealth Press, 1951). See also Epperson, *Peddling Bicycles*, for several missing pieces.

2. Edward C.R. Marks, *The Manufacture of Iron and Steel Tubes*, 2nd ed. (Deansgate, Manchester: Technical Publishing Company, Limited, 1903): 5–16; 27–44; 60–64; 83–84; 97–106; 108–113; and 115–119; and Boore, *Seamless Story*, xv–xvii; and 27–32. See also "Manufacture of Seamless Steel Tubes," *Iron Age* 50 (September 29, 1892): 563–566; "Manufacture of a New Seamless Tube," *Iron Age* 61 (June 9, 1898): 12–13, discussing a system devised by the McCool Tube Company of Beaver Falls, Pennsylvania; and "Spirally Welded Tubes," *Scientific American* 58 (June 16, 1888): 377. For the clinching design, see Patent 578,801, titled "Sheet Metal Tube," dated March 16, 1897, issued to Frank A. Wilmot and assigned to the Wilmot and Hobbs Manufacturing Company. See also "The 'Clincher Tube' and Its Manufacture," *Iron Age* 60 (December 2, 1897): 1–5; and "Foundation Patent on Bicycling Tubing," *AW* 9 (May 27, 1897): 50. Samuel Snell, an Englishman who settled in Toledo, devised a method that encased those turned edges with a steel strip, also with turned edges, inserted along the tube's entire

interior length, producing a tube suitable for children's bicycles or inexpensive models; see "New Era in Wheels," *Toledo Blade* (July 17, 1895): 3. The Credenda Tube Co. of Birmingham, England, patented a method of fabricating seamless tubes by first drilling (cold) or punching (hot) a small axial hole in a solid ingot and then forcing a mandrel through the hole of the heated ingot to expand both the internal and external diameters of the tube. Continued drawing of either the heated tube or the mandrel (one remaining stationary) then refined the tube's internal and external dimensions, consolidating the metal in the process.

3. Marks, *Iron and Steel Tubes*, 32–40; 83–86; Boore, *Seamless Story*, 8–9; and "Weldless Tubing," *BWLAWB* 27 (October 13, 1893): 88. See also English Patent 1,167, dated January 27, 1885, and Patent 9,939, dated 1886.

4. Boore, *Seamless Story*, 61; "Drawing Cycle Tubes," *The Wheel* 17 (June 19, 1896): 81.

5. "Two Rumors," *The Wheel* 7 (July 17, 1891): 676; "Rumor of Another American Plan for the Manufacture of Weldless Steel Tubing," *The Wheel* 7 (August 7, 1891): 771; and Cleveland Moffett, "The Marvels of Bicycle Making. Part 2: A Visit to the Works of the Pope Tube Company," *McClure's Magazine* 8 (March 1897): 18–33. In 1896, the Pope Tube Company issued its first catalog, and in later years pasted a list of the companies to which tubes had been sold, some as early as 1882; author's document.

6. In *BWLAWB*, see "Mr. J.L. Yost," 18 (January 18, 1889): 184; "Lozier and Yost Bicycle Co.," 19 (September 6, 1889): 522; "The Lozier and Yost Bicycle Manufacturing Co.," 19 (October 25, 1889): 694; "Same Old Story. Skip This and Read Something New," 20 (February 14, 1890): 347; "News and Comment," 22 (November 4, 1890): 63–64; and "Mr. H.A. Lozier Interviewed," 22 (December 12, 1890): 166. See also Carey Williams, "A Cyclone. The Story of the Springfield Bicycle Company," *The Wheelmen* 85 (November, 2014): 16–32. See also "Lozier and Yost Weldless Steel Tube Company," *BWLAWB* 22 (January 23, 1891): 316.

7. "The Lozier-Yost Seamless Steel Tubing Company are Building a Plant at Shelby, Ohio," *The Wheel* 7 (May 15, 1891): 363; and "American Steel Tubing," *The Wheel* 7 (August 7, 1891): 771. See also "Here and There," *BWLAWB* 24 (December 18, 1891): 199; and Boore, *Seamless Story*, 36–37, 118–119.

8. Moffett, "A Visit to the Works of the Pope Tube Company," *McClure's Magazine* 8 (March 1897): 18–33. See also "Buildings in 1893," *Hartford Courant* (January 15, 1894): 5. See also "Another Bicycle Building," *Hartford Courant* (June 27, 1893): 3; "Enlargement of the Pope Factory," *BWLAWB* 26 (July 7, 1893): 387.

9. "Manufacture of Bicycle Tubing," *Iron Age* 59, Part 1: (January 7, 1897): 1–8; and "Weldless Tubing," *BWLAWB* 27 (October 13, 1893): 88. See also Kathleen Curran, "The German Rundbogenstil and Reflections on the American Round-Arched Style," *Journal of the Society of Architectural Historians* 47 (December 1988): 351–373. In "Biographical Dictionary of Hartford, Connecticut," *Connecticut Historical Society Bulletin* 54 (Winter–Spring 1989): 64, David Ransom attributes the tube factory at Park and Laurel Streets to George Keller, and although Keller's name is not mentioned in newspaper articles announcing construction of the building, the attribution is well-founded.

10. Moffett, "A Visit to the Works of the Pope Tube Company," *McClure's Magazine* 8 (March 1897): 18–33, at 20–21. See also "The Pope-Mannesmann Company, *WCTR* 14 (September 21, 1894): Supplement, iv; "Seamless Steel Tubes," *Hartford Courant* (September 13, 1894): 5; "A New Corporation," *Hartford Courant* (September 20, 1894): 3; Boore, *Seamless Story*, 41–42; and Epperson, *Peddling Bicycles*, 112.

11. "Weldless Tubing," *BWLAWB* 27 (October 13, 1893): 88; Marks, *Manufacture of Iron and Steel Tubes*, 32–33; Boore, *Seamless Story*: 8–9 and 17–24; and Epperson, *Peddling Bicycles*, 111–112.

12. Marks, *Manufacture of Iron and Steel Tubes*, 40–41, 83–87; and Boore, *Seamless Story*, 8–9, 17–24, 47, 115–118, and 132. For Stiefel, see Patent 551,340, titled "Mechanism for Making Tubes from Metallic Ingots," dated December 10, 1895, issued to Ralph Charles Stiefel; and Patent 23,702 (UK), also in 1895.

13. Boore, *Seamless Story*, 8–9, 17–24, 47, 115–118, and 132. For the sale of Pope's shares, see "Consolidation of Seven," *The Wheel* 20 (November 19, 1897): 27.

14. Boore, *Seamless Story*, 118–122.

15. "A Monster Steel Tube Trust," *AW* 9 (May 27, 1897): 43; "The Seamless Tube Consolidation," *Iron Age* 60 (July 8, 1897): 15; and "Consolidation of Seven," *The Wheel* 20 (November 19, 1897): 27. See also Boore, *Seamless Story*, 49–56. For the American Weldless Steel Tube Company, see "Tubing by the Million Feet," *The Wheel* 18 (October 9, 1896): 50.

16. "A Monster Steel Tube Trust," *AW* 9 (May 27, 1897): 43; "The Seamless Tube Consolidation," *Iron Age* 60 (July 8, 1897): 15; and "Consolidation of Seven," *The Wheel* 20 (November 19, 1897): 27. See also Boore, *Seamless Story*, 52–61; 122–124. In *Peddling Bicycles*, Epperson also discusses the origins of the Ellwood Weldless Tube Company at page 115, but the dates used conflict with other sources.

17. Moffett, "A Visit to the Works of the Pope Tube Company," *McClure's Magazine* 8 (March 1897): 18–33; for the chronology of Pope's plans to build tube factories, see pages 20 and 25–26.

18. "Manufacture of Bicycle Tubing," *Iron Age* 59, Part 1 (January 7, 1897): 1–8; Part 2 (January 14, 1897): 1–5; and Part 3:(March 4, 1897): 1–6. See also Moffett, "A Visit to the Works of the Pope Tube Company," *McClure's Magazine* 8 (March 1897): 18–33; and "A Visit to the Works of the Pope Manufacturing Company," *McClure's Magazine* 8 (April 1897): 33–50. See also Moffett and Pope Manufacturing Co., *How a Bicycle is Made*, 2–7. See also "Ready for Business," *The Wheel* 17 (July 31, 1896): 59; Epperson, *Peddling Bicycles*, 109–118; and James E. Howard, "Steel for Bicycles," *Iron Age* 59 (July 9, 1896): 69–70. For Eames, see "Once a Hartford Citizen," *Hartford Courant* (January 14, 1911): 16; he also headed the motor carriage department.

19. "Manufacture of Bicycle Tubing," *Iron Age* 59, Part 2 (January 14, 1897): 1–5; Moffett, "A Visit to the Works of the Pope Manufacturing Company," *McClure's Magazine* 8 (April 1897): 33–50; and Moffett and Pope Manufacturing Co., *How a Bicycle is Made*, 2–3.

20. "Manufacture of Bicycle Tubing," *Iron Age* 59, Part 2 (January 14, 1897): 1–5. See also John G.D. Mack, "Tests of the Efficiency of the Bicycle," *Transactions of the American Society of Mechanical Engineers* 18 (New York: ASME, 1897): 1067–1075. Eames and Souther also tested wheels, and a fifth apparatus measured the ability of hubs, spokes, rims, connections, and tires to absorb shocks.

21. Harold H. Eames, "Considerations on the Material for Bicycle Tubing," *Iron Age* 18 (June 18, 1896): 1425–1426; and James E. Howard, "Steel for Bicycles," *Iron Age* 59 (July 9, 1896): 69–70. See also Moffett, "A Visit to the Works of the Pope Manufacturing Company," *McClure's Magazine 8 (April 1897)*: 33–50; and Moffett and Pope Manufacturing Co., *How a Bicycle is Made*, 2–3.

22. John Fritz, "The Progress in the Manufacture of Iron and Steel in America, and the Relations of the Engineer To It," *Transactions of the Society of Mechanical Engineers* 18 (New York: ASME, 1897): 39–69. See also Andrew Garn, *Bethlehem Steel* (Princeton: Princeton Architectural Press, 1999): 6–24. At Bethlehem, Fritz designed both the machinery and buildings for the new plant, drawing from his avocational interest in architecture for the latter.

23. Fritz, "Progress in the Manufacture of Iron and Steel," *Transactions of the Society of Mechanical Engineers* 18, 39–69. See also Lance Metz, *John Fritz: His Role in the Development of the American Iron and Steel Industry and His Legacy to the Bethlehem Community* (Easton, PA: Center for Canal History and Technology, 1987). See also James E. Howard, "Steel for Bicycles," *Iron Age* 59 (July 9, 1896): 69–70; and "The Manufacture of Bicycle Tubing," *Iron Age* 59, Part 1 (January 7, 1897): 1–8.

24. Trustee's Deed from Charles M. Joslyn, Trustee of the Estate of George M. Bartholomew, Insolvent Debtor, grantor, to Pope Manufacturing Company, a Maine corporation, grantee, dated June 4, 1894, recorded June 6, 1894, in Vol. 233, page 375; and Quitclaim Deed from George Pope, grantor, to Albert Pope, grantee, dated June 30, 1896, recorded July 1, 1896, in Vol. 248, page 60; both in Hartford City and Town Clerk.

25. Walter M. McFarland, "Asa Martens Mattice. A Biographical Sketch," *Cassier's Magazine*, 27 (March 1905):437–440; and "Getting at Value of Old Tube Plant," *Hartford Courant* (May 11, 1910): 6.

26. "Steel and Glass Shop Construction," *Engineering Record* 29 (December 30, 1893): 79; "A Well-Lighted Machine Shop," *Engineering Record* 38 (July 10, 1898): 123; "The Manufacture of Bicycle Tubing," *Iron Age* 59, Part 1 (January 7, 1897): 1–8, at 4. See also Bradley, *The Works*, 149–153. The Berlin Iron Bridge Company also designed and built a similarly tall, one story machine shop of iron and glass for the Fuller Iron Works in Providence, Rhode Island. See also "Pope Company Buys Back Tube Mill," *Hartford Courant* (September 10, 1909): 6.

27. "The Manufacture of Bicycle Tubing," *Iron Age* 59, Part 1 (January 7, 1897): 1–8.

28. *Ibid.*

29. "New Pope Buildings," *Hartford Courant* (July 6, 1895): 3.

30. "Manufacture of Bicycle Tubing," *Iron Age* 59, Part 1 (January 7, 1897): 1–8; *Atlas of Surveys, City of Hartford, Connecticut* (1896), Plate 17; and "Board of Trade Annual," *Hartford Courant* (January 12, 1898): 12. For frame buildings, see "Building Permits Issued," *Hartford Courant* (January 28, 1899): 8.

31. Manufacture of Bicycle Tubing," *Iron Age* 59, Part 1 (January 7, 1897): 1–8, at 4; and Part 3 (March 4, 1897): 1–6, at 1 and 4; Moffett, "A Visit to the Works of the Pope Tube Company," *McClure's Magazine* 8 (March 1897): 18–33, at 26 and 28. See also "Ready for Business," *The Wheel* 17 (July 31, 1896): 59. For Stumpf, see Lance Day and Ian McNeil, eds., *Biographical Dictionary of the History of Technology*, 1178.

32. "Manufacture of Bicycle Tubing," *Iron Age* 59, Part 1 (January 7, 1897), 1–8, at 4; Part 3: (March 4, 1897): 1–6; and Moffett, "A Visit to the Works of the Pope Tube Company," *McClure's Magazine* 8 (March, 1897): 18–33, at 26 and 28. Editors of the *Hartford Courant* reported that a German engineer (not named) traveling extensively in this country had identified the power plant as one of the two finest he had seen; see "Board of Trade," *Hartford Courant* (January 13, 1897): 12.

33. "Billings and Spencer Co. Not to Leave Hartford," *Hartford Courant* (October 4, 1905): 12.

34. "Manufacture of Bicycle Tubing," *Iron Age* 59, Part 3 (March 4, 1897): 1–6; and Moffett, "A Visit to the Works of the Pope Tube Company," *McClure's Magazine* 8 (March 1897): 18–33, at 26. See also "Shelby Tube Works," *Hartford Courant* (March 19, 1901): 3, citing coal in the company's western plants at $1.00 per ton and coal in Hartford at $4.00 per ton.

35. Eckley B. Coxe, "A Furnace With Automatic Stoker, Traveling Grate, and Variable Blast Intended Especially for Burning Small Anthracite Coal," *Transactions of the American Institute of Mining Engineers* 22 (New York: AIME, 1894): 581–606. See also Patent 510,565 titled "Traveling-Grate Furnace," dated December 12, 1893, issued to Eckley B. Coxe. See also "Raising Steam with the Waste Products of Yesterday," *Coal Age* 14 (October 10, 1918): 676–681; and "Ready for Business," *The Wheel* 17 (July 31, 1896): 59.

36. In *Hartford Courant*, see "Billings and Spencer Co. Not to Leave Hartford" (October 4, 1905): 12; "Pope Company Buys Back Tube Mill" (September 10, 1909): 6.

37. Articles of Association of the Pope Tube Company, dated June 19, 1896, filed in the Connecticut Office of the Secretary of State, June 25, 1896. Capital stock $100,000 in cash; $400,000 in land. In the *Hartford Courant*, see also "Articles of Association of the Pope Tube Company" (June 22, 1896): 2; "New Joint Stock Company" (June 22, 1896): 6; and

"City and Vicinity" (July 2, 1896): 3. For title to the land, see Warranty Deed from Albert Pope to Pope Tube Company, recorded July 1, 1896 in Vol. 246, page 153, Hartford City and Town Clerk.

See also "Manufacture of Bicycle Tubing," *Iron Age* 59, Part 1 (January 7, 1897), 1–8; and Moffett, "A Visit to the Works of the Pope Tube Company," *McClure's Magazine* 8 (March 1897): 18–33, at 26. In *Hartford Courant*, see also "Board of Trade" (January 13, 1897): 12; "Promotion of Mr. Bubser" (October 31, 1899): 8; "Hartford Man's Success" (October 2, 1901): 4; and "Obituary" (June 30, 1903): 7.

38. "Manufacture of Bicycle Tubing," *Iron Age* 59, Part 1 (January 7, 1897), 1–8, at 4–5; and Moffett, "A Visit to the Works of the Pope Tube Company," *McClure's Magazine* 8 (March 1897): 18–33, at 26. See also Harold H. Eames, "Considerations on the Material for Bicycle Tubing," *Iron Age* 59 (June 18, 1896): 1425–1426; and "Board of Trade," *Hartford Courant* (January 13, 1897): 12.

39. "Manufacture of Bicycle Tubing," *Iron Age* 59, Part 1 (January 7, 1897), 1–8, at 5; and Moffett, "A Visit to the Works of the Pope Tube Company," *McClure's Magazine* 8 (March 1897): 18–33, at 30–31.

40. "Local Commuter Travels About 300,000 Miles," *Hartford Courant* (January 13, 1924): 8B; "Horace K. Jones Dies at Home," *Hartford Courant* (May 6, 1925): 4; and H.P. Jones, "Tempering and Annealing Steel," *Transactions of the American Society of Mechanical Engineers* 24 (New York: ASME, 1903): 349. See also Patent 427,768 titled "Process of Treating Metals," dated May 13, 1890; and Patent 563,380 titled "Process of Annealing Metals," dated July 7, 1896; both issued to Horace K. Jones. See also "Manufacture of Bicycle Tubing," *Iron Age* 59, Part 1 (January 7, 1897), 1–8, at 3; "Ready for Business," *The Wheel* 17 (July 31, 1896): 59; and Moffett, "A Visit to the Works of the Pope Tube Company," *McClure's Magazine* 8 (March 1897): 18–33, at 25. See also Pope Tube Company, *Catalog* (1896), author's document.

41. In *Hartford Courant* under the respective headings "Imports for the Week," see (January 9, 1897): 5; (January 16, 1897): 3; (January 23, 1897): 4; (February 13, 1897): 7; (March 6, 1897): 3; (May 1, 1897): 3; (May 27, 1899): 7; (June 10, 1899): 16; (August 19, 1899): 5; and (September 23, 1899): 5. In *Hartford Courant*, see also "City and Vicinity" (January 13, 1897): 12; "Decision on Steel Tubes" (April 10, 1900): 7; "Is To Go To the Flint Rubber Works" (October 30, 1899): 5; and "Gift to Mr. Sponsel" (February 28, 1901): 2. See also Boore, *Seamless Story*, 47, and 132–135.

42. Henry Grattan Tyrrell, *A Treatise on the Design and Construction of Mill Buildings and Other Industrial Plants* (Chicago: Myron C. Clark Publishing Co., 1911): 1–3; and *Engineering of Shops and Factories* (New York: McGraw-Hill Book Company, 1912): xv.

43. *Ibid.*

44. In *Hartford Courant*, see "In Tube Trust" (May 19, 1899): 1; "Tube Works to Shut Down" (January 31, 1900): 9; "Shelby Tube Company" (February 12, 1900): 5; "Shelby Tube Works" (March 19, 1901): 3; "In the Steel Trust" (June 24, 1901): 4; and "Tube Works are Sold" (August 9, 1901): 5. Consolidation of the three companies did not occur until August 1889, and transfer of the land not until 1901. See also Warranty Deed from Pope Tube Company to Shelby Steel Tube Company, recorded May 6, 1901, in Vol. 279, page 702; and Quitclaim Deed from Pope Tube Company to Shelby Steel Tube Company, recorded May 6, 1901, in Vol. 279 page 700, both in Hartford City and Town Clerk. Shelby paid $730,856.17 for Pope's company, and the deeds conveyed the company's easement for well and water utility rights. See also Boore, *Seamless Story*: 69–70, 132–135.

45. In *Hartford Courant*, see "Old Tube Works No Longer Idle" (January 1, 1910): 17; "Getting a Value of Old Tube Plant" (May 11, 1910): 6; "Judge Burpee Reduces Tube Plant Valuation" (May 20, 1910): 3; "City and Vicinity" (February 12, 1910): 3; "Pope Company Buys Back Tube Mill" (September 10, 1909): 6; and "Sale of Tube Mills Finally Completed" (September 30, 1909): 5. During the building's extended vacancy, potential buyers rejected the building because it could not be adapted easily to desired uses.

46. In *Hartford Courant*, see "Pope Company to Leave West Works" (August 12, 1913): 3; "Garvan Company to Leave State Street" (January 27, 1915): 3; "Pope West Works Formally Transferred" (February 12, 1915): 9; and "P. Garvan Co. Moves" (May 5, 1915): 5.

47. For Maxim, see "Personal," *Hartford Courant* (November 24, 1906): 7; and "In Hartford Society," *Hartford Courant* (November 8, 1907): 6. See also *Atlas of Surveys, City of Hartford, Connecticut* (1896), Plate 17; and Epperson, *Peddling Bicycles*, 129–131.

48. In *Hartford Courant*, see "New Automobile Company" (April 27, 1899): 5; "Automobile Companies" (September 22, 1899): 5; "Mr. Day President" (July 11, 1899): 5; (Day also became vice president of the allied Electric Storage Battery Company, a subsidiary of Whitney's EVC); "Bicycle Industrial" (July 21, 1899): 8; "W.C. Whitney and Electric Vehicle Company" (February 4, 1904): 12; "City Briefs" (October 31, 1899): 12; "Automobile Plant" (December 12, 1899): 5; and "Electric Vehicle Company" (September 6, 1901): 5.

49. In *Hartford Courant*, see "Electric Vehicles" (October 29, 1900): 10; "Board of Trade" (January 16, 1901): 7; "Eames Leaves Motor Works" (December 11, 1900): 8; "Going to Pittsburgh" (January 23, 1901): 8; "Mr. Maxim to Leave the City" (February 20, 1901): 7; "Mr. Day's New Position" (April 17, 1903): 8; "H.P. Maxim, Auto Expert" (May 4, 1904): 18; and "Maxim to Form New Auto Company" (July 9, 1907): 10.

50. In *Hartford Courant*, see "Board of Trade Elects Directors" (January 17, 1906): 12; "Columbia Cars To Suit All Tastes" (April 14, 1906): 27; "Receivers Named for the Electric Vehicle Company" (December 11, 1907): 1; and "George H. Day Dead" (November 22, 1907): 2. See also *Hartford City Atlas* (1909), Plate 6.

51. In *Hartford Courant*, see "Herman F. Cuntz on Selden Patent" (January 21, 1909): 14; "Auto Company to Change Name" (June 11, 1909): 2; "Electric Vehicle Company May Be Transferred" (June 16, 1909): 6; "Columbia Motor Car Company of Hartford" (June 30, 1909): 12; "Electric Vehicle Company Now Changed Hands" (July 1, 1909): 5; "Result of Selden Patent Decision" (September 23, 1909): 14; "Columbia Motor Company in Big Combine" (February 3, 2010): 3; "Receivers Named for Columbia Company" (September 13, 1912): 1; "Legal Notice" (December 23, 1912): 23; "Columbia Motor Car Company Changes Hands" (January 10, 1913): 9; and "Billings-Spencer Become Owners of Columbia Factory" (July 1, 1914).

52. "The Billings and Spencer Company," *Hartford Courant* (October 25, 1914): 10AA; "To Spend $100,000 Altering Former Columbia Factory," *Hartford Courant* (December 31, 1914): 4; and *Hartford City Atlas* (1917), Plate 7.

53. In *Hartford Courant*, see "Billings and Spencer Co. to Close Tool Division" (September 7, 1962): 1; "Billings and Spencer Co. to Sell Rest of Work Here to Moore" (December 8, 1962): 29; "Page Pied Piper! Dislodged Rats Invading Homes" (September 1, 1965): 35; and "Chain Building Plans To Cost $3.7 Million" (August 3, 1966): 21.

Chapter 7

1. Sheriff's Deed from the Sheriff of Lucas County to Henry A. Lozier, recorded August 6, 1889, in Vol. 151, page 200, Lucas County Recorder's Office. In *BWLAB*, see "Lozier and Yost Bicycle Company," 19 (September 6, 1889): 522; and "The Lozier and Yost Bicycle Manufacturing Company," 19 (October 25, 1889): 694. See also "Wheel Gossip," *WCTR* 4 (August 30, 1889): 10; and "Lozier and Yost Bicycle Manufacturing Company," *WCTR* 4 (October 25, 1889): 1176.

2. "The Lozier and Yost Plant," *WCTR* 7 (August 7, 1891): 772; "Another Bicycle Factory," *Toledo Blade* (December 14, 1891): 5. Journal and newspaper articles are silent on the matter of electric lighting, but the Sanborn-Perris Map Company plan of 1895, Vol. 1, Plate 34, confirms that method of illumination.

3. Quitclaim Deed from Joseph Yost and Anna M. Yost to Henry Lozier, recorded December 15, 1891, in Vol. 173, page 456, Lucas County Recorder's Office. In the *Toledo Blade*, see "Another Bicycle Factory" (December 14, 1891): 5; "Yost's Bicycle Works" (June 15, 1892): 3; and "Yost's Dinner Pail" (June 10, 1895): 5. See also "Mr. Yost Will Go To California," *WCTR* 8 (December 18, 1891): 527; "Trade Talk," *WCTR* 10 (September 16, 1892): Supplement iii; "The Toledo Trade," *WCTR* 10 (December 2, 1892): 30; "Trade in Toledo," *WCTR* 13 (March 16, 1894): 30; "Yost Sells Out," *WCTR* 22 (October 13, 1898): 1898; and "Yost's Successors," *WCTR* 22 (December 1, 1898): 26. See also "Toledo's Cycle Industries," *American Wheelman* 2 (October 29, 1892): 316; "Bicycle Notes," *Iron Age* 56 (December 12, 1895): 1239; "Bicycle Notes," *Iron Age* 56 (December 26, 1895): 1345; and Sanborn-Perris Map Co., *Toledo, Ohio*, Vol. 1 (1895): Plate 39.

4. "Harriott Bicycle Co.," *Toledo Blade* (July 1, 1892): 3; "Toledo's Cycle Industries," *AW* 2 (October 29, 1892): 316; "The Toledo Trade," *WCTR* 10 (December 2, 1892): 30; "Trade in Toledo," *WCTR* 13 (March 16, 1894): 30; and "Bicycle Notes," *Iron Age* 56 (December 12, 1895): 1239. Other Toledo bicycle manufacturers included: Toledo Bicycle Co.; Gendron Iron Wheel Co.; Charles Truman and Co.; Colton Manufacturing Co.; Union Manufacturing Co.; Maumee Cycle Co. (established by Yost); Harriott Bicycle Co.; and Arlington W. Betts and Company.

5. "Handsome New Edifices," *Toledo Blade* (September 15, 1892): 2; and "An Extension to the Lozier Factory," *WCTR* 10 (November 11, 1892): 28.

6. Harvey Scribner, ed., "Norval Baldwin Bacon," in *Memoirs of Lucas County and the City of Toledo. From the Earliest Historical Times Down to the Present, Including a Genealogical and Biographical Record of Representative Families*, Vol. 2 (Madison, Wisconsin: Western Historical Association, 1910): 348–349. Chapman Publishing Company, "Norval Baldwin Bacon," in *Portrait and Biographical Record of City of Toledo and Lucas and Wood Counties, Ohio* (Chicago: Chapman Publishing Company, 1895): 187–188. Edward O. Fallis, "Obituary. Thomas F. Huber," *Journal of the American Institute of Architects* 8 (January 1920): 46. Lawrence R. Stine, Historic Old West End, Toledo, Ohio (Toledo: Old West End Association, Inc., 2005). Eric Johannesen and Allen L. Dickes, *Look Again. Landmark Architecture in Downtown Toledo and Old West End* (Pittsburgh: Ober Park Associates, Inc., 1973).

7. "Handsome New Edifices," *Toledo Blade* (September 15, 1892): 2; "An Extension to the Lozier Factory," *WCTR* 10 (November 11, 1892): 28; Scribner, *Memoirs of Lucas County*, 348–349.

8. For title to the property, see Quitclaim Deed from Henry A. Lozier and Mary M. Lozier to Lozier Manufacturing Company, recorded January 24, 1893, in Vol. 178, page 409; Warranty Deed from Barton Smith as Trustee to Lozier Manufacturing Company, recorded February 27, 1893, in Vol. 186, page 338; Warranty Deed from Barton Smith as Trustee to Lozier Manufacturing Company, recorded February 27, 1893, in Vol. 186, page 338; and Warranty Deed from Charles J. Moore and Mary L. Moore to Lozier Manufacturing Company, recorded May 5, 1893 in Vol. 189, page 92; all in Lucas County Recorder's Office. See also "The Lozier Mfg. Co.'s annual meeting…," *WCTR* 10 (January 13, 1893): 32; "Improvements of the Lozier Co.," *WCTR* 11 (April 28, 1893): 24; and "Enlarging the Lozier Co.'s Plant," *WCTR* 11 (June 16, 1893): 32. For Charles Moore, see Hugh Dolnar (né Horace Arnold), "Bicycle Tools—18," *American Machinist* 19 (February 27, 1896):18.

9. "Loss of the Lozier, *Toledo Blade* (November 30, 1894): 2; "Lozier & Co. To the Front," *WCTR* 14 (December 7, 1894): 26.

10. In the *Toledo Blade*, see "Loss of the Lozier"

(November 30, 1894): 2; "He May and May Not" (December 1, 1894): 1; and "He Is Sure to Stay" (December 20, 1894): 6. See also "Lozier & Co. To the Front," *WCTR* 14 (December 7, 1894): 26.

11. In the *Toledo Blade*, see "Loss of the Lozier" (November 30, 1894): 2; and "He May and May Not" (December 1, 1894): 1. See also "Lozier & Co. To the Front," *WCTR* 14 (December 7, 1894): 26; and "The Remarkable Rise of the New Lozier Factory," *WCTR* 15 Supplement (March 8, 1895): 49. Accounts do not specify whether electrical power drove mill shafting or whether electric motors operated each unit of machinery.

12. Although newspaper accounts do not identify the architects of the reconstructed factory, the following year Lozier erected a second plant in Thompsonville, Connecticut, very similar in design to the Toledo factory, and commissioned Bacon and Huber to prepare plans. See "Thompsonville's Wheel Factory," *Springfield Daily Republican* (July 12, 1895): 9.

13. "Lozier & Co. To the Front," *WCTR* 14 (December 7, 1894): 26; "The Remarkable Rise of the New Lozier Factory," *WCTR* 15 Supplement (March 8, 1895): 49; and "Enormous Demand," *Toledo Blade* (April 6, 1895): 1. Cleveland newspapers reported that the factory had been rebuilt in forty-four days; see "H.A. Lozier & Co., Cleveland Bicycles," *Cleveland Plain Dealer* (November 12, 1895): 6.

14. For the Canadian plant, see "H.A. Lozier & Co.," *WCTR* 15 (August 9, 1895): 40; and "H.A. Lozier & Co., Cleveland Bicycles," *Cleveland Plain Dealer* (November 12, 1895): 6.

15. "Thompsonville's Wheel Factory," *Springfield Daily Republican* (July 12, 1895): 9; "Lozier's Ambition," *Toledo Blade* (June 24, 1895): 3; "New Connecticut Factory," *New Haven Morning Journal and Courier* (July 13, 1895): 3; "The Lozier Manufacturing Company....," *Stafford Springs Press* (June 13, 1895): 2.

16. "Lozier's Ambition," *Toledo Blade* (June 24, 1895): 3; "New Connecticut Factory," *New Haven Morning Journal and Courier* (July 13, 1895): 3; "The Lozier Manufacturing Company....," *Stafford Springs Press* (June 13, 1895): 2. See also Quitclaim Deed from Willis Gowdy, Trustee and the Hartford Carpet Company to Lozier Manufacturing Company, recorded March 17, 1896, in Vol. 40, page 476, Enfield Town Clerk. See also "Thompsonville Now Busy," *Springfield Daily Republican* (November 24, 1895): 3; "Thompsonville Free Library," *Springfield Daily Republican* (April 5, 1896): 3; "Dull in the Wheel Business," *Waterbury Democrat* (June 16, 1896): 1; and "Town May Lose Lozier Business," *Springfield Daily Republican* (August 4, 1898): 9.

17. "H.A. Lozier & Co.," *WCTR* 15 (August 9, 1895): 40; *Toronto Globe* (April 18, 1896): 8. For online reproduction of article, see Vintage C.C.M, http://www.vintageccm.com/content/ha-lozier-co-toronto-junction.

18. In the *Westfield Times and News-Letter*, see "Lozier Company in Sight" (July 8, 1896): 2; "Now for the Lozier Company" (August 5, 1896): 2; "Round and About" (August 13, 1896): 2; "The News About Home" (August 19, 1896): 2; and "The News About Home" (October 21, 1896): 2. In *Springfield Daily Republican*, see "Hampden County. Westfield. Lozier Fund and the Hospital" (March 4, 1897): 8; "Report on the Lozier Company" (December 23, 1897): 8; and "Hampden County. Westfield" (April 23, 1903): 10. For land records, see Warranty Deed from James Noble, Jr., to the Lozier Manufacturing Company, recorded March 9, 1901, in Vol. 622, page 153, Hampden County Registry of Deeds. See also R.S. Dillon & Co., *Westfield Directory* (1898): 249; and "Will Toledo Lose Lozier?" *WCTR* 17 (June 19, 1896): 39.

19. In the *Westfield Times and News-Letter*, see "Round and About" (December 30, 1896): 2; "The News About Home" (January 6, 1897): 3; "More Business for Westfield" (January 27, 1897): 2; and "Affairs at Lozierville" (March 31, 1897): 2.

20. In the *Westfield Times and News-Letter*, see "The News About Home" (February 24, 1897): 3; and "The News About Home" (March 3, 1897): 2. See also "Westfield Won't Accept," *WCTR* 22 (August 25, 1898): 39; and "Westfield Will Not Give Deed," *WCTR* 25 (July 19, 1900): 8. See also "Report on the Lozier Company," *Springfield Daily Republican* (December 23, 1897): 8; and Indenture from Trustee Loring P. Lane to the Westfield Manufacturing Company, recorded August 27, 1915, in Vol. 909, page 241, Hampden County Registry of Deeds.

21. Declaration of Trust by the Cycle Heights Company, recorded October 21, 1896, in Vol. 549, page 565, Hampden County Registry of Deeds; "Plan of Lots Belonging to the Cycle Heights Co., Located in Westfield, Mass.," by Thayer and Magill, Civil Engineers and Surveyors, recorded May 17, 1897, in the Hampden County Registry of Deeds, Plan 601; "A Big Real Estate Deal," *Springfield Daily Republican* (October 22, 1896): 5; and "Lozierville Dwellings to be Boomed," *Westfield Times and News-Letter* (April 21, 1897): 2.

22. "Lozier Factory," dated November 18, 1896, in *Town of Westfield, Surveys and Miscellaneous Notes*, Book 7 (1896): 63. Drew E. Parks and Oren E. Parks were the city's engineers and surveyors at the time. The books are available at the Westfield City Engineers Department. In the *Springfield Daily Republican*, see "Westfield's New Industry" (August 20, 1896): 8; "Westfield and Lozier Company" (August 7, 1898): 5; "Lozier Company Proposition" (August 14, 1898): 5; "Warrant Promises a Busy Day" (March 26, 1899): 13; "Activity at the Lozier Shops" (November 27, 1898): 5; "Thompsonville to Westfield" (April 19, 1900): 12; "The Lozier Proposition" (January 21, 1901): 8; "Hampden County-Westfield" (March 11, 1901): 8; and "Sealed Proposals" (April 24, 1901): 3. Building dimensions identified in newspaper accounts vary slightly from the insurance drawings, and at least one article referred to Building No. 1 as four stories, possibly including a basement. See also Factory Insurance Association, "View of Westfield Mfg. Co., Westfield, Mass.," 1469 and 1469-B, surveyed December 5, 1919, revised October 11, 1921, surveyed by E.G. Kaufmann, drawn by A.H. Anderson. Available at the offices of the Columbia Manufacturing Company. Drawing 1469, undated, probably represents the factory complex

as it appeared in 1919 and Drawing 1469-B probably represents the complex as it appeared in 1921. See also "Round and About," *Westfield Times and News-Letter* (December 30, 1896): 2.

23. In the *Springfield Daily Republican*, see "Westfield Plant To Be Busy" (June 28, 1899): 4; and "Hampden County-Westfield" (July 7, 1899): 8. See also Factory Insurance Association, "View of Westfield Mfg. Co.," 1469 and 1469-B (1919 and 1921). The testing room was later converted to an annealing room, identified by Factory Insurance Association, "View of Westfield Mfg. Co., Westfield, Mass.," 1469, dated December 18, 1933, drawn by E.H. Lisbon. The 1912 *Atlas of Hampden County, Massachusetts* prepared by the Richards Map Company of Springfield, Ma., Section 6, shows Building No. 9 corresponding to Building No. 6, the blacksmith shop and testing room, shown on the insurance plans from 1919.

24. Factory Insurance Association, "View of Westfield Mfg. Co.," 1469 and 1469-B (1919 and 1921).

25. "At Lozier's Westfield Plant," *WCTR* 22 (January 19, 1899): 38; and Ora Stone, *Westfield" Seat of Whips and Bicycles* (Westfield: S.J. Clarke, 1930): 19. Typewritten publication available at the Westfield Athenium. The original dimensions of the office were 40 by 50 feet; the building seems to have been increased to two stories on that same footprint, possibly in 1915, and then enlarged again to 40 by 78 feet by 1921; the bay windows on the front facade appear to date from that second period of change. The stylized keystones above the entrance are a later modification but before 1948. See Factory Insurance Association, "View of Westfield Mfg. Co.," 1469, dated April 29, 1948.

26. During a period continuing from the summer of 1905, when the second Pope Manufacturing Company (New Jersey corporation) began moving all its bicycle production from Hartford to Westfield, where various other models already were being produced, to 1908, when the company reorganized a third time (Connecticut corporation), to 1912, shortly before the company failed for a second time, the Westfield works grew substantially in size, as the Factory Insurance Association drawings from 1919 confirm. See also Richards Map. Co., *Atlas of Hampden County, Massachusetts* (Springfield, Mass., 1912): Section 6, which verifies that most of the buildings depicted on the 1919 insurance drawings existed in 1912, thus narrowing the range of dates for those newer buildings from about 1905 to 1912. However, motorcycle assembly also began in Westfield about 1910; new buildings may have been erected during World War I when the Columbia military bicycle began production; and rearrangement of interior functions probably occurred during this period as well, adding further complexity. For the date of reorganization of the Pope Manufacturing Company (Connecticut corporation), which entered receivership in October 1907, see Indenture from the Pope Manufacturing Company, a New Jersey corporation, grantor, to the Pope Manufacturing Company, a Connecticut corporation, grantee, dated December 19, 1908, recorded December 28, 1908, in Vol. 335, page 626, Hartford City and Town Clerk, referencing a plan and agreement executed by the reorganization committee, dated July 15, 1908.

27. "Round and About," *Westfield Times and News-Letter* (December 30, 1896): 2; "Report on the Lozier Company," *Springfield Daily Republican* (December 23, 1897): 8; and "Activity at the Lozier Shops," *Springfield Daily Republican* (November 27, 1898): 5.

28. In *Springfield Daily Republican*, see "Women in Bicycle Factory" (November 22, 1897): 2; "Lozier Company Agrees" (April 24, 1898): 3; "Town May Lose Lozier Business" (August 4, 1898); and "Westfield-Lozier Company" (August 7, 1898): 5.

29. In *Springfield Daily Republican*, see "Lozier Company Proposition" (August 14, 1898): 5; "Lozier Company Files Petition" (March 9, 1899): 4; "Warrant Promises a Busy Day" (March 26, 1899): 13; "Activity at the Lozier Shops" (November 27, 1898): 5; "Hampden County. Westfield" (May 25, 1899): 8; "Lozier Time Extended" (June 20, 1899): 8; "Westfield and Lozier Company" (June 25, 1899): 5; "Westfield Plant To Be Busy" (June 28, 1899); 4; "The Lozier Proposition" (January 21, 1901): 8; "Thompsonville to Westfield" (April 19, 1900): 12; "Hampden County. Westfield (March 11, 1901): 8; "Sealed Proposals" (April 21, 1901): 3.

30. J. Perc Boore, *The Seamless Story* (Los Angeles: Commonwealth Press, 1951): 211–212; Epperson, *Peddling* Bicycles, 176–178, 192. For transfer of the land in Westfield, see Warranty Deed from the Lozier Manufacturing Company to the American Bicycle Company, recorded November 16, 1899, in Vol. 605, page 553, Hampden County Registry of Deeds. For Toledo, see Warranty Deed from the Lozier Manufacturing Company to the American Bicycle Company, recorded September 30, 1899, in Vol. 234, page 428, Lucas County Recorder's Office, reciting $25,000 consideration. For Thompsonville, see Warranty Deed from the Lozier Manufacturing Company to the American Bicycle Company, recorded September 28, 1899, in Vol. 41, page 288, Enfield Town Clerk, reciting $10,000 consideration. For newspaper reports of a bicycle trust, see "Bicycle Trust Coming," *Boston Globe* (April 18, 1896): 5. "Monster Bicycle Trust to be Formed," *Chicago Chronicle* (April 18, 1896): 5.

31. "Thompsonville to Westfield," *Springfield Daily Republican* (April 19, 1900): 12; "Thompsonville Loses A.B.C. Plant," *WCTR* 25 (April 26, 1900): 12; "Thompsonville Feels Loss," *WCTR* 25 (June 7, 1900): 7; and "Old Lozier Plant to be Sold," *BW* 47 (August 1, 1903): 537.

32. In *Springfield Daily Republican*, see "Hampden County. Westfield" (March 11, 1901): 8; "Sealed Proposals" (April 24, 1901): 3; "Work on Lozier Addition Declared Unfair" (May 14, 1901): 8; "Masons Will Not Leave Work" (May 18, 1901): 8; and "Hampden County. Westfield" (September 4, 1902): 8.

33. For Westfield, see Receiver's Deed from R. Lindsay Coleman, Albert A. Pope, and John A. Miller, Receivers of the American Cycle Manufacturing Company, to the American Cycle Manufacturing Company, recorded August 27, 1915, in Vol.

909, page 236; and Indenture from the American Cycle Manufacturing Company to the Pope Manufacturing Company, a New Jersey Corporation, recorded August 27, 1915, in Vol. 909, page 39, both in Hampden County Register of Deeds. For Toledo, see Warranty Deed from American Bicycle Company to the International Motor Car Company, recorded January 18, 1902, in Vol. 252 page 530, Lucas County Recorder's Office. For Thompsonville, see Receiver's Deed from R. Lindsay Coleman, Albert A. Pope, and Arthur L. Shipman, receivers of the American Bicycle Company, to the Pope Manufacturing Company, a New Jersey Corporation, recorded December 3, 1903, in Vol. 45, page 303, Enfield Town Clerk. See also "Pope Company Buys Lozier Buildings," *Springfield Daily Republican* (April 12, 1903): 10. See also Epperson, *Peddling Bicycles,* 178–182. In *Springfield Daily Republican*, see "Hampden County. Westfield" (October 2, 1901): 8; "Probable Changes at Bicycle Plant" (September 2, 1902): 8; "Hampden County. Westfield" (April 23, 1903): 10; "Westfield Plant To Be Busy" (May 20, 1903): 4; "Death of H.A. Lozier (May 26, 1903): 7; and "Muster a Credit to Chicopee" (June 21, 1903): 14. Charles Moore started his own automobile and auto parts company in Westfield; see "Manufacturing Westfield Automobiles," *Springfield Daily Republican* (December 13, 1901): 8.

34. "Contract for New Building Awarded," *Springfield Daily Republican* (April 17, 1906): 10; "Big Boom for Bicycle Shop," *Springfield Daily Republican* (June 16, 1906): 10; "Pope to Add to Factory," *Bicycling World* 53 (April 14, 1906): 49; and "Pope Additions Will Be Big Ones," *Bicycling World* (April 21, 1906): 87. The article of April 21 lists the dimensions of the two new buildings as 60 by 100 feet, conforming to Building No. 8 on the factory insurance drawings, and 50 by 150 feet, shorter than the insurance drawings (51 by 200 feet) for Building No. 9. However, the article in the Springfield newspaper recites dimensions that conform to the insurance drawings. See Factory Insurance Association, "View of Westfield Mfg. Co," 1469 and 1469-B (1919 and 1921). Former employees of the Berlin Iron Bridge Company established their own company, the Berlin Construction Company, after the American Bridge Company created a monopoly in bridge construction. The factory in Hagerstown may have continued to produce inexpensive models for a short overlapping period; see "Pope to Leave Chicago," *BWMR 3* (May 12, 1906): 179.

35. Factory Insurance Association, "View of Westfield Mfg. Co.," 1469 and 1469-B (1919 and 1921). See also Richards Map Co., *Atlas of Hampden County, Massachusetts*, Section 6. Lozier's emphasis on producing a bicycle of high quality eventually yielded a number of awards, including a gold medal for Cleveland bicycles presented in 1896 at the Innsbruck International Exhibition in Austria. See "Round and About," *Westfield Times and News-Letter* (August 12, 1896): 2.

36. "Pope to Leave Chicago," BWMR 53 (May 12, 1906): 179. In *Springfield Daily Republican*, see "Westfield's Industrial Growth" (April 22, 1906): 17; "Big Boom for Bicycle Shop" (June 16, 1906): 10; "A Strike at Bicycle Factory" (March 6, 1907): 8; and "To Add New Department" (June 4, 1909): 10. See also Stone, *Westfield,* 18–19; and Epperson, *Peddling Bicycles*, 207–213.

37. Westfield Manufacturing Company Charter dated August 20, 1915, Vol. 320, page 555, and Organization, Vol. 328, page 329, Massachusetts Secretary of State. In *Springfield Daily Republican*, see "Mayor Makes Appointments at Westfield" (January 6, 1925): 1; "Spraying Damages Automobiles" (June 25, 1925): 3; "Frank W. Pratt-Superintendent" (January 6, 1925); and "M'Mahon Chosen Department Head" (December 6, 1935): 4. See also "An Absorbingly Interesting Business Romance," *Westfield Journal* (1925), the first in a series of articles focusing on the Westfield Manufacturing Company, from a collection of newspaper clippings about the company, most without dates or pages, available at the Westfield Atheneum. See also Epperson, *Peddling Bicycles*, 213–228.

38. Factory Insurance Association, "View of Westfield Mfg. Co.," 1469 and 1469-B (1919 and 1921). See also Stone, *Westfield*, 18–20, which creates unexplained discrepancies. Stone's account describes large additions constructed in 1917, and factory areas vastly increased in 1918, but all major buildings shown on the Factory Insurance Association drawing of 1919 also appear on the 1912 *Atlas of Hampden County, Massachusetts*, and photographs prior to 1914 establish the height of Building No. 7 at three stories, and the height of Building No. 8 at one story.

39. In *Springfield Daily Republican*, see "An Outstanding Success" (January 13, 1929): 18; "New Issue" (October 9, 1929): 33; "Company Official Explains Delegation of Duties" (September 3, 1931): 3; "Westfield Manufacturing Company Stockholders Name Successor of J.P. Fogarty" (March 23, 1932): 3; and "To Get $1000 A Month" (October 22, 1932): 6. See also "Busy Scenes in Big Bicycle Plant," *Springfield Sunday Union and Republican* (March 16, 1930): 7F. See also Stone, *Westfield*, 18–22; and Epperson, *Peddling Bicycles*, 216–220; and "Interview with Norman A. Clarke, April 5, 1998, North Chatham, Massachusetts," with various typewritten and handwritten correspondence between Mr. Clarke and Mr. Epperson between April, 1997 and October, 1997, courtesy of Mr. Epperson.

40. "Westfield Manufacturing Now Subsidiary of Torrington Company, With Bright Prospects," *Springfield Daily Republican* (December 22, 1933): 6. See also *Minutes, Board of Directors, Eagle Bicycle Manufacturing Company* (May 24, 1899): 74–75, bound volume available at the Torrington Historical Society; and Epperson, "Interview with Norman A. Clarke."

41. Factory Insurance Association, "The Westfield Mfg. Co., 1469" (1933); and letter from Norman A. Clarke to Bruce Epperson dated December 29, 1997, courtesy of Mr. Epperson.

42. In the *Springfield Republican*, see "Industrial News" (September 29, 1935): 6; "Factory Proposes $21,090 Addition" (October 10, 1935): 5;

"Leading Industries Holding Steady" (October 20, 1935): 18; "Labor Organizer Attempts to Form Bicycle Chapter" (August 20, 1936): 9; "Bicycle Workers Union to Meet" (October 1, 1936): 4; "Westfield Company Has 40 Hour Week" (April 29, 1937): 4; "Clarke Promoted" (July 3, 1937): 4; "Social and Personal Affairs of Interest to Westfield People" (June 13, 1937): 14; "Westfield Plant to Maintain Work on a Normal Basis" (August 27, 1941): 8; "Shells for Bazooka" (September 29, 1943): 7; and "Westfield Mfg. Co. Wins Army-Navy E" (May 2, 1944): 2. See also Epperson, *Peddling Bicycles*, 225–226, and "Interview with Norman A. Clarke," courtesy of Mr. Epperson. As to the dates of promotion of Russell Clarke, interviews and newspaper articles conflict. See also Patent 2,434,423 titled "Bicycle Stand," dated January 13, 1948; and Patent 2,715,033 titled "Bicycle Stabilizer," dated August 9, 1955, both issued to Harold Maschin, the latter patent also with Charles J. Fogarty.

43. Factory Insurance Association, "The Westfield Mfg. Co., 1469" (April 29, 1948); "Factory Proposes $21,090 Addition," *Springfield Daily Republican* (October 10, 1935): 5; Epperson, *Peddling Bicycles*, 221–222; and Epperson, "Interview with Norman A. Clarke," See also Biggs, *Rational Factory*, 1–3.

44. Epperson, *Peddling Bicycles*, 221–222; and Bradley, *The Works*, viii–ix.

45. In *Springfield Daily Republican*, see "Overtime Work for Bicycle Plant" (December 22, 1929): 42; and "1940 Was Best in Years for Westfield Industry; Further Gains Expected" (January 12, 1941): 11F. See also Epperson, "Interview with Norman A. Clarke," and specifically the letter from Norman Clarke to Bruce Epperson dated May 7, 1997.

46. Factory Insurance Association, "The Westfield Mfg. Co.," 1469 (April 29, 1948). See also "Factory Proposes $21,090 Addition," *Springfield Daily Republican* (October 10, 1935): 5.

47. Harold F. Maschin, "The Westfield Manufacturing Company. A Short History of the Company, A Guide Booklet, and Products." Unpublished, typewritten manuscript, undated but c. 1952, available at the Westfield Athenium, Westfield, Ma. A later typewritten or mimeographed document also available at the Westfield Atheneum and titled "General Information About the American Bicycle Industry," undated but c. 1972, author's name not provided, repeats some of the information contained in Maschin's article and adds clarity to several of the manufacturing processes.

48. Letter from Norman A. Clarke to Bruce Epperson dated December 29, 1997.

49. Epperson, *Peddling Bicycles*, 216–228, and "Interview with Norman A. Clarke." In his interview, Clarke states that the company started manufacturing school furniture in 1958. However, Maschin's 1952 article identifies the building where the desks were produced.

50. Epperson, *Peddling Bicycles*, 216–228; Epperson, "Interview with Norman A. Clarke."

51. Warranty Deed from American Bicycle Company to International Motor Car Co., recorded January 18, 1902, in Vol. 252, page 530; Warranty Deed from American Bicycle Company, to International Motor Car Co., recorded June 23, 1902, in Vol. 265, page 204; and "In the Matter of the Application of the Willys-Overland Company to Vacate the Plat of Cycledale," recorded July 23, 1912, in Vol. 385, page 208, all in Lucas County Recorder' Office. Toledo resident Todd Paisley managed to salvage some of the window sash and other artifacts and has thoughtfully documented the factory's demise; personal communication with the author.

Chapter 8

1. "The Gazelle," *BW* 20 (February 28, 1890): 394; "Hagerstown Play Role in U.S. Bicycle History," *Hagerstown Daily Mail* (November 29, 1977): 4.

2. For prices of bicycles during the 1890 season, see *WCTR* 4 (February 2, 1890): 467 (Victor); *WCTR* 5 (February 28, 1890): 2 (Perfection); *WCTR* 5 (March 7, 1890): 30 (Columbia); *WCTR* 5 (March 14, 1890): 67 (Little Giant); *WCTR* 5 (March 21, 1890): 108; *WCTR* 6 (December 19, 1890): 94 (Giant); and *WCTR* 6 (February 20, 1891): 692 (Credenda). See also "The Gazelle," *BW* 20 (February 28, 1890): 394; "During our recent visit...," *WCTR* 4 (January 31, 1890): 455; and "People of the Play," *WCTR* 23 (June 22, 1899): 9.

3. "Messer's Crawford and Co.," *BW* 20 (August 1, 1890): 472; and "Trade Notes," *BW* (August 29, 1890): 602. Map of the Hagerstown Manufacturing, Mining, and Land Improvement Co.'s Addition to Hagerstown, No. 1, recorded June 16, 1890, Washington County Registry of Deeds, Hagerstown.

4. "Filings and Forgings," *WCTR* 7 (April 17, 1891): supplement, i; "Crawford and Co.," *WCTR* 7 (May 22, 1891): 403; "Inventor Schindel's Chequered Career," *WCTR* 13 (April 6, 1894): 28; and "Hustling, Thriving Factory," *Hagerstown Herald and Torch Light* (May 4, 1893): 4. See also Deed from the Hagerstown Manufacturing, Mining, and Land Improvement Company to Robert S. Crawford and Henry Calver, recorded in Vol. 96, page 487; Deed from Henry Calver to Robert S. Crawford; and Deed from Robert S. Crawford and Lucy S. Crawford to the Crawford Manufacturing Company, grantee, both recorded June 23, 1891 in Vol. 97, page 302 (referencing the deeds of March 14, 1891 and April 10, 1891); all in Washington County Registry of Deeds Hagerstown. For Updegraff, see Maryland Historical Trust, Architectural Survey File, WA-HAG-110, Updegraff Building; and Karl Kron, *Ten Thousand Miles on a Bicycle* (Springfield, MA: published by the author, 1885–1887): 782. See also Thomas J.C. Williams, *A History of Washington County Maryland, including a History of Hagerstown*, 2 vols. (Baltimore: Regional Publishing Co, 1968; originally published in 1906); Vol. 1: 454; Vol. 2: 638; 1144.

5. "Crawford and Company," *BW* (November 7, 1890): 41; Sanborn-Perris Map Company, *Hagerstown, Maryland, Washington County* (May 1892): Plate 20.

6. "Filings and Forgings," *WCTR* 7 (April 17,

1891): supplement i; "The Trade," *WCTR* 7 (July 17, 1891): 683; "Trade Changes," *WCTR* 14 (October 5, 1894): 31; "Trade Notes," *WCTR* 8 (December 11, 1891): 502. Sanborn-Perris Map Company, *Hagerstown* (May 1892): Plate 20.

7. "Mr. Crawford," *WCTR* 8 (October 16, 1891): 234; "The Crawford Bicycle Co....," *WCTR* 8 (October 30, 1891): 293; "Trade Talk," *WCTR* 8 (January 29, 1892): 767; "The Crawford Manufacturing Co.," *WCTR* 9 (June 10, 1892): 9; and "A Hagerstown, Md. paper....," *WCTR* 9 (July 8, 1892): 19.

8. "The Crawford Manufacturing Co....," *WCTR* 9 (June 10, 1892): 30; "A Hagerstown, Md. paper....," *WCTR* 9 (July 8 1892): 19; "The Crawford Manufacturing Co....," *WCTR* 9 (July 29, 1892): 29; and "The Crawford Mfg. Co....," *WCTR* 10 (November 25, 1892): 20. See also Deed from the Hagerstown Manufacturing, Mining, and Land Improvement Company, grantor, to Crawford Manufacturing Company, grantee, dated August 31, 1892, recorded September 8, 1892, in Vol. 99, page 270, Washington County Registry of Deeds.

9. "The Crawford Mfg. Co....," *WCTR* 10 (November 25, 1892): 20; "Schoverling, Daly and Gales," *WCTR* 10 (January 13, 1893): 24; and "Hustling, Thriving Factory," *Hagerstown Herald and Torch Light* (May 4, 1893): 4. See also Deed from the Hagerstown Manufacturing, Mining, and Land Improvement Company to Crawford Manufacturing Company, recorded September 8, 1892, in Vol. 99, page 270, Washington County Registry of Deeds. In 1893, the company also paid $1,000 for a small parcel north of the property conveyed by the 1892 deed; see Deed from Hagerstown Manufacturing, Mining, and Land Improvement Company to Crawford Manufacturing Company, recorded June 6, 1893, in Vol. 100, page 549, Washington County Registry of Deeds. See also Sanborn-Perris Map Company, *Insurance Maps of Hagerstown, Maryland, Washington County* (September 1897): Plate 25.

10. "The Crawford Mfg. Co....," *WCTR* 10 (November 25, 1892): 20; "Hustling, Thriving Factory," *Hagerstown Herald and Torch Light* (May 4, 1893): 4; and Sanborn-Perris Map Company, *Insurance Maps of Hagerstown* (September 1897): Plate 25.

11. "Trade Talk," *WCTR* 8 (January 29, 1892): 767; "Schoverling, Daly and Gales," *WCTR* 10 (January 13, 1893): 34; "L.B. Whymper Makes a Change," *WCTR* 11 (July 28, 1893): 33; "The Crawford Co.'s New York Branch," *WCTR* 12 (October 13, 1893): 23; "Crawford Manufacturing Company...," *WCTR* 7 (December 22, 1893): 26; "Crawfords 1894," *WCTR* 13 (April 26, 1894): 56; "L.B. Whymper Will Vacate," *WCTR* 16 (August 30, 1895): 38; "Downtown Cycle District," *WCTR* 22 (September 1, 1898): 29; and "Hustling, Thriving Factory," *Hagerstown Herald and Torch Light* (May 4, 1893): 4.

12. "Short Stories of Cycling Folks," *WCTR* 7 (January 12, 1894): 50.

13. "Crawfords. 1894," *WCTR* 13 (April 26, 1894): 56; "We last week...," *WCTR* 16 (September 13, 1895): 24; "Crawford vs. Williams," *Baltimore Sun* (October 31, 1894): 2; "Attached for Lawyer's Fees," *The* [Frederick] *News* (July 23, 1897): 1; and "Distribution of Profits Among Employees," *Baltimore Sun* (August 29, 1895): 2.

14. "Still Reaching Out," *Hagerstown Herald and Torch Light* (September 27, 1894): 8; and "Hagerstown, Md...," *WCTR* 14 (October 5, 1894): 31. See also Deed from Hagerstown Manufacturing, Mining, and Land Improvement Company to Crawford Manufacturing Company, recorded April 2, 1896 in Vol. 104, page 619, Washington County Registry of Deeds. In 1896, Crawford and his wife conveyed a small parcel of land to his company, located between the original acquisition and the land described in the September 22 deed. For what is probably a corrective document, see Deed from Robert S. Crawford and Lucy Crawford to the Crawford Manufacturing Company, recorded July 7, 1896, in Vol. 105, page 284. See also Sanborn-Perris Map Company, *Insurance Maps of Hagerstown* (September 1897): Plate 25.

15. "The New Surbridge Bicycle Works...," *WCTR* 10 (November 25, 1892): 17; "The Surbridge Manufacturing Co....," *WCTR* 11 (May 5, 1893): 48; "Inventor Schindel's Chequered Career," *WCTR* 13 (April 6, 1894): 28; "The Crawford Bicycle Manufacturing Co....," *WCTR* 14 (November 9, 1894): 111; "The Crawford Wheel and Gear Company," *WCTR* 15 (March 1, 1895): 26; and "The Crawford Wheel and Gear Company," *WCTR* 15 (March 8, 1895): 44. See also Deed from the Hagerstown Manufacturing, Mining, and Land Improvement Company, to the Surbridge Manufacturing Company, grantee, recorded September 24, 1892, in Vol. 99, page 305, Washington County Registry of Deeds.

16. "Crawford Bicycle Works," *Hagerstown Herald and Torch Light*" (May 13, 1895): 7. See also Deed from Albert L. Pope and George A. Yule, Receivers of the Pope Manufacturing Company, and the Pope Manufacturing Company, a Connecticut corporation, grantors, to Montross Metal Casket Company, recorded February 2, 1909, in Vol. 31, page 48, Washington County Registry of Deeds.

17. "Crawford Bicycle Works," *Hagerstown Herald and Torch Light* (May 13, 1895): 7; "The Crawford Bicycle Manufacturing Company," *WCTR* 15 (June 21, 1895): 42; "Hagerstown Is Not Asleep," *The Frederick News* (July 10, 1895): 5.

18. "Great Scheme," *WCTR* 15 (July 5, 1895): 37; "Crawford Manufacturing Company, Hagerstown, Md.," *WCTR* 16 (January 10, 1896): 70; and "The Crawford Manufacturing Company...," *Iron Age* 56 (November 7, 1895): 965. See also Tony Hadland and Hans-Erhard Lessing, *Bicycle Design* (Cambridge: MIT Press, 2014): 102.

19. "The Crawford Bicycle Manufacturing Company...," *Baltimore Sun* (August 14, 1896): 2; "Crawford's Contract," *Baltimore Sun* (October 31, 1896): 8.

20. "Trade Changes," *WCTR* 20 (September 3, 1897): 37; "Crawford Moves on New England," *WCTR* 20 (November 12, 1897): 22; "Crawfords in New England," *WCTR* 20 (November 26, 1897): 21; "They Will Control," *WCTR* 21 (March 3, 1898): 31; "McCallister and Van Mater...," *WCTR* 21 (June 23, 1898): 29; and "Board of Trade, by Recommendation to the Directors, Resolves to Quit," *WCTR* 22 (November 24, 1898): supplement ii.

21. Sanborn-Perris Map Company, *Insurance Maps of Hagerstown* (September 1897): Plate 25.

22. "Only a Fake," *WCTR* 20 (November 19, 1897): 45; "Advertisement," *WCTR* 20 (November 26, 1897): 38–39; "Crawfords Choice Offering," *WCTR* 20 (December 3, 1897): 30; "Not True," *WCTR* 20 (December 24, 1897): 61; "Value and Price," *WCTR* 20 (January 14, 1898): 30; "Crawford's Chainless," *WCTR* 21 (February 25, 1898): 30; "Price Remains the Same," *WCTR* 21 (March 24, 1898): 32; Francis P. Prial, "Bicycle Makers in Concert. The Facts, and Sidelights," *WCTR* 23 (March 23, 1899): 45.

23. "Crawford to Increase Facilities," *WCTR* 21 (July 14, 1898): 16; and Sanborn Map Company, *Insurance Maps of Hagerstown, Maryland* (September 1904): Plate 25. See also Williams, *History of Washington County*, Vol. 1: 454.

24. "Board of Trade, By Recommendations to the Directors, Resolves to Quit," *WCTR* 22 (November 24, 1898): supplement ii; "The Crawford Line," *WCTR* 22 (January 13, 1899): 33; "The Crawford Line," *WCTR* 22 (January 26, 1899): 42; and F.P. Prial, "Bicycle Makers in Concert," *WCTR* 23 (March 23, 1899): 45.

25. "Combine Cannot Control the Trade," *Cycle Age* 23 (June 8, 1899): 138; "Total Output," *WCTR* 23 (June 22, 1899): 8; and "People of the Play," *WCTR* 23 (June 22, 1899): 9.

26. "Hagerstown Happenings," *Baltimore Sun* (August 1, 1899): 8; "A.B.C. Committees on Sales to Jobbers and Dealers are at Work," *WCTR* 24 (September 14, 1899): 8; "Crawford Property Transferred," *WCTR* 24 (November 9, 1899): 19, citing recording of the deed in November. See also Deed from Crawford Manufacturing Company, a Maryland corporation, to the American Bicycle Company, a New Jersey corporation, recorded November 6, 1899, in Vol. 110, page 694, Washington County Registry of Deeds.

27. "False Alarm About Subordinate Employees," *WCTR* 24 (October 5, 1899): 8; "Crawford to Leave Hagerstown," *WCTR* 24 (December 7, 1899): 4; "The Eastern Lamb Group," *WCTR* 24 (December 14, 1899): 15; and "A.B.C. Directors Meet," *WCTR* 24 (January 11, 1900): 15.

28. "Crawford Secures Coal Land," 25 *WCTR* (March 29, 1900): 21; "The Crawford Line," *WCTR* 25 (August 2, 1900): 7; "Whymper's Position," *WCTR* 25 (August 2, 1900): 7; and "Maryland Briefs," *Baltimore Sun* (September 2, 1901): 6.

29. Deed from American Cycle Manufacturing Company by R. Lindsay Coleman, Albert A. Pope, and John A. Miller, Receivers of the American Cycle Manufacturing Company, to the American Cycle Manufacturing Company, recorded September 12, 1903, in Vol. 119, page 42, Washington County Registry of Deeds. See also Pope Manufacturing Company, *What It Is, What It Was* (Hartford: Pope Manufacturing Company, 1904), pamphlet available at the Connecticut Historical Society. See also "Crawford Bicycle Works," *Hagerstown Herald and Torch Light* (May 13, 1895): 7.

30. The Horseless Carriage," *Baltimore Sun* (October 25, 1895): 2; "Cars for Glidden Race," *Baltimore Sun* (July 8, 1906): 10; and "Hagerstown Once Noted for Automobile Manufacturing," *Hagerstown Daily Mail* (August 27, 1962): 106. See also Williams, *A History of Washington* County, Vol. 2, 1250–51; and Mary H. Rubin, *Hagerstown. Then and Now* (Charleston, SC: Arcadia, 2010): 37, which may not correctly identify the owner of the stables.

31. Williams, *A History of Washington* County, Vol. 2: 1044–47.

32. Mark Theobald and Keith Marvin, Coachbuilt.com/bui/m/moller_mp/moller_mp.html.

33. Deed from Albert L. Pope and George A. Yule, Receivers of the Pope Manufacturing Company, and the Pope Manufacturing Company, a Connecticut corporation, grantors, to Montross Metal Casket Company, recorded February 2, 1909, in Vol. 31, page 48, Washington County Registry of Deeds. See also Sanborn Map Company, *Insurance Maps of Hagerstown* (September 1904): Plate 25.

34. Sanborn Map Company, *Insurance Maps of Hagerstown, Maryland, Washington County* (1918): Plate 31.

Chapter 9

1. Patent 361,280, titled "Bicycle," dated April 19, 1887; and Patent 433,562, titled "Velocipede," dated August 5, 1890; both issued to Leonard Gaylor. See also "Eagle Bicycle," *LAWB* 6 (January 6, 1888): 7; and Biggs, *Rational Factory*, 1–3.

2. Patent 361,280, titled "Bicycle," dated April 19, 1887, issued to Leonard Gaylor; and Carl Wiedman, "High Wheel Safeties Mechanical Concepts," *The Wheelmen* 36 (May, 1990): 2–16, at 14. See also Carey Williams, "The Flight of the Eagle," *The Wheelmen* 86 (May 2015): 16–28. Thanks to Carey Williams and Glenn Eames for their descriptions of riding Eagle bicycles.

3. Wiedman, "High Wheel Safeties."

4. *Stamford City Directory* (1889–90): 82. "Minutes. Stockholders Meetings, Eagle Bicycle Manufacturing Co." (March 6, 1888): 1–2; and "Minutes, Board of Directors, Eagle Bicycle Manufacturing Co." (July 17, 1888): 1–2; (July 21, 1888): 3; and (September 1, 1890): 59–60. Both are bound volumes available at the Torrington Historical Society. Gaylor's father, Charles Gaylor, was born in 1816 and died in 1902. Gaylor's brother, Charles Henry Gaylor, died in 1870. However, Charles Henry's son and Gaylor's nephew, Charles E. Gaylor, may have been involved with the company. At the time of the vote to sell the business to the American Bicycle Company in 1899, Charles Gaylor voted his eighty shares by proxy; if the elder Gaylor, he would have been eighty-three at the time. See "Minutes. Stockholders Meetings, Eagle Bicycle Manufacturing Co." (May 24, 1899): 74–75; "A Word About High Wheels and Particularly the Eagle," *BWLAWB* 22 (December 1890): 161.

The company founders or their family members were all closely connected to several Stamford businesses including the Citizens Savings Bank (Charles Gaylor), the Stamford Savings Bank (Lounsbury), the First National Bank of Stamford (Charles Gaylor and Isaac Wardwell, Sr.), and the Stamford Gas and Electric Company (Lounsbury, Charles Gaylor, and Ferguson). See Stamford Advocate, *Tercentenary Edition, Town of Stamford, Conn. 1641–1941*, a supplement to the *Stamford Advocate* (Saturday, June 7, 1941): 21, 40, 64–65, 137–138, 147 and 152; available at the Stamford History Center.

5. "Minutes, Board of Directors, Eagle Bicycle Manufacturing Co." (September 1, 1890): 59–60; "Minutes. Stockholders Meetings, Eagle Bicycle Manufacturing Co." (May 24, 1899): 74–75. See also "A Word About High Wheels and Particularly the Eagle," *BWLAWB* 22 (December 1890): 161.

6. "Minutes, Board of Directors, Eagle Bicycle Manufacturing Co." (March 16, 1889): 40; and (September 1, 1890): 59–60. See also Charles Meinert, "From Sea to Shining Sea," *The Wheelmen* 60 (May 2002): 11–21; and "Across the Continent," *BWLAWB* 22 (November 21, 1890): 87.

7. "Minutes, Board of Directors, Eagle Bicycle Manufacturing Co." (March 16, 1889): 40; (September 1, 1890): 59–60; (October 29, 1890): 66-67; and (November 17, 1890): 68-70. The Garden street factory was later occupied by the Blickensderfer Typewriter Company, invented by George C. Blickensderfer, but the company eventually moved to a larger building. See John E. Keeler, "Manufacturing Interests of Stamford," in William T. Davis, ed., *The New England States*, Vol. 2 (Boston: D.H. Hurd & Co., 1879); and Robert Blickensderfer and Paul Robert, *The Five-Pound Secretary. An Illustrated History of the Blickensderfer Typewriter* (Laren, Netherlands: Virtual Typewriter Museum, 2003): 10–11.

8. "Minutes, Board of Directors, Eagle Bicycle Manufacturing Co." (October 10, 1890): 83–84; THS; "A New Industry," *Torrington Register* (October 23, 1891): 3; and "Trade Notes," *WCTR* 8 (October 23, 1891): 266.

9. In *Torrington Register* see "A New Industry" (October 23, 1891): 3; "Wednesday" (December 18, 1891): 3; "Eagle Bicycle Manufacturing Co. Meeting" (January 22, 1892): 1; and "Cycling Notes" (April 5, 1895): 3. See also "Minutes, Board of Directors, Eagle Bicycle Manufacturing Co." (October 10, 1890): 83–84; and (August 3, 1896): 112–113. See also "Trade Notes," *WCTR* 8 (October 23, 1891): 266.

10. In *Torrington Register*, see "Trip to the Eagle Works" (March 18, 1892): 2; and "In the New Eagle Factory" (February 21, 1896): 4.

11. In *Torrington Register*, see "We mentioned several weeks ago...." (August 12, 1892): 1; and "Debut of the New Eagle" (October 28, 1892): 1. See also "Where Eagles are Made," *WCTR* 10 (November 18, 1892): 23; and "Erie's Progression," *WCTR* 16 (February 14, 1896): 104. In 1901, after ABC had acquired the Black Manufacturing Company, Gaylor became general manager of the Waltham Manufacturing Company in Massachusetts, maker of Orient bicycles; see "Gaylor Succeeds Metz," *BWLAWB* 44 (October 17, 1901): 41.

12. "Eagle Bicycle Manufacturing Co.," *WCTR* 12 (January 12, 1894): 47; and "Minutes, Board of Directors, Eagle Bicycle Manufacturing Co." (February 23, 1894): 101. In *Torrington Register*, see "Another one of our concerns...." (March 16, 1894): 3; "The Eagle Bicycle Manufacturing Co." (November 30, 1894): 1; "In the New Eagle Factory" (February 21, 1896): 4; and "Torrington Bicycle Show" (March 27, 1896): 1. See also "The Eagle Factory," *BW*. 30 (April 12, 1895): 933.

13. In *Torrington Register*, see "Successful Welding of Aluminum" (March 22, 1895): 1;_"Friday" (April 5, 1895): 2; and "In the New Eagle Factory" (February 21, 1896): 4. See also "Aluminum Trade Notes," *Aluminum World* 1 (June, 1895): 161; "Minutes, Board of Directors, Eagle Bicycle Manufacturing Co." (July 9, 1895): 107; "The Eagle Bicycle Manufacturing Co.," *WCTR* 15 (August 2, 1895): 33 (two articles); and "The Eagle Bicycle," *Scientific American* 74 (January 11, 1896): 1, 20; See also Warranty Deed from Achille F. Migeon to the Eagle Bicycle Manufacturing Company, a Connecticut corporation, recorded October 17, 1895, in Vol. 38, page 339, Torrington Town Clerk. Migeon later conveyed a second parcel sixty feet in width adjoining the southerly boundary of the company's lot; see Warranty Deed recorded January 31, 1898, in Vol. 42, page 349, Torrington Town Clerk. See also Patent 509,021 titled "Wheel Rim," dated November 1, 1893, issued to C.S. Dikeman.

14. "Minutes, Board of Directors, Eagle Bicycle Manufacturing Co." (July 9, 1895): 107; and "In the New Eagle Factory," *Torrington Register* (February 21, 1896): 4. Company owners may have received recommendations for Peck from Waterbury businessman George Lilley, who became governor of Connecticut in 1909 and who probably knew Peck's work in Waterbury.

15. "Minutes, Board of Directors, Eagle Bicycle Manufacturing Co." (July 9, 1895): 107. "In the New Eagle Factory," *Torrington Register* (February 21, 1896): 4.

16. "The Eagle Bicycle Manufacturing Company," *WCTR* 15 (August 2, 1895): 33; "In the New Eagle Factory," *Torrington Register* (February 21, 1896): 4; and Theodore Peck, "Factory for the Eagle Bicycle Manufacturing Co., Torrington, Conn.," Plan Nos. 1, 2 and 6, Torrington Historical Society.

17. Peck, "Factory for the Eagle Bicycle Manufacturing Co., Torrington, Conn.," Plan No. 5.

18. "In the New Eagle Factory," *Torrington Register* (February 21, 1896): 4; Peck, "Factory for the Eagle Bicycle Manufacturing Co., Torrington, Conn.," Plan No. 1 and Plan No. 2; and Sanborn-Perris Map Co., *Torrington, Litchfield County, Connecticut* (September 1896): Plate 1. The factory's power plant was installed by M.J. Daly of Waterbury; electric lighting and phones by E.A. Perkins; plumbing and iron piping by A.D. McCarty, and standpipe by the P. Pryibil Machine Co. based in New York City.

19. Robert McCullough, "Bicycle Factory Remnants: The Heritage of 19th and 20th Century Cycling," in *Cycle History 20. Proceedings of the 20th International Cycling History Conference, Freehold, New Jersey (July 30 to August 1, 2009)*, Gary W. Sanderson, ed. (Cheltenham, England: Quorum

Print Ltd. for the John Pinkerton Memorial Publishing Fund, 2010): 206–218; and "Wheels of Fortune: The Bicycle Boom, Trinity Cycle, and its Keene Factory, *Historical New Hampshire* 67 (Fall–Winter 2013): 52–80.

20. "The Eagle Bicycle," *Scientific American* 74 (January 11, 1896): 1, 20; "In the New Eagle Factory," *Torrington Register* (February 21, 1896): 4; and Peck, "Factory for the Eagle Bicycle Manufacturing Co., Torrington, Conn.," Plan No. 1 and Plan No. 2.

21. Mechanic's Lien by A.D. McCarty, recorded in Vol. 36, page 444; Mechanic's Lien by Hotchkiss Bros. & Co., recorded December 6, 1895, in Vol. 36, page 453; and Mechanic's Lien, recorded December 6, 1895, in Vol. 36, page 454–455; all in the office of the Torrington Town Clerk. Whether the general contractor, C.D. Janssen, had received payment from the Eagle company's owners and had failed to pay the subcontractors, or whether disputes about the quality of work developed, the matter was eventually resolved in July 1896. In *Torrington Register*, see "Torrington Bicycle Show" (March 27, 1896): 1; and "1897 Wheels" (December 4, 1896): 3. See also "Come Into Line," *WCTR* 19 (July 2, 1897): 21; and "Nothing Unexpected," *WCTR* 19 (July 2, 1897): 25.

22. "1897 Wheels," *Torrington Register* (December 4, 1896): 3; "Eagle Bicycle," *L.A.W. Bulletin and Good Roads* 27 (March 11, 1898): 224; and "Cycling," *Outing* 31 (March 1898): 618–626, at 623. See also "Minutes, Board of Directors, Eagle Bicycle Manufacturing Co." (August 3, 1896): 112–113; Sanborn-Perris Map Company, *Insurance Maps of Torrington, Litchfield County, Connecticut* (October 1901): Plate 13; "Board of Trade," *WCTR* 21 (June 23, 1898): n.p.; and Bird's Eye Bits," *WCTR* 21 (Supplement, June 23, 1898): ii–iii.

23. "President Garford's Report," *WCTR* 20 (January 21, 1898): iii; "Minutes of the Board of Directors, Eagle Bicycle Manufacturing Co." (August 1, 1898): 122–123; "More Eagle Bicycles Sold in 1898 Than Ever Before," *WCTR* 22 (August 18, 1898): 1; and "Editorial Gossip," *WCTR* 22 (December 15, 1898): 17.

24. "President Garford's Report," *WCTR* 20 (January 21, 1898): iii; "More Eagle Bicycles Sold in 1898 Than Ever Before," *WCTR* 22 (August 18, 1898): 1; and "Minutes of the Annual Meeting of Stockholders, Eagle Bicycle Manufacturing Co." (August 9, 1899): 79–84.

25. "National Board of Trade of Cycle Manufacturers Still Alive," *WCTR* 22 (December 15, 1898): 17; "End of the Board of Trade," *WCTR* 22 (January 5, 1899): 21; "The National Board's Dissolution," *WCTR* 22 (February 2, 1899): 21; "The Chicago Show," *WCTR* 22 (January 12, 1899): 30–38, i–iii; and "The New York Show," *WCTR* 22 (January 26, 1899): 36–40, i–x. See also Epperson, *Peddling Bicycles*, 171–174.

26. "American Bicycle Company. Trust Items," *WCTR* 23 (June 29, 1899): 7–9; "The Combine—A Comparison of Outputs," *CATR* 23 (June 8, 1899): 138; and "People of the Play," *WCTR* 23 (June 22, 1899): 8–9. See also Epperson, *Peddling Bicycles*, 171–174.

27. "Minutes of a Special Meeting of Stockholders, Eagle Bicycle Manufacturing Co." (May 24, 1899): 74–78; and "Minutes of the Annual Meeting of Stockholders, Eagle Bicycle Manufacturing Co." (August 9, 1899): 79–84. Meeting minutes do not identify the provisions of Spalding's initial offer that the directors found objectionable.

28. "Minutes of the Board of Directors, Eagle Bicycle Manufacturing Co." (August 8, 1899): 127–130.

29. "Editorial Gossip," *WCTR* 22 (December 15, 1898): 17; "National Board of Trade of Cycle Manufacturers Still Alive," *WCTR* 22 (December 15, 1898): 17; "End of the Board of Trade," *WCTR* 22 (January 5, 1899): 21; "The National Board's Dissolution," WCTR 22 (February 2, 1899): 21; "The Chicago Show," *WCTR* 22 (January 12, 1899): 30–38, i–iii; "The New York Show," *WCTR* 22 (January 26, 1899): 36–40, i–x; "A.B.C. Almost Ready," *WCTR* 24 (August 24, 1899): 9; "Monarch In, Eagle Out," and "Formally Floated," *WCTR* 24 (August 31, 1899): 9. See also "Minutes of the Board of Directors, Eagle Bicycle Manufacturing Co." (August 9, 1899): 131; and "Minutes of the Annual Meeting of Stockholders, Eagle Bicycle Manufacturing Co." (August 1899): 79–84. During discussions, shareholders of the Torrington Co. objected to "the clause in the contract requiring the vendors to agree not to be interested in the bicycle business," suggesting that the provision would give ABC the right to halt the company's ongoing manufacture of bicycle parts; see *Hardware Dealer's Magazine* 47 (June 1917): 1250. A shareholder list dated 1898 and available at the Stamford History Center shows forty-seven shareholders holding 4,000 shares, with percentages held by majority shareholders slightly different than those noted in the minutes of 1899.

30. "Eagle Company Rebels Against the Bottom Bracket Patent," *WCTR* 24 (December 28, 1899): 14; "To Sue the Eagle," *WCTR* 24 (January 11, 1900): 15; and "A.B.C.-Eagle Bottom Bracket Contention. Hartford Looks for a Decision in a Year," *WCTR* 24 (January 25, 1900): 30. See also "Bottom Bracket Bogey," *BWMR* 43 (August 22, 1901): 428. The lawsuit included the H.P. Snyder Manufacturing Co., the Wisconsin Wheel Works, and several others.

31. Patent 631,282 titled "Bicycle," dated August 22, 1899, issued to Charles S. Dikeman; Patent 640,884 titled "Bicycle," dated January 9, 1900, issued to Charles S. Dikeman; Patent 647,812 titled "Bicycle Frame," dated April 17, 1900, issued to Joseph Dikeman; Patent 648,657 titled "Bicycle Frame," dated May 1, 1900, issued to Charles S. Dikeman; Patent 656,950 titled "Handle Bar Pillar for Bicycles," dated August 28, 1900, issued to Joseph S. Dikeman; Patent 662,115 titled "Bicycle Frame," dated November 20, 1900, issued to Joseph Dikeman; Patent 666,187 titled "Bicycle Frame," dated January 15, 1901, issued to Joseph Dikeman; and Patent 686,034 titled "Bicycle Frame," dated November 5, 1901, issued to Charles S. Dikeman. See also "Eagles Surprise," *BWMR* 41 (November 8, 1900): 107; "Dikeman Named as Trustee," *BWMR* 43 (August 1, 1901): 371; and "Eagle Bicycle

Manufacturing Company," *BWMR* 44 (January 2, 1902): 318–319.

32. Warranty Deed from Achille Migeon to the Eagle Bicycle Manufacturing Company, recorded September 6, 1900, in Vol. 46, page 344, Torrington Town Clerk. See also "Boston Is Hard Hit" *BWMR* 41 (September 20, 1900): 469; "Will Make Marine Motors," *BWMR* 41 (March 14 1901): 668; "Prominent Torringtonian Dead," *BWMR* 43 (July 18, 1901): 337; "Eagle Bicycle Manufacturing Company," *BWMR* 44 (January 2, 1902): 318–319; "Walsh Leaves Cycle Trade," *BWMR* 44 (January 16, 1902): 367; "Makers in Session," *BWMR* 46 (November 13, 1902): 141; "Reductions in Eagles," *BWMR* 46 (December 11, 1902): 241; "Eagle Loses Its President," *BWMR* 46 (January 8, 1903): 416; "Coming to Motor Bicycles," *BWMR* 46 (January 15, 1903): 445; "Eagle and Dikeman Part," *BWMR* 47 (August 22, 1903): 607; and "Fire Singes Eagle Factory," *BWMR* 48 (December 12, 1903): 279. See also "National Cycle Trade Association," *Cycle and Automobile Trade Journal* 7 (March 1, 1903): 24. In December 1903, a fire destroyed a wood-frame building used for motor launch construction, and several boats in the building. See also "Minutes of the Board of Directors Meetings, Eagle Bicycle Manufacturing Co." (January 19, 1903): 142; and Epperson, *Peddling Bicycles*, 189–191.

33. "Bottom Bracket Patent is Sustained," and "What May Happen," *BWMR* 51 (July 15, 1905): 389–391; "Bottom-Bracket Decree Entered," *BWMR* 51 (August 12, 1905): 483–484; "End of the Eagle," *BWMR* 51 (September 9, 1905): 574; and "Pope Files Thirty Suits," *BWMR* 52 (September 30, 1905): 5. The decree affected bicycles built during a period beginning six years prior to the start of litigation, 1901. See also Warranty Deed from the Eagle Bicycle Manufacturing Company to the Progressive Manufacturing Company, recorded September 5, 1905, in Vol. 56, page 73, Torrington Town Clerk; and "Minutes of the Board of Directors Meetings, Eagle Bicycle Manufacturing Co." (October 2, 1905): 157–158. See also Carey Williams, "The Flight of the Eagle," *The Wheelmen* 86 (May 2015): 16–28.

Chapter 10

1. My research involving the Keating Wheel Company and its factories began in early 2002 and canvassed patent records; periodicals; newspaper accounts on microfilm; deed records; materials owned by local historical societies; and travel in Westfield, Holyoke, Springfield, and Middletown. The *Springfield Republican*, later digitized, has aided this research greatly. The papers of Arthur Lovett Garford held by the Ohio Historical Society, MSS6, are an especially valuable collection revealing the financial upheavals occurring during the bicycle craze of the 1890s. The historical society graciously allowed me to copy those letters in 2009.

Portions of this chapter appeared previously in an article titled "Bicycle Factory Remnants. The Heritage of 19th and 20th Century Cycling," published in *Cycle History 20. Proceedings of the 20th International Cycling History Conference. Freehold, New Jersey (July 30 to August 1, 2009)*, Gary W. Sanderson, ed. (Cheltenham, England: Quorum Print Ltd. for the John Pinkerton Memorial Publishing Fund, 2010): 206–218.

In 2014, R.K. Keating published a commendable biography, *Wheel Man, Robert M. Keating: Pioneer of Bicycles, Motorcycles and Automobiles* (Jefferson, NC: McFarland, 2014), a very thorough and valuable study of an important figure in cycling history. I have relied on that work to spot gaps in the chronology I developed from newspaper and periodical accounts, and also to reinforce several key topics, notably Keating's experiments with motorcycles and automobiles, as well as the final years of Keating's life. In addition, Mr. Keating (the author) provides a very detailed narrative regarding the design and marketing of Keating wheels, as well as important contextual background for the financial machinations that ultimately caused the company's demise.

2. "Robert M. Keating," in *Biographical Review, Leading Citizens of Hampden County*, Massachusetts (Boston: Biographical Review, 1895): 936–937. Henry D. Taylor, comp., *By-Laws, Rules and Regulations of the Springfield Bicycle Club, Springfield, Mass.* (Springfield, MA: Henry D. Taylor, publisher, 1892): 27. Both documents are available at the library of the Connecticut Valley Historical Museum, Springfield.

3. "Keating," *Biographical Review*, 6; "State of Maine Certificate of Organization of a Corporation," for the Warwick Cycle Manufacturing Company, dated March 15, 1888, recorded in Volume 11, page 221, Maine Secretary of State. See also "The Warwick Perfection Bicycle," *WCTR* 1 (June 29, 1888): 403; "The Overman Wheel Company, the Coventry Machinist's Company, and the Springfield Bicycle Manufacturing Company," *WCTR* 2 (November 23, 1888): 272; "We received a call...," *Bicycling World* 4 (April 7, 1882): 258; "Personal" *Bicycling World* 5 (July 21, 1882): 446; and "Currente Calamo," *Bicycling World* 8 (November 23, 1883): 27. See also "The Story of the Bicycle: The Overman Wheel Company," *Progressive Springfield* 1 (May, 1891): 207–209; and "Reaching After an Industry," *Springfield Republican* (June 20, 1891): 6.

4. Patent 420,805 titled "Velocipede," dated February 4, 1890 (application filed October 4, 1889); and Patent 426,670 titled "Velocipede," dated April 29, 1890 (application filed December 30, 1889), both issued to Robert Keating; Patent 361,280 titled "Bicycle," dated April 19, 1887 (application filed October 28, 1886); and Patent 433,562 titled "Velocipede," dated August 5, 1890 (application filed March 7, 1888); both issued to Leonard B. Gaylor. Although not the only inventor to experiment with spring devices during the early years of safety bicycles, Keating's heavy spring-levers for the front fork are noteworthy, foretelling similarly rugged springs introduced on mountain bike forks roughly a century later.

5. "Looking After Its Rights," *LAWB* 2 (February 26, 1886): 169; and "End of the Bicycle War,"

Springfield Republican (June 27, 1886): 5. See also Patent 559,178 titled "Bicycle Frame," dated April 28, 1896 (application filed November 16, 1894), issued to Robert M. Keating; and R.K. Keating, *Wheel Man*, 345–46.

6. R.K. Keating, *Wheel Man*, 88.

7. In the *Springfield Republican*, see "Westfield. Business Men's Association Formed" (April 14, 1887): 6; "Hampden County—A Promising New Manufacturing Enterprise" (September 11, 1890): 6; "Superior Cycles" (May 27, 1891): 1; and "Hampden County" (June 15, 1891): 6. See also "May Come to Holyoke—A Good Industry for the City," *Holyoke Daily Transcript* (June 29, 1891): 4; *Westfield City Directory* (Westfield, MA: R.S. Dillon & Co., 1891): 111, 180; and "Keating," *Biographical Review*, 936–937. The value of Keating's patents as represented in shares of stock is not known. Industrial buildings survive in the vicinity of 326 Elm Street, but without more information about Keating' occupancy in that factory, identifying any surviving traces is difficult.

8. "State of Maine Certificate of Organization of a Corporation, Keating Manufacturing Company," dated July 2, 1891, recorded July 4, 1891, in Vol. 16, page 411, Office of the Maine Secretary of State, and recorded July 3, 1891, in Vol. 9, page 412, Cumberland County Registry of Deeds; located in File 16–411, Maine Secretary of State. See also "Hampden County—Westfield," *Springfield Republican* (June 10, 1891): 6. In the *Holyoke Daily Transcript*, see "The Stock is Selling" (June 23, 1891): 4; "May Come to Holyoke—A Good Industry for the City" (June 29, 1891): 4; "To Make Bicycles" (July 16, 1891): 4; "The Keating Wheel Company's Plant Purchased" (July 23, 1891): 4; and "Progress of Holyoke's New Industry" (July 23, 1891): 4.

9. "State of Maine Certificate of Organization of a Corporation, Keating Manufacturing Company." See also "To Make Bicycles," *Holyoke Daily Transcript* (July 16, 1891): 4, which lists Whitcomb as president and Clarke as treasurer; adding to the confusion, five directors are listed: Whitcomb, Clarke, Netherwood, Collins, and D.E. Webster, with no mention of Keating and contradicting the articles filed with the Maine Secretary of State. In the *Springfield Republican*, see also "Progress of Holyoke's New Industry" (July 23, 1891): 4; "Features of the Bicycle Factory" (December 28, 1891): 6; "Holyoke" (September 15, 1893): 6; and "C.D. Rood to Rescue Keating Company (October 11, 1893): 6. See also Keating, *Wheel Man*, 30–31, 36, 49–50, for a more thorough discussion of the company's financial structure

10. In *Springfield Republican*, see "Features of the Bicycle Factory" (December 28, 1891): 6; and "The Keating-Wheel Factory To Be Built At Once" (August 6, 1891): 6. See also "The Keating Wheel Co.," *BWLAWB* 24 (January 22, 1892): Supplement, n.p. For Casper Ranger, see William Richard Cutter, ed., "Caspar [*sic*] Ranger," in *Memorial Encyclopedia of the State of Massachusetts*, Vol. 2 (New York: American Historical Society, 1917): 408–410. The factory was built in two sections, one sixty and the other fifty feet wide.

11. In *Springfield Republican*, see "Features of the Bicycle Factory" (December 28, 1891): 6; "A Busy Holyoke Industry" (April 3, 1895): 4; and "Holyoke" (October 5, 1892): 6. See also "To Make a Light Cycle," *Holyoke Daily Transcript* (January 19, 1892): 4. Journalists attributed the grinding machine to a machinist named Horner; both Joseph Horner and E.C. Horner developed grinding machines.

12. "Features of the Bicycle Factory," *Springfield Republican* (December 28, 1891): 6; and "To Make a Light Cycle," *Holyoke Daily Transcript* (January 19, 1892): 4. See also letter from Robert M. Keating to A.L. Garford dated June 23, 1895, Garford Papers, MSS6, OHS, recounting a ten-day closure of the canal.

13. "Keating Wheel Co. Name Change," recorded July 24, 1892, in Vol. 13½, page 52, and "Increase of Capital and Change in Directors," recorded September 24, 1892 in Vol. 13½ , page 70, Maine Secretary of State; located in Folder 16–411. In *Springfield Republican*, see "Holyoke" (August 26, 1892): 6; "Holyoke" (September 5, 1892): 6; "Reorganization of the Keating Wheel Company" (September 20, 1892): 6; and "Holyoke News and Comment" (September 24, 1893): 2. See also "Progress of Holyoke's New Industry," *Holyoke Daily Transcript* (July 23, 1891): 4.

14. In *Springfield Republican*, see "Holyoke" (September 15, 1893): 6; "Auction Sale Announced for Yesterday Postponed Presumably on Account of an Injunction" (October 4, 1893): 6; and "Holyoke" (October 18, 1893): 6.

15. In *Springfield Republican*, see "Holyoke News and Comment" (September 24, 1893): 2;

"Holyoke" (September 28, 1895): 8; and "Holyoke" (October 7, 1895): 6. See also "Keating Wheel Affairs," *Holyoke Daily Transcript* (March 26, 1896): 5; and Keating, *Wheel Man*, 88–89. In 1895, Whitcomb attempted to use the factory to manufacture his own bicycles.

16. In *Springfield Republican*, see "C.D. Rood to Rescue Keating Company" (October 11, 1893): 6; "Holyoke" (October 18, 1893): 6; and "Holyoke" (October 19, 1893): 6. See also letters from Robert M. Keating to Arthur L. Garford, dated December 18, 1896, and December 28, 1896, Garford Papers, MSS6, OHS.

17. In *Springfield Republican*, see "Holyoke" (January 11, 1894): 6; "Holyoke" (January 25, 1894): 6; "Holyoke" (April 6, 1894): 6; "Holyoke" (October 29, 1894): 6; and "Holyoke" (August 9, 1895): 4. Patent 525,081 titled "Tire for Wheels," dated August 28, 1894 (application filed December 13, 1893); Patent 559,178 titled "Bicycle Frame," dated April 28, 1896 (application filed November 16, 1894); Patent 568,767 titled "Crank-Shaft and Bearing for Bicycle," dated October 6, 1896 (application filed December 10, 1895); Patent 581,730 titled "Ball-Bearing-Retaining Device," dated May 4, 1897 (application filed May 23, 1896); Patent 607,175 titled "Wheel," dated July 12, 1898 (application filed May 23, 1896); Patent 607,543 titled "Adjustable Handle-Bar," dated July 19, 1898 (application filed June 1, 1896); Patent 568,768 titled "Crank-Shaft and

Bearing for Bicycles," dated October 6, 1896 (application filed June 1, 1896; and Patent 647,499 titled "Divided Crank-Shaft for Bicycles," dated April 17, 1900 (application filed September 9, 1896); all issued to Robert M. Keating. See also Keating, *Wheel Man*, 75–82.

18. Tony Hadland and Hans-Erhard Lessing, *Bicycle Design* (Cambridge: MIT Press, 2014): 393–395.

19. "What Wheel Willie Winifred Windle Will Ride," *WCTR* 9 (May 20, 1892): 24; letter from Robert M. Keating to A.L. Garford dated June 18, 1896, Garford Papers, MSS6, OHS; and Keating, *Wheel Man*, 88. Keating was among the guests invited to Windle's wedding ceremony in June, 1892. See "County News-Millbury," *Worcester Evening Gazette* (June 3, 1892): 7; and "On A Tandem," *Worcester Daily Telegram* (June 3, 1892): 4.

20. "Keating Wheel May Move," *Springfield Republican* (December 14, 1895): 8; Letter from Robert M. Keating to A.L. Garford, dated June 23, 1895, Garford Papers, MSS6, OHS; "The Middletown Board of Trade," *Middletown Penny Press* (December 12, 1896): 12; and Keating, *Wheel Man*, 98.

21. "Keating Wheel Company to Leave Holyoke," *Springfield Republican* (March 26, 1896): 8; and "Manufacturing Plants," *Engineering News* 35 (March 26, 1896): 105. In *Middletown Penny Press*, see "Agreement Signed" (May 23, 1896): 8; and "Keating Here" (June 9, 1896): 8.

22. Warranty Deed from Rogers and Hubbard Co., a Connecticut corporation, to the Keating Wheel Company, a Maine corporation, recorded June 11, 1896, in Vol. 126, page 57, Middletown Town Clerk; and "Manufacturing Plants," *Engineering News* 35 (June 11, 1896 Supplement): 193–194. In *Middletown Penny Press*, see "Keating Here" (June 9, 1896): 8; and "Contract Awarded" (June 11, 1896): 2.

23. "A Wonderful Cycle Factory," *WCTR* 18 (February 12, 1897): 112; Charles F. Warner, ed., "Casper Ranger," in *Picturesque Hampden* (Northampton, MA: Picturesque Publishing Company, 1892): 148; and Cutter, ed., "Caspar [*sic*] Ranger," in *Memorial Encyclopedia*, 408–410.

24. Letter from M.L. Goss to Arthur Garford, dated May 9, 1898; Garford Papers, MSS6, OHS.

25. "Keating Wheel Affairs," *Holyoke Transcript* (March 26, 1896): 5; Sanborn-Perris Map Co., *Insurance Maps of Middletown, Connecticut* (May 1901): Plate 2. Letter from Arthur Patrick to Arthur Garford, dated December 28, 1898, Garford Papers, MSS6, OHS.

26. "A Wonderful Cycle Factory," *WCTR* 18 (February 12, 1897): 112; "The New Bicycle Factory," *Engineering News* 37 (February 18, 1897): 96; and Letter from Arthur Patrick to Arthur Garford dated December 19, 1898, Garford Papers, MSS6, OHS.

27. Sanborn-Perris Map Co., *Insurance Maps of Middletown, Connecticut* (May 1901): Plate 2; and "Switch Through Factory," *Middletown Penny Press* (July 22, 1895): 8. See also Keating, *Wheel Man*, 107, with an excellent discussion about the transport of sand from Willow Island in the Connecticut River. See also Letter from Arthur Patrick to Arthur Garford dated December 12, 1898, Garford Papers, MSS6, OHS.

28. "A Wonderful Cycle Factory," *WCTR* 18 (February 12, 1897): 112; "The New Bicycle Factory," *Engineering News* 37 (February 18, 1897): 96; "Electric Power in the Keating Bicycle Factory," *Electrical Engineer* 23 (February 10, 1897): 169–170; "Bicycle Factory Operated by Electricity," *Electrical Age* 19 (February 27, 1897): 131–132.

29. *Ibid.*

30. In the *Middletown Penny Press*, see "Important Changes" (August 1, 1896): 5; "Transfer of Title" (September 5, 1896): 2; "The Keating Company" (June 3, 1897): 2; "Machinery Arriving" (June 11, 1897): 8; "Factory Made Ready" (July 9, 1897): 2; "The New Model" (September 2, 1897): 2; and "Keating Wheel Company" (October 28, 1897): 2, and (October 29, 1897): 2 (twice published). For the hand-screw and wire-screw machines from Pratt and Whitney Company, see Lease recorded February 23, 1898 in Vol. 126, page 370; and Lease recorded November 10, 1898, in Vol. 126, page 541, both for six-month terms in the amount of $432; and both recorded with the Middletown Town Clerk; whether those machines operated with electric motors is not known.

For business failures, see "Worcester Cycle Company," *WCTR* 17 (April 10, 1896): 92; "Mortgaged for Half-Million," *WCTR* 18 (October 2, 1896): 2; "Of Royal Lineage," *WCTR* 18 (February 12, 1897): 106; "Worcester Worse," *WCTR* 19 (July 2, 1897): 21; "Defeated After Departmenting," *WCTR* 19 (July 16, 1897): 21; and "Mr. Smith to Borrow," *WCTR* 20 (August 27, 1897): 11. See also Deed to the Worcester Cycle Manufacturing Company recorded August 31, 1896 in Vol. 1518, page 10, Worcester County Registry of Deeds.

31. Memorandum of Notes and Credits, undated but c. June 1989; Letter from R.M. Keating to Arthur Garford, dated December 28, 1896; Letter from R.M. Keating to Arthur Garford dated December 30, 1896; Letter from Arthur Garford to R.M. Keating dated March 5, 1898; and letter from Arthur Garford to R.M. Keating dated March 7, 1898; Garford Papers, MSS6, OHS.

32. "Company Reorganized," *Middletown Penny Press* (October 15, 1898): 2; Letter of Certification from Carroll W. Morrill, Clerk of the Keating Wheel Company, to Byron Boyd, Maine Secretary of State, dated October 31, 1898, recorded November 1, 1898, Vol. 1 of Changes, page 289, File 16–411, Maine Secretary of State. See also Letter from Arthur Garford to R.M. Keating, dated March 5, 1898; Letter from Arthur Garford to R.M. Keating dated March 7, 1898; Memorandum of Agreement between Charles Rood and Arthur Garford dated June 16, 1898, and accompanying Memorandum of Notes and Credits; and Letter from M.H. Crampton to Arthur Garford, dated October 25, 1898; all in Garford Papers, MSS6, OHS.

33. Patent 619,315, titled "Sprocket Chain," dated February 14, 1899 (application filed February 27, 1897); Patent 688,419 titled "Bicycle-Frame," dated December 10, 1901 (application filed September

4, 1897); and Patent 691,147 titled "Back-Pedaling Brake," dated January 14, 1902 (application filed September 13, 1897); all issued to Robert M. Keating. See also Letters from Arthur Patrick to Arthur Garford, dated September 5, 1898, and November 3, 1898, Garford Papers, MSS6, OHS.

34. "To Make Wagons," *Middletown Penny Press* (November 16, 1898): 2. See also Letter from M.L. Goss to Arthur Garford, dated September 9, 1897; Letter from M.L. Goss to Arthur Garford dated May 8, 1898; Letter from Arthur Garford to Arthur Patrick, dated May 7, 1898; Letter from Arthur Garford to Arthur Patrick, dated June 28, 1898; Letter from Arthur Patrick to Arthur Garford, dated September 5, 1898; Letter from Arthur Patrick to Arthur Garford, dated October 24, 1898; Letter from Arthur Patrick to Arthur Garford, dated November 3, 1898; Letter from Arthur Patrick to Arthur Garford, dated December 28, 1898; Letter from Arthur Patrick to Arthur Garford, dated January 11, 1899; Letter from Robert Keating to Arthur Garford dated January 12, 1899; and letter from Robert Keating to Arthur Garford, dated January 20, 1899; all in Garford Papers, MSS6, OHS.

35. In *Middletown Penny Press*, see "Home of Light Wheels" (January 10, 1899): 5; and "The Keating Catalog" (February 24, 1899): 2. See also "Keating Cutting Down," *WCTR* 23 (June 22, 1899): 12. See also letter from Arthur Garford to Arthur Patrick dated June 7, 1898; General Sales Department Letter No. 3, dated November 1, 1898; Letter from Arthur Patrick to Arthur Garford, dated November 29, 1898; Letter from Arthur Patrick to Arthur Garford, dated November 29, 1898; Letter from Arthur Patrick to Arthur Garford dated December 2, 1898; Letter from Arthur Patrick to Arthur Garford, dated December 12, 1898; Letter from Arthur Patrick to Arthur Garford dated December 19,1898; and Letter of George Lytle to dealers, undated but c. December 1898; all in Garford Papers, MSS6, OHS.

36. "American Bicycle Company. Trust Items," *WCTR* 23 (June 29, 1899): 7–9; "The Combine—A Comparison of Outputs," *CATR* 23 (June 8, 1899): 138.

37. In *Middletown Penny Press*, see "Bicycle Combination" (March 25, 1899): 2; and "Plan Considered" (March 25, 1899): 5. See also Keating, *Wheel Man*, 181–184.

38. In *Middletown Penny Press*, see "A New Engine" (January 4, 1899): 2; "Plan Considered" (May 25, 1899): 5; "To Make Automobiles" (July 11, 1899): 5; and "Gasoline Automobiles" (August 22, 1899): 5. See also "Keating Closes Down," *WCTR* (July 13, 1899): 8; and Patent 618,972 titled "Gas Engine," dated February 7, 1899 (application filed April 29, 1898), issued to Charles R. Alsop.

39. Letter of Notification from Carroll W. Morrill, Clerk, to Honorable Byron Boyd, Maine Secretary of State, dated September 15, 1899, recorded September 21, 1899 in Vol. 1 of Changes, page 453, File 16-411, Maine Secretary of State. In *Middletown Penny Press*, see "Increased Capital" (September 16, 1899): 2; "Capital Subscribed" (October 9, 1899): 2; "A Local Automobile" (October 16, 1899): 4; "Delivery Auto Comes" (October 18, 1899): 4; "No Material Change" (October 31, 1899): 2; and "Betts Is Receiver" (July 3, 1900): 4. See also Letter from Robert Keating to Arthur Garford dated November 8, 1899; and Letter from Robert Keating to Arthur Garford, dated November 21, 1899; Garford Papers, MSS6, OHS.

40. In *Middletown Penny Press*, see "Delivery Auto Comes" (October 18, 1899): 4; "The First Automobile" (November 11, 1899): 4; and "A New Automobile" (January 13, 1900): 5.

41. In *Middletown Penny Press*, see "Cost of Assessment" (October 25, 1899): 5; "Orders Coming In" (January 27, 1900): 5; "Plan of Reorganization" (February 7, 1900): 4; and "Betts Is Receiver" (July 3, 1900): 4. See also "Keating Company Bondholders," *Springfield Republican* (February 17, 1900): 5; "Keating Bondholders Skeptical About Receivership," *WCTR* 25 (July 12, 1900): 6; and letter from Arthur Garford to Charles Rood, dated April 25, 1900; Garford Papers, MSS6, OHS. See also Keating, *Wheel Man*, 198–208.

42. In *Middletown Penny Press*, see "Betts Is Receiver" (July 3, 1900): 4; "For Reorganization" (July 7, 1900): 5; "Keating Receivership" (July 16, 1900): 2; and "Keating Company Affairs" (August 28, 1900): 5. See also "Receiver for Keating Company," *Springfield Republican* (July 3, 1900): 3; Letter from Arthur Garford to Charles Rood, dated March 16, 1900; Letter from Charles Rood to Arthur Garford, dated March 19, 1900; Letter from Arthur Garford to Charles Rood, dated March 26, 1900; Letter from Charles Rood to Arthur Garford dated March 27, 1900; Letter from Arthur Garford to Charles Rood dated June 22, 1900; and letter from Arthur Garford to Joseph Merriam, dated July 2, 1900; Garford Papers, MSS6, OHS. See also Keating, *Wheel Man*, 207–215.

43. In *Middletown Penny Press*, see "Appraisers' Work" (November 12, 1900): 2; and "Keating Co. Claims" (March 2, 1901): 2. See also "Mr. Rood's Claim Allowed," *Springfield Republican* (June 23, 1901): 16; and "Fire Insurance Assets," *Hartford Daily Courant* (December 26, 1900): 4. Garford's status was that of an unsecured creditor, but his loans were made through his saddle company; see letter from Arthur Garford to the Keating Wheel Company, dated November 7, 1899, Garford Papers, MSS6, OHS. However, Rood, Coffin, Merriam, Coles and Burrows held a security interest in the company's chattels; see Quitclaim Deed recorded January 16, 1902, in Vol. 132, page 543, Middletown Town Clerk. See also letter from Charles Rood to Arthur Garford dated March 27, 1900; Letter from Arthur Garford to Charles Rood, dated July 5, 1900; and Trust Agreement between Robert M. Keating and O. Vincent Coffin dated June 28, 1898; Garford Papers, MSS6, OHS. See also Keating, *Wheel Man*, 235.

44. In *Middletown Penny Press*, see "Keating Company Affairs" (August 28, 1900): 5; "Keating Bonds" (November 19, 1900): 2; and "Ready for Market" (November 15, 1900): 2. See also "Middletown," *Hartford Daily Courant* (January 19, 1901): 12. See also Patent 675,387 titled "Motor Bicycle," dated

June 4, 1901; Patent 675,388 titled "Motor Bicycle," dated June 4, 1901; Patent 675,389 titled "Motor Bicycle," dated June 4, 1901; Patent 675,390 titled "Battery-Casing for Motor Bicycles," dated June 4, 1901; Patent 675,391 titled "Bicycle Frame," dated June 4, 1901; Patent 675,392 titled "Pedal-Brake and Controller for Motor-Cycles," dated June 4, 1901; Patent 695,562 titled "Bicycle-Motor," dated March 18, 1902; Patent 785,808 titled "Carburetor for Hydrocarbon-Engines," dated March 28, 1905; all issued to R.M. Keating but assigned to the R.M. Keating Motor Company. See also Keating, *Wheel Man*, 221–232; 245–249; 253–255; and 310–317.

45. In *Middletown Penny Press*, see "Keating Plant Sold" (June 15, 1901): 5; and "Order of Sale Passed" (June 22, 1901): 5; "Bonds First Mortgage" (June 26, 1901): 5; "The Keating Property" (August 1, 1901): 2; "Forfeited $10,000" (August 3, 1901): 5; "Bondholders Met" (October 21, 1901): 5; "The Agreement" (November 14, 1901): 5; and "The Keating Shop" (November 12, 1901): 4. See also "All for Bondholders," *Bicycling World* 43 (June 27, 1901): 284; "Keating Property Sold" *Hartford Daily Courant* (January 17, 1902): 2; and Keating, *Wheel Man*, 266–275.

46. In *Middletown Penny Press*, see (July 29, 1902): 3; (July 11, 1902): 5; (July 26, 1902): 2; (January 6, 1903); (December 30, 1903): 2. See also Receiver's Report. Letter from Arthur Garford to Henry M. Earle dated March 30, 1900; and Keating, *Wheel Man*, 284–285.

47. Quitclaim Deed from Trustees O. Vincent Coffin, George A. Coles, and Seth H. Butler, to Frederick A. Betts, Receiver of the Keating Wheel and Automobile Company, recorded January 16, 1902, in Vol. 132, page 540; Quitclaim Deed from O. Vincent Coffin, Joseph Merriam, George A. Coles, William H. Burrows, Charles H. Rood, John Bolt, P.B. Phelan, and the Middlesex Mutual Assurance Company, to Frederick A. Betts, Receiver of the Keating Wheel and Automobile Company, recorded January 16, 1902, in Vol. 132, page 543; Warranty Deed from Frederick A. Betts, Receiver of the Keating Wheel and Automobile Company, to the Eisenhuth Horseless Vehicle Company, recorded January 16, 1902, in Vol. 132, page 541; Trustee's Deed from George T. Shull, Trustee in Bankruptcy of the Eisenhuth Horseless Vehicle Company, to Everett J. Esselstyn, recorded May 1, 1907, in Vol. 137, page 300, pursuant to a sale at auction on March 22, 1907, for $21,000; and Bill of Sale recorded May 1, 1907, in Vol. 137, page 298; all in Middletown Town Clerk. See also Letter dated March 3, 1903, to Byron Boyd, Maine Secretary of State, regarding dissolution of the Keating Wheel and Automobile Company. In *Middletown Penny Press*, see (July 29, 1902): 3; (July 11, 1902): 5; (July 26, 1902): 2; (August 8, 1902): np; (January 6, 1903) np; and (December 30, 1903): 2. See also Keating, *Wheel Man*, 274–278, 280–285.

48. Quitclaim Deed from Everett J. Esselstyn and Sarah B. Esselstyn to The Noiseless Typewriter Company, a Connecticut corporation, recorded June 30, 1909, in Vol. 142, page 155. See also Quitclaim Deed from the Noiseless Typewriter Company, a Connecticut corporation, to Joseph Merriam, recorded July 20, 1914, in Vol. 149, page 275, pursuant to a U.S. District Court order dated April 16, 1914. See also Warranty Deed from the Noiseless Typewriter Company, a Connecticut corporation, to the Noiseless Typewriter Company, Inc., a Delaware corporation, recorded January 5, 1922, in Vol. 163, page 385; signed by Charles Colby, president, attested by Joseph Merriam, Secretary.

See also Warranty Deed from the Noiseless Typewriter Company, Inc., a Delaware corporation, to Remington Noiseless Typewriter Corporation, a New York corporation, recorded June 5, 1924, in Vol. 168, page 177; and Warranty Deed from Remington Noiseless Typewriter Corporation, a New York corporation, to Remington Typewriter Company, a New York corporation, recorded July 14, 1927, in Vol. 178, page 216.

See also Warranty Deed from Remington Typewriter Company, a New York corporation, to Remington Rand, Inc., a Delaware corporation, recorded April 13, 1931, Vol. 186, page 448; Warranty Deed from Remington-Rand, Inc, a Delaware corporation, to Andover Kent, Inc., a Delaware Corporation, recorded January 23, 1941, Vol. 202, page 347, for $315,000; Warranty Deed from Andover Kent Aviation Corporation, a Delaware corporation, to Remington Rand, Inc., a Delaware corporation, recorded April 14, 1952, in Vol. 245, page 172; Certificate of Name Change by Remington Rand, Inc., changed the corporate name to Sperry Rand Corporation, effective June 30, 1955, recorded April 15, 1970, in Vol. 368, page 629; and Quitclaim Deed from Sperry Rand Corporation, a Delaware corporation, to Public Health Foundation for Cancer and Blood Pressure Research, Inc., a Delaware corporation, recorded April 17, 1970 in Vol. 368, page 631, conveying a portion of the property in question. All in Middletown Town Clerk.

49. In *Hartford Daily Courant*, see "City News in Brief" (August 4, 1906): 6; "Keating Estate Closed," *Hartford Courant*, August 21, 1906: 14; and Keating, *Wheel Man*, 288–290; 299–317.

Chapter 11

1. Patent 315,094 titled "Wheel for Vehicles," dated April 7, 1885; Patent 322,221 titled "Bicycle," dated July 14, 1885; Patent 328,987 titled "Tool for Making Hollow Rims for Bicycle Wheels," dated October 27, 1885; all issued to George Tho. Warwick. In *Springfield Republican*, see also "Springfield" (April 4, 1888): 6; and "Decline of Wheeling Locally" (April 8, 1888): 9.

2. "The Warwick Perfection Bicycle," *WCTR* 1 (June 29, 1888): 403; "Decline of Wheeling Locally," *Springfield Republican* (April 8, 1888): 9; "The Warwick Perfection Bicycle," *BWLAWB* 17 (October 19, 1888): 480; and "Way Down East," *WCTR* 2 (November 23, 1888): 270.

3. In the *Springfield Republican*, see "A South-End Blaze" (August 5, 1886): 3; and "Sudden Death of D.L. Swan" (April 14, 1895): 2. See also

By-Laws, Rules and Regulations of the Springfield Bicycle Club, Springfield, Mass. (Springfield: Springfield Printing Company, 1887): 24; available at the Connecticut Valley Historical Museum Library.

4. "State of Maine Certificate of Organization, Warwick Cycle Manufacturing Company," dated March 10, 1888, recorded March 22, 1888, in Vol. 11, page 221, Maine Secretary of State; "The Warwick Cycle Manufacturing Company," in *Inland Massachusetts Illustrated. A Concise Resume of the Natural Features and Past History of the Counties of Hampden, Hampshire, Franklin and Berkshire* (Springfield: Elstner Publishing Company, 1890): 92–93; "A New Firm in the Bicycle Manufacturing Business," *BWLAB* 16 (April 13, 1888): 405; "The Warwick Perfection Bicycle," *WCTR* 1 (June 29, 1888): 403; and *By-Laws, Springfield Bicycle Club*, 25. In the *Springfield Republican*, see also "A New Bicycle Factory" (April 4, 1888): 6; and "A Fine New Bicycle Factory" (May 16, 1891): 3.

5. Patent 399,454 titled "Bicycle," dated March 12, 1889; and Patent 434,615 titled "Velocipede," dated August 19, 1890; both issued to George Tho. Warwick. See also "The Warwick Perfection Bicycle," *BWLAB* 17 (October 19, 1888): 480–481; and "Way Down East," *WCTR* 2 (November 23, 1888): 270.

6. In the *Springfield Republican*, see "Springfield" (October 21, 1889): 6; and "A Prosperous Wheel Company" (July 2, 1890): 5. See also "Reorganization of the Warwick Cycle Mfg. Co.," *WCTR* 4 (October 24, 1889): 176; "Warwick Cycle Mfg. Co.," *WCTR* 8 (November 27, 1891): 423; "The Warwick Cycle Manufacturing Company," in *Inland Massachusetts*, 92–93. 423; and "Built Upon Honor," *Progressive Springfield, Massachusetts*, George S. Graves, ed. (Springfield: G.S. Graves, 1913): 9. Conceivably, Warwick may have developed a working relationship with the Springfield Foundry Company during his early years in that city.

7. Concerning the reorganization, in the *Springfield Republican* see "Springfield" (October 21, 1889): 6; and "Springfield" (October 28, 1889): 6. See also "Reorganization of the Warwick Cycle Mfg. Co.," *WCTR* 4 (October 25, 1889); and "Warwick Cycle Manufacturing Company," *WCTR* 8 (September 18, 1891): 108. For biographical information about the owners, in the *Springfield Republican* see "Notice" (March 23, 1888): 1 (Bill); "Springfield" (June 25, 1891): 6; "Death of George L. Bleloch" (November 25, 1891): 6; "Some Nominees for the Legislature" (October 29, 1891): 6 (Brewer); "G.D. Chamberlain Dies at His Home, Long Active Here" (February 21, 1944): 1; "A Local Publishing Company" (June 9, 1888): 6 (Graves); "The Phelps Publishing Company" (June 6, 1891): 3 (Graves and Myrick); "A Business Man as Candidate" (November 28, 1893): 6 (Russell); "Sudden Death of D.L. Swan" (April 14, 1895): 2; and "Death of Dr. Vaille" (July 16, 1885): 6 (Wallace and Bill). In the *Springfield Republican*, see also "City Fathers Resume Business" (September 3, 1889): 8; and "Springfield. The Board of Trade Committees" (April 21, 1890): 6. See also *By-Laws, Springfield Bicycle Club*, 25–29. D.L. Swan likely influenced the company's new direction by his ties to some of the investors, those representing the paper and publishing industries for example. In addition, he may have been related to George Chamberlain by marriage (Swan's wife was Lydia Chamberlain of Holyoke).

8. "Warwick Cycle Manufacturing Company," *BWLAWB* 22 (November 1889): 78.

9. "Reaching After an Industry," *Springfield Republican* (June 20, 1896): 6.

10. Patent 420,805 "titled Velocipede," dated February 4, 1890; and Patent 426,670 "titled Velocipede," dated April 29, 1890; both issued to Robert M. Keating.

11. In the *Springfield Republican*, see "Busy Times at a Bicycle Factory" (March 27, 1890): 6; "A Prosperous Wheel Company" (July 2, 1890): 5; and "A Fine New Bicycle Factory" (May 16, 1891): 3.

12. In the *Springfield Republican*, see "Springfield" (January 29, 1889): 6; "Meeting of the Wheelmen's League" (February 18, 1890): 8; "Hampden County—A Promising New Manufacturing Enterprise" (September 11, 1890): 6; "A Fine New Bicycle Factory" (May 16, 1891): 3; and "The City Marshalship" (December 15, 1894): 7. See also see "Wheel Gossip," *WCTR* 3 (March 1, 1889): 9; "George R. Bidwell's 1889 Catalog," *WCTR* 3 (April 12, 1889): 134; "George R. Bidwell's 1890 Prospectus," *WCTR* 5 (May 2, 1890): 278; and "The Last of the Cits," *WCTR* 7 (March 27, 1891): 140. For Hendrick's appointments, see also "Built Upon Honor," in *Progressive Springfield*, 9–14.

13. "Warwick Diamond Safety," *BWLAWB* 22 (December 5, 1890): 140; and "Warwick Cycle Manufacturing Company, *BWLAB* 23 (September 18, 1891): 677. See also "A Fine New Bicycle Factory," *Springfield Republican* (May 16, 1891): 3.

14. "Warwick Cycle Manufacturing Co. Increase of Capital," dated July 23, 1890, recorded September 12, 1890, in Vol. 13, page 325; and "Warwick Cycle Manufacturing Co., Decrease of Par Value," dated November 12, 1890, recorded November 15, 1890, in Vol. 13, page 369; both in Maine Secretary of State. In the *Springfield Republican*, see "Busy Times at a Bicycle Factory" (March 27, 1890): 6; "A Prosperous Wheel Company" (July 2, 1890): 5; "Hampden County—A Promising New Manufacturing Enterprise" (September 11, 1890): 6 (Keating); "Bicycles for Government Letter Carriers" (November 1, 1890): 6; and "A Fine New Bicycle Factory" (May 16, 1891): 3.

15. Warranty Deed from Mary E. Heywood and Sarah E. Hovey to the Warwick Cycle Manufacturing Company, a Maine corporation, recorded May 27, 1891, in Vol. 478, page 375; and Quitclaim Deed from Gurdon Bill to Warwick Cycle Manufacturing Company, a Maine corporation, recorded July 31, 1891, in Vol. 480, page 175; both in Hampden County Registry of Deeds. In *Springfield Republican*, see also "A Fine New Bicycle Factory" (May 16, 1891): 3; and "Springfield" (July 17, 1891): 6. See also Sanborn-Perris Map Company, *Insurance Maps of Springfield, Massachusetts* (1896): Plate 82.

16. "A Fine New Bicycle Factory," *Springfield Republican* (May 16, 1891): 3. A drawing of the

factory that accompanies the article clearly shows a four-story building. Although the article itself refers to the building as three stories, it also describes the brick panel that divides the first and second stories, as shown on the drawing, with two additional stories above. Conceivably, Seabury intended the ground level floor as a substitute for a basement, and Richmond's subsequent introduction of a basement beneath the three-story building's easterly half is consistent with that explanation. In any case, the drawing shows a full story at ground level.

17. "A Fine New Bicycle Factory," *Springfield Republican* (May 16, 1891): 3.

18. *Ibid.*

19. "Springfield," *Springfield Republican* (June 6, 1891): 6; and "Built Upon Honor," in *Progressive Springfield*, 9–14.

20. Sanborn-Perris Map Company, *Insurance Maps of Springfield, Massachusetts* (1896), Plate 82.

21. "Built Upon Honor," in *Progressive Springfield*, 9; and Sanborn-Perris Map Company, *Insurance Map of Springfield, Massachusetts* (1896), Plate 82.

22. "Built Upon Honor," in *Progressive Springfield*, 13.

23. "A Fine New Bicycle Factory," *Springfield Republican* (May 16, 1891): 3.

24. "Warwick Cycle Manufacturing Company," *WCTR* 8 (September 18, 1891): 108.

25. "A New Home for the Bicycle Club," *Springfield Republican* (May 16, 1891): 9. For Gardner's books, see for example *Farm Architecture: Houses and Barns* (Boston: Rand, Abery and Co., 1881); and *Town and Country School Buildings* (New York: E.I. Kellogg and Co., 1888). Either George Gardner or George Pyne probably designed the clubhouse because the elder Gardner was in Atlanta during the time recovering from illness.

26. In the *Springfield Republican*, see "Special Notices" (May 25, 1890): 3; "Special Notices" (May 26, 1890): 3; "Bright Papers in the Morning" (August 13, 1891): 4; and "Death of F.R. Richmond" (November 6, 1907): 4. Richmond later formed an association with another architect, J.W. Donahue; see "Local Intelligence," *Springfield Republican* (August 28, 1897): 8. See also "A New Church and Two New Chapels in Springfield," *Springfield Republican* (July 29, 1882): 6, and "The Christian Workers," *Springfield Sunday Republican* (March 7, 1886): 5.

27. In the *Springfield Republican*, see "Special Notices" (May 25, 1890): 3; "Special Notices" (May 26, 1890): 3; "Bright Papers in the Morning" (August 13, 1891): 4, and "Death of F.R. Richmond" (November 6, 1907): 4.

28. "Warwick Cycle Manufacturing Company," *BWLAB* 23 (September 18, 1891): 677; "Warwick Cycle Manufacturing Company," *WCTR* 8 (September 18, 1891): 108; "The Warwick Cycle Manufacturing Company's New Factory," *WCTR* 8 (January 29, 1892): 770; and "Built Upon Honor," in *Progressive Springfield*, 9–14. The Ames company manufactured some of the new machinery for the Warwick firm; see "Chicopee," *Springfield Republican* (December 24, 1891): 7.

29. "Warwick Cycle Manufacturing Company," *BWLAB* 23 (September 18, 1891): 677; and "Built Upon Honor," in *Progressive Springfield*, 9–14. Descriptions of the office arrangements vary.

30. In the *Springfield Republican*, see "The Firemen's Hard Struggle" (October 28, 1891): 6; "Retirement of George Warwick" (November 18, 1891): 5; and "Warwick Cycle Manufacturing Company" (November 19, 1891): 5. See also "Warwick Cycle Mfg. Co.," *WCTR* 8 (November 27, 1891): 423.

31. In the *Springfield Republican*, see "Personal and Social Mention" (October 21, 1894): 8; and "G.D. Chamberlain Dies at His Home; Long Active Here" (February 21, 1944): 1; "Springfield" (April 19, 1879): 5; "Educational" (July 10, 1879): 3; and "Springfield" (August 13, 1881): 5.

32. In the *Springfield Republican*, see "The Warwick Model for 1892" (January 21, 1892): 3; and "Springfield" (March 16, 1892): 6. See also "The Warwick Cycle Manufacturing Company's New Factory," *WCTR* 8 (January 29, 1892): 770; and "Built Upon Honor," in *Progressive Springfield*, 14. Chamberlain eventually rejected the name "Puritan" to avoid confusion with Columbus models being sold by the Simmons Hardware Company; see *WCTR* 9 (June 10, 1892): 30.

33. In the *Springfield Republican*, see "A Suit Against George Warwick" (March 24, 1892): 5; and "Chicopee" (December 24, 1891): 7. See also Patent 472,005 titled "Bicycle," dated March 29, 1892, issued to Samuel Vale and assigned to George Warwick. See also "Two Bicycle Factories," *Toledo Daily Blade* (December 15, 1891): 3.

34. In the *Springfield Republican*, see "Important Verdict for Warwick Company" (May 2, 1892): 5; and "Springfield" (February 10, 1893): 6. See also Patent 383396 titled "Velocipede," dated May 22, 1888, issued to George Illston of Birmingham, Warwick County, England; Illston secured English Patent 4,606 on November 12, 1879.

35. "The Bicycle Manufacturers," *Springfield Republican* (September 15, 1893): 3; "A Sterling Jersey Firm," *BW* 29 (October 12, 1894): 818; "The Warwick-Stockton Company," *WCTR* 14 (October 12, 1894): supplement iv; and "Warwick Wins His Suit," *WCTR* 19 (May 28, 1897): 25. For the building, which has not survived, see Warranty Deed from Charles S. Stockton and Martha A. Stockton, grantors, to Stockton Manufacturing Company, grantee, dated April 12, 1898, recorded April 14, 1898, in Vol. P31, page 10, Essex County Registry of Deeds; and *Robinson's Atlas of the City of Newark*, Vol. 3, Plate 8 (Newark, NJ: Elisha Robinson: 1927). For Warwick's inventions, see, for example, Patent 693472 titled "Coaster and Brake Mechanism for Cycles," dated February 18, 1902; or Patent 959825 titled "Screw Machine," dated May 31, 1910; both issued to George T. Warwick.

36. "The Warwick Cycle Mfg. Co. Changes Officers," *WCTR* 10 (September 6, 1892): 26; and "The Warwick Company," *Springfield Republican* (September 7, 1892): 6.

37. "The Warwick Cycle Mfg. Co. Changes Officers," *WCTR* 10 (September 6, 1892): 26.

38. In the *Springfield Republican*, see "Down Go

the Bicycle Prices" (May 26, 1893): 5; and "The Break in Bicycle Prices" (May 29, 1893): 4.

39. "Meeting of Warwick Cycle Co.," *BWLAWB* 26 (July 28, 1893): 429; and "Warwick Cycle Manufacturing Company," *BWLAB* 26 (August 4, 1893): 439. In the *Springfield Republican*, see "Down Go the Bicycle Prices" (May 26, 1893): 5; "Hendee Declines the Presidency" (July 26, 1893): 6; and "New Manager of the Warwick Company" (August 2, 1893): 6. Between 1888 and 1893, Warwick, Brewer, Chamberlain, Rood, Bill, and Hendrick filled the office of president; Warwick, Chamberlain, Rood, Very, and possibly both Bill and Hendrick filled the vaguely-defined role of business manager.

40. "Mr. A.O. Very...," *BWLAWB* 20 (January 10, 1890): 224; and "We take pleasure...." *LAWB* 24 (March 25, 1892): 681. See also Patent 413,770 titled "Needle for Sewing Machines," dated October 29, 1889; and Patent 526,333 titled "Adjustable Handle Bar," dated September 18, 1894; both issued to Alpha O. Very.

41. In the *Springfield Republican*, see "New England News Items. Hampden County" (February 2, 1867): 8; "The City Marshalship" (December 15, 1894): 7; "Career of Joshua Stevens" (January 23, 1907): 12; and "Original Home of the J. Stevens Company is Being Torn Down" (July 23, 1933): 37.

42. In the *Springfield Republican*, see "Reduced Prices for Bicycles" (December 2, 1893): 6; and "Warwicks are Built on Honor" (September 11, 1894): 10. See also "Warwick Cycle Manufacturing Company," *BWLAWB* 26 (August 4, 1893): 439; and "The Warwick Factory," *BW* 30 (January 4, 1895): 261.

43. In the *Springfield Republican*, see "Warwick Cycles" (February 24, 1894): 8; "Local Intelligence" (March 3, 1894): 6; "Springfield" (March 3, 1894): 6; and "Springfield" (April 25, 1894): 6. See also Deed in Trust from the Warwick Cycle Manufacturing Company to the Springfield Safe Deposit and Trust Company, recorded April 16, 1894, in Vol. 520, page 321; the lender's interest was reconveyed simultaneously by Quitclaim Deed recorded April 16, 1894 in Vol. 520, page 324; both in Hampden County Registry of Deeds.

44. In the *Springfield Republican*, see "A Businessman as Candidate" (November 28, 1893): 6; "Springfield" (March 21, 1894): 6; "The City Marshalship" (December 15, 1894): 6; "The City Marshal Selected" (December 15, 1894): 7; and "Enameling Oven Explodes" (April 12, 1895): 6.

45. "In and About Springfield," *Springfield Republican* (November 10, 1895): 8; "The Warwick Factory," *BW* 30 (January 4, 1895): 261; "Very Good," *WCTR* 16 (November 8, 1895): 80; and "Warwick Company Attached," *WCTR* 20 (December 3, 1897): 21.

46. In the *Springfield Republican*, see "In and About Springfield" (November 10, 1895): 8; "Bicycles" (May 2, 1896): 4; "Springfield" (February 9, 1897): 8; and "New England Cycle Show" (February 21, 1897): 2.

47. "Warwick Company Attached," *WCTR* 20 (December 3, 1897): 21; and "Assignees Are Appointed," *WCTR* 21 (March 17, 1898): 23. In the *Springfield Republican*, see "A Heavy Attachment Made" (November 25, 1897): 4; "Springfield" (November 30, 1897): 8; "Conference on Warwick Affairs" (December 1, 1897): 8; "Society and Personal Mention" (December 19, 1897): 8; "Springfield" (December 21, 1897): 8; "Warwick Stockholders to Meet" (March 3, 1898): 4; and "Suit Against Second National" (December 18, 1901): 5.

48. "Warwick Company Attached," *WCTR* 20 (December 3, 1897): 21; "Warwick's Debts," *WCTR* 21 (March 10, 1898): 23; and "Assignees Are Appointed," *WCTR* 21 (March 17, 1898): 23. In the *Springfield Republican*, see also "Will Probably Sell at Auction" (November 29, 1898): 4; and "Suit Against Second National" (December 18, 1901): 5.

49. Scott Molloy, *Irish Titan, Irish Toilers. Joseph Banigan and Nineteenth-Century New England Labor* (Durham, NH: University of New Hampshire Press, 2008): 27, 60, 64–65, 81, 83–84, 203–211.

50. Molloy, *Irish Titan*, 230, 248.

51. Warwick's Debts," *WCTR* 21 (March 10, 1898): 23; "Assignees Are Appointed," *WCTR* 21 (March 17, 1898): 23; "Warwick Closes Down," *WCTR* 21 (August 4, 1898): 15; and "Warwick Company's Affairs," *CATR* 20 (January 27, 1898): 140. In the *Springfield Republican*, see "Warwick Stockholders to Meet" (March 3, 1898): 4; and "Will Probably Sell at Auction" (November 29, 1898): 4. See also Assignment in Insolvency, from Charles S. Long, Judge of the Court of Insolvency, Assignor, to Alfred S. Clarke and Joel H. Hendrick, Assignees, recorded March 16, 1898, in Vol. 577, page 315, Hampden County Registry of Deeds.

52. In the *Springfield Republican*, see "Will Probably Sell at Auction" (November 29, 1898): 4; and "A New Warwick Company" (February 19, 1899): 10. See also "Vale, Warwick!," *WCTR* 24 (November 23, 1899): 34.

53. See Assignee's Deed from Alfred S. Clarke and Joel H. Hendrick to Daniel B. Wesson, recorded November 27, 1899, in Book 611, page 216, Hampden County Registry of Deeds. See also "Vale, Warwick!," *WCTR* 24 (November 23, 1899): 34; and "Warwick Plant Transferred," *WCTR* 24 (December 7, 1899): 13.

54. In the *Springfield Republican*, see "Dwight Street Rail Case" (March 30, 1899): 4; "A Few Little Warwick Claims" (December 21, 1899): 5; "Against Warwick Directors" (December 31, 1899): 10; "Deputy Sheriff Walter S. Miller...," (January 3, 1900): 3; "Salary Awarded A.O. Very" (June 3, 1900): 4; "Dividend For A.O. Very" (March 7, 1901): 12; and "Suit Against Second National" (December 18, 1901): 5. See also "Warwick Dividend Due," *BWMR* 44 (February 27, 1902): 551.

55. "The New Warwick Automobile," *Springfield Republican* (November 24, 1900): 12. See also Patent 681,522 titled "Muffling Device," dated August 27, 1901; Patent 681,523 titled "Starting Device for Internal Combustion Engine," dated August 27, 1901; and Patent 737,887 titled "Vehicle Body," dated September 1, 1903; all issued to Alpha O. Very.

Chapter 12

1. "History of the Iver Johnson's Arms and Cycle Works," a typewritten manuscript, undated and unsigned, c. 1950 (presumably prepared by a family member); "On Iver Johnson History," an undated, unsigned, single-page typewritten list of important dates with handwritten annotations; and an untitled list of products manufactured by the firm from the date of its inception, also typewritten and undated, but circa 1933. All are available at the Fitchburg Historical Society. In *Worcester Daily Telegram*, see "Transfer of Steel Works" (October 5, 1895): 5; and "Willie Windle's New Wheel" (August 8, 1895): 8. See also "Two New Factories in Worcester," *WCTR* 15 (July 5, 1895): 24.

2. "Is Adjudged to be Insolvent," *Worcester Daily Telegram* (April 15, 1896): 1; "Tonight's Dedication," *Keene Evening Sentinel*, November 11, 1897, 6; "An Auspicious Dedication," *Keene Evening Sentinel* (November 12, 1897): 6; and "A fire occurred…," *The American Stationer* 40 (August 20, 1896): 293. Regarding the Worcester Cycle Company, newspaper and journal accounts reported that the company acquired the idle plant of the New England Steel Works, which may have been a former tenant of property owned by the Worcester Steel Works or John Byrne; see Limited Warranty Deed from Elizabeth M. Byrne to the Worcester Cycle Manufacturing Company, recorded October 4, 1895, in Vol. 1491, page 11, Worcester County Registry of Deeds. See also "Large Suits by Creditors," *Worcester Daily Telegram* (June 23, 1897): 2.

3. "Munger Locates in Worcester," *WCTR* 16 (September 6, 1895): 50; "Starters Ready, Timers Ready, Go!" *Worcester Telegram* (May 9, 1896): 1. Ritchie, *Major Taylor*, 48–50, 54–55.

4. William Richard Cutter, comp., *Historic Homes and Places and Genealogical and Personal Memoirs Relating to the Families of Middlesex County, Massachusetts*, Vol. 4 (New York: Lewis Historical Publishing Company 1908): 1754; and *Worcester City Directory* (Worcester: R.L. Polk and Company, 1892): 460. See also Permit dated April 27, 1891 for one-story horse shed on Winona Street issued to J.C. Speirs, in *Record of Building Permits—New Buildings, City of Worcester* (January 10, 1889 to April 19, 1892): 54; and Permit No. 489 dated June 18, 1891, for office and storehouse issued to J.C. Speirs, in *Record of Building Permits—Repairs and Additions, City of Worcester* (January 16, 1889 to April 30, 1896): 26; both projects built by Ward and Blanding. See also Sanborn Map Company, *Insurance Maps of Worcester Massachusetts* (1892): Plate 41; and "New Bicycle Factory," *Worcester Daily Spy* (January 24, 1892): 8. See also Warranty Deed from Horace H. Bigelow and Adelaide E. Bigelow to John C. Speirs and Arthur L. Moore as copartners, recorded October 30, 1890 in Vol. 1338, page 263; Warranty Deed from Arthur L. Moore and Amelia L. Moore to John C. Speirs, recorded October 30, 1890, in Vol. 1338, page 267; all in Worcester County Registry of Deeds. See also "Certificate of Organization, Speirs Manufacturing Company," recorded January 25, 1892, in Charter Book 27, page 4803, Corporation No. 4803, Massachusetts Secretary of State. See also "Small Strike at Speirs," *Worcester Telegram* (August 28, 1895): 6.

5. "New Bicycle Factory," *Worcester Daily Spy* (January 24, 1892): 8; and Sanborn Map Company, *Insurance Maps of Worcester Massachusetts* (1892): Plate 41.

6. "A Change of Ownership," *Worcester Daily Spy* (January 26, 1893): 2; "Working in Worcester," *WCTR* 21 (March 10, 1898): 1898; "Lovell Wins on Both," *Boston Globe* (July 12, 1899): 7; *Speirs vs. Union Drop Forge Co.*, 180 Mass 87 (1901).

7. Patent 536,301 titled "Method of Making Wrenches," dated March 26, 1895; and Patent 536,403 titled "Saddle," dated March 26, 1895; both issued to John C. Speirs and the latter assigned to the Speirs Manufacturing Company. See also "Small Strike at Speirs," *Worcester Daily Telegram* (August 28, 1895): 6; and "The now rapidly decreasing element…," *WCTR* (September 3, 1897): 1897. See also Permit No. 354 dated June 17, 1897, for addition to shop issued to J.C. Speirs, in *Record of Building Permits—Repairs and Additions, City of Worcester* (May 1, 1896, to March 31, 1903): 12.

8. "Speirs Stops," *WCTR* (April 28, 1898): 21. See also Mortgage from Speirs Manufacturing Company, a Massachusetts corporation, to Julian F. Bigelow, Samuel Winslow and George Stevens, recorded March 31, 1892, in Vol. 1378, page 3; Deed in Trust from Speirs Manufacturing Co. to John F. Bicknell and Charles D. Clark, recorded in Vol. 1574, page 515; and Deed of Trust by John C. Speirs to Daniel S. Pratt and William H. Inman, recorded May 12, 1898, in Vol. 1577, page 364; all in Worcester County Registry of Deeds.

9. Trustees Deed from John F. Bicknell and Charles D. Clark to Speirs Manufacturing Company, recorded February 11, 1899, in Vol. 1600, page 545; Deed of Assignment from Speirs Manufacturing Company to Horace H. Bigelow, recorded February 11, 1899 in Vol. 1600, page 546; Quitclaim Deed from Horace H. Bigelow to Speirs Manufacturing Company, recorded February 10, 1899 in Vol. 1602, page 376; and Warranty Deed from John C. Speirs and Nellie E. Speirs to Locomobile Company of America, recorded August 18, 1899, in Vol. 1619, page 484; all in Worcester County Registry of Deeds. See also "Speirs Furnishes Complete Line," *WCTR* 24 (January 18, 1900): 58.

By 1910, the frame foundry and machine shop built by John Speirs in 1891 had been replaced by a brick shop that continues to stand today. However, Worcester's *Record of Building Permits-Repairs and Additions* and *Record of Building Permits—New Buildings* between 1891 and 1899 show only permits for wood buildings issued to Speirs individually, and thus the existing brick shop likely was built after 1899. See Sanborn Map Company, *Insurance Maps of Worcester, Massachusetts* (1910), Vol. 2, Plate 145.

10. John C. Speirs and Charles Fletcher built an electric runabout in 1895. "The propulsion was an electric motor, and power was generated by 40 special accumulator cells. The car was designed to carry

two people ... and it was run at a maximum speed of 20 miles an hour." "The Automobile in Worcester," *Worcester Magazine* 11 (1908): 91–99. See also Design Patent 32,749 titled "Engine Frame," dated May 29, 1900; Patent 671,782 titled "Tube Sheet for Boilers," dated April 9, 1901; Patent 671,783 titled "Steam Engine," dated April 9, 1901; Patent 685,230, titled "Hydrocarbon Burner," dated October 22, 1901; all issued to John C. Speirs and all assigned to the Locomobile Company of America.

11. Various deeds from the Speirs Manufacturing Company, grantor, to Horace H. Bigelow, grantee, recorded April 29, 1901, in Vol. 1682, page 336; recorded May 11, 1901, in Vol. 1684, page 257; and recorded November 13, 1901 in Vol. 1701, page 39; and Deed from Horace H. Bigelow, grantor, to the Cartwright Borden Company, recorded November 13, 1901 in Vol. 1701, page 593; all in Worcester County Registry of Deeds. See also Patent 687,346 titled "Bolt," dated November 26, 1901, issued to John C. Speirs; and Patent 768,200 titled "Universal Joint," dated August 23, 1904; issued to John C. Speirs and Harry E. Dey and assigned to the Autocar Company. See also "Prospectus. National Chain Motor Service Corporation," issued by Bailey and Company, Boston, in *Boston Post* (July 21, 1920): 20; and "John C. Speirs," *Hartford Daily Courant* (June 5, 1932): A5.

12. "Two New Factories in Worcester," *WCTR* 15 (July 5, 1895): 24. See also Patent 546,954 titled "Velocipede," dated September 24, 1895, issued to William L. Decker and assigned to the Decker Cycle Company.

13. Patent 571,753 titled "Crank and Pedal," dated November 24, 1896; Patent 587,710 titled "Chain Adjustment for Bicycles," dated August 10, 1897; and Patent 587,711 titled "Saddle Support for Bicycles," dated August 10, 1897; all issued to William L. Decker. See also *The American Stationer* 40 (August 20, 1896): 293.

14. Sanborn Map Company, *Insurance Maps of Worcester Massachusetts* (1892): Plate 18.

15. In *Keene Evening Sentinel*, see "Tonight's Dedication" (November 11, 1897), 6; and "An Auspicious Dedication" (November 12, 1897): 6. The story of the Windle and Trinity bicycle companies was published previously; see Robert McCullough, "Wheels of Fortune: The Bicycle Boom, Trinity Cycle, and its Keene Factory," in *Historical New Hampshire* 67 (Fall–Winter 2013): 52–81.

16. In *Worcester Daily Telegram*, see "Willie Windle's New Wheel" (July 23, 1895): 6; and "Willie Windle's Wheel" (August 8, 1895): 8. See also "From High Bicycle Champion to Bank President," *Worcester Sunday Telegram*, September 7, 1930, Section 5, front page. For Berlo, see Daniel J. Dwyer, ed., *Prominent Wheelmen and Bicycle Club Directory of Massachusetts, 1894* (Boston: Garfield Publishing Co., 1894): 55. Windle's bicycle offered an exceptionally strong but light frame with the insignia W.W.W. in gold letters on the head. For Windle's cycling accomplishments, see "Back in the Arena," *WCTR* 16 (October 11, 1895): 40.

17. In *Middletown Penny Press*, see "Keating Here" (June 9, 1896): 8; "Contract Awarded" (June 11, 1896): 2; and "The Middletown Board of Trade" (December 12, 1896): 12. Keating was among the guests invited to Windle's wedding ceremony in June 1892. See "County News—Millbury," *Worcester Evening Gazette* (June 3, 1892): 7; and "On A Tandem," *Worcester Daily Telegram* (June 3, 1892): 4.

18. "Willie Windle's Wheel," *Worcester Daily Telegram* (August 8, 1895): 8. The Garver Manufacturing Co. in New York supplied machinery; see "Windle's Factory," *WCTR* 16 (August 23, 1895): 49. Journalists reported that the building held 15,000 square feet (100 feet by 50 feet), but that estimate conflicts with depictions of the mill on the 1898 *Atlas of Worcester* and the Sanborn Map Company's *Insurance Map of Worcester*, Vol. 1 (1910): Plate 76. See also "The Windle Cycle," *Keene Evening Sentinel* (November 19, 1896): 6 for conflicting descriptions.

19. In *Worcester Daily Telegram*, see "Willie Windle is Cut Adrift" (February 1, 1896): 8; and "Again in Hands of the Trustees" (April 4, 1896): 4. For Batchelder and Lane, see Keene History Committee, *Upper Ashuelot: A History of Keene, New Hampshire* (Keene, NH: Keene History Committee, 1968): 242, 266–68, 272, and 477. The Worcester newspaper referred to the buyers from Keene as A.P. Batchelder and A.T. Lane. The Keene newspaper correctly identified them as A.T. Batchelder and E.F. Lane.

20. In *Worcester Daily Telegram*, see "Again in Hands of the Trustees" (April 4, 1896): 2; "New Owners are Enjoined" (April 7, 1896): 1; and "Is Adjudged To Be Insolvent" (April 15, 1896): 1. In *AC* 8, see "Windle Cycle Co. Failure" (March 6, 1896): 894; and "The Lapham Failure" (May 1, 1896): 1291.

21. Regarding Fowler, see "$200,000," *WCTR* 16 (January 10, 1896): 112; "Frank T. Fowler and L.E. Crandell...," *WCTR* 16 (August 23, 1895): 50; "The Fowler Cycle Manufacturing Co...," *WCTR* 16 (September 27, 1895): 42; "Pullman Road Race," *WCTR* 9 (May 20, 1892): 18; "Chicago Races," *WCTR* 10 (August 26, 1892), 28; and "Big Plans," *WCTR* 11 (March 10, 1893), 33.

22. "Fowler Brings Suit," *WCTR* 18 (October 16, 1896): 25; "Munger Company Quit," *WCTR* 17 (July 3, 1896): 37; "Fowler Plants Himself," *WCTR* 18 (October 18, 1896): 29; "Deal is Off," *WCTR* 18 (November 13, 1896): 25; "Windy City Man Buys," *WCTR* 18 (November 19, 1896): 1; and "Where Windle Was," *WCTR* 18 (November 27, 1896): 29. In the *Worcester Daily Telegram*, see also "Will Make the Windle Bicycle" (May 21, 1896): 7; "Still Undecided" (September 22, 1896): 8; "Good Men Come in Big Droves" (November 20, 1896): 1; and "Building an Addition" (November 26, 1896): 5.

23. Shareholders included Francis Faulkner and Harry Colony. In *Keene Evening Sentinel*, see "The Windle Cycle" (November 19, 1896): 6; "Stock Subscriptions Needed" (December 3, 1896): 6; "Appeal for Funds" (December 5, 1896): 8; "Still $3,000 Short" (December 7, 1896): 8; "Prospects for Bicycle Factory Favorable" (December 8, 1896): 6; "Enough Money Promised" (December 9, 1896): 6; "The Bicycle Enterprise" (December 10, 1896): 6; "Mr. Fowler in Keene" (December 11, 1896): 6; "Exemption

Granted" (December 12, 1896): 3; "Cycle Company Organizes" (December 17, 1896): 3; and "The City Councils Vote to Exempt the Trinity Bicycle Factory" (June 21, 1897): 6. See also corporate charter, Frank T. Fowler Manufacturing Company, December 11, 1896, recorded December 12, 1896, New Hampshire Secretary of State.

24. In *Keene Evening Sentinel*, see "Mr. Fowler in Keene" (December 11, 1896): 6, and "Cycle Company Organizes" (December 17, 1896): 3.

25. In *Keene Evening Sentinel*, see "City News" (January 23, 1897): 3; "Treasurer of Trinity Cycle Co." (January 25, 1897): 3; "The Bicycle Factory" (February 25, 1897): 6; "President Frank T. Fowler...," (February 27, 1897): 8; "President Frank T. Fowler" (April 26, 1897): 6; "A Large Manufactory" (June 18, 1897): 6; and "Deal Consummated" (June 19, 1897): 8. See also "Fowler Finishes," *WCTR* 20 (September 17, 1897): 13. For the newsletter see *Trinity Chimes* 19 (February 19, 1897): 79; and "Wady With Fowler," *Trinity Chimes* 20 (February 4, 1898): 58 (Clifton Wady prepared the newsletter illustrations).

26. In *Keene Evening Sentinel*, see "Deal Consummated" (June 19, 1897): 8; "Architect Nourse of Worcester...," (June 22, 1897): 6; "Making Good Progress" (July 21, 1897): 3. In *Keene Evening Sentinel* under the heading "City News," see (June 22, 1897): 6; (August 5, 1897): 6; (August 16, 1897): 3; (August 17, 1897): 6; (August 23, 1897): 6; and (August 27, 1897): 3.

27. Bradley, *The Works*, 30–35. See also George H. Hutchinson, "Mill Building Construction with Details from Practice," *Engineering Record* 26, pt. 1 (October 22, 1892): 330–332; pt. 2 (October 29, 1892): 347–48; the journal incorrectly stated the author's name as George Hunt Robinson. In *Keene Sentinel*, see "City News" (August 27, 1897): 3; "A Well-Constructed Building" (September 10, 1897): 6; and "New Buildings in 1897" (December 31, 1897): 6. The 1924 Sanborn Map Company's *Insurance Map of Keene* shows that iron columns and steel beams had been installed by that date, probably to strengthen the floor system for heavier or faster machinery.

28. In *Keene Evening Sentinel*, see "Electric Light and Power" (June 23, 1897): 3; "Ten days more...," (September 20, 1897): 6; "City News" (October 2, 1897), 3; "A Defective Foundation" (October 11, 1897): 6; "City News" (October 15, 1897), 6; "City News" (October 16, 1897): 3; "City News" (October 20, 1897): 3; "City News" (October 27, 1897): 6; "City News" (November 2, 1897): 6; "City News" (November 17, 1897): 6; "City News" (November 23, 1897): 6; and "City News" (November 30, 1897): 6. Walter Nourse worked in partnership with Albert Barker, as Barker and Nourse. See *Worcester City Directory* (1892), 458, 460.

29. In *Keene Evening Sentinel*, under the title "City News," see (November 17, 1897): 6; (December 9, 1897): 3; (December 14, 1897): 3; (December 15, 1897): 6; (December 22, 1897): 3; and (January 5, 1898): 3. See also "At the Trinity Factory," *Keene Evening Sentinel* (January 26, 1898): 6. For the sprinkling system, see Sanborn Map Company, *Insurance Maps of Keene* (1902): Plate 13.

30. "Trinity Cycle Company," *Keene Evening Sentinel* (September 29, 1897): 6. Notes from the shareholders' meeting reveal that the company sold at least one thousand Windle bicycles, along with numerous Trinity wheels manufactured at the Worcester plant.

31. "Moffat Cycle Co.," *WCTR* 7 (July 31, 1891): 738; "Moffat Cycles for 1892," *WCTR* 8 (November 27, 1891): 423; "The Lincoln Cycling Club...," *WCTR* 8 (February 12, 1892): 884: "Moffat Cycle Co. Succumbs," *WCTR* 9 (August 18, 1892): 25; and "George Moffat Sues the Hill Cycle Co.," *WCTR* 12 (December 8, 1893): 20.

32. For Fowler and Hill, see "The Fowler Safety," *WCTR* 10 (November 4, 1882): 25; "Two New Factories," *WCTR* 11 (March 10, 1893): 32; "The Hill Cycle Manufacturing Company...," *WCTR* 11 (April 14, 1893), 30; "A Successful Chicagoian [*sic*]," *WCTR* 12 (September 29, 1893): Supplement page iii; "Fowler Leaves the Hill Co.," *WCTR* 13 (April 6, 1894): 46; "Mark Hill Dead," *WCTR* 13 (April 20, 1894): 22; "Good Things in Fowler Bicycles," *WCTR* 14 (December 14, 1894): 42 (an advertisement for the Hill Cycle Mfg. Co.); and "George Moffat Sues the Hill Cycle Co.," *WCTR* 12 (December 8, 1893): 20. For Fowler's sale of his interest, see "$200,000," *WCTR* 16 (January 10, 1896): 112. This article reported that Fowler's company had earned $300,000 the preceding year, driving share value up from $100 to $800, but whether those figures are accurate is unclear. The buyers also agreed to purchase the shares held by Fowler's mother-in-law, and for the litigation that resulted from that part of the sale, see "Fowler Brings Suit," *WCTR* 13 (October 16, 1896): 25.

33. For transactions involving the Fowler Company in Chicago, see "Fowler Company Fails," *WCTR* 20 (October 29, 1897): 17; "Cited to Appear," *WCTR* 20 (November 5, 1897): 15; "Fowler Debits and Credits," *WCTR* 20 (November 19, 1897): 21; and "Fowler's Full Hand," *WCTR* 20 (January 7, 1898), 24. Reinforcing the unlikelihood of burdensome debts, Chicago papers reported in September 1897, that upon Fowler's return to that city he began purchasing trotting horses and formed the Westside Trotting Association. See "Fowler Favors Trotting," *WCTR* 20 (September 24, 1897): 16.

34. "The City Councils Vote to Exempt the Trinity Bicycle Factory," *Keene Evening Sentinel* (June 21, 1897): 6. The lease from Jones to the Trinity company was never recorded in the Cheshire County Registry of Deeds, and Jones and Fowler declined a request by the council to examine the lease.

35. "The City Councils Vote to Exempt the Trinity Bicycle Factory," *Keene Evening Sentinel* (June 21, 1897): 6.

36. Christie Russell, "Reynold Janney: Educator and Inventor," *Clinton* [Ohio] *Chronicle* 13 (April 2002): 29–32. For Janney's inventions related to bicycle parts, see Design Patent 26,412 titled "Design for a Foot-Piece for Pedals," dated December 15, 1896; Patent 625,449 titled "Dust-Proof

Bearing," dated May 23, 1899; and Patent 628,941 titled "Adjusting Washer," dated July 18, 1899, which permitted the tightening of bearings by hand and without special tools; all issued to Reynold Janney.

37. "The Cycle Trade Outlook for 1898: New Models Illustrated and Described," *Outing* 31 (February 1898): 513–20. For Boston rims, see Alexander James Wallis-Taylor, *Modern Cycles: A Practical Handbook on Their Construction and Repair* (London: Crosby Lockwood and Son, 1897), 111–12.

38. *Catalog, Trinity Cycle Manufacturing Co., Worcester, Massachusetts, Builders of the Trinity, A Genuine Bicycle.* (New York: Trow-Wheatley, 1897): 3.

39. *Catalog, Trinity Cycle Manufacturing Co.* (1897): 3–5, 10, 21, 23.

40. *Catalog, Trinity Cycle Manufacturing Co.* (1897): 11–12, and "It Leads Them All," *WCTR* 15 (February 22, 1895): 27.

41. Bruce Epperson, "Failed Colossus," *Proceedings of the 9th International Cycling History Conference, Ottawa, Canada. August 19–21, 1998* (San Francisco: Van der Plas Publications, 1998): 93–108, and *Pedaling Bicycles*, 106–12. The Corson Cycle Manufacturing Company was incorporated on January 1, 1896; see New Hampshire Secretary of State, Corporation Division, File B50500. A firm of machinists, Newhall and Stebbins, working near Keene in Hinsdale, also may have built bicycles or bicycle parts. See the Sanborn-Perris Map Company, *Hinsdale, Cheshire County, N.H.* (1892): Plate 1.

42. In *Keene Evening Sentinel* under the heading "City News," see (December 14, 1897): 3; (December 22, 1897): 3; (January 18, 1898): 6; "At the Trinity Factory" (January 26, 1898): 6; (February 8, 1898): 3; (February 24, 1898): 3; (March 9, 1898): 3; (April 2, 1898): 3; (April 16, 1898): 8; and (December 19, 1898): 6. In *Keene Evening Sentinel* see also "A New Bicycle Brake" (January 18, 1898): 6; and "The 1898 Trinity Ready" (February 2, 1898): 6. The origin of the bicycle orders is not known. Between the 1897 and 1898 seasons the Keating firm in Middletown, Connecticut, lost all its sales agents in northern New England: two in Maine, seventeen in New Hampshire, and twelve in Vermont. This reduced the number of bicycles Keating sold in those three states from 527 in 1897 to 21 in 1898. Although a great many factors contributed to these developments, competition from the Trinity company may have accounted for at least some of the losses. See letter, with accompanying table, from Arthur Patrick to Arthur Garford, September 5, 1898, box 1, folder 10, Garford Papers, MSS6, Ohio Historical Society.

43. "City News," *Keene Evening Sentinel* (April 5, 1898): 6; "Trinity Chimes," *WCTR* 19 (February 19, 1897): 79; and "Trinity Trade in Chicago," *WCTR* 22 (October 6, 1898): 18.

44. *Catalog, Trinity Cycle Manufacturing Co.* (1899), and "The 1899 Cycle Models Illustrated and Described," *Outing* 34 (April 1899): 96–101. In *Keene Evening Sentinel* under the title "City News," see (August 19, 1899): 8; (September 29, 1899): 3; (October 30, 1899): 6; and (December 13, 1899): 3. For the decline in bicycle manufacturing, see "Some Bicycle History," *WCTR* 24 (October 19, 1899): 17. For information about the Little-Janney wheel hub, see Patent 665,569 titled "Interchangeable Hub," dated January 8, 1901, issued to Edward W. Little and Reynold Janney. See also "The Combine—A Comparison of Outputs," *CATR* 23 (June 8, 1899): 138.

45. In *Keene Evening Sentinel*, see "City News" (December 13, 1899): 3; "New Automobile" (July 4, 1900): 1; "The Transit" (February 10, 1902): 3; and "Business Absorbed" (June 19, 1902): 6. At the Cheshire County Historical Society a file folder titled "Transportation, Automobiles," box 17, folder 52A, contains a typewritten account of the manufacturing of automobiles at the Keene plant, as well as photocopies of related articles. Citing the *Keene Sentinel* of February 13, 1901, the anonymous author of that account indicates that the Steamobile Company of America acquired the Keene business in February 1901. In March, Janney successfully applied for a patent concerning a vehicle brake for automobiles and assigned it to the Steamobile Company. See Patent 684,259 titled "Vehicle Brake," dated October 8, 1901, issued to Reynold Janney and assigned to the Steamobile Company of America.

46. Russell, "Reynold Janney," 29–32.

47. "The Fowler Cycle Works," *Outing* 35 (March 1900): 645. See also "Frank Fowler's New Policy," *WCTR* 22 (October 6, 1898): 14; "Boomer from Boomersburg," *WCTR* 22 (October 13, 1898): 30; "Frank T. Fowler, President," *WCTR* 22 (January 19, 1899): 60; "Frank T. Fowler, Alderman," *WCTR* 23 (April 20, 1899): 18; and "Fowler is a Sailor Now," *WCTR* 24 (November 9, 1899): 30.

48. "Millbury Wants Wheel Factory," *Worcester Daily Telegram*, June 23, 1897, 7; "From High Bicycle Champion to Bank President," *Worcester Sunday Telegram*, September 7, 1930, section 5, p. 1; and "Speirs Stops," *WCTR* 21 (April 28, 1898): 22.

Chapter 13

1. Patent 305,226 titled "Building Construction," dated September 16, 1884, issued to Ernest L. Ransome. See also "A Large Monolithic Factory Building," *Engineering Record* 38 (1898): 188–189. "Reinforced Concrete Construction in a Factory Extension at Bayonne, N.J.," *Engineering Record* 50 (July 2, 1904): 16–10; George P. Carver, "Reinforced Concrete Building Work for the United Shoe Machinery Co., Beverly, Mass," *Engineering News* 53 (May 25, 1905): 537–546; and Reyner Banham, "Ransome at Bayonne," *Journal of the Society of Architectural Historians* 42 (December 1983): 383–387.

2. Patent 623,686 titled "Machine for Molding Hollow Concrete Building-Blocks," dated April 25, 1899; Patent 674,874 titled "Concrete Wall for Buildings," dated May 28, 1901; Patent 727,428 titled "Machine for Molding Hollow Concrete Building-Blocks," dated May 5, 1903; all issued to Harmon S. Palmer. See also Carl Condit, *American*

Building Art: The Twentieth Century (New York: Oxford University Press, 1961), 166–177.

3. "New Corporations," *Buffalo Courier* (February 2, 1904): n.p. In a series of newspaper articles published in 1970 under the column heading "Faces and Places," and sub-heading "The Emblem Bicycle Company Series," town historian Donald D. Cook recounted the company's history. Clippings of those articles, which do not include the publication's name and mostly are without dates, are available at the Evans Historical Society. The articles are most useful for providing the names of many company employees. See No. 2, "The Heil Barn-Bicycle Factory," and No. 10, "The Ball Park and Race Track." In my interview with Village Trustee William G. Houston, whose father worked for the bicycle company, Mr. Houston stressed the vital role that the company had played as the tiny community's largest employer (July 11, 2008); see for example "High School Commencement," *Angola Record* (June 22, 1927): 1.

4. Cook, "Emblem Series," No. 1: "The Idlewood Plants"; the spelling of Glass's name also appears as Glas.

5. Cook, "Emblem Series," No. 3: "Mr. Schack Meets Mr. Pierce." Cook states that Schack purchased the machinery, stock, good will, and marque of Pierce bicycles from George Pierce, who was in the process of selling his bicycle business. However, in *Buffalo's Bicycles. Reflections on Buffalo's Colossal and Overlooked Bicycle Heritage* (Orchard Park, NY: Pedaling History Bicycle Museum, 2001): 103, author Carl Burgwardt explains that Pierce continued to manufacture bicycles until bankruptcy forced sale of the business to the Emblem firm in 1915. Reconciling those two opposing accounts may not be possible. Burgwardt's research is thorough but Cook interviewed both Schact and Heil and his account thus carries weight. See also "W.G. Schack," *Buffalo Sunday Times* (April 30, 1922): 72; and "New Corporations," *Buffalo Courier* (February 2, 1904):

6. In the *Angola Record*, under column heading "Talk of the Town," see (January 4, 1906): 1; and (August 30, 1906). See also Burgwardt, *Buffalo's Bicycles*, 100–104; and Cook, "Emblem Series," No. 4: "The First Emblem Plant in Angola."

7. Warranty Deed from Julius M. Schwert and Louisa E. Schwert to Emblem Manufacturing Company, recorded October 6, 1906, in Vol. 1045, page 410; Erie County Registry of Deeds; the parcel is 1 and 4/125 acres. In 1912, the company acquired a parcel of adjoining land to erect workers houses; see Quitclaim Deed from James H. McIntyre and Delia M. McIntyre to Emblem Manufacturing Company, recorded October 6, 1906, in Vol. 1192, page 525, Erie County Registry of Deeds. In the *Angola Record*, under column heading "Talk of the Town," all on page 1, see (February 1, 1906); (March 29, 1906); (April 12, 1906); (May 17, 1906); (June 7, 1906); (July 26, 1906); and (September 20, 1906). See also Cook, "Emblem Series," No. 6: "Emblem Task Force About 1915." Cook cites 1908 as the year that the company moved into the building, but the news accounts in the *Angola Record* are likely reliable. See also the advertisement "Penn-Allen Portland Cement," *Angola Record* (January 2, 1908): 4.

8. In the *Angola Record*, see "Talk of the Town (July 18, 1912): 1; "Ten Years Ago This Week" (April 29, 1920): 3; "Ten Years Ago This Week" (September 16, 1920): 5; and "Fifteen Years Ago—1910" (September 17, 1925): 7.

9. Patent 375,377 titled "Machine for Molding Building-Blocks," dated December 27, 1887, issued to Harmon S. Palmer. See also Note 4 above.

10. S.B. Newberry, "Hollow Concrete Block Building Construction in the United States," *Concrete and Constructional Engineering* 1 (1906): 118–125. See also Pamela H. Simpson, "Cheap, Quick and Easy: The Early History of Rockfaced Concrete Block Building," *Perspectives in Vernacular Architecture* 3 (1989): 108–118.

11. Newberry, "Hollow Concrete Block Building Construction."

12. The Warwick factory was demolished very recently, but window sash may have been 54 inches by 106 inches.

13. Cook, "The Emblem Bicycle Company Series," No. 5: "The New Emblem Bicycle Plant"; and No. 8: "The Emblem Office and Staff." See also Simpson, "Cheap, Quick and Easy"; and "A Long Span Concrete Girder Pierce Arrow Motor Car Co.," *Engineering Record* 62 (November 5, 1910): 529. See also Grant Hildebrand, *Designing for Industry: The Architecture of Albert Kahn* (Cambridge: MIT Press, 1974), 34–43; the Trussed Concrete Steel Company also participated in the design process for the Pierce complex.

14. "Motorcycles," *Buffalo Courier* (April 14, 1907): 32. See also Cook, "Emblem Series," No. 6: "Emblem Task Force About 1915"; and No. 9: "Meet the President" (September 17, 1970). See also "Creditors Get After Pierce Cycle Company" (August 10, 1910): 1; "In Bankruptcy No. 3743. District Court of the United States. In the Matter of Pierce Cycle Company, Bankrupt," *Buffalo Commercial* (September 20, 1912): 5; and "Emblem Mfg. Co., Angola, N.Y.," *Bicycle News* 2 (November 1916): 10.

15. Letter to Hon. D.S. Alexander, dated December 22, 1908. *Tariff Hearings Before the Committee on Ways and Means of the House of Representatives*, 60th Congress, 2nd Session (1908–1909), Vol. 3, House of Representatives Document No. 1505 (Washington, D.C.: GPO, 1909): 2724–272. See also "Bicycle Orders Strain Angola Plant to Limit," *Buffalo Times* (1936): 6-D, undated photocopy available at the Town of Evans Historical Society.

16. Cook, "Emblem Series," No. 8: "The Emblem Office and Staff." See also "Bicycle Orders Strain Angola Plant to Limit," *Buffalo Times* (1936): 6-D; "Five Years Ago This Week (May 25, 1922): 2; and "Emblem-Pierce Team Swamps Farnham," *Angola Record* (October 21, 1920): 1.

17. "Motorcycles," *Buffalo Courier* (April 14, 1907): 32; Cook, "Emblem Series," No. 6: "Emblem Task Force About 1915"; and No. 9: "Meet the President" (September 17, 1970). See also Burgwardt,

Buffalo's Bicycles, 101–104; "Bicycle Orders Strain Angola Plant to Limit," *Buffalo Times* (1936): 6-D; and "W.G. Schack," *Buffalo Sunday Times* (April 30, 1922): 72. In *Angola Record*, see "Local and Personal" (November 5, 1931): 1; "Emblem Resumes Work" (February 23, 1933): 1; "Return of Bicycle Increases Production at Emblem Plant" (June 15, 1933): 1; "Local and Personal" (September 18, 1930): 1; "Local and Personal" (September 10, 1931): 1; "Talk of the Town" (August 8, 1912): 1.

Chapter 14

1. Patent 94,187 titled "Sewing Machine," dated August 31, 1869, issued to Job Davis. In the *Dayton Daily Journal*, see "The Watertown Works" (January 8, 1889): 3; "Watertown Visitors" (February 8, 1889): 4; "The Davis Sewing Machine Surely Coming" (February 12, 1889): 4; "The Davis Sewing Machine Works" (May 7, 1889): 4; "The Corner Stone" (July 11, 1889): 4; and Howard Burba, "When 'The Davis' Came to Dayton" (October 9, 1932): 41. See also "The plans…," *Watertown Daily Times* (February 27, 1889): 4. See also Warranty Deed by George P. Huffman et al. to the National Improvement Company, recorded October 2, 1889, in Volume 165, page 581; and Warranty Deed by the National Improvement Company to the Davis Sewing Machine Company, reciting $150,000 consideration and recorded December 21, 1889, in Volume 167, page 38; both in Montgomery County Registry of Deeds. See also W. Anthony Huffman, "The Huffy History," typewritten manuscript available at the Dayton Metro Library, Local History Reference (1996), and telephone interview with Tony Huffman on October 15, 2009.

2. In the *Dayton Daily Journal*, see "The New Industry" (March 15, 1889): 4; Howard Burba, "When 'The Davis' Came to Dayton" (October 9, 1932): 41. See also "We today furnish…," *Watertown Herald* (January 11, 1890): 4; and Sanborn-Perris Map Company, *Insurance Maps of Dayton, Ohio* (1897–1898): Vol. 2, Plate 77. Among four articles describing building dimensions, no two are the same.

3. "The New Industry," *Dayton Daily Journal* (March 15, 1889): 4; Sanborn Map Company, *Insurance Maps of Dayton, Ohio* (1918): Vol. 3, Plate 343.

4. "The Davis Sewing Machine," *Dayton Daily Journal* (September 21, 1889): 4; "The Dayton" *WCTR* 15 (August 9, 1895): 32; "Ohio Articles of Incorporation, Davis Sewing Machine Company," recorded August 5, 1895, in Vol. 67, page 427; and "Certificate of Subscription, Davis Sewing Machine Company," recorded August 20, 1895, in Vol. 62, page 486; both in the Ohio Secretary of State and found in File 11721. See also Deed from the Davis Sewing Machine Company, a New York Corporation, to the Davis Sewing Machine Company, an Ohio Corporation, recorded October 31, 1895 in Vol. 205, page 399, Montgomery County Registry of Deeds; and Sanborn-Perris Map Company, *Maps of Dayton, Ohio* (1897–1898): Vol. 2, Plate 77. See also "Dayton Bicycle. America's Finest Wheel," *Classic Bike* 3 (1997): 1–7; and Huffman, "Huffy History."

5. Telephone interview with Tony Huffman on October 15, 2009. For platted subdivisions by the National Improvement Company, see Plats A through F, in Plat Book B, pages 309, 323, 322, 351, 332, and 329, respectively; Plat of National Improvement Company, Plat Book B, page 327; and Plat of National Improvement Company, Plat Book C, page 4; all dated either 1889 or 1890. See also Plat of W.P. Huffman, et al., Plat Book B, page 176, dated 1886; and Plat of Huffman Heights, Plat Book I, page 18, dated 1906. Plat books are available at the Montgomery County Archives in Dayton. See also *Atlas of the City of Dayton, Ohio, City of Oakwood and Adjoining Territory, 1940* (Philadelphia: E.E. Brownell Engineering Company, and Dayton: Cellarius Map and Atlas Company, 1931 and 1940).

6. "The Combine-A Comparison of Outputs," *CATR* 23 (June 8, 1899): 138; "Dayton Bicycle," *Classic Bike* 3, Issue No. 1 (1997): 1–7; Warranty Deed from Gustav W. Sauder, Trustee, to Davis Sewing Machine Company recorded October 25, 1900, in Vol. 233, page 435, Montgomery County Registry of Deeds; and "Resolution" by the Davis Sewing Machine Company, dated July 6, 1903, recorded July 7, 1903, in Vol. A30, page 1137, Ohio Secretary of State, File No. 11721. See also Huffman, "Huffy History."

7. Sanborn Map Company, *Insurance Maps of Dayton Ohio*, Vol. 3 (1918): Plates 343 and 344.

8. "Dayton Bicycle," *Classic Bike* 3, Issue No. 1 (1997): 1–7.

9. Sanborn Map Company, *Insurance Maps of Dayton Ohio*, Vol. 3 (1918): Plates 343 and 344.

10. "New Yorkers Buy the Davis Plant," *Motorcycle Illustrated and the Bicycling World* 10 (November 11, 1915): 15; "Yale and Snell Lines of Bicycles Go to Dayton," *Bicycle News* 2 (April 1916): 11. See also Patent 1,378,041 titled "Process for Manufacturing Bicycle Forks," dated May 17, 1921; Patent 1,388,961 titled "Bicycle Construction," dated August 30, 1921; and Patent 1,403,611, titled "Process for Manufacturing Bicycle Frames," dated January 17, 1922; all issued to Elmer M. Lewis and all assigned to the Davis Sewing Machine Company. See also Receiver's Deed from Earl H. Turner, Special Master Commissioner, to the Davis Sewing Machine Company, recorded February 27, 1924, in Volume 513. See also Huffman, "Huffy History."

11. Quitclaim Deed from Horace M. Huffman to Huffman Manufacturing Company, dated February 23, 1928, recorded April 28, 1928 in Vol. 628, page 25, Montgomery County Registry of Deeds; and Huffman, "Huffy History."

12. Sanborn Map Company, *Insurance Maps of Dayton Ohio*, Vol. 3 (1918) and (1950): Plates 343 and 344.

13. "Huffman Bicycles. Leaders of Luxury and Style," *Classic Bike* 3, Issue 2 (1997): 1–14.

14. Huffman, "Huffy History."

15. Huffman Bicycles," *Classic Bike* 3, Issue 2 (1997): 1–14; and Huffman, "Huffy History."

16. *Ibid.*

17. Huffman Bicycles," *Classic Bike* 3, Issue 2 (1997): 1–14; "The Huffy Corporation," in Bruce W. Ronald and Virginia Ronald, *Dayton, The Gem City* (Tulsa: Continental Heritage Press, 1981): 192; and Huffman, "Huffy History."

18. *Ibid.*

Chapter 15

1. Chester Liebs, *Secrets of Japanese Cities the World Admires* (Tokyo: Yousensha, 2011). Liebs observes that while bicycle parking at congested transit stations presents problems, many quiet neighborhoods in cities such as Tokyo prohibit bicycle parking for no good reason other than impressions by urban planners that parked bicycles are disorderly, rather than eco-friendly.

2. "Wanted to Contract," *Dayton Herald* (February 27, 1888): 4, a request for 600,000 bricks; "A Moral Agent," *Dayton Daily News* (May 6, 1899): 10; Judith Sealander, *Grand Plans: Business Progressivism and Social Change in Ohio's Miami Valley, 1890–1929* (Lexington: University of Kentucky Press, 1988), 18–28.

3. "A Moral Agent," *Dayton Daily News* (May 6, 1899): 10.

4. Sanborn-Perris Map Company, *Insurance Maps of Dayton, Ohio* (1897): Vol. 1, Plates 29 and 30. The Stewart Street and Rubicon Street bicycles houses are shown on the 1897 Sanborn map, as is the wheelman's clubhouse.

5. In *Dayton Evening Herald*, see "The National Cash Register Company...", (July 13, 1893): 16; "Notice" (January 20, 1899): 2; and "The Growth and Development of the National Cash Register Industry" (February 1, 1902): 10. See also "An Honor to Dayton," *Dayton Daily News* (June 20, 1899): 27; and "F.M. Andrews Dies. A Noted Architect," *New York Times* (September 3, 1948): 19.

6. John C. Olmsted, "Report on Dayton Land Scheme" (October 25, 1895), Library of Congress, Olmsted Associates Records, Series E, Box E-5, Volume 3, Folder 4, Page 149. See also "Plan of NCR Co.'s Works" (January 9, 1896), Plan No. 280–1; and "Planting List, J.H. Patterson, Dayton Ohio" (March 3, 1896), File 00280–01–03, both in Records of the National Park Service, Frederick Law Olmsted National Historic Site. In *Dayton Herald*, see also "Fair Grounds" (October 15, 1898): 1; and "Professor John C. Olmsted...," (July 1, 1899): 3.

7. "Sketch of Proposed Vine Clad Pergola Connecting Dormitory and Dining Hall" (September 15, 1904), Plan No. 280–112, Records of the National Park Service, Frederick Law Olmsted National Historic Site. See also Sealander, *Grand Plans*, 42.

8. "A Moral Agent," *Dayton Daily News* (May 6, 1899): 10.

9. Sanborn-Perris Map Company, *Insurance Maps of Dayton, Ohio* (1897), Vol. 1, Plate 29. Patent 620,863 titled "Bicycle Rack," dated March 7, 1899, issued to H.L. Wilcox; and Patent 646,053 titled "Bicycle Rack," dated March 27, 1900, issued to W.H. Humphrey. See also Bicycle Manufacturers Association, Joseph Goodman, ed., *The Bicycle: Admittedly the Lowest Cost Means of Transportation Between Two Given Points* (Hartford, CT: Bicycle Manufacturers Association, 1919); and glass plate negative 34/97 showing removal of bicycle sheds in 1899 for construction of Building No. 3, Dayton History Archive Center.

10. Sanborn Map and Publishing Company, *Insurance Maps of Dayton, Ohio* (1887): Plate 11.

11. "Plan No. 19, Design A" (Fall 1900); "Specimen Detail Planting Plan of House Lots" (August 14, 1900): National Cash Register Company; and "Design for Proposed House Located on South Side of Lot"; all in Records of the National Park Service, Frederick Law Olmsted National Historic Site.

12. Alexandra Celia Kelly, *Consuming Ivory: Mercantile Legacies of East Africa and New England* (Seattle: University of Washington Press, 2021).

13. Sanborn Map Company, *Map of Essex, Middlesex County, Connecticut* (February 1914): Plate 7.

14. Michael J. Wells, *From Bicycles to Buicks. The Story of Behrens and Bushnell* (Essex, Connecticut: Essex Historical Society, 1997): 17–21; Sanborn Map Company, *Map of Essex, CT Count 6, Connecticut* (February 1914): Plate 7.

15. Patent 562,629 titled "Bicycle Support," dated June 23, 1896, issued to Walter J. Smart; Patent 565,0757 titled "Bicycle-Rack," dated August 4, 1896, issued to Henry Westphal; and Patent 573,171 titled "Bicycle Rack," dated December 15, 1896, issued to Henry Westphal.

16. Patent 585,739 titled "Bicycle-Support," dated July 6, 1897, issued to Howard D. Brundage; Patent 581,585 titled "Bicycle-Rack," dated April 27, 1897, issued to George Hirschman, Sr., and George Hirschman, Jr.; Patent 620,863 titled "Bicycle Rack," dated March 7, 1899, issued to Henry L. Wilcox; and Patent 615,264 titled "Bicycle Carrier," dated December 6, 1898, issued to Thomas Coleman DuPont.

17. "A Prize Plan for a Bicycle Storage House," *Engineering News* 39 (March 31, 1898): 215.

18. *Ibid.*

19. "An American System of Bicycle Storage," *Engineering News* 39 (May 5, 1898): 282.

20. Bicycle Manufacturers Association, *The Bicycle.*

21. *Ibid.*

22. Sanborn Map Company, *Atlas of the City of Hartford and the Town of West Hartford* (1917): Plate 7; and Bicycle Manufacturers Association, *The Bicycle.*

A Selected Bibliography

By far, the primary sources used to construct the company histories offered in this work included newspaper articles; published accounts in cycling's numerous periodicals and trade journals; articles from various other periodicals; archival records from local and county historical societies or libraries; corporate archives; patents; deed records from county registries of deeds or town clerks' offices; and Sanborn-Perris Insurance Company maps. The sources that follow represent works that either provide contextual background, offer biographical accounts of important individuals, were used extensively to fill gaps in historical records or to develop thematic threads throughout this work, or offer continued reading for those who wish to explore these topics in greater depth.

Arnold, Horace. "Modern Machine Shop Economics." *Engineering Magazine* 11, Part 2 (May 1896): 263–298.

Banham, Reyner. "Ransome at Bayonne." *Journal of the Society of Architectural Historians* 42 (December 1983): 383–387.

Biggs, Lindy. *The Rational Factory: Architecture, Technology, and Work in America's Age of Mass Production.* Baltimore: Johns Hopkins University Press, 1996.

Boore, J. Perc. *The Seamless Story.* Los Angeles: Commonwealth Press, 1951.

Boston Manufacturers Mutual Fire Insurance Co. *Report No. V, Slow Burning or Mill Construction.* Boston: published by the author, 1902, 1904, and 1908.

Bradley, Betsy Hunter. *The Works: The Industrial Architecture of the United States.* New York: Oxford University Press, 1999.

Burgwardt, Carl. *Buffalo's Bicycles: Reflections on Buffalo's Colossal and Overlooked Bicycle Heritage.* Orchard Park, NY: Pedaling History Bicycle Museum, 2001.

Condit, Carl W. *American Building Art: The Twentieth Century.* New York: Oxford University Press, 1961.

______. *The Chicago School of Architecture: A History of Commercial and Public Building in the Chicago Area, 1875 to 1925.* Chicago: University of Chicago Press, 1964.

Connecticut Board of World's Fair Managers, Publications Committee. *Connecticut at the World's Fair. Report of the Commissioners From Connecticut of the Columbian Exhibition of 1893 at Chicago. Also Report of the Work of the Board of Lady Managers.* Hartford, CT: Case, Lockwood and Brainard Company, 1898.

Coxe, Eckley B. "A Furnace With Automatic Stoker, Traveling Grate, and Variable Blast Intended Especially for Burning Small Anthracite Coal," in *Transactions of the American Institute of Mining Engineers* 22 (New York: AIME, 1894): 581–606.

Curran, Kathleen. "The German Rundbogenstil and Reflections on the American Round-Arched Style." *Journal of the Society of Architectural Historians* 47 (December 1988): 351–373.

Cutter, William Richard, ed. "Caspar Ranger," in *Memorial Encyclopedia of the State of Massachusetts*, Vol. 2 (New York: American Historical Society, Inc., 1917): 408–410.

______. *Historic Homes and Places and Genealogical and Personal Memoirs Relating to the Families of Middlesex County, Massachusetts*, Vol. 4. New York: Lewis Historical Publishing Company, 1908.

Dolnar, Hugh, né Horace Arnold. "Bicycle Tools-1," *American Machinist* 18 (October 3, 1895): 781; to "Cycle Tools-31," *American Machinist* 19 (September 24, 1896): 894.

Dwyer, Daniel J., ed. *Prominent Wheelmen and Bicycle Club Directory of Massachusetts, 1894.* Boston: Garfield Publishing Co., 1894.

Epperson, Bruce D. "Failed Colossus." *Proceedings of the 9th International Cycling History Conference, Ottawa, Canada. August 19–21, 1998* (San Francisco: Van der Plas Publications, 1998): 93–108.

______. *Peddling Bicycles to America. The Rise of an Industry.* Jefferson, NC: McFarland, 2010.

Fritz, John. "The Progress in the Manufacture of Iron and Steel in America, and the Relations of the Engineer To It," in *Transactions of the Society of Mechanical Engineers* 18 (New York: ASME, 1897): 39–69.

Gardner, George. *Farm Architecture: Houses and Barns.* Boston: Rand, Abery and Co., 1881.

______. *Town and Country School Buildings.* New York: E.I. Kellogg and Co., 1888.

Garn, Andrew. *Bethlehem Steel.* Princeton: Princeton Architectural Press, 1999.

Goodman, Joseph, ed. *The Bicycle: Admittedly the Lowest Cost Means of Transportation Between Two Given Points.* Hartford, CT: Bicycle Manufacturers Association, 1919.

Graves, George S., ed. *Progressive Springfield, Massachusetts.* Springfield: G.S. Graves, 1913.

Hadland, Tony, and Hans-Erhard Lessing. *Bicycle Design: An Illustrated History.* Cambridge: MIT Press, 2014.

Hildebrand, Grant. *Designing for Industry: The Architecture of Albert Kahn.* Cambridge: MIT Press, 1974.

Hounshell, David. *From the American System to Mass Production, 1800 to 1932.* Baltimore: Johns Hopkins University Press, 1984.

Hubbard, Guy, comp. "Geneaology of the Machine Industries of Windsor, Vermont" (1922). Large wall chart available at the American Precision Museum, Windsor, Vermont.

Huffman, W. Anthony. "The Huffy History," typewritten manuscript available at the Dayton Metro Library, Local History Reference, 1996.

Johannesen, Eric, and Allen L. Dickes. *Look Again. Landmark Architecture in Downtown Toledo and Old West End.* Pittsburgh: Ober Park Associates, 1973.

Jones, H.P. "Tempering and Annealing Steel," in *Transactions of the American Society of Mechanical Engineers* 24 (New York: ASME, 1903): 349.

Kanigel, Robert. *The One Best Way—Frederick Winslow Taylor and the Enigma of Efficiency.* New York: Viking Press, 1997.

Keating, Robert K. *Wheel Man: Robert M. Keating, Pioneer of Bicycles, Motorcycles and Automobiles.* Jefferson, NC: McFarland, 2014.

Keeler, John E. "Manufacturing Interests of Stamford," in Davis, William T., ed., *The New England States,* Vol. 2. Boston: D.H. Hurd & Co., 1879.

Kelly, Alexandra Celia. *Consuming Ivory: Mercantile Legacies of East Africa and New England.* Seattle: University of Washington Press, 2021.

Kidder, Frank, and Harry Parker. *Architects' and Builders' Handbook.* New York: John Wiley & Sons, 1882, and 18th ed., 1931.

Kron, Karl. *Ten Thousand Miles on a Bicycle.* New York: Karl Kron, 1887.

Liebs, Chester. *Secrets of Japanese Cities the World Admires.* Tokyo: Yousensha, 2011.

Marks, Edward C.R. *The Manufacture of Iron and Steel Tubes,* 2nd ed. Deansgate, Manchester: Technical Publishing Company, 1903.

Metz, Lance. *John Fritz: His Role in the Development of the American Iron and Steel Industry and His Legacy to the Bethlehem Community.* Easton, PA: Center for Canal History and Technology, 1987.

Moffett, Cleveland, "The Marvels of Bicycle Making," in *McClure's Magazine.* The series consists of four articles that are part of a special series under the general heading "Great American Business Enterprises," prepared as supplements under the magazine's editorial supervision but with expenses paid by the subject companies. The articles are paginated separately from the editorial and advertising sections, with page numbers continuing consecutively from the preceding article, and are not always included in bound volumes of the magazine. The four articles relating to bicycle manufacturing are Part 1, "A Visit to the Hartford Rubber Works," Vol. 8 (February 1897): 1–16; Part 2: "A Visit to the Works of the Pope Tube Company," Vol. 8 (March 1897): 18–33; Part 3: "A Visit to the Works of the Pope Manufacturing Company," Vol. 8 (April 1897): 33–50 (also titled "A Visit to the Columbia Bicycle Works"); and Part 4: "A Visit to the Hartford Cycle Company," Vol. 9 (May 1897): 51–58. The Pope Manufacturing Company printed a condensed version of Moffett's articles in pamphlet form under the title "How a Bicycle is Made. One of America's Great Industries," but without date, and it is available at the Connecticut Historical Society.

National Fire Insurance Company of Hartford, Connecticut. *A Quarter Century's Fire Underwriting. 1871–1896.* New York: De Vinne Press, 1897.

Norcliffe, Glen. "Bridging the American System and Mass Production: Albert Pope's System of Bicycle Manufacture," in *Tools and Technology. Newsletter of the American Precision Museum,* Summer 1997 (Windsor, Vermont): n.p.

Perkins, Robert. "A Marvel of Mechanical Engineering." *Engineering Magazine* 9 (May 1895): 281–301.

Pope Manufacturing Company. *An Industrial Achievement.* Hartford: Pope Manufacturing Company, 1907. Printed pamphlet available at the Connecticut Historical Society.

______. *What It Is, What It Was.* Hartford: Pope Manufacturing Company, 1904. Printed pamphlet available at the Connecticut Historical Society.

Ransom, David F. *George Keller, Architect.* Hartford: Hartford Architecture Conservancy and The Stowe-Day Foundation, 1978.

Ruskin, John. *The Stones of Venice,* Vol. 2. New York: John W. Lovell Company, 1872.

Rybczynski, Witold. *A Clearing in the Distance.* New York: Simon & Schuster, 1999.

Sealander, Judith. *Grand Plans: Business Progressivism and Social Change in Ohio's Miami Valley, 1890–1929.* Lexington: University of Kentucky Press, 1988.

Simpson, Pamela H. "Cheap, Quick and Easy: The Early History of Rockfaced Concrete Block Building." *Perspectives in Vernacular Architecture* 3 (1989): 108–118.

Stoddart, Judith. *Ruskin's Culture Wars.* Charlottesville: University Press of Virginia, 1998.

Stone, Ora. *Westfield. Seat of Whips and Bicycles.* Westfield: S.J. Clarke, 1930. Typewritten publication available at the Westfield Athenaeum.

Stone, Ora L. *History of Massachusetts Industries: Their Inception, Growth and Success,* Vol. 1. Boston: S.J. Clarke, 1930.

Tyrrell, Henry Grattan. *Engineering of Shops and Factories.* New York: McGraw-Hill Book Company, 1912.

______. *A Treatise on the Design and Construction of Mill Buildings and Other Industrial Plants.* Chicago: Myron C. Clark Publishing Co., 1911.

Wallis-Taylor, Alexander James. *Modern Cycles: A Practical Handbook on Their Construction and Repair.* London: Crosby Lockwood and Son, 1897.

Wells, Michael J. *From Bicycles to Buicks: The Story of Behrens and Bushnell.* Essex, CT: Essex Historical Society, 1997.

Williams, Thomas J.C. *A History of Washington County Maryland, including a History of Hagerstown,* 2 vols. Baltimore: Regional Publishing Co, 1968; originally published in 1906.

Index

Numbers in ***bold italics*** indicate pages with illustrations

www.ingramcontent.com/pod-product-compliance
Ingram Content Group UK Ltd.
Pitfield, Milton Keynes, MK11 3LW, UK
UKHW051929100926
8556IPUK00022B/1455

9 781476 6